The Papers of
WILLIAM HICKLING PRESCOTT

Wm H. Prescott

The Papers of
WILLIAM
HICKLING
PRESCOTT

Selected and Edited by

C. HARVEY GARDINER

The University of Illinois Press

Urbana : 1964

===

Other works concerning William Hickling Prescott

by C. Harvey Gardiner

Prescott and His Publishers (1959)

*William Hickling Prescott: An Annotated Bibliography
of Published Works* [1959]

William Hickling Prescott: A Memorial
(co-editor and contributor, 1959)

The Literary Memoranda of William Hickling Prescott (edited, 1961)

Prescott's *History of the Reign of Ferdinand
and Isabella the Catholic* (edited and abridged, 1962)

and

eight essays in journals of the United States,
Mexico, Ecuador and Spain

*A grant from the Ford Foundation has helped to defray
the cost of publishing this work.*

Foreword

———

As HISTORIAN and man of letters, William H. Prescott has earned and won a niche in the pantheon of American greatness. The *History of the Reign of Ferdinand and Isabella, the Catholic* (3 vols., Boston, 1838 [1837]) gained for him the first international reputation accorded an American historian. His histories of the conquests of Mexico and Peru contributed toward the initiation of Anglo-American awareness of Latin America. Under Prescott's hand history assumed such readable form that it vied successfully with three-decker novels for the attention of the general public.

Prescott, however, was not historian and scholar to the exclusion of all else. In his family life he was dutiful son, loving husband, doting parent. His social circle knew him as one loyal to his club, an inveterate diner-out, a connoisseur of wines, a witty conversationalist, and one with unfailing ways with the ladies—a gentleman. In the broader community he was spiritually sensitive and close to his church, politically firm in his loyalty to party, and genuinely humane in his support of charitable institutions. As investor and man of the world of business, he left his heirs a larger estate than he inherited. So affable were his ways and so kind his nature that everyone loved him as a man even as they hailed his genius as historian. He was a remarkable, a complex person. Perhaps it remains for Prescott and his contemporaries to tell that which has been left untold so long—the fullness of his nature, the diverseness of his life.

These selected papers, which aggregate a scant 10 per cent of the available material, adhere to many broad patterns evident in Prescott's life: (1) he wrote few letters during his first thirty years, and those prior to 1820 were strictly family letters; (2) during the 1820's the papers pivoted on his search for a career and his final determination of the direction that his scholarly interest would take; (3) the 1830's widened his correspondence but it, focused on his researches and the publication of his first book, still was almost completely restricted to Americans; (4) with the 1840's came a tremendous increase in volume and a widening of the range of correspondents, with this the best decade for sensing, through his papers, the total man; and finally (5) the 1850's demonstrated the tireless letter writer, enjoying his friendships and memories, his visitors and married children—most of it to the exclusion of serious scholarly labor. Throughout the decades there was a focus on his family—his parents, his wife, his children, his grandchildren.

Prescott's correspondents represent a remarkable range of occupations: such aides as Alexander Burton, Alexander Hill Everett, Edward Everett, Theodore Fay, Martín Fernández de Navarrete, Charles Folsom, Pascual de Gayangos, Jonathan Goodhue, Arthur Middleton and Obadiah Rich; such women as Fanny Calderón de la Barca, Fanny de Gayangos, Lady Mary E. Lyell, Lydia H. Sigourney and Anna Ticknor; such publishers as Richard Bentley, James Brown, Harper & Brothers, Phillips, Sampson and Company and George Routledge; historians such as George Bancroft, Brantz Mayer, John Lothrop Motley, Patrick Fraser Tytler and Robert Anderson Wilson; such politicians as Joel Roberts Poinsett, James K. Polk and Daniel Webster; such clergymen as William Ellery Channing, George E. Ellis, Henry Hart Milman and Alexander Young; such novelists as Charles Dickens, Maria Edgeworth, Edward Maturin and Mary Elizabeth Wormeley; such biographers as John Church Hamilton, Washington Irving and John Gibson Lockhart; such scholars as Cornelius Conway Felton, Richard Ford, Albert Gallatin, Joaquín García Icazbalceta, Francis Lieber, William Stirling and Peter Stephen DuPonceau; such poets as Fitz-Greene Halleck, Oliver Wendell Holmes, William Henry Leatham and Henry Wadsworth Longfellow; such intimate friends as William Howard Gardiner, George Stillman Hillard, Theophilus Parsons, John Pickering, Jared Sparks, Charles Sumner and George Ticknor; and such nobodies as Lucilla Stanley Lincolne and R. Augustus Wight. In addition, his papers related Prescott to literary agents, diplomats, translators, critics, humanitarians, philanthropists, learned societies, military men, educators, nobility, printers, booksellers and jurists.

Approximately 21 per cent of the selections relate to foreign correspondents: English, Spanish, French, Italian, German and Mexican. Because all of his books were published in English editions, because he sought and won high regard in English literary circles and because he traveled and had many delightful friends there, the English contingent of Prescott's contacts was the most important foreign one, by far. For similarly sound reasons, it being the fountainhead of indispensable materials for his researches, the contacts with Spaniards were next in importance abroad.

To anyone tempted to insist that the selections have been made with an eye to identifying Prescott with significant figures, let it be said, first, that Prescott's career is legitimately related to the activities of hundreds of significant persons, and second, that scores upon scores of those figures are not met in the items presented in this volume.

The twenty-four nonepistolary items, representing approximately 7 per cent of the collection, include: an itemized accounting of house repairs on Prescott's mansion; agreements with two of his reader-secretaries; memoranda on maxims for composition, religious beliefs and a course of study; invoices covering books shipped from Europe; memoranda concerning his vision, work schedule, expenses, income, landscaping plans, a son's allowances and publishing contracts; a poem; and a will.

In sum, in terms of the range of Prescott's correspondents and papers, as well as the range of his activities, this collection is broadly representative, not definitive in reference to any person or matter.

. . . .

Two circumstances implement the desire to depict William H. Prescott through his papers. There was a bit of the pack rat in Prescott—he dutifully preserved paper with writing upon it: deeds, receipts, tax assessments, statements of income, lists of expenses, agreements, invoices, wills, memoranda on many matters—all these as well as personal journals, commonplace books and incoming correspondence. By-products of his impaired vision, draft copies of the letters which Prescott sent to far quarters of the earth, are also available. From the age of twelve to a moment shortly before his death, Prescott's life can be traced through his own writings and those of his contemporaries.

Selected primarily as an account of the total range and nature of William H. Prescott's career and personality, this collection of papers is structured so that approximately 76 per cent of the materials is by Prescott. The remaining items, written to him or between intimates of his, are significant because they increase and sharpen our perspective on Prescott, as well as add an awareness of those who constituted his intimates.

Every letter by Prescott that is utilized is printed in its entirety. Fewer than 2 per cent of the items have been printed previously in their entirety and less than 7 per cent of these papers have been printed either completely or partially. Whenever an item has been printed, either completely or in significant proportion, that publication is duly mentioned.

. . . .

Previously published papers of William H. Prescott deserve some attention. George Ticknor's *Life of William Hickling Prescott* (Boston,

1864) is cast in the well-known "life and letters" format of that day. Despite heavy incorporation of letters, Ticknor rarely presents complete texts, and his deletions promote an unbalanced view of Prescott which is long on chiseled grandeur and short on warmly human aspects. Both Rollo Ogden (*William Hickling Prescott*, Boston and New York, 1904) and Harry Thurston Peck (*William Hickling Prescott*, New York and London, 1905), while producing better synthesized biographies than that by Ticknor, continue his practice of employing extracts rather than complete papers.

Roger Wolcott's *The Correspondence of William Hickling Prescott 1833–1847* (Boston and New York, 1925) is a rich and accurately transcribed sampling of Prescott papers. Indispensable though it is to the student of Prescott, this work knows these limitations: it treats only the climactic period of Prescott's career as historian; fewer than 5 per cent of the Prescott letters therein are given in their entirety; and the selection of papers is restricted to a single, albeit the finest, collection. Clara Louisa Penney's *Prescott: Unpublished Letters to Gayangos in the Library of the Hispanic Society of America* (New York, 1927) admirably complements, for the years through 1847, Wolcott's volume. For the period 1848–59 the Penney volume offers for the first time the complete texts of numerous letters by Prescott to his principal European aide.

Complete texts of Prescott papers, in appreciable quantities, also have appeared in the following works by the present editor: *Prescott and His Publishers* (Carbondale, Illinois, 1959), wherein complete publishing agreements, in particular, are found; and *The Literary Memoranda of William Hickling Prescott* (2 vols., Norman, Oklahoma, 1961), wherein the complete texts of Prescott's literary notebooks (1823–58) are published.

Minor sources of published Prescott materials, by which it is meant that they commonly offer isolated items and those frequently in extracted form, include the *Proceedings* of the Massachusetts Historical Society and biographies of many of Prescott's contemporaries, including, for example, George Ticknor, Charles Sumner, Fitz-Greene Halleck, Henry W. Longfellow and Samuel Rogers.

Even as the published sources of valid Prescott papers are noted, two kinds of confusion which have led to the exclusion of certain items require attention. Lawyer William Prescott, father of the historian, has been confused repeatedly with William H. Prescott. For example, the lawyer, not the historian, wrote the letter to William Ellery Channing on September 5, 1837, which Fulmer Mood and Granville Hicks published in the *New England Quarterly*, V (July, 1932). A second area of confusion, indulged in by collectors and librarians, is that which repeatedly finds the correspondence of Dr. William Prescott of Concord, New Hampshire, grouped with that of the historian.

In addition to selecting the materials, the editor has adopted certain editorial practices and similarly has rejected others. The chronology of Prescott's life with which this foreword closes is intended as a guideline reference.

Letters by Prescott are always given in their entirety. Most of the letters to Prescott, however, are not presented completely, centered leaders indicating any and all omissions. Explanatory notes, appended to relevant letters, occasionally refer to and summarize materials which are not otherwise contained in this collection.

Whenever possible, in Prescott's letters, the abbreviations and contractions, some of which are irregular as well as inconsistent, are expanded silently. This includes the ampersand and the thorn. However, the form "&c." is retained. Representative of the abbreviations that are expanded are w. (with), mog. (morning), p. (past), m. (minutes), N.A.R. (*North American Review*), yr. (your), dlls. (dollars), evg. (evening) and L C (Letter of Credit). Proper names reduced by Prescott to initials pose, on occasion, an insurmountable problem. Their expansion or retention reflects the capacity of the editor to identify positively the individuals concerned. Superscript is lowered. Nothing, however, that might affect the meaning is undertaken by the editor.

Excessive use of the dash is replaced by commas and other appropriate punctuation in Prescott's letters. When dashes between punctuated sentences appear to indicate paragraphing, paragraphing is introduced.

In the letters to Prescott, the capitalization, grammar and spelling—except for abbreviations, which are expanded—remain as found in the original manuscripts. Because the overwhelming majority of letters by Prescott were penned by others, various members of his family as well as numerous professional reader-secretaries, a different procedure is adopted for them. Except for the first two letters, which were written before his vision became impaired and his dependence on others set in, the errors of spelling, capitalization and grammar are corrected silently. The headings and inside addresses occasionally found at the bottoms of letters are moved to the tops of the letters.

Gaps in the text are handled as follows: (1) when one or two words or parts thereof which are not conjecturable are illegible or missing, that fact is indicated thus: [. . .], with [. . . .] employed at the end of sentences; and (2) for more extended illegible or missing passages, explanatory notes are introduced. Materials supplied by conjecture or deduction are placed inside square brackets. Doubtful words or passages are designated thus: [?]. The employment of [*sic*] has been reduced to a minimum.

The omission of two types of information generally found in published collections of papers of prominent men deserves explanation. Because of the weakened and fluctuating state of his vision, Prescott's personal role as letter writer varied considerably. In a small percentage of instances his letters are ALS in nature. Many times he simply signed the letters which, originally drafted by him on his noctograph, were penned in fair copy by his reader-secretary or some kinsman. On numerous occasions Prescott garnished his aides' fair copies with closing phrases or sentences, personalized complimentary closes and postscripts. So numerous and varied are the epistolary tidbits in Prescott's own hand that any effort to identify them would defy normal bibliographical categories and prompt editorial pedantry. Accordingly the individual items are not identified in terms of their being ALS, LS, etc. Every item, however, is understood to be derived from the fair copy original manuscript unless otherwise identified. For related reasons, no mention is made of the styling of envelop addresses.

Exhaustive annotation is intended to assist the reader. Those individuals who are not identified in notes are either sufficiently identified in the text as to obviate it or they are so minor or shadowy as to defy it.

ACKNOWLEDGMENTS

This collection of the papers of William H. Prescott is based upon the generous cooperation of many individuals and institutions.

Mr. Roger Wolcott, of Boston, a great-grandson of William H. Prescott and the owner of the largest and most significant collection of Prescott papers, once more has accorded the present editor the widest access and the most unrestricted use of the papers of his famous kinsman. Mr. Wolcott's cooperation, indispensable to the fulfillment of this project, is deeply appreciated.

Similar sentiments of indebtedness and gratitude are directed to the Massachusetts Historical Society, the depository of this richest collection of materials about Prescott. In the Society's library the William H. Prescott Papers are admirably supplemented by almost a dozen other collections which impinge upon Prescott's career. For access to and for assistance while working with these materials, thanks are directed to the Massachusetts Historical Society, Director Stephen T. Riley, Winifred Collins, John D. Cushing, Malcom Freiberg and Warren G. Wheeler.

At Harvard University, where numerous other collections touch Prescott's career, words of appreciation are extended to William A. Jackson, Librarian of Houghton; to Carolyn E. Jakeman, in charge of the reading room of The Houghton Library; to Kimball C. Elkins, Senior Assistant in the Harvard University Archives; and to the photographic services of Harvard College Library.

Boston Public Library, another holder of multiple collections related to the life of Prescott, is deserving of sincere expressions of thanks. Foremost there among those who aided the present project are: Zoltán Haraszti, late Keeper of Rare Books; John Alden, Acting Curator of Rare Books; Edith A. Wright, Editorial Assistant; Sarah W. Flannery and Marjorie G. Bonquet, Deputy Supervisors of Reference and Research Services; and B. J. O'Neil, Coordinator of General Reference Services.

In addition to the three leading despositories of Prescott papers, the assistance of the following institutions and individuals is gratefully acknowledged: The Academy of Natural Sciences of Philadelphia and Venia T. Phillips, Manuscript Librarian; the American Antiquarian Society and Clifford K. Shipton, Director; the American Philosophical Society, Whitfield J. Bell, Jr., Associate Librarian, Gertrude D. Hess, Assistant Librarian, and Murphy D. Smith, Manuscripts Librarian; the Bowdoin College Library, Richard Harwell, Librarian, and Dale C. Gresseth, Assistant Librarian; the British Museum and T. A. J. Burnett, Assistant Keeper, Department of Manuscripts; the Brown University Library, John R. Turner Ettlinger, in charge of Special Collections, and Mary W. Ranby, Manuscript Assistant; the University of California General Library, Donald Coney, University Librarian, and Eliza Hart Pietsch, Rare Books Department; the Chicago Historical Society and Archie Motley, Manuscript Librarian; the William L. Clements Library, The University of Michigan, and Howard H. Peckham, Director; the Colby College Library, Edwin Arlington Robinson Treasure Room, F. Elizabeth Libbey, Associate Librarian, and Richard Cary, Curator of Rare Books and Manuscripts; The Connecticut Historical Society and Thompson R. Harlow, Director; the Dartmouth College Library, Edward Connery Lathem, Associate Librarian, and Kenneth C. Cramer, College Archivist; Charles E. Feinberg, Detroit; the Georgia Historical Society and Lilla M. Hawes, Director; Harper & Brothers and Dorothy B. Fiske; the Haverford College Library, A. T. Haakinson, Supervisor of The Treasure Room, and Thomas E. Drake, Curator; The Hispanic Society of America and Clara L. Penney; The Historical Society of Pennsylvania and R. N. Williams, II, Director; Houghton Mifflin Company; the Humanities Research Center, The University of Texas, and Ann Bowden, Librarian; the Henry E. Huntington Library and Art Gallery, Robert O. Dougan, Librarian, and

Helen S. Mangold, Assistant, Department of Manuscripts; the University of Illinois Library and Robert F. Delzell, Library Administrative Assistant; Professor Joseph Jones, Department of English, The University of Texas; the University of Kansas Library, Special Collections Department; the Margaret I. King Library, University of Kentucky, and Jacqueline Bull, Archivist; the Lehigh University Library, James D. Mack, Librarian, and Robert S. Taylor, Associate Librarian; The Library Company of Philadelphia and Lillian Tonkin; The Library of Congress and David C. Mearns, Chief, Manuscript Division; The Lilly Library, Indiana University, Doris M. Reed, Curator of Manuscripts, and E. L. Craig, Reference Librarian; the Maryland Historical Society, Archives, and John D. Kilbourne, Librarian; the Massachusetts Institute of Technology, Microreproduction Laboratory; The Pierpont Morgan Library, Frederick B. Adams, Jr., Director, and Herbert Cahoon, Curator of Autograph Manuscripts; Professor Samuel Eliot Morison, Boston; the Morristown National Historical Park, Morristown, New Jersey, and Francis S. Ronalds, Superintendent; the National Library of Scotland, the Trustees of the National Library of Scotland, and J. S. Ritchie, Assistant Keeper, Department of Manuscripts; The New-York Historical Society and James J. Heslin, Director; The New York Public Library, Robert W. Hill, Keeper of Manuscripts, and Paul R. Rugen, First Assistant, Manuscript Division; The New York Society Library and Sylvia C. Hilton, Librarian; the New York *Times;* the Peabody Institute of the City of Baltimore and Frank N. Jones, Director of Library; the Perkins School for the Blind, Edward J. Waterhouse, Director, and Nelson Coon, Librarian; The Phillips Exeter Academy, Davis Library, and Rodney Armstrong, Librarian; the Probate Court, Suffolk County, Massachusetts, Louis F. Musco and John F. Collins, Registers, and John A. Griffin and Arthur A. Kelly, Assistant Registers; the Redwood Library and Athenaeum, Newport, Rhode Island, and Donald T. Gibbs, Librarian; The Rhode Island Historical Society and Clarkson A. Collins, III, Librarian; The University of Rochester Library, John R. Russell, Director of Libraries, and Ruth Hollis; the Rosenberg Library, Galveston, Texas, Charles O'Halloran, Director, and Mildred Stevenson, Reference Librarian; the Rev. Herbert Boyce Satcher, D.D., Philadelphia; the Southern Illinois University Library, Ralph E. McCoy, Director of Libraries, Ralph Bushee, Rare Book Librarian, and Alan M. Cohn, Humanities Librarian; The State Historical Society of Wisconsin, Josephine L. Harper, Manuscripts Librarian, and Margaret Gleason, Reference Librarian; the Wellesley College Library and Hannah D. French, Research Librarian; and the Yale University Library, David R. Watkins, Chief

Reference Librarian, and Dorothy W. Bridgwater, Assistant Head, Reference Department.

A BIBLIOGRAPHY OF MANUSCRIPTS

The contribution of each institution, collection and private collector to the present work is indicated in the following tabulation of items utilized:

The Academy of Natural Sciences of Philadelphia (1)
American Philosophical Society (2)
    Archives (2)
Boston Public Library (27)
    Mellen Chamberlain Autograph Collection (3)
    A[bram] E. C[utter] (comp.) Autograph Letter and Engraved Letter and Engraved Portraits of William H. Prescott the Historian (1)
    Charles Folsom Papers (22)
    Rare Book Department (1)
British Museum (2)
    Add. MS. 34625 (1)
    Add. MS. 40690 (1)
Brown University Library (1)
    Wayland Papers (1)
University of California (1)
    Rare Books Department (1)
William L. Clements Library (1)
    Hughes Collection (1)
Colby College Library (1)
    Edwin Arlington Robinson Treasure Room (1)
The Connecticut Historical Society (1)
    Sigourney Papers, Hoadley Collection (1)
Dartmouth College Library (2)
    Archives, Ticknor Collection (2)
Charles E. Feinberg (1)
Georgia Historical Society (1)
    Letters of Honorary Members and Officers, vol. I (1)
Harvard College Library (35)
    Autograph File (2)
    Richard Bentley Papers (9)
    Henry W. Longfellow Papers (2)
    Jared Sparks Papers (15)
    Charles Sumner Papers (7)
Haverford College Library (2)

Charles Roberts Autograph Collection (2)
The Hispanic Society of America (3)
The Historical Society of Pennsylvania (6)
  Gratz Collection (2)
  Meredith Papers (1)
  Joel R. Poinsett Papers (2)
  O. D. Wilkinson Collection (1)
The Huntington Library (9)
  S. Austin Allibone Papers (2)
  Francis Lieber Papers (7)
University of Kansas Library (1)
  Special Collections Department (1)
The Library of Congress (3)
  Oliver Wendell Holmes Papers (1)
  James K. Polk (1)
  Joseph Story Papers (1)
Massachusetts Historical Society (206)
  George Bancroft Papers (8)
  George E. Ellis Papers (1)
  A. H. Everett Papers (1)
  Edward Everett Papers (3)
  William H. Gardiner Papers (5)
  Miscellaneous bound (2)
  William H. Prescott Papers (184)
  Shattuck Papers (1)
  Wormeley-Latimer Papers (1)
The Pierpont Morgan Library (1)
Samuel Eliot Morison (1)
National Library of Scotland (1)
  MS. 935, no. 43 (1)
The New-York Historical Society (2)
The New York Public Library (5)
  DeCoursey Fales Collection (1)
  Miscellaneous Papers—Wm. H. Prescott folder (4)
The New York Society (2)
  Goodhue Papers (2)
Perkins School for the Blind (2)
  Letters, 1838–39 (2)
Probate Court, Suffolk County, Massachusetts (1)
The Rhode Island Historical Society (1)
  Channing Autographs (1)
The University of Rochester Library (1)

E. G. Miner Collection (1)
The Rev. Herbert Boyce Satcher, D.D. (1)
Southern Illinois University Library (1)
The State Historical Society of Wisconsin (1)
　Draper-Wisconsin Historical Society Correspondence (1)
Yale University Library (4)
　E. B. Pierce Papers, Historical Manuscripts Collection (1)
　Yale Collection of American Literature (3)

William Hickling Prescott

A CHRONOLOGY

=====

1796—May 4—Born at Salem, Massachusetts. Son of lawyer William Prescott and Catherine Greene Hickling Prescott

1799—November 12—Birth of sister Catherine Elizabeth Prescott

1803–8—Attended various private schools in Salem

1804—January 2—Birth of brother Edward Goldsborough Prescott

1808—September 17—Family moved to Bumstead Place, Boston

1808–11—Attended classes conducted by the Rev. Dr. John S. J. Gardiner and others in Boston

1811—August 22—Entered Harvard as a sophomore

1812–13—Left eye injured at college during junior year

1814—August 24—Commencement Day, A.B. degree

1815—January—Inflammation of eye

September 26—Sailed for the Azores, wintering with grandfather Thomas Hickling, the U.S. Consul

1816—April 8—Sailed for England

May–July—Eyes examined and treated in London

August 3—Crossed to France

October 18—Entered Italy

1817—March 12—Departed from Italy

March 30—Returned to Paris

May 14—Returned to London

September—Returned to Boston, family residing in Pond Street (renamed Bedford Street in 1821)

1818—June 13—Prime founder of the literary-social organization "Club"

1819—September 28—Sister Catherine Elizabeth married Franklin Dexter of Boston

1820—March–July—Editor of *The Club-Room;* author of three selections therein

May 4—Married Susan Amory, daughter of wealthy merchant family of Boston

1821—October—"Byron's Letter on Pope," first review article, in *North American Review*

1822—April—"Essay Writing" in *NAR*

1823—January—"French and English Tragedy" in *NAR*

1824—July—"Mr. Sprague's Prize Poems" in *NAR*

September 24—Birth of first child, Catherine Hickling Prescott

October—"Italian Narrative Poetry" in *NAR*

October 12—"Cui Bono?" in *The United States Literary Gazette*

1825—July—"Da Ponte's Observations" in *NAR*

August 1, 15—"Romance in the Heroic and Middle Ages" in *The United States Literary Gazette*

1826—January 19—The reign of Ferdinand and Isabella chosen as subject of historical research and writing

January 27—Birth of first son, William Gardiner Prescott

April—"Leisure Hours at Sea" in *NAR*

June—James Lloyd English, first significant professional reader-secretary, assists Prescott

July—"Scottish Song" in *NAR*

1827—July—"Novel Writing" in *NAR*

1828—April—First trip to Washington, D.C.

July 27—Birth of second daughter, Elizabeth Prescott

October—"The Life and Writings of Molière" in *NAR*

1829—February 1—Death of eldest child, Catherine Hickling Prescott

October—"Irving's Conquest of Granada" in *NAR*

1830—January 25—Birth of fourth and last child, William Amory Prescott

July—"Asylum for the Blind" in *NAR*

September 11—"Obituary Notice of the Rev. Dr. Gardiner" in *Columbian Centinel*

1831—June–July—First trip to Niagara Falls

July—"Poetry and Romance of the Italians" in *NAR*

December 31—"Edinburgh Review" in *The New-England Galaxy*

1832—April 7—"North American Review" in *The New-England Galaxy*

July—"English Literature of the Nineteenth Century" in *NAR*

1833—January 12—"For the New-England Galaxy" in *The New-England Galaxy*

1834—"Life of Charles Brockden Brown" in J. Sparks (ed.), *The Library of American Biography*, I

1837—July—"Sales's Don Quixote" in *NAR*

October 4—"A Close Parallel" in *Boston Daily Advertiser*

December 25—*History of the Reign of Ferdinand and Isabella, the Catholic*, 3 vols., Boston. The London edition appeared January 17, 1838

1838—January—"Tales from the German" in *NAR*

April—"Sir Walter Scott" in *NAR*

1839—April—"Kenyon's Poems" in *NAR*

October—"Chateaubriand's English Literature" in *NAR*

1841—January—"Bancroft's United States" in *NAR*

1842—April—"Mariotti's Italy" in *NAR*

April–May—Trip to New York City

1843—"Preface" in Madame Calderón de la Barca's *Life in Mexico*

January—"Madame Calderón's Life in Mexico" in *NAR*

October—*A History of the Conquest of Mexico, with a Preliminary View of the Ancient Mexican Civilization*, 3 vols., London. The American edition (New York) appeared December 6–21

1844—April 11—Death of brother, Edward Goldsborough Prescott

June—Trip to Niagara Falls

September 17—"Catherwood's Ancient Monuments of Yucatan" in *Boston Courier*

December 8—Death of father

1845—Purchased, remodeled and moved into 55 Beacon Street

August 16—*Biographical and Critical Miscellanies*, London. The American edition (New York) appeared in early December, 1845

1846—March–April—Trip to Washington, D.C.

1847—May 17—*A History of the Conquest of Peru, with a Preliminary View of the Civilization of the Incas*, 2 vols., London. The American edition (New York) appeared June 22, 1847

1848—March–May—*Memoir of the Honorable John Pickering, LL.D.* Commissioned by the Massachusetts Historical Society

June 9—Contracts for services of reader-secretary John Foster Kirk, his last such aide (1848–59)

1850—January 1—"History of Spanish Literature" in *Boston Daily Advertiser*

January—"Spanish Literature," last review article in *NAR*; "History of Spanish Literature" in *Bentley's Miscellany*

April—Last trip to Washington, D.C.

May–September—Second and last trip to Europe

1851—June–July—Last trip to Niagara Falls

November 6—Son William Gardiner Prescott married Augusta Peabody of Salem

1852—March 16—Daughter Elizabeth married James Lawrence of Boston

May 17—Death of mother

1853—June—Summer residence shifted from Nahant to Lynn, Massachusetts

October 6—"New and Interesting Work," in *National Intelli-gencer*

1855—October 30—*History of the Reign of Philip the Second, King of Spain,* vols. 1 and 2, London. The American (Boston) edition appeared December 10, 1855

1856—January–February—"Memoir of the Honorable Abbott Lawrence" in *National Portrait Gallery;* also published separately

December 8—*The History of the Reign of the Emperor Charles V* (to William Robertson's work, Prescott added "The Life of Charles V After His Abdication"), 3 vols., Boston. The London edition appeared the same month

1857—December—"The Battle of Lepanto" in *The Atlantic Monthly*

1858—February 4—First apoplectic stroke

September–October—Last of the annual visits to the rural residence at Pepperell

December—*History of the Reign of Philip the Second, King of Spain,* vol. 3

1859—January 28—Apoplectic stroke, and death, at 55 Beacon Street

"John Sylvester John Gardiner, D.D." in William Buell Sprague's *Annals of the American Pulpit,* V (written in 1848)

1871—"Ticknor, George, LL.D." in S. Austin Allibone's *A Critical Dictionary of English Literature and British and American Authors,* III. WHP's portion of this, limited to page 2416, was written in 1855

Contents

FOREWORD . . . . *v*

1808

1. To Catherine Elizabeth Prescott, 10 May . . . 3

1811

2. To William Prescott, 23 August 4

1816

3. To William and Catherine Prescott, 15 March . . 5
4. From William Prescott, 10 June 12
5. To William and Catherine Prescott, 21 July . . . 14
6. From Catherine Prescott, 29 November 17

1817

7. From William Prescott, 4 January 17
8. To William and Catherine Prescott, 12 January . . 18
9. From Catherine Prescott, [late January–early March] . 20
10. From William Prescott, 2 March 21
11. To William Prescott, [c. 29 April] 22

1819

12. Poem Sent to Susan Amory, August 30

1820

13. To Jared Sparks, 9 February 31
14. To Fitz-Greene Halleck, 15 March 32
15. To Francis W. P. Greenwood, [c. March] . . . 33
16. Timothy Swan to Charles Wells, 23 April . . . 33
17. To Theophilus Parsons, 3 May 34
18. To Jared Sparks, 29 June 34

1821

19. Commonplace Book, Maxims in Composition, [early in year?] 35
20. Commonplace Book, Religious Beliefs, 4 April . . 36
21. Commonplace Book, Course of Studies, 30 October . . 37
22. Commonplace Book, Memorandum, [autumn?] . . 38

1822

23. To Gorham Parsons, 7 March 38
24. Commonplace Book, Studies, [early in year] . . . 40
25. Commonplace Book, Musings, [early in year?] . . 40

1823
26. To George Ticknor, 17 December 41
1824
27. To Theophilus Parsons, 25 September 44
1826
28. To Theophilus Parsons, 2 January 44
29. To Jared Sparks, 22 February. 45
30. To George Bancroft, 16 November 46
31. To Alexander Hill Everett, 26 December . . . 48
1827
32. From Alexander Hill Everett, 3 January . . . 49
33. To Alexander Hill Everett, 13 July 51
34. Invoice from Obadiah Rich, 21 July 53
35. To Edward Everett, 13 November 54
1828
36. To Obadiah Rich, [January] 54
37. To George Bancroft, 25 February 56
38. To Susan Prescott, [21 April] 56
39. To Susan Prescott, 27 April 58
40. To Obadiah Rich, 25 June 60
41. To Edward Everett, 25 July 62
42. To Jared Sparks, 28 September 63
1829
43. To Obadiah Rich, 6 February 66
44. To Obadiah Rich, 20 October. 67
45. To Obadiah Rich, 28 December 69
1830
46. To Jared Sparks, 17 February 71
47. To Jonathan Goodhue, 14 April 72
48. Invoice from Obadiah Rich, 15 December . . . 73
1831
49. To Obadiah Rich, 11 March 74
50. To George Bancroft, 30 April 76
51. To Susan Prescott, 2 July 77
52. William Amory to Susan Prescott, [12 July] . . . 79
53. To Obadiah Rich, 10 September 79
54. Invoice from Obadiah Rich, 10 December . . . 81
1832
55. To Obadiah Rich, 13 February 83
56. To Obadiah Rich, 10 March 83

57. To Obadiah Rich, [10] July 85
58. Invoice from Obadiah Rich, 18 December . . . 86

    1833
59. To Obadiah Rich, 11 March 87
60. To George Bancroft, 16 March 88
61. To Jared Sparks, 8 May 90
62. To Jared Sparks, 1 August 91
63. To Obadiah Rich, 13 August 92
64. To Obadiah Rich, 19 October 95
65. To Jared Sparks, 24 December 96

    1834
66. To Obadiah Rich, 17 January 97
67. To Obadiah Rich, 17 September 98
68. To Obadiah Rich, 25 November 99

    1835
69. From Obadiah Rich, 20 January 100
70. From Cornelius Conway Felton, 31 January . . . 101
71. To George Bancroft, 17 June 101
72. To Obadiah Rich, 22 July 103
73. To Jared Sparks, 23 July 105

    1836
74. To Jonathan Goodhue, 29 July 106

    1837
75. From Jared Sparks, 24 February 107
76. To Jared Sparks, 25 February 107
77. To Jared Sparks, [1 March] 107
78. To George Bancroft, 6 March 108
79. To Jared Sparks, [22 March] 109
80. To Charles Folsom, [15 April] 110
81. To Charles Folsom, [c. 20 April] 111
82. From John Pickering, 1 May 111
83. To Colonel Thomas Aspinwall, 20 May 112
84. To Thomas G. Bradford, 29 May 113
85. To Charles Folsom, 23 August 113
86. To Charles Folsom, 11 September 114
87. To Charles Folsom, 2 October 115
88. To Richard Bentley, 4 October 117
89. To William Howard Gardiner, 4 October . . . 118
90. To Charles Folsom, 19 October 119
91. To Charles Folsom, [25 November] 120

92. To Charles Folsom, 6 December 121
93. To Charles Folsom, [12 December] 121
94. To Jared Sparks, 25 December 122
95. To Charles Folsom, 25 December 124
96. To Joseph Story, 27 December 124

1838

97. To Charles Folsom, 16 January 125
98. To Charles Folsom, [20 January] 126
99. To Alexander Young, 14 March 127
100. To Charles Folsom, [19 March] 127
101. To Charles Folsom, [17 April] 128
102. To Franklin Bache, 28 April 129
103. To Dr. George C. Shattuck, 16 June 130
104. To William Ellery Channing, [c. spring] 130
105. To Francis Lieber, 22 September 131
106. To William Sullivan, 21 December 132

1839

107. To Joel Roberts Poinsett, 8 January 133
108. To Joel Roberts Poinsett, 26 January 134
109. To Charles Folsom, 30 January 137
110. To Joseph G. Cogswell, 18 February 138
111. To Richard Bentley, 11 June 139
112. To Israel K. Tefft, 23 July 141
113. To Charles Folsom, 5 August 141
114. To Samuel Gridley Howe, 3 September 142
115. To Charles Sumner, [c. 5 October] 143
116. To Martín Fernández de Navarrete, 12 October . . 144
117. To Samuel Gridley Howe, 11 November 145
118. To Little and Brown, [23 November] 146
119. To Francis Lieber, 26 November 147
120. From Pascual de Gayangos, 1 December 149
121. To Washington Irving, 24 December 152

1840

122. To Francis Lieber, 10 February 154
123. From Patrick Fraser Tytler, 24 February 155
124. From Colonel Thomas Aspinwall, 29 February . . 156
125. From Richard Bentley, 3 June 158
126. To Thaddeus William Harris, 22 June 159
127. To Fanny Calderón de la Barca, 15 August . . . 159
128. To Charles Sumner, 16 October 165
129. From Arthur Middleton, 4 November 166

130. To Pascual de Gayangos, 28 November 167
131. To Francis Lieber, 31 December 170

1841

132. From Fanny Calderón de la Barca, 19 January . . . 172
133. From William Henry Leatham, 27 March 173
134. To James Brown, 26 May 174
135. To Francis Lieber, 3 June 174
136. To Pascual de Gayangos, 27 October 177
137. To Richard Bentley, 15 November 181
138. To Luigi Mariotti, 15 November 182
139. From John P. Richardson, 29 December 183
140. To Henry Wadsworth Longfellow, 30 December . . 184

1842

141. To Francis Lieber, 5 January 185
142. Memorandum Concerning Eyes, 28 April 187
143. To Susan Prescott, [29 April] 189
144. From Richard Ford, 5 June 192
145. To Charles Sumner, 12 July 194
146. To William Gardiner Prescott, 25 August . . . 194
147. To Charles Dickens, 15 December 196

1843

148. To Charles Folsom, 9 January 197
149. To William Gardiner Prescott, 6 February . . . 197
150. To William Gardiner Prescott, 27 February . . . 199
151. From Harper & Brothers, 3 April 200
152. From Colonel Thomas Aspinwall, 17 April . . . 201
153. To Harper & Brothers, 2 June 202
154. Robert Cooke to Colonel Thomas Aspinwall, 8 June . 204
155. To George Nichols, 19 June 205
156. To William Howard Gardiner, 24 June 206
157. To Metcalf, Keith and Nichols, 19 August . . . 206
158. To Charles Folsom, 4 September 207
159. To William Gardiner Prescott, 24 September . . . 208
160. From Josiah Quincy, 12 October 209
161. From Colonel Thomas Aspinwall, 3 November . . 209
162. To Harper & Brothers, 19 December 210
163. To Peter Stephen DuPonceau, 23 December . . . 211
164. To Theodore Sedgwick Fay, 23 December . . . 212
165. From William Howard Gardiner, 27 December . . 212

1844

166. From George Stillman Hillard, 1 January . . . 213

167. From Lord Morpeth, 23 January 214
168. To Jared Sparks, 18 March 216
169. From Harper & Brothers, 25 April 216
170. To Albert Gallatin, 9 May 217
171. To Grenville Mears, 27 June 218
172. To Brantz Mayer, 24 July 218
173. To Dr. Samuel Cabot, 11 September 219
174. To Harper & Brothers, 28 October 220
175. From Count Adolphe de Circourt, 6 November . . 221
176. From Colonel Thomas Aspinwall, 9 December . . 221
177. From David Sears II, 24 December 222

1845
178. To Edward Maturin, 27 January 223
179. To Gales and Seaton, 31 January 224
180. To François Auguste Marie Mignet, [March] . . . 224
181. To Macvey Napier, 15 May 225
182. To Francis Lieber, 6 August 226
183. From Richard Ford, 6 August 227
184. Catherine Prescott to Susan Prescott, 25 August . . 228
185. To William Gardiner Prescott, 8 September . . . 229
186. To Henry Wadsworth Longfellow, 16 September . . 230
187. To Mary Elizabeth Wormeley, 7 October [?] . . . 230
188. To Fletcher Harper, 8 December 231

1846
189. From Mary Elizabeth Wormeley, 3 February . . . 232
190. Accounting of House Repairs from George M. Dexter,
    March 234
191. To President James K. Polk, [April] 236
192. To Harper & Brothers, 12 December 237

1847
193. From Colonel Thomas Aspinwall, 3 February . . . 238
194. To Harper & Brothers, [24 April] 239
195. To Charles Folsom, 26 April 240
196. To Joseph G. Cogswell, 12 May 240
197. Agreement with Robert Carter, [c. mid-year] . . . 241
198. To Harper & Brothers, 30 June 242
199. To Christopher Hughes, 30 June 244
200. From Colonel Thomas Aspinwall, 3 July 244
201. From Maria Edgeworth, 28 August 245
202. From Catherine Prescott, 24 September 248
203. To Harper & Brothers, September 249

204. From Richard Bentley, 31 December   249

     1848
205. To Caleb Butler, 28 January   250
206. To Obadiah Rich, 25 February   250
207. Agreement with John Foster Kirk, 9 June .   .   .   251
208. To William Gardiner Prescott, 7 August .   .   .   251
209. To Albert Gallatin, 14 August   253
210. Memorandum Concerning Personal Regimen,
    1 September   255
211. To William Gardiner Prescott, 1 October .   .   .   255
212. From General William Miller, 10 November .   .   .   258
213. To Edwin Percy Whipple, 28 November .   .   .   260
214. To William Gardiner Prescott, 3 December   .   .   260
215. From Frances de Gayangos, 15 December .   .   .   262

     1849
216. From Dr. H. Eberty, 8 January   263
217. To Lydia H. Sigourney, [c. January]   264
218. To William Gardiner Prescott, 5 February   .   .   265
219. From William Stirling, 8 February   267
220. To Richard Bentley, 9 February   268
221. From John Church Hamilton, 28 April .   .   .   268
222. To William Gardiner Prescott, 1 May .   .   .   269
223. From George Bancroft, 10 May   272
224. To Daniel Webster, 20 June   272
225. To Charles Sumner, 3 July   273
226. To Francis Bowen, 22 October   275
227. To William Gardiner Prescott, 28 October   .   .   276
228. From Richard Bentley, 8 November   278
229. To William Gardiner Prescott, 2 December   .   .   279

     1850
230. To Isaac Lea, 22 January   281
231. To William Gardiner Prescott, 3 February   .   .   282
232. To Richard Bentley, 4 February   285
233. To Susan Prescott, [11 April]   286
234. To William Gardiner Prescott, 28 April .   .   .   287
235. To Charles Sumner, [c. 30 April]   290
236. From Harper & Brothers, 7 May   291
237. To William Gardiner Prescott, 14 May .   .   .   291
238. To George Bancroft, 14 May   292
239. From Edward Everett, 20 May   293
240. To William Howard Gardiner, 18 July .   .   .   294

241. To William Amory Prescott, 29 July 296
242. To Charles Sumner, 2 September 297
243. To William Howard Gardiner, 30 September . . . 299
244. To Henry Wadsworth Longfellow, 7 October . . . 299
245. To John Gibson Lockhart, 26 November . . . 300
246. To Ángel Calderón de la Barca, 19 December . . . 301
247. From Richard Ford, 23 December 304

1851
248. To Richard Bentley, 20 May 305
249. From Richard Bentley, 22 May 306
250. To Lady Mary E. Lyell, 14 July 306
251. To Rufus Wilmot Griswold, 24 September . . . 309
252. From Pascual de Gayangos, 22 October 309
253. From Abbott Lawrence, 12 December 310

1852
254. To Jared Sparks, 19 February 311
255. From Lady Mary E. Lyell, 1 July 312
256. To Pascual de Gayangos, 11 July 313
257. From Henry Hart Milman, 31 July 315
258. From William Stirling, 8 November 316
259. To Richard Bentley, 26 November 317
260. Memorandum Concerning Expenses, [c. 31 December] . 318

1853
261. To Lady Mary E. Lyell, 1 March 319
262. From Colonel Thomas Aspinwall, 11 March . . . 321
263. To Lady Mary E. Lyell, 28 March 322
264. From R. Augustus Wight, 11 April 323
265. To Mary Elizabeth Wormeley, 1 August 324
266. To Lady Mary E. Lyell, 13 September 324
267. From Fanny Calderón de la Barca, 3 November . . 326
268. To Lady Mary E. Lyell, 25 December 328
269. From Harper & Brothers, 28 December 331
270. Memorandum Concerning Income, [c. 31 December] . 331
271. Memorandum Concerning Expenses, [c. 31 December] . 333

1854
272. To Lady Mary E. Lyell, 26 February 334
273. To Alexander Burton, 26 February 336
274. To Richard Bentley, 15 May 337
275. To Fanny Calderón de la Barca, 17 July 338
276. From Harper & Brothers, 29 July 340

277. To Harper & Brothers, 7 August 341
278. From Richard Bentley, 11 August 341
279. To George Bancroft, 23 August 342
280. To Lady Mary E. Lyell, 4 November 344
281. To George Stillman Hillard, 15 November [?] . . . 346
282. To S. Austin Allibone *et al.*, 28 November . . . 347

1855
283. From Anna Ticknor, 1 January 348
284. To S. Austin Allibone, 20 March 348
285. To Joaquín García Icazbalceta, 26 April 349
286. Memorandum Concerning Landscaping, 4 September . 350
287. To Harper & Brothers, September [?] 351
288. From Russell Sturgis, 17 October 351
289. Memoranda Concerning Allowances for Sons,
   2 November 352
290. From Richard Ford, 29 November 354

1856
291. Memorandum Concerning Publishing Contract,
   14 January 355
292. From Clements Robert Markham, 5 March . . . 356
293. To Charles Sumner, 13 March 357
294. From Lucilla Stanley Lincolne, 25 March . . . 357
295. To Charles Folsom, [c. 9 April] 358
296. To Lady Mary E. Lyell, 9 June 359
297. To Lord Wensleydale, 13 June 362
298. To Richard Bentley, 4 August 363
299. To Josephine Augusta Prescott, 15 October . . . 364
300. From George Routledge, 31 October 366
301. To Richard Chenevix Trench, 3 November . . . 367
302. To Edward Everett, 18 November 368
303. To George Routledge, 19 December 368
304. To William Gardiner Prescott, 29 December . . . 369

1857
305. To Lady Mary E. Lyell, 9 February 372
306. To Josephine Augusta Prescott, 17 February . . . 375
307. To Robert Anderson Wilson, 8 April 377
308. To Lyman C. Draper, 28 May 378
309. To George E. Ellis, 1 June 379
310. To Moses Dresser Phillips, 21 August 382
311. To John Lothrop Motley, 8 September 383

312. Memorandum Concerning Publishing Contract,
    11 December 384
313. From Moses Dresser Phillips, 30 December . . . 384

        1858
314. To William Gardiner Prescott, 31 January . . . 385
315. From George Bancroft, 18 February 387
316. From R. H. Major, 20 February 388
317. To Charles Summer, 26 February 388
318. To George Bancroft, 17 April 389
319. To Charles Folsom, 22 April 389
320. To William Gardiner Prescott, 26 April 390
321. From Moses Dresser Phillips, 12 June 391
322. To Charles Folsom, 30 June 392
323. To George Routledge, 20 September 393
324. To William Howard Gardiner, 30 October . . . 394
325. From Richard Bentley, 9 November 395
326. To Oliver Wendell Holmes, 28 December . . . 395
327. From Lady Mary E. Lyell, 30 December 396

        1859
328. To George Routledge, 11 January 397
329. To William Amory Prescott, 22 January 398
330. To Sir Charles Lyell, 23 January 399
331. To William Amory Prescott, 25 January 401

    APPENDIX
332. Last Will and Testament of William H. Prescott . . 402

    INDEX 429

The Papers of
WILLIAM
HICKLING
PRESCOTT

THE PAPERS OF

William Hickling Prescott

══

1. ### To Catherine Elizabeth Prescott[1]
    (WHP Papers, Mass. Hist. Soc.)

[Salem,] May 10th 1808

My Dear Sister:

As you have been in Boston some time, & as I am desirous of receiving a letter from you, I now take up my pen to write a few lines to you, in hopes, that you will return me a speedy answer. I understand by your letter, and those of Cousin Clifford, that Dr. Randall has extracted a few of your *grinders,* which I am very glad to hear; I also congratulate you, that you conducted yourself so much like a *heroine,* whilst under the painful but useful operation of the Doctor's instruments. I very well remember, how I behaved when Dr. Treadwell, two or three years ago, took a couple of tusks out of my jar; I now think, that I shall be perfectly willing, when necessity requires it, to have a handful of my teeth nipped out by *Dr. Randall,* but by *no one* else. Yesterday, my Father, Mr. Knapp, Capt. Peabody, Augustus,[2] and myself went up to the Circus, where I was both delighted and astonished, by the dangerous and extraordinary feats of horsemanship which the members of the Circus performed. But time will not allow me to scribble any more, therefore I must conclude with desiring you to remember me kindly to all our friends—and believe me your affectionate brother[3]

WM. H. PRESCOTT

1. Catherine Elizabeth Prescott (1799–1864), WHP's only sister to attain adulthood, was Lizzy to her friends. She married lawyer Franklin Dexter of Boston in 1819 and bore him four sons. There was always an exceptional bond of affection between her and WHP.

2. Jacob Newman Knapp, known as "Master Knapp," was one of WHP's teachers in Salem, Massachusetts. Subsequently, in Boston, Knapp conducted a school which WHP's brother attended.

Captain Joseph Peabody, a Salem shipping magnate, was a close friend of the Prescott family.

Joseph Augustus Peabody (1786–1828), son of Captain Joseph Peabody and father of Josephine Augusta Peabody, WHP's future daughter-in-law, was a boyhood friend of WHP.

3. In September, 1808, the Prescotts moved from Salem to Boston. Apparently this is the oldest extant letter by WHP.

2.   To William Prescott[1]

(WHP Papers, Mass. Hist. Soc.; and extracts in George Ticknor, *Life of William Hickling Prescott* [Boston, 1864], pp. 14–15, and in Harry Thurston Peck, *William Hickling Prescott* [New York and London, 1905], p. 26)

                                                    Boston, August 23, [1811]

Dear Father

I now write you a few lines to inform you of my fate. Yesterday at 8 o'clock I was ordered at the President's, & there together with a Carolinian Middleton[2] was examined for Sophomore. When we were first ushered into their presence; they looked like so many judges of the Inquisition; & were ordered down into the parlour most frightened out of our wits, to be examined by each seperately; but we soon found them quite a pleasant sort of chaps. The President sent us down a good dish of pairs, & treated us very much like gentlemen.[3] It was not ended in the morning, but we returned in the afternoon, when Proffessor Ware examined us in Grotius on Religion.[4] We found him very goodnatured, for I happened to ask him a question in Theology, which made him laugh so, that he was obliged to cover his face with his hands. At 1/2 past 3, our fate was decided, & we were declared Sophomores of Harvard University. As you would like to know how I appeared, I will give you my conversation verbatim with Mr. Frisbie,[5] when I went to see him after the examination. I asked him, Did I appear well in my examination, Sir? Ans. Yes. Question—Did you think that I appeared very well, Sir? Ans. Why are you so particular young man? Yes you did yrself a great deal of credit. I feel to-day 20 pound lighter than I did yesterday. I shall dine at Mr. Gardiner's to-day. Mr. & Mrs. Gardiner both say that on me depends Wm's going to college or not;[6] if I behave well he will go. If not that he certainly shall not go. P. Mason[7] has asked me to dine with him on Commencement day as he gives a dinner. I believe I shall go. As I have but little time & thought it best to tell a long story & write it badly, than a short one written well. I have been to see Mr. Hale[8] this morning—no news. Remember me to yr fellow-travelers, C. & M. &c., &c. Love to mother, whose affectionate son I remain

                                            WM. HICKLING PRESCOTT

P.S. Edward is in fine health,[9] & they say a real pleasure & no trouble at all to them at Aunt Callahan. I met Andrew Thorndike in town to-day—looked in excellent health. Yr affectionate son[10]

                                                WM. H. PRESCOTT

1. William Prescott (1762–1844), son of Colonel William Prescott of Bunker Hill fame, father of WHP and one of the ablest American lawyers of his generation.

2. Arthur Middleton (1795–1853), a Harvard classmate of WHP, served as secretary and chargé of the U.S. legation in Madrid for eight years, during which time he aided WHP's scholarly projects.

3. John Thornton Kirkland (1770–1840), a Unitarian clergyman, served as president of Harvard between 1810 and 1828.

4. Henry Ware (d. 1845) was Hollis Professor of Divinity at Harvard for forty years. In the Latin, this work was *Grotius de Veritate*.

5. Levi Frisbie (d. 1822).

6. John S. J. Gardiner (1765–1830), educator and Episcopal clergyman (Trinity Church, Boston), instilled in WHP his love of classical learning.

William Howard Gardiner (1797–1882), son of John S. J. Gardiner and lifetime friend and confidant of WHP, graduated from Harvard in 1816. He and WHP named their firstborn sons for each other.

7. William Powell Mason (1791–1867), who distinguished himself as lawyer and reporter of the U.S. Circuit Court.

8. Probably Nathan Hale (1784–1863), the journalist and lawyer who later owned and edited the *Boston Daily Advertiser* and helped to found the *North American Review*.

9. Edward Goldsborough Prescott (1804–44), the only brother of WHP to attain adulthood. He successively was lawyer, soldier, orator, politician, editor, businessman and clergyman. For many years he was Ned to family and friends.

10. This is the last letter so completely the product of WHP's own labors that it is presented as written, with its abbreviations, errors of spelling, etc.

Despite an injury to his left eye during his junior year, WHP graduated in 1814. For months he studied law, but in January, 1815, his sight deteriorated, interrupted his studies and forced him into a darkened bedroom. His slow recovery, plus the desire to avoid the rigors of the New England winter and to consult eye specialists, led to his voyage to Europe, via the Azores.

3.   To William and Catherine Prescott[1]
                   (WHP Papers, Mass. Hist. Soc.)

                              St. Michael's [Azores] 15 March 1816

I cannot but regret, my beloved parents, that the opportunities of writing have not been more frequent; for, although it would be cruel to inform you of distresses, while actually existing, which it was not in your power to alleviate, yet it is so soothing to the mind to communicate its griefs, that I doubt I could refrain from it.

The windows at Rosto de Cão are constructed on much the same principle with our barn doors. This uncharitable quantity of light, and a slight cold, increased the inflammation with which I landed to such a degree that, as I could not soften the light by means of blinds, which are unknown here, I was obliged to exclude it altogether by closing the

shutters. The same cause retarded my recovery for, as the sun introduced himself *sans ceremonie* whenever I attempted to admit the light,
I was obliged to remain in darkness until we moved into the city, where
I was accommodated with a room which had a northern aspect, and, by
means of different thicknesses of baize nailed to the windows, I was
again restored to the cheering beams of heaven. This confinement
lasted from the 1st November till the 1st February and during six weeks
of it I was in such total darkness it was impossible to distinguish objects
in the room. Much of this time has been beguiled of its tediousness by
the attention of Amelia and Harriet,[2] particularly the latter, who is a
charming creature and whom I regard as a second sister.

I have had an abundance of good prescriptions. Grandfather[3] has
strongly urged old Madeira as a universal nostrum; and my good Uncle
the doctor no less strenuously recommended beef-steaks. I took their
advice for it cost me nothing; but, as following it cost me rather too
dear, I adhered with Chinese obstinacy to bread and milk, hasty pudding, and gruel. This diet and the application of blisters was the only
method I adopted to preserve my eye from inflammation.

I have not often, my dear parents, experienced depression of spirits,
and there have been but few days in which I could not solace my sorrows with a song. I preserved my health by walking on the piazza with
a handkerchief tied over a pair of goggles, which were presented me by
a gentleman here, and by walking some hundred of miles in my room,
so that I emerged from my dungeon, not in the emaciated figure of a
prisoner, but in the florid bloom of a *bon vivant*. Indeed every thing
has been done which could promote my health and happiness; but
darkness has few charms for those in health, and a long confinement
must exhaust the patience of all but those who are immediately interested in us. A person situated as I have been can be really happy no-
where but at home, for where but at home can he experience the affectionate solicitude of parents. But the gloom is now dissipated, and my
eyes have nearly recovered their former vigour. I am under no apprehension of a relapse, as I soon shall be wafted to a land where the windows are of Christian dimensions, and the medical advice such as may
be relied upon.

The most unpleasant of my reflections suggested by this late inflammation are those which arise from the probable necessity of abandoning
a profession congenial with my taste, and recommended by such favourable opportunities, and adopt one for which I am ill qualified and have
but little inclination. It is some consolation, however, that this latter
alternative, should my eyes permit, will afford me more leisure for the
pursuit of my favourite studies. But on this subject and every other

relative to my eye, I shall consult my physician and will write you his opinion. My mind has not been wholly stagnant during my residence here. By means of the bright eyes of Harriet, I have read part of Scott, Shakespeare, travels through England and Scotland, the *Iliad, Odyssey* and what is of more importance than all the rest, I have been three times through a good part of Dufief,[4] by which I have learnt most of the phrases and technical colloquial terms and can converse with the Portuguese who are acquainted with the language, without the least difficulty, although when I arrived, I found it impossible. Amelia has read some of the Grecian and Roman histories, and I have cheated many a moment of its tedium by composition which was soon banished from my mind for want of an amanuensis.

I am now fortified with a very redoubtable one, James Collis, Esq. who arrived here 9th January from London as my grandfather's clerk. And as there is little business this year, lest his fingers should become torpid for want of exercise, I have taken compassion on them and installed him as my private and confidential secretary. But since contrary to all laws of criticism, I have consumed the greatest part of my letter in talking of my own sweet self, I will change so poor a subject for one much nearer my heart. The petition I shall lay before you, though only the second time of writing, will, I hope, be granted without opposition.

Last year, my dear parents, Elizabeth requested that you would have your portraits taken. I was not then aware how important this might be to our future happiness, for it is absence only that evinces how dear are our friends to us. Let me beseech you not to refuse our united request. God forbid that I should ever behold the time when the colours of the painter shall be the only remains of parents so beloved. But should this period ever happen to any of your children, what a solace would they derive from this. I recollect, my dear mother, saying something *en badinage* of your profile which I have since often regretted. If you have any affection for us, therefore, do not deny a favour which can be of so little consequence for you to bestow, and may be of so much importance for us to receive.

Mrs. Treadwell and suite[5] arrived here 10th December and if the climate was as efficacious for repairing the brains as it is for mending the constitution, she would have every reason in the world to be satisfied, for her son's health is perfectly reestablished. They now occupy the house at Rosto de Cão. I received by them letters from my good friends, a file of newspapers, and two files of domestic gazettes. This fireside intelligence is particularly interesting; it transports me into the bosom of my family and revives every good feeling of the soul. It is impossible to be too minute. I was much depressed by the death of my two friends. Randolph's I had anticipated.[6] His fate, poor fellow, was peculiarly severe. His dying eyes were closed by foreign hands and the last melancholy offices performed by those who could feel no particular attachment to him. I hope to shed a few tears over his grave, for his virtues are fresh in my memory. A mutual love of classical literature often associated us in our studies, and I had hoped to have seen him attain a distinguished rank in the senate of his country. Pickman's death inexpressively shocked me.[7] When I parted from him, I little thought it was for the last time. I lived with him for two years in all the freedom of social intercourse, and the sprightliness of his wit has enlivened many an hour. But these joys will return no more.

I was much concerned that the complaint of our excellent friend Mr. Thacher had returned,[8] and no less rejoiced to learn by your subsequent dispatches (Captain Davison) that he was convalescing. I lately received a letter from Petty Vaughan, Esq., advising me of the most favourable season to visit England. This unexpected act of kindness prognosticates much benefit from his acquaintance.

I intend to have the family arms engraven in London. I wish you would send me a fac-simile of them, which may be easily obtained from Dr. Prescott,[9] for I am acquainted only with the crest and, as people of the same name often have the same crest but different bearings, I might confound my genealogical tree with some others, which would be a great pity, as I should wish to ascertain if "our blood"
      "Has crept through scoundrels ever since the flood"[10]
or if it has not flowed through some more illustrious channels. There is something extremely ominous in the crest which, you know, is the bird of night.

While in confinement, my dear parents, I made myself acquainted with the administration of these islands and since my emancipation, I have endeavoured to initiate myself into their habits and customs. Whatever opinion I had formed of the Portuguese, I could have no idea of the debasement which our capacities may suffer when crampt by an arbitrary government and Papal superstition. Indeed I believe there is an original inferiority in the nature of the Portuguese and if it were possible to dissect the soul, I suspect in three-fourths of the nation the anatomy would be composed solely of knavery and stupidity, with an equal chance which of these two ingredients should predominate.

It is impossible in the closet to form an adequate conception of the mummeries of the Romish Church. The religious rites are no doubt performed with much greater splendour in Italy, but I doubt they are accompanied with more bigoted zeal and veneration in any quarter of the globe, for the pomp of majesty is never so imposing as when viewed at a distance.

The governor presides over the military department only. The executive consists of three senates of four members each residing in distinct provinces of the island and regulating their internal economy. The judiciary consists of three magistrates, each presiding over separate provinces, and accountable to a supreme judge or corregidor. Before a criminal can be punished, he must be convicted at this court, sentenced at Terceira, and confirmed at Lisbon, thus justice flows through so circuitous a channel that when obtained, it is with the utmost difficulty and procrastination. Monopolies, as in all despotic countries, are very numerous and many expensive articles of commerce declared contraband, while their manufacture is confined to a few individuals to the prejudice of the community. In these islands there is a petty species of nobility founded solely on landed property. The members are termed *morgados,* which signifies literally an inheritor of an entailed estate. As these entailments are very frequent, they form a sort of monopoly of landed interest, whose pernicious consequences in so small a place as this are obvious on the least reflection.

Provisions are so dear and labour so extremely cheap that the wretched condition of the poor can scarcely be exceeded. They live in the same room with their cattle and have no windows and most of them no chimneys to their houses. They subsist principally on corn bread and vegetables and their clothing is so scanty that at every mile you meet a hundred little *sans culottes* without even a shirt to their backs. Another cause of this extreme poverty is the great number of *jours de fête* in these Catholic countries, where there are almost as many saints as sinners, and where the Saints' days are held in such veneration that, although you may play, it is sacrilege to work. There are no less than 50 festivals independent of Sundays in which there is a total stagnation of industry.

In the common acts and conveniences of life, they are centuries behind us; but they certainly must have made great progress in cleanliness since my dear mother was here. It is true, I know some families who, when the sheets are changed, sew the clothes to the bed to save the trouble of making it anew, but this is uncommon for they generally perform this operation every morning. The Scotch fiddle[11] is now quite out of repute among people of fashion, and as to fleas, I have not been troubled with more than seven or eight at the same time.

The natural fecundity of the soil remedies, in some measure, the indolence of the husbandmen. Indeed it must be confessed that almost all the arable land is cultivated, and such is its fertility that they frequently obtain two crops in a year. Perhaps these advantages of soil and climate are unfavourable to much energy of character, as the uncommon activity of nature renders this virtue almost superfluous in the inhabitants. However this may be, there are certain characteristics which mark the Portuguese nation, and which have mixed with their blood from time immemorial.

Jealousy, pride and ignorance seem to be virtues inseparable from their constitutions. In the intercourse of social life they have much ceremony and little comfort, and the only passions which engross their attentions are the love of woman and the love of money.

From a people in whom I find so little to respect, I can part without much reluctance; but I feel that I shall experience all the pangs of a second departure from home when I leave the family in whose bosom I have been cherished with the warmest kindness. In my grandfather I have found the affection of a parent, and in my charming Harriet that of another sister. When my dear mother and Lizzy write to her, I am sure they will do it in the strongest terms of gratitude and affection. For these two I feel a particular regard but indeed my kind grandmother and my uncles and aunts, without exception, have concurred in expressing the same solicitude for me which they have for one another. As thanks are the only poor return you can make, I am sure you will bestow them liberally upon every individual of this excellent family, since I have been inexpressively [sic] to all. Should it be possible, I shall certainly visit them on my return to America, since my *heart* is bound to them with the strongest ties of gratitude and affection. Before I conclude I will give you a bulletin of my present health.

When in Brookline,[12] I had by no means recovered the same vigour of constitution and the same quantum of flesh which I enjoyed before my illness. On my voyage I parted with a few more pounds of mortality, but since my liberation from confinement, I have been strong enough to ride more than 30 miles in a day on jackback without experiencing the least fatigue, am in such good care that my coat actually refuses to button, a phenomenon which happened formerly only after dinner. I ascertained my weight the other day, which was exactly *154* pounds, but some allowance must be made as this operation was performed after dinner and with my Havannah chapeau on my head, for whose brim you may very safely deduct a couple of pounds, at least.

As to spirits, the thermometer has been so high that were I not to decamp very soon, I should feel some apprehension of being confined as *non compos*. My eye is somewhat debilitated by the late inflammation and has not the same degree of strength as when I left America.

It is doing very well, however, and could I be insured against colds, I might laugh at fortune. As you mention nothing of grandmother, I presume she is as comfortable as when I left her.[13] Pray be more particular in this respect for the future.

I wish, my dear parents, you would be more circumstantial in regard to your own health. As you are both valetudinarians, you cannot be equally well at all times; and general assurances of good health amount to nothing.

Give my warmest affections to dear Aunt A's family—how often do I think of them, to Aunt Callahan's and to all my other good friends. The want of time has prevented my answering all their kind letters. Tell them I shall not fail to do it the next opportunity, when I shall also fulfill my engagements with Gray and Lyman.[14]

You must address your next letters to the "tight little isle," where I hope to arrive by the latter part of April. Remember me to every individual of our family. I look forward with pleasure to the day when I shall put their blood once more in motion. And now, my beloved parents, without the usual apologies of candles in their sockets, midnight hour, dinner bell or any other epistolary excuse, I shall conclude this *olla podrida* of nonsense in which I have consumed as much paper as will suffice a very recent batch of family pies and which, while you are eating them, if you have no better amusement, may remind you of your sincerely affectionate son

WILLIAM

P.S.—April 4.

Since the above was written, I fortunately received the letters, trunk, and crackers which were sent by Captain Winter. I am extremely obliged to Dr. Jackson, and more than I can express to Mr. Perkins for their kind attentions.[15] As I cannot find my goggles anywhere, I presume they have wound upon their laces before me. I have been disappointed of my expectation of sending you these letters and shall probably take them with me to England, for which I have already procured a passage on board the brig "Charles," Captain Connell, under the auspices of Mrs. Treadwell. Would that it were my dear Harriet, but since the match of Barnes has been dissolved, it has been thought inexpedient for her to visit England. Barnes is a dashing young fellow of very good family, and with person and manners so engaging that he was permitted to pay his address to Harriet until his pretensions should be examined. Upon investigation, however, it was found that early extravagancies had so deeply involved him that he has been very wisely discarded.

Mrs. Treadwell would have gone a month sooner but I prevailed upon her to procrastinate her voyage. We shall embark, however, on Monday the 8th April. Once more, adieu, my beloved parents. I cannot bear to dwell on separation so painful to my soul.

P.P.S.—London, June 9, 1816

As I mentioned goggles, I must inform you I wear no such paraphernalia in England. My physician prefers glasses with silk, as I formerly wore them in America, and he intends I shall soon even discard the silk appendage, that I may obtain a freer circulation of air.

1. Catherine Greene Hickling Prescott (1767–1852), daughter of merchant-consul Thomas Hickling, wife of lawyer William Prescott and mother of WHP, enriched several charitable institutions of Boston by her services.

2. Amelia and Harriet Hickling, young aunts of WHP, were daughters of Thomas Hickling by his second wife. Harriet later married John White Webster of the Harvard faculty.

3. Thomas Hickling, maternal grandfather of WHP, combined the roles of merchant and U.S. consul for several decades in the Azores.

4. Nicolas Gouïn Dufief (1776?–1834) published works on language study which were adapted especially to French and Spanish.

5. Of Boston.

6. Theodorick Tudor Randolph (d. 1815).

7. Haskett Derby Pickman (d. 1815).

8. Samuel Cooper Thacher (1785–1818), Unitarian clergyman, had succeeded John T. Kirkland (q.v.) in the pulpit of the New South Church, Boston, at which the Prescotts worshiped.

9. Dr. Oliver Prescott (d. 1827).

10. Alexander Pope, *Essay on Man,* Epis. iv, l. 209.

11. The itch.

12. In this suburb of Boston WHP had convalesced during mid-1815.

13. Widowed Mrs. William Prescott (d. 1821), then eighty-three years old, continued to live near Pepperell, close upon the Massachusetts–New Hampshire line.

14. Theodore Lyman (d. 1849) and either Francis Calley Gray (1790–1856) or his brother John Chipman Gray (1793–1881). The Grays were sons of a Salem shipowner and lifelong friends of WHP. Francis, or Frank to his friends, was lawyer, traveler, scholar and philanthropist. John Chipman became WHP's traveling companion in France and Italy in 1816–17.

15. Dr. James Jackson (1777–1867), a leading physician of Boston for decades, served as family doctor for the Prescotts for a half-century. His published writings detailed WHP's case of impaired vision.

4.   From William Prescott
                  (Extracts, WHP Papers, Mass. Hist. Soc.)

                                              Boston, June 10th 1816

My dear William

. . . .

You will now have an opportunity of writing to us every fortnight and I beg you to keep us regularly advised of the state of your health, your present occupations and amusements, and your views and intentions for the future, and whether your health, particularly your eye, continues so much impaired and so tender as to render it necessary to pass the next winter in a milder climate than this.

. . . .

Don't *trust yourself to quacks* nor suffer *anything* to *be done which shall endanger the sight you now have* from the maimed eye.

. . . .

If your eyes will permit, we shall wish you to give us an account of the men and things you see, and the occurrences which happen, that you think will be interesting to us. Recollect that we are confined to our chimney corners and that we expect you to explore and observe for our benefit and amusement as well as your own.

. . . .

Endeavour to inform yourself while there of every thing worth knowing or which you will be likely afterwards to wish you had learnt. Leave no room for vain regrets.

. . . .

Some of the principal objects which will attract and probably engage most of your attention and consideration are the two Houses of Parliament, the judicial courts, the literary institutions and the manufactures.

. . . .

It will be very useful to you to obtain some information respecting their great manufactories. They are the first that are or ever were in the world. You can't leave England without visiting some of them. In the 24th Number of the *Quarterly Review* for January 1815 there is a review of a work by Colquhoun on the wealth, power and resources of the British Empire.[1] This Review is well worth your reading before you leave England.

I hope you will be able to pick up the books I gave you a list of cheap. You must take a little pains for it for they are all old editions and probably out of print.

. . . .

Genl. Brooks is governor[2] and both branches of the legislature are Federal. The probability is that nothing decisive will be done respecting the separation of Maine until the wish of the District is better ascertained.

. . . .

For the next four years both our Senators in congress will be federal.[3]

. . . .

Altho I have made you an allowance, I am sure you will be as economical as possible, remembering that your means and mine are very limited and that what you spend now will so far diminish the little assistance I shall be able to afford you on your return.

. . . .

Your affectionate father
WM. PRESCOTT

[P.S.] Be on your guard against sharpers—American friends who may want your money.[4]

1. P. Colquhoun's *A Treatise on the Wealth, Power, and Resources of the British Empire.* . . . (London, 1814) was reviewed therein, pp. 393–433.

2. John Brooks (1752–1825), soldier, physician and politician, had defeated General Henry Dearborn for the governorship of Massachusetts. His administrations (1816–22) were the "Indian Summer of Federalism" in that state.

3. In June, 1816, Massachusetts' senators were Joseph B. Varnum and Eli Porter Ashmun.

4. Many aspects of the discipline which gradually came into WHP's life derived from his father's example and counsel.

5. To William and Catherine Prescott
(WHP Papers, Mass. Hist. Soc.)

London, 21st July, 1816.

My dear Parents,

As Captain Tracey, I understand, sails tomorrow, I cannot let the opportunity escape without writing you, but my principal dispatches will proceed in the "Minerva," (Magee), in the course of this week. I was grieved to learn from your letter by the "Milo" that you had experienced so much anxiety on account of my silence. I hope, however, you will consider this a sufficient explanation of it. During the first week after my arrival, as my eyes were not in very good trim, I was unwilling to write till I could give you the opinion of some oculist. The remainder of the month I was under the care of Cooper and Farre,[1] neither of whose opinions were at all satisfactory to me. Besides I heard of no opportunity for Boston, and was in daily expectation of the departure of my friend Ray and of Mrs. Perkins. These circumstances were the cause of my procrastination; pray do not suspect me of neglect or forgetfulness, most of the letters were already written. I still continue under the care of Sir William Adams[2] and pursue the same regime as before, except that he thinks blisters do not benefit me, and that when my eye is the least inflamed, the most efficacious and instantaneous remedy is cold water. My eyes have certainly acquired considerable strength. As an evidence of this, I could not bear candle light when I arrived here, and although I never expose myself to the theatres, operas, or evening parties of any kind, yet at a late dinner I have two or three times found myself in the society of ten or a dozen candles, without experiencing the least inconvenience. This is an experiment, however, I dislike, and I always retreat as soon as possible. Sir William Adams is certainly very clever. We may always suspect men of quackery who rise suddenly into reputation, but I am convinced he may be relied upon. As his applications may be made as easily when travelling as when resident, and as I wish to eradicate the rheumatism by migrating to a warm country before it is late in the autumn, I shall go over to Paris the first of next month, where I have made all the necessary arrangements with my friend Gray for an excursion to Italy. My physician has given up the idea of sea-bathing, and thinks that with prudence I shall do very well. He, however, intends to fortify me with written directions, and as I shall revisit England before I return to America, I shall then receive my final instructions. We shall pursue our tour with as much rapidity as is consistent with health and improvement. I need not assure my beloved parents that my heart bounds forward with rapture to the moment that shall restore me once more to my native home. As to the future, it is too evident I shall never be able to pursue a profession. God knows how poorly I am qualified and how little inclined to be a merchant, indeed I am somewhat puzzled to think how I shall succeed in this without eyes; and I am sadly afraid I shall never be able to draw up my mind to any large amount. Since I have been in London I flatter myself I have seen most of those things, both in the town and its environs, which would compensate the curiosity of a stranger. I have lately returned from an excursion to Windsor, Hampton Court, Pope's residence, Twickenham, Sir William Herschell and his telescope, for an account of which lions I shall refer you to my dispatches in the "Minerva." Pray send me no more letters by private conveyance. Those entrusted to Brookes have not yet arrived, and as Miss Hinckley has gone down to Derbyshire, her proteges will no doubt make the tour of the spar mines of Derbyshire before I see one of them. The only sure conveyance is the letter-bag of the vessel. Kiss dear Lizzy, Ned and Will[3] for me. I shall write her by the "Minerva." I wish you would give her a good lecture, for the short letters she writes me. They are absolutely nothing but postscripts. Since I have wooed the French muse on her account, however, I hope she will shake off her diffidence. Remember me most affectionately to grandmother, dear Aunt A's petite coterie, Aunt Callahan's, and particularly to Caroline Preble,[4] my regards to Mrs. S. Perkins. I owe her many obligations for her kindness, and feel a warm friendship for her. Pray remember me to our good household, and to all my worthy friends, masculine and feminine. Whenever I make a rural excursion, it reminds me of Brookline and I wish with a sigh that you were present to enjoy it. I believe Sir William Adams thinks me half a woman for I told him the other day (I don't know what conversation led to it) I should never think of travelling again without my parents, or at least a wife and half a dozen children to accompany me. Sir William has, of course, been very polite, and invited me to My Lady's concertos, and eight o'clock dinner parties, which I no less politely declined. Adieu my much loved parents, believe me ever   Your very affectionate

WILLIAM

P.S. I have given Mr. Butterworth directions to purchase many of the books you ordered. The prices are reasonable. Those might be expected more than the ancient cost, as the year books cannot be had under £12. I shall not decide until I hear from you. As you probably are not in immediate want of them, I shall bring them home when I return. I sent last week half a dozen letters to St. Michael. Pray when you write, urge Harriet to spend a year or two with us. There can be no reasonable obstacle, and you will find her a charming companion.

Hoc scripsit my good clerk McCandlish.[5]

1. Sir Astley Paston Cooper (1768–1841), surgeon, was then Professor of Comparative Anatomy at the Royal College of Surgeons.

Dr. John Richard Farre (1775–1862) was a founder and physician of the Royal London Ophthalmic Hospital.

2. Sir William Adams (afterwards Rawson), oculist extraordinary to His Royal Highness, was credited with successful new and improved modes of curing various species of cataract and the Egyptian ophthalmia.

3. William Hickling, a son of Thomas Hickling and a youthful uncle of WHP, was Ned Prescott's schoolmate in Boston at this time.

4. Caroline Preble, daughter of Ebenezer Preble of Watertown, Massachusetts, was one of WHP's youthful sweethearts. She later married a British naval officer and bore him three literary-minded daughters.

5. On August 3, WHP entered France at Calais and on October 7, accompanied by John Chipman Gray, he departed from Paris. En route to Italy they visited Lafayette at La Grange.

6.   From Catherine Prescott
(Extracts, WHP Papers, Mass. Hist. Soc.)

No. 26   Boston, November 29, 1816
An arrival from Havre to New York has brought us yours, my beloved son, of the 5th of October, which gave us great pleasure.

.   .   .   .

As to the Leghorns, we all depend upon some nice ones. I should like you should get 6 white, and 6 black leghorn hats with crowns, as good as can be procured. You mentioned marble and alabaster being very reasonable. We should like some neat chimney ornaments, if you can get them without giving a great price, and they can be packed so as to come without injury. As you are in the midst of those things, you can judge best what would be most useful, as money is not the most plenty [sic] article with us, we should like what is most worth the cash. Nice kid gloves, and a piece of linen cambrick it would be well to get in France. You will no doubt stock yourself well with pocket handkerchiefs, and silk stockings, as they are cheaper there than here.[1]

.   .   .   .

1. These were neither the first nor the last such instructions received by the traveler.

7.   From William Prescott
(Extract, WHP Papers, Mass. Hist. Soc.)

Boston, 4 January 1816 [1817]
Our last letters from you, my dear William, were under date of 6th of October. You will probably have visited and perhaps taken leave of the fallen but once proud mistress of the world before this finds you. Tho' fallen, dilapidated and plundered, she yet contains much to gratify the curiosity and reward the industry and diligence of its literary visitors. If your health has permitted, I doubt not this will have been a busy winter. I hope you have been able in this short time to lay in a stock upon which you will be able in future to draw for the benefit and pleasure of yourself and your friends. I recommend to you

during your travels to avail yourself of every proper opportunity of conversing with respectable natives of the countries you visit. It will perfect your knowledge of their languages, and give you a better knowledge of the country, its institutions, laws, customs and manners than you can get from foreigners. Remember that one hour is more precious while you are on this tour than two will be at home.

.   .   .   .

8.   To William and Catherine Prescott
                    (WHP Papers, Mass. Hist. Soc.)

Rome, January 12th 1817.

Tomorrow, my beloved parents, we have fixed our departure from the *septicollis urbs*. I quit Rome with regret[1]—but it is for the classical scenery of Naples. It will ever be dear to my recollection for the gratification it has afforded me, and your letters have not a little contributed to these pleasant moments. I have just received the Nos. 21, 22[2] which, thank God, met with no obstacle, as they were entrusted to no private opportunity. It was with pleasure I again traced the well-known characters of my dear father. Be assured I sincerely sympathize with your afflictions. It is but little consolation that they contribute to health; it is purchasing it with too great an expense of comfort. You mention my expenses—I have adverted to them in a preceding part of the letters. Those of physicians and medicines amount to about one hundred pounds—it is heavy but if they were to be consulted, could not be avoided. I have now made half of my continental tour. My clothes and every other article included I have somewhat exceeded my allowance. The remaining half will add to them but the rigid economy which I shall practice during five or six weeks residence in Paris will enable me to liquidate the overplus. During my former residence there, from my ignorance of the city, and of the expense of such a town, I did not economize with the same rigour I shall upon my return. I have incurred no superfluous charge, but the gowns in Paris, and the prints at Florence.[3] I hope you will condemn neither. From the former I could not refrain. The latter, as good specimens of the best engraver in the world, were cheap, and will command more than their original price. I feel that I need no inducement to convince me of the propriety and necessity of economy. We may reach Paris by the latter part of March. I should not like to venture across the channel before May. The English climate has too much asperity. June and July will be consumed in the tour. These are bad months for returning—they are unfavourable to

short voyages, abound in calms and bright suns—and I am convinced
would be exceedingly pernicious to me. Mr. Hinckley expects the
"Triton" and the "Milo" in the autumn. I should be fortunate to embark in either of them—perhaps it may be in the society of Mr. Hinckley and his fair daughter. My dear mother expresses a wish to know the
nature of the Vatican. I have given some account of it in my letter to
Elizabeth, but as it may be illegible, will repeat it. The Vatican is a
palace of the pope—his winter residence. It is built, like most of the
Roman houses, of brick, covered with plaster, and distributed into
large hollow squares adorned with piazzas. It stands near the church
and connects with the colonnade of St. Peter's—but as the structure is
irregular, and is somewhat concealed by the immense portico of St.
Peter's, it has nothing imposing in its external appearance. It has un-
dergone many modifications from the different popes, and from its
situation and the beautiful view it commands is also called the Belvedere—whence the denomination of the statues it contains—Apollo de
Belvedere, Torre de Belvedere &c. Part of the interior is devoted to the
apartments of the pope, and is consequently not visible. We have been
offered, by the bye, a presentation at the levee of His Holiness[4]—but
as it would require an appropriate dress, cut in such a manner as would
render it useless for any other purpose, we thought it not worth the
expense. The rest of the interior is devoted to a library containing
many ancient manuscripts, long galleries and spacious saloons filled
with valuable relics of antiquity, superb statues, and exquisite paintings. The walls are encrusted with marble, the floors of the same material, the ceiling glowing in frescoes of the best makers, and supported
by columns of verd antique, alabaster, and oriental jasper. These are
arranged so as to produce the most surprising effect—every where the
eye resposes upon magnificence of materials and perfection of art. It is
these chefs-d'oeuvres, these columns and statues and paintings, to
which the Vatican owes its celebrity, and not to any intrinsic merit of
the building. Thank dear Lizzy for her letter; I have no small compunc-
tions for having so unjustly taxed her with silence. I was gratified with
the boys' letters—much improved in writing and composition. I hope
Edward does not make his debut next year. Two years with Dr. Gardiner would give him a more extensive acquaintance with the classics,
than he may gain at any subsequent period. Should he even continue
under Mr. Knapp, he would be qualified for a Sophomore before the
[. . .] and would be much more likely to appreciate the importance of
his time. The Freshman duties are so trifling that a boy with common
capacity, and indolent habits, will easily find opportunity for indulging
them. Boys at this tender age have not ordinarily sufficient understand-

ing to comprehend the more abstract studies—have not the ambition which would frequently be awakened at a later period—are not sufficiently matured to have a fair chance in the competition of college honours—and are easily seduced by those who are older and more mischievous than themselves. It is an error of which the English are never guilty—and I believe nine times out of ten the experiment proves fatal. The boy graduates as puerile in every thing but years as when he entered—but one lucky combination of youth, industry and genius too frequently overbalances a whole system of calculation. Once more my ever beloved parents adieu.

I was surprised to learn [of] the death of Mr. Sears.[5] C. Thorndike has been very unwell—but I am glad to find from his last letter is convalescent. Pray inform Mr. S. Perkins that I have put his seal under the special protection of Mrs. Bowdoin, and will enclose an impression of it when I return to Rome. I should have had the pleasure of writing Mrs. Perkins, but I am ashamed that hieroglyphics like these should be seen out of the family. I must expect you will find my letters replete with the grossest errors, of all descriptions. But consider, my dear father and mother, the situation of one who writes without seeing the motion of his pen. I hardly know how, where, or what I write.[6]

1. WHP had arrived in Rome on November 23, 1816.

2. Much as diplomatic correspondence, the Prescott letters were numbered so that records of their receipt, loss, etc. might be more readily kept.

3. In the course of two visits to Florence, WHP purchased fifteen engravings by Rafaelle Morghen (1758–1833).

4. Pius VII.

5. David Sears of Boston.

6. This unsigned letter was written on the wired device, the noctograph, which WHP had purchased in London.

After visiting Naples and its environs, WHP and Gray returned northward via Rome, Siena, Florence and Pisa. On March 12, 1817, they sailed from Leghorn, for Marseilles. Two weeks of hurried travel between that port and Paris put them in the French capital on March 30.

9.   From Catherine Prescott
                    (Extract, WHP Papers, Mass. Hist. Soc.)

             [from a fragmentary letter written at intervals between
                          late January and early March, 1817]

                    .   .   .   .

We are now very busy, in making repairs in the house in Pond Street,[1] whither we shall remove in the course of a month. I think, my dear

Will, you will be pleased with our situation. It is a good house, tho'
old-fashioned. You and Elizabeth are to have the two front upper chambers, which I think very pleasant. Your father will take the kitchen
chambers for his library, which will accommodate him finely. We are
having the whole house papered and painted, and every thing done to
make the house comfortable and pleasant. There is a large yard attached to it, with a brick stable, all which will be convenient. The
street is not so good as this,[2] but I have no doubt it will improve as
houses are built in it, and it is quite a central situation.[3]

.   .   .   .

1. Within a few years Pond Street was renamed Bedford. WHP lived in this
house until 1845.
2. Before the change to Pond Street, the Prescotts lived on Summer.
3. With ailing eyes, WHP wrote of his new room on May 1, 1817, "I hope it
has blinds, shutters, and curtains, that the Sun never has the audacity to enter
it, that it has a fireplace, or a stove, which is a much more sensible contrivance,
that the bed is furnished with curtains and the floor with a carpet. You will
think me whimsical, but these requests may be all resolved into bad eyes and
the rheumatism."

10.   From William Prescott
                    (Extracts, WHP Papers, Mass. Hist. Soc.)

                                        Boston, March 2d 1816 [1817]
My dear Son,

.   .   .   .

We have been now full five months without a line from you. I trust
we have some copious letters on the way. We are all expecting and
looking for them with great solicitude. The last we heard of you was
that on the 12th of November you were at Florence. This was by a
letter from your companion Mr. Gray to his father.

.   .   .   .

I hope you have been able to get some knowledge of the Italian language and of the different governments in Italy, as well as of the commerce carried on from their different ports. Your love of the classics
will have prompted you to explore and examine the ruins of Roman
grandeur. I don't understand by your letters before you left Paris how
long you intend to stay there on your return, nor whether Mr. Gray
will return with you. There is much to be learnt and more to be
avoided in that great city. It disguises vice and gives it more the sem-

blance of virtue and presses a young stranger with more alluring and seductive temptations, I believe, than any of the places you have visited in the south of Europe.

.   .   .   .

While in France it will no doubt be your endeavour to perfect your knowledge of their language and to obtain what knowledge you can of their history—of the late revolution—its causes—characters of the leading men in it and the strength and stability of the present government and also of the commerce and manufactures of this great, active and ambitious nation. I know well that a thorough knowledge of all these can't be acquired in a few months, but with an active inquisitive mind much may be learnt in a short time on the spot by observation, conversation and books. If your eyes will allow, I think even a very brief diary or memoranda book, containing only hints which would serve to remind you of what you have seen and heard, would prove useful.[1] You must remember that much will be expected of you when you return. Every one will not reflect, as I do, that the great object of your visit to Europe was the recovery of health.

.   .   .   .

I feel entire confidence, my son, that your knowledge of my circumstances and your own prospects will lead you to practise the strictest economy in every thing. It is, you may be assured, very necessary—much more so than if *you* and *I* both enjoyed good health—but I will not preach long on this *not* very entertaining subject, trusting to your practice without.

.   .   .   .

1. This suggestion was both late and unnecessary. WHP's journal for this trip covers his movements from his departure from home on September 26, 1815, to a moment in midsummer of 1817 when he was preparing to sail home from England. The entries are not in WHP's hand. Apparently McCandlish and other short-term secretaries wrote it up for him.

11.   To William Prescott
                     (WHP Papers, Mass. Hist. Soc.)

                                          [Paris, c. April 29, 1817]
Statement of expenses.[1]
   In London I was allowed £50 per month, and during the three months, May, June, and July, which I spent there, I drew for the whole

amount. When I return I shall live upon half the sum. The cause of this expenditure was the expensive apartment which Sir William Adams advised me to take upon the Regent's Park. Secondly, their immense distance from the greater part of my friends, five or six miles, and as I frequently dined or spent the evening with them, my coach hire was no small expense. Thirdly, the necessity of riding in the evening (when other people walked), to avoid the night air. This consideration, however, is not of so much importance for I usually walked six or seven miles a day. I should have been too much fatigued to have extended my promenade in the evening, had I been inclined. Fourthly, I am not ashamed to own my ignorance and inexperience, which led me into several expenses I should now avoid—one thing is due to myself, I have never been guilty of an extravagance of which I was conscious at the time. Lastly, the expense of boots, hosiery and clothes of all descriptions, which cost me no less than 60 pounds, and which I could not have afforded if I had not landed with near 40 pounds. Most of the clothes are in perfectly good order, although I have worn them constantly for a year. One article was a waterproof boxcoat, it cost 11 guineas. It will last me all my life, and I have already had eleven guineas worth of good out of it. The expenses of my physicians and medicines were heavy, but they will not recur again in London, unless I should be afflicted again with some unforeseen disease. I paid £60 to Sir William Adams, £10 to Mr. Cooper and Dr. Farre, 10 guineas to a Mr. Marshall for attending my feet. Perhaps you recollect that the ridiculous custom of wearing tight boots in college had caused excrescences on the insteps of both my feet. These were so increased and inflamed in London that I could neither wear boots nor high shoes. This was a serious calamity. Mr. Cooper could do nothing to them, Mr. Marshall had paid a particular attention to this part of the anatomy, and cured me after an attendance of two months. I believe I should have suffered all my life in America. It is well enough to mention this anecdote to the boys, if they have the same childish vanity, and squeeze the overgrown family feet into Chinese shoes. The bills of my apothecary and chemist were about 25 pounds, the whole amount £105. Sickness is too expensive to be suffered twice in London. When I quitted London for Paris, I thought myself justified in drawing for £50 to answer the additional expenses of the journey. When I reached the Continent, I found that with travelling I could not hope to reduce myself within £37, your allowance. I determined, therefore, to adopt what was possible, and to use every effort not to exceed £40 for £37. I must beg, therefore, that you will have the charity to read £40. 20 shillings sterling at the average rate of exchange is worth about 24 francs. £40 are consequently equal to 960 francs, or 31 francs and a half per day. I did not spend this income in Paris, but saved a good part of it. Of the expenses of travelling I could form no accurate idea, as I could not travel like most other young men, in a calash. A calash is an open vehicle something like our chaise, which would have exposed my eye to the glare and dust of the roads, to keen winds, to wet and damp weather, to the rays of the sun, and to the night air. Any one of these causes would have produced an inflammation. It might have answered for a journey of two or three days, but I could not reasonably have expected to reach Lyons. The only vehicle adapted to my situation was a chariot, lined throughout with green, with the front blind always pulled up, so that we had a perfect view of the country, but from the side windows only. A chariot was an enormous additional expense, not only in the prime cost, but, as I afterwards found, in the increased rates of posting. We purchased a chariot for 2000 francs, 1000 francs each or £41.13. It was also necessary to take a servant, as I could not have attended to the luggage in the evening when we arrived at the inns, and indeed for many other obvious reasons a person in my situation could not have travelled without one. It is fortunate that in both these expenses, which I should never have incurred had it been optional, my friend Gray was perfectly willing to join with me, for motives of comfort and convenience, and he has shown the same accommodating disposition in every other expense which the peculiarity of my situation has rendered necessary. The posting in France is regulated by the number of persons. As there were three of us, we were obliged to have three horses and one postilion, at 130 sous each, or 6 francs, equal to 5 shillings sterling, per post. A French post is five miles. Travelling in France, including tavern bills, averaged rather more than 100 francs per day, 50 francs each. In northern Italy we had the same number of horses, but a post was 7 miles and a half and the rates were 50 sous to each horse and postilion. Thus for half the greater distance we paid two-thirds a greater price. This was a sensible addition to our expenses; but it was not until we crossed the Apennines and entered the dominions of His Holiness and the King of Naples that we were ground to the very marrow. By the most unjust tariffs in the world the only distinction which is made is between covered and opened carriages, classing light chariots under the same denomination with berlins and barouches, heavy double coaches. By this wise provision, we were never suffered to travel with less than four horses and two postilions, 300 sous per post, or 15 francs equal to 12 shillings and a half sterling and where there was the least ascent, which occurred three or four times a day, we were compelled to take six horses and three postilions, 450 sous per post, about 18s. 8d. sterling. Mr. Hinckley has grumbled and fought his way through Italy in an English chariot, and complains bitterly that they harnessed so many horses to his nutshell that it required a spy-glass to reach the forward postilion. A calash would have travelled in France with two horses, in Lombardy with the same number, and in southern Italy with three horses and one postilion, never more than four horses and two postilions. As our expenses had been so great, we had hoped to have economized during our three months' residence in Naples and Rome, but we miscalculated. The English have so overstocked every part of the Continent that the Italians have assured me the price of everything relative to travellers has been doubled within the last two years. My infirmities would not allow me like other young men to live at ordinary inns, and dine at traiteurs upon Italian mixtures. We were obliged to live at the most expensive hotels, because it was there only we could obtain good and simple food. These circumstances, combining with the usual expenses of cicerones &c., prevented my living within my income. We returned to Paris by the first of April. My draughts upon Mr. Welles had commenced the 1st of September, a period of seven months. My allowance would therefore have entitled me to 6720 francs or £280. I found that the sum total of my draughts was 9400 francs, about £390. The balance against me, therefore, was £110. I hope to account for a part of this sum upon principles unconnected with the posting. In the first place, by deducting the expenses of physicians, medicines and articles purchased solely in relation to my disease. Secondly, the reimbursement which I shall derive by a sale of the carriage, a positive liquidation of expense. Thirdly, in the exclusion of such articles as have been purchased for my friends and not for myself. I paid Dr. Robertson something more than one hundred francs, the medicines which I purchased during two months' residence in Paris, and a large quantity which I laid up for my tour, including certain medical apparatus, a pair of sheets, and a pair of large green silk curtains to protect me from the sun in the carriage, to hang up in the windows of inns which were unfortified with blinds or curtains, and to soften the light in an inflammation, amounted to 270 francs. I was obliged to replenish my store of medicines at Naples, and as I use none but what are manufactured in England, I found them much more expensive than at Paris. Par exemple, for eighteen ounces of Epsom salts Mr. Reilly charged me 8 dollars, about 40 francs, partly from the heavy duties, and in part, I suspect, an imposition. My medicines in Italy cost me 80 francs. The sum total is 450 francs, or 19 pounds. For the chariot we have been offered 1200 francs. We shall consequently not take less, probably not get more. By selling my share for 600 francs,

I sustain a loss of 400. Had it been a calash, in the same proportion I should not have lost more than 150 francs. Tempis pour moi 600 francs are just 25 pounds, a positive reimbursement. The gowns which I bought in Paris amounted, as near as I recollect, to 270 francs, the prints of Florence to 180 francs. I know not if you consider the last extravagant. I purchased them as the best specimens of this fine art. I knew they were rare in America, and concluded that if you were disposed to part with them, you could obtain much more than the original cost. I am confirmed in this opinion when I consider the comparative price of Morghen's prints at Florence and at Paris. I inquired by accident the other day the price of the Apollo with the houris dancing round his chariot and preceded by Aurora, copied from the inimitable fresco in the Ruspigliosi palace. For this print I paid 15 francs to Raphael Morghen, and it sells for 63 francs in the shops of Paris. These sums united amount to 450 francs, 19 pounds. The sum total of these three exceptions is £63 which, subtracted from £110, leaves a balance against me of £47. But, you will say, this is a charming method of paying off the national debt. I made an exclusion in favour of physicians and medicines, and you seem to have annexed your linen drapers, mercers, and fifty other bills which have not the least connection with one or the other. I must answer that your allowance was made for a man in health; that it was formed from an inquiry of sensible men who had made the tour of Europe some ten years before what money was sufficient to enable a man to travel like a gentleman. The allowance they assigned was liberal, and would have been adequate, even in the increased price of things, to the reasonable wants of a man in health, independent of his purchases. But I was an invalid, and the peculiarities of my disease plunged me into a sea of expense, upon which it was impossible to calculate—the enormous rates of posting, the most expensive hotels where I could find good and nutritious food, and the frequent recurrence of petty expenses such as the hiring of hackney coaches when other people could have walked but when I was prevented by the windy, wet or sunny weather or exposure to the night air. But you might have staid at home—had I adopted this plan, an object which would have consumed five hours might have detained us as many days, and neither my friend Gray nor any other friend would have consented to any such detention and I should have omitted many interesting objects though actually in the same town. It was a fortunate thing for me that Gray, with an accommodation I should have found no where else, was willing to make every expense mutual which my infirmities obliged me to incur. These united expenses, from which a man in health would have been exempt, were enormous, but as they are also indefinite, I have taken them upon my own shoulders. It is but fair then that I should appropriate as extra expenses not only physicians and medicines, but such articles as were purchased solely in consequence of my disease, and would not have been purchased otherwise, such as the sheets, silks, &c. The chariot requires no explanation, as I have deducted simply the reimbursement. I could not refrain from purchasing the gowns, and I presumed you would approve of it although it [was] independent of my income. The prints will ever maintain more than their original value. I knew they were to be had with difficulty in America, and as I was upon the spot, it seemed barbarous to neglect them. I expended 100 francs in Rome, but as it was for myself, I could not charge you with it. The balance against me was, therefore £47 or 1120 francs. I determined, upon my return to Paris, to retrench myself within 11 francs, by which I should save 20 francs per day, and the course of seven weeks, which I intended to reside here, should have liquidated the whole debt within a small amount. This was not a chimerical scheme. The first six days I was confined by an inflammation but, exclusive of medical expenses, did not exceed the allowance I had prescribed. For three or four days I enjoyed an interval of health and during that period lived, and should have continued to live, upon less than 10 francs a day. This I effected by entering into cheaper apartments, dining upon one plain and simple dish without wine, abandoning the luxury of a fire and keeping myself warm by exercise and a great-coat, and privations of this kind were not ungentlemanly as they were merely solitary. I calculated also upon two or three weeks residence with Mr. [Daniel] Parker at Draveil,[2] but as all my hopes have been blasted, so these, my economical schemes, were thwarted by unforeseen disease. I might say it is true that, independent of expenses incurred by my fever, I still live within the limits I had assigned. But this distinction is merely nominal, the expense to you remains the same. I merely wish to convince you that I have not only been anxious to reduce myself within your allowance, but that I should have effected this had I not been baffled by circumstances which it was not in my power to control, and which were not induced by imprudence or excess. In my present situation, the expense of five weeks in Paris and one at Mr. Parker's, inclusive of everything—apartments, food, physicians, servant, and medicines &c., will not exceed £50. The purchases which I have made, including commissions, your French books, and a few classics which I have taken the liberty to buy for myself as my friend Ticknor[3] assures me they are now as cheap here as in any part of the world. Also different articles of dress upon principles of economy for my family and myself, exclusive of Lizzy's watch, will not

exceed £50. I can reduce my expenses in London to a pretty sure calculation. The tour of six weeks to Scotland will not, at the outside,
exceed £100 each.[4] This is £25 more than my allowance within that
period. If I am not again disappointed by disease, I shall not, at the
utmost, exceed £25, per month, for my private expenses while I reside
in London. Suppose that I reside in England the four months, May,
June, July and August, inclusive of my Scotch tour, my private expenses
will not exceed £160. To these we may add £10 for physicians. I think
I shall be obliged to throw away no more upon them. I shall also spend
£60 upon boots, flannels and clothes. This I should do from obvious
economy. Clothes, you well know, are infinitely cheaper and better
made than with us; and boots, although somewhat dearer in the original price, are nearly three times as cheap, as from the superiority of
both upper and under leather, they will last more than three times as
long. This I know from experience, a pair of English boots which I
bought near a year since and have worn constantly are now in good
order. A pair of American boots, with the same service, would not have
lasted me more than three months. I have thrown three pairs of American boots that I brought with me into the trunk, and I shall never
again put them on. They are constructed upon such delicate Chinese
dimensions. I hope you will commission me to purchase some clothes
for you; the whole amount of these expenses will be £230. To these
we will add 50 guineas for my passage, and we will throw in the remaining £18 for possibilities, and for one or two books, Mitford's *Greece,*
Gibbon's *Memoirs,* &c., if they are reasonable. The sum total is £300.
To these we will add £305 which I spent during my previous residence
in London. £390 for my travels on the Continent, and £100 during this
my last residence in Paris, sum total £1095, say £1100. Eleven hundred
pounds, therefore, exclusive of the passage money you paid Captain
Lindsey, of Elizabeth's watch, and of your law books, in which I shall
not exceed the prices you have stipulated, will be the sum total of my
expenses of every description, from the time I quitted America until my
return. From this we will deduct the expenses of physicians, medicines
&c. £105 spent previously in London, £19 upon the Continent. During
my last illness, simply my physicians and medicines will not amount
to less than £25 and £10 I have allowed the faculty upon my return to
London. The sum total of medical expenses is £159. If to these we add
the sums expended upon commissions and upon articles purchased for
others and myself, upon principles of economy, and as far as relates to
myself this will be perfectly just, since you will make a proportionate
deduction in my future income—£19 for the gowns and the prints. I
have not deducted the £25 for the carriage, as the alabaster ornaments

and Leghorn hats will nearly amount to that sum. £25 for these, therefore, £50 for purchases in Paris, £60 in London, the sum total is £154 which, added to the £159, amounts to £313, say £310, which subtracted as extra expenses from the £1100 leave £790 for my private expenditure. Allowing me, therefore, eighteen months, from the time I landed in England until I reach America, supposing I arrive in October, and allowing 50 guineas for the time I am upon the ocean, considering that I have drawn for eight months upon England and eight more months upon the Continent, I shall not have exceeded my allowance £10.

You will probably be disappointed in the sum total of this heavy expenditure but when you look into the details I hope you will be convinced that I have not only been anxious to circumscribe myself within my allowance, but that I have effected it, independent of reasonable extra expenses. When you consider the great additional expenses which the peculiarity of my situation have compelled me to incur, all of which I have met without exceeding my allowance, I hope you will believe that I have always consulted economy as far as my health would justify, and that you have no reason to repent the confidence reposed in me. You will excuse me for adding that I have entered upon no pecuniary transaction of any importance without previous reflection, and there is none upon retrospection which I regret. Should I unfortunately not find in you a coincidence of opinion, you will consider my errors as the errors of misjudgement, and not of willful extravagance. I shall be anxious to receive an answer to this letter, and beg you will favour me with one as soon as you have read it. Pray be explicit and unequivocal in your criticism upon my conduct. I should consider myself very fortunate should I receive this answer before my embarkation. I have given you the average rate of exchange, between London and Paris it varies considerably, and has lately been much in favour of London, in consequence of the loan made to the French government. The exchange was very different in different parts of Italy. We generally found honest bankers, but suffered not a little from a knave in Rome. He had the effrontery to charge me 12 dollars for the postage of my letters while I resided there. I could not expose the imposition upon the spot but when I compared the accounts of my bankers in Florence, I found that several times where they had charged me two parcels for postage, something less than two francs, he had charged two dollars. A man must shrug his shoulders and make as small draughts upon such scoundrels as possible. Perhaps you will find some mistakes in my mathematics, the reduction of pounds into francs, and of francs into pounds is somewhat complicated, and, as the calculation has been made wholly in my mind, without any reference to figures upon paper, you may perhaps detect some errors, though I believe they must be very few, and of little consequence, I have repeated it so often. I unfortunately could not be assisted by my secretary who, though a very good scribe, will never make a Newton. He thinks, however, and I am half of his mind, that it is the easiest thing in the world to convert pounds into francs and requires no assistance. Fribourg[5] has just drawn the warming pan from the bed, and my eyes begin to be as hermetically sealed as they were wont to be when I had been digging for cubic roots, or searching for unknown quantities. I shall soon be beyond the regions of calculation, so I wish you, beloved father, a good night and a *bon repos.* Your truly affectionate son

WILLIAM

Hoc scripsit mon secretaire Busson.[6]

1. This statement probably accompanied WHP's forty-nine-page letter of April 29 to his parents.

2. This wealthy American lived in splendor in the country not far from Paris.

3. George Ticknor (1791–1871), the scholarly friend and confidant whose interest in Spanish culture first directed WHP toward Spanish historical themes, had just completed his studies at Göttingen.

4. The projected trip to Scotland never materialized.

5. Swiss-born Fribourg had served WHP and Gray on the long trip from Paris to Italy and return. In addition to serving as valet, he handled baggage, bargained with hotelkeepers, etc.

6. On May 13, 1817, WHP sailed for Brighton from Dieppe. After consultation with Sir William Adams in London, he went to Oxford, Blenheim, the Cotswolds, Tintern Abbey and the River Wye, Bristol, Bath and Salisbury on one excursion, and to Cambridge on another. At end of summer he was sailing for America.

In Boston WHP again suffered inflammations and rheumatism. Following a slow recovery, he increasingly entered society.

12.   To Susan Amory[1]
                 (WHP Papers, Mass. Hist. Soc.)

                                              August, 1819

                       Souvenir
                    W. H. P. to S. A.

                        — —

     And sweetly did the pages fill
        With fond device and loving lore,
     And every leaf she turn'd, was still
        More bright than that she turn'd before.
                                         Moore[2]

1. Susan Amory (1802–69), daughter of merchant Thomas Coffin Amory, married WHP in 1820 and bore him four children, three of whom reached adulthood.

2. WHP was nearly perfect as he set down the third quatrain of Thomas Moore's "To Mrs. Bl——, written in her album." In the first line "sweetly" should read "daily." In addition to these sentiments of the Irish poet, WHP also sent Susan lines from Byron and Ossian.

13. To Jared Sparks[1]
(Jared Sparks Papers, Harvard College Library)

Boston, February 9th 1820

My dear Sir

I send you a copy of the *Club-room*,[2] a paper which is to be furnished out of the wits of the Tuesday evening Club,[3] of which you were a member. You will perceive that [it] is miscellaneous, and we have no subscription, and do not intend to pledge ourselves for its periodical appearance. As the literary merits of most of our members have already been decided by their public performances,[4] we have little reason to doubt our ability to support such a work. If you can assist our cause by your recommendations, or in any other way for which you have inclination and leisure, (although I suspect you are but poorly off for the last) you will much oblige the Club in general, and me in particular as the editor. The pieces in this Number were written in the following order by Warren, Parsons, Dexter, Ware.[5] I am dear Sir Yours very truly

WM. H. PRESCOTT

1. Jared Sparks (1789–1866), clergyman, editor, biographer, historian and college president—through all of which he was a close friend and confidant of WHP. In 1820, Sparks was serving as a Unitarian minister in Baltimore.

2. Between February 5 and July 19, 1820, four issues of this literary publication, all edited by WHP, appeared in Boston.

3. "Club" first met on June 13, 1818, under WHP's leadership. Its original membership of nine expanded to twenty-four, all of whom were initially related to the Boston scene. A combination of social and intellectual interests, Club remained important to WHP throughout his life.

4. Several members of Club had published items in the infant *North American Review* and in some more ephemeral publications of the area.

5. Henry Warren (d. 1869) graduated from Harvard in 1813, one year before WHP.

Theophilus Parsons (1797–1882), author, editor, lawyer, teacher and friend of WHP.

Franklin Dexter (1793–1857), a scholarly and distinguished lawyer and WHP's friend and brother-in-law.

John Ware (1795–1864), physician, editor and educator.

14.   To Fitz-Greene Halleck[1]

(Miscellaneous bound, XIX, Mass. Hist. Soc.; and printed, with alterations, in
James Grant Wilson, *The Life and Letters of Fitz-Greene Halleck* [New York,
1869], pp. 238–39)

Boston, March 15, 1820

To the author of 'Fanny'[2]

The author of 'Fanny' will be somewhat surprised at this abrupt
communication from an unknown correspondent. I take the liberty of
sending him the last number of the *Club-Room*, a paper lately set on
foot by a knot of gentlemen in this town, most of whom are habitual
contributors to the *North American Review*, which you have probably
met with. We have been in the habit of meeting together for social
and literary purposes once a fortnight, and as it was thought it would
be a good exercise for us, if not for the town, to give vent to some of
our speculations, we have adopted this form to do it in, and we make
our paper a miscellaneous budget of light and serious matter, in prose
or poetry, as may be convenient.

Your pieces, if, as I suppose, you are the author of those signed
'Croaker,' have been read in the newspapers with great interest, but
'Fanny' is of a higher order, and for its easy conversational wit, and
poetry of description, must go alongside of Lord Byron's and Mr. Rose's
productions in the same way.[3] It is the admiration of your poetical
talents which has led me to make this communication to you, and to
request, if you feel inclined to give your pieces a circulation among
your Eastern brethren, you would sometimes select the *Club-Room* as
the medium of communication. I find no difficulty as the editor in obtaining compositions in prose; but it is otherwise in poetry, which,
as it is not necessary to publish, we feel unwilling to publish unless it
is particularly good; and I know of no source from whence I could be
so likely to obtain this as from the author of 'Fanny.'

I hope you will not consider this communication as impertinent on
my part, as I am perfectly aware that a refusal to comply with it would
be very reasonable and is to be expected, but I am willing to make it
even upon an improbable chance of success.[4] I am, sir, with great respect, Your very obedient servant,

WM. H. PRESCOTT

1. Fitz-Greene Halleck (1790–1867), the distinguished Connecticut-born
poet.

2. Published about the beginning of 1820, this, Halleck's longest poem, sati-
rized the fashionable and political follies of the day. Enjoying great success, it
appeared in many editions.

3. Probably William Stewart Rose (1775–1843), the Scotch poet, scholar and translator.

4. More indicative of WHP's love of poetry than of his success in soliciting manuscripts, this communication did not produce the desired result.

15.   To Francis W. P. Greenwood[1]
           (The Rev. Herbert Boyce Satcher, D.D., Philadelphia)

Pond St., Friday [c. March, 1820]

My dear friend

I send you two copies of the *Club-Room* No. 2. The printer made a most whimsical mistake in the "Grave-yard,"[2] which was not in either of the proof sheets, by displacing the letter c. in the word clump. I looked over the sheets again after they were printed. I detected it, and as I thought a "lump of pines" would be considered rather an extraordinary figure for a serious piece, I had the unlucky c. prefixed, so that it hobbles rather lamely, but better so than a mistake in the sense, and an impeachment of good taste. I am sorry you have such bad weather for your exercise, although I suppose such weather is sun shine to the *Club Room*. Your truly affectionate

W. H. PRESCOTT

1. Francis William Pitt Greenwood (1797–1843), a literary-minded classmate of WHP at Harvard, won renown for his pulpit eloquence.
2. The full title was "The Village Grave-Yard."

16.   Timothy Swan to Charles Wells
              (WHP Papers, Mass. Hist. Soc.)

Boston, April 23, 1820

Mr. Charles Wells
Sir,

All the copies of the Pamphlet entitled *Club Room* No. 3 being about 500 pamphlets which I delivered to you to be bound are the property of Wm. H. Prescott, he having employed me to procure the same to be printed and bound and to sell them for him. I hereby request you to deliver the same to him or his order on demand.

TIMOTHY SWAN

I accept the above order, and agree to deliver all the aforesaid Pamphlets to the said Wm. H. Prescott or his order on request.

April 23, 1820   CHARLES WELLS

17.   To Theophilus Parsons
        (Mellen Chamberlain Autograph Collection, Boston Public Library)

Pond St., May 3, 1820

Dear Theop:[1]

It is so long since the bet became due that I ought to pay interest, but such a thing, I believe, is contrary to the code of honor, and is still more contrary to the laws of love, which have a right to preside over our bet. However if I have lost my money I have got my wife, and I am very willing to pay it as a discount upon the high prize.[2] Yours ever affectionately

W. H. PRESCOTT

1. WHP often employed this nickname.
2. His marriage to Susan Amory took place the following day, and it was time for WHP to pay a bet concerning his bachelor status.
The newlyweds lived with the bridegroom's parents.

18.   To Jared Sparks
            (Jared Sparks Papers, Harvard College Library)

Boston, June 29, 1820

My dear Sir

I am very sorry to give you so much trouble about the affairs of Club and the best apology I can find is that as you were one of the founders, you no doubt take as much interest as any one else in the success of its enterprises. Swan, who first published the *Club-room,* has failed and I have now put the work into Cummings' and Hilliard's hands. Swan is a young man and my principal motive for putting the work into his hands at all was to benefit him. In town it has taken care of itself, and each number has considerably more than paid its expenses —but out of town it has not been well managed. The agent in Baltimore knew nothing and cared nothing about Swan and seems to have paid little attention to his orders. Cummings and Hilliard have put the work into the hands of Cook and greater numbers into those of Cushing and Jewett. They are associated in the profits of the work and as they are better known probably their wishes will be attended to. You will much oblige me if in some of your perambulations that way you would call upon these gentlemen and request them to advertise the numbers and give them a fair exposure on their counters, and if you are disposed to assist us in any way that will not cost you too much time and trouble, Club will take it very kindly of you. The third number was made up by [John C.] Gray, [Franklin] Dexter, [John] Ware,

Everett, Dr. Fisher[1] and myself. The fourth will be published in the course of a week.[2] I am dear Sir Yours very truly

W. H. PRESCOTT

1. Edward Everett (1794–1865), orator, statesman, diplomat and educator, later assisted WHP's projects on numerous occasions.

Dr. J. C. Fisher and Edward Everett were the only contributors who were not members of Club.

2. With this issue, in July, the publication ceased.

19. Commonplace Book,[1] Maxims in Composition
(Pp. 81–83, WHP Papers, Mass. Hist. Soc.)

[early 1821?]

Maxims in Composition

I. The composing:

Turn over the subject *generally* in my own mind, in order to get *original* views of it, and also, to *direct* my course of *reading,* that it may not be wasted. *Read for facts;* not for *reflections* on my subject, especially in current books, and read whatever may furnish the former. *Minute down* useful *facts;* and also *quotations:* afford some time in looking up the last; when happy they are serviceable. Reflect on my subject, or on *parts* of my subject, again, in the course of this reading— but as before, only *generally,* and on the *facts,* the *pith.* All this time nothing but *matter,* leading ideas, facts &c. have been thought of. The subject, however, being now sufficiently matured, go over the whole in one *rapid* sketch, *ideas* and *images, not dressed in their* precise *language,* but *mistily seen* and *sketched.* When you are to write, *run over* all you are to write on *that day* first, and then *sit down,* and *keep your chair* all the rest of the day you are composing.

Write nothing that does not contribute to the purpose—however *fine,* I shall be dissatisfied with it. No *words, epithets,* that do not make it *clearer, or stronger. Figures* I dislike—unless they conduce highly to both these ends. *Gentle allusions* are very agreeable, if they conduce to either. Write clearly—but do not bind your fancy down *to too strict a literality.* But on the other hand be always *definite,* not loose, and overrun with mere verbiage. Endeavor to produce a *harmony* in the whole piece, and a *proper keeping* in every part of it—never trying to be *eloquent* out of place. Where there is no peculiar beauty, use the most common expression.

As to correction, write off freely, correct last—i.e. the correction is more likely to be just, then, than it would be when composing—at any rate, on all subjects such as Arts, &c.: write with full swing.

Write freely, boldly in manner, without fear of bad taste. You will know when all is finished—William Howard Gardiner [and] Franklin Dexter will at any rate, whether what you have written is bombast &c. When writing, *think (Never think, except alone* and unliable to *interruption, from your own occupation,* or from other *people* or *things) deeply,* or you will do badly. Get *7 hours* uninterrupted if you can— that is enough, if well used. *Never* try to write under *1 hour* after a *moderate* dinner. Never *review* more than *2 pages* of the *preceding day's* work, or I shall be too *familiar* with my piece to correct it. *Copy no manner, nor style.* It is impossible to make another man's coat fit your own body.

Be cautious, very, very doubtful about correcting in cold blood—i.e. after *dwelling on a passage.* And do *not correct,* unless a striking defect, *in print.* Place no great stress on verbal alterations. Nor waste time— they take most time, and produce little effect.

N.B. You can write, after proper reflection, from 1 to 2 pages of the *North American Review* in a day.[2] *I ought to write two.*

It may be well, perhaps, for the sake of illustration, quotation, &c. to read your favorite, rich, and eloquent *poets,* one or two days before composing.[3]

1. This record by WHP covers a miscellaneous array of themes and activities between early January, 1820, and early July, 1822.

2. Between 1821 and 1850, the dates of his first and last contributions to that quarterly, WHP contributed many articles to the *North American Review.* Here, however, the reference is not to articles but rather to a unit of work which he had adopted. Pleased, apparently, with the format of the *North American Review,* which then contained forty-two lines and approximately 450 words per page, WHP calculated his own labor in terms of multiples of that page size.

3. For additional rules on composition, see William Hickling Prescott (C. Harvey Gardiner, ed.), *The Literary Memoranda of William Hickling Prescott* (2 vols., Norman, Oklahoma, 1961), I, 50–52, 86–87, 114–16, 184.

20.   Commonplace Book, Religious Beliefs
(Pp. 84–85, WHP Papers, Mass. Hist. Soc.)

April 4, 1821

I believe after due examination[1]

1. In the truth of the Christian religion.

2. That there is much authority for believing in the inspiration of the Apostles, and I believe in it.

3. There is much authority for relying on the authenticity of the whole Pentateuch, and I am willing to rely on its authenticity.

4. There is much reason for receiving the divine legation of Moses as shown in an examination of the four last books of the Pentateuch.

5. As to the doctrine of the Trinity, there is much in the Old and New Testament to bear it out, and in its ancient reception in the Church. But the general spirit of the volume seems to accord with the Unitarian faith, and upon the whole such are my feelings on the subject that although I am not satisfied of the fallacy of the Trinity, I am not convinced of its truth, and as I have been accustomed to an intelligible creed, my mind naturally revolts at a mystery, and yet this is no argument against it in these matters. How necessary is Charity then upon subjects of so much doubt.

6. The dispute about two natures of Christ seems to be purely verbal. Both with Unitarians and Trinitarians Christ must have been possessed of different faculties here, from what he enjoyed in a previous state of existence.

7. Whether eternal punishment is eternal pain, according to our notions of pain, or a diminution of pleasure, at any rate there is every ground to believe that the unfortunate wicked shall forever feel the effects of his wickedness.

8. We have every reason both from the assertions and references of the Apostles, and of Christ, to believe in the inspiration of the prophets of the Old Testament.[2]

1. WHP assessed his religious beliefs on a number of occasions; for a more detailed examination of them, see Prescott (Gardiner, ed.), *The Literary Memoranda,* I, 105–14.

2. WHP was a staunch Unitarian and his wife Susan was an equally orthodox Episcopalian. They attended both churches.

21. Commonplace Book, Course of Studies
(P. 18, WHP Papers, Mass. Hist. Soc.; and printed in Ticknor, *Prescott,* p. 62)

Memorandum October 30, 1821

Course of Studies[1]

Memorandum   Remark on each author

1. Principles of grammar, correct writing &c.

2. Compendious History of North America.[2]

3. Fine prose writers of England from Roger Ascham to present day. Principally with reference to their mode of writing. (Not including historians except as far as requisite for an acquaintance with their style.)

4. Latin classics, 1 hour a day.

1. Aiming at a gentlemanly career in letters, WHP began to discipline himself.

2. This did not immediately command his attention. Throughout his career, as one might expect, WHP's projected programs differed considerably from those that he put into practice.

22.   Commonplace Book, Memorandum
(P. 17, WHP Papers, Mass. Hist. Soc.)

[Autumn, 1821?]

Memorandum

I will write a review no oftener than once in three Numbers of the *North American Review*[1]—*no oftener,* and *print* only what I think will *add* to my reputation. I may write in succession when what I have previously written is not good enough to print.

In the interim I will follow a course of reading, and make the subjects of my reviews, as far as I can, fall in with this course, or with what I have before read.

Provide for the next subject so as to allow 3 months preparation.

Pursue this course until I am thirty—that is if I intend to write the Number, next but one.

Memorandum—I will never engage to write for a Number.

1. WHP's first review article in the *North American Review*, "Byron's Letter on Pope," appeared in the issue of October, 1821.

23.   To Gorham Parsons
(Miscellaneous bound, XIX, Mass. Hist. Soc.)

Boston, March 7, 1822

My dear Sir,

I hope you will not consider me impertinent if I request your opinion upon a subject, on which I know no one so well qualified to give advice as yourself. I have been appointed one of a Committee of Managers of the Boys' Asylum,[1] to enquire into the expediency of removing the institution from Boston into the country. The hopes of diminishing the expenses by employing the boys in a more lucrative occupation than what they can have in town is the principal object proposed by it. As the funds of the institution are small, however, there is an unwillingness to hazard them in an experiment, which would not be attended with almost certain success; and as the gentlemen who superintend the institution at present are but little acquainted with agriculture, they are incompetent to form any notion of the probable success of such a scheme. I will, (with your permission,) state to you such particulars as I have collected, of the *funds,* the *expenses,* and the *present earnings* of the institution, that you may be enabled to form some judgment on this matter.

The property consists in a house, and land at the North End, (the old mansion of Sir William Phipps[2]) which are worth $8000.—bank stock to the amount of $4000. The income is principally derived from subscribers, who paid last year $1900. Add to this $200, the interest upon the bank stock—and the whole annual income is $2100. *40 boys* are maintained in the Asylum; 17 of them at the present moment between 5 and 9 years of age, and 22 of them between the age of 9 and 13. The whole earnings of these boys (which are derived from knitting stockings, pasting covers for bookbinders, and making steel chains) do not exceed $100 per year. No better occupation can be provided for them in town. These boys are superintended by a woman who receives high wages.

Their *consumption per quarter* amounts to 82 bushels of meal, 435 quarts of milk, 1 large tierce of rice, 910 pounds of meat, 234 pounds of fish, 91 quarts of beans, 22 bushels of potatoes, also, about *500 weight of pork per annum.*

You will perceive my dear Sir, from this statement, that although these boys average 10 years of age they earn individually not more than 2 dollars per annum—while they cost each 50 dollars per annum. We have thought that by removing them to a farm in the country they could be more profitably employed upon it, raising vegetables, or in tilling the ground—some way or other—and their diet might be accommodated to what they would raise. The occupation, were the expense equal, would be obviously more healthy, manly and useful than the present. There would however be the *increased expense* of an intelligent superintendent, and the difficulty of finding one. And without such a man the scheme would probably be a ruinous one. Will you have the goodness to take this into consideration, my dear Sir, and to let me know, if not inconvenient to you, the next time you are in town, when and where I may have an opportunity of seeing and conversing with you on this subject.

I should like to learn your opinion respecting its feasibility—as I suggested the scheme to the Managers, I feel the more desirous to show that it is expedient, if it really is so.[3] I am, dear Sir Most respectfully Your Obedient Servant

W. H. Prescott

1. The Boys' Asylum was patterned after the Boston Female Asylum, an

organization to which WHP's mother had already given much time. This is the first, but not the last, identification of WHP with humanitarian causes in his home community.

2. Sir William Phipps (1651–95), the first Royal Governor of Massachusetts.

3. The outcome of this suggestion is not known, nor is there any additional record of WHP's service on behalf of the Boys' Asylum.

24.   Commonplace Book, Studies
(P. 48, WHP Papers, Mass. Hist. Soc.)

[early 1822]

STUDIES

I am now 26 years of age (nearly). By the time I am 30, (God willing) I propose, with what stock I have already on hand, to be a *very well read English scholar,* to be acquainted with the *classical* and useful authors (prose and poetry) in *Latin, French,* and *Italian*—especially *History.* I do not mean a critical or profound acquaintance. The two following years, 31–32, I may hope to learn and to have read the classical *German* writers—and the translations (if my eye continues weak) of the *Greek.* And this is enough for *general discipline.*[1]

HOURS—A.M. Serious Study—P.M. Lighter.

1/2 past 7–8   1/2 past 8–11   1/2 past 11–10 minutes past 2; or to 25 minutes after 2.   1/2 after 4–6   10 minutes past 6–10 minutes past 7.[2]

1. Except for dropping the German writers, WHP adhered to this general program. In late 1824 he began to study Spanish.

2. In other periods and places, WHP's daily work schedules varied. See Prescott (Gardiner, ed.), *The Literary Memoranda,* I, 180, 185, 242–43, and II, 134, 233, 248–49.

25.   Commonplace Book, Musings
(Pp. 45–47, WHP Papers, Mass. Hist. Soc.)

[early 1822?]

Musings

History has always been a favorite study with me;[1] and I have long looked forward to it as a subject on which I may one [day] exercise my pen. It is not rash, in the dearth of well-written American history, to entertain the hopes [of] throwing a light upon this matter—especially with the rich materials which are now buried in pedantic lumber, and foreign languages, in the Ebeling Collection.[2] This is my hope. But it requires time and a long time, before the mind can be sufficiently prepared for this department of writing. 1° An easy style, and familiarity with composition must be first obtained by practice. Skirmishing occasionally in the Reviews is the best discipline for this purpose. A review is the proper gymnasium of a writer, in which he may try his strength before he comes into the world upon his own credit. 2° The understanding must be ripened by reflection and experience. Poets may be born, but historians are made. 3° The memory must be enriched and the taste improved by a wide cultivation of polite letters; (I do not mean a critical or profound acquaintance with them.) 4° When all this is attained, and not till then, the man is prepared to investigate the *particular* subject of his intended history. After this, some years of careful, deep, and accurate research into whatever has a relation to this subject can alone authorise him to come before the public as an historian.

These are at least my notions upon the matter. I think 35 years of age full soon enough to put pen to paper. The preceding years may be devoted to the objects above enumerated. Gibbon and Hume[3] were both more than 40 years old when they commenced their great histories —and Robertson[4] was, I believe, nearly of the same age. I have said nothing of traveling, though I think, from obvious reasons, every historian should be personally acquainted with the country concerning which he is to write.[5]

1. Two libraries, those of the Prescott household and the Boston Athenaeum, and one teacher, John S. J. Gardiner, did most to develop this interest. Harvard then offered the undergraduate exceedingly little history.

2. Harvard had recently acquired the library of C. D. Ebeling (1741–1817) of Germany.

3. The great history by Edward Gibbon (1737–94) was *The Decline and Fall of the Roman Empire,* and the masterwork of David Hume (1711–76) was his *History of England.*

4. Among the principal titles by Scotch Whig historian William Robertson (1721–93) were his *History of America* and his *History of the Emperor Charles V.*

5. Correct though he was in this matter, WHP did not practice what he preached. He never set foot in Spain, Mexico or Peru, the settings for his own histories.

26.   To George Ticknor
(Rare Book Department, Boston Public Library; and extracts printed in Ticknor, *Prescott,* pp. 67–68)

Bedford St., December 17, 1823.

Dear George

I think better of snowstorms than I ever did before, since though it keeps a man's body in the house, it brings his mind out. I suppose if it had been fair weather yesterday, I should have not had the little dissertation upon Madonna Laura which instructed as well as amused me. As to the question respecting the real existence of Madonna, I can have but little to say, because my only documents, all that I have ever read in relation to it, are Ginguené's and Tiraboschi's lives of him,[1] and his Italian poetry. I read a review some time since about him in the *Edinburgh* [*Review*], but I don't recollect which way it ran, if it entered into the question. One thing seems to me clear, that the *onus probandi* is with those who would deny the substantiality of Laura, because she is addressed as a living person by Petrarch,[2] and because no contemporary unequivocally states her to have been an ideal one. I say unequivocally because the remark you refer to, of one of the Colonna family, seems to have been rather an intimation or a gratuitous supposition which might well come from one who lived at a distance from the scene of the attachment—amour, or whatever you call this Platonic passion of Petrarch's. The *idealists,* however, (to borrow a metaphysical term) would shift this burden of proof upon their adversaries. On this ground, I agree with you that internal evidence derived from poetry whose essence, as you truly say, is fiction, is liable to great misinterpretation. Yet I think that although a novel or a long poem may be written, addressed to, and be descriptive of some imaginary goddess &c. (I take it there is not much doubt of Beatrice or of the original of Fiammetta), yet that a long series of separate poems should have been written with great passion under different circumstances, through a long course of years, from the warm period of boyhood to the cool retrospective season of gray hairs, would, I think, be in the highest degree improbable. But when with this you connect one or two external facts, e.g. the very memorandum to which you refer written in his private manuscript of Virgil, intended only for himself as he expressly says in it, with such solemn unequivocal language as this—"In order to preserve the melancholy recollection of this loss, I find a certain satisfaction mingled with my sorrow, in noting this in a volume which often falls under my eye, and which thus tells me there is nothing further to delight me in this life, that my strongest tie is broken &c &c." Again, in a treatise "De Contemptu Mundi" a sort of confession in which he seems to have had a sober communion with his own heart as I infer from Ginguené, he speaks of his passion for Laura, in a very unambiguous manner. These notes or memoranda, intended as they were for his own eye only, would, I think, in any court of justice be admitted as positive evidence of the truth of what they assert. I should be willing to rest the point at issue on these two facts.

Opening his poetry, one thing struck me in support of his sincerity, in seeing a sonnet which begins with the name of the friend you refer to
"Rotta e l'alta Colonna d 'l verde Lauro"
Vile puns, but he would hardly have mingled the sincere elegy of a friend with that of a fictitious creation of his own brain. This I admit is not safe to build upon and I do not. I agree that it may be highly probable [that] investigators, Italian, French and English, have feigned more than they found, have gone into detail where only a few general facts could be hoped for, but the general basis, the real existence of some woman of the name of Laura, who influenced the heart, the conduct, the intellectual character of Petrarch, is, I think, not to be resisted. And I believe your conclusion does not materially differ from this. I return the *Poeti del Primo Secolo*. Though prosaic, they are superior to what I had imagined, and give me a much higher notion of the general state of the Italian tongue at that early period than I had imagined it was entitled to. It is not more obsolete than the French in the time of Marot, or the English in the time of Spenser.[3] Petrarch, however, you easily see infused into it a warmth and richness, a splendor of poetical idiom which has been taken into and incorporated with the language by succeeding poets. But he [is] the most musical, most melancholy of all. Sismondi[4] quotes Malaspina, a Florentine historian, as writing in 1280 with all the purity and elegance of the modern Tuscan. But I think you must say, *Sat prata biberunt*. I have poured forth enough, I think, considering the little I know of the controversy.

I have got a long morning again as I dine with a lady party at 4 o'clock at shrimp. So if you will let me have Cary,[5] I think it may assist me in some very knotty passage—though I am aware it is too fine [print] to read much.

Give my love to Anna,[6] who, I hope, is none the worse for last night's frolicking. Yours affectionately

W. H. PRESCOTT

[P.S.] It did not occur to me you may want Dante[7] as you read him with G. If so, I can borrow Frank's,[8] who, I am pretty sure, owns one.

Do you know of a larger edition of Cary's translation in town?[9]

1. In this period WHP was reading Pierre Louis Ginguené, *Histoire littéraire d'Italie*, and Girolamo Tiraboschi, *Storia della letteratura italiana;* see Prescott (Gardiner, ed.), *The Literary Memoranda*, I, 22–23.

2. Francesco Petrarca (1304–74).

3. Clément Marot (1495–1544), poet; and Edmund Spenser (1552?–99), author of the *Faerie Queene*.

4. Jean Charles Léonard Simonde de Sismondi (1773–1842), the Swiss author of *De la littérature du Midi de l'Europe,* which, in 1823, appeared in English under the title *Historical View of the Literature of the South of Europe*.

5. Henry Francis Cary (1772–1844) won renown for his English translation of Dante's masterwork.

6. Anna Ticknor, Mrs. George Ticknor, was one of the ladies of Boston whom WHP held in highest esteem.

7. Dante Alighieri (1265–1321), author of the *Divina Commedia*.

8. Probably Francis Calley Gray.

9. WHP's love of poetry, especially Italian poetry, persisted, as did the intellectual influence of Ticknor in his life.

27.   To Theophilus Parsons
(Mellen Chamberlain Autograph Collection, Boston Public Library)

12 o'clock, Boston, September 25, 1824

Dear Theop:

I can let you have on Monday morning, if you desire it for your next *Literary Gazette,* a rambling essay on the Cui Bono? to the amount of about seven of your columns. If that is too long, it can be better shortened than divided. I wish you would let me know and I will make a fair copy for your devils.[1]

Miss [blank] Prescott, aged 22 hours (9 lb. weight),[2] sends her love to the learned editor of the *U.S. Literary Gazette.*[3] All are doing well. *Valete et plaudite.* Your affectionate friend

WM. H. PRESCOTT

1. "Cui Bono" was published in the issue of October 15, 1824, pp. 200–203.

2. The daughter, WHP's firstborn, was named Catherine Hickling Prescott (1824–29), in honor of his mother.

3. In August, 1825, a second essay by WHP appeared in the *United States Literary Gazette,* by which time his sixth contribution to the *North American Review* had been published. The literary apprenticeship continued apace.

28.   To Theophilus Parsons
(Mellen Chamberlain Autograph Collection, Boston Public Library)

Bedford St., Boston, January 2, 1826

Dear Theop:

I cannot buy the shares for the same reason you cannot keep them. There never was so great a greediness for money in Boston, owing to the assessments on man and stock falling due, from individuals who hold more than they are actually worth in it, and from the banks refusing to discount until they have made their returns to the Legislature.

I have offered your shares to my father, to William Eliot, and to Dwight.[1] They decline purchasing, unless, as Dwight says in a note to me, you are disposed to sell at 35 or 40 per cent advance, in which case he thinks it not difficult to find a purchaser, meaning perhaps himself. But then he says two shares are too small a number to buy, and his remark was predicated on the supposition that you should sell the whole.

I cannot advise this. Several shares were sold by J. Thorndike, Jr. about six weeks since, at 50 per cent advance. There is no reason why they should not be worth as much now, except from the present distress for money. You might give a credit for the greater part of the money, perhaps. You are obliged to offer them to the County at the market price, you know, in preference to any other purchaser, and if they decline, you had better put them in the hands of a broker, to sell for you. My poor services I hope you will command on this or on any other occasion you may find them convenient.[2] Yours ever

WM. H. PRESCOTT

1. Probably William Havard Eliot (d. 1831), a member of Club, and Henry Dwight (d. 1848), both of whom had graduated from Harvard with Parsons in 1815.

2. From the time of his marriage, at least, WHP owned and managed properties which demanded his awareness of economic conditions.

On January 19, 1826, WHP determined that the reign of Ferdinand and Isabella would be the historical theme to which he would dedicate his scholarly energies.

29.   To Jared Sparks
(Jared Sparks Papers, Harvard College Library)

February 22nd 1826

My Dear Sir,

I send you the notice of the Midshipman's Poems, which I brought to Club last night for you. They are of that mediocre kind that I could not find in my heart to praise, and yet so amiable that I can still less find in my heart to abuse them, so I have contented myself with something negative or neutral, which I hope the selflove of the author will mistake for praise, but which I am sure no body else will.[1] Why were you not at Club last night?

We canvassed your character pretty freely, I can assure you. You have lately been so punctual in attending the meetings of that august body that you are looked upon as one of its pillars. I have been seduced by an apparent improvement of my eye into too liberal use of it, which has again thrown me back. I know not when the foul fiend will leave me.[3] Yours ever

WM. H. PRESCOTT

1. This notice appeared in the April, 1826, issue of the *North American Review,* pp. 453–55. As reviewer, WHP always belonged to the "be-kind-to-the-author school of criticism."

2. In the course of compiling a list of books that he needed for his history project, WHP had strained his eyes the previous month. Considerably depressed, he was unable to resume serious work until June, 1826. At that time his reader-secretary was James Lloyd English (d. 1883).

30.   To George Bancroft[1]
               (George Bancroft Papers, Mass. Hist. Soc.)

                                       Boston, 16 November 1826

My dear friend

A letter from me, who am so little given to the art epistolary, is a thing so uncommon that you will hardly know what to make of it, so I will proceed to explain the matter immediately. Mr. Lunt,[2] who at present you know reads to me, will next August be admitted to the bar and leaves me without eyes.

I am desirous to replace him by some gentleman who is acquainted with the French and Spanish languages, as a knowledge of these will greatly facilitate my enquiries into the period of Spanish history, concerning which I believe I have spoken to you.

Some improvement in the state of my own eyes, which I can use without injury an hour a day and which I trust will continue, will I am convinced, with the assistance of one who is acquainted with these languages, enable me to prosecute my undertaking for which I shall possess such original authentic materials.

Ticknor, knowing these views, thinks no one would be as well adapted to my purpose as Mr. Walker, one of your present instructors. He is informed that this gentleman intends to quit you the next autumn, in order to pursue his own professional studies. If so, the proposals I am willing to offer him may be as much for his interest as mine. I offer him $250. a year for 3 or 4 years (I prefer a longer term and could not agree for less than 3 years) and his professional education in my father's office, provided he will during the same period read or write for me, (but of writing he will have very little comparatively) 6 hours a day, (Sundays of course excepted).

This will leave him master of 3 or 4 hours a day for his own studies and his time as a student will all be allowed to him. My father's law library is second to none in town and his private library is, you know, respectable.

I think that the terms are liberal, and they are very much more than

I have ever engaged to one who has hitherto read to me. I make this on the ground that Mr. Walker knows or will know the French and Spanish languages, I do not mean as a critic or scholar, but as a gentleman; in short, well enough to read the common writers of history, &c with ease. I will only add that if the propositions I have made do not hold out a sufficient inducement, it will not be in my power to make any better.

I enclose a letter to Mr. Walker from Ticknor who, as personally acquainted with him, has written to him, and another from Lunt, who, as he has been with me a year, may make Mr. Walker acquainted with the nature of his situation and relations to me, &c. My object in enclosing these as well as in writing to you is that, if there has been any misapprehension in this business, or if this proposal of mine in any way interferes with your or Cogswell's arrangements, you may return them to me instead of communicating them to Mr. Walker and all negotiation on my part shall be at an end. If, however, you think these proposals for Mr. Walker's benefit and mine, I wish you to make them known to him.[3]

We have nothing new in town, except weddings and wedding visits. You surprised me by your account of Walsh's journal; who is there in Philadelphia to keep the mill agoing? I should doubt the capacity of our reading public to digest two quarterlies, and I prognosticate a violent death, as has been the case with most of Mr. Walsh's magnificent plans.[4]

Sparks has several irons in the fire besides his journal. He has made the circuit of all the old States after original papers, letters, &c. of Washington; and this has brought into his possession such a large quantity of unpublished documents relating to the Revolution that his labours, I have no doubt, will end in an entire history of that event. His materials, he says, will cost him over 2000 dollars; and he has a trip to England in view at some future day for the purpose of turning over their archives.[5]

Adieu my friend; commend me to Cogswell[6] and believe me Truly yours,

WM. H. PRESCOTT

1. George Bancroft (1800–1891), educator, politician, statesman and historian, was a lifelong friend and confidant of WHP. At this time Bancroft was in the midst of his Round Hill School experiment at Northampton.

2. George Lunt (d. 1885).

3. Walker never served WHP as reader-secretary; in due time J. L. English resumed that duty.

4. In 1827 Robert Walsh introduced *The American Quarterly Review;* it

continued publication until 1837. For a fuller statement concerning the publisher and his publication, see Frank Luther Mott, *A History of American Magazines, 1741–1850* (New York, 1930), pp. 129, 271–76.

5. Jared Sparks soon surrendered his editorship of the *North American Review*. The researches cited later resulted in *The Writings of George Washington* (12 vols.) and *The Diplomatic Correspondence of the American Revolution* (12 vols.). In various ways he served WHP's interests while abroad in 1828–29.

6. Joseph Green Cogswell (1786–1871), trained for the law by WHP's father, became a bibliophile and librarian. In various ways he assisted WHP's historical labors. In 1826 he was Bancroft's partner in the operation of Round Hill School.

31.   To Alexander Hill Everett[1]

(Draft, WHP Papers, Mass. Hist. Soc.; and extracts in Ticknor, *Prescott,* p. 77, and in Rollo Ogden, *William Hickling Prescott* [Boston and New York, 1904], pp. 30–32)

Boston, December 26, 1826

My dear Sir

I had just written my preceding letter to you when I received yours of the 16th of September last, which from some impediment or other, has been more than three months on its passage to me. I cannot express my sense of your kindness in thus readily promoting my undertaking. Amid so many important public as well as personal concerns, which necessarily engage you, I had no right to claim this, though I confess I did expect it. I entirely agree with you, that it would be highly advantageous for me to visit Spain, and to dive with my own eyes into the arcana of those libraries which you say contain such ample stores of history; and I assure you, that as I am situated, no consideration of domestic ease would detain me a moment from an expedition, which after all would not consume more than four or five months.[2] But the state of my eyes, or rather eye, for I have the use of only one half of this valuable apparatus, precludes the possibility of it. During the last year, this has been sadly plagued, with what the physicians are pleased to call a rheumatic inflammation, for which I am now under treatment from Dr. Jackson, under the general direction of Mr. Trevors, an eminent oculist in England. I have always found traveling, with its necessary exposures, to be of infinite disservice to my eyes, and in this state of them particularly I dare not risk it.

You will ask, with these disadvantages, how I can expect to succeed in my enterprise? I answer that I hope always to have a partial use of my eyes, and for the rest, an intelligent reader, who is well acquainted with French, Spanish and Latin, will enable me to effect with my ears what other people do with eyes. The only material inconvenience will be a necessarily more tedious and prolonged labor.

Johnson in his life of Milton says that no man can compile a history who is blind.[3] But, by the blessing of God, if my ears are spared me, I will disprove the assertion. Although I should lose the use of my vision altogether, an evil not in the least degree probable, my chronicle, whatever other demerits it may have, shall not be wanting in accuracy and research. If my health continues thus, I shall necessarily be debarred from many of the convivial, not to say, social pleasures of life, and consequently must look to these literary pursuits as the principal and permanent source of future enjoyment. As with these views, I have deliberated, taken up other projects, and my progress, since I have begun to break ground, entirely satisfies me.[4]

The following is a duplicate answer to your letter of the 16th of September, 1826, which answer is dated December [blank], 1826. If you have received the original, therefore pray take no trouble to read this.

1. Alexander Hill Everett (1792–1847), diplomat, political writer and editor. While U.S. Minister to Spain he became the first of a considerable number of American diplomats to further WHP's historical projects.

2. Although he never set foot inside an archive, WHP was soon disabused of the idea that his materials could be collected in a matter of months.

3. Speaking of Milton, Johnson had written, "To compile a history from various authors, when they can only be consulted by other eyes, is not easy, nor possible, but with more skilful and attentive help than can be commonly obtained; and it was probably the difficulty of consulting and comparing that stopped Milton's narrative at the Conquest; a period at which affairs were not yet very intricate, nor authors very numerous." See Samuel Johnson, *Lives of the English Poets* (2 vols., London, 1925), I, 73.

4. The weak and fluctuating state of his vision repeatedly caused WHP to toy with the idea of discarding his Spanish project.

32.   From Alexander Hill Everett
                 (Letterbook, A. H. Everett Papers, Mass. Hist. Soc.)

Madrid January 3, 1827

Wm. H. Prescott Esq.

My dear Sir

Soon after I had the pleasure of writing to you, Mr. [Obadiah] Rich returned from London, and immediately undertook the execution of your order for the purchase of books. They are now on their way to Cadiz and will, I think, prove satisfactory to you. We thought it more convenient for the purposes of package and transportation to consider your order and that of Mr. Ticknor as a joint concern. The cases are accordingly directed to the Boston Athenaeum.[1] You will of course find no difficulty in separating the articles intended for you, whether for the payment of duties or of the cost, which you can if you please reimburse to Mr. Ticknor as I have not made use of the draft you sent me on London.

Mr. Rich possesses the two MSS. named in your list. They can be copied at the price you mention of two reales a page and will cost at that rate about fifty dollars each. I have directed Mr. Rich to put that of Carbajal in hand.[2] Considering from your second letter that your project was still in some degree unsettled, we concluded to defer the copying of the other until I should hear from you again. You will therefore have the goodness to let me know your intentions in this respect. I think it not improbable that I could procure for you copies of the Quincuagenas of Oviedo,[3] mentioned in my last letter. They are dispersed through the different Royal libraries; but by the aid of [Martín Fernández de] Navarrete,[4] with whom I am on good terms, I suppose I could have the use of them for this purpose. Let me know therefore whether you would like to have them. You will see in the memoirs of the Academy the manner in which they are spoken of by Clemencin.[5] I have no further information respecting them than what he gives, but should judge from his description that they would afford very copious and valuable materials for a view of the state of society which seems to be your principal object.

I trust that your eyes are now in good order and that you are prosecuting your enterprise with vigor. I assure you that I feel great interest in it and should be truly happy to aid you to the extent of my power. I beg you therefore to command me without reserve and am with great respect Yours very truly and faithfully

1. At this time both Prescott and Ticknor were subscribers of the Boston Athenaeum, and Ticknor, serving as a trustee, was also concerned with book purchases for that growing collection.

2. The manuscript of Dr. Lorenzo Galindez de Carbajal (b. 1472) was his "Anales del Rey Don Fernando el Católico."

3. Very important to WHP in his research for his first book was Gonzalo Fernández de Oviedo y Valdés' manuscript "Las quincuagenas de los generosos é ilustres é no menos famosos reyes, príncipes, duques, marqueses y condes et caballeros, et personas notables de Espana."

4. Martín Fernández de Navarrete (1765–1844), a distinguished Spanish scholar, assisted WHP's pursuit of documents for his historical themes and also helped accord him recognition.

5. Diego Clemencin (1765–1834), Spanish literary and political figure, wrote *Elogio de la Reina Isabel la Católica,* which was published in the sixth volume of the *Memorias* of the Real Academia de la Historia.

33.   To Alexander Hill Everett
                      (Draft, WHP Papers, Mass. Hist. Soc.)

                                               Boston, July 13, 1827
My Dear Sir

The second convoy of Spaniards[1] reached us about three weeks since, and all in excellent condition. The great work *España Sagrada*, I find, as I anticipated, I might have dispensed with; but on the whole I must consider it exceedingly fortunate that there should be no more supernumeraries in an order made up by me from such imperfect sources. Among the books sent to the Athenaeum is the sixth volume of the *Memorias* of the Spanish Academy. I have never seen it before, which will account to you for my ignorance respecting the Quincuagenas of Oviedo. This sixth volume is indeed invaluable for my purposes, since it is wholly devoted to my subject, filled with very sensible reflections by Señor Clemencin, and with abundance of historical illustrations and authentic documents taken from the public archives in Spain. This, together with my own books supply all the information I can desire, respecting the proper choice of authors necessary to my design.

The archives of Simancas appear to be rich in documents relating to this period, and if I were to visit Spain myself, I might, perhaps, make some pertinent extracts from them. Upon the whole I believe this has been done sufficiently for my purpose in this 6th volume of the Academy. In addition to the works ordered by me from Mr. Rich April 25, 1827—of which I have sent a duplicate, I shall be obliged to you if you will request him to get for me—

Alonso de Palencia—Cronica de Henrique IV—or his Annals, if they do not come unreasonable. Also the sixth volume of the *Memorias* of the Royal Spanish Academy of History. I should like very much the extracts from the Quincuagenas of Oviedo—the manuscripts—marked Y, 59 and K, 81, particularly the former, appear to be preferable—vide *Memorias* Royal Academy t. VI, p. 224. The work of Carvajal, cited with the greatest praise by Señor Clemencin, appears to be the Memorial or Registro &c. I suppose this therefore to be preferable to the Annals—vide *Memorias* Royal Academy p. 65 note. If I can obtain the works which I last ordered from Mr. Rich, (all of which, with the exception of Quintanilla et Mendoza's work, appear to me indispensable) together with these above cited, I believe I shall have no further reason to trouble you with my importunity.

You will confer a great obligation on me by advising Mr. Rich of the contents of this letter.

You have doubtless heard that our friend Sparks is busily engaged with the epistolary remains of Washington. And very substantial remains they are. Who would have thought that this great general &c in the midst of his multitudinous avocations would have found time to have concocted seventy folios of letters—yet so it is. Sparks has also been authorized by Congress to publish the diplomatic correspondence between the president and that body and our foreign ministers during the Revolutionary War—from all which the excellent editor of the *North American* will doubtless gain much credit and certainly a great deal of money.[2]

The last number of his Review is thought the best that has appeared for a long while. I am glad of it, for setting aside personal regard for Sparks I should be very sorry to have the *Southern Quarterly*[3] conducted with more spirit than our own. There appears to be little danger of this at present. Nothing can be more meagre than the two numbers already ushered into the world; criticism without a spark of philosophy and done up in a style, half florid, half pedantic, which might better suit the columns of the *National Gazette*.[4] If it does not go up, however, it will not be for the want of a gentle puff or two from the editor. Mr. Walsh made us a visit lately. He told me there were 60 writers in Philadelphia who could furnish as able contributions as those already published. I heard incredulous; but since I have read his numbers, I believe him perfectly. Mr. Walsh has made another bend in his politics, and has given up chanting paeans to the cold virtues of Mr. Adams. This, however, surprises nobody. The reason he assigns is that Mr. Adams does nothing and will do nothing for the Federal party, being altogether under the influence of his western counsellor Mr. Clay. As this is not the season for Court or Congress, there is little business of a public nature stirring. Mr. Webster has been transplanted from the House to the Senate,[5] which considering the numbers and ferocity of the opposition there, may be called "casting Daniel into the lion's den." The many-headed monster has not decided on his successor, probably Mr. Gorham, possibly Mr. Frank Gray.[6] Our own private circle has been a little startled by the unexpected secession of the Reverend President Kirkland from the faction of old bachelors, who, as you may have perhaps heard, will lead to the hymeneal altar, as the newspapers have it, the blooming fair, so long known as Miss Betsey Cabot, somewhere about the latter end of September. There has been a prodigious mortality among the older gentlemen and spinsters during the last two years, who seem to have taken the hint from your new views of Mr. Malthus' problem.[7]

Adieu, my dear Sir—I beg you will present my respects to Mrs. Everett and believe me[8] Ever yours with great respect

1. Here the reference is to the second shipment of materials from Spain.

2. In his estimate of the rewards awaiting Sparks, WHP was doubly mistaken.

3. A somewhat confusing reference to *The American Quarterly Review*. To the Bostonian anything south of New York was southern.

4. Robert Walsh's newspaper in Philadelphia.

5. Despite a political outlook that mirrored most of that of the statesman, WHP never counted Daniel Webster (1782–1852) among his friends.

6. Benjamin Gorham (1775–1855) won this election.

7. Politics and society often evoked WHP's humor, but fluctuations in the economy never did.

8. For many reasons, including the assistance of his reader-secretary, slowness of communication and the cost of postage, WHP commonly wrote long letters to his transatlantic correspondents.

34.   Invoice from Obadiah Rich[1]
(WHP Papers, Mass. Hist. Soc.)

Alvar Gomez, De rebus gestis a Franc.		
Ximenio Cisnerio. Compluti, 1567	f⁰	300
Ordenanzas Reales de Castilla.		
Burgos, 1528 B. L.		100
Leyes de la Hermandad, Burgos, 1527 B. L.	f⁰	100
Leyes del Quaduno nuevo hecho en la vega de		
Granada. Salamanca, 1550		40
Leyes de Toro gloradas por Cifuentes.		
Medina, 1555		60
Zurita, Historia de Hernando el Catolico.		
2 Vols. Zaragoza, 1580		120
Blancas, Coronacion de los Reyes de		
Aragon &c. Zaragoza, 1646		60
Box, packing, land-carriage &c., shipping		
charges		80
E. E. Madrid Received the amount of A. H.	Reales	860 $43
Everett Esqr. July 21st 1827		

O. RICH

1. Obadiah Rich (1777–1850), bookseller, bibliographer and consular official. He was indispensable in the building of WHP's historical library; many such shipments came to grace his shelves and to aid his research.

35.   To Edward Everett
          (Prescott's Letters 1827–58, Edward Everett Papers, Mass. Hist. Soc.)

                                              November 13 [1827]

Dear Sir,
     Your grace is so ample that I could hardly find a pretext for not
furnishing some twenty pages of tittle tattle for your July number. If
you should meet with any very dull or lively book on your return from
Washington that you would like to have noticed and will send it to
me, I shall be obliged to you.[1] Yours respectfully

                                              WM. H. PRESCOTT

     1. No item by WHP appeared in the July, 1828, issue of the *North Ameri-
can Review.*

36.   To Obadiah Rich
               (Draft, WHP Papers, Mass. Hist. Soc.)

                                              [January, 1828]

Dear Sir
     I am happy in being able to inform you that the two boxes of Span-
ish books arrived here about a month since in a vessel by Bilbao, where
I suppose they must have been detained a good while. The printed
volumes are good copies, and in excellent condition. The manuscripts
of the Catholic Kings are well and legibly copied, particularly the first
half of Carvajal, which I suppose to be a Spanish hand. These Annals,
however, are, I am sorry to find, without punctuation. Alonso de Palencia's Chronicle comes very opportunely[1]—indeed by my last letter to
Mr. Everett, I requested a copy of it. The chirography of this however
is so crabbed and enigmatical that I shall have it again copied here.
From the infirmity of my eyes, the greater part of my Spanish is now
read to me—and a difficult manuscript would add new delays to my
necessarily very snail-like progress. On the whole I have great reason
to be satisfied with your kindness and attention in procuring me all
that I had ordered, some of these works being by their rarity such as I
had no right to count upon—and I am very much obliged to you for
these good offices.
     I informed you, I believe, when in Spain that I had ordered such
other books as related to my subject from Paris. Mr. Herbert [?] Colles-
ton [?], who has been making large purchases for the Athenaeum, was
my agent. He has partially complied with my instructions—but I have
written to him, in New York, where he now is, that I shall put into your

hands the collection of the remainder—and at the close of this letter I will annex a catalogue of such works as I wish you to procure for me on the Continent, as, of course, even if they could be had, they would come too dear in London. I am not precise in regard to the editions specified, and you will remember my general request respecting print and paper to you formerly.[2] In a letter written to Mr. Everett but for me, I requested you to get for me the 5th and 6th volumes of the *Memorias* of the Spanish Academy of History, also Navarrete's late publications. I wrote to Mr. Everett the other day, repeating this request. Will you, when you write to Spain, see that this be done. You may add—

The manuscript of Henry IV—will amount to 48 dollars (I believe) at the rate of the others. I know not whom to send this to. Will you advise me how I am to pay for this, and for the books you may hereafter send me—perhaps you will prefer a bill of exchange direct. I suppose I am not to expect any extract from the Quincuagenas of Oviedo. The dog-in-the-manger hauteur of the Spaniards in regard to their unpublished manuscripts would not be unworthy of the Chinese.

I have complied with your request, in mentioning you to those of my friends whom I have thought might have occasion for your literary services. The Trustees of the Athenaeum have commissioned you, as you are already aware, to make purchases for them. The necessities of the Athenaeum will, like that of all similar institutions, increase with the growth of it—but its funds, though ample in comparison with what they have been hitherto, are by no means commensurate with its wants. All such institutions should undoubtedly contain those works which are too bulky and expensive for a private library. It falls somewhat heavy upon a writer here, that he must make a collection for himself of such works as in other countries are already prepared for him in the public libraries.

The following is the list of books I wish purchased for me. I do not desire any very unreasonable prices to be given, as with the exception of Jovius, I here have in my possession all that is indispensable. I have marked with an asterisk those works of which I am most desirous, and with a cypher those which I care the least for—and which you need not purchase, unless they come cheaper.

Judging from the prices quoted, I presume the above books may be had for less than $200, which sum I should not at any rate wish to exceed.[3]

1. WHP's published estimate of this source, which he used considerably, is in his *History of the Reign of Ferdinand and Isabella, the Catholic* (3 vols., Boston, 1838), I, 136–37.

2. For his working historical collection, WHP never sought books in the rarest of editions and finest of bindings. He always instructed his aides and agents to secure good serviceable printings, preferably of large type size on excellent paper.

3. The draft copy of this letter is not accompanied by the promised list of books.

37. ## To George Bancroft
(George Bancroft Papers, Mass. Hist. Soc.)

Boston, February 25th 1828

My dear Friend,

I this second received your copy of Peter Folger's Remains,[1] whose splendid execution in chirography, gilding, binding &c &c does equal honour to all parties concerned. I shall send it straightway to London and doubt not that it will be much more acceptable than the dilapidated old Pamphlet which we have mourned over so long. I am glad you have got up a translation of Everett's *America;* it will serve to draw out the sting which Walsh gave him,[2] which, I assure you, made him feel very sore, as he bitterly complained in a letter to me about three months since from Madrid. I shall welcome with pleasure your translation from Heeren, as by it we shall gain at the same time a learned German and an English classic.[3] If this does not earn me a copy gratis, I don't know what will. Please to make my regards to your wife and Cogswell and believe me now and ever Yours affectionately

WM. H. PRESCOTT

1. Probably Peter Folger (1617–90), the Nantucket pioneer who wrote on religious intolerance in New England.

2. Alexander H. Everett's *America* was translated into Spanish by an instructor at the Round Hill School and published at Northampton in 1828. The original edition, published in Philadelphia in 1827, was reviewed in *The American Quarterly Review*, I, 2 (June, 1827), 494–520.

3. Many of the works of Arnold Hermann Ludwig Heeren (1760–1842), admired by Bancroft, were translated and published by him in America and England. In 1828 the title involved was the *History of the States of Antiquity.*

38. ## To Susan Prescott
(WHP Papers, Mass. Hist. Soc.)

Monday, 10 A.M., [April 21, 1828] Washington[1]

I arrived here, dear Susan, yesterday at noon, after a rather fatiguing journey from Philadelphia, which we left on Saturday at twelve. We proceeded about 50 miles down the Delaware, whose scenery, though occasionally beautiful on the Pennsylvania coast, was inferior to what we had seen higher up the river. We landed at New Castle and rode across Maryland to French Town, over a vile road of ruts and stones for about 30 miles. I am glad that father did not venture upon the journey.

We took the steamboat again at French Town, near Elkton, and crossed the head of the Chesapeake during the night, reaching Baltimore at 3 in the morning. The night was dark as Egypt, and a smart thunder squall in the course of it gave us all a good shaking. I slept more comfortably, however, than I had done in the "Chancellor Livingston."

We had orators, Jacksonites and Adamsites, aboard the boat, who kept us awake spouting speeches till near midnight—when we were all gathered to our rest. In the morning the sight of some forty or fifty personages, in white shirts and white handkerchiefs round their heads, popping up one after another out of their beds looked like resurrection day. We landed at 8 o'clock, so dark and stormy that you could not tell the land from the water; and there was a most charming confusion in pulling out trunks, bags, coats &c—for we could hardly make out who our own legs and arms belonged to.

We left Baltimore at 4 in the morning and were 8 hours traveling 40 miles through a green country where isolated farm houses and broken fences exhibited the greatest poverty and indolence. Tell Kitty I am among the "negers" now. You can hardly open your eyes without seeing a score of them. They are so civil and attentive, however, that I begin to think better of slavery.

We went to see Mr. Clay last evening[2]—who is as worn and thin as a dyspeptic—he is killed by care and anxiety. His manners, though far from graceful, are very amiable. We then proceeded to Mr. Vaughan's, the English minister's. A very well-bred, well-informed personage who gave us much entertaining gossip about high life in England. He has engaged us to dine with him sociably today and I anticipate an agreeable afternoon.

I slept like a top last night, as you may well believe, having got only 3 hours the night previous, and having walked with Mr. Webster out to Georgetown in the afternoon, an affair of six miles—for we went also to the Capitol, in the opposite direction—while George more wisely took a nap.

At eleven we shall go to the House—and I am now going to pay my respects to the king of men, for the present at least.[3] So you may wonder how I can condescend to talk with such little personages as you. I shall

write you and father from Washington. I am beginning to have a sec-
ond attack of home-sickness and while sad sit now facing homewards.
Kiss Katie and Will.[4] Love to father, mother &c &c. My eye is fairly.
I shall read all you write. Your affectionate[5]

WM. H. PRESCOTT

1. On this, his first American trip of consequence, WHP was accompanied
by George Ticknor.

2. Henry Clay (1777–1852) was then Adams' Secretary of State.

3. Writing, on April 22, of his call upon the President, WHP told Susan, "I
called to see Mr. Adams, in his princely residence, which formed somewhat of
a contrast to the occupant. He was dressed in checked waistcoat, blue trowsers,
yarn socks, and clod-hopper shoes." WHP had first met John Quincy Adams in
London in 1816.

Of his visit to Congress, WHP wrote in the same letter, "The members of
the Senate make a very respectable appearance. Those of the House are somewhat mottled. I saw one gentleman rolling about drunk . . . another blow
his nose with his fingers. . . ."

4. Catherine, the daughter nearing her fourth birthday, is alternately Kitty
and Katie. Will was the two-year-old son, William Gardiner Prescott (1826–95),
who later attended Harvard, studied but never practiced law, married Josephine Augusta Peabody of Salem, and fathered four children.

5. During this, his first extended absence since his marriage, WHP established the lifelong habit of writing detailed letters to his stay-at-home wife.

39.   To Susan Prescott

(WHP Papers, Mass. Hist. Soc.)

Sunday, 10 A.M. Baltimore, April 27, 1828

We arrived here, dear Susan, yesterday at 1 o'clock. I dined at Dr.
Stewart's in the country, where I saw Margaret G. and had a hospitable
welcome, and sufficiently [...] family dinner. The environs of this
place are very beautiful—and the grounds of Dr. Stewart, about 2 miles
from town, command a fine view of a very extensive landscape and
water scape.

In the evening I was introduced to a phrenological society in Baltimore—composed chiefly of doctors, who, after reading a very satisfactory (to themselves) lecture on the science of craniology, proceeded to
a careful examination of my pericranium. They measured it with a
variety of instruments, until they had ascertained a complete map of my
scull, with all its flats and elevations. When what do you think was the
result?

The organ of *firmness* was found predominant above every other. Far
above that of Mr. Webster's, of which they had a scale. I was very low
in the development of *parental affection*. So you will not accuse me of

loving Kate too much again. And the organ of *secrecy* was found in high perfection. The other qualities came pretty right.

I told them they were never more mistaken in their lives—that I was totally destitute of *firmness,* being remarkably weak of purpose on most occasions; and that I never kept a secret in my life. They were a good deal annoyed, and insisted upon it that I did not know my own character.

There were lying upon the table the sculls of five or six pirates—who had been executed at Norfolk, who had certain developments not unlike mine. So much for this profound science.

Today we dine at Mr. Oliver's and pass the evening at Mr. Carroll's,[1] and tomorrow embark at 5 A.M. in the steamboat for Philadelphia, which we shall reach in the evening—and where we shall probably stay till Saturday.

The hotel, Barnum's, at which we are staying, is on the greatest scale of any we have met with—and well kept.

I have just received Mother's letter of the 23d. (I will look up one of our bloody cousins, dear Mother—and if she or he be within the liberties of Philadelphia it will be hard but I shall find them out. I am happy to learn that you and father are going [on] a little journey. It is of great importance to you to escape the vile east wind. I wish you could have the balmy breeze that I am now enjoying. But you can obtain it only by a very fatiguing journey. Baltimore in its general aspect reminds me of Boston. It has few fine public buildings, but the dwelling houses, with shining white marble steps, have an air of neatness and beauty quite attractive. The people are busy and cheerful, and all mad for their great railroad, to which they have subscribed more than 4 millions, in this city.[2] Yet things had shockingly depreciated here, and a house which in Boston would rent for $600 may be easily had for 300. The sanguine anticipations from this railroad have, however, given every thing a start again. This is their last chance.

So it seems you were near being burnt out. What a satisfaction it must be to you to have two such active personages in the family in times of fire as Edward and Susan. I think the premiums in Bedford Street should be reduced one-half at least. George is stretched on a sofa reading *Cyril Thornton*[3]—and I am preferring to gawk about the town with all my eyes—so adieu, dear Mother.)

Pray continue to write me, dear Susan, of the little chicks. They may be sure of the whip and the work box—and a kiss or two into the bargain. I must not forget that I dreamed about you more than an hour last night, which I mention as a proof of my attention to you. Love to father, mother, Elizabeth, Edward, Frank and family, your mother and family &c &c. I miss the children so. Your affectionate

                                                    WILLIAM H. PRESCOTT

P.S. I read all the letters I received with my own eyes. You write a good-sized, fair hand, and that is all I want.

1. Charles Carroll (1737–1832) of Carrollton, last surviving signer of the Declaration of Independence.
2. In February, 1827, the agitation began for the railroad which resulted in the Baltimore and Ohio Railroad.
3. Captain Thomas Hamilton's novel *The Youth and Manhood of Cyril Thornton* was published initially in Edinburgh in 1827.

40.   To Obadiah Rich
(Draft, WHP Papers, Mass. Hist. Soc.)

                                          Boston, June 25, 1828

O. Rich Esq.
  London
Dear Sir

I received your letter of the 12th of March in due season. You mention in it your intention of revisiting Madrid for the purpose of removing your family to London—an exchange of residence by which you will be much the gainer if the reports I have heard of the low state of society and civilization in the old Spanish capital be correct.

The books which you sent me came in very good condition. And I am much obliged to you, for the little manuscript biography of Ximenes which I shall doubtless make useful to me in spite of the hieroglyphics in which it is written. I must thank you, also, for the kind interest which you take in the success of my proposed work, and for your liberal offer of any other materials in your possession that may have relation to it. I inclose a list of a few more books, which I wish you to purchase for me, as from their titles they would seem to be pertinent to my subject. With regard to most of them, however, this is but conjecture on my part, and if upon examination you should find it otherwise, you can omit such books. Those which may be underscored I wish sent at any rate.

Notwithstanding that through your aid I have assembled such a rich body of materials, there are still some desiderata left, but which perhaps cannot be supplied. Notwithstanding the copiousness of details with which I am furnished, I have very few works which discuss my subject, or any portion of it, in a philosophical manner, which can aid me by their general reflections, and the extended views which they present. You may say, indeed, that if I am furnished with the facts, it is my province to deduce from them correct general results &c. and that if the ground is wholly new, so much the better for me. Yet it might be confessed that the speculations of a sensible writer who may have glanced however incidentally at my subject, might furnish me with some useful hints, present some inaccuracies with which I might otherwise [. . .], and put me sometimes upon a different train of thought from what I should have entered of my own accord. I have found such aid, for instance, in Hallam's *Middle Ages;* in Varillas' *Policy of Ferdinand the Catholic;* in Gaillard's *Rivalité de la France et de la Espagne* —a good work which I have borrowed, until I receive a copy from you. But I am still in want of works which may throw similar light on the domestic policy of the Catholic Kings (for I am well enough off in regard to their foreign polities): on the domestic policy of Charles V and Philip 2d—which I would contrast with theirs in Robertson's history, principally to the external relations of Spain under Charles; on the civil constitution, social conditions and genius of the Arabs, especially of Spain; on the permanent influence of the Inquisition on Spain, and on the character of the nation. Investigations like these, which make up the philosophy of history, are to be expected only from French or English or German writers—and would be very acceptable to me, whether they come in the form of a book, a pamphlet or a review. The London and Edinburgh Quarterlies are very meagre on these heads, though I have met with some scattered notices in them. The influence of the discovery of America on Spain, and on the world generally, and the colonial policy of the Spaniards as originating with the Catholic sovereigns are topics that have been amply discussed by various authors which are accessible to, or possessed by me. I presume I have most of the native authors who have touched upon the constitutional history of Spain, and who too often seem to have had their tongues tied under the system of intellectual oppression which has so long prevailed in that unhappy country. Marina's *Theory of the Cortes* is an honourable exception to this.

As you live in the very centre of literary circulation and have access to catalogues and collections which I have not, you may perhaps meet with some such works as I have adverted to, either recently published or ancient; and your wider acquaintance with Spanish history may suggest to you some others.

I accompany this letter with a catalogue of such rare French and English works pertinent to my subject as I have already in my possession or under my control, in order that you may not unnecessarily buy them for me.

I smile at the offer you make me, of arranging for the publication of my book with some English bookseller.[1] Had I as many eyes as Argus, I have not the wit nor the experience that would enable me to turn off a work in the rapid style of Scott or Irving.[2] But working as I do a great part of the time, with another person's eyes, you may judge, where there are so many authorities to study, how necessarily snail-like must be my progress. In the meantime there is no hurry. I am not likely to be forestalled in my subject by any other adventurer—and as it affords me both occupation and amusement, I care not how long, within a reasonable compass, it may take me. I mean to make myself master of my subject, in all its remote relations before I begin to write upon it. I must make amends by novelty of materials and notarial accuracy, for any want of originality in the reflections. I shall be satisfied if I can bring the whole to a conclusion in five years from the present time. But I have talked too long about my *chateaux d'Espagne.*

I have made a remittance of £50, being £10 more than you desire, to Mr. Everett, and when you send me any books in addition to those on my last order, you will be pleased to let me know the additional amount I am to pay therefor. I do not wish you, however, to exceed £20, in addition to the £50 which I have now remitted to you, for the purchase of books on my account. As it will be obviously of importance to me to collect all my sources of information together as soon as possible, you will oblige me by transmitting such works as you may purchase for me as soon as you can conveniently do it.[3] I am, dear Sir, truly your obliged servant

1. Eight years passed before WHP tried to take advantage of this offer.
2. Sir Walter Scott (1771–1832) and Washington Irving (1783–1859), two of the most popular authors of the day, were special favorites of WHP.
3. The draft copy of this letter is not accompanied by any lists of books.

41.   To Edward Everett
(Prescott's Letters 1827–58, Edward Everett Papers, Mass. Hist. Soc.)

Boston, July 25, 1828

My dear Sir

I send you an article which will take up some 25 or 30 pages of your journal. I should not have been so slow with it, but that I carried the book, which I had intended to have reviewed, into the country, and forgot to take it out of the coach, so that it went on, the Lord knows where, to Canada, I suppose. As there was no other copy of it here, I waited in hopes of its return, till so much of this month had elapsed, that I had no time to waste. And so for want of a better work, I have taken Taschereau's *Life of Molière,* which unluckily was reviewed by Sir W. Scott in No. 3 *Foreign Quarterly.*

On comparing them, you will find, as you would anticipate, some resemblance in the selection of the anecdotes, but none whatever in the mode of relating them, or in the general reflections at the beginning and end of the article—would that there had been more.

My pieces come round like the spots in the sun. I promised Sparks to furnish him about this amount annually. If you do not like it, I trust you will make no ceremony in returning it. If you do, I beg that you will make what excisions or emendations you think best. I doubt not I shall be a gainer by them. And you will further oblige me by sparing my eyes the trouble of revising the proofs.[1] Yours with great truth

WM. H. PRESCOTT

1. Of this article WHP wrote (Prescott [Gardiner, ed.], *The Literary Memoranda,* I, 92), "I wrote at the rate of 3 pages per day, & could with eight hours labor have written from 4 to 5, it being chiefly narrative." This review appeared in the October, 1828, issue of the *North American Review,* pp. 372–402. For the next four years WHP contributed one article annually to the Boston quarterly.

42.   To Jared Sparks
(Jared Sparks Papers, Harvard College Library)

Pepperell, September 28, 1828

Dear Sparks,

You see I write from the old manse at Pepperell, where we are passing the fall, as, in consequence of my Father's having been troubled with a bad cough, we passed the heats of the summer at Nahant, and opened the campaign here rather late.[1] Next year we may hope to have the pleasure of your society, and talk over, at leisure, your adventures in the land of wonders. I must acknowledge the receipt, in due season, of your two letters dated June 4 and July 9—which I should have sooner answered—but I never had any character as a correspondent.

We were all exceedingly pleased that you have succeeded so well in your application to the official functionaries in England; and I hope you will not meet with the obstacles you anticipate in France. It must be a very mistaken jealousy and altogether worthy of the Chinese, which would lead them to throw obstacles in your way to your arriving at a knowledge of facts that occurred fifty years ago. You will, by these researches, get into your possession such a body of authentic materials as will ensure you perfect success in your ultimate work on American history, which, after all, as it will be an original composition, will be the most important result of your labors, as regards your own reputation.

We were all much gratified that you found Charles Amory[2] so promising a young man. He has excellent natural dispositions and required only what he was fortunate enough to find in his brother William,[3] a competent friend and adviser, as he was entering into life. He began rather wildly; but I have no doubt of the manner in which he will finish.

The letter you enclosed from Lockhart[4] was very satisfactory to me I can assure you; for I should have been not a little chagrined to have gone so far out of my way as to write for a foreign journal and to have had my article returned on my hands, a catastrophe which from an ominous passage in your first letter did not appear to me very improbable—so that I began to regret that I had sent the piece. But it is all *comme il faut* and I am much obliged to you for the part you have taken in forwarding my designs.[5] We have little news here.

The great presidential question begins to make more sensation as it draws nearer to a determination. The Jacksonites are more sanguine than the Adamsites, but it is difficult to form any well-grounded calculations as to the result—there are so many lies and misstatements in circulation.

The lesser presidential question of Harvard College has not been much stirred of late. The corporation, it is understood, is in a quandary. Everett and Ticknor are the two most prominent candidates, and the discussion has raked up all the animosities and personal feelings that have ever been entertained against either of these individuals. It seems highly probable, in the opinion of the knowing ones, that the corporation will resort to some third party, as the best means of settling the difficulty, perhaps Dr. Ware, the present temporary incumbent in the office—as they sometimes choose the candidate who is nearest to the grave for the chair of St. Peter, when the conclave are at fault in regard to a successor. I am surprised that Alexander Everett has not been more currently spoken of. He has many qualities admirably suited to the place.[6]

In consequence of a visit which I paid to Washington last spring, I did not furnish my article for the old North[7] last July. I have written one of about thirty pages for the ensuing October number, on Molière, which I hope you will like. I had worked up another topic, but the book which I was bringing to Pepperell was accidentally left by me on the coach, and passed on to Canada and did not return till it was too late to make use of it. Walsh told me in Philadelphia that he intended to write an article for the *North American* on the political influences of the Catholic and Protestant religions, or some such topic—I am perhaps not precisely accurate in the subject. You once mentioned to me that he had before spoken of this to Everett. I imagine it will end with intention; though he expresses great good will to the journal and lauds it, *cum grano salis,* in his Gazette as usual.

If you see Mr. O. Rich, I wish you would ask him if he received in London a bill of exchange for £50, together with a new order for several works relative to my subject, from me this summer, and tell him I shall receive a supply of books from him, as soon as he can muster them, with much pleasure.

I am creeping along as fast as my eyes will let me, but that is not much faster than Parry travelled over his polar ice.[8]

All your friends continue well. William Eliot's busily occupied with building a spacious hotel on the land opposite your old quarters, so you have well escaped a record siege of noise and brick dust. I believe he will get out of the scrape without much loss, which is more than I once feared.

Adieu, my dear friend. Pray write, should you remain in Europe beyond this year, to Your sincere friend,

WM. H. PRESCOTT

1. To escape the heat of Boston, three generations of Prescotts often went, in this period, to the ancestral farm at Pepperell in May, transferred to their cottage at Nahant in July and returned to Pepperell in September.

2. Charles Amory (1808–98), Susan Amory Prescott's brother and her junior by six years, was twelve years younger than WHP.

3. William Amory (1804–88), intimate friend and brother-in-law of WHP, married Anna Sears of Boston and fathered five children.

4. John Gibson Lockhart (1794–1854), son-in-law and biographer of Sir Walter Scott, edited the *Quarterly Review* for many years.

5. This article never appeared in the English journal and the entire matter is shrouded in considerable secrecy, a by-product of its author's disappointment.

6. In his report and speculation WHP was partly right, partly wrong. Kirkland's successor at Harvard was Josiah Quincy, who, assuming the presidency on January 29, 1829, held the post for more than sixteen years.

7. A favorite appellation for the *North American Review,* it was often employed by WHP.

8. Sir William Edward Parry (1790–1855), English arctic explorer.

43.   To Obadiah Rich
                (Draft, WHP Papers, Mass. Hist. Soc.)

                                    Boston, February 6th 1829

Dear Sir,

  I have received your parcels by the "Java," which had the incredible
passage of nearly three months, and by the "Amethyst," in good condition. I am much obliged to you for your prompt attendance to my
wishes. Most of the books have been obtained at prices which I could
not have expected in London, and the print, which is of so much importance to me, is large and clear. On looking over the catalogue sent
to Mr. Ticknor I find several works which I had supposed might not
be very easy to meet with, although not quoted by Brunet at high
prices. Perhaps you had better give a little more for them at such a sale
in order to make sure of them. The edition of the *Classici Italiani* is
to be had so much cheaper on the Continent than in England that it
had undoubtedly better be bought there, unless you can meet with a
copy nearly as cheap at an auction sale. The copies of this collection
are executed very differently, some being clear and others very much
blurred, a circumstance which I will thank you to attend to. I add two
or three books, which you may buy for me at reasonable prices. Some
of them I see are on Hibbert's catalogue.

  Brunetto Latini—*Il Tesoro*—Mr. Ticknor tells me he has stated the
price which he should be willing to give for this. If it goes above his
mark, and not exceeding 20 shillings, I should like it.

  Forteguerri's *Ricciardetto*—translated by Lord Glenbervie

  Catalogue des livres de compte MacCarthy, with the prices—2 volumes

  Catalogue of the library of William Roscoe, with the prices

  Delices de l'Espagne—Leiden—6 volumes in 3

  Raynouard—*Poésies des Troubadours*

  Bowring's Translations of Spanish Poetry

  Lays of the Minnesingers—London, 1825

  Depping—*Histoire de l'Espagne*—Paris, 1811

  A. W. Schlegel—*Observations sur la langue et la littérature Proven-
çales*—Paris, 1818

  Peyron—*Essais sur l'Espagne*

  I should like to have the travels of some intelligent modern English
or French traveller in Spain, if you know of any.

  I have no book and can find none in the Ebeling Collection in
Harvard College containing the ordinance of Ferdinand for the establishment of the Council of the Indies or the laws enacted under him

for the government of the Spanish colonies. The *Recopilación de las leyes de las Indias,* a work referred to by Robertson in his *America* and in the College library, with one or two trifling exceptions contains no provision of a more ancient date than the reign of Charles V. The several excellent codes which you have sent me relate only to the domestic government of Spain under the Catholic Kings. Can you supply this deficiency?

You mention drawing upon me at 60 days sight. This will suit me as well as any other, and if you find this not so convenient, I will make you the necessary remittances upon your notifying me of it.

Mr. Irving's *Moorish Chronicles* is in the press here. From a short extract which I have seen from it, it looks like something betwixt romance and history. Can you tell me whether he is likely to occupy himself further with a discussion of the period on which I am engaged? A person will fare poorly who comes after such a writer.[1]

1. Irving's successive works on Spanish themes kept alive WHP's fears that his subject might be gutted by the fast-working, popular New Yorker.

The death on February 1, 1829, of Catherine Hickling Prescott, his eldest child, was a blow from which WHP's historical labors did not recover fully for months.

44.   To Obadiah Rich
(Draft, WHP Papers, Mass. Hist. Soc.)

Boston, October 20, 1829

Dear Sir,

I am happy to acknowledge the receipt of the parcels by the "Amethyst" and the "Caroline." They are purchased at very reasonable prices. The copy of Tasso I consider an excellent bargain. The Novellieri, though very neat, are unfortunately so small as to the type that I must request you to buy me another copy of Bandello's novels of larger print.

I feel some embarrassment about returning the manuscripts which you were kind enough to take the trouble to send me. But the two *comunidades* are later than my period, and the one on the Medina Sidonia family, which I should else have retained, would make me blind were I to read two pages of it. The manuscript of Alonso de Palencia, which you may remember to have sent me from Spain, I was obliged to have wholly transcribed in large characters at an expense equal to its original cost to me. The little Cartapacio &c., which is written beautifully and concerns my subject, I have kept. The others

I have sent to your correspondents Gray and Bowen[1] to be forwarded to you in the first parcel.

I see you are not aware of the wretched quality of my eyes, or rather, I should say eye, for I have but one, the sight of the other having been extinguished by an accidental blow in College, which is the source of all my troubles. The remaining eye is liable to inflammations—to the degree that for five years I was debarred from using it as many hours,[2] besides having endured two applications of the knife to it, and repeated confinements in dark rooms. I thank God, however, I have of late years with some interruptions enjoyed a fair use of it. Yet I scarcely read a word during the whole of 1826–7, but was obliged to be read to. And this last summer, as you may have noticed in rather a gloomy letter I wrote from Nahant, I have lost four months use of it. But I have since been able to go on with my labors, and I have no doubt with prudence I shall complete in a few years what I am now some way advanced in. Excuse these personal details—I give them for once as a justification of what may seem to you a singular and vexatious particularity on my part.

I hope you have been able to supply some of the deficit on the Spanish order at Paris—as well as the Italian—though I do not desire any inexpedient haste in the last. If you can get my books half-bound in England as reasonably and handsomely as the Thierry *L'Angleterre par les Normands* you sent me, I think you had better have it done to all books of the size of small quartos, octavos and under, which may be *shabbily bound* or *in papers*—not those in *new boards* and the same to such large quartos and folios as may be *in papers*. It costs me twice as much to get it done here, and not so well either. Indeed, several times the binding has cost me more than the work. I will thank you to send me in addition to former orders—

Bandello's *Novelle*
Wiffen's *Garcilaso de la Vega*
Dante and His Times (one of Murray's Library)
Southey's *Peninsular War*—if in octavo
Barante, *Littérature Française in XIX siècle*—I have that on the XVIIIe
Turner's *History of Edward VI, Mary and Elisabeth,* octavo
Massuchelli, *Vita de Aretino*
Life of Alexander the Great (Murray's F. Library)
Villers, *Essais sur l'influence de la reformation &c.*

I wish also you to send me as it comes out the "Library of Entertaining and Useful Knowledge"—half binding, two volumes in one. I wish you also to send the *Foreign Review* (not the *Foreign Quarterly Re-*

view) beginning with the ninth number. I have the 8 preceding numbers. These need not be bound.

Touching Foscolo's manuscripts, I think I had better not meddle with them. They are probably the refuse of his commentaries on Dante, and at any rate, I don't see that they could be of service to me.

I have received the following books—viz. a copy of Dante, 3 tom. 4to Roma 1791, a duplicate of Wiffen's Tasso—3 tom. 8vo. and Massieu, *Histoire de poésie française,* 1 tom. 12mo not mentioned on any invoice to me or Mr. Ticknor. I have sent the Tasso and Massieu to Mr. Gray to sell on your account—have kept the Dante. I wish you would rectify this mistake and advise me if I have done right.

I received your draft for $250. in favor of Baring Brothers & Company bearing date August 19, 1829 and paid the same to their agent Mr. Ward.

I shall attend to your request respecting the Congress Library[3] when I see Mr. Everett, whose brother Alexander is now expected. I suppose I may expect soon to have an answer in some shape or other from Mr. Lockhart. I remain truly yours

WM. H. PRESCOTT

1. Probably Francis C. Gray and Francis Bowen (1811–90). The latter, a philosopher and author, owned and edited the *North American Review* for more than a decade, beginning in 1843.

2. On the score of his physical ailments, WHP's capacity for self-pity was enormous, so much so that it occasionally, as here, led him into gross exaggeration.

3. Desirous of widening the area of his American operations as bookseller, Rich asked WHP to recommend certain purchases to the Library of Congress. WHP complied with the request.

45.   To Obadiah Rich
(Draft, WHP Papers, Mass. Hist. Soc.)

Boston, December 28, 1829

Dear Sir,

I hasten to acknowledge the receipt of your letter of November 18, for I find I am likely to have a large fraction of my Italian library twice over. Mr. Amory writes me November 1 that he has shipped from Leghorn complete sets of the *Classici Italiani,* 250 volumes—half bound 160 dollars, and also of the XVIII secola 130 volumes, $110—purchased at Florence. Pray, therefore, do not go on with your purchases of these works, and such as are now bought you had best dispose of as you can in London. I could not sell them for half their cost.

I am much chagrined with the fate of my last article to Mr. Lockhart, if fate it can be called when I know not what has become of it. You omitted to say anything of it in your last letter, so that I am ignorant whether Mr. Lockhart has yet received it, but I suppose not. I cannot but think that my letter to him must have miscarried, as it is inexplicable, when he invited me to send him a list of such articles as I would undertake for him, that he should have paid no further attention to my reply to him. I have written him another letter (inclosed to you is a duplicate of this letter) which I will thank you to let him have and also the article along with it, if not already sent. I have requested him in this letter to return the Spanish article to you, in case he does not like it, and also the first Italian article, if he does not intend to use it. I will thank you if either or both are returned to you to retain them until Mr. Amory comes to London. I will advise him to call for them. I am extremely sorry to trouble you so much in a business foreign to your vocations, and which I fear must be vexatious to you. But you have kindly consented to undertake it, and this must be my apology. The articles are now sufficiently stale, and I am almost vexed that I ever wrote them.[1]

I am sorry to find that you were not fortunate in completing the deficit on my orders in Paris, and I hope to meet with a copy of the *Epistolae Traversarii* by Mehus, a book not in this country, though essential. Would you not stand a better chance of supplying the Italian department by sending direct to your correspondent?

I wish you also to purchase the following books:

Salazar de Mendoza—*Crónica del Gran Cardenal &c* 1625—Salva's Catalogue No. 3923.

Salazar—*Origen de las dignidades seglares de Castilla &c.* 1794—Salva's Catalogue No. 3924.

Saggio Istorico Critica della Comedia Italiana—da F. Salfi 1829.

These volumes of Constable's Miscellany—I, II, III, IV, V, VI, VII, X, XI, XII, XV, XVI, XVIII, XIX, XX, XXI, XXII (for 1827, also that for 1828), XXIII, also *History of the Rebellions in Scotland under Montrose, Dundee and Mar in 1689 and 1715* by Robert Chambers, 2 volumes.

Laborde, *Itinéraire Descriptif de l'Espagne* 5 tom. 8vo., *not his work called Voyage Pittoresque.*

Xth volume of Ginguené's *Histoire littéraire d'Italie*, continued by Salfi.

As they come out—Di Lardner's Cabinet Cyclopedia, viz. *History of Scotland* 2 volumes, *History of Maritime Discovery* 2 volumes, *Lives of*

British Statesmen 3 volumes, *Treatise on Astronomy* 1 volume, *History of England* 3 volumes, *History of Ireland* 1 volume, *Lives of Eminent British Lawyers* 1 volume.

Allacci, *Drammaturgia*

Butler's *Life of Erasmus*

The two first works of Salazar de Mendoza are, I see, to be got in London and I should like them by the first opportunity as they will be of little use to me unless I can get them in the course of three or four months. The edition of Dante de Romanis, which I sent for, has a 4th volume published separately, which I should like to have in addition to the earlier edition of Roma 1791 which I have taken from you in lieu of the Romanis edition.

I wrote you October 20, 1829 advising you of my acceptance of your bill of exchange and specifying some works, chiefly English, which I should like and which, together with the bulk of this order, can be soon procured. I then requested you also to have such books as are in boards half-bound—it is good economy. I have not yet seen the books arrived by the "Liverpool." Trusting that I may soon have some better accounts of my stray articles, I remain Truly your friend and servant

[P.S.] I send a duplicate of this letter from Boston in order to make sure of stopping the purchase of the *Classici*.[2]

1. All of these articles which went to Lockhart failed of publication in England, and they remain shrouded in mystery.

2. A conscientious builder of his library in this period, WHP demonstrates, in his correspondence with Rich in 1829, his two-pronged nature as historian–man of letters.

46.   To Jared Sparks
(Jared Sparks Papers, Harvard College Library)

Bedford St., February 17, [1830]

Dear Sparks

Can you accommodate me with ten or twelve pages in the next number of the *North American* (your last, I understand)? I want to recommend to the public an Asylum for the Blind, which we are organizing in this town. I will endeavor to have it ready by the 1st of next month.[1]

Will you have the goodness to lend me, by the bearer, the 1st and 2d volumes of Mr. Poinsett's *Español*? Truly yours

W. H. PRESCOTT

1. This article appeared in the July, 1830, issue of the *North American Review*, pp. 66–85. WHP's personal identification with the resulting institution,

which has grown to be the world-famous Perkins School for the Blind, extended across the ensuing decade.

47.   To Jonathan Goodhue[1]
                 (Goodhue Papers, The New York Society Library)

                                                        Boston, April 14, 1830

Dear Sir,

I am about to ask a favor of you in behalf of a public institution,
which, I fear, may cause you more trouble than I should feel authorized, notwithstanding your friendship, to expose you to on my own
account.

We are getting up in Boston an Asylum for the Blind, on something
of a similar plan with that in Liverpool; and it is of great importance
to the institution that the first instructors should be persons not only
fully competent to their offices, but also heartily interested in the cause
—the good effects of which have been seen in the Deaf and Dumb
Asylum at Hartford.[2] We are particularly desirous to get a teacher who
is able to instruct the pupils in the mechanic arts. If he could also teach
them the elementary branches of mental education—reading, writing
&c., he would answer our purpose so much the better. Our funds are not
very large, but as we hope to get assistance from the state, and mean to
make the labors of the pupils contribute to their support, we trust we
shall succeed in our undertaking.

My object in writing to you is to ask if you can give us, or can obtain
for us in Liverpool, any information respecting the probability and
expense of procuring as a teacher some person who has had experience
in the business and would be able to advise us how to proceed, and
especially, who would take an interest in promoting the end we have
in view. Whether he should be blind or not, I cannot tell, but should
rather think not. You will oblige me by writing me your opinion and
the result of your inquiries on this matter.

Mr. Brooks[3] has written Mr. Thornely on the subject, and also to
Mr. Freem, both of whom you may be acquainted with, and from whom
you could probably obtain such information as we are in want of.

I trust you will excuse this liberty, which I should not take were I
not well acquainted with your disposition to promote all benevolent
enterprises; and no foreigner can understand our wants so well as one
of our own countrymen.

If, however, your stay in Liverpool should be too short to allow you to attend to the subject, or the inquiry is likely to be attended with inconvenience to you, I beg you will treat me with sufficient candor to pay no regard to this letter, as I shall know that you have the will, if not the ability, to assist us.[4] Believe me, dear Sir, Very respectfully Your friend and servant

WILLIAM H. PRESCOTT

1. Jonathan Goodhue (1783–1848), a Salem-born friend of the Prescott family, centered his successful mercantile interests in New York City, from which place he often assisted WHP with transatlantic shipments.

2. WHP's admiration for the Hartford operation included his repeated, but unsuccessful, efforts in 1830 to induce the Rev. T. H. Gallaudet to move from Hartford to Boston to undertake the direction of the institution for the blind; see Rev. Heman Humphrey, *The Life and Labors of the Rev. T. H. Gallaudet, LL.D.* (New York, 1857), pp. 236–43.

3. Edward Brooks (1793–1878), another of the thirty-one original incorporators of the institution for the blind, was assisting WHP in the effort to acquire its first personnel.

4. In 1831 Samuel Gridley Howe (1801–76) became the first director of the Boston institution.

48. Invoice from Obadiah Rich

(WHP Papers, Mass. Hist. Soc.)

Wm. H. Prescott Esqr.   To O. Rich   Dr.[1]

1830				
Jan. 1	To balance due on last year's account			£33.17. 0
	" Books pr Julian pr Invoice		20. 9.	
30	" Paper parcel pr ditto—with			
	Salazar Cronica del Gran Cardenal	12.		
	— Dignidades de Castilla	12.		
	Allacci Drammaturgia	5.		
	Garuba Serie di Verti	15.		
	Library Entertaining Knowledge:			
	2 volumes and binding	9.		
	Manni Veglie piacevole	3.		
	Commission 5/ charges 2/	7.	3. 3.	
Feb. 18	To Sundries pr Clematis f. 375-10		15.	
March 5	To Sundries pr [blank]			
	Lombardi Volume 3	8.		
	Dante Opere minore Volume 1	7. 6		
	Vesti di Lengua	4.		
	Sade Vie de Petrarque	1.18.		
	Raccolta di Novelle 3 volumes			
	and binding	15.		
	Il Pecorore 2 volumes	9.		
	Constable's Miscellany 21 volumes	2.15.		
	Commission 17/ Charges 5/	1. 2.	7.18. 6	
17	To Sundries pr Liverpool			
	Scott's Scotland 2 volumes	9.		
	Library Entertaining Knowledge			
	Volumes 3, 4 and binding	9.		

	Foreign Review No. 10	4. 7		
	Salfi Saggio	1. 6		
	Commission and charges	4. 6	1. 8. 7	
April 17	To History of the Jews			
	3 volumes and binding	15. 6		
	Boccaccio Opere Volume 6	4. 6		
	Cesare Esame	1. 6		
	Butler's Erasmus	6.		
	Muller's Romancero	3. 6		
	Roscoe's Lawyers	4. 6	Omitted but now sent	
	Commission and charges	6.	2. 1. 6	
May 25	To Books sent Gray and Bowen			
	Panizzi Orlando Volume 1	9.	Will you have it continued?	
	Court and camp of Bonaparte			
	and binding	5. 3	14. 3	
June 20	" Comedias de Cervantes			
	and Commission		16.	
	Butler's Sermons and Analogy 2			
	and binding	15.		
	Foreign Quarterly No. 11	4. 7		
	Commission and charges	3.	1. 2. 7	
	Amount carried forward		£52.13. 5	£33.17. 0
	Amount brought forward		52.13. 5	£33.17. 0
July 4	To Ginguené Volume X	7.		
	" Mackintosh's England Volume 1	4. 6		
	" Ottimi Commento &c. 8° 3	16.		
	" Romanis Dante Volume 4	13.		
	" Binding 3 8vo and 1 4to	10.		
	" Commission 6/ Charges 1/	7.	3.17. 6	
Dec. 10	" In a box to F. C. Gray Esqr.			
	Travesarii Epistolae f° 2 volumes	1.16.		
	Binding ditto	14.		
	Taylor's German Poetry Volume 3	11. 3		
	Commission 5/6 and charges 2/	7. 6	3. 8. 9	
15	" Postage to date		14. 4	60.14. 0
				£94.11.
	Cr.			
	By my draft to Baring Brothers and Company	£50.		
	" balance to next year's account	44.11.		94.11.
	Errors excepted			
	London December 15, 1830			

O. RICH[2]

1. Annual statements, such as this one, were supplemented by individual ones for separate shipments. WHP's requests for some of the items listed herein may be traced in items 44 and 45.

2. WHP's endorsement of this invoice reads, "Received February 1831."

49.   To Obadiah Rich
(Draft, WHP Papers, Mass. Hist. Soc.)

Boston, March 11th 1831

Dear Sir,

I inclose you the second of a set of exchange for £75 on Mr. Wiggin of London, of which the first was sent about the middle of last month. I have just received your letter by the "Roscius" bearing date January 20th. The books have not yet been taken out of the vessel. I fear that Lord Guilford's sale will not have done much to complete the deficit in my Italian order. I wish you to send me out the London weekly paper called the *Spectator,* to which I should like to subscribe as it appears to me to contain the most interesting political and social gossip, in a compact form, of any of the London newspapers that I have seen, also the 9th number of the *Foreign Review,* I having lost mine. I hope you will be punctual in transmitting the newspaper and the future *Foreign Reviews.* I wish you also to send me the following viz:

Chalmer's *Political History of the United States*

An English translation of Laplace's *Exposition du système du monde* (I saw a copy of this at one of our booksellers)

Grahame's *History of the United States*

I told you in my last that I had written to Mr. Poinsett[1] respecting the Mexican antiquities. I have received an obliging answer of which I subjoin a copy. You will perhaps think it best to open a communication direct with Mr. Poinsett should Lord Kingsborough[2] incline to avail himself of his offers. Should you prefer, however, to conduct the correspondence through me, or make use of me in any other way relative to the matter, I will attend to it with much pleasure. Truly yours

W. H. P.

Here a copy of Mr. Poinsett's letter.[3]

P.S. Since writing the above I have received the books by the "Roscius," all in excellent order. I take the liberty to return you the manuscript of the Italian life of Ximenes through the hands of Gray and Bowen, 1st because as I know not what authority it possesses I do not see well how I can quote it, 2d because I am obliged to read now *wholly* with the eyes of another, and have been indeed for nearly a year, I find it takes me six times as long to get at the contents of a manuscript as of the same quantity of printed matter. I must thank you, however, for your kindness in offering me the manuscript. Yours &c.

W. H. P.

1. Joel Roberts Poinsett (1779–1851), first U.S. Minister to Mexico, corresponded with and assisted WHP on several occasions.

2. At this time Rich was assisting the British nobleman Lord Kingsborough in assembling the materials which eventually went into the mammoth work *Antiquities of Mexico* (9 vols., London, 1830–48).

3. Poinsett's letter was dated February 22, 1831.

50.   To George Bancroft
                  (George Bancroft Papers, Mass. Hist. Soc.)

                                                  Boston, April 30, 1831

My dear friend,

I know not whether this letter will hit you in Northampton as you are probably most of the time on the wing during the vacation. My purpose in writing it is to say a few words respecting Mr. Cunningham, who, I believe, was invited some time since to connect himself with your Unitarian church in Northampton. My brother[-in-law] Mr. William Amory, who is his intimate friend, has given me to understand that Mr. Cunningham regrets he did not avail himself of the opportunity of forming this connexion. Next to a Boston parish, which I suppose he would naturally have preferred, there is no place so much to his own taste as Northampton, and the lady of his heart, who has been bred in the country, would far prefer it even to Boston. Knowing such to be the feelings of Mr. Cunningham, the regard which I have for him has led me to open the matter candidly to you as one who is interested and will probably have most influence in determining the opinions of the congregation. I have never heard Mr. Cunningham preach but once. His sermon then was far superior to what it has been often my fortune to hear from the Boston clergy, most of whom I cannot help thinking he excels both in capacity and attainments. My private opinion can be of no value to you, who have doubtless had much more frequent opportunities of forming your own judgment respecting his merits than I have had. I hope you will not consider this interference as impertinent on my part, to which I have been led by a desire that no ignorance of the state of feeling between the parties should prove a barrier to [a] connexion which, I believe, would be beneficial to both.

We jog on in much the same way here and, as we are none of us Jacksonists, care little for the upsetting of cabinets or any other mad pranks, which doubtless keep you awake at Northampton; for I perceive you are doing as many a misguided man has done before you, quitting the sweets of letters for the thorny path of politics. I must say I had rather drill Greek and Latin into little boys all my life than take up with this trade in our country. However so does not think Mr. E. Everett, nor Mr. A. H. Everett, nor Mr. &c. &c. &c. who are much better qualified to carry off all the prizes in literature than I can be —or indeed than they are in politics. Your article on the Bank of the United States produced quite a sensation, and a considerable contrariety of opinion.[1] Where will you break out next? I did not think to see you turn out a financier in your old age.

I have just recovered from a fit of sickness, which has confined me to my bed for a fortnight. I think the weather will confine me to the house another fortnight. Do you mean to make a flying trip to our latitude this vacation? We should be glad to see you. In the meantime I must beg you to commend me to your wife and believe me Most affectionately your friend

WM. H. PRESCOTT

1. Bancroft's article appeared initially in the *North American Review,* XXXII (January, 1831), 21–64. Subsequently it was printed separately.

51.   To Susan Prescott
                    (WHP Papers, Mass. Hist. Soc.)

Montreal, Saturday, July 2, 1831[1]

Dearest Susan

I returned last evening with William [Amory] from Quebec, having consumed just 44 hours in a journey of 380 miles, and devoted half a day to the fortifications, Plains of Abraham and all that sort of thing, and traveled over the city till I know it as well as Montreal. Now if there was ever a lion knocked on the head in better style, I should like to see the man who has done it.

Out of the last eight nights, six have been passed in steamboats, four of them without taking my clothes off. I have got to be quite attached to this way of life, and to the bustling, jovial magnificence of these great leviathans of the rivers which sweep along (at least the one we went in to Quebec did) at the rate of 15 and 18 miles an hour, and have accommodations equal to any hotel in the country.

On our return we were very glad to find that Mrs. Sears[2] had so far recovered that we shall resume our retrograde march on Sunday, and, returning by way of Lake Champlain, Lake George, Saratoga, North River and New York again, reach home by Sunday (or beginning of the week) in all probability, and very glad shall I be to greet your sweet faces once more. I shall have done up traveling enough to last for ten years to come, and to vindicate myself from the Colonel's sneers at my lethargic propensities.

Quebec is a spectacle well worth the trouble I took to see it. The *coup d'oeil* is on the whole finer in its way than anything I recollect, perhaps, except the bay of Naples. The precipice covered with fortifications frowning over the city, and the undulating river, studded with

shining villages on the opposite coasts, and a superb backbone of mountain ridges, are above all eulogium in the landscape way.

Niagara Falls, Trenton ditto [i.e. Falls], and Quebec are the three
ineffaceable points for the memory to respose on after this tour is
wound up. We made some pleasant acquaintances on our trip, among
others that of a Mr. Prescott, a son of the Halifax doctor, a very intelligent, genteel personage whom I was very willing to see bearing the
family name. Through him we became acquainted with an English
officer who procured admission for us into the works, which, as we were
out of season, would have been otherwise inaccessible for us.

The Canadians remind one of the French, especially of that part of
France which borders on the English Channel. They are of a lazy, cheerful temper, with the same habits, tastes, modes of cultivation which
have descended from their ancestors, very dirty but with plenty of all
that they seem to care for, and most of them as ignorant as one could
imagine. They are loyal, I am told, in their feelings, and the present
Governor General, Lord Aylmer, is an affable sort of a man who con-
ciliates the good-will of the people, which had been ruffled a good deal
by the aristocratic airs of Lord Dalhousie.

We returned in the boat in company with a Sir John Caldwell, a
social old gentleman who, we found, had been in Boston and knew
your father very well and who gave us considerable information about
affairs in Canada. On the whole, William and I concluded, though it is
a secret, that more was to be picked up in this independent bachelor
way of traveling than as the attaches of a coterie of ladies. What a pity
that profit and pleasure can't go together.

The roofs of the houses here and in Quebec are plated with tin which
glitters like molten silver in the sunbeams, giving a striking effect on
the whole to the towns en masse and particularly soothing to the eye.
I have a church under my window whose sloping roof of metal reflects
a ball of [fire] appalling to the stoutest eye when the sun glances on it.

On the whole, I am very glad that I have penetrated into Canada—
it has opened to me a new world, both of man and nature, i.e. scenery,
&c. But I am weary of this vagabond life and wish to become once more
a fixture in Bedford—or rather Nahant, where you are all now, I suppose. I bought a watch for William in Quebec, and Anna has this
morning bought a Lyon crape, with my money, for you in Montreal.[3]

I am sorry Uncle Hale appears in no better health—and am very
glad that you assisted him. You always do what's right. Goodbye, dear
Susan, love to father and mother and Elizabeth and Edward and kiss
the children. Your affectionate

WILLIAM H. PRESCOTT

1. In a mixed party of fellow Bostonians, WHP was off to Niagara Falls and other scenic places.

2. Mrs. David Sears.

3. The watch was for William Gardiner Prescott; the shopper was Anna Sears, who soon married William Amory.

52.   To Susan Prescott
(Extract from postscript by William Amory, WHP Papers, Mass. Hist. Soc.)

New York, Tuesday, 3 P.M. [July 12, 1831]

.   .   .   .

This William [i.e. WHP] . . . seems quite sentimental and homesick, talks of nothing but his wife and Betty and knows as little how to take care of himself as his son the Colonel.[1] He changes his pantaloons and coat every time the wind changes and wears from five to ten pair of drawers, according to the thermometer. He finds his trunk enormous and unwieldy, can find nothing but what is on top and grooms every time he opens it.[2]

.   .   .   .

1. Betty was Elizabeth Prescott (1828–64), the only daughter of WHP to attain adulthood. In 1852 she married James Lawrence of Boston.

Apparently William Amory Prescott (1830–67), second son and youngest child of WHP, so resembled his paternal great-grandfather that he was nick-named the Colonel at this time. Later he was called the Judge because of his resemblance to WHP's father.

2. With due allowance for William Amory's fun-poking account, one still glimpses WHP as the expression of sartorial elegance that he was throughout his life.

53.   To Obadiah Rich[1]
(Draft, WHP Papers, Mass. Hist. Soc.)

Boston, September 10th 1831

My dear Sir,

I must acknowledge the receipt of your letters [of] May 16, June 6, and June 22d, with the books accompanying, excepting the last by the "Pedlar" which, I understand, has put into Halifax in distress. With regard to the fears which you express in one of your letters of your friends and correspondents here having diminished their confidence in you, as far as I can learn, they are without foundation. No person has been appointed to supply the college library[2] but yourself, nor is any other contemplated, as Mr. Ticknor ere this has assured you. This latter gentleman is as much your friend as ever and if Mr. Gray has not written, it is purely accidental. Gray and Bowen complained to me indeed a little of your not letting them know why you did not procure, and in such case what probability there was of your ultimately procuring such books on their orders as you did not send to them. I suppose most of your correspondents too may have suffered a little by your absence in Spain. For myself I can truly say that I am now and ever have been influenced only by a hearty desire to serve you as I have shown here on more than one occasion both in public and private, and indeed considering the variety and in many instances the rarity of the books which you have purchased for me, it would be unfair in me to do otherwise. The Spanish order I find almost wholly answered. The Italian has yet some lagging which I should think you might supply in Italy. Agreeably to your request, I now send you a catalogue and the dates when ordered of such books previously ordered as have not been received, and which I should like to have. I will make one or two remarks. My reason for preferring 8vos to 4tos is solely the difference of price. Where a 4to can be afforded, therefore, at not much greater expense than an 8vo, pray buy it. With regard to rare books, I do not wish to give extravagant artificial prices, where augmentation of price amounts to three or 4 dollars only for an article, particularly if it is rare, although the original cost be much less than this it is of no great consequence [sic]. I have underscored those works which I most desire and of course should be willing to give something extra for them.

With much regard, believe me, Sir Truly yours

Order of September 10th 1831

Comparative View of Social Life of England and France by the editor of Madame du Deffand's letters.

Life of Sir William Herschel by J. F. W. Herschel (Cabinet Library)

Scott's (Sir Walter) *Letters on Demonology and Witchcraft*

The Life and Death of Lord Edward Fitzgerald by Thomas Moore 2 volumes 8vo.

Some of these orders, as those of the Cabinet Library &c, relate to books yet unpublished. I must add that such books as are in the course of publication, of which I have received only part of the series, such as Boccaccio's *Opera*—Panizzi, MacIntosh's *England* &c., must, of course, be continued to the end although I may not have specified them.

1. In terms of WHP's intellectual life, Rich was easily his most significant correspondent and aide in the early *1830's*.

2. I.e. Harvard.

54. Invoice from Obadiah Rich

(WHP Papers, Mass. Hist. Soc.)

W. H. Prescott Esqr   To O. Rich   Dr.

1831						
Jan.	1	To Balance of account sent				44. 7. 9
	14	" Petrarcha Opera f° 2		1. 1.		
		" Tales of a Grandfather 12°				
		12 volumes		1.12.		
		" King's Life of Locke 8° 2	3. 6	1. 1.		
		" McCrie's Reformation in Italy	1. 9	8.		
		" Butler's D'Agnesseau	1. 9	5.		
		" Irving's Conquest of Granada	4. 6	18.		
		" Bowring's Spanish Poetry	1. 6	3. 6		
		" Cabinet Cyclopedia Maritime				
		Discovery 1 and 2		9.		
		" Cabinet Cyclopedia Herschell's				
		Introduction		4. 6		
		" Boccaccio Opera tom. 7, 8		9.		
		" Cancellieri sopra Dante 12mo	1. 6	4.		
		Binding	14. 6	14. 6		
		Commission 19/7 Charges 3/6		1. 3. 1	8.12. 7	
April	1	Simond's Tour in Italy	2.	10.		
		Library Entertaining Knowledge				
		3 volumes [...]		13. 6		
		Panizzi, Ariosto Volumes 2, 3, 4		1. 7.		
		Commission		3. 6	2.14.	
	13	Foreign Quarterly 12 and 13		9. 2		
May	5	ditto 14		4. 7		
		Foreign Review 9		4. 7		
		Commission and charges		3. 8	1. 2.	
	16	Chalmer's Political Annals 4to		1.10.		
		Graham United States 8° 2	4.	18.		
		La Place System of the World 2	4.	1. 1.		
		Priestley's Corruptions 2		16.		
		Bunyan Pilgrim's Progress	3. 6	16.		
		Davy's Agricultural Chemistry	1. 6	11. 3		
		Lord John Russell's Europe	4. 6	12.		
		Soame Jenym works 4		16.		
		Lettre Inedite 2	3.	8.		
		Poemata Italorum	1. 6	3. 6		
		Poesia di Trovatore	2. 6	6. 9		
		Cabinet Cyclopedia Maritime				
		Discovery Volume 3		4. 6		
		Cabinet Cyclopedia Macintosh				
		England 2		4. 6		
		Constable's Wilson				
		Volumes 1 and 2		5. 6		
		Petrarca Poesie minore Volume 1		4. 6		
		Lombardi Letteratura Italiana				
		volume 4		7. 6		
		Retrospective Review				
		Volumes 11 and 12		15.		
		Binding 24/6 Commission 27/6		2.12.		
		Annual Retrospect				
		2 volumes omitted		7. 6	12.19. 6	
		Amount carried forward			25. 8. 1	44. 7. 9
		Amount brought forward			25. 8. 1	44. 7. 9

June 8		To Walpole's Correspondence 8° 4	10.	1. 4.	
		Walton's Life and Memoirs 8° 2		10.	
		Hughes on Insurance	2. 6	16.	
		Library Entertaining Knowledge Arch. of Birds	1. 6	3.	
		Stewart's Life of Robertson		5.	
		Binding	14.	14.	
		Commission 10/6 Charges 2/6		13.	4. 5.
		Villemain Cours de Litterature 8° 5	7. 6	1. 9.	
		Guizot Cours d'histoire 5	7. 6	1. 9.	
		Boccaccio Opere tom. 9		5. 6	
		Wordsworth's Excursions		8.	
		Binding	15.	15.	
		Commission		9.	4.15. 6
July 26		Constable's Wilson Volume 3		2. 9	
		Sarmiento Poesia Española 4to		6.	
		Croker Boswell's Johnson 8° 5	12. 6	2. 2.	
		Captain Hall's Fragments 12° 3	3. 9	11. 3	
		Library Entertaining Knowledge History &c.	1. 6	3.	
		Southey's Nelson	1. 3	3. 9	
		Companions of Columbus	1. 3	3. 9	
		Chatham's Letters	1. 3	2. 3	
		Hutchinson's Ethics		4. 6	
		Priestley's Correspondence		7.	
		Binding	1. 1. 6	1. 1. 6	
		Commission		11. 6	5.19. 3
Aug. 2		Foreign Quarterly No. 15		5.	
9		Fall of Nineveh		3.	
		Commission 10/6 [. . .] 3/6		14.	3.14.
Oct. 8		Priestley's Heathen Philosophers		6.	
		Vita Nova di Dante	1. 6	3.	
		Foscolo Orazione etc.	1. 6	3. 9	
		Appendice al Dante		3.	
		Vita Dantis	1. 6	3. 9	
		Salfi Ristretto 12° 2	3. 6	4. 6	
		Secolo di Dante	2.	8.	
		Foscolo Tragedia	1. 9	3.	
		Pechio Vita di Foscolo	1. 9	3.	
		Binding	13. 6	13. 6	
		Commission		5.	
		Foreign Quarterly No. 16		5.	3. 1. 6
		Carried forward		£47. 8. 4	44. 7. 9
		Brought forward		47. 8. 4	44. 7. 9
Dec. 10		Sundries via Dromo Panizzi, Ariosto Volume 5	12.	9.	
	1. 3	Scott's Demonology	5.	3. 9	
	7. 6	Ariosto Opere f° 2 in 1	20.	16.	
	8.	Walpole's last 10 years 4to 2	5. 5	1. 1.	
		Sismondi Histoire des Francais 13–15		1. 2. 6	
		Priestley's early opinions 8° 4	30.	1. 1.	
	4. 6	Coxe's Memoirs of Walpole 2	26.	18.	
	2. 6	DeFoe's Robinson Crusoe 12° 2	10.	7. 6	
	3.	Comparative view of social life &c. 2	20.	15.	

1.6	To Albrizzi Ritratti	6. 6	5.	
3.	Moore's Lord Edward			
	Fitzgerald 2	21.	16.	
	Petrarca Opere minore			
	Volume 2	7.	5. 3	
3. 9	Library Entertaining Knowledge			
	3 volumes	12.	9.	
	Constable's Wilson Volume 4	3. 6	2. 9	
	Cabinet Cyclopedia Donovan			
	Domestic Economy	6.	4. 6	
1.15.			£8.16. 3	
	Commission on £13.12.		1. 7. 3	
	Binding		1.15.	
	Past expenses		5.	12. 3. 6
	Alfieri Tragedie for Mr. Amory			5.11.
	A roll of prints for ditto			
	Spectator April 9th to			
	December 31	38.		1.18.
	Postage from Boston			
	January to December		9.	67. 9.10
				£111.17. 7
	March 21 By remittance			75.
	Balance to New Account			£36.17. 7
	Errors excepted			
	London December 10, 1831			

O. RICH

55.   To Obadiah Rich
(Draft, WHP Papers, Mass. Hist. Soc.)

Boston, February 13, 1832

My dear Sir

I must acknowledge the receipt of two of your letters dated October 31 and December 14, 1831. Your account for the last year appears to be perfectly correct. The balance against me is, I find, nearly £37. I enclose you a bill of C. J. Cazenove & Company's on P. Wiggin for seventy pounds. The "Dromo" has not yet arrived, we may expect it, I suppose, every day. On its arrival I shall write you more fully. You are this time, I suppose yet in Spain. I have only to add now that I wrote you a letter on January 4 containing a few additional orders. Truly yours

56.   To Obadiah Rich
(Draft, WHP Papers, Mass. Hist. Soc.)

March 10, 1832

My dear Sir,

I enclose you a draft, being the second bill of exchange on P. Wiggin

Esq. for £70, which is rather more than £30 beyond the balance against me in your yearly account, which as far as I can see is correct. I enclosed the first in a letter dated February 13, since which the "Dromo" has arrived with the books &c—in very good order. The Walpole memoirs is a good bargain, or else it was a bad one for those who bought them when they first came out. Cannot some other English quartos that I have ordered be got at or nearly at an 8vo price, now that their novelty is worn off? I suppose I shall hear before long of the Italian books ordered by you from Molini. I am glad to find that you have obtained the agency of so many public institutions in various parts of this country. Our Athenaeum has run a little ahead of its means, however, so that it must limit its supplies, for the present at least, to new publications.[1] I wrote you a letter containing a few additional orders January 4. I will thank you also to send me the following—

Panizzi's *Ariosto,* being volume 6. This I order as probably containing a biographical notice of the poet. It is not worth while to send the remaining volumes of the text, they are scarcely worth the cost.

Rose's translation of the *Orlando Furioso*

Miss Mitford's *Stories of American Life*

Roscoe's Novelists Library, those volumes containing *Humphrey Clinker, Roderick Random*

Ventouillac, *French Librarian or Literary Guide*

Stebbing, *Lives of the Italian Poets* 3 volumes

Foreign Quarterly Review Number 15. I have lost the one you sent me.

Lardner's Cabinet Cyclopedia—Macaulay, *France from Accession of the Bourbons*

Sustenance's *Laconics* (I know nothing about this book but presume it is a good selection of English quotations.) I have been in no hurry to send this letter, believing that it would at any rate reach England before your return.

Believe me, Truly yours

[P.S.] In addition to the foregoing I wish Charles Lyell's *Principles of Geology.* I should also like to get engravings of the heads of Roscoe, Hallam, Gibbon, Sismondi, Thomas Moore, and Madame de Staël. I should not want the engravings unless they were likenesses and about the size of Lord Byron's head by Westall, or Scott's by Raeburn, which I have. I doubt if most of these heads have been engraved—at least of the size I want. Mr. Ticknor has a print such as I should like of Madame de Staël, with a turban on her head and I think, though I am not sure, leaning on her hand. If handsome prints of a frameable size of Shakespeare, Voltaire, Ariosto and Cervantes can be obtained, I should like to have them as representatives of their different literatures. I do not care for one, therefore, unless I get the other three.

1. In 1832, and for some years thereafter, WHP's awareness of the affairs of the Athenaeum exceeded that of a mere subscriber because in this period he was also serving as a trustee of that institution.

57.   To Obadiah Rich
                        (Draft, WHP Papers, Mass. Hist. Soc.)

                                                    Nahant, July [10] 1832
Dear Sir,
    I have received two letters from you since writing my last, bearing dates April 14 and May 21. The prices in the last show considerable deduction from the original costs. You do not acknowledge the receipt of one written by me in March, although by the purchase of two of the books ordered in it, I perceive it has come to hand. I do not understand why you did not complete the order, as the books are all of common occurrence. I must confess I was in hopes ere this to have got some more of the balance of my old Italian order, which you said would come from Molini. Pray let me know if any unexpected impediments occurred in reference to it. The new Italian order, as you write me, I may daily expect from France.
    I wish you would send me
        Sismondi's *Italian Republics.* Lardner's Cabinet Library
        Diary of an Invalid
        Moore's *Life of Byron* duodecimo 4 volumes
        Conversations on Vegetable Physiology 2 volumes
        Conversations on Chemistry 2 volumes 12mo. with plates by Lowry,
            both these by Mrs. Marcet
        Conversations on Natural Philosophy, with engravings by Lowry
        Southey's *History of the Moors* when published
        Irving's *Alhambra* to accompany the English edition of his other
            works as previously ordered (except *Columbus* and *Chronicle of
            Granada*)
    Mr. Irving, as you perceive, has returned to live with us. Mr. Newton has engaged himself to an American lady, daughter of Mr. William Sullivan, a lawyer of eminence in our town. He returns to Europe in the fall, but with a design in two or three years of permanently establishing himself here.
    Believe me truly yours

58. Invoice from Obadiah Rich

(WHP Papers, Mass. Hist. Soc.)

W. H. Prescott Esqr.   To O. Rich   Dr.

1832					
Jan. 1st	To balance of last year's account				36.17. 7
Feb. 22	" Cabinet Cyclopedia Volume 21 Eminent Statesmen		6.	4. 6	
	" Library Entertaining Knowledge parts 27 and 28 Paris		4.	3.	
March 1	" New Monthly Magazine and Blackwood		6.	4. 9	
	" Foreign Quarterly Number 17		6.	4. 7	
April 1	" New Monthly and Blackwood		6.	4. 9	
	" Laborde Itinéraire 6 volumes and Atlas				2. 5.
22	" Boccaccio Opere volumes 10 and 13		12.	9.	
	" Foreign Quarterly Number 15		6.	4. 7	
May 1	" Blackwood and New Monthly		6.	4. 9	
12	" Foreign Quarterly Number 18		6.	4. 7	
16	" Chalmer's Mary Queen of Scots 8° 3	4. 6	2. 8.	1. 4.	
	" Crombies Natural Theology 2	3.	1. 1.	16.	
	" Ventouillac's French Librarian	1. 6	18.	12.	
	" Remains of R. White 8° 2	3.	1. 4.	12.	
	" Romance of History 12° 3	4.	18.	12.	
	" Laconics 3		12.	9.	
	" Porterage 1/ Binding	16.		17.	
June 1	" Blackwood and New Monthly		6.	4. 9	
July 1	" ditto ditto		6.	4. 9	
24	" Rose's Orlando 8 volumes	16.	3.16.	2.12. 6	
	" Stebbing's Italian Poets 3	6.	1.11. 6	1. 4.	
	" Irving's Tales of a Traveller	8.	1. 4.	12.	
	" " Bracebridge Hall	8.	1. 4.	12.	
	" Il Dittamondo 12mo	1. 6	5.	4. 6	
	" Roscoe's Humphrey Clinker and Roderick Random		12.	9.	
	" Moore's Life of Byron 6 volumes		1.10.	1. 3.	
	" Binding	1.19. 6		1.19. 6	
Aug. 2	" Blackwood and New Monthly		6.	4. 9	
Sept. 1	" ditto ditto		6.	4. 9	
	" Foreign Quarterly Number 19		6.	4. 7	
30	" Reports on Common law 3 volumes in 2		1.10.	1. 1.	
	" Irving's Alhambra 8° 2	8.	1. 4.	16.	
	" Diary of an Invalid	1. 6	15.	6.	
	" Abercrombie on Truth	1. 6	10. 6	6.	
	" Lyell's Geology 8° 2	3.	1. 7.	1.	
	" Conversations on Chemistry &c. 5	6. 3	1.16. 6	1. 7. 6	
	" Sismondi's Italian Republics	1. 3	6.	4. 6	
	" Charges 3/ Binding	1. 1. 6		1. 4. 6	
	Forward		29. 0. 6	23.12. 1	39. 2. 7
	Brot forward		29. 0. 6	23.12. 1	39. 2. 7

Oct.	1	" Blackwood and New Monthly	6.		4. 9	
	22	" Boccaccio volume XI	6.		4. 6	
		" L'Aventurero Ciciliano 8°	12.		9.	
Novr.	1	" Blackwood and New Monthly	6.		4. 9	
		" Foreign Quarterly Number 20	6.		4. 7	
	6	" Roscoe's Spanish Novelists 8° 3	1. 7.		1.	
Decr.	1	" Blackwood and New Monthly	6.		4. 9	
	4	" Macintosh England volume 3 in George Ticknor's parcel	6.		4. 6	
	31	" Spectator 1 year			2.12.	
		" Court Journal from February 18			2. 6.	
		" Expense on 12 monthly parcels			12.	
		" Postage			9. 5	
		" Rota Poesie 2 volumes omitted July 24	10.		4. 6	
					32.12.10	
		Commission on	£33. 5. 6		3. 6.	35.18.10
		To Invoice from France				17. 6. 8
						£92. 8. 1
		Cr. By Cash pr draft			70.	
		" balance to New Account			22. 8. 1	92. 8. 1
		Errors excepted				
		London December 18, 1832				
						O. Rich[1]
		Romancero de Romances			fr. 5	
		Obras de Moratin 8 in 6 and binding			60	

1. This accounting is endorsed: "Received February 7, 1833." While these annual invoices are excellent indices of the growth of the Prescott library, they cannot be construed in terms of WHP alone. His father, in retirement, spent hours daily among books, and the family reading circle that involved all members of the family also led to the acquisition of many titles.

59.   To Obadiah Rich
(Draft, WHP Papers, Mass. Hist. Soc.)

March 11, 1833

Dear Sir,

I enclose the second of a bill of exchange for Baring, Bros. & Co. for £50, the first of which I sent you by a letter of February 21, since which date I have received nothing from you. I am now engaged on Gonsalvo's Italian campaigns,[1] and should find it extremely convenient if you could procure me the French "Vie de Gonsalve de Cordoüe" by Duponcet, which I ordered some years since, as well as Richard, "Parallèle du Cardinal Ximenes et du Cardinal Richelieu" Rotterdam, 1705. I have seen the former of these works referred to frequently, and if they can be got, I am sure you will be able to mouse them out for me without loss of time. I have only to add that I wish you to discontinue the *Court Journal* and substitute the *Athenaeum,* a number of which you sent me the other day.

I have conversed with Mr. Everett again concerning your agency for the *North American.* He appears sensible of the importance of your services, but this part of the business is placed under the direction of Mr. Bowen. Your arrangements with him, you know, of course, better than I do, and I hope you will be able to come to a better understanding with him.

I see you are agent for a number of our public libraries, though I suppose the purchases for most of them are to no great amount, except perhaps for Harvard College and Congress. The Athenaeum is too low in funds to afford much prospect of increasing its orders at present. At the last meeting of the Trustees, there was some complaint that the periodicals have not been sent with sufficient promptness, of which, I suppose, you have been informed before this, as a committee was appointed to communicate it to you.

Believe me, Truly your friend and well wisher,

1. The day before he wrote this letter, WHP reminded himself, "Finished reading for the two first chapters of Part II of my history. A long while has been spent, but not misspent, as it has included a survey & estimate of all the ground to be taken up in my future operations." See Prescott (Gardiner, ed.), *The Literary Memoranda,* I, 156. In terms of its organization and total wordage, WHP was at the midpoint of his first history.

60.   To George Bancroft

(George Bancroft Papers, Mass. Hist. Soc.)

Boston, March 16, 1833

My dear Bancroft

I have been invited with my Father to take stock in a bank about to be established in Louisville, Kentucky. The charter promises well and it would seem, to judge from the business done by the U.S. branch established there, to be a shewy place for such an institution. The capital authorized amounts to two millions. My object in writing you is to ascertain if you can throw us any light on the matter, in regard to the character and objects of the persons who set it afoot, and who will probably have the management of it. I suspect that both this and the Cincinnati bank are predicated on the belief of the determination of the Charter of the U.S. Bank, which looks less probable than it did. Will you have the goodness also to inform me if you know any further particulars of the Cincinnati bank and, in short, which of the two, if either, you would prefer to embark in.[1]

I am sorry to disturb your historical labors in this way, but you will not require apology for a labor of love.

How goes on the immortal work? I find Ticknor and Sparks have both conceived a favorable opinion from what they heard of it.[2] But of one thing rest assured, if you foreswear your own soil and settle in Philadelphia,[3] it will be damned to a certainty in the *North American,* that we are resolved on; and you know there is no appeal from that tribunal. One thing more, for which you will be damned, I beg you to understand, (at least in this world,) that is, if you do not render ample justice to the memory of my grandfather—who scarcely got bread during his lifetime, and it seems, is not likely to get a stone after his death[4]—and who has had half his honors filched from him by gulls of historians whose eyes have been fascinated by the apparition of General Warren because he had the good luck of being shot on the battlefield. Excuse this little burst of—patriotism—nothing but patriotism— a mere love of country, which makes me desire to have all its great points of history put in the true vein.[5] Have the goodness to answer by return of post.

Now if this is not a pistol at your breast—surrender your thoughts *nolens volens.* Susan desires to be remembered to you—pray give my regards to your wife, and believe me Yours ever faithfully

WM. H. PRESCOTT

1. No record remains of any investment by either Prescott in either bank. Ordinarily Prescott investments did embrace banks, chiefly Boston banks, but it was doubly unlikely they turned to the West at this time: they neither knew nor liked the developing West, and they were hostile to the policies of the Jackson administration.

2. Bancroft was then fast at work upon the first volume of his *History of the United States.*

3. Because of the social ostracism which he experienced in aristocratic circles in Boston due to his espousal of the Democratic party and the Jackson administration, Bancroft was seriously considering his departure from the Hub city area. He did not leave Boston at this time. WHP, although he detested George's politics, was Bancroft's friend for life.

4. Even then the Bunker Hill Monument Association, in which WHP, his father, mother and brother were all active, was striving to complete the monument for which the cornerstone had been laid on June 17, 1825. When finally dedicated on June 17, 1843, the monument included a statue of Colonel William Prescott, the "stone" desired by WHP.

5. Twenty-five years passed before Bancroft wrote his account of the Battle of Bunker Hill. Bancroft sent WHP, early in 1858, the proof sheets of his account of that action. Anyone reading the *History of the United States,* VII, 423–31 knows that WHP was pleased with Bancroft's verdict.

61.   To Jared Sparks

(Jared Sparks Papers, Harvard College Library)

Boston, May 8, 1833

My dear friend,

I received your letter respecting Brown in good time.[1] The last ten days I have been spinning round like a teetotum in consequence of a donation which Colonel Perkins[2] took it into his head to present to the Blind, of whom I am an unworthy guardian, *(unoculus inter caecos)* on conditions which have given us work enough, I assure you, to comply with. These were to raise 50,000 dollars, and such is the public spirit of the good town, that, in little more than a week, we have raised within five or six thousand of the whole amount. I don't believe any other city in the Union would have done this thing in such style, with the prospect, too, of the balance of the Bunker Hill monument on our backs, which must be provided for within this month. Well, just as I had washed my hands of the Blind business, and was settling down quietly on my own accounts, going on with a little campaign which I was in the depths of when the Colonel made his grand assault, comes your epistle, making my very hair stand on end. A pretty piece of work it cuts out for the dog days, when the height of a man's ambition is to draw a long breath in quiet. I do not know exactly what to answer. I don't like to say nay to any request of yours. I am engaged now on a campaign in Italy with my Spanish fellows, and I must see them through at all events, before I meddle with anything else. This will take me nearly all the rest of the month. So if you can get any one to do your business to your satisfaction, and let me off to the third volume, I should like it better. If not, however, I will undertake for fifty pages, more or less, to be furnished any time after July, only requesting you to let me know the latest date I may be allowed, and also to refer me to a sample of the kind of page to be printed, that I may form some estimate of quantity, before I cut my cloth.

So poor Gray,[3] you perceive, has lost his election. Pity that he was set up. The politicians are sadly at fault for want of a candidate. I do not think they will pitch on Everett,[4] though I think he ought certainly to be the man. The truth is there is such a thing as speaking and writing one's self out of favor, as well as into it, and this too although the matter be excellent. If Mr. Everett had done half as much for the public, he would have done twice as much for himself.

I suppose you are buried up to the eyes in proofsheets. I rode by your quarters the other morning before breakfast.[5] Everything looked quiet as a Sabbath day, which it was not. So I concluded you did not allow the sweet sounds and sights of the country to disturb your morning's nap. I envy your escape from this Babel of bricks and horrid human [...] which begins to grow intolerable as the weather grows hot. Had my wife been well enough, we should have taken flight to Pepperell. As it is, we shall go early to Nahant. I hope Mrs. Sparks continues in health and spirits. I saw a little bijou of hers at the Fair, for which the Blind and the blind guides have to thank her. Pray, present my regards to her, and believe me, Now and ever, your friend

WILLIAM H. PRESCOTT

1. Sparks had just requested WHP to write an appraisal of novelist Charles Brockden Brown (1771–1810) for the first volume of the projected series entitled *The Library of American Biography*.

2. Thomas Handasyd Perkins, merchant-philanthropist. The school for the blind now honors his memory.

3. Francis C. Gray.

4. Edward Everett.

5. Despite the number of falls from horses which are recorded in his papers, WHP was an excellent horseman. He often galloped out to the Jamaica Plain district to watch the sunrise and to give tone to his body because of his otherwise sedentary activities.

62.   To Jared Sparks

(Jared Sparks Papers, Harvard College Library)

Nahant, August 1, 1833

My dear Sparks,

I have written a life of Brown of about fifty *North American* pages in length.[1] I am very sorry to send you such sorry trash. But it was not written *con amore*—though I have done it as well as I could. I have praised him twice as much as I think he deserves,[2] and I am afraid the reader will find that out. The truth is, Brown should be worked up by some one that *feels* him, as Walsh and Edward Channing appear to have done. If Mrs. Sparks has New York kindness for his memory, she could, if she could find leisure and spirits, make a much better memoir than I have done out of the facts I have given. If she will do this, or if she or you will look over and make a refacimento more to your taste of what I have done, I shall feel not a little pleasure, and the public will be much the gainer. If, as you were pleased to think, my name as a contributor can be of any use, can it not be mentioned among a list of contributors in the Preface, instead of being obliged to father this child of dulness in particular.[3] At any rate don't print it, or at least put my name to it, if it will discredit me. You will be candid with me in this, I know.

I will send it to you the first time Palfrey[4] lights on us here—which [happens] every two or three days.

I hope you and Madame continue in health. The heat has not been oppressive or even great here. But every house in the island is stuffed full to overflowing, and it is as difficult to settle one's brains in such an atmosphere of noise and nonsense as it would be in a windmill. I believe you found that out once. Pray give my regards to your wife, and believe me Ever sincerely yours,

WM. H. PRESCOTT

[P.S.] Thursday evening—Mr. Amory has taken the manuscript to Boston and will leave it at Gray and Bowen's for you—where you can get it.

1. The essay on Brown is in Sparks (ed.), *The Library of American Biography*, I (Boston, 1834), 117–80.

2. To himself, on July 29, 1833, WHP confided, "His [Brown's] defects as a fictitious writer are so annoying that I could not have finished one of his novels, unless as a job." See Prescott (Gardiner, ed.), *The Literary Memoranda*, I, 164. Later critics have tended to exalt Brown. The fiction that WHP read was overwhelmingly English fiction. In fact, aside from Irving, he read very few American writers of prose fiction.

3. Although WHP, by this time, had published at least twenty-three articles, his name had never accompanied one of them. His name did appear with the biographical sketch of Brown.

4. John Gorham Palfrey (1796–1881) was teacher, editor, public official and historian, as well as WHP's friend. Between 1835 and 1843 he edited the *North American Review*.

63.   To Obadiah Rich

(Draft, WHP Papers, Mass. Hist. Soc.; and extracts in Roger Wolcott, *The Correspondence of William Hickling Prescott 1833–1847* [Boston and New York, 1925], pp. 1–2)

Boston, August 13, 1833

My dear Sir,

It is some months since I have heard from you, your last letter, not reckoning the one or two printed notices with the parcels, bearing date February 14, in which you speak of your proposed visit to Spain in the autumn. I write this now, in hopes that it will overtake you before you set out on your expedition. In my last of March 11, I requested you to get for me Duponcet, "Vie de Gonsalve de Cordouë," and Richard, "Parallèle du Cardinal Ximenes et du Cardinal Richelieu," Rotterdam, 1705, old orders, which if they can be procured, would come very pertinent to my personal necessities. I suppose you have received my letters requesting you to discontinue all periodicals whatever, except the *Foreign Quarterly* and the *Athenaeum*. I see Herschel's *Astronomy* (Cabinet Cyclopedia) is out. I suppose I shall get it soon. There is a manuscript in the Royal Library at Madrid in 3 volumes folio, entitled "Batallas & Quincuagenas por Gonzalo Hernández de Oviedo," which contains much matter, I am persuaded, of the most useful and authentic kind for the illustration of Isabella's reign and as yet never drawn upon by historians. I wish I could get an extract from certain parts of it in any way, copied in a plain, good-sized, legible hand. As I cannot expect any one, if he had the knowledge, to hunt it over and select the essential parts, I think I can venture to select myself the passages to be copied. If you will turn to the 6th volume of the *Memorias* de la Real Academia de Historia, you will find the following references: p. 226, Dialogues 8, 23, 28, and 36—p. 227, Dialogues 1, 2, 3, 5—p. 229, Dialogues 2, 4, 9—p. 230, Dialogues 29, 43, 44—p. 231, Dialogue Don Alonso de Silva—p. 233, Dialogues relating to Cisneros, Talavera, and Deza—p. 234, Dialogue relating to Mendoza and Dialogue 6. I know nothing of the length of these dialogues, having seen only extracts from them. I do not wish a larger quantity transcribed than would make the expense fifty or sixty dollars. I shall be much disappointed if you cannot get them for me.

My work, if ever finished, will take up, as I before stated, three octavos. I have completed nearly two, and have had three copies of the manuscript printed in order to correct it under my own eye, and to prevent typographical errors in the book when printed, as I intend to have it, in London. You will think this a queer whim but the printing these 3 copies will not cost me more than double what it would to have a fair manuscript transcribed.[1] *Au reste*, I go on leisurely, taking care that the book shall be an amusement and not a burden to me. I see you and the old North have shaken hands and parted, so much the worse, I fear, for the latter. I have heard nothing from Italy as yet, and indeed there is not much remaining to hear on that score. I have felt half a mind when I had knocked their Catholic Highnesses on the head to take up Philip II's reign, whose domestic history, at least, has been superficially treated by Watson.[2] I suppose, if need be, the rich old hives in Spain would furnish me abundance of material unexplored. Yours very truly

WM. H. PRESCOTT

P.S. You may send me as soon as convenient the following—

Robert Blakey's *History of Moral Science* 2 volumes
Life of William Roscoe by Henry Roscoe 2 volumes
Percival's *History of Italy* 2 volumes
German History of Italian Literature and Poets by Dr. Genthe, see *Foreign Quarterly,* Number 22, p. 533.

Do not send more of the *Library of Entertaining Knowledge;* except related to British Museum.

Rose's *Orlando Furioso*—volumes 7, 8 bound in dark blue and gold, like the former six. I have English copies of Scott's novels as far down as the *Fortunes of Nigel,* inclusive, published in 12mo form by Archibald Constable & Co., Edinburgh and Hurst, Robinson & Co., London, 1822. For the sake of uniformity, I should like to have all his *subsequent novels* of this same edition which I suppose will come very reasonable now the last more complete edition, with notes, of most abominable type, is in fashion. Be careful not to get any preceding *Nigel,* which you know came after the *Pirate, Kenilworth, Ivanhoe, Abbot, Monastery* and all the old Scottish novels. Have them neatly bound in calf but not all uniform. So much for England. There is one thing I am very desirous to have you procure for me in Spain.

As neither the English nor American public are familiar with the portraits of eminent Spaniards, I should be very glad to adorn my pages with the likenesses of Ferdinand, Isabella, Gonsalvo de Córdova and Columbus, all of whose biographies fall entire within my history.[3] The two former, to be prefixed to two of the volumes, of the usual half length size. The 3 latter[4] merely heads like those in Roscoe's *Lorenzo de Medici.* I should not choose to spend more than 50 guineas on this affair, which I fear would not pay for anything beyond the portraits of Ferdinand and Isabella. The engravers here tell me it would be enough for that, in the best style. Isabella's prefixed to the sixth volume of the *Memorias* de Academia de Historia would furnish a most authentic model for her. Can you not get an engraving of Ferdinand as correct, or a sketch from the best likenesses of him to serve as a model to an engraver in England? Perhaps good portraits of the other 3 persons may be found in books or elsewhere, but I fear you will think I am putting my £50 on rather severe duty, so I leave it to you what can be done within those limits. I would not give a fig for anything but a copy of an original executed in the best manner. I should add the engravers tell me here that heads alone well finished like those I allude to in Roscoe could be executed for 5 or 6 guineas apiece, and reduced sketches of portraits for as many dollars each, by a competent artist.

1. This printing by Dickinson eventually cost WHP $456.10, "an expense," he said, "*I shall never incur again.*" His handling of this printing is discussed in Prescott (Gardiner, ed.), *The Literary Memoranda*, I, 162, 188, 190, 214.

2. WHP's opinion of the study of Philip II by Robert Watson (1730–80) was widely held.

3. Portraits of every one of these individuals appeared in WHP's published history.

4. Referring to five persons, but only naming four, WHP seems to have omitted the name of Cardinal Ximenez de Cisneros.

64.   To Obadiah Rich
(Draft, WHP Papers, Mass. Hist. Soc.)

Boston, October 19th 1833

Dear Sir,

I have come butt up against a passage of my history in which I find myself deficient in a capital authority. This is a work by Luis del Marmol Carvajal, entitled "Historia del Rebelión y Castigo de los Moriscos del Reyno de Granada," printed at Málaga, 1600 and subsequently at Madrid and, I believe, Paris. A book of high authority and no doubt attainable without much difficulty in England as well as Spain, as it is repeatedly quoted. Pray send it to me as soon as you can get it.[1]

I wish also Sempere, *Considerations sur la Grandeur &c.* You may also send me *The History of Spain and Portugal* published in Lardner's Cabinet Cyclopedia in 5 volumes. It has plenty of learning and talent in it, though dashed off in the usual style of book making now a days. Pray inform me who is the author. He refers repeatedly, I see, to the Acts of the Cortes. Are they printed as such? And if so, cannot you send me those embraced under Ferdinand and Isabella's reign. The only acts I have knowledge [of] which have been collected are in the various Spanish codes, which I possess. I trust you got my letter of September 20, requesting Robles and Pulgar's and Poza's lives of Ximenes, as I have daily occasion for them. The old manuscript life of this worthy which you may remember to have sent me some two or three years ago, whose author I think I can trace altho anonymous, I have turned to good account. Since writing you last, I have received "Parallèle de Ximenez" and the life of Gonsalvo, for which I am much obliged to you. I doubt, however, if they prove of much value to me.[2]
Yours

1. WHP made heavy use of this title as he wrote the sixth and seventh chapters of Part Second of his history.

2. For WHP's assessment of the sources related to the career of Cardinal Ximenez de Cisneros, see his *Ferdinand and Isabella*, II, 398–400.

65.   To Jared Sparks
                    (Jared Sparks Papers, Harvard College Library)

                                              Boston, December 24, 1833

My dear Sparks,

    I will be frank with you. I have neither credit nor cash in hand; the
former being used up to get a note for five thousand dollars renewed
which falls due on the first of January, and the last being required for
manufacturing assessments for the 15th of January, to meet which I
have put my last bank shares in the broker's hands. I believe I can
arrange it, however, satisfactorily for you and me. I have two thousand
dollars in the Firemen's Insurance Company,[1] and I will transfer five
hundred dollars of it to you and you shall agree to replace the same
six months or a year hence, as most convenient. This is the only dis-
posable stock that I have, and I hope it will answer your purpose, and
you see it will be attended with no inconvenience whatever to me.[2]
    I am sorry for your bump, though I dare say you have mistaken its
nature, and that if you had let a Spurzheimite overhaul your cranium,[3]
he would find it to be nothing but an oversized historic development,
made out of your overworking this last year. Indeed, if you do not
moderate a little, I should not be surprised if your whole body should
be turned into one historic bump. I had Bancroft in my library till
almost eleven last evening, discussing the forefathers and a' that. I suppose you know he has broke ground with the printer. He has taken
my hint of a double column and made a very fair page to the eye. I
see your *Washington* has got into the world, it will not be easy to
beat it in beauty of execution.[4] Pray give my regard to Mrs. Sparks
and to the little duodecimo which I suppose will be the fairest of all
your works. Believe me Faithfully Your Friend

                                              WM. H. PRESCOTT

    1. Railroads soon became conspicuous in the Prescott investment portfolio,
but at this time, following the lead of his father, WHP's investments were in
real estate, banking, manufacturing and insurance.
    2. WHP often did his utmost to aid financially embarrassed friends, and
inasmuch as he was able to do this without jeopardizing a friendship, he was
doubly successful.
    3. In this period of great popularity for phrenology, the reference is to
phrenologist F. J. Gall's gifted pupil John Gasper Spurzheim.
    4. WHP's interest in books included their physical form, and in his desire
that his own book be particularly attractive in its format, he used Sparks's
work as a model.

66.   To Obadiah Rich
                  (Draft, WHP Papers, Mass. Hist. Soc.)

                                        Boston, January 17, 1834
Dear Sir,

   I must acknowledge the receipt of your letter of September 30, which came to hand about two months since. I have been so much occupied of late that I have suffered a long while to pass without answering it. I stated what I wanted of the Waverley Novels somewhat inaccurately to you. I will make it clear now. I own them all as far down as the *Fortunes of Nigel* inclusive, some in octavo, some in duodecimo form, and these last not of an uniform edition. What I now want is the remainder of the series since the *Fortunes of Nigel* of any edition or editions, uniform or not no more,[1] always excepting the last from its being such abominable sized type. They may be neatly bound in full calf without much ornament as they will correspond better with what I have. I am something like the old lady who wanted the largest sized print in the smallest sized Bible. I am obliged to you for having written so promptly for the Quincuagenas of Oviedo. I hope you will be able to procure the extracts for me, as they would be extremely valuable I am convinced. Pray follow the thing up if you do not go to Madrid in person, so that there may be no delay. I am glad to hear that authentic portraits of my principal characters can be easily procured and at a reasonable price. I shall no doubt request your services therefor at some future time. I took the liberty to mention what you said in your letter to Mr. Everett and Bowen, hoping that it might lead to a better understanding on the subject of the *North American*. Mr. Everett seems personally to have the most friendly feelings towards you. I cannot but hope that things may be brought back into the old train. The *American Monthly*, you will have learnt before this, has changed hands, and become absorbed indeed in another journal.[2] I am glad that you receive increased orders from our large towns. I know not what the College may do; I think the Athenaeum may enlarge its orders a little the current year, as the funds [are] in somewhat improved condition. So much for your last letter. I will repeat some books ordered in my letter dated September [blank] and October 19, '33 as you have not acknowledged the receipt of them. *I wish you to send* Poza, Pulgar, Raidin [?]. I ordered Robles inadvertently, I find I have it, [. . . .] Is there any manuscript history of Ximenes I can easily [get] except Marmol? I am obliged to [. . .] a portion of my work [. . .] Sempere's *History of Spain and Portugal*. I find Acts of Cortes referred to by the author of the last, who is he?[3] Are they printed as such independent of the codes of laws?

If so, can you send those relating to Ferdinand and Isabella's reign?
You may also send Irving's abridgment of his *Columbus*, Family Library.[4]

1. Apparently "more" should read "matter."
2. *The American Monthly Review*, published in Boston by Hilliard and
Brown and others, had known two calendar years of life. In December, 1833, it
was combined with Buckingham's *New-England Magazine*.
3. Juan Sempere y Guarinos (1754–1816), Spanish political historian.
4. Years later, when he was faced with the necessity of abridging his own
first history, WHP found Irving's abridgment helpful.

67.   To Obadiah Rich
                  (Draft, WHP Papers, Mass. Hist. Soc.)

                                        Boston, September 17, 1834
My dear Sir

I have not heard from you since February 28, 1834, since which I
have sent you two letters dated May 12 and August 22. The object of
the last letter was solely to make sure of the *extracts from the Quincuagenas of Oviedo*,[1] for which purpose I enclosed you a letter to a
friend of mine, Mr. Arthur Middleton, secretary of legation at Madrid,
who may probably have the means as he certainly will have the inclination to forward my views. In case of the miscarriage of these letters
to you, I shall be obliged to you if you will write to Mr. Middleton
stating my request if you think he can do anything to promote it. I have
set my heart on these extracts.

I find the following books on my list ordered within the last year
and not yet received. (Repeat the orders) By my letter of May 9[2] I requested you to get me an engraving of Leslie's "Sancho before the
Duchess,"[3] and also of Wilkie's "John Knox Preaching,"[4] if published.
I wish you to send me also the following new works (Refer to list ordered September, 1834 [1833]). These *Chronicles of the Canongate* you
omitted by some inadvertence to send in the complete collection of
Scott's novels.

I have nothing to add but that I mentioned in my last the receipt of
Varilla's *Louis XI and XII*, Changenie [?] d'Italie and the *Foreign
Quarterly* Number 24, which had been missing all winter. They were
safely deposited in the bookstore of Mr. Burdett who had no orders
where to send them.

I know of nothing new here that would particularly interest you. Mr.
Edward Everett has resigned his seat in Congress, having found out,

after holding it nine years, that politics was a poor game enough in the present condition of the country. It is understood that he will take charge of the *North American Review,* and that he is its proprietor.

1. Extracts of the letter of August 22, 1834, are in Wolcott, *Correspondence of Prescott,* p. 4.

2. Extracts of the letter of May 9, 1834, are in *ibid.,* p. 3.

3. This work, usually titled "Sancho and the Duchess," is by Charles Robert Leslie (1794–1859).

4. This work, usually titled "Preaching of John Knox," is by Sir David Wilkie (1785–1841).

68.   To Obadiah Rich
(Draft, WHP Papers, Mass. Hist. Soc.)

November 25th 1834

My dear Sir

My last date from you is February 18. So long an interval has elapsed that I should doubt if you were in the land of the living if I had not evidence to the contrary in a letter I saw of yours the other day to Mr. Ticknor mentioning my Ségur and Boulay-Paty as having been shipped.[1] One or two English books ordered last May might have reached me before this, but I am most disappointed in not having got yet either Pulgar or Poza's *Ximenes* or Sempere's *Consideration &c.*— ordered more than a year since, but above all the extracts from Ovie-do's *Quincuagenas.* I fear some ill luck has betided me there. You doubtless received my letter to Mr. Middleton, the American secretary of legation. Pray have the goodness when you receive this to let me know how the thing stands. Inform me also what are the *Acts of Urbis* cited by Dunham,[2] and whether they are printed and accessible in regard to Isabella's reign. One other work I have most inadvertently omitted, which I must get if it be any way possible—i.e. the edicts passed under this reign commonly called *Pragmáticas de Ramírez* of which several editions—for which if necessary I refer you to *Memorias de la Real Academia de Historia VI,* p. 216—appear before 1550. I have completed Isabella's reign, being this very moment occupied with her funeral. The rest of the journey, which may last me a year, I must travel on as[3] her Catholic spouse alone.

In addition to the books ordered in my last, September 17, easily procured, I wish you to send me Miss Burney's *Memoirs* of her father[4] and also the *Edinburgh* and *London Quarterly Review* as regularly and expeditiously as they come out. They have ceased to reprint them here in a tolerable form. The *Edinburgh* beginning with Number 121 and the *Quarterly* with Number 103.

I see by Mr. Ticknor's letter that you have been in France and by the public prints that you are made Consul of Minorca. What is to become of the bibliopolical business in England? I feel much concerned to know. I shall depend on receiving a line in answer to this—and believe me Very truly yours

[P.S.] I suppose the difficulty of getting Spanish books is much enhanced by the present state of the country.[5] You have shown too much interest in my concerns, however, to allow me to doubt they will be overcome if you can do it.

1. Probably Louis Philippe comte de Ségur (1753–1830), author of numerous historical works, and Pierre Sébastien Boulay-Paty (1763–1830), author of treatises on commercial law.
    2. Samuel Astley Dunham (d. 1858), author of *History of Spain and Portugal* (5 vols., 1832–33).
    3. For "as" read "with."
    4. I.e. *Memoirs of Dr. Burney* (1832).
    5. The regency on behalf of youthful Isabella II, who had ascended the throne in 1833, intensified the political ills besetting Spain.

69.   From Obadiah Rich
(WHP Papers, Mass. Hist. Soc.)

London, January 20, 1835

Dear Sir

In a box for Russell Odiorne & Co. I have sent a few books for you, some of which should have been sent to you long ago. I shall have a few more to send you by the next vessel for Boston. The principal excuse that I have for the delay in sending these books is the unfrequency of having anything to send to Boston. I trust you will have received the *Pragmáticas* before this reaches you. I am so little satisfied with the results of my exertions to serve my countrymen here that I contemplate with much pleasure my retirement to the pleasant little island of Minorca.[1] I am trying to find some one with as good a will and a better head, to take my place in the "Bibliopolical business;" and shall be much gratified if I can meet with such a one.

The Acts of the Cortes which you enquire about, I have in my possession in 20 folio volumes; they commence in the year 1020; all before the year 1523 are manuscript; they were never printed. I am in treaty with the British Museum for these and about 30 more printed volumes

of Ancient Legislation, of great rarity. I ask for the whole 200 guineas.
A similar collection (described in Salva's Spanish Catalogue part 2,
which I believe Mr. Ticknor has) was sold here a few years ago for
£500; bought for the Spanish Government.

I remain very sincerely Yours

O. RICH

1. WHP was appalled at the prospect of losing Rich's assistance. Time would
demonstrate, however, that WHP, with numerous aides in various places in
Europe, never would need to depend upon any one person so much as he had
depended upon Rich for more than half a decade. Rich found he could not
completely turn his back upon books, even while he served as U.S. Consul in
Minorca.

70.   From Cornelius Conway Felton[1]
                    (WHP Papers, Mass. Hist. Soc.)

Cambridge January 31, 1835

Wm. H. Prescott Esq.
Dear Sir

I am directed by the committee of the Phi Beta Kappa Society[2] to
invite you in their name to deliver an oration on their next anniversary, in this place.

I cannot forbear expressing a strong hope and wish that you may
be willing to accept the invitation and favor the society with an address on that occasion.[3]

With high respect I am very truly Yours

C. C. FELTON
Corresponding Secretary of Φ. B. K.

1. Cornelius Conway Felton (1807–62), a classical scholar of unusual intellectual breadth and genial human qualities, both of which endeared him to
WHP.
2. WHP had been elected to Phi Beta Kappa during his senior year at
Harvard.
3. No record exists of any address by WHP during his entire adult life.

71.   To George Bancroft
                 (George Bancroft Papers, Mass. Hist. Soc.)

Pepperell, June 17, 1835

My dear Bancroft,

How are you and how are you employing yourself this summer?
Building up the *"monumentum perennius,"* or evaporating in news-

paperials?[1] The last I heard of you was in this form. I wish for the sake of good taste, if nothing else, you would forswear such thin potations, as this periodical and party scribbling and speechmaking, and stick to your one great object, too great for any man yet to have done well, though you seem to be in a fair way for it—the history of your country. Such ample scope that affords for every thing save theories, which I trust will never find their way into it.

I have just returned from a Bunker Hill celebration[2] in our good town of Pepperell. The Prescott guards, a dapper little company, have had an oration—the orator was my brother Edward[3]—so of course we all turned out. The house was decorated with various patriotic emblems &c. There were two or three pews stuffed full of survivors; who I suppose will be carted about the country as long as their bones hold together, as the appropriate ornament of such festivities. Four of them had been in the Bunker Hill shock—and one eighty-six years of age is on the eve of encountering a still greater shock, being about to be married next week to a flourishing spinster of the same date. The whole affair went off well enough; and the audience were brought into the Niobe vein by the patriotic reminiscences of the orator.

You know, of course, our friend Ticknor and family are half on their way to Europe—for a residence of four years—a sad gap in my circle. The death of his little boy gave his wife a shock from which she found it so difficult to rally, that he determined on this expedient. The excitement occasioned visible good effects before their departure. They will pass their time chiefly in the large cities, with occasional excursions, in the most civilized and comfortable parts of Europe. My old correspondent Rich has had an appointment in Minorca, which I fear will withdraw him from the bibliopolical business. He sent me the other day a beautiful octavo 500 pages *Bibliotheca Nova Americana,* being a complete catalogue of books relating to America, published in the 18th century, with careful notices and criticisms each by himself. He had only a few copies printed for distribution. It occurred to me the work might be of use to you; if so mine is at your service when and as long as you want it.

I find the country as usual favorable to the historic muse.[4] I am so near the term of my labors, that if I were to remain here six months longer, I should be ready to launch my cockboat, or rather gundalow, for it is a heavy 3 volume affair, into the world. A winter's campaigning in the metropolis,[5] however, will throw me back, I suppose, six months further. I have little more to do than bury and write the epitaphs of the Great Captain, Ximenes and Ferdinand. Columbus and

Isabella are already sent to their account. So my present occupation seems to be that of a literary sexton, and I begin to weary of it. Pray let me know how you get on—at what part of your narrative you have arrived—when you expect to finish your next volume and what success your sales of the first have had. The trumpet of fame has blown a loud blast in your favor. Pray take its clear healthy ringing tones, instead of the penny trumpet squeaks of *fungus popularitas*, as a schoolfellow of mine once rendered the old phrase "mushroom popularity." You see, by the bye, your friend Everett has got to the upper round.[6] What will become of the old North and its present pilot?

Pray give my regards to your wife, and believe me, dear Bancroft, Very sincerely your friend,

WM. H. PRESCOTT

1. Herein the former refers to his work on his *History of the United States* and the latter to Bancroft's political writings in the newspapers. Newspaperial is a WHP original.

2. This letter is dated on the sixtieth anniversary of the battle.

3. In this period Edward Goldsborough Prescott, soon to turn clergyman, was winning popularity for his orations on historical occasions. On occasion he was the designated orator of the city of Boston on Independence Day.

4. Two days earlier, on June 15, WHP had written, "During the five weeks I have been at Pepperell, I have accomplished about sixty pages print—nearly two pp. per diem." See Prescott (Gardiner, ed.), *The Literary Memoranda*, I, 179.

5. In Boston the social side of WHP always found him yielding to time-consuming temptations of society.

6. In 1835 Edward Everett was elected Governor of Massachusetts by a combination of Whigs and Anti-Masons. He held that post four consecutive terms, 1836–39.

72. To Obadiah Rich

(Draft, WHP Papers, Mass. Hist. Soc.; and extracts in Wolcott, *Correspondence of Prescott,* p. 5)

Boston, July 22d 1835

My dear Sir,

I received yours of May 2d in due season, together with the inter-linear school books and some others ordered by me. I have little further to add now except to request that before leaving London, you will find time for the various things mentioned in my letter of March 13th, which, when I have obtained them, will complete all that will be necessary for the illumination of my historic labors. I shall hope to receive them early in the winter, as should they come later they can be of little other use than mere reference. By next spring I shall have disposed of my whole drama and must request particular advice of you, what way I shall take of putting it into three good English octavos.[1] As I shall send out one of my fair printed copies, the merits of the work can be more readily judged of by a bookseller, and I think it will be clearly for my advantage to interest a bookseller more or less in the publication. You see I endeavor to avail myself of your friendly offices as well as your professional ones.

I see Alison's *French Revolution* 3d and 4th volumes are out, which I wish you would send me—also the continuation of Sismondi's *Histoire des Français* subsequent to tom. xv. Also, if they can be got separately, in Baudry's collection of ancient and modern novels, those of Mackenzie, Radcliffe, Godwin, Smollett and Richardson. I have some notion of writing a life of Cervantes when I have nothing better to do,[2] which might fill a little volume, and occupy a year agreeably. I own his works with Pellicer's edition of *Don Quixote*—but I should like whatever would be of subsidiary service to his biography, as Navarrete's *Vida* among other things. My head runs a little too on Philip II. Have you any unpublished documents and good original materials for a domestic history, for Watson has written a foreign one of his reign.

My present history of Ferdinand and Isabella, whatever deficiencies it may have in point of execution, embraces in its plan a thorough view of the literary and social, as well as the political condition of Spain at this period, and I believe over great part of the ground has the merit, to the English reader at least, of novelty. Sparks advises me to print it here—I may perhaps do so conjointly with the publication in London.

I must thank you before closing this letter for the *Bibliotheca Nova Americana,* which you did me the favor to send me. It is a beautiful specimen of bibliography, exhibiting wider research, I suspect, than any other scholar can boast in this way.[3] Its compendious criticisms must be of great value to any person engaged in these studies, and I do not well understand how you found time for them. I mentioned in my last that I would make the necessary remittances to whom ever you left in charge of your affairs, though I suppose, if I want Spanish books, I shall be able to communicate with you at the place of your destination.

Believe me, dear Sir Very truly yours

WM. H. PRESCOTT

1. See item 40 *supra*, p. 62.
2. The nearest WHP ever came to doing a biography of Cervantes was his

review of Sales's *Don Quixote* in the July, 1837, issue of the *North American Review*.

3. WHP had received the first of two volumes entitled *Bibliotheca Americana Nova; or, A Catalogue of Books in Various Languages Relating to America, Printed Since the Year 1700.* The second volume appeared in 1846.

73.   To Jared Sparks
(Jared Sparks Papers, Harvard College Library)

Nahant, July 23, 1835

My dear friend

It is with the sincerest sorrow I have learnt the fatal termination of your wife's illness. Although from what I heard some time since, I feared there was small chance for her recovery. I had not the pleasure of knowing her intimately but I knew her well enough to feel the charm of her delightful manners, and her gifted and cultivated mind. Her death is indeed a most deplorable event for you—the more so, considering your retired pursuits and her capacity and tastes for entering into them. I wish I could offer consolation that might mitigate your sorrows, but there is none to be derived from words, or indeed from anything but the conviction, which you have, of a future existence, and the knowledge that the friend you have lost possessed too much moral perfection not to be happy in it. It is impossible, however, to be so disinterested as to surrender our own griefs, even to suit a delightful and animating conviction. You have met with one of those blows which loosens the hold on life more than any worldly calamity. In the same degree, however, they strengthen the hope with which we look forward to the future, by multiplying the objects of interest in that better world.

It is the death of dear friends, of pure and virtuous spirits, which disarms death of its terrors for ourselves, making it, as it were, the beginning of a new life, where we are to rejoin in nobler forms of existence, what we have most loved on this frail, perishable earth. There is indeed inexpressible consolation in the thought that it is the outward form alone, the senseless, material part that has perished, and that the soul, all you have ever prized and loved, still exists, and will continue to exist, in a more pure and glorious condition of being forever.

I am glad for your sake, that your mind will not be allowed leisure to recoil on itself, by excessive—for alas! useless repining. You have occupations which demand your time, and they are fortunately of that ennobling and useful kind which will not jar on your feelings. You have lost one, indeed, who shared and sympathized most in your labors. But you have friends left, believe me, who strongly sympathize in them, and who only regret that their sympathy can do so little.

All our family desire to be remembered to you in the kindest manner —and believe me, dear Sparks Yours most truly and affectionately

WM. H. PRESCOTT

74.   To Jonathan Goodhue
              (Goodhue Papers, The New York Society Library)

Nahant, July 29, 1836

My dear Sir

I am about to ask a favor of you, which I do with the more reluctance as I fear it will put you to some trouble. It is two years since I requested Mr. Middleton, Secretary of Legation at Madrid, to procure for me a copy of some manuscripts in the Royal Library. He did it, but was unable to find a safe conveyance for them till now; when last week I received a letter from him, informing me that he had availed himself of the return of one of Mr. Van Ness's[1] servants to forward this parcel on to New York, to J. J. Roosevelt Esq., giving a draught on me for the amount—about 92 dollars. As I have received Mr. Middleton's letter, I presume the manuscripts have arrived by the same conveyance and are in Mr. Roosevelt's possession. I have not the pleasure of knowing that gentleman, and I shall be much obliged to you, if you will take the trouble to send for them, and pay the bill on my account, and send me the papers by some safe conveyance, to our house Bedford Street, Number 22. If Mr. Ward[2] is in New York, I have no doubt he will be kind enough to take charge of the papers for me, and bring them at once to Nahant, and if he will pay the amount, I can reimburse him at once. But, of course, any way you point out, I will attend to for repaying you.

I hope you will not think I take too great a liberty in asking this favor, but I know no one in New York whom I can apply to so willingly, except indeed Mr. Cogswell, and I doubt whether, as it is vacation time, he may be there.

With much regard, believe me, dear sir, Very truly yours

WM. H. PRESCOTT

1. Cornelius Peter Van Ness (1782–1852) served as U.S. Minister to Spain from 1829 to 1837.

2. Samuel Ward (1814–84) was a warmhearted New York financier. As gourmet and socialite, he had a wide circle of intimates in Europe and America.

75.   From Jared Sparks
                      (WHP Papers, Mass. Hist. Soc.)

                                    Cambridge, February 24th, 1837

My dear Sir

I propose to go into town on Tuesday next, and will be with you at
1/2 past 2, and talk about the book.[1] Mr. Longfellow[2] will go, as you
requested.

I have read several chapters, and am reading more. The book will
be successful,—bought, read and praised.[3] Most truly yours

                                            JARED SPARKS

1. Sparks was one of several individuals to whom WHP submitted prepublication copies of *Ferdinand and Isabella* for critical evaluation.
2. Henry Wadsworth Longfellow (1807–82). As poet, student of Spanish culture and friend, he meant much to WHP.
3. In October, 1836, WHP had sent one of the copies of the prepublication
printing of his book to Thomas Aspinwall, who, at the suggestion of Obadiah
Rich, assumed the role of WHP's literary agent in London. See Wolcott, *Correspondence of Prescott,* pp. 6, 8.

76.   To Jared Sparks
                      (Jared Sparks Papers, Harvard College Library)

                                    Bedford St., February 25th [1837]

Dear Sparks

We shall be very glad to see you and Mr. Longfellow on Tuesday.
Pray tell him we dine at three. I shall ask nobody to meet you but
William Amory. Do not you make it later *than ½ past two*—at furthest
—since I wish to consult you fully as to the best way of getting out the
book—the size of the volumes &c &c. I count on you for all the information relative to the mysteries of the trade.[1] Ever yours

                                            WM. H. PRESCOTT

1. For WHP it was easy to make and keep friends, and the flattery in this
closing statement guaranteed Sparks's fullest cooperation.

77.   To Jared Sparks
                      (Jared Sparks Papers, Harvard College Library)

                                    Wednesday morning, [March 1, 1837]

Dear Sparks

Volume 2d of the History was not in the parcel.[1] I mention it that it may not be mislaid. You can send it in or bring it when you come. I have no occasion for it now. The more I think of the stereotyping, the better I am pleased with the arrangement[2]—if I can secure the services of a good midwife to bring my bantling into the world. Ever yours

WM. H. PRESCOTT

1. Apparently Sparks had completed his reading of WHP's *Ferdinand and Isabella*.

2. Every book by WHP was introduced to American readers via author-owned stereotype plates.

78.   To George Bancroft
(George Bancroft Papers, Mass. Hist. Soc.)

Boston, 6 March, 1837

Dear Bancroft,

I have at length finished the rigging of my bark, and am preparing to launch her on the mighty deep.[1] I cannot do better than take counsel of you, who have gone through the perils of the voyage and come off victorious, happy and glorious, from it. My work will take up three volumes, which I intend to throw into the octavo form, to be executed in a manner very like yours. Now what is the best mode of bringing it before the public? Would you advise me to stereotype, if I can make a bargain with the Stationers' Company, or with Gray & Hilliard,[2] they finding the paper &c and allowing some trifle a volume, and I, of course, providing the plates? Or would it be better to print an edition of 1000 copies, in the usual way, and employ some publisher to dispose of them on my account? I suppose the last would reimburse me soonest. But which would spread the book most effectually, and make it known? My object, you know, has not been gain, but an honest reputation; and I should prefer, unless it was very disadvantageous in a pecuniary way, to take that course which would most certainly circulate the book. I do not deceive myself with expectations of profit. If that had been my object, I should have taken another subject. If I publish it on my own account, will it not require a good deal of supervision and personal interference, to insure its proper distribution, from which I should be excused in the other course? Will you have the goodness to let me know, in a few words, what your stereotyping costs you, and what agreement you have made with Bowen?

I will thank you to respond to these queries as soon as convenient and with all befitting seriousness—as I am somewhat perplexed in my present predicament. I hope this string of interrogatories will not reach you when you are up to your neck in your own composition—if they do, you will wish the querist at the antipodes. But I will trust to your good nature. We are all well here, and have been looking for some time, for your second bantling, to divide, not diminish, the laurels of the first. Your volumes will scarcely stop short of the number of the Muses.

I received a letter from Ticknor the other day. He is in Italy—and Cogswell and Frank Gray are now with him. He sent me a long account of an interview with Metternich—in which that canny statesman dropt some things that a Yankee politician might pick up with profit. Sparks is bringing his *magnum opus* to a close. He is bound by contract to complete the last, i.e. first, volume, the life of Washington, in April. This writing against time is not to my taste—and sometimes, though it is not likely to be the case with him, proves quite as hard to the reader as the writer.

Adieu, dear Bancroft, I hope your family continue all in good health. Pray present my regards to your wife, and believe me Yours faithfully

WM. H. PRESCOTT

1. Behind the nautical allusions which crowd WHP's writing—books and correspondence—two things should be noted: the sea that he contemplated romantically from the cottage at Nahant, he loved; the sea that he sailed repeatedly, he detested.

2. Both were Boston companies, the former being newly established, the latter well known and reliable.

79.   To Jared Sparks
(Jared Sparks Papers, Harvard College Library)

Wednesday evening, [March 22, 1837]

My dear Sparks

I enclose you your Contract for which I am much obliged to you.[1] I am sorry that my Index-monger is so exorbitant. But it will be better to come to his terms than to hunt further. So I will trouble you to arrange it so with him.[2] He should complete it so as to be stereotyped when the rest of the work is printed by Folsom, without delay.[3] Ever truly yours,

WM. H. PRESCOTT

1. Apparently WHP was comparing the terms of one of Sparks's contracts with those tendered him by the Stationers' Company. See Wolcott, *Correspondence of Prescott*, p. 13.

2. John Langdon Sibley (1804–85), a classmate of WHP's brother at Har-

vard. He long served as librarian of that institution, and he executed indexes for successive histories by WHP.

3. The stereotype plates were produced by Folsom, Wells and Thurston of Cambridge, as was the printing.

80.   To Charles Folsom[1]
(Charles Folsom Papers, Boston Public Library)

Saturday morning [April 15, 1837][2]

My dear Sir

I have concluded to alter the caption or running title of chapter I and indeed have changed the principle somewhat on which all the titles are to be made. Instead of Ferdinand and Isabella on one page, and the general title of the chapter on the other, I now propose to give a general title on the left page, and a more particular one on the opposite. This will give much more variety. The Granada War, for instance, runs through half a dozen chapters. The Italian through as many—the same unvarying title will weary the eye of the reader. Instead of that I would put War of Granada on the left—Conquest of Málaga, War of Granada —Surrender of the capital—and so on.[3] The captions for chapter I had better be

Left page   *Right page*
     Reign of John II of Castile   Birth of Isabella

I will complete a catalog of the whole for you.

As to the length of the captions, Bancroft, I find, frequently gets from 35 to 40 letters. A sentence not exceeding thirty—if set close—will not appear cumbrous.

I wish to make a suggestion about the postscripts as I call them. What think you of letting them run across the page rather than double column? In that case they might each have its side note explaining the subject of the biographical sketch[4]—and they would not require a running line of text for the effect—as in the other case.

I shall not take any decision in this point till I have had your counsel, who are my Magnus Apollo in these perilous concerns.[5] Truly yours

WM. H. PRESCOTT

1. Charles Folsom (1794–1872) meticulously applied his editorial and proof-reading skills to successive manuscripts by WHP. In the process of converting manuscripts into books, Folsom was WHP's most regular aide.

2. A few day earlier, on April 10, WHP had contracted for the publication of his book in America; see C. Harvey Gardiner, *Prescott and His Publishers* (Carbondale, Illinois, 1959), pp. 21, 53.

3. The running heads of the published book incorporated this proposal.

4. Biobibliographical essays rather than postscripts, these portions of the manuscript were printed in double columns.

5. Again the generous compliment which encouraged the recipient's maximum cooperation.

81.   To Charles Folsom
(Charles Folsom Papers, Boston Public Library)

I send this at 12 o'clock [c. April 20, 1837]

Dear Sir

I have run over the proofs—and written with each the alterations which I wish. I have broken the text in two convenient places into paragraphs—thinking the length would appal the reader at the outset. When you find paragraphs too long, have the goodness to break them up—always—unless the subject is very *cohesive,* a page would be long enough—in general. You may think it best to raise the side note[1] of Rise of Alvaro de Luna a line or two to suit the paragraph. As to Spanish capitals—I think it is best to conform to our English rules—though a quotation might seem to stand on somewhat different grounds—but it is best to be uniform. My object in seeing these proofs is to overlook the affair at its starting—and chiefly the references. As to the text, I hardly glance at it—except in regard to the paragraphs to see the general effect.

I am sorry the references require so much correction. But the first will be the worst. Of course when a work is a manuscript you will always add MS. in the reference—through the whole. Yours

W. H. Prescott

P.S. You will bear in mind the length of the page—now about a line too long—though not too many lines. Its width is very nearly right.

1. The side notes, however helpful to the reader, did not appear on all printings made from these stereotype plates.

82.   From John Pickering[1]
(WHP Papers, Mass. Hist. Soc.)

Beacon Street, May 1, [1837]

My dear Sir,

Being uninterrupted last evening, I had an opportunity to finish the few pages that remained of your work—and I now return the volumes, with many thanks.

I cannot, however, take leave of them without again expressing the high satisfaction I feel, that our country should have produced such a work—a work, which, unless I am greatly mistaken, will live as long as any one produced by your contemporaries either here or in England.[2]

I am, my dear Sir, with the warmest regard Very truly yours

JN⁰ PICKERING

1. John Pickering (1777–1846) was a friend of the Prescott family from days in Salem, Massachusetts. He repeatedly encouraged WHP in his intellectual endeavors. At this time he is returning a prepublication copy.

2. In "Prescott's Reign of Ferdinand and Isabella," *The New-York Review*, II (April, 1838), 308–41, Pickering placed his praise of the book before the public. More than 150 editions, printings and translations of WHP's first history tend to substantiate Pickering's verdict.

83.   To Colonel Thomas Aspinwall[1]
(Draft, WHP Papers, Mass. Hist. Soc.)

Boston, 20 May 1837

My dear sir

I send you, for Mr. Bentley,[2] the duplicate corrections of Part 2d of the History. Should he use the American proofs, he will have no occasion for these. At all events, I don't see that it will be necessary to trouble you more in the affair, since the proofs, if he desires them, will go direct to him. I mentioned to you that they would go through the hands of Baring Brothers & Co., Liverpool, subject to your orders. I have not received yet a copy of your agreement with Bentley.[3] I trust the squally aspect of the times will not postpone operations in England. It will not, at any rate, retard the printing here, and I have no reason to suppose it will the publication. Things go on rather more easily now under our paper system—whether more securely remains to be seen. I think, however, measures will be taken by the leading banks throughout the country, for limiting issues within proper bounds, with a view to returning as soon as possible to a specie basis. But we are far enough from it at present. Even what little we had for the ordinary purposes of circulation is gradually sliding out of the market—a circumstance which occasions much inconvenience.[4] So much for experiments and speculation.

With sincere regard, I am dear Sir,

1. Thomas Aspinwall (1786–1876), a veteran of the War of 1812 and for several decades Consul-General of the United States in London, served as literary agent for numerous American authors, including WHP. He had concluded a contract on March 20, 1837, for the publication of WHP's book by the firm of Richard Bentley.

2. Richard Bentley (1794–1871), a leading London publisher in mid-nineteenth-century decades, published five titles by WHP.

3. The text of this contract is reproduced in Gardiner, *Prescott and His Publishers,* p. 283. In this half-profits arrangement, Bentley assumed all the production expenses for a printing of unstated size.

4. In addition to his continuing opposition to Jacksonian financial policies, WHP was witnessing the early stages of the Panic of 1837.

Additional letters related to the theme of this one are in Wolcott, *Correspondence of Prescott,* pp. 17–20.

84.   To Thomas G. Bradford[1]

(Samuel Eliot Morison, Boston; and in William H. Prescott [Samuel Eliot Morison, ed.], *History of the Conquest of Peru* [New York, 1957], p. xxviii)

Pepperell, May 29 [1837]

My dear Sir:

I understand from Mrs. Dexter[2] that you wished to borrow a Latin book of me. She did not mention the name—but as you once spoke of Peter Martyr *(Epistolae)* I suppose it may be that worthy. If so, if you will take the trouble to mount up into my attic, you will find him, snugly ensconced among some old Spaniards, on the lower shelf, middle compartment of the bookcase, western side of the room. That or any other work, which I have, is entirely at your service, only I will trouble you to leave a memorandum of the same, with the 'genius loci'—or, in other words, the old words, the old lady you will find in the kitchen.[3] Yours very truly,

W. H. PRESCOTT

1. Thomas Gamaliel Bradford (d. 1887), teacher and writer, was a lesser member of the intellectual community of Boston during the lifetime of WHP.
2. I.e. WHP's sister.
3. A frequent borrower, WHP was also a generous lender of books.

85.   To Charles Folsom

(Charles Folsom Papers, Boston Public Library)

Nahant, August 23, [1837]

My dear Sir

It is so long since I have heard from you, that I begin to fear some of your presses must have broken down under the superincumbent mass of mind or matter. I can give you, I think, three very good reasons for quickening operations. In the first place, I have not heard, and doubt if I shall hear from Bentley; so long a time has elapsed it makes it probable that he will depend on your sheets, as I wrote him word that they would be regularly forwarded unless I was advised to the contrary. Secondly, I wish my reviewer may have a fair copy of the whole during his leisure season, which will continue only a few weeks longer.[1] Thirdly, I should be very glad to have the Introduction turned off before I go to Pepperell. The variety and character of its contents makes it much to be wished that I should have access to my library during its revision. If you can turn off the work by the 7th of September I can postpone my departure to Pepperell till that date. There you see are reasons plenty for going straight through the thing—and I cannot conceive of one for twaddling along as if we had peas in our shoes—which we have been doing the last fortnight.[2] Very truly yours

WM. H. PRESCOTT

1. The prospective reviewer of whom WHP was so solicitous was William Howard Gardiner, whose review eventually appeared as "History of the Reign of Ferdinand and Isabella, the Catholic," *North American Review*, XLVI (January, 1838), 203–91.

2. Folsom was already well known for the time-consuming care that he bestowed upon semicolon, adjective and synonym.

86.   To Charles Folsom

(Charles Folsom Papers, Boston Public Library)

Pepperell, Monday evening, September 11, [1837]

I send you the *Title page—Dedication—Preface—*and *Introduction Section* 1—Section 2d to follow the next day.

The *Contents* consisting of our little notes printed in column, you will print of course before the Introduction—each volume having its own Contents.

I think with you much of a handsome symmetrical *Title page.* The names Ferdinand and Isabella might be printed in a deeper, broader and blacker character a *little* larger than the rest. What do you think of Old English for the cognomen The Catholic? I defer to you on typographical taste and perspicacity. I should like, however, *to see a copy of the printed Title page* before it is fixed in immortal bronze.

As to the *Preface*—I do not conceive a larger type than that of the text of the body of the work for it—like Sparks's *Washington.* I think a slight distinction between them may be well obtained by scabb (hang the word, I don't know how to spell it for printers)-arding a shade wider—giving it a little more dainty and gentleman-like aspect. Could you not send me a specimen before casting, with the Title page?

I observe you don't say any thing about 'stereotyping' in Sparks's book—but simply 'printed by.' Don't you think mentioning the stereo-type gives an air of expected popularity &c., to a considerable extent? If so had it not better be omitted? I have no such foolish expectations, I assure you.

I saw Gardiner the other day. He is setting seriously about the affair. I am very desirous, as he is, that he should have the balance of the work in his hands. Now is his time for haymaking—and the Preface and Postscripts and the last chapter, which he has not seen, are indispensable to his understanding the ground. He had *none* of the third volume. Pray feed him while the steam is up.

The time of publication is settled—December 1st—without further delay. You will hear soon, if you have not heard, from Russell.[1] I suppose I may write a letter to go in the packet of October 1 to Bentley, telling him my engagements are performed, and that he may bring out the work from a complete copy executed under the eye of our American Aldus.[2]

Can not Mr. Sibley send me at once the Index for revising? I have already had the part relating to the Introduction and the first, and I believe the whole or a great part of the second, volume. Pray give heed to these suggestions and queries. Yours truly

W. H. P.

[P.S.] The mail comes daily.

Would it not be well to advertise the book, *in a plain manner,* in the Old North, as coming out on the first of December?

1. John B. Russell of the American Stationers' Company, WHP's publisher.
2. The sobriquet the Cambridge Aldus was often applied to Folsom. The reference, of course, is to the famed Italian printer Aldus Manutius (1450–1515).

87.   To Charles Folsom
(Charles Folsom Papers, Boston Public Library)

Pepperell, 2 October, 1837

My dear Sir:

When a man has once set up for a scribbler, there is no knowing where his pen will run, or rather where it will stop. In the present instance you will, I doubt not, commend its activity; and under that impression I must ask a favor and some trouble of you. I have written for Hale a brief critique on Sparks's recent work, as no better hand has appeared to take it up in his columns. I have said nothing but what is plainly true, I believe—but in touching on the embarrassments under which his task has been performed, I have been led insensibly, from a

certain feeling of indignation, which I suppose all his friends partici-
pate in, into some allusion to the causes of them. Although, as I have
said, I believe I have not exaggerated, or indeed told half the matter,
yet, on reflection, I entertain some doubts as to whether the strictures
on the government thus expressed would be approved by him. As the
facts are notorious, and he is not a party to the communication, I can
not see any objection. There may be such in his mind, however, that in
desiring to help I may, after all, in his view of things, be only hurting
him. Yet I do not choose to omit any strictures, without such be the
case. And on the other hand, I wish to get his opinion without his having any privity to the criticism, so that he might be able to say, if
necessary, it was done without his knowledge. For a man may be very
willing to have the truth told by another, without his participation,
while he would decline to have it done with it. For this reason I could
not send him the communication, and thus leave it to him to decide for
himself—to say nothing of the awkwardness of sending a man his own
praises—all reeking in the manuscript. Now it occurs to me that the
end may be obtained through a common friend, without committing
him. I wish, therefore, you would, when you see the good gentleman,
ascertain if he would have any scruples as to its being intimated in a
friendly newspaperial notice of his book, that "Congress, though urged
on the subject, had declined aiding the work by taking a number of
copies;" and secondly, "that, the manuscripts having been purchased
by [the] government, during the progress of his work, had been required
from him, and that the residue of his labors had been performed with
this requisition over his head."

That is the sum of the doubtful matter. If he objects to both, then
be pleased to strike out all after the words "avowed patronage of the
nation" page 4 line 3, to the end of the paragraph. If he objects to the
second query only, then strike out all after the words "from pecuniary
loss," to the end of the paragraph—as the concluding remarks will
be too heavy for the first head alone. If from what he says you find any
inaccuracies in my statements alluded to, which is possible, and if he
does not object to noticing the circumstances, have the goodness to correct such inaccuracies. He, not knowing that any communication has
been made, only answering the questions in the abstract, may truly say,
if need be, he was not privy to the affair.

Now is not this a mighty comboberation[1] about a penny trumpet
twaddle in the newspaper! But *volat irrevocabile verbum—immedica-
bile* when once fled—and I had rather write a quire in manuscript than
print a word that should harm or displease a friend. And as I know you
agree with me in this I will make no apologies for inflicting such a

prosy scrawl on your good nature. I will only add, that I shall be obliged to you to seal the letter, and let it find its direction. I would not, for obvious reasons put it in the Cambridge Post Office—though you might in the Boston.[2]

With respect to their Catholic Highnesses, you have nearly washed your hands of me, it seems. I am very glad that we came up to the mark proposed—as nothing would have chagrined me more than to fall short of my own voluntary engagements. I suppose you will forward the *duplicate* of the last pages the week after the first parcel, and you can add the few errata in the first part of volume 3d that I have just inspected. There were not many errors or alterations. I made three (change of as many words) in the stereotyped copy I returned to you on Saturday. I have written Bentley, and told him we should be out here probably in December. I have also written to Russell in favor of Peabody's paper;[3] and I should hope it might be made in season for our intended publication by December 1. I shall be glad to hear from you touching these points—and when you write, as I suppose you are behind the curtain, could you let me know the authors of the articles in the Old North—the last number? I suppose you think I can't indite a sentence without a note of interrogation at the end of it—but the time is coming when you will not be plagued with many more queries of mine to answer. Ever yours,

WM. H. PRESCOTT

1. Like newspaperial, comboberation is another WHP original.
2. WHP's article, praising Sparks's *Washington* and condemning the Democratic administration in Washington, appeared in the *Boston Daily Advertiser,* October 4, 1837, over the signature "Historicus."
3. In due time this superior paper went down to Boston from Salem.

88.   To Richard Bentley
(Richard Bentley Papers, Harvard College Library)

Boston, October 4, 1837

Sir,

I have now performed what I proposed—as my printer informed me he has forwarded the last parcel of Ferdinand and Isabella to London. I hope they will be found of the service I anticipated in saving the English printer time and trouble. As I thought it desirable the work should appear at nearly the same time, in both countries, I have arranged with the publishers here that the book shall not come out till December. My friend, Mr. Ticknor, now in France, will be in London in the winter, and will take eighteen or twenty copies to distribute among persons whose good opinion would be desirable. And as this will be a mutual benefit, I hope you will not think it unreasonable to let him have them at a moderate price.

As I have not had the pleasure of receiving an answer to my former communication to you, I felt some doubt whether you meant to rely on the American proofs. They have gone out regularly, I presume, however, but you will oblige me by informing me on receipt of this, whether they have all come safe to hand,—and when it is your intention to bring out the book in London. Very truly your obedient servant

WM. H. PRESCOTT

89.   To William Howard Gardiner

(William H. Gardiner Papers, Mass. Hist. Soc.)

Pepperell, October 4, 1837

My dear William:

I propose making a descent on the metropolis on Wednesday, the 11th, and shall pass Thursday in town. I think it proper to notify you of this important movement, agreeably to my agreement when we last met, though, as to the reunion we then talked of, I am not sure that we should not do better with a quiet tête-a-tête, round the family ingle. But one or the other, I look to, to wind me up for the next month. Though, as it may very well be that your engagements will make neither convenient for you, you will not hesitate to say so—only have the goodness to send a line to the house for me,[1] advising me what to do on Thursday, and leave word that the note be not forwarded to Pepperell, but wait there for me. Excuse my precision, but a mistake in the matter would be no joke to a friend from the country.

I lead a most quiet, homespun sort of life here, plenty of leisure for reading and scribbling, and wiping off old scores to correspondents. I have sent, by the by, this morning, a little critique on Sparks's *Washington,* to the respectable Daily.[2] A gentle puff, even from the country, may help to swell his sails for a fair offing. In truth, he deserves a good word from his friends; and every American should be his friend for concocting a work so truly national, and so honorable to the nation. Far from it, however, the government, who should have been the foremost to testify their sense of his merits, have refused in Congress to aid the work by subscription, but have menaced him with repeated requisition of the Washington manuscripts, which have become their property by purchase. Their patriotism and their literature are about on a par. Mr. Van Buren, I remember, seriously told Sparks once, that he had never read a page of Shakespeare! The republic has no need of scholars, I suppose he thinks.

The last number of the *North* has found its way into our woods. I have only glanced at it, but it looked uncommonly weak and waterish. The review of Miss Martineau, which is meant to be double spiced, is no exception.[3] I don't know how it is, but our critics, though not pedantic, have not the business-like air, or the air of the man of the world, which gives manliness and significance to criticism. Their satire, when they attempt it, which can not be often laid at their door, has neither the fine edge of the *Edinburgh,* nor the sledge-hammer stroke of the *Quarterly.* They twaddle out their humor, as if they were afraid of its biting too hard, or else they deliver axioms with a sort of smart, dapper conceit, that looks like a little parson laying down the law to his little people. I suppose the paltry price the *North* pays[4] (all it can bear, too, I believe) will not command the variety of contributions and from the highest sources, as with the English journals. Then, in England, there is a far greater number of men highly cultivated, whether in public life or men of leisure, whose intimacy with affairs and with society, as well as books, affords supplies of a high order for the periodical criticism. For a' that, however, the Old North is the best periodical we have ever had, or, considering its resources, are likely to have for the present.[5]

Now there is a batch from a country gentleman. Adieu my dear friend—love to Caroline,[6] and believe me Ever thine,

WM. H. PRESCOTT

1. I.e. the house in Boston, at 22 Bedford Street.

2. The *Boston Daily Advertiser,* whose Whiggish outlook matched his own, was the only hometown newspaper that WHP read regularly.

3. WHP refers to the review of Harriet Martineau's *Society in America* in the *North American Review,* XLV (October, 1837), 418–60.

4. The quarterly then paid $1.00 per page to its contributors.

5. On the subject of reviewing, WHP's actions, as well as his opinions, had changed with the years. He was no longer writing reviews with any regularity.

6. I.e. Mrs. William H. Gardiner.

90.   To Charles Folsom
                (Charles Folsom Papers, Boston Public Library)

Pepperell, October 19, 1837

Dear Sir;

I return you the proofs, with some corrections—two or three of them on account of some inaccuracies in my own statements. I have inserted

one *side note* at the close of the 2d Section of the Introduction, which
should also be introduced into the Contents, if there is room—if not,
it is of no consequence. Page xxxix, 2d column of notes, line 9 from
bottom, I see a reference to Masdeu, *"supra."* I don't know what it
means—had it been *sup.* I should have supposed supplement. The
book is in the College Library, and if you are there perchance you can
turn to it; if not, let it run—*n'importe.* You will find a much larger
number of corrections for broken types in the first section of the Introduction than usual; and yet I think your own eye may detect many
more. The truth is, the types, especially for the notes, have become a
good deal damaged in the course of the war; so that the vestibule will
not afford quite so attractive an appearance as the rest of the edifice. I
wish you would look over the ground yourself, and remedy it as far as
possible. I wrote, immediately on my return here, to F. Peabody, urging
excellence of paper, sizing, and despatch. Pray look to the matter yourself, as the best memories want jogging. I intimated to you in a former
letter that I would rather you would not state the book to be stereotyped, but only printed by you. The word stereotyped will add nothing
to the credit of your press, and I don't like the ostentatious appearance
it has, in the first place, and in the second, it would make the title of a
further edition, should one be called for, of even less value than it would
otherwise be—which I confess, as things are managed now-a-days, is
not much. I have myself forwarded to Bentley the corrections made in
these last proofs. I send this by a private opportunity—but know of
none to return. We shall be in town by November 10. Yours truly

WM. H. PRESCOTT

[P.S.] Since writing the above I have received a letter from Mr.
Peabody, which I inclose. We seem to be in very good luck in that
quarter. You see if the execution is not first class at whose door the sin
will lie. My mother goes down on Wednesday, and returns on Saturday,
and will bring any parcel that you may have occasion to send. We shall
all be down on the tenth.

October 23.—I was disappointed in sending this on the 19th.

91.   To Charles Folsom
                (Charles Folsom Papers, Boston Public Library)

Saturday, [November 25, 1837]

Dear Sir

I should like very much to get a copy of my work—one of those on
the purple paper—if I could for Mr. John Pickering who *between our-*

selves proposes to review my book for a New York journal. He asked me to let him have a copy. I shall be in Cambridge to examine the classes on Monday,[1] and I will try to see you in your office—when you can let me know about this. Yours

W. H. P.

1. At this time WHP was serving Harvard in the only capacity in which he ever served that institution, as an examiner in modern languages.

92.   To Charles Folsom
                (Charles Folsom Papers, Boston Public Library)

Bedford Street, December 6, [1837]
My dear Sir

How do you like the wood-cut—I think *à merveille.* I am in truth quite agreeably disappointed. But can't judge till it is incorporated into the Title page.[1] *When shall I have one?* Time gets on with noise-less—but certain tread. I hope the printing is in advance of him. *Pray let me know*—and how you dispose of the *Title and the Motto.* The review is now it seems [in] your hands.[2] The book ought to be in the shops here and at the south—when the Review appears, according to all the rules of good policy. Pray jog Mr. Thurston[3] if he needs it —which I suppose he don't [*sic*]. Yours truly

WM. H. PRESCOTT

[P.S.] I will return the Index tomorrow or next day.

1. This woodcut depicts the arms of Castile and León before they were quartered with those of Aragon.
2. I.e. the one written by William H. Gardiner for the *North American Review.*
3. Of the printing firm of Folsom, Wells and Thurston.

93.   To Charles Folsom
                (Charles Folsom Papers, Boston Public Library)

Tuesday evening, [December 12, 1837]
My dear Sir

Mr. Andrews[1] proposes to visit you today—and to get a copy of as much as is printed—which I want for Bancroft.[2] In thinking over the Title page—I think you may dispense with In Three Volumes—if you think it *much preferable.* Use your own discretion.

Mr. Palfrey threatens to cut off all the extracts in Gardiner's article. He may as well cut my head off. Who will believe half the fine things said of the book without a voucher. The article is somewhat *lengthy*,[3] to be sure, but it is a learned and elaborate one, I am sure, and the extracts will be as new to his reader as the review. People will certainly think they were afraid to quote me. It is so very unusual an occurrence —in this sort of article. Pray remonstrate with our Aristarchus[4]—and believe me Yours

W. H. P.

1. Of the publishing house of American Stationers' Company.

2. Eventually Bancroft's review, "Prescott's Ferdinand and Isabella," appeared in *The United States Magazine and Democratic Review,* II, 61 (May, 1838), 160–66. To help Bancroft to an awareness of certain matters which the author thought should be covered in the review, WHP wrote the would-be reviewer a detailed letter; see "Promoting a Book: Prescott to Bancroft, December 20, 1837," *The Papers of the Bibliographical Society of America,* LI (Fourth Quarter, 1957), 335–39.

3. Instead of somewhat, Gardiner's article was exceedingly, lengthy; it ran to eighty-nine printed pages, possibly an all-time high in the pages of the *North American Review.* Sparks at once dubbed it the fourth volume of the history; see Wolcott, *Correspondence of Prescott,* p. 21.

4. WHP compares editor Palfrey with the Greek grammarian and critic Aristarchus of Samothrace (d. 150 B.C.?).

94.   To Jared Sparks
(Jared Sparks Papers, Harvard College Library)

Christmas Morning, 1837[1]

Dear Sparks:

I have great pleasure, at last, in sending you their Catholic Highnesses, who keep their Christmas in Boston; and a merry Christmas I hope it will prove to all concerned. I think you will admit that Queen Isabella herself would have been gratified to have seen herself exhibited in so beautiful a dress, in these barbarous regions, discovered under her patronage. The whole *physique* of the book is equal to an English [one]. I fear it will be thought too good for the intellectual.

You were kind enough to say you would notify the Company to what Southern editors they might send copies, the *Intelligencer, New York American, National Gazette,* &c. I think you mentioned Gilman in Charleston. Your opinion, with these people, will do more for me than any thing else. Would it not be well to secure room from the editors of the newspapers for a few extracts, at times, which might recommend the book to purchasers? If you think so, Andrews has one or two unstitched copies in his possession, from which he could easily forward such extracts occasionally, to the printers. It seems to me that a judicious use of the scissors is, after one or two good notices, an effectual way to recommend the book.[2] But you have had most experience. I only hope the Company will sustain no loss by the publication. Mr. Pickering has undertaken to review the work for Henry's journal in New York. In Philadelphia I am least provided for; and if you think it best, I should thank you to write a line to Warton, the editor of the *American Quarterly*,[3] whom I think you know, calling his attention to the book, and directing the Company to send a copy to him. You will excuse my troubling you on this point, I know; for when a man's ship is to be launched, especially if it be his first, he feels rather extra-anxious to have wind and tide in his favor. Once fairly out, with a fair offing, it is his own fault if he can't weather the storm.[4]

I have written to Rich, requesting him, when the book comes out, to send a copy to Bowring.[5] I should send him one of ours, as I am sure it will be better than the one from the English press, but that I fear copies arriving before the publication there might affect the copyright, or Bentley might have some reason to complain. Ever thine

WM. H. PRESCOTT

P.S. The Postscript is the gist of the letter. *Club* celebrates with me tomorrow evening. Supper half past eight. So take this for a notice, and come early. When you have a fit of the vapors, I would prescribe a visit to School Street, to learn how your book sells. It has risen far above the atmosphere of puffs. A neat advertisement has been put in at the end of my book—which I hope you will like to see there.

P.P.S. Bancroft is in town, he told me he should go out to see you. You had better see him here. I have sent a note to Palfrey and should like to have you and him come and dine with me on Thursday at 4 o'clock and I will ask Bancroft and Gardiner in to meet you.[6] Yours

W. H. P.

1. Publication day for the *History of the Reign of Ferdinand and Isabella, the Catholic.* The title page, however, bore the date MDCCCXXXVIII.

2. WHP always thought that well-chosen sizable extracts baited the interest of the review reader and converted him into a potential purchaser.

3. Even as he solicited aid, WHP knew exactly where he wanted it in Philadelphia.

4. WHP marshaled reviewers and review media as systematically as he gathered data for his writing. One discussion of this theme is in C. Harvey Gardiner, "William Hickling Prescott: Launching a Bark," *The Americas*, XV (January, 1959), 221–34.

5. Sir John Bowring (1792–1872), linguist, writer and traveler. As editor (*Westminster Review*) and as author, especially on certain Spanish literary and historical subjects, his appeals to WHP were several.

6. For months, aside from seeing his book through the press, WHP had en-

gaged in what he termed "literary loafing"; now it was time for celebration. Only in the new year would he return to serious scholarship.

95.   To Charles Folsom
            (Charles Folsom Papers, Boston Public Library)

                        Bedford Street, December 25, [1837]

My dear Sir

Club celebrates with me tomorrow evening—and I hope you will come in. Supper at 1/2 past eight. Their Catholic Highnesses keep their Christmas in Boston—and I shall have the pleasure to send you a copy so soon as I can conveniently get one. The binder is very diligent—but cannot turn out more than twenty-five a day—and the company has made such arrangements that they would rather have me wait a few days.

Your title page is beautiful, unencumbered—and yet full. The book may safely stand along side the best English productions of this class —in all that relates to the typography and paper and general effect. I shall send out a few copies to England, as a sample of our achievements in this way. Bancroft, who is here, is delighted with it. I should not be surprised if he were hereafter to enter into negotiations with you for printing his future volumes.

Andrews wishes to have one or two copies, if he could, of *Gardiner's article*—to make use of it, for advertising and recommending the book at a distance.[1] If you have the proofs, cannot you furnish them to him. He would like to have them soon—and will not show them to any one, of course. Yours

                                        WM. H. PRESCOTT

    1. The January issue of the *North American Review,* in which this would appear, was not scheduled for release before the first of January.

96.   To Joseph Story[1]
            (Joseph Story Papers, The Library of Congress)

                        Boston, December 27, 1837

My dear Sir

Allow me to offer you the copy of a work which has occupied my leisure for some years. Your own familiarity with general literature, in spite of engrossing professional studies—and the friendly interest you have always shown in the success of younger men in all liberal pursuits, have led me to believe you would take an interest in the fruit of some study on my part. I feel it is to the approbation of writers like yourself that I must look for the best reward of my labours.[2]

With the greatest respect, believe me, dear sir, Truly yours,

WM. H. PRESCOTT

1. Joseph Story (1779–1845), the renowned associate justice of the United States Supreme Court, was a friend of the Prescott family.

2. Countless such presentation copies made WHP his publisher's best customer.

97.   To Charles Folsom
(Charles Folsom Papers, Boston Public Library)

Boston, January 16, 1838

Dear Sir:

Owing to your note's remaining in the rooms of the Stationers' Company, I did not receive it till yesterday morning. I trust you are in the full tide of the Second Edition. The book has continued, and still continues, to go off in a marvellous sort of way. I hope it won't all turn out what a boy I remember in Dr. Gardiner's school rendered into his classical Latin as a *"fungum popularitatem."* It is obvious now, however, that the publishers much miscalculated, as to the size of the edition.[1] Andrews takes a hundred copies with him to the South on Wednesday—rather scanty grist, if the book sells at all, for New York, Philadelphia and Washington. There will remain not more than five and twenty copies in the locker to supply the trade here. I suppose you will be able to throw two hundred more into the binder's hands in the course of ten or twelve days. But then the detention of the paper, &c will make it a "far cry" to the balance of the edition—and Andrews wishes to feel his way, at the South, before ordering the paper.

An advertisement has been prepared, which will be sent out to you by Mr. Andrews for the new edition. I suppose you will print it on a leaf to be inserted between the bastard title and the portrait. Of this you can judge. You will also have to bother your brains for the interpolation of "Second Edition" on the title page. I confide in your resources. Would it hurt the effect, think you, to lengthen the page by a line? I doubt if it would be observed.

Now with respect to the errata.

Introduction p. cvii, n. 60 l. 5 for "Cerden" read "Cerdan"
     "   " cxvii n. 82 1st column last line—for "Faviller" read "Fiveller"

Volume I p. 24 l. 9 from bottom for "confounds" read "confound"
"   " " 48 last line—for "formidble" read "formidable"
"   " " 160 delete side note "Gallant defence of Perpignan"—also
delete in the Contents.
Volume I p. 308 n. 47, last line but two—for "Fabricus" read "Fabri-
cius"
"   " " xxxix, n. 14 2nd column l.9 from bottom—for "supl.
1, 8" read "supl. 18."
Now for Petrarch—poor murdered Petrarch—for "Now" read "chè"
and for "anco" read "ancor"[2] Truly yours,

W. H. Prescott

1. The first edition consisted of 500 copies.
2. Corrections, stemming from errata lists supplied by many friendly readers, are reflected in numerous early American editions of the history.

98.   To Charles Folsom
                (Charles Folsom Papers, Boston Public Library)

Saturday, P.M. [January 20, 1838]

My dear Sir;

My own eyes have not been in trim to look through or indeed to look
into that renowned History, since it has come from the press. The errors, such as they are, have been furnished me by others; and that they
have been able to point out no more must arise, I conceive, either from
the immaculateness of your press, or quite as probably from the circumstance that the readers have not been able to get on further than the
first volume. However that may be, I shall make inquiries, and, if I
hear any thing further, straightway inform you. You speak of the scant-
iness of the second edition. I shall never consent to have that name
limited to the two hundred copies you are now striking off. It must
cover the balance of what I have sold to the Company. I hope, by the
by, the said two hundred will be deposited by the first of February in
the binder's hands. Pray look into the Advertisement, and see if the
word "large" had not better read "copious"—if so alter it accordingly.
Andrews has gone to New York with the books—yesterday.[1] Ever yours,

Wm. H. Prescott

1. WHP continued to concern himself with the publication and perfection
of his first work, but that was not enough to consume all of his energy. Considering the conquest of Mexico as a likely theme for his next effort, he set
about building the collection required for that research; see Wolcott, *Correspondence of Prescott*, pp. 22–23.

99.   To Alexander Young[1]
(Rare Books Department [Tuthill Collection], University of California)

March 14th [1838]

My dear Sir

Mr. Folsom has informed me that you were kind enough to promise him some corrections for the next edition of *Ferdinand and Isabella*. Tomorrow he begins with the balance of the second edition[2]—and if you can furnish him or me with any such errata as have occurred to you, you will oblige. Yours with much regard

WM. H. PRESCOTT

1. Alexander Young (1800–1854), a scholarly Unitarian clergyman (New South Church, Boston), possessed antiquarian and historical interests.

2. Planned for 750 copies—to complete the total of 1250 for which the American Stationers' Company had contracted—this edition stuttered forth in February and March and possibly ran to 800 copies; see C. Harvey Gardiner, *William Hickling Prescott: An Annotated Bibliography of Published Works* (Washington, [1959]), pp. 3–4, 5.

100.   To Charles Folsom
(Charles Folsom Papers, Boston Public Library)

Monday Morning, [March 19, 1838]

My dear Sir

I send you an addition which I wish you to insert at the end of the Postscript to Part II, chapter 15, volume III, p. 168. The Spanish Minister Don Calderón de la Barca[1]—I suppose not a descendant of his great namesake who was in orders—though by the bye that is not conclusive against it—has sent me several volumes relating to early Spanish history and among them one on the life of the Great Captain—a reprint of 1834 from an old and as I had supposed, and as the Spanish scholars generally have thought, long since lost. The little communication I have had with Spain of late years owing to the troubles of the country has prevented its reaching me. It is of no moment, as far as new light or facts are concerned but would have furnished another good reference as a contemporary document. As such it should be noticed—and there is just room for what I have written—pray measure it mathematically. I suppose there will be no great difficulty in splicing the columns, so as not to set up again the old matter.[2]

His Excellency—now no longer his Excellency, by the by, since he has just resigned his office, in consequence of refusal to subscribe to the new constitution—told Mr. Goodhue he should, had he continued in office, have presented a copy to the queen himself—and Mr. Goodhue adds that he talks of translating the work into Spanish.[3]

Praise Ben Jonson! that would be a feather in our caps my masters. Ever yours

W. H. P.

1. Ángel Calderón de la Barca (1790–1861), distinguished Spanish statesman, held, among other posts, diplomatic assignments in Washington and Mexico City. On March 23, 1838, he wrote WHP, "I think it the duty of every Spanish lover of literature to show his gratitude to one who like yourself has expended so much time and money to perpetuate for posterity, with the mastery that you have shown, the memory of the most glorious and interesting period in the history of Spain—perhaps of the world." See Wolcott, *Correspondence of Prescott*, p. 24.

2. On some occasions WHP found it impossible to fit desired additions into the straitjacket represented by the stereotype plates.

3. The diplomat's friendship and assistance repeatedly redounded to WHP's advantage, but his repeated promises to translate first one and then another Prescott title came to naught.

101.   To Charles Folsom
         (Charles Folsom Papers, Boston Public Library)

Tuesday Morning, [April 17, 1838]

My dear Sir:

I am disappointed in not being able to meet you tonight, as I wished to commune with you very much. If you ever come in town, cannot you give me a call? Mason, who was to have taken the Club for Hale today,[1] has unexpectedly decamped to Walpole, and left us all in the suds. When will the Catholic Highnesses reappear from your press? I suppose you lose no time, but I am sustaining a very serious injury by the delay, unavoidable though it be. You promised me, you know, half a dozen copies for the Spanish Minister by the 25th, i.e. Wednesday week. The fulfilment of this promise is of the last importance, as the diplomatists say, to me, as they are to be my credentials for getting what I am now sending for to Madrid, and De Calderón leaves New York in the packet of May 1.

What an unlucky business is this of the Editor and the Collector.[2] I sincerely regret that controversies of this kind should be brought before the public. I don't know how it is, but letters seem to me to afford as much ground for differences as politics, or any other subject—more's the pity. Truly yours,

WM. H. PRESCOTT

[P.S.] In a letter received from Mrs. Wormeley[3] the other day, she says Bentley acknowledges the American edition of *Ferdinand and Isabella* to be equal to his own, with the exception of one of the engravings. Mrs. Wormeley says that her husband had seen Bentley, who said that "the book would be *the work* of the times, and the sale had exceeded even his expectation." Captain Marryat[4] tells me for my comfort that "the publishers in England are all a set of d—d rascals, without exception—and Bentley, though rather more plausible than the rest, is not a whit better." If that is true, I shall be worse off than Peter Pindar's razor-seller.[5]

1. William Powell Mason and Enoch Hale (d. 1848).

2. The political controversy between George Bancroft and John Gorham Palfrey was indicative of the widening ostracism imposed on the former in Boston.

3. Caroline Preble Wormeley was the former Caroline Preble of Watertown, Massachusetts.

4. Frederick Marryat (1792–1848), naval officer and novelist, spent 1837–38 in Canada and the United States, recording his impressions in *A Diary in America, with Remarks on Its Institutions.* He was neither the first nor the last English literary tourist with whom WHP became acquainted.

5. John Wolcot (1738–1819), satirist and poet, employed the pseudonym Peter Pindar. In Ode III of the Farewell Odes, for MDCCLXXXVI, one meets the peripatetic razor-seller to whom WHP refers.

Within the week, on April 21, WHP wrote three letters to Spain in pursuit of materials for his new project; see Wolcott, *Correspondence of Prescott*, pp. 24–32.

102.   To Franklin Bache
(Archives, American Philosophical Society)

Boston, 28 April 1838

Franklin Bache, Esq.
Secretary of the American Philosophical Society[1]
Sir:

I have received your notice of my election as a member of the American Philosophical Society of Philadelphia. I know no honor which could be conferred on me, more grateful to my feelings, than to be allowed to form one of so ancient and highly respectable an association; and I regard it as a flattering testimony, from those whose good opinion I covet, that my own efforts, however humble, in the cause to which the Society is devoted, have not been wholly useless.

I am Sir, very respectfully Your obedient servant,[2]

WILLIAM H. PRESCOTT

1. One of the earliest of more than a score of such honors, this honorary

membership was all the more welcome because it came from the nation's oldest learned society.

2. This letter is endorsed: "Read, St. Meeting, May 4, 1838." Later it became WHP's practice to send a copy of his latest work along with such letters of acceptance.

103.   To Dr. George C. Shattuck[1]
(Shattuck Papers, Mass. Hist. Soc.)

Pepperell, 16 June, 1838

Dear Sir:

I understand from Mr. Ticknor that your son was kind enough to let him have a copy of *Ferdinand and Isabella,* which he had carried out with him to Paris.[2] I am happy in the present opportunity of replacing it with a copy of the second edition, which I believe you will find to be better executed, and on better paper, than the preceding.

Believe me, dear Sir, very respectfully and truly, Your friend,

W. H. PRESCOTT

1. George Cheyne Shattuck (1783–1854), a physician and philanthropist of Boston.
2. Either Ticknor had exhausted his supply of the English edition or he simply wanted a copy of the American edition to show to his European literary friends.

104.   To William Ellery Channing[1]
(Channing Autographs, The Rhode Island Historical Society)

Bedford Street, Thursday Morning [c. spring, 1838]

Rev. Dr. Channing

My dear Sir:

I have read the letters you have sent me, and I must confess, with some surprise. I have, indeed, noticed Dr. Dunham in two or three places in my history, and in some instances, as on page 269 of the third volume, in a manner which led me to think he would not feel much obliged to me; and as I knew he was a regular writer in the periodicals, and held rather a sharp pen, I was prepared to see it dipped in gall, if he should speak of me. It seems, however, I have been fortunate enough not to beget ill-will in the only quarter where I had reason to fear I had given occasion for it.[2]

With respect to the Doctor's situation, it is much easier to commiserate than to relieve it. It is of some importance, at all events, to know something of his personal character, independently of his literary qualifications, which are, beyond question, great. I will take the liberty, under your favor, therefore, to communicate the correspondence to our friend Mr. Ticknor, who knows, I believe, something of him; and will wait on you on Saturday at noon, unless I hear from you to the contrary.

Believe me, dear Sir, Yours with great respect,

WM. H. PRESCOTT

1. William Ellery Channing (1780–1842), eloquent Unitarian clergyman and vigorous writer.

2. Samuel A. Dunham had written the review of WHP's book which appeared in the *Athenaeum* for January 20, 1838.

105.   To Francis Lieber[1]

(Francis Lieber Papers, LI3028, The Huntington Library, San Marino, California. Reproduced by permission)

Boston, September 22, 1838

Dr. Francis Lieber
My dear Sir:

I have perused your volume on Political Ethics[2] with so much pleasure, and, I hope, edification, that I cannot refrain from giving you my judgment, in compliance with your request, though on a subject on which my opinion is worth very little. Your work seems to me admirably adapted for an elementary book, while it affords ample matter for reflection to those who have more thoroughly studied the subject. The occasional dryness (or what would appear dryness to a youthful tyro) of some of the topics, is well relieved by the stores of pertinent illustration, which you have drawn from the widest range of observation and study. In this particular, it reminds one of Malthus's manner of conducting his celebrated investigation, and which gives it an interest of a different character from that of an abstract philosophical inquiry. Your sentiments are not merely liberal, but are distinguished by a warm philanthropy, and a reliance on the capacities and good principles of our nature. Your first chapter, on the debatable ground of the selfish principle, as a motive of action, is an example of this. And in the same spirit are conceived your benevolent thoughts on civilization, on the connection of sound morals with public policy, and your suggestions for the amelioration of the penal code, which you have expanded elsewhere in greater detail. The part which treats of the State seems to me full of sound, and often original, thinking. The tenth and eleventh chapters, particularly, are well worthy of study by the American statesman; and it is no light result, that in the discussion of so many delicate topics, which, in one way or another, have become the scandal and stumbling-blocks of politicians, you have had the courage to write what you honestly believe; showing that you have written, not for a party, but for the eye of posterity.

I shall say nothing of the style of the book, which, although an occasional departure from the English idiom may be detected, is a wonderful achievement for a foreigner. I recollect no foreigner, unless Motteux, in his translation of *Don Quixote*,[3] who has handled the English language more skilfully.

Such are some of my impressions on rising from your book—which, however, I may well feel a diffidence in offering to you. I can only wish that it may meet with the currency it deserves—for the sake of my countrymen, quite as much as yourself.

Believe me, dear Sir With much truth yours[4]

WM. H. PRESCOTT

1. Francis Lieber (1800–1872), a vigorous Berlin-born professor of history and political economy in South Carolina.

2. A reciprocating exchange of presentation copies of their books found WHP with the first volume of Lieber's *Manual of Political Ethics*, the second volume of which appeared in 1839.

3. Peter Anthony Motteux's five-volume translation of Cervantes' masterpiece had been published in Edinburgh in 1822.

4. WHP and Lieber quickly formed a two-man mutual admiration society in reference to each other's writings. They corresponded, sporadically, for decades.

106. To William Sullivan[1]
(Wayland Papers, Brown University Library)

Bedford Street, December 21, [1838]

My dear Sir:

I have the pleasure to send you the engraving of Columbus, of which I spoke yesterday, and another of Gonsalvo de Córdova, executed in a very inferior style to the first. If you will take the trouble to send them to Bradley, the binder, in Washington Street, two doors north of Court Street, he will insert them in the proper places in your second and third volumes. They were sent me by Bentley, as I believe I mentioned to you, a short time since.[2]

Believe me, dear Sir, with great respect Your friend and servant

WM. H. PRESCOTT

1. William Sullivan (1774–1839), a Boston lawyer with literary and historical interests.

2. Having adopted several English illustrations as superior to those used in the American edition, WHP thus improved his friends' copies of his book; see Wolcott, *Correspondence of Prescott*, p. 34.

107.   To Joel Roberts Poinsett

(Joel R. Poinsett Papers, The Historical Society of Pennsylvania)

Boston, January 8, 1839

Sir:

I feel much hesitation in writing you, who have so many important affairs on your hands,[1] about a matter which concerns only myself. But there is no one, I believe, who can afford me the information which I need, so well as you, and I rely on your liberal feelings and the interest you take in letters, to excuse me. I have for some time meditated an account of the expeditions of Cortés and Pizarro, with a thorough preliminary view of the previous civilization of the countries they conquered. The subject has been so often treated that its principal value now must be derived from the novelty and authenticity of the materials on which it is to be founded. My own library furnishes me with some works relating to the period, not easy to be found. For the rest I have made a considerable remittance (£300) to Madrid, for the copying of manuscripts which I had reason to believe were in existence there. I find I was right, and that my orders are now in rapid progress of execution there.[2] I hope thus to assemble a body of authentic and hitherto unpublished documents, relating to the Conquest, that shall exhibit it, if not in a new, at least in a light which can be established as the true one. I am desirable, however, to add to this collection any thing germane to the matter, which I can meet with in Mexico itself; and there are several manuscripts pointed out by Humboldt[3]—one, especially, showing the condition of the capital immediately after the Conquest, and compiled at that time. I propose, therefore, to remit five hundred dollars, which I suppose will be all that is requisite, to Mexico, to procure the few things that can be met with there. There are, if I am not mistaken, many manuscripts there, some in the Castilian, but chiefly in the Indian languages, which relate to an earlier period of the national history, and which, unless they come down to the Conquest, I shall probably not have occasion for. I have been favored with letters by my friend Mr. De Calderón, the Spanish Minister, to two gentlemen there, Count Cortina, and Mr. Gorostiza,[4] to whose cooperation I must look, for ascertaining what manuscripts should be copied, as well as to have them copied. The misfortune is, that the whole country is in such a state of bouleversement, that it is very difficult to hold any communication with the capital; and I cannot be sure that either of the above gentlemen is resident there at the present moment. It would be desirable, if I could, therefore, to find some other person permanently resident there, who might deliver my letters to the parties, and, in case of their absence, execute my orders. Will you have the goodness to inform me if you know of such a person, who would be likely to attend to such an affair. And, secondly, whether there is any channel now existing, through the government, or whether there is likely to be any soon, by which I could communicate with Mexico. With the letters, I should like to send copies of a late work for which I have become responsible, the *History of Ferdinand and Isabella,* as vouchers for my historical fidelity, to those of whom I ask such favors. I should be sorry to have this attempt to communicate with Mexico miscarry, as, though not essential, it is important to my general plan.

I must confess, on concluding this long epistle, I feel even more doubtful than when I began, of the propriety of imposing it on you. But my friend Mr. Bancroft has encouraged me to do so, and the pleasure, and I trust I may add profit, that I have derived from perusing your own account of a country in which I have now become interested,[5] makes me feel that I have some acquaintance with, though I have not the honor of being personally known to you.

Believe me, Sir, with great respect,[6] Your obedient servant,

WM. H. PRESCOTT

1. At this time Poinsett was serving as Secretary of War under President Van Buren.

2. For reports from and instructions to Arthur Middleton and Friedrich Wilhelm Lembke in Madrid, see Wolcott, *Correspondence of Prescott,* pp. 38–40, 41–54.

3. The reference is to Baron Alexander von Humboldt's (1769–1859) *Essai politique sur le royaume de la Nouvelle Espagne* (5 vols., 1811), which had already been translated into several other languages.

4. José Gómez, Conde de la Cortina, was an expatriate Spaniard who was prominent in Mexican political, literary and social circles; Manuel Eduardo de Gorostiza (1790–1851) was primarily a dramatist.

5. Poinsett's *Notes on Mexico, 1822,* published in 1824, was the first American travel account of independent Mexico.

6. WHP did not take into account the fact that Poinsett's stay in Mexico had resulted in such bitter enmity being entertained by many toward him that his ability to assist the historian knew considerable limitation there.

108.   To Joel Roberts Poinsett
(Joel R. Poinsett Papers, The Historical Society of Pennsylvania)

Boston, 26 January, 1839

Dear Sir:

I received your very kind letter in due season; and if I have not sooner replied to it, it was not from insensibility to the very frank and courteous offer of assistance, which you have made me, but from the desire to arrange matters so as to secure a certain communication, as far as in my power, with Mexico, with as little trouble as possible to the parties concerned. I believe I have now done this, and I will take the liberty to explain it to you.

I have obtained, through Mr. Ward of this city, agent of the Barings, a credit on that house for six hundred dollars, in the hands of Manning & Marshall of Mexico, who have a branch of their house also at Vera Cruz. I forward to your care a letter to them, and also letters from Mr. De Calderón and Mr. A. H. Everett to Count Cortina, and to Mr. Gorostiza—besides others from myself to these gentlemen. To these you will oblige me by adding the letter of which you spoke to Mr. Pakenham.[1] I have instructed Manning & Marshall (to whom Mr. Ward has also written fully) to present the letters to Count Cortina, if he should be in Mexico; and if not, then to Mr. Gorostiza; and in case both are absent, yours to Mr. Pakenham. I would not have them deliver the letters to more than one, to save confusion, as well as unnecessary inconvenience. The letter of credit directs Manning & Marshall to pay the drafts of whichever of these gentlemen shall take charge of the affair.

I have ordered my bookseller to put all three copies of *Ferdinand and Isabella* in a box, and it will be sent tomorrow by the rail-road, directed to Frank Taylor, bookseller, in Pennsylvania Avenue, for you. I have explained to Manning & Marshall how to dispose of these copies. These gentlemen, being permanently resident there, have afforded me a good *point d'appui* for my little operations, which, from the great uncertainty as to which of the parties may be in Mexico, seem to be ridiculously complex.

I shall avail myself of your obliging offer, by asking you to do me the favor (1) To write a letter to Mr. Pakenham, briefly explaining to him the nature of the aid I request of him, viz. to obtain some suitable person to select and superintend the copying of such manuscripts as are germane to my subject, and to use his influence to procure permission for such copies to be made for me. Perhaps Dr. Alamán[2] may assist me in this way. I have inclosed a paper of instructions to the agent, whoever he may be, which I will thank you to inclose in your letter to Mr. Pakenham. I should hope it would be an affair of a few weeks only. I think you may point out to him Messrs. Manning & Marshall, as persons who would aid him in any inquiries or in executing any commission for me; and who will pay his drafts for the expense incurred. I have ordered one of the copies of *Ferdinand and Isabella* to be presented to Mr. Pakenham provided he shall be applied to at all. (2) To forward my parcel of letters, with yours, and the box of books, to Mexico, so that they may pass into the hands of Manning & Marshall—which, if you think best to address them to Mr. Jones, the Consul, can be done by him. I have ordered the cover of the box to be screwed so that it can be taken off in Washington, and on the reverse side another address written, according to your orders.

Thus you see I have frankly taken you at your word; and I trust it will not impose greater inconvenience on you than you anticipated. Should the box not come to hand, you will oblige me by advising me of it, as the miscarriage of this part of the apparatus can easily be rectified.

The credit I have obtained may appear rather limited to you. But as my inquiries relate to the Conquest and its immediate period, I do not think there will be a large mass of materials to collect, though I know there are some. If I were to go deep into the antiquities of Mexico I should, doubtless, find an ocean of manuscripts. But I shall content myself, for these, with the accounts I can gather from printed works; my design, in this respect, being, to give such a view of the previous civilization of the Mexicans, as will interest the reader in their fortunes; and not to involve myself in the mesh of speculation which has bewildered so many wiser and more learned heads than mine. But I do wish to place the Conquest both of Mexico and Peru on a perfectly authentic basis.

Another reason for not appropriating a larger sum for Mexico, is the expense already incurred by me. I have made it a point to assemble every printed work relating to the early Mexican history, including Lord Kingsborough's, and the magnificent work *Antiquités Mexicaines* published a few years since in Paris.[3] Besides this, I have allowed three hundred pounds for my manuscripts from Madrid; so that I am like to pay quite as much for my whistle as it is worth.

You will be gratified to learn that my application to Madrid has been perfectly successful. I received letters last week, informing me that the Royal Academy of History, the great depositary of the public records, by virtue of their office of national historiographer, have thrown open their archives to me, and allowed copies of every thing in their collection having any bearing on my subject. This was brought about by the application of their President, Navarrete, who has offered to me all the documents in his own possession for the same purpose. One of the members of the Academy has been appointed to superintend the selection and copying of the manuscripts, and a letter from him informs me that he has found materials sufficient to occupy four copyists, who have been engaged since July in the work, and that he thinks he shall be able to supply me such a body of unpublished and authenticated documents, as will put both the Mexican and the Peruvian Conquest in a point of view both new and true.[4] I hope he may not be too sanguine—but he is a man of learning, a German, the author himself of a history of the earlier period of Spain, well known on the Continent. For all these favors I stand not a little indebted to the influence and recommendation of my kind friend, Mr. De Calderón.[5]

And now that I look back on this long gossip about my own concern to one who is personally a stranger to me, and whose time is so fully occupied with matters of real importance, I must confess I feel some doubt whether I have not taken something like an unwarrantable freedom. I can only hope that the friendly tone of your own communication, leading me to believe that you took an interest in the success of my literary scheme, will be sufficient apology in your eyes. If it is not, I shall indeed be greatly troubled. Relying on this, I am, my dear Sir, With sincere respect,[6] Your obliged and obedient servant

WM. H. PRESCOTT

1. Sir Richard Pakenham (1797–1868) served as the English Minister to Mexico between 1835 and 1843. In the middle 1840's he was Minister to the United States.

2. Lucas Alamán (1792–1853), Mexican statesman and historian. He became a friendly and helpful correspondent of WHP, as well as the annotator of a Mexican edition of WHP's second history.

3. By Guillaume Dupaix, this work was published in Paris, 1805–7.

4. See F. W. Lembke to WHP, November 22, 1838, in Wolcott, Correspondence of Prescott, pp. 41–46. Volume I of Lembke's work, Geschichte von Spanien had been published in Hamburg in 1831.

5. Despite the fact that considerable naïveté attends WHP's thinking about research in archives, he was always able, thanks to friends, money and a knowledge of what he wanted, to serve his purposes from a distance.

6. For a full and unified statement of WHP's contacts in Mexico, in this period and later, see C. Harvey Gardiner, "Prescott's Ties with Mexico," Journal of Inter-American Studies, I (January, 1959), 11–26.

109.   To Charles Folsom
                (Charles Folsom Papers, Boston Public Library)

                                        Boston, 30 January, 1839
Dear Sir:

I intend to send out a copy of Ferdinand and Isabella to Bentley, with such emendations and additions written therein as are too ponderous to bring into stereotype. The paper of the fourth edition is too cottonish to write well upon; and in fact it is a paper that I don't cotton to myself at all[1]—and feel quite ashamed to send it abroad. Will you inform me 1. Whether the paper of the fifth edition is more highly glazed, and decidedly superior to this? 2. If so, when I shall be able to have a copy for my purpose?[2] Yours truly

WM. H. PRESCOTT

[P.S.] I wish you could produce a better effect in your title pages. They look all "pale and mealy" like Joanna Baillie's ghost,[3] by comparison with the English—which, I suppose, must be divided between the cut of the types and the color of the ink—as it would be treason to doubt the skill of our American Baskerville.[4]

1. Prone to punning from boyhood on, WHP did not limit it to oral exchanges.

2. The text of WHP's contract with Little, Brown and Co., concluded on May 14, 1838, after the financial collapse of the American Stationers' Company, is in Gardiner, *Prescott and His Publishers,* pp. 284–89. The third edition of *Ferdinand and Isabella,* the initial one by the second American publisher, appeared in August, 1838, and the fourth edition emerged in November of that year. The fifth American edition was published in February, 1839. All of these editions were 500-copy impressions.

3. Works by Joanna Baillie (1762–1851) probably had been read in the family reading circle that embraced all generations of Prescotts.

4. Playing off each of his publishers against the other, WHP was able to better his book in both Boston and London as successive editions appeared.

Bestowing high praise upon his American printer, WHP likens him to the famous John Baskerville (1706–75), renowned for his type face as well as his printing.

110.   To Joseph G. Cogswell
(British Museum, Add. MS. 40690, f. 88)

Boston, 18 February, 1839

My dear friend:

I inclose you one of the miseries of Editors, a letter from an anatomical subject, who has a natural aversion to being skinned in his own lifetime. He has probably not been so accustomed to it as some of his brethren may have become by this time; and I suppose the first time is the one *qui coute.*[1] I have a sort of fellow feeling for him, just now, from seeing that I am pulled over coals in the last *Edinburgh;* but in what manner, as the Review has not come to hand, I cannot tell. "I guess, and fear"—as Burns says. All I can say is, that it is a shame that you critics should canter over the ground that a poor laborer in the vineyard has been planting and watering with the sweat of his brain for years, and knock it all to pieces in a jiffy with your iron hoofs.

Touching our friend Mr. Young, I hope, if it be true that he is treated in the coarse manner he suggests, that this communication will not come too late for your consideration; as he is an excellent and amiable man, whose feelings we should all regret to see wounded.

I have received, thanks to your kind offices,[2] a very frank and friendly letter from Irving, leaving the battlefield open to me, in a manner which makes the goodnatured act doubly acceptable. Since you were here, I have received letters from Madrid, informing me that the Royal Academy of History have thrown open their archives to me, and appointed one of their number to superintend the collection and copying of all manuscripts in their possession, relating to the Conquest of Mexico and Peru. The gentleman thus employed is a German, Dr. Lembke, who has himself written a work of established reputation on the early Gothic history of Spain. He writes me that he has employed four copyists, since July, in the good work, and that he has collected a mass of unpublished documents relative to the Mexican Conquest, which will throw an entirely new light upon it, and is now going on with the Peruvian, in which the library appears to be equally rich. He has sent a box already to Cádiz, and I cannot but hope, as I see a vessel arrived at New York from that port, that my manuscripts may be in it. Is not this rare luck? I was nine years trying to get a single document for my purposes, when concocting their Catholic Highnesses. I should not take up your time with this twaddle about my own affairs, but that I know you feel an interest in all relating to us.

All your friends here are well. Gray is delivering a beautiful course of lectures on the formation and early progress of the English language —which he illustrates by reading passages from the ancient writers. The lectures are not written, and are delivered with uncommon spirit.

My wife and mother desire remembrances, and believe me, I am always Faithfully yours,

WM. H. PRESCOTT

1. In reference to this somewhat obscure episode two things might be borne in mind: Cogswell was then editing the *New York Review;* Prescott, as ever, was the friendly supporter of any Boston writer.

2. Initially Cogswell had played the role of intermediary between WHP and Irving. Washington Irving's magnanimity in surrendering the Mexican conquest theme and the happy circumstances which made the acquisition of materials in Spain so much easier than before combined to stimulate WHP's labors on his second history. In the spring of 1839 WHP continued to correspond with workers in Spain, received some of the desired transcripts and again talked of studying Philip II; see Wolcott, *Correspondence of Prescott,* pp. 57–59, 61–70.

111.   To Richard Bentley
(Richard Bentley Papers, Harvard College Library)

Boston, 11 June, 1839

Dear Sir:

My correspondence with you is rather of an Irish character, in which the correspondence is all on one side. This is the fourth letter I have written since I have had the favor of an answer. And besides the letters, I have forwarded to you a print of the good Queen Isabel, a corrected copy of my History, and subsequently a parcel of additional notes and illustrations, of the safe arrival of which I have had no intimation from you; a circumstance which has left me in much doubt and perplexity as to whether they have not all or at least some of them miscarried. I really think Lord Melbourne, with the nation on his shoulders, would have found time for a line or two, under these circumstances;—especially as he finds it for scribbling answers to maids of honor and their dowager mammas.[1]

I see by your advertisement that the second edition of *Ferdinand and Isabella* is nearly ready,[2] and I infer from the style of the notice that my parcels have come to hand. I am desirous to see a copy of it somewhat sooner than I did of the first edition, which was six months in reaching me; and I have ordered Rich to get me two copies. I suppose it is usual with you to allow the author a certain number on every new edition. Here I get one per cent. I will trouble you to advise me what number you will place at my disposal. Colonel Aspinwall writes me that you have told him you would settle the account for the former edition with him in a few days. This is all right, and I have no doubt it will be adjusted perfectly satisfactorily. At the close of March I sent a small parcel to you, to the care of Rich. I fear, through some inexplicable blunder of his, it has miscarried. It contained an article on *Ferdinand and Isabella,* by Count Circourt, in a French review, which, as an able critique, I thought you might like to see.[3] This is of no consequence, however; but it also contained a letter, in which I asked you to let me have 2,000 more engravings of Columbus and Gonsalvo, each, as those I had have been *all* worked up—the last batch having been just sent to the printer. Notwithstanding this rapid consumption, I think the market must be now so well filled that the second lot of 2,000 will last me several years. Should it be a larger number, however, than you care to have struck off, I will thank you for five hundred till I can gain time to have the plates engraved for me in London, which I would rather do than have the American purchasers hereafter disappointed. If you will have them sent to Rich, he will take charge of them for me. In your answer to this letter, which I flatter myself I may count upon, I will thank you to mention *the number of copies printed for the second edition;*[4] and also it would rejoice me [. . .] much to learn from you what may be the present standing and prospects of the work on your side of the water; for, though I am just now up to the elbows in other matters, for which I believe I have told you the Spanish

Academy furnished me ample materials, I feel a greater interest in the fortunes of their Catholic Highnesses, as my first born.

Believe me, with much truth Your obedient servant

WM. H. PRESCOTT

1. William Lamb, second Viscount Melbourne (1779–1848), English statesman.

2. The second edition appeared in London on June 26, 1839; see Gardiner, *Annotated Bibliography*, p. 7.

3. Count Adolphe de Circourt (1801–79) of France published a massive five-installment review of WHP's book in the *Bibliothèque universelle de Génève* between 1838 and 1840. A lengthy correspondence between author and reviewer followed.

4. It consisted of 750 copies.

112.   To Israel K. Tefft[1]

(Letters of Honorary Members and Officers, vol. I, Georgia Historical Society)

Boston, 23 July, 1839

I. K. Tefft, Esq.

My dear Sir:

I have received your letter advising me of my election as an Honorary Member of the Georgia Historical Society. Such a testimonial of approbation from so respectable an association, in so distant a part of my own country, is particularly grateful to me; and I beg you to present my acknowledgments for the honor conferred on me.

I have ordered my publishers to forward, by the first opportunity, a copy of the *History of Ferdinand and Isabella,* for the Society, which you will oblige me by placing on the shelves of its library.[2]

Believe me, with much respect, Your obedient servant,

WM. H. PRESCOTT

1. Israel K. Tefft was Corresponding Secretary of the Georgia Historical Society and WHP's occasional correspondent.

2. Ten days later, on August 2, Calderón de la Barca wrote WHP, "I enclose herewith the official communication of your admission to the Academy of History." See Wolcott, *Correspondence of Prescott,* p. 84.

113.   To Charles Folsom

(Charles Folsom Papers, Boston Public Library)

Nahant, 5 August, 1839

Charles Folsom Esq.

My dear Sir:

I have at length received a summons from Little and Brown to prepare for the Sixth Edition;[1] and I send you the fruit of sundry corrections by kind friends, since the last. I begin to be aweary of correcting, and shall let their Highnesses run for the future, I believe, unless I detect something worse than a cacophony, at least. I don't know but I have already supplied you with a large part of these corrections; but none of them, at all events, have been printed. Add one correction more, by substituting the verb *lend* for "loan" about the bottom, I should think, of the third page of chapter 21, Part II. I have nothing to refer to here but Bentley's second English edition, which is not paged exactly like the American. It contains a most beautiful portrait of the good Queen, very gracefully finished. It is copied, in its text, and notes, and references, all exactly from the last American. It is printed with a very similar type to the last, but with more on a page.

I have also received the last *Quarterly,* containing a long paper on their Catholic Highnesses, well sprinkled with pepper, sugar, and salt —the last not of the true Attic, certainly. He has found out that I hate stars and garters, and am little better than a loco-foco, God help us! Also, that I love the French overmuch, and have formed my sesquipedalian style on Dr. Channing in the text, and Dr. Dunham in the notes! He might as well have said Dr. Johnson and Dr. Ollapod. He calls me to account, moreover, for blunders which I have exposed myself in others, and thus enabled him to charge on me. This is too bad— but *secundum artem.* The fact is, he is a regular humbug, with a good deal of the wag, not to say blackguard; and withal, I have no doubt, meant to do the civil thing by me, on the whole, for he has said as nice things of me as any other of the genus. So much for good Master Ford.[2]

I suppose your period of gestation will not be short of three months. The paper must not be inferior to the last. I have not yet seen it. Pray remind the publishers of this, when you see them. Yours truly,

WM. H. PRESCOTT

1. This 500-copy edition appeared in October, 1839; see Gardiner, *Annotated Bibliography,* p. 7.

2. Richard Ford (1796–1858), critic, author and connoisseur, was a leading English authority on Spanish culture. Despite this frosty beginning he and WHP became devoted correspondents and warm friends.

114.   To Samuel Gridley Howe
(Letters, 1838–39, #169, Perkins School for the Blind)

Tuesday Morning, Nahant, September 3, 1839

My dear Sir:

I regret very much it will not be in my power to meet the Trustees on

Thursday; but we are just on the wing for Pepperell, where we pass the autumn. I am the more sorry not to meet you, as the subject of printing is to be discussed. I entirely agree with you as to the paramount importance of going on with it, somehow or other. Whatever else we do is limited in its consequences to our Institution; but the printing reaches every institution in the country, and has its influence in Europe, even. It certainly has done more than any thing else to raise the character of our Asylum, at home and abroad, and to place it on a ground much higher than that of a mere charitable institution. The improvements made by you well entitle it to this rank; and it would be a great pity indeed, if, now that we have all the apparatus, skill, and experience requisite for going on with it, we should be obliged to abandon it, and let others reap the fruits of our, or rather your, discoveries. It will be rather difficult, however, I fear, to bring the public into the giving vein so soon after the late call on them. Can not some way be devised for raising the wind by means of public exhibitions and musical performances at the Institution, or in the different towns? Would it not be better even to take part of the funds provided by the state and help the printing along till we can raise enough in some other way? We have the right to reserve all over what is necessary to maintain twenty pupils, and it would be a less evil to postpone the education of a few individuals, than to abandon what is of such extensive and useful application as the printing. I dare say you have thought of the ways and means, however, much more than I have; though I am sure you cannot appreciate the importance of the subject more. I am only sorry I cannot be with you, to act on the matter.

Believe me, dear Sir Yours faithfully

WM. H. PRESCOTT

115.   To Charles Sumner[1]
                  (Southern Illinois University Library)

Saturday Morning, [c. October 5, 1839]

Better late than never, dear Sumner. When you work to Greece—if you can *remember* it, pray advise me of it. Your memory is not a full development.

I have received a thousand dollars worth of manuscripts by the Steamer—for the money a very small heap—but diamond dust—in my eyes.[2]

When I see Ticknor I will mention the Edgeworth.[3] Yours affectionately

WM. H. PRESCOTT

1. Charles Sumner (1811–74), orator and statesman, was then touring Europe. Upon his return to America a warm friendship ripened between Sumner and WHP.

2. Concerning the Spanish materials which had recently arrived, see WHP to Arthur Middleton, September 12, 1839, in Wolcott, *Correspondence of Prescott*, pp. 95–96.

3. Maria Edgeworth (1769–1849) was widely known in America for her novels. Her admiration for WHP's works promoted a correspondence between them.

116.   To Martín Fernández de Navarrete[1]
(Draft, WHP Papers, Mass. Hist. Soc.)

October 12, 1839

My dear Sir,

I wrote to you in January last, thanking you for the kind offices you had rendered me in procuring documents relative to the conquests of Mexico and Peru. I have now to thank you for your very kind letter in which you have taken the trouble to point out various authorities for my narrative, most of which are fortunately in my library. But how can I express my sense of your great kindness in the aid which you have constantly afforded Dr. Lembke in making his collection for me, by your judicious counsels, and now by the permission to make copies of your valuable manuscripts? I can only hope that the work I am now engaged upon will not prove unworthy of these great favours, as I am certainly deeply sensible of them. The second box of manuscripts has arrived in Boston for me, though my absence in the country has prevented me from seeing it yet. My diploma from the Academy is in it, I understand. I receive it with great pleasure, as the mark of the approbation of this distinguished body, and it adds much to my gratification that my nomination should have come from you.[2]

The materials for the Peruvian history are not near so copious as those for the Mexican. I regret very much that Dr. Lembke has not been able to obtain a copy of the third part of Oviedo's work relating to Peru. I cannot but hope that it may still be found by him in some quarter. The manuscript of Pizarro which you have been kind enough to send me will be no doubt of much value, as the work of one of the actors.

When I shall have disposed of the conquests of Mexico and Peru, which I think, should not occupy more than four years,[3] I had intended to have employed myself on the reign of Philip II, a noble subject, and never yet satisfactorily treated in English. It would require, however, ample and authentic materials to undertake it with any prospect of success. There is no doubt, abundance of such materials in Spain, if one could get access to them. Unfortunately the death of the venerable Señor González⁴ will make it difficult to explore the contents of Simancas, or even to know what its archives contain. Still I do not give up the hope that Dr. Lembke may collect sufficient materials to justify me in undertaking the work, especially as I believe I can obtain valuable supplies for the subject from the libraries of Paris, London, and Vienna. I shall not make any attempt in these quarters, however, unless I can succeed in obtaining materials from Spain, as the basis of my operations.⁵

A new edition of my *History of Ferdinand and Isabella* in England contains a very beautiful print of the good queen copied from the sixth volume of the *Memorias de la Academia.* As this edition is also somewhat more complete than the last published here, I shall have the pleasure of sending you a copy of it through Mr. Middleton when I return to Boston, which will be sometime in November, and I hope the execution of the portrait will please you.

I pray you to accept the assurances of the distinguished consideration with which I have the honour to be Your much obliged and obedient Servant

1. In this period the Spanish scholar's assistance was critically important to WHP.

2. Later, when a few choice honors were listed on WHP's title pages, his honor from the Royal Academy of History at Madrid was always included.

3. Eight years would have been a more correct estimate, it being 1847 when WHP concluded his labor on Peru.

4. For WHP's effort to win archivist Tomás González' assistance, see Wolcott, *Correspondence of Prescott,* pp. 24–25.

5. On October 14, two days after writing this letter, WHP wrote the first page of his *History of the Conquest of Mexico;* see Prescott (Gardiner, ed.), *The Literary Memoranda,* II, 46.

117.   To Samuel Gridley Howe

(Letters, 1838–39, #202, Perkins School for the Blind)

Boston, November 11, 1839.

My dear Sir

I beg leave to communicate through you my intention to decline being a candidate for reelection as a Trustee at the next annual meeting. My absence in the country six months of the year,¹ added to the other accidental causes of absence, when in town, have prevented my attending to the duties of the office in a proper manner for the last two years, and I do not think it right, or feel willing to continue in an office where I do not perform my share of the labors. I have now been connected with the Institution for ten years—from its first humble beginnings, when it went about like a pauper suing for a protector, until I have seen it established in its present magnificent quarters, and flourishing under the goodwill and liberal patronage of the community. Its reputation, during this time, has kept pace with its fortunes, and it has been the means, through your instrumentality, chiefly, of extending a better system and some important facilities for instruction to the most distant parts of our own country, and even to Europe. These are results for which we all have deep reason for gratitude to Providence, who has conducted the Institution safely through those dark times when some, who wished it well, could "see no sign to guide us,"—an expression which some of the Trustees of that day will readily call to mind. I, for one, feel a real gratitude, and, I may say, an honest pride, that I have been so long the associate of a body (though I have done so much less than some others in it) which has had charge of the interest of the Institution. I beg you will express to the Trustees these feelings on my behalf, and that you will allow me to add that if my cooperation (extra officially) can, in any way, be of service to you, hereafter, you will not hesitate to call on me without reserve.[2]

Believe me, dear Sir, with much truth Your friend and servant

WM. H. PRESCOTT

1. This is a slight exaggeration. In this period WHP's annual combined stays at Pepperell and Nahant approximated 140 days, or somewhat less than five months.

2. Despite Howe's remonstrance, WHP terminated his official relationship with the institution. Privately his interest in it continued, as did his financial support of it. WHP wrote this letter on the day of his return to Boston from Pepperell. In the country the children had interrupted his work, and in town he anticipated the customary social demands upon his time. Apparently in his desire to throw himself into his Mexican project, he was taking steps to protect his time for his research.

118.   To Little and Brown

(Miscellaneous Papers—Wm. H. Prescott folder, The New York Public Library)

Bedford Street, Saturday Morning [November 23, 1839]

Messrs. Little and Brown

Dear Sirs:

I am glad you are going to take time by the forelock; as I believe, with one exception, there has not been an edition of the work got out yet before the market was emptied. There will be no danger of it this time, I suspect. Pray be particular about the paper—you may depend upon it, the getting up of the work is half the battle; and I would not, on any account, have it lose the credit, and with it, *in the long run, the profit,* of being regarded as the best specimen of book-making (I mean as to mechanical execution) that the country has produced. I have two or three trifling alterations, which I will send the printer. With regard to the date of the notes,[1] it is very reasonable that they should date from the time when the edition begins to be sold—which will not be, of course, till the fourth is exhausted; and I am agreed to have the edition printed with this understanding. Yours very truly,

WM. H. PRESCOTT

1. For each of the 500-copy impressions in this period, WHP customarily took the note of his publisher in the amount of $844.25; see Gardiner, *Prescott and His Publishers,* p. 289.

119.   To Francis Lieber

(Francis Lieber Papers, LI3030, The Huntington Library, San Marino, California. Reproduced by permission)

Boston, November 26, 1839

My dear Sir,

I have received your obliging letter of the twelfth of October, and since then, the second volume of your *Political Ethics,* for which I heartily thank you. I have read several chapters in it, which show me that it is conducted with the same liberal spirit and sound views, which distinguish the other part. It is remarkable that you should have brought together such a variety of pertinent illustration from all sources, familiar as well as recondite, by which you have given life and a popular interest to your philosophy. It is a book so full of suggestion that the reader has done only half his work when he has read a chapter, for it puts him on a train of thinking for himself, which he must carry on after he has closed the volume. I think you have every reason to be satisfied with the attention it has awakened, which, considering the sober character of the topics and the patient study they demand, was not to have been counted upon so soon.

Touching the movement for the introduction of a copyright law—I can truly say, I feel sincerely interested in it; as well I may, now that I enter my fillies for the plate. But, in truth, I am a dull hand in action, and am too much taken up with a confounded hard job of extracting civilization from the semi-civilized races of Anahuac to be able to do more than follow in this business. Irving is the person, undoubtedly, to conduct it, but I think there is too much to be said, in order to interest him in it properly, to be managed by correspondence. An hour's talk would do more than a week's writing. Should I, at any time, visit New York, I shall make it a point to see him. But it really requires something more than a passive memorial, and some one should take care of it, and follow it to Washington, to suggest answers and explanations on points which a strong opposition will undoubtedly raise. Where shall we find such a person?

Were the trade all as reasonable as Little & Brown, there would be no difficulty. But I fear it will be hard to persuade those worthy gentlemen who live by skimming the cream of other people's wits so easily, to have a conscience.

I see a project broached for publishing the new popular works in newspaper sheets, of such a size that each sheet shall contain two volumes, to be afforded at eight cents! It will not be easy to persuade either buyer or publisher of this precious trash that he will be a gainer by a fair copyright law. We stand in relation to British literature pretty much as we do in reference to their marine. As the language is the same between the two nations, we shall never want pretexts for helping ourselves, without ceremony, to the books of the one, and the sailors of the other. It is a game at which the weaker party, to a superficial eye, that looks only at first results, has too manifestly the advantage. Still I do not despair of an enlightened appeal to principles of equity, and to a more enlarged view of our real interests.[1]

Your friend Hillard has come out with his Spenser,—a very good edition, and on a very good plan.[2] The introduction and notes written by him contain much excellent matter, handsomely expressed. It has a thorough glossary at the bottom of the text, and I suspect it will do more to *popularize* the old bard than any preceding edition has done.

Your fair friend Miss Mary Appleton is to become in due time, as you know, the rib of Mr. Mackintosh, a quiet, reserved gentleman, of plain good sense, and without a trait, I understand, in common with her. Addio—

Believe me, my dear Sir Very faithfully yours

WM. H. PRESCOTT

1. The future would expand and confirm WHP's interest in international copyright; it also confirmed, on that score, the truth of his admission, "I am a dull hand in action. . . ." WHP's relation to the issue is detailed in Gardiner, *Prescott and His Publishers,* pp. 101–34.

2. George Stillman Hillard (1808–79) was a scholarly lawyer and a devoted friend of WHP.

120.   From Pascual de Gayangos[1]

(Extracts, WHP Papers, Mass. Hist. Soc.; and in Wolcott, *Correspondence of Prescott*, pp. 102–8)

9 Burton St., Burton Crescent, London
December 1st, 1839

Dear Sir:

I have to apologize for not answering sooner your two kind letters of the 30th March and 6th July, but a long visit to Oxford, whither I had gone for the purpose of consulting the Arabic manuscripts in the Bodleian, and, on my return to London, a severe indisposition have hitherto prevented my fulfilling the agreeable duty imposed upon me; the desire, too, of entering fully on the topics treated in your letter and giving you a detailed account of the papers and manuscripts in my possession made me delay longer than I should otherwise have done the completion of my task.

I can assure you Dear Sir, that nothing could be so gratifying to me as to enter into a correspondence with the author of *Ferdinand and Isabella;* I had long wished for that honour; more than once, since I had first the pleasure of reading your work, did I take the pen resolved to address you on the subject and communicate to you the intelligence contained in my manuscripts, but the formality of English manners, and the fear of being thought an intruder, invariably made me desist from my undertaking. However, encouraged by two countrymen of yours, Messrs. Ticknor and Sumner, whom I had the pleasure to meet at my friends, I was on the point of breaking the rules of English *bienséance* and addressing you on the subject, when I was told at Holland House[2] that you had written to me, and soon after I received your very kind letter of the 6th July.

The papers in my possession formed once a collection of twelve folio volumes, if I am to judge from the numbers on the vellum binding, which run thus—volume II, IV, VI, IX, XII. They are entitled *Papeles varios tocantes á la historia de España.* Two more volumes belonging to the same collection are in the British Museum, but, although I had them in my house for some time before they were sold by a friend of mine to that establishment, I could not ascertain whether they occupied any of the numbers wanting between one and twelve, or whether they were marked with higher ones, as they had both been deprived of their original vellum bindings and dressed in calf. Of this, however, I am certain, namely that they once made part of the same collection, some volumes of which are now in my possession.

I now proceed to give you an account of the contents of each of my volumes.

.   .   .   .

Let me now explain to you how this splendid collection of historical documents came thus to be scattered and how and when I came to own five volumes of it.

.   .   .   .

You will naturally inquire to whom did the collection belong before it was placed in the Library of the Convent of Santo Domingo; and I will answer that in my opinion it must have been made either by Zurita or by Gerónimo Blancas.[3] Numerous marginal notes and references prove that the volumes were once the property of a chronicler of the Kingdom of Aragon, and the documents which they contain are also chiefly relating to the affairs of that *corona* or to the countries conquered by, or dependent upon it. But as I have no means here of identifying the handwriting I cannot say positively whose they are.

The correspondence between Gonzalvo and Ferdinand—for I have found in the same volume four or five dispatches or orders addressed by the latter to the former—I consider by far the most valuable part of my collection, as they are calculated to throw much light upon the history of the Italian wars, as well as upon the personal character of Gonzalvo. When I first came to this country in 1836, I had some intention of publishing the *Crónica de Bernáldez,* with a few illustrations and notes upon the last wars of Granada, intending further to give as an Appendix my letters of the Great Captain, but unluckily, although I took some steps towards it, I found no publisher in London who would undertake printing the work at his own expense, and I was therefore obliged to desist. The publication of your history has since given me the death-blow and I have now given up entirely all idea of publishing them for the present. I only wish I had had the pleasure of becoming acquainted with you sooner, you might with the aid of my papers have cleared up some doubts which hang still over the life and actions of the great man.

I need not tell you that this and every one of the historical manuscripts in my collection is at your service, and that you must from this moment consider yourself at full liberty to have any you like transcribed, although I must not conceal from you that the copying, or rather the decyphering of the letters of the great Captain is a very arduous task—and one not to be accomplished by a common scribe. Your hero knew how to wield the sword better than the pen, he was besides very little of a grammarian and made no scruple of introducing a French or Italian word whenever the equivalent Spanish did not come soon to his mind. I send you a facsimile of part of a letter, and a transcript of another, that you may judge at once of the difficulty of the reading, and of the great man's bold and graphic style.

.   .   .   .

I am, however, ready to atone for my *crime* by undertaking for you, as soon as I am more disengaged, an entire transcript of Gonzalvo's correspondence; I have likewise began a very full index *raisonné* of all the documents respecting Ferdinand's reign in my possession, which I fully expected to send you along with this letter, but I am sorry to say that my task, interrupted by a severe indisposition and the fagging work of correcting the press of my work, where I have occasionally given the original text, has hitherto retarded its completion. As soon as it is finished I shall certainly take the earliest opportunity to send it to you.

.   .   .   .

Allow me to put an end to this long and irksome letter by assuring you that nothing could have been more satisfactory to me than to become acquainted with a gentleman whose literary pursuits have so well illustrated the most brilliant period of the history of my country, and whose future labours are calculated to shed light upon another no less important subject. Excuse me if I felicitate you upon the manner in which your arduous task has been executed, and if I say, from the bottom of my heart, that I am at a loss what to admire most in your work, whether your exquisite erudition and extensive reading, or your profound philosophy,—or that most difficult as well as most rare quality in an historian—freedom from all political as well as religious bias.

Hoping that our acquaintance will last, and that you will employ me in whatever you may deem useful,[4] I have the honor and the pleasure to subscribe myself, Dear Sir, Your obedient servant

PASCUAL DE GAYANGOS

1. Pascual de Gayangos (1809–97), collector, translator, bibliographer, writer and much more, was WHP's most persistent aide in Europe during the 1840's. Delighted by Gayangos' review of his book in the *Edinburgh Review* (January, 1839), WHP had addressed letters of appreciation and inquiry to the Spanish scholar.

2. Lord Holland's place in Kensington was distinguished for its social-literary gatherings and for its wealth of manuscripts, many of which related to Spain.

3. Jerónimo de Zurita y Castro and Gerónimo Blancas y Tomás, royal historiographers of Spain in the sixteenth century.

4. This friendship ended only with WHP's death. Gayangos became his most indefatigable and most indispensable aide. A full statement of Gayangos's services is in C. Harvey Gardiner, "Prescott's Most Indispensable Aide: Pascual de Gayangos," *The Hispanic American Historical Review*, XXXIX (February, 1959), 81–115.

121.   To Washington Irving[1]

(Yale Collection of American Literature, Yale University Library)

Boston December 24, 1839

My dear Sir

I received some weeks since a letter from Dr. Lieber, of Columbia College, in which he informed me that measures were to be taken in Congress, this session, for making such an alteration in our Copy-right law, as should secure the benefits of it to foreigners, and thus enable us to profit in turn by theirs. He was very desirous that I should write, if I could not see you personally, and request your cooperation in the matter. I felt very reluctant to do so, knowing that you must be much better acquainted, than I was, with the state of the affair, and, of course, could much better judge what was proper to be done. My indefatigable correspondent, however, has again written me, pressing the necessity of communicating with you, & stating in confidence, as he says, that Mr. Clay is to bring in a bill, this session, and that Mr. Preston is to make the speech, &c.[2] Mr. Preston told him that it would be very desirable to have a brief memorial, signed by the names of the persons most interested in the success of the law, and that you were the proper person to prepare it. If any thing be done, there can be no doubt that you are the one, who, from your literary position in the country, should take the lead in it. Whether any thing effectual can be done, seems to me very doubtful. Such a law is certainly demanded by every principle of justice. But, I suspect it is rather late in the day to talk of justice to statesmen. At all events, one of those newspapers, which they are now turning out every week here, and which contain an octavo volume, each, of the new publications, at sixpence a piece, will, I am afraid, be too cogent an argument in favor of the present state of things, to be refuted by the best memorial, ever drafted. Still, we can but try—and while the effort is making by the best men in Congress, it may be our duty to try. Of all this, however, you can best judge. I can only say, that if you will prepare a paper, I shall be very glad, when it has been signed in your city, to do all in my power, to get such signatures to it here, as will give it most weight. I trust I shall not appear officious in this matter, nor seem like a dun, abhorred of Gods and men—to you, as I do to myself—for I can well understand, from my own feelings, how distasteful this sort of work must be to you.

It will give you pleasure, I flatter myself, to know that I have completely succeeded in my negotiations in Spain. Señor Navarrete with whom you were acquainted in Madrid, has very liberally supplied me with copies of his entire collection of MSS. relating to Mexico and Peru, which, it is improbable from his advanced age, that he will ever publish himself. Through his aid I have also obtained from the Academy, copies of the collection made by Muñoz,[3] and by the former President, Vargas Ponce, making, altogether, some 5000 pages, all in fair condition,—the flower of my Spanish veterans. From Mexico, through my good friend Calderón, who has now gone there, you know, as Minister, I look for further ammunition,—though I am pretty independent of that now. I have found some difficulty in collecting the materials for the preliminary view, I propose, of the Aztec civilization. The works are expensive, and Lord Kingsborough is locked up in Chancery.[4] I have succeeded, however, in ferreting out a copy—which, to say truth, though essential, has somewhat disappointed me. The whole of that part of the story is enveloped in twilight—and I fear, I shall, at best, make only moonshine of it—I must hope that it will be good moonshine. It will go hard with me, however, but I can fish something new, out of my ocean of manuscripts. As I have only half an eye of my own, my progress is, necessarily, no more than a snail's gallop.

I should be very glad to show you my literary wares, but I fear you are too little of a locomotive in your habits, to afford me that great pleasure. Though I cannot see you bodily, however, I am sitting under the light of your countenance—for you are ranged above me, (your immortal part) in a goodly row of octavos,—not in the homespun garb, but in the nice costume of Albemarle and Burlington Streets.[5] My copy of the Sketch Book, by the by, is the one owned by Sir J. Mackintosh, and with his pencillings in the margin.[6] It was but last evening that my little girl read us one of the stories, which had just enough of the mysterious to curdle the blood in the veins of her younger brother,[7] who stopped up both his ears, saying "he would not hear such things just as he was going to bed,"—and as our assertions, that no harm would come of it, were all in vain, we were obliged to send the urchin off to his quarters, in good earnest—with—I fear, no very grateful feeling towards the author.

Pray excuse this long talk about my own [. . . .][8]

1. Washington Irving (1783–1859), essayist, novelist and historian, popular-

ized one Spanish theme after another. No vigorous correspondence resulted, but he and WHP, admiring each other, did exchange letters occasionally.

2. William C. Preston (1794–1860) was then the junior Senator from South Carolina.

3. Juan Bautista Muñoz' indefatigable researches produced a documentary mass which many historians, including WHP, have liberally employed.

4. The publication of Lord Kingsborough's multivolume *Antiquities of Mexico* had brought financial ruin to that British nobleman.

5. Referring to the heart of the publishing district of London, WHP reiterated his respect for English bookmaking.

6. Sir James Mackintosh (1765–1832), British statesman and historian.

7. WHP's daughter, Elizabeth, was then somewhat more than eleven years of age and her younger brother, William Amory, was not quite ten years old.

8. The remainder of this letter is wanting. Irving's endorsement reads: "Answd Jan 21, 1840."

122.   To Francis Lieber

(Francis Lieber Papers, LI3031, The Huntington Library, San Marino, California. Reproduced by permission)

Boston, February 10, 1840

My dear Dr. Lieber,

I feel, in taking up my pen to write to you, like a person paying a visit which he ought to have paid a month before. I fear you have begun to suspect, by this time, that I belong to that numerous, and, I hope, respectable class of persons who are better at receiving letters than at answering them. But I have not been altogether so negligent as you may think. Soon after receiving yours, I plucked up courage and wrote to Irving—who not long since returned me an answer, in which he excused himself from taking any lead in the matter, on the ground of his habitual procrastination; but professed himself willing to cooperate with his name and influence. He referred me to a note written by him in the last *Knickerbocker,* which you may have seen, expressing his conviction of the importance of a copyright law. I conversed on the subject with Mr. Webster, before his departure; and he promised to support the bill, if introduced in the Senate. The Committee, however, have made such a report on it that I fear nothing is to be passed, this session, nor have I much hope, in any other. The *apparent* interests of the public are too much in the same scale with those of the publishers, and they, no doubt, persuade themselves that it is a greater good for the country to make the British authors work for us for nothing, than to put a little money into the pockets of the few, who drive the trade of authorship, among ourselves. As to appealing to higher motives, one must have more faith in the stuff that statesmen are made of, than I have, to think they will weigh against the little calculations of selfishness. I am very sorry to think so, as independently of the principle of national equity, and the real benefit to the country, by the proposed act, I think an English copyright, (which, you know, is contingent upon reciprocity) would be of worth to the sort of books of historical research which I am employed on.

These are not very palmy times for books, or any thing else. All whom I have heard speak of your book, praise it, but I should think its sales must be much short of what you can expect in better times—at least, [you] fare as others do. So we must put up with glory, instead of money. I received a diploma from the Royal Academy of Science, of Naples, this week, and as the venue, as the lawyers say—of my story lies partly in the Neapolitan territory, they ought to be good judges.[1] At all events, I shall consider them so. The work is now translating in Rome,[2] and I should think some passages would stick in some of their Catholic crops. At present, I am pretty busy—in my way—with my barbarous friends the Aztecs. You have, doubtless, heard of your countryman, poor Dr. Follen's loss, in the Lexington; which adds another to the black catalogue of disasters, by flood and fire, to which the cupidity and carelessness of our people daily subject us. Your other friends are all well here —Mrs. Mackintosh has flitted south, and passes her winter at Washington. Adieu my dear Dr. Lieber, with much haste believe me Sincerely your friend

Wm. H. Prescott

1. WHP's election to associate membership in the Royal Academy of Science of Naples, in 1839, inspired correspondence between him and Count Camaldoli. On July 26, 1840, the Count wrote WHP, ". . . I have just induced the Herculanean Academy of Archaeology to elect you a member." See Wolcott, *Correspondence of Prescott*, p. 143.

2. The blind Marquis Gino Capponi (1792–1876) of Florence initiated the move to convert *Ferdinand and Isabella* into Italian. After numerous delays and changes of translator, the Italian edition appeared in Florence in 1847–48.

123. From Patrick Fraser Tytler[1]

(WHP Papers, Mass. Hist. Soc.)

London
34 Devonshire Place
Monday February 24th 1840

My dear Sir

I trust you will pardon my so addressing you, but it is impossible for me to use any colder terms in acknowledging your letter, and the accompanying present of your history of Ferdinand and Isabella. To the high merit of the work and to the place it has now confessedly taken in European literature, I was no stranger, but to receive it as a mark of your approbation, and regard, and to be addressed from the new world as a brother labourer greatly enhances the gift—I am indeed much encouraged, when I find that any thing I have done, or rather attempted to do, has given you pleasure, because I can sincerely say that I feel the value of your praise. You are indeed a lenient critic and far overate [sic] my labors, but it will I believe be generally found that they who know best, and have most successfully overcome the difficulties of historical research, are the readiest to think kindly of the efforts of a fellow labourer.

I trust that you are again engaged on some high historical subject and sincerely hope that your employing an amanuensis is not indicative of any return of that severe calamity which you so cheerfully and magnanimously overcame in your Ferdinand and Isabella—At present I am intently occupied with the last volume of my history of Scotland, which embraces the painful and much controverted period of Mary. I have been fortunate in recovering many letters and original papers hitherto unknown, and hope to be able to throw some new light on the obscurer parts of her history, but it is full of difficulty, and I sometimes despair. Such as it is, I shall beg your kind acceptance of it and my other volumes as soon as it is published.

Believe Me Dear Sir With Every feeling of respect and regard Most Truly Yours

PATRICK FRASER TYTLER

P.S. Your parcel only reached me on the afternoon of Saturday the 22d February—The extreme beauty of the mechanical part of the work —the good taste shown in the whole "getting up" as the booksellers I believe term it, are very remarkable. As far as my experience goes I think it handsomer than any thing lately produced in this country.

1. Patrick Fraser Tytler (1791–1849), Scotch historian, was renowned for his multivolume *History of Scotland*.

124.   From Colonel Thomas Aspinwall
                (WHP Papers, Mass. Hist. Soc.)

London, 29 February 1840

My dear Sir,

Mr. Bentley's bill for £100 was duly paid and I shall soon call on him for a settlement of the account for the first edition of your work. He is always busy and I do not think it quite politic to spur him too hard especially as you are so much disposed to consider the pecuniary part of your concerns with him as of secondary importance.

With respect to my commission my feeling is much like your own. My exertions for the accomplishment of your wish to have the work published here were not prompted in the slightest degree by any thought of the "luck penny" that might come afterwards, nor since it has been generously placed at my discretion by your kind confidence, do I find it an easy matter to allow the *père de famille* to have a vote in determining the amount. But as it so happens that I have mouths to feed and as you will feel your delicacy relieved in some degree by my treating the present as an affair of business I venture to state that the usual rate of commission in ordinary cases of this nature is ten per cent on the proceeds of books published on half profits.[1] You will accordingly find on the next page the account so far made out on that principle. But I frankly tell you that I care not one farthing about it, and if you think I have "jewed" you, I pray you in your next to call me "Hunks" and tell me you will only repay the postage incurred.

You may therefore draw for the balance of the account subjoined, or any other balance which you may consider to be nearer the mark.

I am much obliged for your friendly attentions to my son.[2] I think all the better of him for your good opinion of him. It will be a great comfort to me, if he continues to enjoy it.

Pray remember me most kindly to Mrs. Prescott and your excellent parents and believe me to be

My dear Sir, Ever faithfully yours

THOS. ASPINWALL

Recd. Amount of Bentley's note £100

Postage as per minute at foot	£ 3. 2. 9
Commission at 10%	10. –. –
	13. 2. 9
Balance	£86.17. 3

1836		Feby 3	3. 2	May 9	. 3
Decr. 2	£–. –.11	10	2. 6	" 19	1. 7
8	1. 7	March 4	. 3	" 31	7.11
12	1. 8	20	. 3	June 10	. 3
15	4. 8	April 22	3. 2	" 12	9. 6
16	2. 6	Carried	£1. 1. 2	" 14	2. 2
31	. 3	forwd.		" 19	2. 6
		1837		July 22	1. 4
1837		Amount	£1. 1. 2	" "	2. 6
Jany 20	. 3	April 24	2.11		

1838		May	17	. 3	Octr	9	1. 7
Feby 14	1. 7	June	25	[. . .]	1840		
Carried	£2.13. 8	"	28	[. . .]	Jany	13	. 8
forwd.		July	22	[. . .]	Feby	29	. 3
Amount	£2.13. 8	"	30	[. . .]	Total		£3. 2. 9
1839		Septr	2	. 3			
April 18	1. 4	"	13	1. 4			

1. WHP accepted this proposal and always, for subsequent titles as well as *Ferdinand and Isabella,* paid Aspinwall a 10 per cent commission on his English earnings.

2. William Aspinwall (1819–92) was completing the studies which resulted in his Harvard LL.B. in 1840.

125.   From Richard Bentley
                        (WHP Papers, Mass. Hist. Soc.)

New Burlington Street, June 3, 1840

H. Prescott Esqre
My dear Sir

I have delayed writing to you from time to time until I should have something agreeable to communicate. The Second Edition of your *History of Ferdinand and Isabella* will, I think, be absorbed in the course of a few months, and therefore I should be glad to receive any corrections and additions which you may deem proper to make, whenever it is convenient to you.[1] We appear to be very slow coaches in England in regard to the sale of your book when compared to its circulation in United States; but the fact is that frivolous reading is, I fear, more patronized than the useful or elegant. Nevertheless we make sure although a slow progress; and your book has assuredly taken its stand with the classics of our language. The medal which Mr. Ford was so obliging as to lend me of Gonsalvo is in the hands of the engraver, but is not yet completed, and I now propose to keep that as well as the two maps you forwarded to me until a new Edition shall be required.

I was glad to hear that you were engaged upon another historical work; and hope for the sake of literature independently of the great gratification I should feel in introducing it to English readers that health may enable you to accomplish your purpose.[2] In your hands, from your indefatigable research, the subject in itself so full of interest would derive great additional value.

Pray accept my best acknowledgments for your kind expressions in regard to the matter of accounts. I trust shortly to forward to Colonel Aspinwall another statement of the continued sale of your work.

Believe me to be, Dear Sir, Yours faithfully

RICHARD BENTLEY

1. Bentley was overly optimistic about the early absorption of the second London edition; the third did not appear there until February, 1842.

2. The eager publisher was far ahead of the author; WHP was then slogging his way through the fifth chapter of the Introduction to his work.

126.   To Thaddeus William Harris[1]

(E. G. Miner Collection, The University of Rochester Library)

Boston, June 22, 1840

My dear Sir

I return you the maps with my thanks.

I still have Cogolludo's *Yucatan,* which I take the liberty to retain—under the presumption that this will be permitted me. It is the only authority relating to my subject not in my own library. And it so happens that I am now engaged on a part of my work of which Cogolludo relates, and which I cannot postpone as my work must be completed by [blank].

Under these circumstances, as it is known that I am responsible for it, I trust there will be no objection to my retaining the volume for a few weeks.[2] Yours very truly

WM. H. PRESCOTT

1. Thaddeus William Harris (1795–1856), librarian at Harvard as well as physician and naturalist, served WHP's scholarly needs on numerous occasions.

2. Two days later WHP was off to Nahant for his summer sojourn. At the approach of commencement, the librarian normally bent every effort to get every book back on the shelves of the library.

127.   To Fanny Calderón de la Barca[1]

(Draft, WHP Papers, Mass. Hist. Soc.; and extracts in Wolcott, *Correspondence of Prescott,* pp. 146–51)

15 August 1840

My dear Madame Calderón

I received a letter yesterday from your husband inclosing a document relating to the burial of Cortés, &c., for which I wish you would thank him. And I must thank you for the good long letter you were kind enough to send me last June. Commend me to a lady correspondent—i.e. some few ladies. They are the best letter-writers in the world, and go to it as naturally as they would a good gossip over a dish of tea, mixing up a little acid, throwing in a character or two, and flavoring the whole with that agreeable kind of wit which makes altogether the most delicious compound. There is nothing like the letters of the French women, except, indeed, Horace Walpole's—and he was a kind of a Betty, you know, with a little too much malice on the whole for the true epistolary, in which the sting should carry no venom. He had plenty of it, it must be confessed. But I think I had better talk to you of the living than the dead, whom we neither of us care a fig for.

I have met with a few commonplaces in an *omnium gatherum,* which I put down here. Your friend Mrs. Ritchie,[2] who has become an 'inseparable' of my sister Mrs. Dexter, has gone on an excursion to Springfield with her father for a few days. The Ticknors are at Wood's Hole passing the summer. It is far beyond New Bedford, near Martha's Vineyard, and we write to them as the Toads in a Hole. Indeed they might well be in the heart of a stone, like some of those poor toads that we read of in the natural history journals, for all that their friends ever see of them in their hermitage. The Appletons are in a pretty place, that belongs to W. B. Lawrence,[3] near Newport, where Fanny's bright eyes waste their glances on the cold billows, with many a tear between for Mary. That separation has cost her a heartache—the only one I suspect she has ever known, for she still walks 'in maiden mediation, fancy free,' and free in fact, I suspect, in spite of all poor Longfellow's prose and poetry.[4] Her friend, and I don't know but yours, Mrs. Butler,[5] has been in town, or rather at Roxbury on a visit to Mrs. Cleveland,[6] who has a grand passion for her. And from all accounts she is a very attractive person intellectually, though somewhat too independent, perhaps, for this critical world. She has a manuscript tragedy in her desk which she does not publish, it having been thought by some fastidious friends rather too untameable in some of its expressions for the sensitive public. I have neither seen the manuscript nor the lady, though we have exchanged greetings. I believe you will agree with me her writings are full of talent, and her verses of picturesque beauty. She has thrown off several little poems which have been caught up by the newspapers, that you may have seen, besides her more elaborate efforts in the dramatic. She is full of the olden times and steeped up to the eyes in the Elizabethan Age, which gives a beautiful colouring of the antique to her dramatic pieces, whatever the critics may say.

We are all at present—or rather the *beau sexe,* to speak more correctly—are all over head and ears catering for a great Fair, for the purpose of completing the Bunker Hill Monument, which at present is a monument of our poverty rather than our patriotism. It is to be held in

Quincy Hall. It is all got up by the ladies;[7] it seems very fitting that the guerdon for the brave should come from the hand of beauty. At all events it is well to look on it as a matter of sentiment, though it is an indifferent compliment to our patriotism that our legislature did not see the thing through themselves, as it was one in which the honour of the state is so nearly interested. But our good people would rather pay for their independence with their blood than their dollars. Your old friend Mrs. H. G. Otis[8] has just returned—quite in time, as she has a genius for fairs, you know—though I have not heard that she has taken a table. She brings home her little family—some of them indeed full fledged, and accomplished up to the eyes. With all this they are preparing to enter Harvard College. This seems to be an odd finale to a transatlantic education, to bring them only to the beginning of our own. The oldest boy goes into the Law School there. I am very sorry I cannot give you any gossip that would be worth a sixpence to you. But your friends are all out of town, and so are we too, for the matter of that. We are perched on our cliff at Nahant, 'Fitful Head' we call it,[9] where we see the huge leviathan gamboling about, and scattering the spray all over the piazza. We can almost fish from our balconies at high tide, and want only the rocking to persuade ourselves as we sit at table that we are on board a frigate, or a steamer at least. Among the visitors here is General Miller[10] who saw you lately at Mexico, and gives us very agreeable accounts of you, and a very interesting one of the country. He has given me many details relative to South America and Peru, which is to form one of my subjects if I should live so long. He is a fine fellow, and if the patriots had more such, they would not be playing pranks to make Heaven weep, as they now do. He desires me to remember him to you and your husband. When he left Mexico he did not expect to come here, at least not directly.

I left off writing here, having just received a letter from Mrs. Ticknor who tells me she is living in delightful loneliness at Wood's Hole, where the inhabitants know much more of the islands in the Pacific than they do of Boston, as they are all whalers. Their quiet is something of a contrast to this spot, where the house is like a wind-mill—buz-buz-buz, for we are but a stone's throw from the steamboat landing, and an arrow's shot from the hotel. Commend me to a fashionable watering place for demolishing the sublime and beautiful at a blow. Nature is here in her wildest and most touching dress—or rather undress—for we are as naked of trees and verdure as the grand plateau where you are. But still she is awful in the might of her waves and huge mountains of granite. But when I look out from my eyrie, and see the frightful little figures in loose gowns and oil-skin caps that are dabbling in the waters, and dandies, belles and troops of nurses with musical babies in their arms talking small talk to the winds and waters, I feel there is but one step from the sublime to the ridiculous. Now do you not think this a lovely place for concocting histories and the like? Especially with three or four children about one, working their way through the flowery path of knowledge, and calling on you to give them a helping hand every five minutes in the morning. Yet in this hurly-burly I am occupied not only with my new work, but with corrections and revisions without end, of my old sins in this way. Bentley informs me that he has a new edition in the press of *Ferdinand and Isabel* and asks for errata, &c. Another edition is also in the press here, and by a letter from Florence this week I am requested to send corrections for an Italian translation going on there, under the auspices of the Marquess Gino Capponi, a scholar whose reputation you may know. So you see their Catholic Highnesses do not yet go to bed with the Capulets. And that, I flatter myself, will give you and my kind friend, your husband, pleasure.

I suppose in the course of your excursions round the valley that you will visit Tezcuco, the capital of the rival state of the Aztecs with which they were so long associated in peace and in war. If you have a copy of Clavigero by you,[11] he will give you as well as any the account of these matters, and I dare say you have read them. Some of Bustamante's[12] publications, especially his 'Tezcuco en los últimos tiempos, etc.,' and also his Alamedas, relate particularly to them. He has edited and perhaps written some useful matter, though I suspect from the character of his remarks one might write him down an ass. But perhaps I wrong him. He is a bigot at all events, quite worthy of the dark ages and furious against the old Spaniards as if come down straight from Guatimozin. By the bye, will you be good enough to inform me whether there are any descendants of Montezuma or of the Tezcucan line of monarchs now living in Mexico? Should you visit Tezcuco I hope you will give me some account of the appearance of things there. And I wish you would tell me what kind of trees are found on the table land and in the valley. In describing the march of the Spaniards I am desirous to know what was the appearance of the country through which they passed, and although there may be some changes in the vegetable productions raised by men, the great features of nature and the forest scenery are no doubt much the same. And I should be sorry to put the trees on one level that will only flourish on a lower or higher one. Your road I believe lay to the west of the great mountains Iztaccihuatl and Popocatepetl of melodious sound. Cortés passed between them. Are they not magnificent mountains? And Orizaba, which I suppose you saw in the distance after leaving Perote, must look splendid in its wintry snow. I believe I could make out my way to the capital if I were set down at Vera Cruz, but I believe I shall not try, though your presence there is a sore temptation; and as Miller says, if one escapes having his neck broken by the jolts, or being stripped by the gentlemen of the road, one will find it very pleasant travelling—should he get through the *vómito* region safely. It is strange that [that] disease, by the bye, should not have been known on the coast in the time of Cortés. But the tropical climate must produce a miraculous vegetation in the *tierra caliente*. Is not the road bordered with flowers and the trees bent under a load of parasitical plants of every hue and odour? I should like to get a peep into this paradise. But I go on stringing idle questions. There is one I shall be obliged by your thinking of again. Bullock,[13] the traveller, speaks of a monument to Cortés in a chapel of the Hospital of Jesus, surmounted by a bronze bust of the hero. Could you get me a little sketch or give me a description of it, and also copy the inscription on the monument? This I could work in with some effect.[14]

I shall trouble you no more. I am ashamed to give you so much trouble as I have already, but when I write I ask you and your husband whatever comes into my head, and if it is difficult to answer or to do, pray dismiss it without ceremony. I am sure I may take the will for the deed, but I do not know here what things are most easy or difficult for you there. Pray thank your husband for his kind thoughts of my hobby, when he has so much of his own business to think of. Do not let him vex himself about papers for me, which I dare say will be copied in good time, though the *mañana* disease in Mexico is as bad as the *vómito* in Vera Cruz. If he succeeds in getting the portrait, do not hurry to send it by a doubtful conveyance, as I shall not want it for my work for a good while, and I would not run the risk of losing it. He does not say anything in this note to me about the daguerreotype. Has it not arrived? Or does it not work well? I shall be as much chagrined if it does not as he must be about his plaguing suit. I sent to get the best advices thereon from Curtis yesterday and he has written to me the following—[blank]

Aug. 20. Another P.S., or rather P.P.S. I have just received a letter from New York advising me of the arrival of a box of paintings for me from Madrid, and last evening a letter came from Middleton telling me that the box contains portraits of Ferdinand, Isabella, the Great Captain, Ximenes and Cortés, all but the last copied from originals by the best artists in Madrid.[15] Shall I not be transported to the days of the Catholic Kings in earnest? The Cortés is a copy from one in Toledo, which was itself taken from the one in Mexico. Droll enough. As I have now attained the object, I shall not want a duplicate from Mexico. But if it is begun, or your husband has made arrangements for copying it, of course you will get it finished, and I will find a place for it by sending it to an engraver in London for the English edition. So he will not task himself about the matter, in any event. I hope my collection relating to documents for Philip 2d's reign is also going on prosperously. Pray tell me. I have a scholar in Paris transcribing in the archives there,[16] and Middleton says I shall probably have access to Simancas as there is a friendly disposition towards my views—and old Navarrete in particular shows quite an interest in them.

Middleton soon leaves Spain, being supplanted by a Chargé, Mr. Vail. I wish when your husband writes to any person in Madrid who may be likely to have influence in opening to me the archives there he would take the trouble to mention my views, and if he will tell me to whom he recommends them, I will write to my agent Dr. Lembke— a member of the Academy and a resident in Madrid—that he may avail himself of their assistance.[17]

1. Frances Erskine (Inglis) Calderón de la Barca (1804–82), born in Scotland and for a time a resident of Boston, was the wife of Ángel Calderón de la Barca, the first Spanish Minister to Mexico. Gossipy letters passed between WHP and Fanny for decades.

2. Mrs. Andrew Ritchie, wife of Andrew Ritchie (1782–1862), was the former Sophia Harrison Otis, daughter of Harrison Gray Otis of Boston.

3. William Beach Lawrence (1800–1881), lawyer and politician, served as governor of Rhode Island.

4. Frances Elizabeth Appleton, Fanny to her friends, married Henry Wadsworth Longfellow in 1843.

5. A writer of plays and reminiscences, Mrs. Pierce Butler was the former Frances Anne Kemble (1809–93).

6. Mrs. Henry Russell Cleveland, the former Sarah Paine Perkins, lived in the suburban Jamaica Pond district.

7. No one worked more diligently for the success of this fair, which netted about $30,000 for the monument, than did WHP's mother.

8. Mrs. Harrison Gray Otis, the daughter of Boston merchant William Boardman, was one of Boston's leaders of society.

9. Lovers of Scott's writings, the Prescotts had lifted the name for their cottage from his novel *Pirate*.

10. General William Miller (1795–1861), an English soldier of fortune, had figured conspicuously in the Peruvian war of independence. For WHP's profit from his friendly criticism, see Prescott (Gardiner, ed.), *The Literary Memoranda*, II, 56–58.

11. Francisco Xavier Clavigero (1731–87) published his *Storia Antica del Messico* in 1780.

12. Carlos María de Bustamante (1774–1848), Mexican historian and politician.

13. William Bullock, English antiquarian and museum operator, published his *Six Months Residence and Travels in Mexico* in 1824.

14. Many of Fanny's letters from Mexico enriched WHP's *Conquest of Mexico*. Some of them, treating many things in addition to Mexico, are in Wolcott, *Correspondence of Prescott*, pp. 128–33, 167–70, 220–23, 247–54, 263–66, 284–88.

15. See Middleton to WHP, July 17, 1840, in *ibid.*, pp. 140–42.

16. F. W. Lembke had gone there from Madrid.

17. Lembke, not in Madrid, was not to return there. In some manner he had so offended Spanish authorities that he was *persona non grata*. He soon ceased to serve WHP as a research aide.

128.   To Charles Sumner
                (Charles Sumner Papers, Harvard College Library)

                                                 Pepperell, October 16, 1840

Thank you, dear Sumner, for your obliging note informing me of Milnes'[1] good intentions. I suppose we shall get a *'florilegium yankiense'* in time, which all may take a leaf from. One would be glad to avoid isms of any kind. But I shall be glad if the time should ever come when we can assert our independence of these island pedagogues. It is a hard case for letters here. We are obliged to write a language which is not spoken around us, are brought before foreign tribunals, tried by foreign laws, while even the venerable authority of ancient British precedent is over-ruled. We have achieved only half our independence.[2]

Here we are in our mountain solitudes, watching the fading leaf of autumn. The year dies like the dolphin—as his Lordship says of the day—each hue more lovely than the last. The Ticknors are with us, helping us meditate—not the thankless Muse, but the dying glories of the season. But I forget—I am not writing to a fair correspondent—but a strapping limb of the law. By the by, a fair correspondent writes word that you are dividing your homage between Themis and the lovely Fanny. Whose smiles do you like best? What a pow-wowing the newspapers have made about the donation of the latter lady! As if none but Vestals were to be allowed to be charitable. As to nationality, we are more fastidious than our fathers, who borrowed the German swords to fight their battles. We prefer, however, to have the *trophies* all our own. For my own part, I do not see how the fair dancer's noble benefaction could have been refused without great discourtesy.

Fare thee well.[3] May all good angels wait on thee—that is, good fat clients—a lawyer's angels—and crown thee with glory, and, the ripe honours of a chancellor's wig. Faithfully yours

                                                    WM. H. PRESCOTT

1. Probably Richard Monckton Milnes (1809–85), poet, reviewer and literary patron.

2. WHP's love of English literature and concern about English criticism were always tempered by his desire for the achievement of American intellectual independence.

3. In this period Edward Everett and Jared Sparks, both of whom were in Europe, were prowling in archives in behalf of WHP's research interests; see Wolcott, *Correspondence of Prescott,* pp. 161, 170–72.

129.   From Arthur Middleton
(WHP Papers, Mass. Hist. Soc.)

Madrid, November 4, 1840

My dear Prescott,

I have just sent off to Cádiz[1] another small box with a couple of books bought by Lembke and more copies on the Conquest—the fragments were found at last by looking for them under the title you suggested—the detached papers were hunted up by our indefatigable friend Navarrete. He says that he can discover nothing more worth sending—so that I suppose you will now content yourself with what you have. I have transcribed our little account on the next page and to make one business of it will send you an order for the amount $30 by Mr. C. P. Van Ness of Vermont, our late minister, on whom I am going to draw a bill in a day or two. I do not draw upon Barings because Lembke writes me word from Paris that the credit has been transferred to him—on the supposition that I had already left Madrid. This I shall do now in a few days as Mr. Vail is on the road, but my place, as it regards your views, will be amply filled by Lembke. He writes me that you have given him full powers [to] ferret out Don Felipe Segundo—and I think he may promise himself complete success on his return to this place. The men now brought into power by the late movement are animated by more liberal views in general, as well as by a friendlier feeling towards our country, than their predecessors —with regard to the enquiry you make of Lembke. Madrazo[2] tells me that the original is in Venice, but the author unknown. I suppose this will find you "up to the ears" in the blood of your Conquest. I wish you well through the slaughter, and hope you will find a good excuse for it. Your *Isabels* I am going to dispose of according to the tenor of your wishes—to distinguished literati. I speak of my own copies—the others have already been received by Messrs. Navarrete and Cortés.

My six months chargé-ship here has given me an opportunity of witnessing and recording the closing scenes of the civil war and the opening of a new era. This luckless people have now a chance of tasting the sweets of constitutional liberty. The chains still hang, perhaps, about the bleeding limbs, but the spell that rivetted the links is broken. Adieu my dear Prescott and believe me Ever yours truly

                                                        ARTHUR MIDDDLETON

Account between A. Middleton and W. H. Prescott

Dr.	Cr.	
To balance and amount of bill drawn 20 of July of which $150 was sent to Lembke — and account rendered in my last — $ 2.70	By amount paid to López for copies July 21 —	$11.20
	By amount paid Mr. Burton at Cádiz for expences of boxes of books to and from America —	6.63
	By amount paid López for copies August 15 —	14.00
	By amount paid for carriage of boxes to Cádiz —	1.00
		$32.83

                                        $32.83
                                      — 2.70
Balance due me $30.13

1. Spanish shipments to WHP moved increasingly via Cádiz once it was realized that Alexander Burton, a kinsman from Pennsylvania, was the American consul at that port.

2. José Madrazo y Agudo (1781–1859), court painter in the reign of Ferdinand VII.

130.   To Pascual de Gayangos

(The Hispanic Society of America; draft, WHP Papers, Mass. Hist. Soc.; and extracts in Wolcott, *Correspondence of Prescott,* pp. 180–82, and in Clara Louise Penney, *Prescott: Unpublished Letters to Gayangos in the Library of the Hispanic Society of America* [New York, 1927], pp. 24–26)

                                        Boston, November 28, 1840

My dear Mr. Gayangos,

I am much obliged by your very kind letter of the 15th of October,[1] together with the sheets containing part of the Index of your manuscripts. I track my way along in them, and am pleased to find an occasional confirmation of views and inferences drawn by me from other less authentic sources. For instance I had intimated the fact of Ferdinand's having the French ministers, especially the Cardinal d'Albi, secretly in his pay, during the Roussillon negotiations; and I find this strongly confirmed by the evidence of a private correspondence between this personage and the Spanish government. When I have examined the whole index, I may ask the favour of a few papers, if not long, to be copied at your leisure—but a very few only. I impose on your liberality more than enough. I have examined the catalogue very carefully, and done my best to verify your doubtful dates, and should be very happy to detect an error that you may see what attention I have given to it. But I find none. My means of ascertaining them are, however, very limited, since the titles of the letters are necessarily too brief to afford much of a clue, and the incidents are very often too minute or inconsequential to have attracted the notice of the general historian. When the rest of the index comes, with the volume of your new work, which you are so kind as to promise me, I shall have the pleasure to write you again. I look for the book with much impatience.[2] Spanish-Arab literature is such a rich field, and so little cultivated hitherto, that a scholar, who has devoted as much attention to it as you have, cannot fail to have communicated much that will be of value to letters. Conde is, I believe, the only Spanish writer who has thought of making the Arabic historians speak for themselves[3]—and his work, with much merit, is far from satisfactory. But he died before completing it, and we must be grateful for what he did accomplish. If his selections had been illustrated by explanatory notes, like those he has added to the Nubian geographer, it would have contributed much to its value.

As to the Mexican documents, it does not grieve me that you do not meet with more of them; though, if they existed, I should like to have them. But my shelves are well stocked with materials for this part of my labours; and the researches which, through my friend Calderón, have been made for me, in the archives of Mexico, have added but little to the rich collection gleaned by the industry of Muñoz, Vargas Ponze[4] and Navarrete from all the repositories in the mother country and in the colonies.

Among the manuscripts noticed by you in the British Museum, Zurita, or Çorita, on the Lords of Mexico, is one of the series translated by Ternaux.[5] It is a valuable compilation by an old lawyer of Philip 2d's court, who came out to Mexico. The only manuscript I think I should desire a copy of is the one entitled 'De las Inscripciones, medallas, edificios, templos, antiguedades, y monumentos del Perú.' I shall *not* want a copy of the correspondence, &c with Dr. Robertson,[6] which is bound up with it. Touching Las Casas,[7] I have received from Madrid only a small portion of his great work, and only two of the three volumes of it exist in the libraries there. The parts copied for me, as I only desired those relating to Mexico, are libro 3, capítulo 27 and capítulos 113 to 123 inclusive. This brings the Conquest up to the mission of Montejo and Puerto Carrero to Spain, an early stage of the proceedings. I shall be obliged by your seeing if there are any subsequent particulars of Cortés and his expedition &c in the volumes in the British Museum, and by letting me know it. My Spanish agent, Dr. Lembke, has been in Paris, where he has had some copies from Ternaux's manuscripts, and it is possible he may have added the deficit from Las Casas, of which Mons. Ternaux has, I believe, a complete copy. So I will not order the extracts, if you find any, till I hear from him.

You are certainly very right in the estimate you make of the difficulties of Philip 2d's reign as an historical subject. Some passages in it must remain more or less under a cloud. But it affords a noble range, and materials are abundant if they can be reached. I shall not decide till I learn what success I am likely to meet with in Madrid. If I set about a collection, I shall wish to confer with you upon it. The heirs of the archivero Gonzales offered me the manuscripts you speak of for the moderate sum of 3000 dollars. But to a man who wants original documents, it would scarcely be worth as many reals. I fear there are other difficulties to the investigation of the archives of Simancas, besides that of the disorderly state of their contents.

I have received lately copies, from original portraits, of Ferdinand and Isabella, Ximenes, Gonsalvo de Córdova, and Cortés. The copies have been executed by the best artists in Madrid, Gutierrez[8] and Madrazo, whom perhaps you may know, and several of the paintings, especially Isabella and Gonsalvo, are admirable. They are of the size of life; and, as they hang up on the walls around me, I feel myself transported to the glorious land of chivalry, in the day of her [. . . .] Gonsalvo's portrait is wholly unlike the poor print engraved by Bentley— from [I do] not know what source, and I think I shall have an engraving taken from [it] it is so characteristic of the great man. But I will not take up more of your time, only to add that Mr. Ticknor desires his kind remembrances to you. I enclose you a notice from the Quincuagenas of Oviedo, of the Garcilasso de la Vega whose letters you have in your collection—the father, you know, of the poet. Perhaps, however, you have Oviedo's manuscript. Adieu, my dear Mr. Gayangos.[9] Believe me with the most grateful sentiments for your kindness Yours most truly and affectionately

WM. H. PRESCOTT

[P.S.] Since the above was written I have learnt [of] Lord Holland's death—a sad loss indeed—for I believe no English nobleman possessed a more cultivated taste or generous heart. I believe he was loved and honoured by all who knew him—or were acquainted with his character.

1. An extract from this letter is in Wolcott, *Correspondence of Prescott,* pp. 165–67.

2. *History of the Mohammedan Dynasties in Spain,* a two-volume work, appeared in 1840–43.

3. José Antonio Conde's (1765–1820) *Historia de la dominación de los Árabes en España* was published in 1820–21.

4. José de Vargas y Ponce (1760–1821).

5. Henri Ternaux-Compans (1807–64), French historian and collector. Many of his manuscripts came to America, permanently, in the 1840's. WHP, having initiated correspondence with Ternaux-Compans in March, 1839, had received assurances of the widest cooperation from him; see Wolcott, *Correspondence of Prescott,* pp. 60–61, 74–75.

6. William Robertson (1721–93), Scotch historian, had been the most recent significant British student of Spanish history.

7. Bartolomé de la Casas (1474–1566), churchman, humanitarian and propagandist. The work cited was not printed until 1875.

8. José Gutiérrez de la Vega (d. 1865).

9. WHP soon determined that after his books on the conquests of Mexico and Peru he would dedicate his talents to a history of the reign of Philip II. Most of Gayangos' assistance related to that project.

131. To Francis Lieber

(Francis Lieber Papers, LI3034, The Huntington Library, San Marino, California. Reproduced by permission; and extracts in Thomas Sergeant Perry [ed.], *The Life and Letters of Francis Lieber* [Boston, 1882], pp. 146–47)

Boston, December 31, 1840

Francis Lieber Esqr.

I should have sooner thanked you for your friendly letter, my dear Lieber—I will not say Doctor, since that is a title you eschew, though you are very willing to shower it on the heads of your friends, it seems.[1] I have not that aversion to it, and indeed, have enjoyed the glory thereof for some three months, though I think it will be long before you will see that or any other academic laurel garlanding my name on a title page. Still such honours are a gratifying testimony of good will and good opinion, from the highest quarters, to which I think no scholar can be indifferent. As to your twitting me with my blindness, the historian's work is a blind business, at best. I have one eye, though a poor one, but if I can claim to be *unoculus inter caecos,* my ambition will be satisfied.

We are all moving here in the usual paths of pleasure, or profit—the last is the high road, the golden road, indeed, of pleasure, in our money-making community. I wish we had a little more of the liberal tastes shown by John Bull, when his bags are well lined. I had a letter from Sparks, a day or two since, informing me of a visit he had paid to a worthy baronet in Worcestershire, Sir Thomas Phillipps,[2] who divides his time between rural sports and letters. He has a great estate; and a splendid library; for one item, eleven thousand volumes of manuscripts! —the largest private collection, I suppose, in Europe. Among them are some curious Spanish ones, of which he offers me copies. He has a private press in his establishment, from which he turns off curious antiquities, printing only some five and twenty copies of a work. This is the very cream of civilization, when fox hunters find a relaxation in pleasures so intellectual. Our rich men go on heaping up the gold dust, to be scattered into infinite atoms at their deaths again. I know several young men of good estates here, whose ambition is satisfied by the noble post of head of a cotton factory—I mean young men who have received our best academic education. Yet this is better than the lethargy which so many millionaires fall into in other parts of our country, and in Europe, too. It is an active development of the powers, though in a grosser form —a *material* civilization—better suited, perhaps, to the circumstances of the country, where so much is to be created, than the intellectual civilization, which belongs to a nation, who has already done much, and reached the period of retrospection—contemplation. The exciting condition of things in a new and changing community like ours, impels us forward; we have no time to reflect—little to study—except as this last prepares us to act. Go ahead, is the motto—a confounded uncomfortable one for a quiet, sedentary body, who likes repose in an armchair.[3]

Sparks has succeeded beyond his hopes in getting access to materials, and in discovering them, and will return in the spring from his tour to London and Paris, where he has been buried in the libraries, public and private, with a rich freight of manuscripts—the true ammunition for the historian. Bancroft does not set so much store by them, and places more stress on the manner of working up the article, than on its original quality. Both are indispensable. His last volume meets with a great sale.[4] He will now come on the Revolutionary ground, along side of Sparks. The field is a wide one, and they need not jostle each other.

But I will spare you any further twaddle, begging you to believe me —now and ever Faithfully your friend

WM. H. PRESCOTT

1. Upon Lieber's recommendation, South Carolina College later awarded WHP an honorary degree.
2. Sir Thomas Phillipps (1792–1872).
3. This paragraph is one of WHP's best statements on this subject.

4. Returning Bancroft's kindness, WHP reviewed George's latest volume for the *North American Review* (January, 1841).

132.   From Fanny Calderón de la Barca
                (Extract, WHP Papers, Mass. Hist. Soc.)

                            Mexico [City], 19th January, 1841

                    .   .   .   .

However, I now have about ten minutes before Mr. Ellis[1] puts up his despatches which I must employ in begging you *upon no account* to pin your faith to Waldeck[2]—whose work even by the most Mexicanised of Mexicans is considered a tissue of exaggerations—his sketches very fine, but also painted like a poet. It is a great pity that travellers will so exaggerate—whether in over- or underrating every country that is not well known. Lord Kingsborough's immense work is about the greatest curiosity in the Museum here—where indeed there is little to be seen. Calderón is to write and send you different things by the next Habana packet. He is as you may suppose by no means *enchanted* with the state of Spanish affairs. How far Espartero's[3] ambition may lead him, remains to be seen. Some think he will take Iturbide[4] for his model, in which case there is little to fear—except for himself. In all cases, I think it most probable that all the foreign Ministers will renounce, Calderón amongst others—but this is in *confianza*. I *ought* to be very sorry, but the idea of returning homewards *balances* matters rather equally. I shall however be sorry to leave many persons in Mexico—for it is impossible to have met with more kindness; and I am inclined to think they will be sorry to lose *us*—at least the Spaniards will regret Calderón—who has worked hard for them and their rights. I wish you could look in upon my Saturday *tertulias,* which are very pleasant. I was assured that these sort of soirees were impossible in Mexico—but I have now given eight, and they are more crowded each time. We have music, dancing, whist and écarté—refreshment tables and I have even induced the ladies to come without their diamonds—in simple muslin dresses—and to spend from eight p.m. until one in the morning without smoking! I must send you along with Calderón's packets by the Habana, a letter upon *earthquakes,* written by Count Cortina to a very pretty Mexicana, who had been dreadfully frightened by the last one. It is so characteristic of the writer, that it is worth reading. We have had a magnificent mass here given in the Cathedral by a rich Senator, who some years ago made a vow, that every *noche buena* in honour of our Saviour's birth, he would

give this musical mass. A number of the first ladies in Mexico sang, and
I was *cajoled* into playing the Incarnatus on the harp! It was a most
brilliant affair; and all *léperos* being kept out by the soldiers, it was
what they call here *una concurrencia muy lucida*. I had a letter from
Alexander[5] who seems as is natural, very sorry to leave Boston—though
I hope the step he has taken will be for his advantage. My ten minutes
are *out,* and I must send this to Mr. Ellis *luego, luego.* When you see
Mrs. Ritchie, pray give her my best love—also to Fanny Appleton, and
muchas memorias to Mr. and Mrs. Ticknor. Calderón sends his best
regards, and I remain very sincerely yours—

FANNY CALDERON DE LA BARCA

1. Powhatan Ellis (1794–1844), American Minister to Mexico from 1839 to
1842. Early in Ellis' stay in Mexico City, WHP had corresponded with him;
see Wolcott, *Correspondence of Prescott,* p. 110.

2. Jean Frédéric, Comte de Waldeck, published his *Voyage pittoresque et
archéologique dans la province d'Yucatan pendant les années 1834 et 1836* in
1838.

3. Baldomero Espartero (1793–1879) ousted Queen Regent Christina and
assumed the post of regent for Isabella II himself.

4. Agustín de Iturbide (1783–1824) served briefly as Emperor of Mexico
in 1822–23. Upon his return from exile in 1824, he was executed.

5. Fanny Calderón's brother, Alexander Inglis.

133.   From William Henry Leatham[1]
          (WHP Papers, Mass. Hist. Soc.; and in Ogden, *Prescott,* pp. 120–21)

Wakefield, Yorke, March 27, [1841]

Sir,

The perusal of your admirable History of the Reign of "Ferdinand
and Isabella—the Catholic"—has suggested the composition of the enclosed little drama entitled the "Siege of Granada." As I have printed
but a very limited number of copies a new edition is not improbable.
Would you allow me to dedicate my next, and I trust more corrected
Edition, to yourself?[2]

I am sir, with all respect—Your most obedient servant

WM. HENRY LEATHAM

1. William Henry Leatham (1815–89), member of the British Parliament
and author, is representative of the poets, dramatists and novelists, in America
and England, who drew inspiration from successive titles by WHP.

2. No second edition of this work ever appeared. Soon, however, Leatham
drew inspiration anew from WHP's second history; see Wolcott, *Correspondence of Prescott,* pp. 461, 504–7.

134.   To James Brown[1]
        (Yale Collection of American Literature, Yale University Library)

                                    Bedford Street, May 26, 1841

My dear Sir—

I send you the letters to Bentley and Rich.[2] And when you deliver
them, you had best make a point to see them. I have offered the Abridgment[3] to Mr. Bentley on the same terms that he has the greater work.
And I have asked him to sign an agreement therefor with Colonel
Aspinwall, with whom he arranged for the other—as I think it best to
make one account of it. So there will be nothing further for you to do
but to give him the letter, and you may as well learn from him what he
thinks of it for London. I fear if he does not take it, some one else will
rob us both of the profits of it.

In the letter to Rich I have asked him to get engravings of the Montezuma—which I wish you to deliver him—and of *Columbus*. And you
can tell him you will bring home the plate and proofs of the last when
you return, if you come by way of London. I have asked him to get this
plate done first.

When you have seen Bentley, get as correct a notion as you can of his
dealings with me—and write me your opinion.[4] It shall go no further.
Yours very truly

                                    WM. H. PRESCOTT

    1. James Brown (1800–1855), partner of Charles C. Little in the firm of
Little, Brown and Co., published WHP's first history between 1838 and 1844.
    2. Soon to embark for England, Brown had been supplied with letters of
introduction by WHP.
    3. Frightened by rumors of a forthcoming unauthorized abridgment of his
history, which never materialized, WHP prepared his own abridgment, which
he never published.
    4. WHP's lurking distrust of Bentley stemmed from several factors: his
feeling that publishing was "the slippery trade"; his belief that Bentley had
charged exorbitant sums to advertising; and his belief that behind somewhat
befuddled accountings Bentley was trying to cheat him of part of his earnings
in England.

135.   To Francis Lieber
(Francis Lieber Papers, LI3036, The Huntington Library, San Marino, Cali-
                    fornia. Reproduced by permission)

                                    Boston, June 3, 1841

Dear Lieber,

    I should have answered your friendly epistle sooner, but have just
returned from an excursion to Connecticut with my parents and the

Ticknors. Never did I see more beautiful scenery in New England, or Old—such magnificent elms, rich meadows, and the broad silver lining of the Connecticut, the queen of waters. The people, which is not often the case in our country, seem to have caught something from the genius of the place, and instead of wretched buildings, or great staring roads that cut up the beauties of the turf, show as much taste as we find among the peasantry of England—humouring, not spoiling, the pretty face of Nature. But I forget I am not writing to a boarding school miss, but to a grave doctor, learned in ethical and political philosophy, and a' that, and a' that. I read at Springfield an article on the said doctor's learned lucubrations, in the last *Edinburgh*. What a kind, courteous, and complimentary tone the writer has. What good luck he has in finding ground to make battle on. And when he has agreed by chance, it is like Pope's honest man.

Did it by stealth, and blushed to find it *praise*.[1] This is the true spirit of reviewers of the present day, at least, of foreign reviewers, who have no bowels for us on this side the waters. The article in question—*quantum valeat*—is in one sense highly complimentary to your work, since it shows by its length and ratiocinatory spasms, that the critic girded up his loins for a great fight—*magnum certamen,* truly. On the whole an elaborate article in one of the principal foreign journals is beneficial to the sale and reputation of a work, in whatever spirit the paper may be written. Such is the prejudice, silly prejudice, still lurking in the public, in regard to this contemptible kind of writing; the school in which sciolists skirmish, humbuggers twaddle, laugh in the sleeve, and think to lead the much abused public by the nose. I think, however, the gross blunders of reviewers, their manifest incompetency on various occasions, the fallacy of their predictions as proved by results, and, above all, the counter-workings of opposite forces, as of the leading journals, the *London Quarterly* and *Edinburgh*—each claiming infallibility—pope and antipope—have all done much to open the eyes of people—so that those only who are born to be gulled would think of wholly relying on a critical verdict. I often think of Scott's remark in one of his letters, speaking of his own complimentary notice of Southey's *Curse of Kehama*. "Had the order of the day been *pour déchirer,* I should have made quite a different thing of it!"[2] So much for good faith—in the reviewing gentry. As to their literary qualifications, any one who has studied and reflected years on a subject, and reads the butterfly speculations of a fashionable critic on it afterwards can feel no emotion but that of profound contempt. So much for reviewers, of which respectable fraternity having been a member myself, I ought to know something.[3] I never could meet a thoroughbred of the same school without feeling like Cicero's augurs.

Your friend Miss Appleton had a short passage of 13 1/2 days. I have just got a letter from Gray (Frank) who went with her. They met some brilliant specimens of the icebergs, a quarter as big as Boston common, throwing off huge flakes like avalanches, and shining like a wall of diamond in the sun.

We are all here looking with hope to the new policy of the new dynasty. But sudden cures cannot be wrought by any policy, though undoubted Jupiter will be more likely to help those who put their own shoulder to the wheel, and with good faith and political principle—if there be such a thing—we may hope in time to clear ourselves from the slough.[4]

Our literary gentry are industrious in their ways. Ticknor is now hammering with good effect on his Spanish literature. Bancroft has concocted an abridgment. I have undertaken the same task for youth and schools, of my bantling—an infernal job, to pare off the nose and ears and toes of one's own and only begotten, to sweat down the muscles and sinews to a mere skeleton—an unsightly little abortion of one tome 12mo—stunting and dwarfing ideas as well as paragraphs down to the calibre of schoolboys. But what can one do? I would never do the dirty deed, but I am driven to it, and it is better to do up your own than leave it to another to do at your expense. It completely interrupts for the season my Mexican campaigns, in which I was going on swimmingly.[5]

Many thanks for your friendly exertions to clothe me in the same respectable titles with yourself. Although I eschew the title, I am gratified with the compliment from so respectable an institution. Sumner is in good order, and quite in a legal career again, getting weaned from his transatlanticism.

I suppose you duly received a letter which I wrote you last winter. I am too bad a correspondent to afford to have any of my letters miscarry. Adieu my dear Lieber.

With sincere regard, believe me, most faithfully yours

WM. H. PRESCOTT

1. Pope's exact words were: "Do good by stealth, and blush to find it *Fame*," "Epilogue to the Satires," Dialogue I, l. 136.

2. Scott meant, of course, that he had reviewed Southey's poem from the standpoint of friend and literary ally of that author.

3. Except for friends who turned author, WHP, by this time, had stopped writing reviews.

4. Some of his limited political optimism stemmed from the fact that, Whig that he was, he welcomed the Harrison victory of 1840.

5. Prescott (Gardiner, ed.), *The Literary Memoranda,* II, 73–76, details the labor on the abridgment.

136.   To Pascual de Gayangos
(The Hispanic Society of America; draft, WHP Papers, Mass. Hist. Soc.; and extracts in Wolcott, *Correspondence of Prescott,* pp. 266–69)

Boston, October 27, 1841

My dear friend,

I have received your two letters of the 22d of September,[1] in which you mention your loss by the failure of the publisher Knight. I had heard that he failed for a large amount, but had no idea that I should have been pained by learning that any friend of mine was to suffer by him. With regard to the little sum you have in consequence, as you say, allowed Mr. Rich to pay you, I am very glad you have done so, and hope you will not hesitate to call for the balance, when you desire. Be assured I do not consider it as lending you anything, but as a money debt from me to you, which still leaves me your debtor in another, and much more important way, a debt of kindness, which I fear I cannot repay.

Will you allow me to add, now we are on this subject, that if the loan of 50 or 100 pounds can be any accommodation to you, you have only to let me know it, and I shall feel most happy to have it in my power to oblige you, taking your own entire leisure for repayment. I hope, at all events, this offer will not displease you, and that you will take it in the spirit in which it is intended.

The portraits by Señor Carderera[2] that you have sent me are very spirited. That of the Catholic Sovereigns bears evidence of being a most literal copy from the original sculpture. Had I got them earlier, I should have had them engraved. I believe I must restrict my expenditure in this way now to the works that are to come. I shall be very happy to take the two portraits, and Mr. Rich will pay you the four pounds for them, if you will be good enough to send the bill to him. I should be glad if Sr. Carderera will send me, also, his Pizarro and Cortés, and any other portraits whether sketched by himself or engraved, of persons in those two expeditions. I should like, also, any that he may have of Philip 2d, or any distinguished person in that reign. He will oblige me by sending, as he did with those already sent, an account of the source whence they are derived; and any additional information he can give respecting the best portraits of those persons, I shall find very acceptable. He will, of course, name his prices for each, and what I do not incline to take, I will return by the first steamer. I do not care for the sort of illustrations with which the French historical writers sometimes embellish their works, which seem to me better suited to romance than history. But authentic portraits of the great actors in the drama, I shall always try to get. I believe I am provided with two such of Cortés, one from a painting of which I have a copy, taken of him in his latter days, and never engraved.

I am very glad that you propose to write a full account of the *Dominación de los Árabes*. It is a noble subject, and well worthy of you. But I do not like the idea of your African expedition—at least, if it is to carry you out of the reach of civilization. It would be attended with some risk, and much personal privation and suffering. Could the objects not be obtained without such a sacrifice? There were doubtless many manuscripts carried over to Barbary by the exiled Moriscoes. But I should fear they could hardly have survived so many years of barbarism. As to the volumes of your precious store of manuscripts which you talk in that case of sending to me, during your absence, I can only say, it will, of course, give me great satisfaction to see these interesting documents; and I should probably avail myself of their possession to have copies made of those relating to Philip 2d *in extenso*. But I assure you, it would give me serious uneasiness, should any accident happen to them under my care. Though for that they would be as tenderly provided for as my own library is, which is the best I could do. I still hope I shall not have the loan of them, at the cost of your exile in Africa.

Touching Philip 2d, of whom I have before spoken to you, I shall now write more fully. I look to that as the great subject for which I am to buckle on my harness, when I have disposed of Mexico and Peru. The former will be completed, I think, in little more than a year—certainly at the rate at which I have been lately advancing.[3] The other may take two years more—say four in all. Then I propose to give eight or ten years, if necessary, to a thorough anatomy of this great reign, viewed in all its relations, domestic, foreign, and its influence on the intellectual and social condition of the nation; a rich and magnificent theme. You may, perhaps, think this is cutting out rather a rash quantity of work, considering the debility of my eyes, and the limited use I have of them. But if they should break down entirely, I trust my ears will bear me through. But then the materials—I have ascertained where they are to be found. I am quite satisfied that if I get nothing in Spain, I shall be able to procure more than enough in Paris, Brussels and Vienna, in addition to printed works, to give a very complete picture of this reign, in all its internal relations, as well as foreign. The Marquis Capponi in Florence is possessed of the diplomatic correspondence of the Venetian ministers at the court of Philip, and other important papers are in the Medician Archives, both of which are now being copied for me. I mentioned to you, I believe, that my book was translating into Italian, under the auspices of Signor Capponi, a most enlightened and liberal person. Besides him, my friend Mr. Everett, who has been passing the winter at Florence, has taken an active interest in getting me other materials.[4] During his residence in Paris, last year, he examined the public libraries with reference to the same object, and found an immense mass of materials, all systematically arranged, both in the Royal Library and that of the Foreign Archives, under Mignet's[5] care. The latter was, I think, the place where the papers were transferred from Simancas in Bonaparte's time, and many of them have since not been restored, or copies of them taken. The result of his enquiries has convinced me that in Paris alone, I should find an *embarras de richesses* for this reign; and the difficulty will consist in the selection. A collection has been made in Brussels with reference to this very subject, as I learn through the minister from the Netherlands at London, Mr. Van de Weyer[6]—of which I can obtain copies. I have corresponded with the Librarian at Vienna, and have no doubt of getting what I shall want there.[7]

As to Spain, I don't know what to think. The last volume of the *Memorias* of the Real Academia da la Historia contains a considerable mass of documents for illustrating this reign, there first printed. As a Member of the Academy, I can command its papers; but I believe it has no others. Those in the hands of the government at Simancas are, I fear, in high disorder, and not very accessible. But I have made no effort to procure them. I had hoped Dr. Lembke would have superintended this collection of materials for me in Paris and Brussels, and, if he could, in Spain. But I have not heard from him—strange to say— these eighteen months. He made the collection, in a very thorough and judicious manner, almost wholly from the materials of the Academy, though partly in Paris, for my present subject. But what has become of him, I know not. That collection including printed books and manuscripts cost me about 250 pounds, of which about a hundred and twenty-five he took for his trouble. But copying in Spain is very cheap. I have proposed to allow six or seven hundred pounds for the Philip II materials, which, I trust, will be enough.

My object in fatiguing you in this long detail is to learn if it would meet your arrangements, when you have disposed of the engagements you have immediately on hand, to superintend the collection of materials, as far as they can be made in Paris, Brussels and London, and if you have the means, hereafter in Spain. I believe it would not require many weeks of your time, as the materials are all very easily reached.[8]

The British Museum, your own library, and the volume of manuscripts in the late Lord Holland's (of which I should hope there would be allowed me a copy) would afford matter for transcription in London. The task of copying, being assigned by you to others, would leave you the labours of selection and supervision. It is this business of selection which is most important to me, as the excluding of trivial matter will alone enable my appropriation to cover what is really important.

Should you find it convenient to undertake this, it would be well to see Mr. Everett. He will soon (if he is not there already) be in London, as Minister from the United States to the British Court. When he went into public life, some dozen years since, he was one of the most accomplished men in this country, combining with uncommon talents, very large literary acquisitions. He filled the office of Professor of Greek in the best college in our country, at Cambridge, near Boston. I should have much pleasure in making you acquainted with him. He can inform you of everything relating to the collections in Paris, which he carefully examined for me. When you are ready to attend to the matter, I would remit the sums you thought proper, at once, for you to use, and as to remuneration, there can be no difference of opinion between you and me. But I will add nothing further till I hear from you, only that I wish you would be guided in your answer solely by what may be for your own interest and convenience, without any reference to my wishes as expressed here, a caution which the delicacy of your feelings makes it proper for me to give. For much as I should like to effect this under your auspices, I would not for the world do so at any sacrifice on your part.

Believe me, dear Mr. Gayangos, Most sincerely and affectionately yours

WM. H. PRESCOTT

P.S. You speak of a life of the Great Captain by a contemporary, Herrera, as announced in Spain. Should it come to your hands, you will much oblige me by sending it to Rich on my account. I wrote you September 14th a letter which I suppose has reached you, asking you to furnish Bentley with autographs (a line or two of each with the signature) of the five principal persons in my "History of Ferdinand and Isabel." You see I am always ready to tax your kindness.[9]

1. Extracts of one letter are in Wolcott, *Correspondence of Prescott*, pp. 255–56.

2. Valentín Carderera y Solano (1796–1880).

3. At this time WHP was rapidly writing the opening chapters of Book III; see Prescott (Gardiner, ed.), *The Literary Memoranda*, II, 78–79, 243.

4. See Edward Everett to WHP, September 21, 1841, in Wolcott, *Correspondence of Prescott*, pp. 254–55.

5. François Auguste Marie Mignet (1796–1884), historian, served for many years as director of the archives of the French Ministry of Foreign Affairs. WHP knew him through the Institut de France.

6. Sylvain Van de Weyer (1802–74) served as Belgian Minister at the Court of St. James for decades. WHP met him in London in 1850.

7. Ferdinand Wolf (1796–1866), librarian of the Imperial Library at Vienna, had corresponded with WHP as early as October, 1839; see *ibid.,* pp. 99–100.

8. Gayangos was disposed to help, but the time involved greatly exceeded WHP's optimistic estimate.

9. Exceeding the role of selector and supervisor, Gayangos served WHP's purposes in England, France and Spain.

137.   To Richard Bentley
(Richard Bentley Papers, Harvard College Library)

Boston, November 15, 1841

My dear Sir,

I have received yours of the 20th October, and am very glad that the edition which was strangled in its birth, last season, is likely to have a safe delivery this. I am much obliged by your furnishing the copies of the Gonsalvo medallion to Rich, and should like to have a plate of it, as you politely offer, engraved for me, at once; as I suppose the expense would not be much and I prefer to own one myself. I have told you, I think, that I have a fine copy in oils of a Spanish portrait of the Great Captain; but, on the whole, think I shall not have it engraved; as the medallion does him very fair justice, and I must reserve any loose coin for the embellishments for my Mexican bantling. I shall have three or four portraits from originals for that, and have now a full length of the Conqueror—as large as the Vicar of Wakefield's picture—which, you may remember, was too big for any room in his house—from Mexico, which I shall get engraved. I have been doing good work this summer in the country, and believe I shall break my hero's neck in a year or so, if I have good luck. It will probably make three volumes, as good a number as any for a history.

Touching the new edition of *Ferdinand and Isabella*—I am glad you intend to *substitute* Mr. Ford's medal for the old print. They would not keep one another in countenance. I sent you last year two maps for Gonsalvo's campaigns in Italy, and the War of Granada; very convenient for the reader, of the size of a page each. If you have mislaid them, let me know, and I will send you them again, at once, and they can be engraved in a few days. I am glad you keep the book in three volumes, and I believe that good type and paper &c is good economy, if the work itself is worth any thing. Could you not get rather *newer types than the preceding?* I mentioned in one of my letters that soon after my book came out, I was made a member of the Spanish Academy of History. If it would help the sale of the book, you can stick it on my name. Otherwise not. It would not here where I am known, and so I let it alone. If you put it on, say, *"Cor. Member* of the Royal Academy of History, at Madrid, &c &c" which last may stand for a round dozen of other societies which I shall not display, they being nothing to Spanish history. This title is so pertinent, that it may possibly serve as an endorsement of my labours by the highest authority.[1]

I observe Murray advertises a book, Bancroft's *History of the United States,* as the tenth edition. He, in fact, sells an edition printed here, which is the tenth. As I have had eight, also, here, would it help you to put it in your advertisements?[2] Of all these, you can judge best, as if they would not really help the sale, it is not worth while to notice any of them. You will have for this new Edition, a new Preface added to the old one, new notes from original correspondence of the time, two maps, a new engraving, autographs, which Mr. Gayangos will send you if you apply to him, and various emendations.

I dare say I have run over all these things in my previous letters to you. But there never was harm done by a word too much, especially when the party to whom it is spoken may heed it or not, as he likes. So with best wishes for your success in this and all your bibliopolical labours—I am faithfully yours

WM. H. PRESCOTT

1. This Spanish honor, plus other leading European ones, soon graced WHP's title pages in both England and America.

2. For a detailed view of WHP's ideas for the promotion and distribution of his books, see Gardiner, *Prescott and His Publishers,* pp. 167–201.

138.   To Luigi Mariotti[1]
(Miscellaneous Papers—Wm. H. Prescott folder, The New York Public Library)

Boston, November 15, 1841

Mr. Mariotti
My dear Sir,

I returned yesterday from my villeggiatura—having been absent from town these four months. I went to the booksellers, Little and Brown, who have the care of your volumes. I find only two copies remaining. Mr. Brown tells me he conversed with you respecting them, in London. He does not think it would be safe to publish an edition here, but if you have any copies on hand, of your own, he thinks it would be well to send another dozen. Otherwise, it would not be advisable to do any thing more about it. The higher literary criticism, especially of a foreign language, is a luxury rather beyond the standard of our market—at least for a large class of purchasers—at present. But I believe all who have read your book, and they are among the best educated, of course, think and speak very highly of it. I have heard such flattering opinions from more than one, though I have been absent from society, of late; and certainly, I and my own family are much indebted to your eloquent exposition of the beauties of your delightful literature.[2]

You spoke to me of obtaining a place, if possible, in some University, as a teacher, or lecturer. I shall not forget it, should any occasion, in which I can serve you, present itself. But I have not heard of any such place, and when a vacancy occurs, there are many competitors to push their claims on the spot, as you are aware. I shall be very glad, however, should it be in my power to serve you, and in doing so, American scholarship.

With sincere wishes that you may find more flowers in the hard path of exile, than your great countryman Dante could meet with—I am very truly yours

WM. H. PRESCOTT

1. Antonio Gallenga (1810–95), a Piedmontese patriot who employed the pseudonym Luigi Mariotti, had lived in the United States between 1836 and 1839. Very briefly he was a party to the Capponi translation of WHP's book; see Wolcott, *Correspondence of Prescott*, pp. 143, 158.

2. WHP reviewed the London edition of Mariotti's *Italy—General Views of Its History and Literature in Reference to Its Present State* in the *North American Review* (April, 1842).

139.   From John P. Richardson
                         (WHP Papers, Mass. Hist. Soc.)

Columbia, South Carolina College
December 1841

Doctor William H. Prescott
  Boston
  Resolved—That the Degree of Doctor of Laws, be conferred on Mr. William H. Prescott of Boston, in testimony of the high respect felt by this Board for his talents and learning; and that he be informed of the fact, by the President of the Board.[1]

Dear Sir—

I have the honor herewith to transmit the foregoing copy of a Resolution of the Board of Trustees of the South Carolina College; and beg leave to offer you my personal congratulations on receiving a distinction, conferred from so very just and sincere a regard to merit and acquirements. Very respectfully Your Obedient Servant

JOHN P. RICHARDSON

December 29th 1841   Ex Officio President, of the Board of Trustees, of the South Carolina College

1. Francis Lieber's efforts to honor his friend had borne fruit.

140.   To Henry Wadsworth Longfellow

(Henry W. Longfellow Papers, Harvard College Library; and, with modifications, in Samuel Longfellow [ed.], *Life of Henry Wadsworth Longfellow; With Extracts from His Journals and Correspondence* [3 vols., Boston and New York, 1891], I, 411–12)

Boston, December 30, 1841

My dear Longfellow,

I don't know that an old stager in authorship like you, cares for anybody's opinion. And yet I think one is never indifferent to the opinion of a friend. At all events, I am too much your debtor for the beautiful little poems you have just published not to express my pleasure to you. I have read most of them several times, and not with less satisfaction that I recognized now and then an old familiar face. The ballads I never saw before. The hexameters strike me as the most doubtful. Every experiment even by the best hand shows that our language is not nicely enough modulated for them. I don't think either that the original tone of thought in this piece *"de longue haleine"* is of so decided a poetical character as your own writing. You are too good for translation, though you certainly improve your natural vein by the slight infusion into it —I will not say imitation—of foreign and ancient models. In two or three ballads, especially the "Armed Skeleton" and the "Hesperus," you have seized the true colouring of the antique. Nothing better have I seen in this way since the "ancient marinere." The small pieces are touching and graceful—showing that delicate blending of sentiment and poetic imagery, which art must despair to reach. I bought a copy at the same time with our noble friend[1] the other day, who expressed a warm admiration of your writings.

I hope—I do not believe that these remarks will seem intrusive or impertinent to you from, my dear Longfellow Your sincere friend

WM. H. PRESCOTT

1. Probably George William Frederick Howard (1802–64), then Lord Morpeth and subsequently Earl of Carlisle. In 1850 he did much to make WHP's visit to England a memorable one.

141.   To Francis Lieber

(Francis Lieber Papers, LI3037, The Huntington Library, San Marino, California. Reproduced by permission)

Boston, January 5, 1842

Dear Lieber,

Thank you sincerely for your very friendly offices, and interest in my behalf. The LLDship is not a thing which I wish to stick as a cognomen, any more than you do,—but I prize it very much as a testimonial of approbation from one of the respectable literary institutions of our country,—the proper authorities for pronouncing on literary desert. I don't know that I ever told you I had a similar honour a year since, conferred by a college of the same name in New York.[1] You mentioned in a letter, a long way back, that you had furnished the words of a diploma of doctorship for me in one of the universities of Virginia—I forget which. Tell me, if you think of it when you write again, which was the college, and whether you have heard any more of it. Perhaps they did not, like your good-natured board, think me after all worthy of the laurel.[2]

We are jogging along in the old track—dinners, soirees, gossip, any thing but hard study.[3] Commend me to the villegiatura for that. I do more in two months at Pepperell, than I can in six in town. We have lately been much taken up with English visitors, especially the Lyells[4] and Lord Morpeth. The former are now in North Carolina, their southern limit. Madame is a rare specimen of her sex, full of intelligence, and sweet and agreeable in her manners. Her husband is a man of science, bedded in geological strata chin deep, but a very excellent person in every sense. Lord Morpeth is a real gem of the British coronet; unpretending, cultivated, and blessed with qualities of heart and understanding that would "smooth the raven down" of radicalism till it smiled. He is blessed, moreover, with excellent digestive apparatus, and had he staid much longer, would have run me up a private account of dyspepsia, as I assisted him on numerous occasions. Your John Bull has an admirable physique, which puts us "deteriorated races" of the New World to shame. He will visit Charleston, and as it is possible, though not probable, he may Columbia. I have ventured to give him a line to you, that you might do him the honours of the institution. I hope he will visit it, as I am sure the acquaintance would give mutual pleasure.

I have just been reading the article on Hastings in the *Edinburgh*. It is, as you probably know, by Macaulay, traced with his usual pen of fire—words that burn. He writes with great strength and brilliancy, and with most wonderful richness and pertinence of illustration. But—there is always a but—there is wanting that easy, unsolicited grace which gives the last touch to style, beyond the reach of art. He has all that art can give. He is a great mannerist, and repeats words and phrases in a way, which, however emphatic, is much better suited to declamation than writing. Indeed, he always seems to be on his legs addressing an audience—no common audience, it is true. He has great strength—not condensation, however, of thought. He deals too much in striking antitheses, and *effect,* to conciliate entire confidence. He has an air of candour, certainly, but his energetic expression overstates both the *per* and the *contra.* He is a Rembrandt among critics—all lights and shadows—no gentle, imperceptible gradation of tints,—delicate disclosures of character. Everything is forced by violent contrast. The effect, however, is always startling, sometimes really great. He reminds one of Michelangelo, chipping off frightful fragments in hewing out his statues —which come out gigantic, muscular, and admirably proportioned, it must be owned, after all. There is a pitiless pelting of criticism, (worthy of the illustrious *North American*) which you may thank yourself for bringing on your unlucky head by your own remarks. The St. Cecilia lady, by the by, is Mrs. Sheridan, the mother of the beautiful Mrs. Norton, &c. Her name, I think, was Lindley.

We have little news stirring in the literary way. Bancroft is in labour with the first volume of his Revolutionary history. Longfellow has just let off another pretty little volume of odes and ballads. Ticknor is potting down Spanish literature in a quiet regular way. Sumner has written two or three newspaper columns on the right of search, which I have not yet read, but hear much commended.

I am in the capital of Montezuma, staring about at the strange Aztec figures and semi-civilization.[5] I received last month a rich collection of original documents from a learned Spaniard in London, of original correspondence of the epoch of Ferdinand and Isabella. It consists of letters of these respectable persons, and their principal courtiers; also, of contemporary princes—among others Emanuel the Great of Portugal, Maximilian, Charles V &c, &c. It is interesting enough to hold in one's hands the very letter written three hundred and twenty years since, by the celebrated emperor. The handwriting of the Spaniards of that day, was far inferior to that of the Italians, of which I have several specimens. Charles' autograph is in German text.

I spoke some time since to Lowell about the lectures.[6] He decides for himself, taking no counsel, but his own. He spoke highly of you. But whether this really bodes anything, I know not.

Have you a vacancy in your college for a man like Mariotti? He is a very clever linguist, and a thorough Italian scholar, of course, writes English remarkably, well enough for the British journals, and has a good knowledge of history. In a letter I received from him the other day, he expressed a desire to get a situation in some American college.

Believe me, dear Lieber, Yours most sincerely

WM. H. PRESCOTT

[P.S.] Your pamphlet has not yet made its appearance here.

1. I.e. Columbia College.

2. The College of William and Mary conferred an honorary LL.D. on WHP in July, 1841, and apparently failed to notify the recipient.

3. On January 17, 1842, WHP reminded himself, "Each dinner cost me the next day from the mischief to the eyes." See Prescott (Gardiner, ed.), *The Literary Memoranda*, II, 82.

4. Sir Charles Lyell (1797–1875), eminent geologist and frequent traveler in the United States, wrote travel accounts of his experiences in the New World.

Mary E. Lyell, daughter of geologist Leonard Horner, was WHP's principal correspondent during the last decade of his life.

5. WHP was then writing Chapter IX, the last one in Book III of the *Conquest of Mexico*.

6. Probably referring to the lectures established by John Lowell (1799–1836), who founded Lowell Institute in Boston and its program of lectures by leading scholars in all fields of learning.

142. Memorandum Concerning Eyes

(WHP Papers, Mass. Hist. Soc.; and in Wolcott, *Correspondence of Prescott*, pp. 301–2)

New York, April 28, 1842

Came to this place 3 days since to see Dr. Elliott the Oculist.[1] His opinion after a careful scrutiny is, that the *left eye* has a paralysis of the nerve which covers much of the retina with a deposit of lymph in the coats. That the tremulous iris shows the vitreous humour is affected. That the forcing in of the lens by the blow dissolved a portion of this humour which is a cellular substance and cannot be restored. That the paralysis, (which he considers a suspended circulation, not decay,) may be removed, and the eye recover much power of vision and clearness. That I may, unless something untoward occurs, be even able to see letters, but the tremulousness of the iris would prevent reading. To benefit the eye thus would require six months at least, of which as many weeks under his hands. He would not advise the attempt if my right eye were good. Nor does he urge the matter now.

Right eye. Irritability of the iris, and of the retina; or iritis and retinitis. The latter is the most important, and when carried to a great height fatal to vision. The former leads to the latter. He thinks I use it rashly. Rheumatism, colds, over-use, etc., etc., may bring on retinitis, which is apt, after a sharp attack to impair the vision a little—though often scarcely perceptible. He considers that he could restore that eye so as to enable me to bear light freely, and even read in the evening. He does not think I could ever use it safely five or six hours a day. He would require five or six weeks with him, and afterwards a year's application of remedies at home. External unguents and internal medicines simply to put the body and spirits in a right state.

My own conclusions. Dr. Elliott was much too sudden and sanguine in his former remarks on the *left eye*. It is true he wanted the case, as, indeed, he says he should much have liked it. If he succeeds as he expects now, it would be little benefit to me, as if I cannot read, I gain little. Taking into consideration the uncertainty, and in my judgment, improbability of much benefit, and the tedium of the remedies, I without hesitation, or the least doubt, forever renounce the intention of having that eye touched or treated in any way, by him or any other. As to the *right eye,* I believe its powers at present are not much short of those of most of his patients, who consider themselves restored. If I did not want to read more than they, I, too, could go freely into light. My experience of it by constant exposures in New York, now a proof of this. Indeed, I suspect I might accustom the eye to this more than I now do. I now use my eye more hours than he would approve, if it were restored by him. The loss of the evening is, perhaps, a benefit, as a check on my over-use. I don't believe he could enable me to bear the heats and excitement of much company with impunity. I don't think his patients generally could bear this and use the eyes closely in reading, too. I without hesitation, therefore, decide never to put myself in his hands for this eye, till the power of vision or its health in whatever way may be greatly impaired beyond what they now are. As to the risk of injury, I think he would be very careful, that he has a thorough knowledge of the anatomy of the eye, and apparently a skillful mode of treating it. He has certainly given relief in many cases, though nothing is easier than self-delusion with the eye. But he has been certainly successful, and though there are many who call him quack, more than one respectable physician in New York speaks highly of his practice. In case of serious trouble, I should prefer him to any oculist, and should put myself under his hands. My case of the right eye is not uncommon.

And yet I should not be too hasty in putting myself in his hands. He certainly overstates, and unwarrantably excites hopes by a sudden, positive assertion—and in other cases than mine. He has a quackish tone also, in his remarks on the phenomena of diseases. His ideas of paralysis I do not find so different from those of other physicians. He undoubtedly has all the advantage of long and large experience, shrewd sense, and a skilful hand.

He said I could not gain by using his remedies for giving temporary vigor, etc., to the eye. Not safe to use the eye under their influence—immediately. He thought I derived no particular advantage from his spectacles, and that magnifying glasses would try my eye by the greater concentration of light.

1. Samuel Mackenzie Elliott, a New York oculist, examined and treated WHP's eyes on several occasions.

143.   To Susan Prescott
                     (WHP Papers, Mass. Hist. Soc.)

Carlton House, New York, Friday, 10 A.M. [April 29, 1842]
My dear Wife—
So here I am—a week in New York. Shall I give you an account of how the time goes? Rise about 8—toilette—breakfast &c., ready for action by 10. Meet no one at breakfast that I ever saw before. Indeed there is not a soul in the House that I know. No matter I never see them except at breakfast, which is kept open from 8 till 11. Get an hour and a half to myself, which I am now improving. Visiters begin very early, on travellers at least—perhaps to find them in. I get out as soon as I can, and pay visits till 4, the common dining hour. The town is so large that it takes a long while to pay a few. Yesterday I was caught two miles from home and after 4—and I had to dress and go another mile to dine. But cabs and omnibusses are flitting by constantly. Dine at 5. Wind up with a supper or evening party—at least such has been and is likely to be my division of labours. To bed not much before 12.

My eyes stand it beautifully—as I don't draw on them for reading. But a headache all yesterday and a growl today make me full of good intentions as to temperance. I practiced much self-denial yesterday at dinner, which was beautifully got up with many temptations in the way of eating and drinking. I must say a variety and richness of wines. I have seen nothing like New York. Tell that to our friend the Doctor. I have seen no Boston people—though Jonathan Amory called yesterday on me. I have not called any where but where I have been obliged. It takes up the whole day. I have nine visits to make this morning—and I endeavour under Wainwright's[1] pilotage to walk them for the sake of exercise. So you see I spin a good deal of sheet yarn—dirty yarn enough here. I have made one call however—on Mr. Gallatin[2]—spent half an hour with him yesterday—he talking very fast and animated, like a Frenchman, the whole time—about the Toltecs, Aztecs and aboriginals. He is thoroughly at home there, especially in the philological way, on which he has written admirably. He showed me a bit of plaster from the walls of Palenque, stained bright red. It looked like some I have from Herculaneum.[3] He said his memory was gone—the New Yorkers say it is still a miracle. He put mine to shame and when I endeavoured to set his right, fell into one or two blunders myself—so I don't believe he will think the better of my historic business from the talk. He is the precise counterpart in his appearance and physiognomy of Fagen—the old Jew of Cruikshank's sketching in *Oliver Twist.* When Wainwright introduced me as Mr. Prescott from Boston, he received me civilly, and went to talking with the dear Doctor. Presently he said abruptly, "What Mr. Prescott is it?" When Wainwright told him, he jumped up, ran across the room, and seizing my hand, told me how happy he was to see me under his roof. I shan't tell you what things he said about that immortal work of ours. "Very young man," said he, "I thought he was sixty!" My age seems to excite some curiosity among the natives. I was fairly cornered by some inquisitive ladies yesterday and obliged to confess myself six and forty May 4—with a wife and three children—married 20 years or thereabouts—all which I dealt out as if I were on the stand. They wonder you don't like traveling. All New Yorkers do. You would be very kindly welcomed by these hospitable people and I have had offers of bed and board for you and me from more than one. But I always say, "I shall wait till I see Boston State House begin to move!"

There is a good deal of difference in New York and Boston society and in the appearance of the houses. The rooms are larger, much higher, and showily furnished. The dinners more elaborately got up. I have heard little or no politics at table. The talk chiefly anecdotical —in the literary way below us, certainly. The men very attentive to costume—quite troublesomely so. Women dress much—even in the morning—too much for good taste—both. The women are many of them very pretty—manners much more free and easy than ours* (*A lady told me that Arthur Middleton married merely to propagate the name and race of Middleton!)—and with very kind hearts. I am certain, though one can't rely on an outsider you know—and a lady told me last evening that a friend and near relation of hers whom I greatly praised had the temper of a tiger! The young men are rather too brusque and conceited for my taste. Indeed as characteristic defects of

Boston and New York manners, the one are too prim, the other too pert. A more kind hospitable people have never breathed. The man I like best here is Brevoort,[4] a most amiable and accomplished person. He gave me the tale he promised me from the *Sketch Book*—the "Wife" —Irving's own draught—and did it so handsomely too. He has offered me any other if I prefer it. I should one or two others—but don't think it delicate to say so, as he picked this out thinking I should prefer it. His wife is a woman of a good deal of talent—quite enough *a la Française*. Indeed she has lived in France so long that she became discontented with her own country. She is a very lively agreeable woman however, and well enough read, for conversation, at least. Brevoort built her the most magnificent house, it is allowed, in New York. He has a great fortune; and what is better, such a character as is highly regarded by all. I dine with him on Sunday. He does not entertain much, they say. She is averse of trouble, like some of our friends in Beacon Street in great houses. I wind up in the evening with a little party at the parson's, the most interesting with Lord Morpeth here. Mr. Harvey, dying of a consumption. His wife, whom I have dined in company with, a delightful woman.

Among my calls this morning, one will be a respectable spinster who has sent to Wainwright to ask me to call on her as she cannot on me. She enclosed a note received from Lord Glenelg about "Ferdinand," and offers me letters to his family, thinking I may be going to Europe. You heard Susana speak of him. But my eyes are getting tired.

I have now settled to stay till *Tuesday,* and *no longer*—a *decided decision.* I stay Monday to dine with Mr. Hone[5]—a rather conspicuously ridiculous egotist, but very hospitable—with a fine house, fine pictures, and very good company at his table. He has followed me up very kindly, and been twice to Carlton House to get me to name my day—so as the good "Massachusetts" sails on Tuesday, I yielded. He promised to have only half a dozen and ask Chancellor Kent[6] &c. If they did but know it, I had rather any time dine with an agreeable woman than any Chancellor in the land. Though for that matter the good chancellor is very near an old woman—that is, when he is near his wife. Today I dine with Mr. Griffin![7] How shall I survive it! He apologizes for not being able to ask as many as he should desire on so short a notice. I told him his family was more than enough! How many new acquaintances I shall make! Wherever I go I have been introduced to every body, or nearly every body in the room. My head is as full of names as a dictionary. But they all come out wrong. I am to meet Verplanck[8]—first time for twenty years at Mr. Griffin's. He told Brevoort he was coming to see me today. It don't give me particular pleasure. He is a cur, I suspect.

Adieu dear wife. Love to all the family and to Elizabeth Dexter and Anna Ticknor, and believe me most affectionately your husband,

WM. H. PRESCOTT

Kiss each of the bairns for me. I shall depend on a good account of each of them. Ask Betty to write to me. You won't expect another epistle.*

*P.S. William don't deserve this. I have just been to the Post Office and no letter—5th day, and this my 3d.

Tomorrow I dine with Mr. Cary, who has a very good collection of paintings to see.

1. Jonathan Mayhew Wainwright (1793–1854), heard often by WHP in the pulpit of Trinity Church, Boston, had moved to New York City, where he later became Episcopal bishop.

2. Albert Gallatin (1761–1849), eminent statesman and dedicated scholar, had first been met by WHP in Paris in 1816 when Gallatin was serving as American Minister to France.

3. WHP had been a souvenir collector while in Europe during 1816–17.

4. Henry Brevoort (1791–1847), a wealthy New Yorker who counted Washington Irving among his intimates.

5. Philip Hone (1780–1851), wealthy merchant, diarist, prominent socialite and public-spirited citizen of New York City.

6. James Kent (1763–1847), jurist, is renowned for *Kent's Commentaries*.

7. George Griffin (1778–1860), lawyer and writer on religious themes.

8. Gulian Crommelin Verplanck (1786–1870), prominent in New York literary circles for many decades, possessed wide-ranging interests and was renowned as an orator.

144. From Richard Ford
(WHP Papers, Mass. Hist. Soc.)

Gevitre near Exeter
June 5, 1842

My dear Sir

Permit me to offer you my very best thanks for the copy of your last edition of *Ferdinand and Isabella,* which you have been so kind as to direct Mr. Bentley to send me; I have lived so long in Spain and particularly in the Alhambra that the work possesses for me a more than ordinary interest, great as is that which it has inspired to readers of all countries; indeed it is a history of which America, and if you will allow me to say so, England has every reason to be most proud, and of it may be justly said as was said of Gibbon's[1] that although the first to grapple with a vast subject it has left no room for any future attempt.

I hope that having now flecked your pen, you will soon resume it—*nunc in reluctantis dracones*[2]—Our mutual friend Pascual Gayangos has often suggested as an almost virgin subject, the life of Philip II. The poor performance of Watson is beneath notice—what a new and noble field for you—what an object for a tour to Europe, to inspect the rich archives of England, Paris and Simancas, where as I can tell you from personal inspection, the state papers, interlined by Philip himself are most various and numerous.

We have now in England a learned Spaniard Don Bermúdez de Castro,[3] who is making researches on the subject of Antonio Pérez, whose deeds and fate form one episode in that mysterious period.

I am sure that I need not say if ever your pursuits or inclinations might lead you to visit *old* England, how happy I should be to render you any humble assistance. If you extended your trip into the green vallies of Devon, my house would be truly *a la disposición de Vd.* It contains a decent Spanish library and good Valdepeñas.[4]

I am at this moment doing a little *handbook on Spain* for Murray, of which I shall beg your acceptance of an early copy when published. I am afraid however that the exchange of presents will be after the fashion of Diomedes and Glaucus.[5] I can only say as far as I am concerned that the oftener it is repeated the greater will be the pleasure and profit to Your obliged and faithful Servant

RICH^D. FORD

P.S. Should your friend Mr. Sumner be in America, I beg you to present to him my compliments.

P.S. I was lately at Naples and saw the *pseudo* portrait of Columbus. I am certain that it cannot be of him, and I wrote a few reasons why to Mr. Bentley begging him to send them to you for your consideration. It is a pity for it is indeed a noble portrait.[6]

1. *The Decline and Fall of the Roman Empire.*
2. Horace, *Carmina.*
3. Salvador Bermúdez de Castro (1814–83), historian, translator and diplomat, started and abandoned a translation of WHP's first history.
4. In 1850, in London, WHP did enjoy Ford's hospitality, including his good wines.
5. In the *Iliad,* Glaucus exchanged his golden armor worth a hundred oxen for Diomedes' armor of bronze, worth nine.
6. WHP's endorsement reads: "This gentleman reviewed me in the London *Quarterly Review.* He afterwards sent a fine medallion of Gonsalvo de Córdova to be engraved for the *History of Ferdinand and Isabella* in consequence of which I ordered Bentley to send him a copy."

145.   To Charles Sumner
              (Charles Sumner Papers, Harvard College Library)

                              Fitful Head, July 12 Evening, [1842]

My dear Sumner

I mourn for the Historic Muse. But I do not design to be part or parcel of that in Committee—beg—by my Modern Language Committee shot—exempt from all others.[1]

If the Lyells descend on our cliffs tomorrow—why cannot you join them? My father and mother are in the country, but I will give you a good welcome and champagne and chowder—instead of ditto and turtle. We dine at two—the boat leaves at six—and coach for cars at five. I see Morpeth is at Montreal. Yours faithfully

                                        WM. H. PRESCOTT

1. WHP refused this committee appointment which had been made without consulting him. Although his father had served Harvard as Overseer (1810–21) and Fellow (1820–26), WHP limited his identification with the institution to his membership on the Modern Language Committee.

146.   To William Gardiner Prescott[1]
                   (WHP Papers, Mass. Hist. Soc.)

                              Nahant, August 25, 1842

My dear William,

In order that you should have no room for misconception on your part as to my determinations in respect to your expenses, I now put them on paper. I shall retain a copy of this memorandum, also myself. *I never will pay a bill for any object, necessary or not, in Cambridge or Boston, without it is contracted with my previous knowledge and approbation.*

Notwithstanding this was signified to you on your entrance into College, you have run up a bill for riding, and now a bill at the booksellers, another for merchandise, as it is called, and lastly a bill for books on the Term Bill, which books I could in part have supplied you with. I have settled for the riding bill, and shall charge you with ten dollars of it only. I shall *advance* the money for Owen (booksellers') bill, and charge you with it all except a blank book. I had resolved to charge you with the books on the Term bill which I could have given you, as Webster, and the Molière, a wanton waste of money. Your class books for the last term cost me 39.58, a very shameful thing. But I have concluded to pay it. Hereafter *I shall not pay for any books in the Term bill except I authorise the purchase.* You can always consult me beforehand, for you may always know what books are required. *You will owe me for these advances*—10. Stearns' riding bill—8.75 Owen's book bill (.75 being deducted). Also, for the Euripides, which with duties &c must with the preceding much more than exhaust your funds. *For the deficiency,* I shall take your January presents from your Grandfather,[2] till the balance is paid. I am willing that you should have money, on applying to me, for a saddle horse, or half a chaise, *four times in* a term. I am willing to pay for your riding out in the *Omnibus on Saturdays* when you walk in, or vice versa. I am willing to pay for your *shoe shining, fire-making, your washing, your oil;* also, for *your clothes when I am asked about them first.* For all else, I make you what I intend to be an adequate *allowance.* If you think it insufficient, you can represent it so to me, and if I think it reasonable, I shall increase it. I would advise you by all means to keep a *cash book,* in which you may set down *every cent* you expend and for what. I have done it for a great many years. Acquire, if possible, *methodical habits in money matters,* if you would not be a miserable dependent; as you get into the world. Set down what you receive also; and do these things at *the very time.* I do not mean to put you on a level with those young men who are to inherit a million. You are to work for your living. I can do little or nothing for you, for my income is moderate and is necessarily required for the family, of which you are but a small part. Do not deceive yourself. You will depend on your industry, your knowledge, your talents—on yourself, almost wholly, for progress in the world. Yet your condition, so inferior in a pecuniary view to the rich young men with whom you associate, is better than that of most of your class, who with difficulty get through college and have not the means of support when they are acquiring their professions, as you will have. You have *every reason for contentment if you will improve your great advantages and be prudent.* If not, you will incur debts you cannot pay, and fall into the most contemptible of all positions—*I shall not aid you.* It is better you should suffer now than later. *But it will be your own fault.* You are now free of debt.

I believe you have good sense and candour enough to see that I am disposed to do all for you—as regards expense—that I can afford—and all that your future prospects can possibly justify.[3] Your affectionate father

WM. H. PRESCOTT

1. Collegian Prescott was in his seventeenth year.
2. Apparently William Prescott remembered the birthdays of his grandchildren—Will's being January 27th—with cash presents.
3. The future soon brought more troubles at Harvard and more letters and

fatherly concern. Will was sufficiently the playboy that he possibly reminded WHP of his own days at Harvard, some of which he so regretted that he wanted to avoid a repetition of them by his son.

147.   To Charles Dickens[1]
                     (The Pierpont Morgan Library)

                                    Boston, December 15, 1842

My dear Dickens,

I send you the remainder of Madame de Calderón's work, or rather I have sent it by this same conveyance to Mr. Rich, who will at once deliver it to you for your publisher. It contains volume 2nd with the Contents and Preface of volume 1st and two engravings. Now that I have read the book through more thoroughly, I think it must have success. It is very full of spirited anecdote, and contains accounts of society, much fuller and more curious than any which I have seen in other books of travels in that country, with most of which I am tolerably familiar. Indeed, none but a Spaniard, or the wife of a Spaniard could have had such opportunities for observation, and no one, unless well acquainted with the language of the country, could have so well profited by them. I think you will be pleased too with the descriptions of scenery, which are oftentimes very beautiful pictures. It is an awkward way to advertise a book simply by the initials of its author's name, and as it appears from sundry passages in it, that the letters were written by the wife of the first Spanish minister, residing in Mexico 1839–41, as much as this, certainly, might be said in the advertisement. I have put my own name to the preface, which may be used if it is worth anything. I have been guilty, also, of—what I never meant to have been again—an article in the *North American Review* to give the work a lift here.[2] But I don't suppose the *North American's* wise saws will have any weight with John Bull. I don't see any occasion to trouble you further about the affair, and I am heartily obliged to you for having allowed me to do so thus much. I suppose the English publishers, when the book is out, will let Madame de Calderón see how she looks in an English dress.[3]

Your friends, poetical and professorial, are in good health. But as there is a pretty considerable strip of snow lying betwixt me and [. . .] I don't see so much of them just now. I am hammering away on my old Aztecs, and have nearly knocked their capital about their ears. They die game, certainly, and one can't help feeling a sympathy for them, though they did occasionally fricasee a Christian or two—"a slice of cold clergyman," as Sydney Smith[4] says.

I see by the paper of this morning that Longfellow is delivered of his verses on Slavery—a sop for the South. Pray remember me most kindly to your wife and believe me, my dear Dickens Ever faithfully yours

WM. H. PRESCOTT

1. WHP had met Charles Dickens (1812–70) repeatedly during the English author's American visit earlier in 1842. Dickens' willingness to serve WHP's purposes in English publishing circles led the American to turn to him with Madame Calderón de la Barca's manuscript.

2. The review appeared in the issue of January, 1843. *Life in Mexico During a Residence of Two Years in That Country* was published simultaneously in England and America.

3. Of all the friends-turned-author whom Prescott helped, he possibly did most for Fanny Calderón; see C. Harvey Gardiner, "William Hickling Prescott: Authors' Agent," *Mid-America*, XLI (April, 1959), 67–71.

4. Sydney Smith (1771–1845), English clergyman, essayist, reviewer and wit.

148. To Charles Folsom
(Charles Folsom Papers, Boston Public Library)

January 9, 1843

My dear Folsom—

I am sorry that it will not be in my power to shake hands with his Clubship tomorrow. But instead, must request your acceptance of half a dozen bottles of sherry—some I received from Ticknor twenty years since when it was nearly twenty years old. So it is high time it should receive the *coup de grâce*.[1] Yours faithfully

WM. H. PRESCOTT

1. Apparently Folsom was playing host to the WHP-founded group which was nearing its twenty-fifth anniversary.

149. To William Gardiner Prescott
(WHP Papers, Mass. Hist. Soc.)

February 6, 1843

My dear Son,

You have now come to a most important crisis in your life, one that will either make you better or worse, but which I hope, and will not indeed doubt, must in the end have a good effect on your character, by leading you to reflection and to strong resolution.[1]

You well know what pains I have taken with your education, and how far you have disappointed me and been untrue to your self. Fortunately, however, your defects have been negative rather than positive; and it is in your power to retrace your steps, recover your position, and lay the foundation of a useful and honourable character. In your change of condition you should begin by changing all your habits that are bad in themselves, or may lead to what is bad. Guard against your besetting sin, indolence.

Be early at your work, be punctual at your hours; be methodical in the distribution of your time, even for your light reading. Method and punctuality will make every thing go lightly and easily. The first step neglected makes the second difficult; till the studies which would have been a pleasure, become a burden to you. Your own experience proves this. *Obsta principiis* should be your motto, more than that of any one that I know. You are old enough to look beyond the present moment, to reflect on the inevitable consequences of conduct in this world and that which is to come. If you spend your youth, that is the season of preparation, in idleness, you know that you must be ignorant as a man, must feel mortified, lose your self-respect, and probably sink into the indulgence of coarser tastes and of vice.

You know that laziness and vice must incur the loss of good friends, the contempt of society, and if it gives you a momentary, most illusory gratification, must make you in the long run, wretched. You know that our conduct here is to determine our happiness hereafter; and that word *hereafter* has a terrible meaning which you are old enough to reflect upon.

Do, my dear Son, consider that you are sent into this world for some other purpose than to lead a life of wasteful idleness. God has placed you here to fill a certain sphere of usefulness commensurate with your abilities and opportunities, and for these he will certainly call you to a strict account. When you are tempted, reflect this is right, and that is wrong, and *cost what it may, I will do the right.* I say nothing of the distress which your misconduct must occasion your parents; your own heart will say more than I can. May you never have to know that there is no anguish like that inflicted by an undutiful child. Hard must be his heart who can deliberately distress those who have been always ready to sacrifice every thing for him.

With regard to your expenses, you must remember that you have now exhausted all your resources. Your necessary expenses fall heavy on me. During your suspension your allowance will be 50 cents a week, and I shall pay no bills of any description; living in a private family you will have need of none. You do not go to idle, but to make up for lost time; and your leisure hours will be passed, I trust, in that kind of society which will put you to no other cost than that of good manners.

With the most earnest prayers, my dear William, that you may return to us with principles strengthened, good resolutions perfected into good and settled habits, and with your mind enriched with the fruits of diligent study, I remain now, as always—Your affectionate Father,

WM. H. PRESCOTT

1. Rusticated from Harvard, WHP's elder son was going to Boylston, Massachusetts, a small town near Worcester, to be tutored by a man named Sanford.

150. To William Gardiner Prescott
(WHP Papers, Mass. Hist. Soc.)

Boston, February 27, 1843

My dear Son

I avail myself of the pretty large blank which the Judge[1] has left to write a few lines to you. I have been extremely gratified, as we all have, by Mr. Sanford's letter, and by those you have written to your mother and Grandmother. They bear very satisfactory testimony to your diligence and your good conduct, and what is of greater importance, to your correct way of thinking on matters of lasting concern to yourself. Mr. Sanford speaks in very decided terms of your industry and your deportment generally; and augurs very favourably for the future. I trust that he and we shall not be disappointed. Pray thank him, for me, for his letter, and tell him that I entirely agree with him in his opinions respecting the system of instruction to be pursued; *Multum, non multa* is a good axiom, especially for you. It is more important to go deep and thorough, than to cover a wide superficies. Little England, with her few acres and elaborate cultivation, raises more than ten times the same number of acres under the slovenly cultivation of our own country. You do not want to be able to say you have read such an author but to show it by the good fruits. Do not go over anything without perfectly comprehending it. Remember how carefully Gibbon felt his way along in his early and, indeed, his later studies. Do not omit the literary journal, with remarks and criticisms of your own. Exercise your critical powers freely and independently. In this way you will learn to judge for yourself, and not to be a humble dependent on the judgments of others. In short, get knowledge. A man may skim through a library and yet get no knowledge, from want of thorough reflection and research.

I find you make yourself acceptable to the amiable family in which you are placed. It speaks well for you, and will return in blessings on your own head. Endeavour to establish *principles* of conduct. Find out and always respect the *right*. Seek, by self-examination—say every Sunday—it will not take long—to detect your own errors and erroneous propensities. And then ask the aid of Heaven in your morning and evening prayers to correct them. Self-examination leads to self-knowledge, and that with a good will to self-government. If you can feel only that you improve, you will be rewarded. Your virtuous resolves will become habits, and a good *character*—so far as we may be good—will be formed. You will then be able to mix in the world without the risk of being led away by its alluring temptations—at least without the risk of one who is governed by impulses instead of principles. You will then have, for you will deserve it, what I should wish a son to have —my entire confidence. You will have, what is better, your own self-respect from the consciousness of trying to do your duty.[2]

You have forgotten to advise us how we can send parcels to you. Can they be left at Worcester, and if so, at what house? Or will it be safe to direct them to Boylston? Ascertain this and let us know. Your grandmother would have sent you some split peas, (which are not very easy to meet with, I suppose,) with her receipt for Mrs. Sanford, had she known how to get them to you.

Elizabeth is to have a little party of friends this evening in compliment to Martha Peabody,[3] here on a visit. We wish you could be with us for the evening too.

This letter was too long, I found, to connect with Amory's, to which Elizabeth has added her contribution. As it is desirable to spell correctly, I will when I write to you, notice any orthographical errors I may have remarked in your letters. "Meant" you spell "ment." "Obliged" you spell "oblidged."

Believe me, my dear William, Ever your affectionate Father,

WM. H. PRESCOTT

1. WHP's father was commonly called Judge Prescott, and young William Amory Prescott was known as "the little Judge." Here, as the letter later indicates, the reference is to Amory, then thirteen years of age.

2. Far from being abstract platitudes, most of the advice given by WHP to his son in this period stemmed from his own formula for living.

3. Elizabeth was nearing her fifteenth birthday. Martha Endicott Peabody (1826–66), daughter of Francis Peabody of Salem, made many visits to the Prescotts, as Elizabeth did to the Peabodys.

151.   From Harper & Brothers[1]
                    (WHP Papers, Mass. Hist. Soc.)

                                                New York, April 3ᵈ 1843
Dear Sir,

Mr. Stephens having communicated to us the contents of your letter, respecting the publication of your new book,[2] we beg leave to submit the following proposition, &c.

We shall be happy to publish your "Conquest of Mexico," and pay you one dollar and fifty cents per copy, on all that we may sell, for the use of the Stereotype Plates, Engravings, and Copyright. We have no doubt but that the sale would be extended to twelve or fifteen thousand copies within the four years, and that we shall be able to sell seven or eight thousand copies within the first year. We are willing to pay for five thousand copies within three months from the day of publication or the cash, deducting the interest. Notes will be given at three months for each subsequent edition as soon as published, or the Cash if desired, by deducting the interest. We should of course use our greatest efforts to sell as many as possible, not only for our own reputation, but because it would be to our *interest* to do so. The work would be issued in the style proposed, and we would have it retailed in the principal cities at six dollars per copy. Our wholesale cash price, by the quantity, to booksellers, would be Four Dollars and Eighty Cents per copy.[3] Respectfully, Your Obedient Servants,

HARPER & BROTHERS

1. Of the four brothers in the New York publishing house, Fletcher soon became the one best known to WHP.

2. John Lloyd Stephens (1805–52), the explorer and author who did much to direct modern attention to the Maya culture. More than anyone else, he encouraged WHP to turn to Harper & Brothers. For early correspondence between Stephens and WHP, see Wolcott, *Correspondence of Prescott*, pp. 339–43.

3. These terms became basic points in WHP's first contract with the New York house; see *ibid.*, p. 348.

Meanwhile, in England, Aspinwall was negotiating with Bentley; see *ibid.*, pp. 330–31, 337–38, 343–46.

152.   From Colonel Thomas Aspinwall
                (WHP Papers, Mass. Hist. Soc.)

                                                    April 17, 1843
My dear Sir,

I have this day received your two letters of the first instant, together with one enclosed for Mr. Bentley. They came by the hands of Mr. Rich some hours after the other letters by mail of the 1st (Cunard) and as tomorrow is the last post for the return steamer of the 19th I shall not be able to make up my mind as to the first step in the negotiation or in preparing for it and then begin operations so as to inform you by the approaching conveyance.

I can however assure you that I shall zealously exert myself in your behalf, all in good time, and to much greater advantage with the aid of your judicious and ample suggestions, accompanied as they are with an outline of the subject and the sources from which you have drawn your materials. I think with you that Bentley is first to be dealt with. But I think I shall tell him that you are quite astonished at the difference between the results of the two editions or rather publications in this country and the United States.

I may as well mention that Murray's notes for nearly a thousand pounds have been all duly honored and that the account generally given respecting him is favorable as to his credit and standing. Although, it should be stated at the same time, that he is by no means a temperance man, nor, as formerly, a capitalist. Still however, his daily indulgencies at the dinner table and the desserts, do not apparently interfere at all with the regularity of his business, nor with his cautious and prudent mode of conducting it. He is extremely fastidious in adopting his literary proteges, and that circumstance in addition to his being the aristocratic, church and State, high Tory publisher, gives currency as well as character to his publications, while his honesty ensures to authors a fair proportion of profits.[1]

His son is with him in business and he has no bad habits. The Longmans[2] however are much the safest men in the trade, but their extreme caution and the number of partners in the house make it tedious and difficult to come to conclusions with them.

I do not know whether Mr. Bentley would or could curtail your share of profits from *Ferdinand and Isabella,* in the event of the publication of *Mexico* going into other hands. We are always at his mercy, such as it is. Most truly yours

THOS. ASPINWALL

1. John Murray (1778–1843), well-known English publisher, was always highly regarded by WHP.
2. Both the Longmans and Murray had considered and declined the first history by WHP; see Wolcott, *Correspondence of Prescott,* pp. 15–16.

153.   To Harper & Brothers
                    (Draft, WHP Papers, Mass. Hist. Soc.)

Boston, June 2, 1843

Messrs. Harper & Brothers
Dear Sirs,

In regard to the arrangement you propose respecting the publication of the History, I am truly sorry that it is not in my power to accede to it, as I should desire to consult your wishes and certainly should defer to your better judgement in the matter of publication. But before I made the contract with you I offered the work through Colonel Aspinwall to the English publishers and with the understanding that it would appear here in November. By a letter I have received from this steamer from Colonel Aspinwall, I find that he is now negotiating the sale of the copy-right on this ground,[1] and is like to make an advantageous bargain with Bentley or Murray. I feel bound therefore not to have the work come out before November; otherwise I should have at once complied as far as in my power (though I could not have got the book ready as soon as you desire) with your request. My first volume you can have when you wish, except the preface and contents, which, being paged by different numerals from the text, I have not yet prepared, but intended to postpone this, as well as the preparation of a map which belongs to this volume, to the last. My second volume will probably be stereotyped by the last of July; the first half of the third volume will be stereotyped by the last of August—but the whole work will not be completed till the latter part of September or the first of October. At those dates I can, I have no doubt, put these parts of the work into your hands *on the understanding with you that no part of the book shall be published before November.*

As to the manner of getting out the work, I confess I prefer the whole at once as much more respectable in its appearance. But as the burden of the thing falls on you, I will waive my own preference and agree to your bringing out a volume a month beginning with November, if you prefer, and am only sorry that I am so situated that I am not able to comply with your other propositions.

As to interference from other quarters, I think not much of that. Nobody has my documents. Mr. Folsom, by a translation of the printed letters of Cortés, would, no doubt do some harm to the subject by making it too hackneyed. But the translation even of Cortés' letters you would not find very readable matter for the mass of people.[2]

I shall be obliged by your letting me know when you would like the plates put into your hands in order to be in season for publication in November. I send by Mr. Catherwood,[3] who does me the favor to take this, a copy of *Ferdinand and Isabella,* which you will oblige me by accepting, that it may serve as a standard in the execution of the work. Mr. Catherwood is also good enough to take charge of a block on which the arms of Cortés are cut. These arms were sent me from Mexico, and I should like to have them stamped on the back of the volumes, like those of *Ferdinand and Isabella.* They must be cut, you know, on a *brass plate*. If you consider this an extra charge, put it down to me. Yours very truly

W. H. PRESCOTT

[P.S.] Mr. Folsom can show you a note, if he pleases, which I have written to him.[4]

Since writing the enclosed, it has occurred to me that if you desire it, there can be no objection to postponing the publication of the work till Christmas, since the publishing time in London is January. This was the time in which my former history was published. In that case it would be soon enough for you to have the plates of the volumes a month later even than the times above mentioned. I will thank you if you can let me know at once your decision on this matter and also whether you shall conclude to bring out the volumes monthly —as it will affect some of my own arrangements here and I shall take measures accordingly with my English publishers.

1. For Aspinwall it was a hectic negotiation; see Wolcott, *Correspondence of Prescott,* pp. 352–54, 355–56, 357–59, 363–65.

2. George Folsom (1802–69), historian and antiquarian, was a cousin of WHP's aide Charles Folsom.

3. Frederick Catherwood (1799–1844) won renown with his drawings of Mayan monuments, which WHP greatly admired.

4. WHP's letter to George Folsom is in *ibid.,* pp. 361–62. Folsom's edition of *The Letters and Despatches of Cortes* was published in 1843.

154. Robert Cooke to Colonel Thomas Aspinwall
(WHP Papers, Mass. Hist. Soc.)

Albemarle Street, June 8, 1843

Dear Sir

Mr. Murray desires me to present his compliments to you and thank you for your obliging communication respecting the forthcoming work of Mr. Prescott.

The author has already asked Mr. Murray to name the terms he feels disposed to publish it upon and from which Mr. Murray cannot deviate.

There is no copy right in the work and there is no law to prevent any one from reprinting it in this country.

If Mr. Prescott would like to consign copies of the work to Mr. Murray's care at a certain price, he will be very happy to undertake the agency for him. *This is the way adopted by Mr. Stephens and Mr. Murray and which has been satisfactory to both parties.*

Or if Mr. Prescott prefers it and will send Mr. Murray the sheets of the book as it is printing in New York, he will print at his own risque and expense the work in this country and divide the profits with the author, *in a similar manner as he does with Dr. Edward Robinson the American author*—otherwise than this, in the present unprotected state of the law and the depressed state of literature, he cannot do.[1]

I am, dear Sir, for my Uncle, Faithfully yours,

ROBERT COOKE

[P.S.] Mr. Murray is not very well or would have written himself.

1. This proposition was not acceptable. Meanwhile, WHP's intrusion into the negotiation for the publication of his second history in England complicated the labors of Colonel Aspinwall, who found this his most tedious transaction in behalf of WHP. Bentley again emerged as WHP's publisher in London. The text of the contract, dated August 8, 1843, is in Gardiner, *Prescott and His Publishers,* pp. 294–97.

155.   To George Nichols[1]
                (Autograph File, Harvard College Library)

Boston, June 19, 1843

Mr. Nichols
Dear Sir

I regret I could not have seen you before you went to Salem. As I go to Nahant on Friday, I shall not now have an opportunity of doing so before I go. It will be necessary for me to have a map—probably two maps—one of the environs of the *capital* of Mexico—the other of the route of Cortés through the country. My own maps—I mean some which I have of Humboldt's design—together with my History will readily furnish the materials for them—which might be made like those in *Ferdinand and Isabel*—noticing only the places noticed in the work itself. It seems to me that your familiarity with the story will enable you to prepare and to make the maps without much difficulty and I am sure you would do it correctly.

As it will be necessary for me to get some one to do this before I go to Nahant—I shall be much obliged by *you letting me know if you are inclined* and have time to do it. If so I will send my copy of Humboldt's maps to Cambridge for you. And if you can call over and see me at Nahant—while you are at Salem, I will explain my views about them—or I will write you more particularly about them. Yours very truly

WM. H. PRESCOTT

[P.S.] While at Salem you will have to return the proofs to Cambridge as there is no coach at present from the cars to Nahant—I believe.

1. Aid is solicited from a member of the printing firm of Metcalf, Keith and Nichols.

156.   To William Howard Gardiner
(William H. Gardiner Papers, Mass. Hist. Soc.)

Nahant, June 24, 1843

My dear William,

I send you the introductory portion of my work, making, as you see, nearly half a volume. There are two other chapters which I print in the Appendix in the same sized type with these which form a proper conclusion of the subject and which cost me much more labor than anything that I send you. They relate to the sources of the Mexican civilization, the architectural remains of the country &c., &c. Should you see any *blunders,* pray note them down. Defects of taste, bad writing &c., &c., must run for luck. The iron law of stereotype forbids change for lighter causes.[1]

I don't care to have the thing seen by other eyes; and when your own have worked through it, at your entire *leisure,* have the goodness to send it to the house at Bedford Street endorsed to be sent to me at Nahant. Yours always affectionately

WM. H. PRESCOTT

1. Gardiner, whose criticism was always welcome and usually sought by WHP, did not write a major published review of this work. Earlier George and Anna Ticknor had given the manuscript their critical attention.

157.   To Metcalf, Keith and Nichols
(Autograph File, Harvard College Library)

Nahant, August 19, 1843

Messrs. Metcalf, Keith and Nichols,
Dear Sirs,

The Index is now completed, which I return to Mr. Sibley. It now makes between forty and fifty pages. You would oblige me by asking him to swet it down to thirty by dashing in the scissors.

I send you the remainder of the Contents and an account of the maps and illustrations. You have now to print the rest of the Appendix and the Index, making in all about sixty pages besides the Contents, which remain yet to be printed.

This cannot be accomplished in a month at the rate we now proceed. The *latest* period to which the work can be delayed and when I should receive the whole copy of proofs from the plates is *Wednesday, August 30th,* as I must send them to town the next day to go by the steamer of September 1. This makes no allowance—&c—to chance of detention on Wednesday by weather.

I shall be absent from Monday till Friday, i.e. Thursday evening so that proofs may be sent to Nahant Friday morning as usual, as I have twice mentioned to Mr. Nichols. My manuscripts have been sent to town and Mr. Otis[1] will be there to oversee the daily corrections. He will be at the house in Bedford Street by nine o'clock and will have the proofs ready to be returned to Cambridge every afternoon without fail. It will not be necessary for me to see either the Appendix or the Index. I should like to see the Contents, i.e. *one page of them* for the model —but I would not delay the proofs a moment on that account. If I am not here, therefore, to see it, let it be printed on the model of *Ferdinand and Isabella.*

The Index might be printed like that in *Ferdinand and Isabel.* I know no better model. It should be sent to England by September 1 or the printers there will never be able to accommodate it to their edition for October 15.[2] It is unnecessary for me to see the Index at all—as I cannot correct it—even if I am at Nahant.

Yesterday both batches of proofs were returned by mistake. I wish you would send back mine.[3] Yours truly,

WM. H. PRESCOTT

1. Edmund B. Otis was WHP's reader-secretary between 1842 and 1846, the most productive period of the historian's creative life.

2. The reconciliation of the English and American publication schedules gave rise to pressures which WHP found most distasteful.

3. At this stage of the process which converted manuscript into book, WHP was a kind of literary generalissimo.

158.   To Charles Folsom
(Charles Folsom Papers, Boston Public Library)

September 4, 1843

My dear Folsom

I inclose you a check for one hundred and fifty dollars—being the sum which we approved—for your services in revising the *Conquest.* I beg leave to assure you, however, that I do not think that a compensation can be made in money for the services of friendship—as I consider yours. And I am under great obligations to you for the patient good-nature and the conscientiousness with which you have gone over the work.[1] Yours very sincerely

WM. H. PRESCOTT

1. One week later, at Pepperell and about to enter upon another period of literary lounging, WHP summarized, for his future guidance, his recent experience with his second history; see Prescott (Gardiner, ed.), *The Literary Memoranda,* II, 104–7.

159.   To William Gardiner Prescott
            (WHP Papers, Mass. Hist. Soc.)

                              Pepperell, September 24th, [1843]

My dear William,

We were all very glad to have a letter from you and I was pleased to find you could give so good an account of your industry.[1] It was what I had expected, as I knew your intentions were good and I cannot but hope that the events of the last year will have made a permanent impression on you. I am glad to find you associated with so good a scholar as Cary;[2] it will be a help and a pleasure to both of you. I would give close attention to the Greek, and try to understand the beauties of the language. Its various dialects, its melody and strength, and its infinite power of compounding or rather of being compounded into new and significant words give it a superiority over all languages ancient and modern. Then it is the root of modern tongues, and the works written in it are the master-pieces of literature. A knowledge of some Greek is indispensable to a gentleman—and a knowledge of a good deal is essential to a scholar.

Your Uncle and Aunt Ticknor, Miss Austin and Anika[3] have been passing the week with us and leave tomorrow. Your grandmother goes with them to Boston and will stay there till Thursday morning. Our friends have been very agreeable—though your Aunt Ticknor is neither in very good health nor spirits—for her. They were disappointed at not seeing you on one of the Saturdays after we left and before they came up here. Martha Peabody passed a week here also, and was taken off by her father on Wednesday forenoon at five minutes notice—somewhat sudden, as we all expected that he would pass the day with us. She is a delightful girl, and we had some pleasant walks—and she taught your sister to be quite a clever whip—as she has shown, more than once, since her departure.

I expect to have from you bulletins of your conduct and progress—once a fortnight—you know. Remember with you—more than most any one—the maxim is true—*C'est le premier pas qui coute.* I have confidence you will not take the "premier pas."

All the household desires love to you, with whom, believe me, my dear Son Your affectionate Father

                                                W. H. P.

1. Returned to college, Will was entering upon his senior year at Harvard.
2. George Blankern Cary (d. 1846).
3. Emmeline Austin (b. 1808) was the daughter of Samuel Austin of Boston. Anna Ticknor (1823–97), daughter of George and Anna and a special favorite with WHP, was called Anika by the historian, to distinguish her from her mother. To her he was Uncle William.

160.   From Josiah Quincy[1]
(WHP Papers, Mass. Hist. Soc.)

Cambridge, 12 October 1843

William Hickling Prescott LL.D.

Sir

It is to me a great pleasure to be the medium of transmitting the accompanying testimonial of the high and just sense entertained, by the Corporation and Overseers of Harvard University, of your character, talents and virtues.[2]

As no man more highly appreciates them, so no one more sincerely rejoices at every evidence of their being generally known and universally acknowledged, than very truly and respectfully Your friend and humble servant

JOSIAH QUINCY

1. Josiah Quincy (1772–1864), statesman, scholar, President of Harvard (1829–45) and friend of the Prescott family.
2. Harvard had just conferred the honorary degree of Doctor of Laws upon WHP, along with his friends Bancroft and Sparks.

161.   From Colonel Thomas Aspinwall
(WHP Papers, Mass. Hist. Soc.)

London 3 November 1843

My dear Sir,

Yesterday Mr. Rich sent me a copy of Bentley's edition of your *Mexico* for which I beg to return you my sincere and warmest thanks. It is got up in quite as good style as the *Ferdinand*—perhaps better.

I have received the notes of Bentley three each for £216.13.4[1] at the respective terms of 6, 9 and 12 months from the 24th of October.

The difficulty arising from the misnomer was adjusted between Mr. Bentley's solicitor and myself by a memorandum signed by each party at the foot of the other's part of the agreement.[2]

Our excellent friend Mr. Everett is in great affliction for the loss of his eldest daughter. She was a person of extraordinary qualities and

proportionably dear to all her family. He is much admired and respected. I am sorry to learn by the last papers that his removal is
threatened.[3]

Ever my dear Sir most truly yours

THOS. ASPINWALL

1. The contract for the *Conquest of Mexico* provided for outright sale of the
English rights to Bentley for the sum of £650.

2. Trying to expand the middle initial of the historian's name, his agent
and publisher had incorrectly written Henry into the contract.

3. At this time Edward Everett was American Minister to the Court of St.
James.

162.   To Harper & Brothers
                       (Draft, WHP Papers, Mass. Hist. Soc.)

                                      Boston, December 19th, 1843

Dear Sirs

I send you by this mail a *Courier* of Saturday and an *Advertiser* of
yesterday, as it is barely possible you may not have them. The piece
in the *Courier* was written by Professor Felton of Harvard University,
a scholar whose name might possibly be of use to you. He will follow
it up with two similar articles in the *Courier* on the succeeding volumes. The extracts in the *Advertiser* I consider quite as effective a way
of introducing a book to notice as criticism, perhaps more so, though
both may serve to support each other. As they will be ready at your
hand, they might be sent by you to some other paper. There will be a
full notice of the work in the *Advertiser* when the whole work comes
out, by an excellent writer. These two papers are the ones of most importance in this town and indeed in New England. My friend, of whom
I spoke in my last, as to contribute a notice in the morning *Post,* was
anticipated by someone in the paper in an article in which he employed himself in digging up bones of poor old Ferdinand and Isabella,
God bless them, who I thought were quietly at rest in their graves. I
am much obliged to you for the many notices which you continue to
send me. I suppose one cannot judge fairly of the prospect of the sales
until the whole work has been issued some weeks.[1] But I shall be delighted to receive your accounts of them from you; and I am sure I say
this not more on my own account than on yours, for you have made
such efforts and done so handsomely by the work that I shall be chagrined if it does not answer your expectation.

In addition to my twenty-five copies of volume III, I wish you would
send me 16 complete sets of the work as soon as published. They **might**

come in a separate box and if it would be more convenient to you, you can send them on Monday instead of the day of publication. A greater part of them are to go at once abroad, the remainder are for literary societies and a few poor friends who would not be likely to buy the work. A good number of my original copies have been distributed so as to help the work and with one or two exceptions with good results.

I will thank you also to send the entire work as soon as published to the persons and places mentioned in the enclosed slips of paper, putting each slip in its copy as before. That to the American Philosophical Society may be sent to Mr. DuPonceau.[2] That to Mr. Middleton may be sent to Mr. Taylor's bookstore in Washington, in which city he is now staying. That to Dr. Lieber may be sent to Charleston. If you will, advise me what bookseller you send it to there, that I may inform him.

I take this occasion to acknowledge the receipt last week of the whole sum due on the copy-right of 5000 copies.[3]

I think Mr. George Griffin will take charge of the copy to Mrs. Sigourney[4] if not convenient to you to forward it. Remember the broken volume 1st to me and the volume III to my New York friends.

1. Published one volume at a time, the three-volume work appeared in New York between December 6 and 21, 1843.
2. Peter Stephen DuPonceau (1760–1844), soldier, lawyer, scholar and resident of Philadelphia, was respected by WHP for his philological studies.
3. I.e. $7500, WHP's payment being at the rate of $.50 per volume or $1.50 per copy of the work.
4. Lydia Howard Huntley Sigourney (1791–1865), writer of prose and verse which won her wide popularity, lived most of her life in Hartford, Connecticut.

163.   To Peter Stephen DuPonceau
(The Academy of Natural Sciences of Philadelphia)

Boston, December 23rd, 1843

Mr. DuPonceau
My dear Sir,

I have directed my publishers, the Messrs. Harper, to send you a copy in my name of the *History of the Conquest of Mexico*, which you will oblige me by accepting; and you will confer an additional favor on me, if you will be so good as to take charge of another copy which I have requested them to send to you for the American Philosophical Society. Should they not reach you at once, I will thank you to advise me of it.

I sincerely hope the work will have some interest for you, and especially that portion of it in which I have endeavoured to exhibit a full and faithful delineation of the Aztec civilization. There are few so well qualified as yourself to estimate the difficulties, and to decide on the success of such an attempt. And I shall feel that I have failed, if it does not receive the approbation of those few critics who, like yourself, are most competent to decide on its merits and its defects.

With great respect, I am, my dear Sir Your friend and servant

WM. H. PRESCOTT

164.   To Theodore Sedgwick Fay[1]
(Draft, WHP Papers, Mass. Hist. Soc.)

Boston, December 23rd, 1843

Sir,

Will Mr. Fay allow one who is personally unknown to him to ask a favour of him? It has occurred to me that, as I see it stated in the newspapers that Mr. Wheaton[2] is to be in Paris very shortly, he may possibly be absent when this letter reaches Berlin. As an entire stranger I may seem to have small ground for inviting your attention to my concerns. But should Mr. Wheaton be absent, I should be much obliged if you could see that the letters and parcels are sent to the gentlemen to whom they are addressed, and if you could make arrangements to have the copies made, as I have indicated in the letter. Our common friend Mr. Sumner induces me to think that this will not be taking too great a freedom with you; and I trust that you will consider the circumstances under which the request is made an apology for it.[3]

With sincere esteem, I am my dear Sir Your obedient servant

WM. H. PRESCOTT

1. Theodore Sedgwick Fay (1807–98), who served in various European capitals, was, at this time, Secretary of the American legation in Berlin.

2. Henry Wheaton (1785–1848), jurist, diplomat and historian of international law, assisted WHP's researches during his term as American Minister to Prussia (1837–47).

3. Fay became one of WHP's aides, furthering the historian's search for materials in German archives related to Philip II; see Wolcott, *Correspondence of Prescott*, pp. 455, 462, 486–87.

165.   From William Howard Gardiner
(WHP Papers, Mass. Hist. Soc.)

Tuesday, December 27th, 1843

Dear William

With many thanks for so acceptable a Christmas gift, I return your own copy of the *Conquest*, which I found a great solace on my journey.

I have read it through—and have no hestitation in saying that it is destined to be more popular even than its predecessor[1]—not because it is more meritorious (for what do *the people* know about that?)—but because the subject and the manner of treating it make an excellent substitute for one of Scott's best historical novels. It's as good as fiction —which ought to be highly gratifying to the compiler of facts. The *Ferdinand and Isabella* embraced matter which must make it intrinsically a more valuable contribution to literature—but in point of literary execution I consider the *Conquest* a decided improvement. I am particularly pleased to see that you have left out those "I"'s—and diminished the sprinkling of Anglicised foreigners. In short if I held the spiteful pen of a reviewer even, I do not see how I could quarrel with it much. All I fear now is that you will be wholly spoiled by success and bury yourself utterly in old chronicles for the sake of working out new histories that will do to stand on the same shelf with these. I hope you'll not get into a *habit* of exceeding yourself.

As for me, I am a restored man in all senses, and ready now to try a case of law, or a case of claret, as the case may be. I hope to begin today with a sample of the latter in your company—being ever yours

W. H. GARDINER

1. The following figures support Gardiner's prophecy: between 1837 and 1959, *Ferdinand and Isabella* was printed approximately 150 times; between 1843 and 1959, the *Conquest of Mexico* was printed approximately 200 times; see Gardiner, *Annotated Bibliography*, pp. 3–128.

166.   From George Stillman Hillard
(WHP Papers, Mass. Hist. Soc.; and in Wolcott, *Correspondence of Prescott,* p. 430)

Boston, January 1, 1843 [1844]

Dear Prescott

Thanks for your present and your kind—very kind note, which is so characteristic an effluence of that warm heart of yours, which makes those who have the privilege of being your friends entirely forget that you are a great historian and only think of you as a person to be loved. How richly do your golden words repay me for all the time spent upon my article,[1] and how much pleasure do I feel in the thought that my work has satisfied you. If it have any merit, it has come from the inspiration of my theme, and you fairly reclaim it as "your thunder." The book I shall value for its rich flow of eloquence and poetry, but now as your gift. Dr. Johnson said that if you called a dog "Hervey," he should love it, and I am sure that an association with your image would give point to the lines of Blackmore and make Timmerman on Solitude a readable book. I am confident that you will not think that I am playing a flatterer's part when I tell you that I esteem my friendship with you as among the best of my possessions; and though among the latest of your friends, I claim not to be behind the oldest of them in attachment to your person and in sympathy with you in your literary success.

It seems almost a waste of ink to wish you a happy new year, for if you are not happy, who can be?—enriched as you are with such gifts and privileges—among not the least of which I esteem the happiness of having your excellent father and mother spared to you to rejoice in your triumphs and to have the evening of their days gilded with the warm light reflected from the blaze of your fame.[2] Faithfully yours

GEO. S. HILLARD

1. Hillard's review of the *Conquest of Mexico* had just appeared in the January, 1844, issue of the *North American Review*. Later he published a sensitive and detailed description of WHP's homes.

2. As the new year opened, WHP was reveling in complimentary words of more than one hundred newspaper reviews, and he was drawing conclusions about techniques of his about which he had been entertaining doubts. See Prescott (Gardiner, ed.), *The Literary Memoranda*, II, 114–15.

167.   From Lord Morpeth
(WHP Papers, Mass. Hist. Soc.)

Castle Howard January 23, 1844

My dear Prescott,

You will have thought me very much overlong in acknowledging your most gracious and precious gift of your *Mexico,* but I sent you a message that you were not to have a word from me about it till I had quite finished it, and as I read it out loud to my Mother and Sister, this has not taken place so soon as you might have expected.

And now my poor verdict will come after you are saturated with the public applause, and will care mighty little for individual suffrages. Still I will hope that however careless you may be of the approbation, you will not be wholly indifferent to the pleasure, with which our occupation has been attended. Nothing could be more satisfactory than to roll along through your easy, animated, and pictured periods, and your candid and discriminating but unassuming disquisitions, and to have my own interest and approval shared by those to whom I read; and then further to find the wide circle without corroborate our verdict

"And Nations hail thee with a love like mine"[1]

You are probably aware that the Review in the *Quarterly* is by Milman,[2] it does not entirely satisfy me, though I know he intended it to
be entirely cordial. When I began, I intended to note down everything
to which I took exception, and then send this captious catalogue on to
you; but I found the points were so few, and for the most part so
minute, that I soon gave this up. I will just mention all that I have
preserved. To begin with a great criticism, I object to the word gentleman*ly*, instead of—*like*.

Vol. I p. 25. I doubt whether some injustice is not done to the character of the modern Greeks, perhaps the [*sic*] rather after what we have
seen of their conduct in, and since, their last Revolution, of which the
Historian was not cognisant when he wrote; but especially I should
imagine that he underrates their capacity.

p. 135. I think that at the end of the 1st note, there is a slight degree
of speaking to Buncombe.

p. 324. At the end of the page, and now and then elsewhere, I am a
little reminded of my private conversations in your up-stairs library.

I think that for an English classical historian, as I hold you to be,
you permit yourself too frequently the use of French words.

And, for your relief, to conclude, I think one sees throughout your
book the most obvious purpose to be thoroughly just, but at the same
time I think you have a bias, not unnatural, to the Spanish side. You
distinctly acquit Cortés of cruelty, and you inspire one with quite a
strong attachment for Sandoval; but in doing both these things, ought
you to have omitted, though I am aware you have the excuse of its not
being within the period of your following the history up closely, the
slight circumstance of Sandoval, after consultation with Cortés, having
burned 60 Caciques and 400 Nobles? This is quoted by Robertson
from Gómara. I trust that you will not by this time repent of having
sent me your book. I assure you the gift was not misplaced.

Tell Sumner there is of course nothing he may not show to you,
Hillard, or Judge Story, but that of course it must be under the most
sacred confidence. We are getting through the mildest winter almost
ever remembered. Before you receive this, I probably shall be a Member of the House of Commons, a re-entry upon public turmoil of which
I do not at all relish the prospect. Are you beginning Pizarro? How
you must have pleased old Rogers by your mention of him;[3] he will
clearly set you down for a more agreeable man than Judge Story. Pray
give my kindest regards to your family. Believe me ever Affectionately
yours

MORPETH

1. The origin of this line has not been established.

2. See *Quarterly Review,* LXXIII (December, 1843), 187–235. Henry Hart Milman (1791–1868), Dean of St. Paul's and famous as poet and historian, was much esteemed in society. For many years he and WHP corresponded.

3. Speaking of the meeting of Cortés and Pizarro in Spain, WHP had written, ". . . one of the most illustrious of living poets . . . in a brief, but beautiful sketch, has depicted the scene in the genuine coloring of the age" (Prescott, *Conquest of Mexico,* III, 314). The reference was to "The Voyage of Columbus" by Samuel Rogers (1763–1855), who was highly esteemed in both social and intellectual circles in England.

Lord Morpeth, himself, must have been pleased by WHP's use of some of his verses; see *Conquest of Mexico,* I, 341–42.

168.   To Jared Sparks
(Jared Sparks Papers, Harvard College Library)

Boston, March 18, 1844

My dear Sparks

I am very much obliged to you for your friendly present of the volume of American Biography. The New Series opens well, with such good writers and good subjects. I have not yet read Everett's memoir, but I have hastened to the one written by you—with great pleasure. It is a wonderful story of enterprise sustained by a high purpose. You have to be it *con amore.* I knew something of LaSalle's adventures, before, but you have given a new revelation of his character, while you have summed up admirably in the conclusion. One would have liked to see some particulars of his painful journey from the Illinois to Fort Frontenac.

I was offered last month by a Mr. French of New Orleans a quantity of manuscripts relating to the discovery and settlement of Louisiana if I would write the history of it.[1] It is not in my line[2]—but the manuscripts may be in yours. Yours always sincerely

Wm. H. Prescott

1. Benjamin Franklin French (1799–1877), whose publications include *Historical Collections of Louisiana.* His letter to WHP is in Wolcott, *Correspondence of Prescott,* pp. 438–39.

2. In this period WHP was acquiring materials related to both Peru and Philip II—see *ibid.,* pp. 436–37, 439–41, 444, 448–49, 453, 454. Otherwise, WHP was still loafing.

169.   From Harper & Brothers
(WHP Papers, Mass. Hist. Soc.)

New York, April 25, 1844

Dear Sir,

We should be pleased to issue your "Ferdinand and Isabella" in numbers, on the following conditions: You are to furnish the stereotype plates of the said work now used by Messrs. Little & Brown, and also (in addition to those already published in the work) thirty-six engraved illustrations, as proposed by you, all at your own expense. We will publish the work from these plates and Engravings in not to exceed twenty-four numbers at twenty-five cents each at retail, and not to exceed sixteen cents and two-thirds at wholesale. We will pay you in cash (less interest for three months), for the exclusive use of the said plates and Engravings, and the copyright for one year from the time that the work shall be published complete, one dollar per copy for three thousand copies, and at the same rate for the additional copies which we may sell of said work. For those which we may sell in muslin binding we will pay you fifty cents additional, or one dollar and fifty cents per copy. Very respectfully yours &c

HARPER & BROTHERS

P.S. The amount due according to the above proposition would be paid on the publication of the first number.[1]

1. Although the Harpers soon became the publisher of *Ferdinand and Isabella,* this proposed serialization of the work never materialized.

170.   To Albert Gallatin
                     (The New-York Historical Society)

Boston, May 9th, 1844

Hon. Albert Gallatin
My dear Sir,

I send you by Harnden today the volumes of Lord Kingsborough's great work on Mexican Antiquities—volumes 1, 2, 3, 5.[1]

There are seven volumes published. The three first contain all the original Aztec manuscripts published in this work. The fifth volume gives the interpretation in Castilian of the three codices which alone have been explained.

Of the remaining volumes the fourth is devoted to Dupaix and Castañeda's drawings of the ruins of Palenque. The sixth contains the English translation of Dupaix's notes, and of the three Spanish interpretations of the codices contained in volume fifth. In this volume are also the cobweb speculations of Lord Kingsborough which you did not desire.[2] The seventh volume contains Sahagún's Mexican History, of which I send you a copy in a more portable form and equally full and exact.

I well believe there is no man in the world who can so well profit by these materials as yourself; and I am most happy to have it in my power to supply you with them. With the sincere hope that they may afford you some amusement, while they help you to throw light on a very perplexing subject, I remain, my dear Sir, with great respect, Your friend and servant

WM. H. PRESCOTT

[P.S.] Will you have the goodness to drop me a line informing me if the books come safe to hand?

1. Prompting WHP's generosity was Gallatin's continuing study of Mexican ethnology.

2. I.e. Lord Kingsborough's theory on the relationship of the Indians of Mexico to lost tribes of Israel.

171.   To Grenville Mears
                    (Draft, WHP Papers, Mass. Hist. Soc.)

Bedford Street, June 27, 1844

Mr. Grenville Mears
Sir,

I have conversed with my father on the subject of my brother's debt to you; and he has agreed to settle it with you, if you are so disposed, by paying to you fifty per cent on it, if it does not exceed six hundred dollars. This is giving it a preference over every other debt, as none were paid more than eighteen per cent in the final settlement with the creditors.[1] Your obedient servant

WM. H. PRESCOTT

1. Following Edward Goldsborough Prescott's death at sea, the Prescott family was occupied with settling his numerous and sizable debts.

172.   To Brantz Mayer[1]
        (Charles Roberts Autograph Collection, Haverford College Library)

Boston, July 24, 1844.

Brantz Mayer Esq.
My dear Sir,

I am much obliged to you for the *Catholic Review,* which you have been so kind as to forward me. It is written with considerable ability, and in the general tone is encomiastic enough to satisfy a more craving man than, I trust, I am. There is one objection to be sure, and that is a sweeping one. Yet I shall not plead guilty to the charge of *bigotry.*

Universal toleration has always been my creed, and I have strictly endeavoured to make myself one of the age and nation of which I wrote. I have had the satisfaction of being thanked by more than one Roman Catholic for not forcing my Protestantism more strongly on the reader. Yet the Baltimore journal thinks me a blasphemer, and the *Dublin Review* prays in a gentler tone "for my conversion from spiritual error." So I suppose there must be two sides to it, and that I am not quite so liberal as I thought I was.

But this is enough of myself. The Calderóns, with whom I believe you are well acquainted, have returned to this country to take up their residence at Washington again. They seem in good health and spirits and propose to pass the hot weather at Newport.

With much regard, Believe me, my dear Sir, very truly yours

WM. H. PRESCOTT

1. Brantz Mayer (1809–73) served as Secretary of the American legation in Mexico (1841–42) and subsequently as Secretary of the Maryland Historical Society. In 1844 he published *Mexico as It Was and as It Is*.

173.   To Dr. Samuel Cabot[1]
(Edwin Arlington Robinson Treasure Room, Colby College Library)

Pepperell, September 11, 1844.

Dr. Cabot

My dear Sir,

I received a letter today from the New York publishers of Mr. Catherwood's drawings, informing me that their agent was to be in Boston yesterday—on the tenth. I do not know his address there, but I presume you will find no difficulty in getting it from some of the booksellers. It is possible that you may give him some hints that may be for his advantage. I have written a few remarks on the work for the *Courier* and a little notice for the man to take round with the subscription paper.[2] And I am sorry that I cannot be in town while he is there.

Believe me, my dear Sir, Faithfully yours,

WM. H. PRESCOTT

1. Samuel Cabot (1815–85), Boston surgeon and ornithologist, had accompanied John Lloyd Stephens and Frederick Catherwood to Yucatan in 1841.

2. WHP's unsigned puff of Catherwood's *The Views of Ancient Monuments of Central America, Chiapas, and Yucatan*, which had just appeared in London, was carried in the *Boston Courier*, September 17, 1844, p. 2.

On August 12, 1844, WHP did his first writing on his third history.

174.   To Harper & Brothers
                    (Draft, WHP Papers, Mass. Hist. Soc.)

                                        Boston, October 28th, 1844

Messr. Harper & Brothers
Dear Sirs,

I will thank you to send me half a dozen copies of the *Conquest of Mexico,* as soon as you conveniently can.

I have just returned from the country where I have been passing the summer. I see your last edition in the bookstores, but I am sorry to see it look so thin and lank. It looks as if it had fallen into a decline; and the paper has a yellow unwholesome look, very inferior to our standard. I am afraid that the purchaser who compares this edition with the preceding will think twice before he pays for it. I trust, however, that the quality of the paper was an oversight, as I could not consent to have the books deteriorate in execution, unless on a regular plan of a cheaper edition altogether, which might be furnished alongside of a better one for those who prefer this last.

I had hoped before this to have heard from you respecting another edition of "the Conquest." They tell me here they were unprovided with books for some weeks at the bookstores. But I suppose we must not expect the demand for works so expensive as this to be so great as for cheaper ones.

I find but fifty copies remaining here of the last edition of *Ferdinand and Isabella,* and it will be now necessary to make a new contract. You remember, no doubt, your proposition to me last spring to take fifteen hundred copies on precisely the same terms that you took the *Conquest of Mexico,* so soon as the present edition should be disposed of. Although you have not withdrawn that proposition, yet as several months have elapsed, you may have changed your mind, and I shall not avail myself of it, till I hear from you that you now wish to abide by it, when I shall ask Little and Brown's proposals and bring the matter to an issue.[1]

I have now fairly got to work on my next history, and have been digging gold, I hope, out of the Peruvian mountains this season. Whether it is gold, or only pinchbeck, time will show.[2] Yours very truly,

                                        WM. H. PRESCOTT

1. When the Harpers repeated their offer and Little, Brown and Co. failed to match or exceed it, the stereotype plates for the first history shifted from Boston to New York.

2. For WHP's progress on the early chapters of the third history, as well as his comments on an improved method for note-taking, see Prescott (Gardiner, ed.), *The Literary Memoranda,* II, 132–34.

175.   From Count Adolphe de Circourt
                   (WHP Papers, Mass. Hist. Soc.)

                                           Paris, November 6th 1844

My dear Sir,

As, by some unexpected circumstance, the publication of Mr. Chevalier's *second* article in the *Journal des Débats* is somewhat delayed, I
will wait no longer for sending to you my little appreciation. By the
next opportunity, I'll send the second article, which will be soon followed by another criticism of Chevalier in the *Revue de Deux Mondes,*
and a third, from me, in the *Bibliothèque Universelle de Genève.*[1] All
this will be little compared with the value of the work, which in point
of literary art and style, of researches, sound judgment and truly historical philosophy leaves so far behind every thing previously written
on the same subject. Our only regret (I speak for some of our colleagues
here) is that you had not completed your undertaking in giving a short,
but clear account of the subjugation by the Spaniards of Mechoacan,
Xalisco, Guatemala and the remainder of the provinces who, during
the lifetime of Cortés, were added to Charles the Fifth's dominions.
A supplementary chapter, drawn from your copious notes, and written
with your inimitable strength and lucidity, could, in a next impression
of the Work, supply that *desideratum.* One could, perhaps, wish too
that the Contents of the Appendix were transferred to the work itself,
as far as it relates to the Aztec civilisation.[2]

I enclose here the letter written to Chevalier by a literary person who
is proposing to translate your history into French.[3]

Be so good as to transmit to our excellent friend Mr. George Ticknor, the enclosed letter and brochures, destined to him; excuse my
haste, and believe me, my dear Sir, Truly yours

                                           A. DE CIRCOURT

1. With WHP's second history, as with his first one, Circourt was a leading
contributor to the American's widening reputation on the Continent. See also
Wolcott, *Correspondence of Prescott,* pp. 530–33.
2. None of these well-founded suggestions was adopted.
3. The French translation by Amédée Pichot was published in Paris in 1846.

176.   From Colonel Thomas Aspinwall
                   (WHP Papers, Mass. Hist. Soc.)

                                           London 9 December 1844

My dear Sir,

The parcel mentioned in your welcome letter of the 15th ultimo has not yet made its appearance. When it does so, the publication of the Essays shall have my best attention in conformity with your wishes and instructions.[1]

I see that Bentley continues to advertise the 3d Edition of *Ferdinand and Isabella* and I infer from that circumstance that he has not issued a fourth.

The election—what a disappointment to all you sinners of Whigs by nature, and what a pity that you did not know earlier which was the best man. But I suppose you could find out who Mr. Polk was.

Ever yours in perfect truth[2]

T. Aspinwall

1. On January 7, 1845, Aspinwall negotiated a half-profits contract with Bentley for the *Biographical and Critical Miscellanies,* the title under which WHP unified and reprinted various essays. The text of the agreement is in Gardiner, *Prescott and His Publishers,* pp. 297–98.

2. Following the death of his father on December 8, 1844, WHP suffered a prolonged melancholy which interrupted his scholarly activity.

177.   From David Sears II[1]
(WHP Papers, Mass. Hist. Soc.)

Boston, 24 December 1844

My dear Sir,

In answer to your note of yesterday,[2] I have the pleasure to enclose a list of notes taken in 1842, and amounting to $117,032.52, and also our general accounts for the last two years, by which you will find that we have received $30,493.52 of that sum,—less what may be paid for interest, and for sales of land—leaving in round numbers a balance due to us of about $100,000. From the foot of our list of notes it has been my habit to deduct about 20% for losses, failures &c. This is ample on the list I enclose.

We have 6500 acres of land unsold. This is mostly of an inferior quality and may sell for somewhere near $2.00 per acre. This land our agent advises us to sell by Public Auction in the spring. I have requested him to write us on the subject that you may judge of the strength of his reasons. Those he has stated on his list of uncontracted lands, are however in my mind sufficient.

In direct answer to your question, and for the purposes you mention, I should estimate the present amount of your father's *personal* property in Maine at $18,000, and its value owing to the trouble of collection &c at $15,000.

The clause in your father's will puts Mr. Dexter and yourself in his place, *with full powers,* and this I am confident will render our connexion both satisfactory and easy.

The memorandum on Webster's old contract will not serve. Another contract has since been made, and acted on, and my request was intended to be that that form should be examined, and if approved, copied with the necessary changes and executed by ourselves and Webster. But this is of little importance as I have written to him to do the same, extending the time to 3 years from July last, and when he has signed it on his part to send it to us. Very truly yours

DAVID SEARS

1. David Sears II (1787–1871) had been, on occasion, the investment partner of William Prescott.

2. WHP was serving as one of the executors of his father's estate.

178.   To Edward Maturin[1]
                  (Draft, WHP Papers, Mass. Hist. Soc.)

Boston, January 27th 1845

Dear Sir,

In reply to your letter, respecting your Romance of the Conquest of Mexico, I can assure you that it will give me much pleasure to do anything to promote your views. But the state of my eyes is such that I shall be unable to read your manuscript and to have it read to me would be a slow process, and not place me in a good position for estimating its merits. I must frankly say to you, moreover, that my recommendation with the Harpers would carry very little weight with it, in these matters. They are very shrewd men of the trade, as you, probably, are aware, and have persons in their employment on whose judgment they rely, much better qualified than I am, to calculate the chances of a sale for a work of fiction. And this of course is the only scale, on which their proposals can be founded.

You will understand me as saying this, not from any reluctance on my part to accede to your request, but from a sincere conviction that my recommendation, after all, can avail nothing, unless it be to induce them to give the work a more attentive examination. And I should be very happy to write and interest them as far as I can for this purpose if you shall desire it, whenever you are prepared to present the book to them.[2]

With regard to the dedication, with which you propose to compliment me, I need not say that it gives me great pleasure that you should think me deserving of it. Believe me, dear Sir Truly yours

WM. H. PRESCOTT

1. Edward Maturin (1812–81), novelist and playwright, was one of many American writers attracted to Spanish American themes by WHP's publications.

2. Maturin's two-volume historical novel, *Montezuma: The Last of the Aztecs,* was published in 1845.

179.   To Gales and Seaton[1]
(Miscellaneous Papers—Wm. H. Prescott folder, The New York Public Library)

Boston, January 31, 1845

Messrs. Gales & Seaton
Gentlemen—

You will oblige me by sending the *Intelligencer* to me—as a subscriber—in place of my Father—William Prescott—now deceased.

I take this occasion to express my admiration of the principles on which your journal has long been conducted—of the signal ability and constancy with which you have expounded our true Constitutional rights—and your endeavors to inspire the community with the most liberal and intellectual tastes. In the political field, I only regret your labors have not been crowned with more success. Your obedient servant

WM. H. PRESCOTT

1. Publishers of the *National Intelligencer* in Washington, D.C. Joseph Gales (1786–1860), an anti-Jackson, pro-U.S. Bank journalist, wrote the editorials which had endeared the paper to WHP. William Winston Seaton (1785–1866) was the associate editor.

180.   To François Auguste Marie Mignet
(Draft, WHP Papers, Mass. Hist. Soc.)

[March, 1845]

Sir,

I have the pleasure to acknowledge the receipt, through our Minister in London, of my Diploma, as corresponding member of the Academy of Moral and Political Sciences in the Institute of France. I need not say that it is most gratifying to me to have received such a mark of distinction from this illustrious body, and to find myself enrolled among those who have shed so brilliant a light over the various walks of literature and science. Allow me to add, that it gives me additional pleasure to have received this diploma from the hands of one, who, like yourself, occupies so distinguished a post in the republic of letters.

I shall avail myself of the first opportunity of a vessel for Havre to send a set of my historical works to be placed on the shelves of the library of the Institute. Meanwhile, I pray you, Sir, to present my acknowledgments to that body for the honor conferred on me, and to accept the assurances of the &c. &c. &c.[1]

1. Whenever WHP placed any of his honors upon his title pages, his membership in the Institut de France headed the list.

181.   To Macvey Napier[1]
                  (British Museum, Add. MS. 34625, f. 214)

                                        Boston, May 15th, 1845
Sir,

I take the liberty to set you right as to a fact mentioned in a paper on the *History of the Conquest of Mexico,* which appeared in the last number of the *Edinburgh Review.* It is stated in a footnote, that I have been for several years blind. This is a mistake, and I should show very little gratitude to my eyes, or rather eye—for of one, it is true, I have lost the sight—not to acknowledge the essential service it has rendered me in my historical researches. I have been troubled, from an early age, with a tendency to inflammation of the eye, which has happily diminished as I have grown older. While engaged on the *History of Ferdinand and Isabella,* I was so far disabled, that I was repeatedly, for months at a time, obliged to rely wholly on the services of another. But of late years my eye has acquired sufficient vigor to enable me, most of the time, to use it reasonably during the day in study, though in writing I am still obliged to make use of a secretary, who deciphers a very illegible manuscript made by means of a writing-case used by the blind. I mentioned this in my Preface as some excuse for clerical blunders that must necessarily occur in deciphering my hieroglyphics. You may think this talking rather long about an affair which can hardly interest the public; but I feel that the statement of positive blindness gives me a degree of merit beyond what I am entitled to on the score of conquering difficulties; though these certainly have not been light.[2]

I avail myself of this occasion to express the great pleasure I have derived from the very beautiful criticism on my work. The courtesy and cordial tone of commendation, which is certainly much beyond my deserts, is, of course, very grateful to me from so eminent a literary journal, and the analysis of the history contains some very shrewd and original views, which I could wish had occurred to me in the composition.

Believe me, Sir, with sentiments of high respect, Your obedient servant

WM. H. PRESCOTT

1. Macvey Napier (1776–1847), the long-time and distinguished editor of the *Edinburgh Review*.

2. A "correction" was printed in the July issue of the *Edinburgh Review*.

182.   To Francis Lieber

(Francis Lieber Papers, LI3039, The Huntington Library, San Marino, California. Reproduced by permission)

Pepperell, August 6th, 1845

My dear Lieber,

How come you in town, when I am not at Nahant? Do you not think that it is as hot here as in Columbia, or probably in h-ll?

Touching the Harpies[1]—those obscene birds of whom you speak. In good sooth, I have found them birds of the right feather. But my experience is not worth much. I make very simple and explicit contracts with them, and have no complicated accounts, advances &c. They agree to take a certain number of copies of a stereotype work, and pay me so much a copy—(one dollar, fifty cents) therefor. They have paid me punctually. My contracts give them also the right to print as many more copies as they please, within the specified time, they paying at the same rate as before. This puts me to a certain extent in their power, as they certainly may cheat me in regard to the number of copies they strike off. But I do not think there is much danger of such a gross fraud in a house of their standing and character, and where it must be known to the four partners, and to some of the subalterns in the establishment, at least if carried to any extent. This would be supposing rogues to be more plentiful than usual, even among publishers. I have found, too, that the report of the Harpers from persons who have dealt with them, and know them best, has been almost always favorable to their integrity. I have had the opinions of such men as Catherwood and Stephens, who have dealt with them long and largely, and who think them shrewd and sharp in their bargains, but faithful in the execution of them. They have no chivalry, and will not send you a horse or a butt of wine, as Scott's publishers did him, if your book should make a fortune for them. I should recommend you to be precise in your *written contract*—and to leave as little in said contract, as possible, to contingencies. Downright sales for an edition are the best thing. But it is not easy for an author to do the best, always—only the best his publisher will agree to. I should add in conclusion that Mr. Fay of Berlin thinks very ill of the whole concern. His case is a difficult one to explain— and he has another pamphlet on the anvil, he writes me, anent the matter. I should easily believe they could be guilty of considerable blunders in their rapid wholesale way of doing business. But I should be very slow to suspect them of intentional fraud.[2]

So you and Sumner talked, you say, of paying a visit to the country mouse. You would not have found it so formidable as a trip to Columbia or to Germany. I shall see you soon, probably, in the Yankee metropolis, where I shall go in a few days, as I propose to break out in an excursion for cooler air, myself.

Believe me, dear Lieber Faithfully yours

WILLIAM H. PRESCOTT

[P.S.] Pray tell Sumner, when you see him, that his brother George[3] informed me [by] a letter by last steamer that he should remain in Paris some months longer.

1. I.e. the Harpers.

2. WHP's relations with the Harpers, involving numerous editions of several titles and large sums of money over a decade, were uniformly pleasant.

3. George Sumner (1817–63) was a political economist and philanthropist.

183.   From Richard Ford
                          (WHP Papers, Mass. Hist. Soc.)

August 6, 1845
123 Park Street
Grosvenor Square
London

W. H. Prescott Esq.
My dear Sir

I beg your acceptance of my *Handbook in Spain,* which, I trust, should you open it, will be found to be something more than a mere book of *posadas y leguas* a la Starkie.[1] At all events you will see your name often mentioned with due honor. I am anxiously expecting to see Philip II worthily treated, and it is a splendid subject, which has yet to be written. Now that our friend Gayangos is settled in Spain, I have no doubt that you will receive some curious and hitherto unedited documents. Simancas contains a hoard of original and most interesting papers regarding that period, which I remember walking through some years ago. I have ventured, ahem, touching on the Escorial, just to allude to the character of its founder *El Escoralense,* but all Spanish students here hope that you will not keep them much longer waiting to know the truth—the whole truth and nothing but the truth. May I subscribe myself your most faithful Servant

RICH. FORD

1. Ford's book, rich in cultural references, enjoyed considerable popularity and several editions.

184.   Catherine Prescott to Susan Prescott
(Extracts, WHP Papers, Mass. Hist. Soc.)

Monday evening, August 25th [1845]

Dear Susan,

.   .   .   .

I then went to Beacon Street, where I was to meet Lizzie. She had been to her dressmakers and shopping, and had just got to the house.[1] She visited dear father's apartments first, and thought they were just what he wanted, and then William's chamber and her own, which I need not tell you she was charmed with, and hardly knew which to admire the most. The furniture in her room was just what she wanted, every thing was in keeping. She could not express how delighted she was, and grateful for every thing that had been done. I was more than repaid for anything that I had contributed towards her pleasure. I found the work progressing fast, and hope to have Miss Ray on Wednesday to make one carpet, either yours or mine.

.   .   .   .

When I left the Asylum I went to the House where I had Mrs. Hanna cleaning, and William Lewis moving furniture. While I was there, who should come in but Mrs. Appleton.[2] Said she came to see the papers which her husband said were beautiful. She was delighted with everything, and as to the library, she was not willing to leave it. It quite charmed her. . . . I hope to be in the house the last of next week.

.   .   .   .

1. In the spring of 1845, WHP had bought the house at 55 Beacon Street. Throughout the summer and early autumn, while the house was being remodeled extensively under the watchful eye of Mrs. William Prescott, the historian and his wife were in the country, at Pepperell. This was a period of

rapid progress for WHP on his third history. Indeed, it found him at the peak of his powers in that respect.

2. Probably Mrs. William Appleton, a next-door neighbor at the Beacon Street address.

185.   To William Gardiner Prescott
              (WHP Papers, Mass. Hist. Soc.)

Pepperell, September 8, 1845

My dear William —

I send you the balance of your dividend on your Reading Railroad bonds—of which you have had ten dollars advanced by your grand-mother. This dividend with the monies given to you in Newport[1] —and used up by you there, if you own, will amount to little short of seventy-five dollars, a round sum. But I trust you will economise now —and incur no superfluous expenses because you have a little silver in your pocket. It will melt fast enough—do your best.

I am very glad you enjoyed yourself at Newport—if as I doubt not, you passed your time in the ballroom and in the society of ladies— and not in the bar-room among rowdies. But you have had your fun, so now to work—with what appetite you may. The last year, I think, will bear reflection—though some days might have been better im-proved—and lucky the student who has not lost many a day in a year. But you have laid a good foundation of classical scholarship—as things go—for your profession—and I trust you will now plunge head and ears—heart and soul—into your professional studies.[2]

Whatever they may be to some others of your companions, to you they are to furnish the tools for working out your independence in life —and for securing you consideration—and self-respect. Whatever your calling, you will be a gentleman—in feeling and conduct—of that I am sure. But you can't afford to be only a gentleman—lucky for you.

Believe me, dear William Your affectionate Father

WM. H. P.

[P.S.] I presume you will read this before burning it! as *manu mea scriptum.*

[P.P.S.] [by Mrs. William Prescott] Dear William I cannot get the money of Mr. Thayer till your father sends the bond. I returned from Pepperell last night, left all well.

C. G. PRESCOTT

1. WHP had spent the third week of August in Newport.

2. Having received his A.B. degree in 1844, Will was studying law at Harvard.

186.   To Henry Wadsworth Longfellow
(Gratz Collection, The Historical Society of Pennsylvania)

Pepperell, September 16, 1845

Henry W. Longfellow Esq.
My dear Longfellow

I am greatly obliged by your thinking of me—and should have doubtless found Mr. Frost—whom you recommend so highly—just what I could have wished, though rather young.

But I have already engaged a secretary—a scholar who graduated this year at Cambridge—Watson[1]—perhaps you know him. He is an *élève* of Dr. Robbins—and very estimable—I understand—both mentally and morally.

What a sad loss you have met with in Cambridge in the death of Judge Story! The Court, the College, and the country. It is difficult to say of which the greatest loss. Sumner, I see, with his usual generous nature, has strewed the flowers over his grave.[2]

Pray commend me and my wife heartily to yours—and believe me Faithfully yours

WM. H. PRESCOTT

[P.S.] I've just taken a letter from William from the office, in which he mentions having been at your house. I am much obliged to you and your wife for allowing him to visit you. I wish him to be in the best school for manners and morals. But I hope it will not prove too great a tax on the teacher.

1. Thomas Andrew Watson (d. 1892).
2. As friend and former student of the distinguished jurist, Charles Sumner had eulogized Justice Story.

187.   To Mary Elizabeth Wormeley[1]
(E. B. Pierce Papers, Historical Manuscripts Collection, Yale University Library)

Pepperell, October 7, [1845?]

My dear Lizzie

Mr. Ticknor has sent me your manuscript, which is written in a good legible hand, or rather hands, as an author's work should be written to do it justice. I shall set about reading it straightway with my wife—the part of the reading which I shall contribute being ears, which I hope will not prove too long to authorize me to form some opinion of your novel. I assure you I have great pleasure in being able to gratify your wishes in any way, and if you never ask anything more severe of me than to read an interesting work of fiction, I certainly shall have no reason to complain. I shall complete the reading in a fortnight at furthest; but if it would be soon enough, it would be better for me to bring down the manuscript when we return to Boston—on the 26th instant at latest. This would avoid risk; but if you prefer, I will send it by the express to Ticknor, when finished.[2]

With affectionate remembrances to your mother and sisters, believe me, dear Lizzie, Always sincerely your friend

WM. H. PRESCOTT

[P.S.] My wife desires me not to omit her remembrances.

1. Mary Elizabeth Wormeley (1822–1904), daughter WHP's friend Caroline Preble Wormeley (q.v.). In addition to writing novels, she married Randall Latimer of Baltimore.

2. This novel, *Forest Hill, a Tale of Social Life in 1830–1831,* was published by Bentley in 1846.

188.   To Fletcher Harper[1]
                (Draft, WHP Papers, Mass. Hist. Soc.)

December 8th, 1845

Fletcher Harper Esq.
Dear Sir,

I see the *Miscellanies* are out,[2] got up in very neat and pretty style; looking stout by the side of its lean brothers of *Mexico.* I think it would have a pretty effect to bind them in different colors beside the universal black.

Will you burden your memory with sending for me a copy to Dr. Wainwright and Messrs. J. F. Cogswell, John C. Hamilton,[3] Henry Carey,[4] Henry Brevoort, John L. Stephens, Robert Ray, as coming from the author. You know the addresses of these gentlemen better than I do.

The rest of my dozen you can forward to me.

1. Fletcher Harper (1806–77), the youngest of the four brothers in the firm of Harper & Brothers.

2. This volume, which contained thirteen essays, all of which had been

previously published in America, was published in London in mid-August and in New York in early December, 1845.

3. John Church Hamilton (1792–1882), son and biographer of Alexander Hamilton, was one of WHP's social intimates in New York City.

4. Henry Carey (1793–1879), political economist and one-time publisher.

189.   From Mary Elizabeth Wormeley
                    (WHP Papers, Mass. Hist. Soc.)

                              3 Grosvenor Square, February 3, 1845 [1846]
My dear Uncle William

I cannot express to you how much I was obliged by your very kind letter to Bentley on my behalf. The creature thought an immense deal of it;—answered the fair friend of Mr. Prescott most civilly,—really kept his promise of giving it an early consideration, and I am sure you will be glad to hear that he has politely expressed his wish to be my publisher. We are to divide the profits of my work *"should any such arise"*—as he has prudently added, which means, I suppose, that the author may possibly get some thing on the wrong side of a third of them—and at Easter it is to make its appearance in the fashionable world. A day or two ago, however, I received a note from Mr. Bentley, suggesting to me how greatly it would be to the advantage of himself, and myself, and that of my poor "Job"—if I felt authorized to hope that I could induce Mr. Prescott to set his name upon the title page as Editor! I of course returned for answer that Mr. Prescott had never seen a line of my production,—that the case might have been different had I been residing in Boston within reach of his advice, but that as I am at present situated I not only felt that I was totally unauthorized to ask him to let me make use of his reputation, but that I would not for the world risk the loss of his good opinion by my presumption in proposing it.

Bentley bowed and apologized; but I went on to say that although as an anonymous work I had not thought of dedicating it to anybody, that if I did venture to inscribe the name of a friend upon its pages there was no one to whom I could more gladly offer it than to Mr. Prescott. I cannot feel that I am authorized in the usual language of a dedication publickly to assure you of what becomes every day more certain, how widely extended throughout the world is your reputation as one of the three great living historians, but as a token of gratitude for your kindness, and as a souvenir of happy days in Boston (soon I trust in spite of the Oregon[1] to be renewed) I should feel at once very happy and very greatly honoured by being allowed to dedicate "Forest Hill" to you.

Will you give me this permission, my dear Mr. Prescott? and if this request is not too presumptuous will you look over the enclosed prefatory Epistle and scratch out anything that you had rather were not there. You need not be afraid that I have said one unkind word of anything American for I can recall to mind but one line of fault-finding in which I said that I should like to see a morning *toilette* adopted for damask chairs.

Bentley sent me the opinion pronounced on my book by the gentleman who looked it over; it was kind and satisfactory; it prophesied that Job would be generally liked, and pointed out some faults that I am trying to improve. I have therefore some ground to hope that he will not disgrace either his Mamma, or his god-father, if indeed you will stand sponsor for my eldest child. I will not of course impose upon your eyes the task of looking over any closely written preface, but I commend my secret to the keeping of whoever reads it to you. Papa is such a bad repository that I fear it will be out of my power when once he knows I have written a book to keep it quiet amongst my friends here; but I have the greatest dread of being known, and I wish to put off the evil day at least until I ascertain its chances of success.

Job is its pet name amongst us; it is really entitled "Forest Hill—a tale of social life in 1830 and 1831"—or something to that effect,—for it meddles a little with the Duke of Modena and the revolution of Italy. Straws, you know, will tell which way the wind blows; and if you could see the effect that your name produces upon Mr. Bentley, I think it would give you a greater idea of your English popularity than many a more elaborate demonstration could do. I have left but little space for Mamma's message. She desires me to give her kind love to Aunt Susan and yourself,—adding that she has warmly sympathized in your late bereavement. All our letters speak of Mrs. Amory[2] as one whose influence was felt through a widely extended family circle, long after her presence had ceased amongst them. Will you present me, too, most affectionately to Grandmamma Prescott, Aunt Susan, dear Lizzie and the rest of your circle. I shall not be grieved if you refuse my dedication,[3] but I should be if I did not think I might subscribe myself Yours gratefully and affectionately

ELIZ^TH WORMELEY

1. At this time tension was increasing between England and the United States in reference to the Oregon territory.

2. Hannah Linzee Amory, Susan Prescott's mother, died in 1845.
3. WHP acceded to the request, and the novel was dedicated to him.

190.   Accounting of House Repairs
            from George M. Dexter[1]
            (WHP Papers, Mass. Hist. Soc.)

Boston, March, 1846

William H. Prescott Esq.
To George M. Dexter, Dr.
For cash paid for altering and furnishing his house, Beacon St., 1845[2]
To paid

Ward Jackson & Co.	lumber	285.09
Harnden & Co.	frames	41.00
M. Brigaldi	painting	200.00
T. Rich	vault	3.00
Kittridge & Blakes	lumber	70.10
	6.75	
Providence Railroad	freight 1.51	8.26
William Sloane	carpets	330.00
Noel and Decourcy	glass	502.10
	1.51	
Norwich Railroad	freight 1.33	2.84
B. Gardner	china	125.00
Francis Vose	copper	251.46
S. & W. Jacobs	stairs	42.39
Bosworth & Pratt	lumber	34.92
Adams & Co.	freight	2.50
Norwich Railroad	freight	31.61
Isaac Bird	paperhanging	23.00
Geo. Ponsot	furniture	722.00
J. Glynn	bells	56.50
Gas Light Co.	fixtures	31.00
Tiffany, Young & Ellis	fancy articles	27.75
O. Gori	marble (pedestal for busts)	100.00
Tiffany, Young & Ellis	bronze figures	23.50
William Sloane	carpeting	256.81
Ward Jackson & Co.	lumber	39.31
Do.	do.	17.89
R. Lovejoy	carting	.50

C. Brooks & Co.	hardware	116.70
Harris Stanwood & Co.	lantern	24.00
Charles E. Cooke	paper	15.75
J. G. Loring & Co.	coppersmiths	627.64
J. Hall & Sons	lumber	186.65
Noel & Decourcy	mirrors	152.47
Premiums on New York	drafts	.65
Colburn & Eames	stone	27.33
S. Curtis	frame	20.00
John Hoppin	cement &c.	91.90
Morse & Tuttle	silverplate	7.62
Bourn & Leavitt	carpenters	82.19
Cariss & Schultz	fender	30.00
John Hoppin	lime	.90
Gas Light Co.	fixtures	656.86
Harnden & Co.	freight on fender	2.25
J. Clarke & Sons	plumbing	691.06
H. & F. Stimpson	range	11.00
D. Safford & Co.	blacksmiths	105.68
J. H. Rolland	glazing	2.10
Reuben Smith, Jr.	carpeting 175.50	175.75
	.25 prem.	
Samuel Welch	bricks	338.70
Bryent & Herman	grates & furnace	137.09
Ditto	pipe 2.16 grate 3.38	5.54
P. M. Brunt	soapstone	31.72
J. F. Williams & Son	register netting	5.00
S. M. Hurlbert	paperhangings	45.71
J. Templeton	stone & marble	265.00
P. & T. Kelley	plaistering	307.41
R. Herring	slater	8.52
E. Robinson	hardware	170.48
Do.	Do.	2.04
G. B. Wheeler	coppering	74.12
Norwich Railroad	freight	4.10
Cyrus Hastings	painting	987.38
Theophilus Burr	carpenter	1963.18
Lawson & Harrington	upholsterers	1448.03
Harris Stanwood & Co.	hooks	1.00
Theophilus Burr	carpenter	18.09
Nathan Prince	mason	769.26

Geo. Ponsot	furniture	124.00
Curtis & Randall	furnace boiler	160.00
Aqueduct Corporation	repairs	1.50
L. L. Cushing	carving	183.00
		13,307.90
	Com. 5 pr. ct.	665.35
		$13,973.25

Control
By cash   1000
               1000
               1000
               1000
               1000
               5500
Balance   3473.25
           $13973.25

Boston March 10th, 1846 Received of W. H. Prescott Thirty-four hundred and seventy-three 25/100 dollars as balance of above account.

G. M. DEXTER

1. George M. Dexter (1802–73), whose wife was the former Eliza Amory, Susan Prescott's younger sister, was engaged in general contracting.

2. The items which follow illustrate the range and nature of the remodeling of 55 Beacon Street for the Prescotts.

191.   To President James K. Polk
                       (James K. Polk Papers, The Library of Congress)

Saturday evening, [April, 1846]

Mr. Prescott had the honor of presenting to the President, through his private secretary, two letters of introduction—immediately on his arrival in the city, and regrets extremely that he has not been favored with an opportunity of paying his respects personally to the President, which his return this evening to New York to spend a few weeks, now precludes, and he is compelled to adopt this mode of doing so.[1]

1. WHP had done what his gentlemanly nature required of him. Politically he had opposed Polk, voting for Clay in 1844, and in his opposition to the war with Mexico, WHP would roundly denounce it as "Mr. Polk's War." WHP's traveling companion on this leisurely three-week trip to Washington was Charles Sumner.

192.   To Harper & Brothers
                    (Draft, WHP Papers, Mass. Hist. Soc.)

                                        Boston, December 12, 1846

Messrs. Harper & Brothers,
Dear Sirs,

It is a long time since I have heard from you, and I now write to announce the completion of my "History of the Conquest of Peru." It will make, as well as I can estimate, between 1000 and 1100 pages, probably nearer 1100 than the former. It will form a counterpart to the *Conquest of Mexico* and is founded on the same kind of materials —more of the manuscripts than of the other. It has a preliminary view of the civilization of the Incas, followed by the narrative of discovery and conquest by Pizarro and his followers. I have arranged with the printer to have stereotype plates made of it so as to correspond precisely with the other work.[1] I have had engraved plates and several thousand proofs struck off in London of the two principal characters from original paintings; also two maps &c—in short, all the same as the other work. The printing will be completed by the first of April, but as I must allow time to send the last proofs and get the work out in London, it could not be published here before the first of June. This, I fear, is rather late for history; and if I should arrange with you, you may possibly prefer to postpone its publication till October or later. It is all one to me.

I am willing to offer you the work on similar terms with those you gave me with the *Conquest of Mexico,* you to pay me for copy-right $.50 per volume on all copies you publish. You took five thousand copies of that with exclusive right of publication in the United States for one year. I would sell you this work in the same ratio, that is, seven thousand five hundred copies, making the same number of volumes which you bought of the other. As the work will be four dollars, instead of six, and would have a better sale opened for it by the other, I should hope you might get rid of the same number of volumes of it in the same time, but I am willing to extend the right of publication to two years, instead of one, that there may be no doubts on that head. It would be easy to arrange the date of publication if you accept my terms, which I would make in all respects, except those already stated, like those in our contract for the *Conquest of Mexico.* I should, however, be more particular to have the paper of a heavier quality than that in your last editions, and indeed, this should be attended to more carefully in the future ones of *Mexico,* as the work, I am convinced, suffers from it.

Should you accept my proposals,[2] would it not be well for me to furnish you an advertisement of the book, explaining, in a dozen lines, the nature of the subject, and the materials on which it is founded.

Have the goodness, when you write me, to let me know how it stands with the last edition of the *Conquest of Mexico*. It seems to be immortal, and also, do me the favor to tell me whether a communication from me came to hand which I sent you two months since from Pepperell. It contained a translation of part of a French critique on my *Miscellanies*. I thought the publication of it might do the book a good turn. I suppose you thought otherwise but I think you might have had the grace to let me know whether the letter reached you, or had gone on to the dead letter office, which would not, considering its contents, much delight me.

1. An initial portion of the manuscript went to the Cambridge printers, Metcalf, Keith and Nichols, on December 15.
2. The Harpers immediately accepted this proposition, and WHP's contract with them was concluded in less than ten days. Meanwhile, Aspinwall had been alerted to undertake the sale of the English rights in London; see Wolcott, *Correspondence of Prescott,* pp. 613-14.

193.   From Colonel Thomas Aspinwall
                   (WHP Papers, Mass. Hist. Soc.)

London, 3 February 1847

My dear Sir,

I now send you the copy of contract made with Mr. Bentley for the sale of the *Conquest of Peru,*[1] and, at the same time, beg to apologize for an error in the hasty postscript to my last letter of the 19th, in which the terms of payments were stated to be 3, 6 and 12 months,— instead of 6, 9, and 12 months, from the day of publication.

I began my negotiations with the £1000 proposition, as suggested by you, and think you ought, in reality, to have had that sum, but I could not obtain it.[2] I trust however, that you will be resigned to your fate, when you take into view, that the present is not quite so large a work as the *Mexico*, and also, that your own expectations, as intimated in your letters, did not appear to go beyond the price obtained for the latter work.

You will notice in the contract, a stipulation that the extent of copy shall be within 160 pages of the same amount of matter, as in the *Mexico*,[3] and likewise that he shall be furnished with the copy, at such a period, as will enable him to publish it here, before it is issued to the public elsewhere.

He has the two engravings sent by you, as I have already mentioned. I presume there are no others. But if others are to accompany the American edition, he should have them at a very early period. He does not now employ Greatbach so much as formerly. Greatbach has risen in his profession, and is turning his attention to higher subjects, than designs for books. But Mr. Bentley thinks that the forthcoming engravings will be quite as well done as the others.

I am, my dear Sir, Ever faithfully and most truly yours

THOS. ASPINWALL

1. The text of this contract of January 17, 1847, is in Gardiner, *Prescott and His Publishers,* pp. 299–301.

2. The *Conquest of Peru* was sold outright to Bentley for £800.

3. The new history was much shorter than both Aspinwall and Bentley expected and exchanges of correspondence were required before the publisher accepted the reality of that fact.

194.   To Harper & Brothers
                (Draft, WHP Papers, Mass. Hist. Soc.)

[April 24, 1847]

Dear Sirs,

I send you by Harnden & Company's express two boxes, one containing the stereotype plates of the *Conquest of Peru,* complete except the last two boxes, embracing the last of the appendix and index, which I will forward in time so as not to delay you. They are not yet completed for you. The other box contains engraved plates, for two portraits, also for a map and autograph for the work—also six thousand portraits struck off in London, from the two plates, which will supply three thousand copies. These prints, for which you are to reimburse me, cost me £20 in London, or $96.80; and the duties on the prints of twenty per cent cost me $19.36, making a total of $116.16, for which you are to account to me.

By a letter received from Bentley, he expects to bring out the book by the middle of May;[1] so I think we must be prepared to bring it out early in June. You have the stamp of the arms for the back of the book. I have had the stereotype plates, as you will see, executed in every respect as well as those of my former works. I shall depend on your executing your part—the press work, paper, binding, &c in as good style as you did the first edition of the *Conquest of Mexico,* which did you great credit, but which you have never equalled since. As the price of these books makes them suitable for permanent ornaments of libraries, it is very important that they should be handsomely got up. Do you not think that dark green or maroon color, for the bindings, would make an agreeable variety with the everlasting black?

In the accounts you gave me, when in New York, of the sales of my works, you state that I have 996 copies of the *Miscellanies* on hand. In the account which you rendered me on the 19th of June last, you state there were on hand 614 copies in sheets, and 140 bound, making 754 in all. At this rate, we shall have the whole edition back again.[2] Pray explain it, and advise me at the same time, of the safe arrival of these boxes; and also, acquaint me if there be any delay in their coming, that I may attend to it at once.

   1. Bentley published the *Conquest of Peru* on May 17, 1847.

   2. WHP was learning that the *Miscellanies,* far from a financial success, was, on occasion, even being returned by agents who had taken copies on consignment. His third history behind him, WHP entered upon another period of literary loafing, this one being reinforced by weakening vision.

195.   To Charles Folsom
(Charles Folsom Papers, Boston Public Library)

Beacon Street, April 26, 1847

Charles Folsom Esq.
My dear Folsom,

   Your critical services with respect to the *Conquest of Peru* are now terminated; and I thank you heartily for the interest you have taken in improving the work, and for the benefit I have derived from your criticism.

   I enclose you a check for a hundred and fifty dollars, being the same amount, if I recollect right, which I paid you for the *Conquest of Mexico.* No arrangement was made between us, but I trust this will prove satisfactory. If not, you will have the candour to say so.[1] Yours faithfully

WM. H. PRESCOTT

   1. Rendering his customary assistance, Folsom, for this two-volume work, was being paid at the rate of $75.00 per volume rather than $50.00.

196.   To Joseph G. Cogswell
(Miscellaneous Papers—Wm. H. Prescott folder, The New York Public Library)

Boston, May 12, 1847

Dear Cogswell,

   Our friend, Sam Eliot,[1] wrote a little volume which was published here last winter, called "Passages from the History of Liberty." I suppose you have seen it; indeed he tells me he ordered the book to be sent to you. About half the edition—which was 600 volumes—has been sold. This sale has been confined pretty much to this neighbourhood; and he wishes to obtain for it a wider circulation. He rightly thinks the Harpers would be the best medium for effecting this. He has written to see if he could make some arrangement with them. As making any profit from the volume is but a very secondary consideration with him, he has left the terms pretty much to them. I have written to them, recommending the work on the score of its literary merits; but the recommendation of a friend, I suppose, will not carry much weight in their *golden* balances and yet, as they have the book already printed, and will, therefore, be put to no charge for the getting it out, I hope they may be induced to advertise and distribute it. As I know your regard for the author and his family, I write you this, to request you would use your good offices in the matter with the Harpers. Sam Eliot has a longer work in preparation, which may take him some years, and he has endeavoured, by this *avant-courier,* to make his name favorably known among his countrymen.

It is lucky that Lizzy and I did not wait your time for coming on. They would have had enough of us in New York.[2] Always faithfully yours

WM. H. PRESCOTT

1. Samuel Atkins Eliot (1798–1862), a lifelong friend of WHP, was a public servant in reference to collegiate, municipal and national affairs.

2. For two weeks in April WHP and his daughter had visited in New York, Philadelphia and vicinity.

197.   Agreement with Robert Carter[1]
           (WHP Papers, Mass. Hist. Soc.)

[c. mid-1847][2]

It is understood that Mr. Carter will read and write for Mr. Prescott for five hours a day, for two years, the hours to be selected by Mr. Prescott. In return for which, Mr. Prescott agrees to pay him four hundred dollars a year, and all that his board shall cost him, out of Boston,[3] over three dollars a week.

The time of the commencement of this engagement, to be the first day of September, eighteen hundred and forty-seven.

ROBT. CARTER
W. H. PRESCOTT

1. Robert Carter (1819–79), unlike his predecessors as WHP's reader-secretary, had been trained in the world of journalism rather than at Harvard. Despite the term stipulated in the agreement, Carter served the historian only one year.

2. Such contracts, usually negotiated in late spring or summer, commonly became effective in September.

3. "Out of Boston" referred to the annual intervals at Nahant and Pepperell.

198.   To Harper & Brothers
                    (Draft, WHP Papers, Mass. Hist. Soc.)

Boston, June 30, 1847

Messrs. Harper & Brothers
Dear Sirs,

The books have come safe to hand and have been followed very close by those for the public, which I am glad to see are now in the shops.[1] I have not yet distributed my own copies, not choosing to do so till your own were in the market. The work is executed faithfully, *according to your contract—in every particular;* and I am glad to see my historical bantling in such a good dress at his christening. As he grows older, pray be careful that he never has a worse one. In future editions of the *Conquest of Mexico* and of *Ferdinand,* I do not doubt you will bring them up to this mark, which is the true one. The elder brother now looks, by comparison, as if he had gone into a decline. I hope the sale will equal your expectations, and I will venture to say that it will be all the better for the creditable style in which the work is brought out. Brother Jonathan is pretty sharp at calculating, and he will feel, at least as far as you are concerned, that he has got his money's worth.

I have a dozen copies, more or less, which I wish you would send to some of my friends in New York, writing in each of them 'From the Author,' viz:

Robert Ray Esq. corner 9th Avenue and 28th Street
Mrs. Richard Ray, 3 University Place
Rev. Dr. Wainwright, 10 Hubert St., St. John's Square.
Joseph G. Cogswell Esq.
Henry Brevoort Esq. 5th Avenue
Ignacio Cumplido,[2] at Louis Hargous', South St.
*Philip Hone Esq.
*Jonathan Goodhue Esq.

Henry Carey Esq. Beech St., St. John's Square

J. Prescott Hall Esq.[3] Bond Street

Samuel Ward Esq.   "   "

*John C. Hamilton Esq.

*Rufus W. Griswold Esq.[4]

Dr. S. M. Elliott Esq., oculist, 183 Broadway

Washington Irving Esq. Tarrytown

Where I have not filled out the address, you can do so, or correct it if wrong. Where I have put asterisks, I forget the address and you can supply it. Mr. Griswold, when I was in New York, was at the New York House and told me he should stay some time in New York. You had better ascertain, before sending it.

I wish you would also send copies for me (writing in each 'From the Author') to the

Hon. Christopher Hughes,[5] Baltimore, Md.

His Excellency Don A. Calderón de la Barca, Washington

Rev. Dr. Bethune,[6] Philadelphia

Dr. John Beckwith, Petersburg, Va.

J. Edward Calhoun Esq.,[7] care of John E. Bouveau, Factor, Charleston, S.C.

There are twenty copies—quite a lump and if you send them any time in the course of the week, it will answer, though I would not have it later.

Pray you to thank Mr. Saunders[8] for his kind attention to my wishes.

P.S. On Tuesday, also, I shall draw upon you for five thousand dollars. I will defer the payment of the balance, unless you prefer a different arrangement.

1. Publication day was June 22, 1847.

2. Publisher of a Spanish translation of the *Conquest of Mexico* which was published in Mexico City in 1844–46.

3. Jonathan Prescott Hall (1796–1862), lawyer, jurist and author.

4. Rufus W. Griswold (1815–57), journalist and anthologist, included WHP in his *Prose Writers of America* (1846).

5. Christopher Hughes (1786–1849) served in the American diplomatic service in Europe for thirty years. WHP first met him in London in 1816. In later life their paths crossed in Baltimore.

6. George Washington Bethune (1805–62), an eloquent Protestant clergyman with literary tastes.

7. James Edward Calhoun (b. 1826), son of John C. Calhoun.

8. Frederick Saunders, an employee of Harper & Brothers with whom WHP often corresponded, especially concerning the promotion of his books.

199.   To Christopher Hughes
            (Hughes Collection, William L. Clements Library)

Boston, June 30, 1847

Christopher Hughes Esq.

Dear Sir,

The Harpers of New York have given to the world a new historical bantling of mine, the *Conquest of Peru,* and I have directed them to send you a copy which you will oblige me by accepting. Should they omit to do so, you will confer a favor on me by taking the trouble to notify them, or me, and it shall be attended to.

I passed a night a month since in your hospitable city, but as it was only a night, en passant, I had not the opportunity of paying my respects to you. I was glad to learn, however, from Mr. Kennedy,[1] who dined with me here, the other day, that you are in good condition.

Wishing that you may live a thousand years, I remain my dear Mr. Hughes Very faithfully yours,

WM. H. PRESCOTT

1. John Pendleton Kennedy (1795–1870), author and public official, knew many literary men. His home was in Baltimore.

200.   From Colonel Thomas Aspinwall
            (WHP Papers, Mass. Hist. Soc.)

London, 3 July 1847

My dear Sir,

Since my last I have endeavoured to dispose of the copyright of your "Ferdinand and Isabella" to Mr. Bentley, but I am sorry to add without success.[1] His first offer was £250 and his final one £300. He then requested me to say what price you expected. I answered £600. He remarked that he could not give so much. In the first place he considered the copyright of the "Ferdinand" as quite different in legal nature from the others, which had been conveyed to him before the London [American?] publication took place, next he says the sales being gradual, the profits (£240 to 260) of the last edition will be spread over two or three years and lastly that he is very well contented with his present position in regard to the work. I did not tell him anything respecting a minimum price because it was useless and might be prejudicial hereafter, if he should manifest any inclination to meet you half way or at any point nearer your limits.

He informed me that he has printed 2500 copies of the *Peru,* and I have little doubt that they will all be sold within two years. It will perhaps be well to say nothing more on the subject at present at least and perhaps until he brings it up again. But should your own views change, I should like to be apprized of the circumstance, that I may be ready for any new proposition from him.

I am, my dear Sir Most truly and faithfully yours

THOS. ASPINWALL

1. In April, 1847, Bentley had asked WHP if he would care to sell his half-interest in *Ferdinand and Isabella* to his publisher.

201. From Maria Edgeworth

(Extracts, WHP Papers, Mass. Hist. Soc.; and extracts in Ticknor, *Prescott,* pp. 271–73)

Edgeworths Town, August 28th, 1847

Dear Sir

Your preface to your history of the *Conquest of Peru* is most interesting.

Especially that part which concerns the author individually. That delicate integrity which made him apprehend that he had raised praise or sympathy from the world on false pretences converts what might have been pity into admiration—without diminishing the feeling for his suffering and his privations, against which he has so nobly, so perseveringly, so successfully struggled, our admiration and highest esteem now are commanded by his moral courage of truth.

What pleasure and pride, honest proper pride, you must feel, my dear Mr. Prescott, in the sense of Difficulty conquered—of Difficulties innumerable vanquished by the perseverance and fortitude of genius!

It is a fine example to human nature; and will form to great workers genius in the rising generation and in ages yet unborn.

What a new and ennobling view of posthumous fame!—a view which short-sighted, narrow-minded mediocrity cannot reach, and probably would call romantic. But which the noble-minded realise to themselves and ask not either the sympathy or the comprehension of the commonplace mean ones.

You need not apologise for speaking of yourself to the world. No one in the world whose opinion is worth looking to will ever think or call this "egotism" any more than they did in the case of Sir Walter Scott, whenever he spoke of himself it was with the same noble, and engaging simplicity, the same endearing confidence in the sympathy of the good and true-minded and the same real freedom from all vanity which we see in your addresses to the Public.

As to your judgment of the advantages peculiar to each of your histories, the *Conquest of Mexico* and the *Conquest of Peru*—of course you who have considered and compared them in all lights must be accurate in your estimate of the facility or difficulty each subject presented—and you have well pointed out in your preface to *Peru* the difficulty of making out a unity of subject—where in fact the *first* unity ends as we may dramatically consider it at the 3d act—where the conquest of the Incas is effected. But not the conquest of Peru for Spain.

.   .   .   .

I admire your adherence to your principle of giving evidence in your notes and appendices for your own accuracy and leaving your own opinions to be rejudged by your readers—furnishing them with the means of judging which they could not otherwise procure and which you having obtained with so much labor and so much favor from high and closed sources lay before us gratis with such unostentatious candor and humility.

I admire and savour too your practice of mixing biography with history; genuine sayings and letters by which the individuals give their own characters and Spain—which is the thing to be done. You have admirably kept the mind's eye upon this the real end and have thus carried on and prolonged and raised as you carried forward the interest sustained to the last moment happily by the noble character of Gasca with which terminates the history of the mission to Peru.

You sustain with the dignity of a just Historian your mottoes from Claudian and from Lope de Vega[1]—and in doing this *con amore* you carry with you the sympathy of your readers.

The Cruelties of the Spaniards to the inoffensive, amiable, hospitable, trusting Peruvians and their Incas is so revolting that unless you had given vent to indignation the readers natural irrepressible feelings would have turned against the narrator in whom even Impartiality would have been suspected of want of moral sense.

I wish that you could have gone further into that comparison or inquiry which you have touched upon & so ably pointed out for further inquiry.

. . . and I thank you for the quantity of information you give in the *notices* of the principal authorities to whom you refer. These biographical notices add weight and value to the authorities—in the most agreeable manner.

Though I own that I was often mortified by my own ignorance of the names you mention of great men, your familiars. You have made [me] long to have known your admirable friend Don Fernández de Navarrete of whom you make such honorable and touching mention in your preface.

I must content myself, however, and comfortably well I do content myself with knowing your dear friend Mr. *Ticknor*—whom I do esteem and admire with all my heart as you do.

You mention Mr. O. Rich as a bibliographer to whom you have been obliged. It occurred to me that this might be *the* Mr. O. Rich residing in London to whom Mr. Ticknor had told me I might apply to convey packets or books to him—and upon venturing to ask the question Mr. Rich answered me in the most obliging manner, confirming, though with great humility, his identity and offering to convey any packets I might wish to send to Boston.

I yesterday sent to him a parcel to go in his next box of books to Mr. Ticknor. In it I have put addressed to the care of Mr. Ticknor a very trifling offering for you, my dear Sir—which trifling as it is I hope and trust your good nature will not disdain.

Half a dozen worked *Marks* to put in books; and I intended these to be used in your books of reference when you are working as I hope you are or will be at your *magnum opus* History of Spain.

One of these marks—that which is marked in green silk "Maria E. for Prescott's works"!!! is my own handy work every stitch (in my 81st year—82d almost) I shall be 82 the first of June.

I am proud of being able even in this trivial matter to join my young friends in this family in working *souvenirs* for the great historian.[2]

Believe me, my dear Mr. Prescott, your much obliged and highly gratified friend and admiring reader and *marker*

MARIA EDGEWORTH

[P.S.] You speak of the Peruvians using the Lasso—How?—as they had no horses. Did they use it in catching the llamas or which animals.

What an excellent incident that is which you record of the escape of a Spaniard pursued, surrounded by Peruvian enemies who were so astonished by his horse's stumbling and his fall from his horse, from which they conceived that the rider could not be separated, that the crowd opened and let him pass!

1. These writers were quoted on the title page of the *Conquest of Peru*.
2. Due to his expanding reputation and his generosity with presentation copies, WHP's correspondence increased greatly in this period. Bancroft, then American Minister to the Court of St. James, repeatedly urged WHP to come to England.

202.   From Catherine Prescott[1]
                (WHP Papers, Mass. Hist. Soc.)

Beacon Street, September 24, 1847

These few lines, my dear children, I leave to explain why I resign the responsible place I have so long occupied. It is not from any dissatisfaction, or from indolence, but from a conviction that it is time for me to resign family cares. I feel that I am not capable of performing the duties that devolve upon every good housekeeper. You have both been kind and never have required more than I ought to perform, but I am too old to be useful, having already exceeded the term of life assigned to man by ten years.[2] Of course, I can not expect mine will be continued much longer. The mind must partake the debility of the body.

It is proper, my dear son, that your wife should be the mistress of your family. Your children should consider her the head to guide and direct in every thing. Your daughter has arrived at an age when she can share in the domestic cares,[3] and is adequate to any household duties that may devolve upon her, the performance of which will be a lasting advantage to her. I have no doubt you would wish me to continue with you, no place would feel so much like home to me. I fully appreciate the kindness and affection with which both you and Susan have always treated me, particularly since I have been more immediately dependent upon you.

Wherever I live, I chuse to pay my board, and all extra expenses, such as the coal I burn in my own chamber, half the wine, my taxes, hackhire or any other supernumerary I may incur. And in case of sickness, which eventually must come, to pay doctors, nurses, and all other after charges and expenses. I am thus explicit because I hope not to be a burden or expense to my children. This is not a hasty decision, nor formed without due deliberation. I have consulted no person upon the subject, but feel assured it is best for us all. In a pecuniary point I have no doubt you will find the advantage as I am not, nor ever was, an economist. I hope at any time if I can be useful you will not hesitate to call upon me, and remember that though I relinquish all care and responsibility, I shall never lose my interest in anything that concerns you. And one of my last prayers will be for the health and happiness of my children.[4] Most affectionately your mother

C. G. Prescott

1. This letter was addressed to Susan Prescott as well as WHP.
2. Mrs. William Prescott was then seven weeks beyond her eightieth birthday.
3. Elizabeth had celebrated her nineteenth birthday in July, 1847.

4. Thus Susan Prescott, after twenty-seven years as WHP's wife, came to administer for the first time the household in which she lived.

203.   To Harper & Brothers
(Draft, WHP Papers, Mass. Hist. Soc.)

Boston, September [1847]

Gentlemen,

I have had the pleasure to receive your note in which you request me to make proposals to you for the publication of my next History. It is quite uncertain, from the state of my health, if I [shall] engage in another historical work. If I do, the completion of it will be necessarily so long delayed that I should not be wishing to enter into any arrangement for its publication at present.[1]

1. Eagerness on the part of his publishers for another title by WHP was not limited to America. He, meanwhile, had not put a word of his next project on paper, nor would he do so until July, 1849.

204.   From Richard Bentley
(WHP Papers, Mass. Hist. Soc.)

New Burlington Street, [London]
December 31, 1847

My dear Sir

Immediately on receipt of your communication of the 30th ultimo I gave directions about the copies of your portrait. They have been sent to Mr. Rich according to your request, and I trust will arrive speedily on the other side. The sale of the "Miscellanies" has disappointed me. The number disposed of is 500 out of an impression of 1000.

It is gratifying to me to report to you the reception of your new book—"Peru." I think I may shortly require to go into consideration about a new edition,[1] and therefore shall be glad to have any corrections you may wish to make. Although the publication of "Peru" has brought "Mexico" under sale, perhaps from its being a kindred subject, "Ferdinand" moves slowly. "Peru" is a general favorite.

Wishing you most cordially a happy new year I beg to subscribe myself Your most faithful Servant

RICHARD BENTLEY

1. For the publishing history of the early English editions of the *Conquest of Peru*, see Gardiner, *Annotated Bibliography*, pp. 153, 154, 156.

205.   To Caleb Butler[1]
                (Gratz Collection, The Historical Society of Pennsylvania)

                                        Boston, January 28, 1848

My dear Sir,

I am very much obliged to you for the copy of your history, which I have been reading with great interest.[2] It shows a diligent research into the antiquities of Groton and Pepperell; and you have collected many particulars of historical value, for illustrating the character and manners of our fathers, which ought not to be suffered to pass into oblivion. Indeed I have found some curious facts in relation to my own ancestry, of which I was not before aware.

The style of your book appears to be perspicuous and correct. Your sentiments, both in religion and politics, are those which I have always been taught to respect. And I honor the moral independence which you have shown in uttering them, at a time when such sentiments are not too popular, and when those who entertain them are not always courageous enough to avow it.

Believe me, my dear Sir, with much regard Your obliged friend and servant

                                        WM. H. PRESCOTT

    1. Caleb Butler (1776–1854), amateur historian and long-time resident of Groton, where he taught for some years, also published oratorical and genealogical works.
    2. *History of the Town of Groton, Including Pepperell and Shirley* had just been published in Boston.

206.   To Obadiah Rich
                        (Draft, WHP Papers, Mass. Hist. Soc.)

                                        Boston February 25, 1848

My dear Sir

I find that I am destitute of good books of travels on the Low Countries. If I could have two or three good works, giving a particular account of the United Provinces—they would be of service to me. I don't mean those trashy travels which are not worth cutting the leaves open. If such travels went back to the 17th or 16th century it would be so much the better. You may spend five pounds for me in this way, and nothing on the binding, as they are for work not show.[1]

Why do not you forward me your annual account?

    1. Needing titles in preparation for his study of Philip II, WHP found his ace bookseller once more available.

207.   Agreement with John Foster Kirk[1]
(WHP Papers, Mass. Hist. Soc.)

Boston, June 9, 1848

It is understood that Mr. Kirk will read and write for Mr. Prescott, for five hours a day, for five years,[2] the hours to be selected by Mr. Prescott. In return for which Mr. Prescott agrees to pay him four hundred dollars a year for the first year, four hundred and fifty dollars for the second year, and five hundred dollars a year, for the remaining three years, and also, all that his board shall cost him when the parties are out of Boston over three dollars a week.

It is further understood that, in case of Mr. Prescott's death previously to the expiration of this agreement, the contract shall be closed by the payment of a year's salary to Mr. Kirk.

The time of the commencement of this engagement to be the first day of September, eighteen hundred and forty-eight.

J. F. KIRK
WM. H. PRESCOTT

1. John Foster Kirk (1824–1904), author and editor. Among other things, he edited an edition of WHP's complete works after the death of the historian.

2. Kirk, the historian's last reader-secretary, served in that capacity for more than ten years.

208.   To William Gardiner Prescott
(WHP Papers, Mass. Hist. Soc.)

Nahant, August 7th, 1848

My dear Son,

I give you a score of letters, and hope you will be able to deliver them all.[1] But some, I suspect, will not come within your beat. I should prefer that you would not deliver the letters to Sumner, Humboldt, and Thierry,[2] if you have letters, or means of introduction, from any one else. Otherwise you can avail yourself of them, and had better do so. Mrs. Lyell's and your Uncle Ticknor's to Kenyon[3] I would deliver, and would make a point of seeing both before leaving London.

With respect to commissions. You have received from me 25 sovereigns, or $120.00 for purchases. I wish you to lay out fifty dollars in Geneva for a watch like your own for Amory. I wish you to get for me two chimney ornaments in Rome, one consisting of three columns, of the temple of Jupiter Stator, I think; the other, a single column or pillar—I forget of what temple. They may be in *giallo autico*—though the single column might be, if it is not too costly, of *rosso autico*. These will together, I suppose, cost between thirty and forty dollars. Should you with this be able to buy only one, buy the three-column group of Jupiter Stator. The remaining money may purchase little souvenirs for your grandmother and sister.

If you go to Amsterdam, which is not probable, or if you can find it in a bookseller's shop in Belgium, I wish you would get for me the numbers of the translation into Dutch of my *Conquest of Peru* published at Amsterdam.[4] Also in Florence buy for me the numbers of the Italian translation, as far as they have come, of *Ferdinand and Isabella*. These numbers, unbound, will not be heavy, and will not take up much room in your trunk, and you can bring them with you.

Another more important commission in Florence, which I have been waiting for you to execute, is this:—Signor Eugenio Alberi, an eminent professor in that city sent me, some few years since, several volumes of a work now publishing in Florence,—*Relazioni degli Ambasciatori Veneti*. I have as far as Serie 2, volume 3, ending with the Relazione di Bernardo Navagiero. I wish you to get all the remaining volumes, as far as they have been published. If you cannot buy them separately, you must get the whole work for me. But, if there is any difficulty, I wish you would see Sig. Alberi. Probably Mr. Greenough[5] is acquainted with him, and will introduce you. If you see him, present my compliments to him, and enquire if he received a copy of my *Conquest of Peru,* which I sent to him last summer, through Mr. Shaw and the house of Grant & Co., Leghorn. I sent a copy, also, to Gino Capponi. If he did not, I shall have much pleasure in sending him a copy, which I can do by way of Leghorn. If there are but two or three remaining volumes of the work, you can put them in your trunk.

Whatever expenses you are at for the books on my account, I shall indemnify you at your return.

Lastly, with respect to your correspondence, I shall expect you to write me a letter the first day of every month, or as near as you can, and I will write you as often. Also, to write to some one of the household, every other fortnight. In this way, we shall get direct intelligence of you once a fortnight. You cannot trust to friends to give your family this information. When hurried, you can write a note, telling your whereabouts. When settled in a town you can write more at large. And your letters will serve as a journal, detailing your movements and observations. Write, also, the day you arrive in Liverpool, without fail, if only a line. You must reflect how unhappy we shall be if you neglect to write to us promptly and punctually, especially in the present troubled state of affairs in Europe, where, what with war, insurrection, and cholera,[6] you will have to take heed to your steps. Your mother will be miserable if she has fears about you, and you only can make her easy.

You will keep a good account of your drafts and your expenditures, arranging it all with your bankers in London, a thing which now requires the greatest care and precision. Your funds will enable you to see what is most important and interesting, and in the way you would like to do so.

Before we leave Pepperell in October, 1849, I trust, my dear son, you will be permitted by Providence to return to us in safety and health, with a mind enriched by travel, and well prepared to enter faithfully into the real business of life.[7] Always your affectionate Father

WM. H. PRESCOTT

INSTRUCTIONS[8]

1. His professional studies completed, WHP's elder son was setting out on an extended tour of Europe prior to entering upon his career.

2. George Sumner, Charles' brother.
Baron Alexander von Humboldt (1769–1859), naturalist, humanist, philosopher, statesman and writer, was an outspoken admirer of WHP's histories.
Jacques Nicolas Augustin Thierry (1795–1856), blind French historian, long inspired WHP.

3. John Kenyon (1784–1856), poet and philanthropist, moved in circles in London which included many literary figures. He belonged to WHP's long list of British correspondents.

4. Translated by G. Mees and published by P. Kraaj, this Dutch edition appeared in Amsterdam in 1847.

5. Horatio Greenough (1805–52), noted American sculptor, resided in Italy for many years. His brother Richard executed a bust of WHP.

6. Pestilence had been joined by the revolutions of 1848.

7. Intended to last one year, this trip occupied two.

8. This entire letter, crowded with instructions, might well have borne this as its heading. However, employed at the close of the letter, it possibly was intended to remind the recipient to retain and refer to these instructions.

209.   To Albert Gallatin

(The New-York Historical Society)

Boston, August 14th, 1848

Hon. Albert Gallatin

My dear Sir,

I believe the steps necessary to be taken to secure a copyright in England are few and simple. The author obtains a certificate, and gives a dozen copies of his works to certain specified institutions. But I cannot give you the particulars; nor, indeed, do I know if it be permitted to a foreigner to take out a copyright there. I have always sold the copyright to the English publisher, considering this as safer and much more simple than to enter into long accounts with him for the sales. If this arrangement is not made, the next best thing, in my judgment, is to publish the work on shares with the publisher. The least eligible mode for the American writer is to have his book published on his own account. The publisher, having nothing to lose, and little to gain, will not be likely to take much interest in the matter.

To secure the copyright in England, the work must be brought out there a short time—say a couple of weeks—before it is published elsewhere. To secure the copyright in this country at the same time, it is necessary that a certificate should be filed in the district clerk's office before the work is published *anywhere*. The second requisite is that copies be deposited in the clerk's office and with the Congressional and Smithsonian libraries, within three months after the date of its publication—the place of publication not being prescribed. This is the opinion given me privately, not juridically, by Judge Story. Thus it is easy for an American to get the benefit of a copyright both in this country and England.

It must be confessed, however, that the copyright of an American work does not stand on the firmest foundation in England. Murray wrote me word that he did not think the English courts would sustain it; and the uncertainty of this diminishes the marketable value of such copyright very sensibly. The great publishers, however, from courtesy, and probably from the uncertainty of any right on their part, have hitherto refrained from interfering with the right claimed by the original publisher of a foreign work. So the case, not having been litigated, remains unsettled.[1]

As to the publishers, any one of the great houses, Murray's, Longman's, Bentley's, Colburn's, &c is a most respectable, and, I suppose, trustworthy medium for bringing out a work. But it is better to employ some agent on the spot, familiar with the business, to negotiate the terms for the publication of a work. Such a person is Colonel Aspinwall, our consul in London—upright and sagacious, and well acquainted with the leading publishers of London. He has had the care of my works, for the sale of which he has charged me a commission of ten per cent. Some of his negotiations in the earliest of the works were attended with a good deal of difficulty, and the compensation was not too much.

There is still another mode of coming before the British public—by having the printed sheets sent out from here, to any amount that may be thought prudent, and sold by the publisher there. This is more feasible where the work is stereotyped. It was the course pursued by our friend Mr. Stephens, who can give you the particulars of it.

I have been rather prolix in my answer—thinking in this case brevity would not be a virtue. Yet I have not answered your precise question, nor can I give you any answer in respect to a copyright on the Continent. The translations of my own works there have been made for the benefit and at the risk of the translators.

With the sincere wish that Heaven may long preserve you in the same health of body that you have of mind, I remain, my dear Sir, With great respect, Your friend and servant

WM. H. PRESCOTT

1. The unsettled international copyright situation plagued WHP in later years.

210. Memorandum Concerning Personal Regimen
(Extract, WHP Papers, Mass. Hist. Soc.)

Nahant, September 1st 1848
Also 1849[1]

Want no Seltzer water at Nahant or Pepperell.

Drunk one bottle of *old* Sherry and three of *old* Madeira.

Pantaloons—wore 1 lb. 6 oz. three days out of four. For coldest days 1 lb. 9 oz. For warmest days 1 lb. 4 oz.

Drawers—those with black marks on the backs worn every day.

No *green glasses*, except twice on piazza at noon.

Gaiters morning and evening walks, rest of time white socks.

Hours. Rise at 6 o'clock, walk an hour, breakfast 8 o'clock. Reader 1/2 ten to two with 1/2 or hour's intermission at twelve. In the afternoon 1/2 past 4 to a quarter of 7, when walk one hour.

Brought down my morocco chair and prince regent.[2]

1. Apparently this record of 1848 served also as a recommendation for 1849.
2. These notes are accompanied by many others on similar subjects for various years.

211.   To William Gardiner Prescott
(WHP Papers, Mass. Hist. Soc.)

Pepperell, October 1st, 1848[1]

My dear William,

Here we are in the shades of the Highlands; and I steal a half-hour from the guests, whom I have left chatting on the piazza, to have a more agreeable chat with you.

Last week we had the Peabodys and Anna Robbins, who, with the help of Amory, made the week pass off merrily enough—at least for them. This week the Perkins, Mrs. Hauteville, and Samuel Eliot are here—with Amory also, and Miss Willing. So we still have a houseful of merry guests, who put up with bad weather with great philosophy. The month of September was uncommonly cool, but October begins with the glass at summer heat, and, what we could dispense with at this moment—an equinoctial storm. But the party indemnify themselves by amusements indoors. Last evening they got up some *tableaux-vivants,* which, with the aid of shawls, old hats, &c., &c., produced a good effect, as seen through a gauze before the door of the dining room. This morning we went decently to church, and tomorrow, if the skies relent, they go to Massapaug Pond. The next day the comers will be goers, and we shall have the rustic solitude all to ourselves for the rest of the season. I am content; for what better company is there than Nature in her autumn trim? Yet we have all enjoyed their visits very much. The only thing wanting, as we all felt, and often said, was your cheerful tones to swell the chorus. Amory has become quite a sporting character—shoots, angles, &c., &c., without harm to himself or anything else—at least so far. He and Edward Perkins,[2] after an excursion of half a day, brought home, as they boasted, a mess of pickerel. It was brought to table under a dainty napkin, which, when removed, displayed to our longing eyes an old salt-fish! Such are the harmless pranks of the Highlands. But you shall have their own missives.

Mary Chadwick will not visit us this summer. The family are greatly afflicted by Mrs. Gorham's death. But it is possible Cora may pass some days with Elizabeth. Should you be surprised to hear that Martha was engaged? I should not be surprised if you were to hear so before the autumn was out. But I may be mistaken. I think it will not be with the Speaker, but with the other more fortunate candidate from her own town.[3]

I have not heard lately from the Ticknors. Your Aunt wrote me a kind letter about you, as I sent her an extract from your letter to me. Your mother, true to her promise, will not read your letters to the company. But Elizabeth read them to Ellen, as I thought she might, and they pleased her much. I cannot tell you how delighted the family are —all generations included—when they find an epistle from over the water at the post office. It is a white day for us, and your grandmother is instantly advised of the contents, as she is very anxious to have them. I suppose you are now revelling in the rich scenes of the Alps; and I am glad to observe you have found out that Switzerland is a hilly country. This shows the good of travelling. You have been over some interesting ground from local recollections. Indeed it would be impossible to go far in the Old World without waking up historic recollections of some sort or other. What a meaning that gives to localities!—sadly wanted here. I hope you thumb the guide-book well, so as to understand the full import of every spot that you tread. This is the way to stamp it indelibly on your memory. I am glad you like the German character. The more you are thrown among the people of the country where you are travelling, and the better you understand their ways—their nationality—the better you will like them. You will find out something peculiar to be liked in every nation; and this is only to be found out on a near intercourse. Your route will be along the edge of the warpath after you have crossed the Alps. But you will soon leave it behind, on your passage to the south, and I trust all will be quiet on your return in the spring.

We are all in health and spirits at the manse, where we shall stay till this last week in October. I like the new farmer and his family very well. He understands his business, as his wife the dairy. We have not seen the Dexters, but I hope we shall see one of the boys before we return. Were you not surprized to hear of Edward's stump oratory?[4] He laughs at it, I am told, as a joke. But when a man has once listened to the music of his own voice in public, he will not be likely to remain mute, for the future.

I received a note, brought me by Macready,[5] from Mr. Kenyon, speaking very kindly of you, and of his pleasure at seeing you. I hope you will find him in London on your return. He has gone to Scotland, I believe, where he will travel with Hillard. I was much obliged by your thinking of the Amsterdam translation of *Peru*, which shows you will heed your commissions.

With constant love from your mother and me, I remain, my dear Son, Your affectionate Father

WM. H. PRESCOTT

[P.S.] October 3d. You have their sign manuals—characteristic—the anonymous, Miss Willing. Rain, rain—last evening acted charades—also Negro melodies—and toasted cheese. Merry indoors all yesterday. Amory an excellent merry-ander—glad I have found out his *forte*. They flit today—and leave us to repose.[6]

1. WHP was quite regular in fulfilling his promise of a letter to Will at the beginning of each month.
2. Edward N. Perkins (1820–99), art lover and philanthropist.

3. Martha Endicott Peabody married Richard Dennison Rogers.

4. Edward Dexter, son of Elizabeth and Franklin Dexter and WHP's nephew, had graduated from Harvard in 1845.

5. William Charles Macready (1793–1873), famous in the theater as a tragedian, repeatedly performed in Boston.

6. Below WHP's postscript, numerous guests crowded their own, all of which are omitted here. Several weeks later, as he prepared to depart Pepperell, WHP wrote: "The last three weeks been lounging thro' the *purlieus* of my subject. Is it to be mine?" (Prescott [Gardiner, ed.], *The Literary Memoranda,* II, 184).

2 1 2.   From General William Miller
              (Extracts, WHP Papers, Mass. Hist. Soc.)

Honolulu, Woohoo, November 10, 1848

William H. Prescott Esqr.

My dear Prescott

I cannot thank you enough for your *Conquest of Peru,* or sufficiently express how highly I prize the gift, which, with your *Ferdinand and Isabella,* and *Mexico, Washington's Life and Writings* by Sparkes, [*sic*] and the *Duke's Despatches,* occupies the best and favourite Shelf of my Library.

I had previously read I believe pretty well all that had been published about Peru, and it is now saying very little to assure you that the perusal of your Work on that Country has given me a far better Insight into and more lasting knowledge of, the principal Characters and succeeding Events described, than I before possessed. Your description of the Suspension Bridges, Vestiges of Ancient Roads, and of the Scenery of the Andes is, as far as my judgment in the matter goes, singularly graphical and correct. What much pleases me also is the Justice which you bestow upon Pizarro whenever he merits it. His Religious zeal, or Bigotry, and consequent cruelty, are much less to be wondered at, and infinitely less deserving censure, I think, than the Fanaticism, and ambition for personal aggrandizement, displayed by some of the Teachers of the Gospel now a days scattered on the South Sea Isles, and who, if they were permitted, would outdo Valverde all to nothing.

If I were sitting along side of you in Boston, as I wish I was, and you required me to point out any Passages that did not altogether concur with my knowledge of facts, all I should have to observe would be:—

1st. The Climate of Cuzco I consider raw and dreary in general: it rains there *á cantaros* during five or six months in the year, although of course with intervals of sunshine; the roads are cold, slimy, and slippery: the Streets of the City are filthy, and the Rooms of the Houses have no fire places, so that it is usual for the people to wear *capes* in as well as outdoors.

2ndly. Although Islay, Quilac, and Mollende are Ports belonging to the Department of Arequipa, the City of Arequipa itself stands upwards of thirty leagues from the Sea Shore, and the River running through its Centre and emptying itself into the Pacific at Quilac, is not navigable even for a Canoe, excepting at a few places; therefore the Galleys (Volüp 289) were most probably constructed at some other place than that you seem to indicate.

3. Why do you call the *Temple* of the Sun, the *House* of the Sun? Is it because the New Englanders still preserve the opinion of the Pilgrims that it would be profanation to admit that a *Temple* for Holy Worship could exist in Heathen Lands?

But these remarks you will say, and with reason, are upon very trivial points. I make them principally to show that I have not been [able to] discover any thing like Paste or British [. . .] in the Diamond Production.

The Revolution of Tupac Amaru, which commenced in 1780 and lasted about three years, is an Event that will deserve Historical Record, and I wish some one, whose Peru was half as good as yours, would write it. It would be, *me parece,* an excellent Link between the Conquest and the War of Independence.

Before proceeding farther I must thank you for the mention or quotation you make of certain Memoirs which, *segun mi modo de ver las cosas ahora,* do not merit such honorable notice.[1]

The Mexicans have fallen far below what was expected of them, and their conduct during the late War has confirmed the opinion I came to long ago, namely, that they are a very inferior People to the *South* Americans. It was lucky for the Invaders that they had not Gauchos, Guasos, Llaneros, or even Lambayeguanos [?] of Peru, to contend against. I firmly believe that a couple of bold and cool-headed *Caudillos* who knew how to do their work properly, each at the head of about 500 followers, might have sufficed to have prevented the go-a-head Volunteers, and hand-ful of Regulars, from entering the Capital of Montezuma, or if they did enter it, to prevent their escape. But, *dios sólo sabe lo que ha de suceden en estos tiempos,* and I confess frankly that my Predictions have turned out totally erroneous: General Scott has performed wonders not only in fighting his way as he did, but in being able to manage at all the very independent but certainly very brave sort of Gentlemen under him. I believe that no one but a true born American could have done any thing with them. How shamefully he appears to have been treated. *Vivent les Republiques!*

. . . .

Yours ever most affectionately

WM. MILLER

1. The writer refers to his own *Memoirs of Gen. Miller,* which WHP cited several times in the fourth chapter of his *Conquest of Peru.*

213.   To Edwin Percy Whipple[1]
            (Yale Collection of American Literature, Yale University Library)

Beacon Street, November 28th, [1848]

My dear Mr. Whipple

I am much obliged to you for your two elegant volumes, in which I recognize some old familiar faces—not the less welcome to me that they are familiar.[2] It is a goodly brotherhood; and I am glad you have proclaimed its parentage to the world as it cannot fail to do you honour.

With my best wishes for your success, I remain Sincerely yours

WM. H. PRESCOTT

1. Edwin Percy Whipple (1819–86), author and lecturer, published many volumes of essays and was intimate with many literary figures.
2. Among the "old familiar faces" in Whipple's *Essays and Reviews* were that writer's reviews of titles by WHP.

214.   To William Gardiner Prescott
                (WHP Papers, Mass. Hist. Soc.)

Boston, December 3d, 1848

My dear William,

Thanksgiving day has come and gone, and I suppose been kept by you in imagination, as I believe you were advised of its date. We had the Ticknors, Miss Wadsworth and brother, the Dexters—(except your Aunt and Arthur, the latter of whom has not recovered from his typhoid fever) and the Wormeleys—horse, foot, and captain. The captain was in full glee and chorus, and cut up his turkey so as to serve a score of appetites, which, you may remember, was an ancient boast of his. We wanted only you to make the set complete. Many a kind word and wish was expressed about you, and a hearty health was drunk by the whole table to the "Yankee Wanderer." In the evening we had some romping games, and all went off soberly at the canonical hour of ten.

Boston is not very merry this winter in the soiree and ballet line.

Mrs. Deacon is getting up a waltzing party at her house, which Amory patronized last week, and the ladies, with Cora at their head, have arranged a whist club, at which the gentlemen are to appear after cards. This is a freak! Lizzy finds some occupation in Salem, where there has been a wedding, as you probably have heard, and Mr. Tot Peabody begins housekeeping in a very nice house which cost only 4000 dollars. So domestic happiness may be bought at a much more reasonable price in Salem than in our town—the very dearest spot in the world, I suspect.

I was last evening at Mrs. Sears's, and saw David looking very well. He dined with us the other day, and spoke of your quarters in Paris, which he eulogized extremely. I hope you get them at a revolution price, which I suppose is half price. By the bye, your mother and Elizabeth have sent to you for some lace. I do not know how you will get it to them without the duty, which is too grinding. I shall remit a hundred and forty dollars extra, on your account, to the Barings, to pay for it.

We have a steamer now due, which, I trust, will bring me a good letter from you, informing us of the state of things in the most giddy of capitals. I shall depend on a full account of things there, as what we glean from the newspapers, &c is little to be trusted. The writers for the press have usually some purpose to serve besides that of telling the truth. Have you given your letters as yet? One of the best of them, to Count Circourt, will fail you, I fear, as he was in Switzerland at the last advices.

Talking of letters, Mrs. Hauteville told me today that you were "a humbug," and desired me to tell you so. She says she does not know if she would answer you now. Surely you ought to write to her without delay. You don't know how much a letter is enhanced by coming from a friend on the other side of the water. The distance lends enchantment to it. Pray write to her, and before long, a longer letter to your Aunt Anna, your steady friend, and one never weary of proclaiming your virtues. You have been well employed since your residence in Paris; and, what with study and sight-seeing, I have no doubt the day runs off glibly enough. But if you would but seize on an hour as it goes, occasionally, for these purposes, it would be an hour well spent.

We are here now just recovering from the bustle of the presidential election. I suppose you have heard the result, and that the Whigs, for a wonder, have triumphed. So now there is great rejoicing, and every one expects to find a panacea for all the ills under which the country has been labouring, and some of which, I suspect, are to be charged more on ourselves than on our rulers. But our chance will be certainly

better with a good pilot at the helm; and all accounts of Taylor represent him to be such. We expect Major Graham here this evening (Sunday) who was with him in Mexico, an intelligent and modest officer—
and also Mr. Power, the Irish player (son of the celebrated Power lost at
sea). He called on me last week, and I invited him here for the evening.
Cora and her spouse, Mr. Hillard, your Uncle William and wife, will
make up an evening. Mr. Hillard and Longfellow were here this morning. The former enjoyed his tour very much. He says Rogers has a
most kind personal regard for me; so I think you will find him your
friend, and a better you cannot well have in London. I do not think
Hillard saw much of Lord Morpeth, now Lord Carlisle. Cabinet ministers have little time for hospitalities.

Amory told you that Pres. Everett has at length resigned[1]—to leave
at the end of the term. The public speculate on his successor. Mr.
Samuel Eliot is mentioned, but the knowing ones give it to Sparks.[2]
Mr. Everett goes out in the odour of sanctity—that is, in much better
odour than he has lived in there, for the scholars have just begun to
appreciate his good qualities.

Your grandmother, mother, and each of us, are in good health, and
send any quantity of love and good wishes to you. Your coming letter
will tell us more of your plans. Only keep clear of *cholera* and *revolution,* and believe me, my dear Son, Always your affectionate Father

WM. H. PRESCOTT

[P.S.] Amory is also looking for a letter from you today or tomorrow.
He says you are very much in his debt.

1. Edward Everett served as President of Harvard between February 5, 1846,
and February 1, 1849.
2. Jared Sparks succeeded Everett, serving until February 10, 1853.

215.   From Frances de Gayangos[1]
                  (WHP Papers, Mass. Hist. Soc.)

Calle de Barquillo 4
Madrid December 15, 1848

My dear Mr. Prescott

Your kind letter to my husband dated Boston November 13 has been
opened by me in his absence. He has been in Andalusia all the Autumn,
and has extended his journey to Tangiers—Tetuan and Tarifa! but
returns this month with regret at not being able to visit Fez and
Morocco. He is charmed with every thing and has purchased some interesting manuscripts. All the Consuls have paid him the kindest

attention and he has been out Boar hunting with Mr. May the British Consul—a great sportsman. We have been this summer at a country house two leagues from Madrid where we have a garden full of vegetables, fruits and flowers, all growing together and a shady veranda covered with a vine of jessamine. Myself and two dear children are quite well from the mountain air we have been breathing so long. My girl is near 12 but is very forward in every thing and speaks three languages—my dear boy is fine and now goes to a day school here. He is very like his father. How I should like to see yourself and family! We think a new ambassador-minister will come over next year—it seems so appropriate to have *you* named that I shall be disappointed if it is not so.[2] The 2nd volume of the translation of *Peru* is out, Mr. de Gayangos will forward them when he comes. Wishing yourself and family a happy Xmas, I remain Yours very truly

FRANCES DE GAYANGOS

P.S. I have Mr. Ticknor's letter safe to give Mr. de Gayangos on his arrival home.

1. English-born wife of WHP's ace assistant Pascual de Gayangos.

2. She was disappointed. In terms of the prior appointment of a literary figure, Washington Irving, she had reason to expect WHP in Spain, but in terms of his complete abhorrence of politics, it was impossible.

216.   From Dr. H. Eberty[1]
(WHP Papers, Mass. Hist. Soc.)

Berlin, 8 January 1849

Dear Sir,

You undoubtedly have waited since a long time for the appearance of my German translation of your admirable last work, *History of the Conquest of Peru*. But I would not send it to you before its complete publication; and as the second volume has appeared before some days only, I have the honour to present it to you, together with the first volume, which already had been published last spring. I wish that you may receive this labour with the same fondness as you did my precedent ones, and as a feeble token of the unbounded esteem which both your character and your wisdom inspire me.

I am very anxious to hear whether the state of your eyes has permitted you to continue your historical writings, and especially the Life and Reign of Philipp II, which you intended to write some years ago. I have a double interest in the affirmation of this question, because, besides the sincere part I take on your fate, I am jealous of the honour to be the only German translator of all the works, with which your pen enriches the European literature.

As soon as the first volume of your above-mentioned work, or of any other of yours appear, pray, send it me without delay, in order to begin immediately the translation of it.

I reiterate the assurance of the highest consideration, with which I have the honour to be, Dear Sir Your most obedient servant

H. EBERTY

1. A retired German physician, Dr. Eberty translated WHP's first three histories into German. Although he possessed no financial interest in any translation of his books, WHP was endlessly cooperative with the translators. They helped him to one thing he much desired, international recognition.

217.   To Lydia H. Sigourney
(Hoadley Collection, Sigourney Papers, The Connecticut Historical Society)

[c. January, 1849]

Mrs. Sigourney

I will now reply to your private note which my wife, who is my secretary in private matters, read to me, and now answers, and I assure you her opinion and mine are one.

I am much pleased that you should have communicated so frankly with me on the subject, as I certainly should not have hesitated to do the same with you in similar circumstances. I have but a slight acquaintance with Mr. Bowen, who is both editor and proprietor of the *North American Review;* and, indeed, as he lives at Cambridge, have not set eyes on him these two years or more.[1] But my relations with him are very friendly, and I shall be most happy if I can be useful to you in this matter. It certainly was a great oversight in him not to have made your popular works the subject of an express article; but his attention, I suppose, is more immediately called to the votaries of Apollo in his own neighbourhood—a lame reason.

I think the best way will be for me to present him a copy (if you will authorize me) in your name, and I will write to him to draw his attention to this publication, urging your undoubted claims, and requesting him to have them fairly canvassed in his journal. It will give me great pleasure to do this; and if his silence has proceeded from accident, as probable, my application may have some effect.[2]

But whether it has or has not, is, after all, of but little moment to one in your position. Your country has long since passed upon your literary claims, and has given you a name among her children—as you must be well-aware—that is to form part of the national inheritance to all future times.

With great regard, my dear Mrs. Sigourney, believe me, Yours

WM. H. PRESCOTT

1. Six years had passed since WHP's last review in the *North American Review.*

2. A review of Mrs. Sigourney's *Illustrated Poems* appeared in the April, 1849, issue of the *North American Review.*

218. To William Gardiner Prescott
(WHP Papers, Mass. Hist. Soc.)

Boston, February 5th, 1849

The month comes round again, dear William, and with it my letter, which I must write and send at once, as a heavy snowstorm makes it probable that the cars will be longer than one day in working to New York.

Last week we received your welcome letter from Paris, of 9th of January. It gives us, however, as much pain as pleasure, for it told us how you had suffered again from your old enemy, who takes you by the throat in one country as well as another. It is a good thing in one respect, however, as a reminder of home. A traveller never thinks of home and the friends that love him best so much as when he is stretched on his back, and instead of seeing sights sees only the walls of his chamber, and the forms of those far off, his imagination peoples them with. But all's well that ends well.

And so you are off for Italy. Here's another *contretemps,* however. Why did you ask me to let you prolong your stay, and yet run away before you got my answer? You did not directly make the request till your letter of the [blank], which I answered by the first steamer, and, as you will have learned before this, assented to. I therein said, and repeat it for fear of mis-carriage, that I am content you should prolong your absence till some time in the spring of 1850, and shall remit 250 pounds more for you, for that purpose. I shall thus allow you 850 pounds, instead of 600 pounds for your tour, and shall further remit 140 dollars on Elizabeth's account, and 12 dollars on Amory's. I enumerate the sums here, that you may know exactly your resources. I have already remitted four bills, for which I paid 500 dollars each, and of whose exact amount you have been notified, no doubt, by the Barings. This hasty departure from Paris will defeat some of the objects proposed by your longer residence. You will be obliged still to run over

Italy *en courier,* and at the worst state of its affairs. You should be in London by the first of May, to see the people. It is very unlucky, but you must mend it as you can. Bancroft writes me so cordially of you that I hope you will be in London while he is minister.

With regard to the secretary of legationship—I think of it as I did when you were here. To a man who is to stay long abroad, and in one country, and who cannot find access into good society there, it might be of advantage. But this is not your case. In London you are well provided with letters, and you can cut and run when your humour takes you, which you could not if you were tied to the tail of an embassy. Then to what does it lead in our country? Literally nothing; not even to consideration, unless you could get the appointment of a full minister, which is only to be bought by service—and sacrifice that many a man would shrink from. Lastly, I have no influence, if I had the wish, to get you into a diplomatic post. "Kissing goes by favour" at Washington—and I have no claims of electioneering services to show. When Mr. Webster was Secretary of State, he told me, if I would recommend a secretary of legation for Spain, it would meet with attention. Dr. Howe, hearing of this, got me to recommend him, and that was the end of it. They have too many debts to pay at the White House to have anything to bestow *gratis;* and it will be long before I shall ask any favour on my own account.

But you will get through the letter without what ought to be its staple—news from home. The best news is that there is little or nothing new, which shows we are all well. The town began to be wide awake about three weeks since. Three different lady-clubs have been set on foot, to supply the dearth of dances and merrymakings. I am going to one at your Aunt Ticknor's tomorrow evening. It is called the *sans cérémonie,* and each lady invites a couple of gentlemen and a lady. I believe they card it first, and then dance. It is all one to me, who do neither. They chose me honorary member of one of these clubs, but I declined the honour, having more visiting on hand than I care for already. On Wednesday I dine with a lady party at our neighbour Appleton's, and last week dittoed at Mrs. Sears. By the bye, Ellen is much pleased that you at last have thought of her, and says she shall not be more than half as long in answering you. They are mighty busy in getting up *tableaux,* borrowing all the pictures round for subjects. Just now we have Shakspere readings from Mrs. Butler—crowded by all sexes and ages—*a l'outrance.* One has to take his seat an hour and a half before the time.

Since my last, Mr. Sparks has been duly confirmed by the overseers as President of Harvard. Mr. Everett, it is said, talks of passing some months abroad for his health, leaving his family still in Cambridge. His friends say he means henceforth to devote himself to letters, and write a book. Perhaps his friend Macaulay's fame has stimulated him. We shall see. Macaulay's book is like all that comes from his pen, both in manner and matter—rich, brilliant, antithetical, full of striking and original views, showing various reading and a prodigious power of illustration. His style is too set, emphatic, almost affected,—too declamatory for essay, much more for history. It is a clever book, and will no doubt raise his reputation.

Your Aunt Anna[1] was charmed with your letter. Pray remember poor Amory, who begins to feel mortified. He wrote four pages yesterday, and then tore them up. Your mother, grandmother, Elizabeth and Amory all send their love to you, to which add that most truly, my dear son, of Your affectionate Father

WM. H. PRESCOTT

[P.S.] In your next inform me of your proposed plans, as far as you can.

1. I.e. Anna Ticknor.

219.   From William Stirling[1]
                        (WHP Papers, Mass. Hist. Soc.)

Keir, Dunblane, N.B.
February 8, 1849

William H. Prescott Esqr.
Sir

As one of the multitude who have been instructed and delighted by your works, and as a cultivator of a corner of the same Spanish field, I venture to beg your acceptance of the accompanying volumes.[2] No English writer has done so much as yourself for the history of Spain. I venture therefore to hope that few readers of English will feel more interest in the Annals of her Artists. Of this, at least, I am sure, that there is no critic on either side of the Atlantic, whose opinion I should value more highly than the opinion of the author of *The History of Ferdinand and Isabella.*

I have heard it so frequently said that you are engaged in writing the History of Philip II, that I cannot help taking leave to say that I hope the rumour is well-founded, and that you have sufficiently recovered from the infirmity of eyesight (alluded to in the Preface to the *Conquest of Peru*) to enable you to prosecute that great undertaking with ease and satisfaction. But in whatever studies these lines may happen to find you engaged, accept of the earnest good wishes, as well as of the hearty admiration of Sir, Your obedient servant

WILLIAM STIRLING

1. William Stirling (1818–78) was a pioneer among Britons in his love of Spanish art. WHP met Stirling in London in 1850 but they corresponded for years, both before and after that date.

2. *Annals of the Artists of Spain* (3 vols., 1848).

220.   To Richard Bentley
                    (Richard Bentley Papers, Harvard College Library)
                                                      Boston, February 9th 1849
Richard Bentley Esq.
My dear Sir,

My friend and townsman Mr. Samuel Eliot has been engaged for some time in the composition of an historical work of which he has now completed two volumes. He wishes to have the book brought before the English public at the same time that it appears here and I have mentioned you to him, as a publisher under whose auspices, should you take the work, it would be desirable to have it come out.

Mr. Eliot is a young man who has a high reputation among us for his talents and literary acquisitions. The work submitted to you is of a comprehensive nature, and—from the glance I have had of it—shows scholarship and careful meditation. You will the more easily judge of its literary merits since he sends out the printed proofs—so much more legible than manuscript. What may be his views in regard to the publication, he will doubtless explain to you more fully when he sends the sheets.[1]

I am glad to see another edition of the *Peru* advertised; and I hope before long to have some good report of the goings of the Catholic Kings.

With great truth, my dear Sir, I remain Faithfully yours

WM. H. PRESCOTT

1. Bentley published Eliot's *History of the Liberty of Rome* in mid-1849.

221.   From John Church Hamilton
                         (WHP Papers, Mass. Hist. Soc.)
                                                      New York April 28, 1849
W. H. Prescott Esq.
   Boston
My dear Mr. Prescott

I have great cause of complaint against you that you passed thro our city without apprizing me of your being here—I only learned thro my daughter who got it from Mrs. Astor Jr. that you had been in town.

I now write to introduce to you Mr. Ditmars of Pennsylvania. He has come on here moved by the wishes of a number of gentlemen in his state and also by his own enthusiastic feelings to urge the preparation of a biography of our distinguished friend General Scott.

In pursuit of this object he now visits you—hoping you may be induced to undertake a history of the Campaign in Mexico. His friends have looked at the subject in various lights and all unite in the belief you are the person to do it.

Warm, as you know, my interest in you is—I beg you to reflect well before you decide definitively not to do it.

You will have no labor of collecting documents or explanatory matter. All will be done to your hand and most authentically and minutely. I will be in this subordinate relation your coadjutor with all my industry, for with me it will be a labor of love.

Listen then, I pray you, favorably to Mr. Ditmars' suggestions and write me soon on the subject.[1] Yours truly

J. C. HAMILTON

1. WHP was repeatedly requested to write what some of the interested parties referred to as the history of "the second conquest of Mexico." For numerous reasons, not least of which was his desire to avoid the hurly-burly of politics, he declined to undertake the task.

222.   To William Gardiner Prescott
(WHP Papers, Mass. Hist. Soc.)

Boston, May 1st, 1849

My dear William,

Since my last to you I have made a tour,[1] with Lizzie and Amory to New York and Philadelphia. We passed four or five days in the former place and a couple in the latter—long enough for Amory and me to see the streets and the theatres, and for Elizabeth to see her dear friend Miss Willing. So we have seen two great capitals that you, with all your travels, have never seen yet.

At New York we dined and danced, and Amory was spinning round with the belles of the New Amsterdam—as Knickerbocker calls it—till three in the morning, and three hours after was up for the cars. Since his return, poor fellow, he has been laid on his back with a scarlet fever. It has, after a week, nearly left him—somewhat the worse in point of strength. But on the whole he has got on—so far, at least—for it is a treacherous disorder—very well; and we have much reason to be thankful. His appetite is good, and he rejoices in an occasional cup of soup extracted from a potato and an onion.

When in New York I dined in company with Mr. Coote at Mr. Ray's. Mr. Coote told me much of you, and seems to like you very well. He was kind enough to offer to assist you in selecting a pair of candelabras for me. I think they should be of about the size of a pair which he brought home to his sister, and of a pattern somewhat similar, to judge from his description of them. You understand they are for the table and mantlepiece. I do not want a marble base, but wish the candelabras to be gilt bronze, with a figure of bronze not gilt, and not very large, supporting them. He told me the expense without the clock would not exceed probably 700 francs, and I would not exceed 800. Pray ask him and Mrs. Coote to aid you in the selection, and I am sure it will be in good taste. And be very careful to have them securely packed for the voyage. You can execute this commission the first time you are in Paris after receiving this. Only take care to advise me when they are shipped for Boston or New York, as the case may be. If you will also state to me the exact damage you incur, I will make it good with your bankers.

At Mr. Astor's, in New York, I dined with Washington Irving. He looked very well, and told me he had been industrious of late. I see the evidence of it in Murray's advertisement of two new works of his. You will see that our friend Samuel Eliot's book in 2 volumes is adver- tized by Bentley as in the press. It is quite a feather in Sam's cap, and I hope will help him to get the professorship of history made vacant by the reorganisation of Mr. Sparks—whose inauguration, by the bye, comes off in June. When in London you will not fail to see Bentley, as I have written him you would call on him, and I believe I gave you a note to him. I should like to know how you find my publisher. He writes me there is a plan for pirating the *Ferdinand and Isabella*. He may tell you about it, and I should like to know what he will do. The English copyright of that work does not stand on so sure ground as my later histories.

Macaulay's book has had a prodigious sale here, as well as in Eng- land. I hope you will have an opportunity of meeting with him in London. I suppose you will reach that metropolis of Christendom before the end of May. Though in your last, to your grandmother, you say nothing of your movements; and you write as calmly in Rome as if half of Italy were not at that very time upside down—as the other half, I suppose, will be before long. I shall be glad when you are out of it. I suppose you cannot have penetrated further than Florence. Perhaps you may be able next winter to make another escapade from

Paris, and strike across the plains of Lombardy. You will have time for it, if you think it worth while.

If you ever make another long tour, I trust you will be fortunate in your companions. It is an inestimable benefit to have those who are necessarily so much in our society and personal intimacy qualified by their own character to act well upon ours. How different a lesson do we get from our travels when we see the things that are strange to us through the medium of an enlarged and cultivated mind, sound principles, and a correct taste. Such a tour brings with it a lasting improvement, when the running commentary is in unison with the noble object of study and contemplation. I fear you have not had the great benefit of such influences, and perhaps have had to encounter, in some degree, the opposite—and, at best, that you have had to rely wholly on yourself. It is fortunate that I have such reliance on your principles and education that I do not doubt you have got nothing but good from your wanderings—though not all the good you might have got under happier auspices. I wish you had had my luck.[2] Pray, hereafter, rather travel alone than in company that you would not have selected from their own intrinsic good qualities.

When in England you will have enough to do to keep your wits wide awake. You will live a year in a month and you will turn it to good account. Colman's *Letters*,[3] which I have just bought, may give you a good idea of society and manners as they now exist in the best circles of London.

Your friend Ritchie is to be married on May 2d. Gordon Dexter[4] is a groomsman. Ritchie has been absent through the winter, as you know, and will not probably return to his business till the autumn. I doubt whether a New York belle will make the best wife for a Boston lawyer. It may very like, convert him, in time, into a New York one. Great doings are going on at the Sears's in expectation of the double wedding. Grace's comes off in about a fortnight, and the whole *famille* Rives will be soon en route from Virginia.[5] David goes to New York for his bridals. But I have used up my paper, and with love from your mother and all the household, I remain, my dear son, Ever your affectionate Father

WM. H. PRESCOTT

[P.S.] I enclose you a letter for Mills, with the address Edmund Dwight gave me. Edmund is a thorough man of business, and in one of the old firms. I spoke to Sumner about some letters; but as none are forthcoming, I shall say no more. I suspect he feels he has drained his credit. I very seldom see him. Mills's address is the *Oxford and*—something, perhaps *London* or *Cambridge Club,* which you will easily find.

1. In mid-April, 1849.

2. Harking back to his Italian excursion of 1816–17, WHP remembers the companionship of classically educated John Chipman Gray.

3. Henry Colman (1785–1849) had published his *European Life and Manners; In Familiar Letters to Friends* in both England and America in 1849.

4. Gordon Dexter, son of Elizabeth and Franklin Dexter, was WHP's nephew.

5. This is the family of William Cabell Rives (1793–1868), politician and diplomat. He served twice as American Minister to France, the second interval being between 1849 and 1853.

223.   From George Bancroft
(WHP Papers, Mass. Hist. Soc.)

1 Upper Belgrave St.
London 10 May '49

W. H. Prescott Esq.

Boston

My dear Prescott

Lady Emmeline Stuart Wortley, the daughter of the Duke of Rutland, is on a visit to the United States.[1] I cannot consent to her visiting Boston, without making to you the request of assisting with Mrs. Prescott to give her a welcome in Boston. Her example of undertaking a tour in our country will be imitated, and I trust that soon a tour to Niagara and the Alleghanies will be almost as common in the fashionable world in England, as a trip to Switzerland and the Appenines. With best regards to Mrs. Prescott I am ever my dear Prescott Faithfully Yours

GEORGE BANCROFT

1. Lady Emmeline Stuart-Wortley (1806–55) published her *Travels in the United States, etc. During 1849 and 1850* in 1851 in both England and America.

224.   To Daniel Webster
(Meredith Papers, The Historical Society of Pennsylvania)

Boston, June 20, 1849

Hon. Daniel Webster

My dear sir,

I have lately had my attention drawn to an affair, in which, I trust, you will take some interest as well as myself—my own not being founded on any personal acquaintance with the subject of it.

Mr. Hawthorne[1] has been recently removed from his place of survey of the port of Salem; but no successor has been named, and the administration, as I understand, have learnt some particulars which have led them to reconsider the subject, and may perhaps prevent any change, after all, being actually made in the office. I wish it may be so; for many respectable Whigs here do not see any good grounds for the removal.

Mr. Hawthorne, I am assured, has not mixed himself up with political matters, and indeed has taken so little interest in them that it has been a subject of reproach to him from the more zealous of his party. In discharging the duties of his office, he has conducted himself, I am told, very acceptably to those who have been brought into contract with him. His private life is beyond reproach, and he has certainly done honor to the country by his writings, which, however, have not sufficed for the support of himself and his young family.

For these reasons, it was with much concern that some who best know the circumstance of the case, and in whose judgment I have great confidence, have witnessed his removal from office. It will, they say, bring odium on the government, and on our own party, as inconsistent with the liberal principles which have been avowed in reference to appointments, and hitherto pursued. And if the real state of the affair were understood at headquarters, I cannot think that the measure would be persisted in. Will you allow me, therefore, to request your interest in his behalf?[2]

With great respect, I remain, my dear Sir, Sincerely yours

WM. H. PRESCOTT

1. Nathaniel Hawthorne (1804–64). The Salem period of his life was of immense importance to his writing.

2. Webster forwarded WHP's letter to Secretary of the Treasury William M. Meredith. Hawthorne, however, was soon relieved of his post.

225.   To Charles Sumner
                (Charles Sumner Papers, Harvard College Library)

Nahant, July 3d 1849

Charles Sumner Esq.
My dear Sumner,

I have read your eloquent oration with the attention which the subject and the manner of treating it well deserve. You afford your readers —as usual—much information drawn from books, as well as from long and ripened meditation; and few among them, I think, will be disposed to contest the soundness of your moral axioms.

Your parallel between public and private war is well put, and the inference is inevitable. I see nothing in which to differ from you, in regard to the question of right, now that you concede the right of self-defence, which, in its most extended sense, must cover that of asserting our political liberty. The great question is, as in the case of slavery, not whether the institution can be defended on moral grounds—still less on those of expediency—but as to the remedy—what is the practicable remedy? Those which you suggest of Congresses and Courts of Arbitration are the most obvious. But how are we to find a guaranty for their faithful and independent action? By what argument can we expect to prevail on the strong man to give up his strength and come down to the level of the weak!—to persuade Russia to disband her armies and England her navy? The term Commonwealth of Nations is somewhat illusory, where there is such a conflict of interests, races, languages, religions, &c. The municipal communities—the towns, counties, states, &c—to which you compare these independent nations, do not afford a fair parallel. The great state of Pennsylvania might consent to enter on equal terms into a compact with the little state of Delaware or Rhode Island, because each has need of greater strength—to be obtained only by such coalition. The State of Pennsylvania, though large as a *state,* would have been little as a nation. But the great powers of Europe have no need of buttresses to support them; and it is only a great moral conviction that would lead France or Russia to refer her disputes with a petty neighbor to a common tribunal. What would have induced Great Britain to refer her quarrel with her colonies to a third party?

And yet the time of the millennium may come, and the great empires of Christendom, which have no need of protection, and no need therefore of acknowledging a supreme tribunal with ultimate jurisdiction, may yet, from high moral considerations be led to adopt such a one, and to surrender their independent exercise of authority. You and I will not live to see it—that is very certain. But there is no reason why the way should not be cleared for such a desirable consummation by all that eloquence, argument, and moral persuasion, can enforce. You have done your work well in the cause, and deserve, and will receive the thanks of every friend of humanity—even those who have least confidence in the results.

One word respecting your personal affairs. You say it is two years since I have entered your office. I am surprized at it; and yet I have not been in Hillard's, or Gardiner's, or that of any other of my friends in that time—unless purely on matters of business. You ought to have known there could be no meaning in this. My intercourse with you, I rejoice to say, has never been ruffled by an unfriendly word or act; and where I may have differed from you as to some of your sentiments, or as to your manner of expressing them, I have always done justice to the elevation of your views and to the integrity of your motives. And this is well known both to your friends, and to some who are not your friends. But enough of this.[1]

I asked Hillard the other day to come down with you and dine with me at Nahant. Why cannot you both do this when Dr. Bethune is in town, and bring him with you. He will like to exchange the heats of Boston for the breezes of the ocean. I never ask more than three here for my fare is but simple—a plain piscatory banquet, and a cool and not bad glass to wash it down with. In short, cool air, cool drink, a warm dinner and a warm welcome. This is adjusting the temperatures rightly I believe. Only give me notice a day before, that you may find all things in order and me at hand.[2]

I remain, dear Sumner, as ever affectionately yours

WM. H. PRESCOTT

1. As Bancroft had done earlier, Sumner was estranging most of his Boston friends. WHP, within his circle in Boston, was a rarity in that he remained the friend of both men.

2. On July 19 WHP began to compose the opening passages of *Philip the Second*.

226.   To Francis Bowen
(Charles Roberts Autograph Collection, Haverford College Library)

Pepperell, October 22, 1849

Francis Bowen Esq.
My dear sir,

I have completed an article on Ticknor's *Spanish Literature*—to the tune of some sixty pages; including extracts to the amount of seventeen or eighteen. It is quite a heap, you see—probably more than you wanted—especially as it is rather thin porridge, I fear. But the plums from the book are big enough, and good enough, I trust, to make it go down. In truth, it is a very important work, and remarkably full of material. The book is to come out by Christmas—so it will be neck and neck with the Review. It would be a good thing if the Review should come out first! It nearly happened in the case of my maiden work—*Ferdinand and Isabella*. The extracts will be, therefore, as new to the public as this article—and a *trifle* better.

When shall I send it to you? It requires to be fairly copied—with a little trimming, and polishing off the rough. Will it answer your purposes by the latter part of next week, as I am rather busy just now in another way?[1] Very truly yours

W. H. PRESCOTT

1. Writing his first major review article in seven years, WHP helped to launch Ticknor's book, this review appearing in the *North American Review* of January, 1850, pp. 1–56. This proved to be WHP's last contribution to that periodical.

227.   To William Gardiner Prescott
                         (WHP Papers, Mass. Hist. Soc.)

Boston, October 28, 1849

My dear William,

Here we are in Beacon Street again! We returned day before yesterday, leaving the Highlands in all the melancholy beauty of the fading year. The foliage has been magnificent; but it has now taken the dull coloring of the European landscape—of this season. The town seems warm and comfortable. But I have enjoyed the bracing air of the hills in my morning walks—having walked about seven or eight miles a day. Amory has become very expert in wood-craft and water-craft. He and Edward Dexter have shot all over the country, and killed, I believe, a brace of woodcock between them. He has also launched a famous boat on the Nissitisset—well accommodated with cushioned seats—in which the ladies have all taken particular pleasure, and our quiet river has been explored through all its windings.

Well, here we are again in the haunts of men!—bustle, brick, and business; and the first days of transition are to me, who love order, a horror. But we are coming to rights again.

The Leghorn venture has arrived—the Italian translation and the marbles. The last have shared the fate of everything else in Italy. Half the columns are broken. Provoking enough; but as, fortunately, they do not appear to be compound fractures, I have no doubt I can get them mended. They are very pretty; and your little vase—an antique lamp, I should think—gives great delight to your mother—for more reasons than one.

What a fine time you are having in the country! English country life is the best phase of society in England—probably in the world.[1] The respectable character of the pursuits and the elegant way of living—and the regard for religion constantly shown by them—cannot be too much praised. I am truly glad you have so good an opportunity of seeing how these noble establishments are conducted. You seem to fall into country sports very well. It is something for a Yankee not to open the gates, but to take them at a leap. I fancy you did not go over a five-barred gate. If you did, I think you wanted the discretion which is the better part of valor. For a fall would be no joke to a traveller, who wants all his limbs in good order; and I know from experience how hard it is, without a good deal of practice, to keep one's saddle in a running leap. At all events, I am glad you did not come off like Commodore Trunnion, whose horse ran away with him, and then spilt him in a quagmire. How very kind the Marshalls have been to you. It tells pretty well for you that they should have put up with you so long. I shall look for your account of your visit to Sir James Graham,[2] and to Mr. Stirling—in the last of whom I feel much interest. You will be in Borderland, I suppose, which is not altogether strange land to you.

When shall you set out for the land of the Don? You will have received, before you get this, a nice lot of letters to the best people in Madrid. Make the most of them, as I know you will. Your French will put you on an equality with the Spaniards—both meeting on a foreign ground for conversation. I hope you will be able to get to Granada. But you will see when in Madrid what you can do. You have read Mr. Ford's book, no doubt, and might, if you have time, look into Gil Blas again *Don Quixote*. Spain in the 19th century is not so very different from Spain in the 17th.

Your Uncle Ticknor has arranged with Murray and with the Harpers. The last take 3500 copies of him at once—a great offer. I have concocted a long paper for the *North American*—rather twaddling but I hope it will do the book some service. I have made honorable mention in it both of Mr. Ford and Mr. Stirling—as I had occasion to mention them and their doings, and did it now *con amore,* for their kindness to you. When in London you will see Ford again, and also Mr. Rogers, and Mr. Lawrence,[3] of course. Bentley, I see, advertizes a smaller edition of all my historicals. As he keeps a large one on hand too, I am inclined to think it may be best for my credit, as well as his pocket.

Have you heard that Mr. Norton is very ill?[4] They feel much alarmed, though more encouraged the last day or two. The cause is a diarrhoea, to which he is constitutionally subject. Every one else that you know, I believe, is well. Next Tuesday, Tom Perkins leads the fair Lilly to the altar. A long wooing! Elizabeth and Amory to be present. The week after Mr. Winthrop[5] does the like by Mrs. Welles—the widower and the widow. So wags the world with us. I met your friend Harry Ritchie this morning, and his bride—all blooming. They are deposited in one of the houses in the Milldam. The more flowers we can transplant from New York the better.

Your Uncle and Aunt Ticknor always take the kindest interest in you, and in your doings.

With love from your mother and all the household (your grandmother, by the bye, made an escapade this morning to Philadelphia, with Gordon Dexter, to be gone a fortnight—pretty well for more than fourscore years!)

I remain, my dear Son, Your affectionate Father,

WM. H. PRESCOTT

1. Within a year WHP would take a trip which confirmed anew this estimate of English life.

2. Probably Sir James Robert George Graham (1792–1861), English statesman.

3. Abbott Lawrence (1792–1855), merchant, manufacturer, statesman, philanthropist and diplomat, had replaced Bancroft as the American Minister at the Court of St. James. His son James married WHP's daughter Elizabeth.

4. Andrews Norton (1786–1853), theologian and scholar. WHP knew him as tutor, lecturer and librarian at Harvard.

5. Robert Charles Winthrop (1809–94), a handsome member of a family of prestige, served in Congress between 1840 and 1851, and an even longer time as President of the Massachusetts Historical Society. WHP knew him in all his capacities. Winthrop's second wife was Laura Derby Welles.

228.   From Richard Bentley
(Extracts, WHP Papers, Mass. Hist. Soc.)

New Burlington Street, November 8, 1849

W. H. Prescott Esq.

My dear Sir

I beg to acknowledge the receipt of your letter of the 22nd ultimo with regard to the new and cheaper Edition of "Ferdinand." I saw so clearly that some attempt would be made to invade the copyright of that work, that I should have been wanting in due care if I had not anticipated the pirates. I should have fought them at a disadvantage if they had been first in the field; for law is a long, tedious and unsatisfactory affair even at the best, and I might *not have been able to maintain my ground* after all. As it is, the measure has been hailed as a wise and enterprizing step; and I have no doubt that profit will follow as well as praise. You will perceive my sincerity in the move by my also publishing *Mexico* and *Peru* in a similar form. Of the latter of which work I had only recently reprinted a large edition. I trust the library editions will continue to sell for both our sakes. Your son when he did me the favor of calling here explained to me the error into which you had fallen in regard to the copyright question.

.   .   .   .

I hope shortly to see your son again on his return from Scotland, whither he went on his return from Switzerland.

I remain, my dear Sir Yours most faithfully

RICHARD BENTLEY

[P.S.] I have sent two copies of [the] new Edition of *Ferdinand* and I shall have great pleasure in sending you as many more as you desire.

229.   To William Gardiner Prescott
                  (WHP Papers, Mass. Hist. Soc.)

Boston, December 2d, 1849

My dear William,

By the mail of last week we received yours dated from Frampton House—a very agreeable letter, giving us a very pleasant peep into country life in Dorsetshire. You are most fortunate in having this opportunity of seeing English society under its most original aspect, and, I should imagine, its most attractive. Your accounts of it are some of the best parts of your correspondence. But I suppose before this reaches you, English country, and cities too, will have nearly faded from your view, or at least that you will be preparing for your departure for the land of the Cid. When you are in Paris, you will attend to the candelabras—when in Madrid, to the fans. Brooks desires me to say that he would not exceed forty dollars for both that you are to get for him, that is twenty apiece, and would be glad to have them cheaper. Let me know the cost of your several commissions, and I will remit the money to the Barings.

I have now disposed of gossip, that I may have the rest of the letter for something of a serious nature. You were told by Elizabeth that we were to have our dance on the coming Wednesday. But it is now postponed—probably till your return. Our thoughts have been occupied with an event of too shocking a nature to allow any room for merriment. You have most probably learnt, by rumor at least, of the mysterious disappearance of Dr. George Parkman[1]—the father of your late travelling companion. The last accounts of him were of an appointment with Dr. Webster[2] at the Medical College in Boston. This was between one and two, on Friday the 23d of November—ten days since. A large reward was offered for his discovery, by Mr. Shaw, but ineffectually till, day before yesterday, a small portion of a dead body was found in a vault of the College, which had connection only with Dr. Webster's laboratory. This and some other suspicious circumstances led to Dr. Webster's arrest as the probable murderer! This occurred on Friday evening, the 30th of November. Some bones of the head, &c were also found in the furnace, nearly destroyed by fire. Since then a still larger fragment of the body, on which some wounds appear, has been discovered in the laboratory, covered up with tan and with minerals in a box. I don't know the whole amount of evidence against the unhappy man. But there are other corroborative circumstances, such as his having had a constant and very unusual fire in the furnace the last week.

He owed Dr. Parkman a small sum of money—as well as myself. Dr. Parkman was very peremptory in requesting punctual payment. This is understood to have led to some rough language between them before this; and if the deed was done by Dr. Webster, it was doubtless the result of some such angry altercation—as the meeting had reference to the payment of money.

But I trust that Dr. Webster will be able to show his innocence. His deportment for the week following before he was apprehended was so perfectly cheerful and every way natural, without gloom on the one hand or over-acting on the other, as would be scarce possible in a man of so very excitable a temperament, who had been betrayed into the commission of so horrid a crime. The Medical College, though not that part of it, is devoted to anatomy, and subjects are frequently brought there. Nor is it possible, I suspect, in the burnt and mutilated condition of these remains—in which the head and hands are wanting —to identify them with Dr. Parkman. Yet Dr. Parkman was seen to enter the College, with the intention of soon returning home, and was never seen to leave it.

The coroner has now the case under consideration, and medical examinations of the remains are going on. The inquest will not be held till Wednesday (I write on Sunday). We shall see that the unhappy man has good counsel to defend him. Your Uncle Dexter,[3] who has looked carefully into the case, thinks he will not be convicted; but alas! if that be all, what will life be to him? I have seen him twice in prison—the first time, much overcome; the second, tranquil—protesting his innocence. I was today at Cambridge with his distressed family —distressed, indeed, though firmly believing his innocence—their only comfort. Their friends are all most ready to show their sympathy. They have great need of it.

Your grandmother is much disturbed by the event, as, indeed, every one is greatly shocked by it. The whole town is talking of nothing else

—the mass of the people wrought up to the greatest indignation. But Dr. Webster has had friends in his adversity who have striven to encourage him by assurances of confidence in his ability to vindicate his character. The talk is so much about these horrid details as to throw quite a gloom over the town, such as I never before witnessed. It is not probable that the trial will come on before January. We will keep you informed of every thing material that occurs in relation to it.

I am truly sorry to be obliged to fill my letter with such a dark tale of domestic woe. But I thought it better to write you fully than to leave you to glean your knowledge of it through the uncertain and incorrect channels of the newspapers.

We are all well, and all desire loving remembrances to you. We go on as usual, only not at this time with extra-ordinary demonstrations of gaiety, for we are akin to the family, though not to the Doctor himself, and the commiseration for them is universal.

But I hear the bell which summons me to the library. Mr. Twisleton[4] —brother of Lord Say and Sele, a very intelligent Englishman, is to pass the evening here. He reminds me of Lord Carlisle. Adieu, my dear boy. With many blessings on you, I remain now and always Your affectionate Father

WM. H. PRESCOTT

1. Dr. George Parkman was a prosperous Boston physician. Following his graduation from Harvard, in 1809, he had studied medicine at Aberdeen.

2. John White Webster (1793–1850), professor of chemistry at Harvard for a quarter of a century, had married Harriet Hickling, Mrs. William Prescott's half sister. Convicted of the murder of Dr. Parkman, he was executed in 1850.

3. I.e. Franklin Dexter.

4. Edward Turner Boyd Twisleton (1809–74), English politician, traveler and socialite, knew WHP both in America and England.

230.   To Isaac Lea[1]
(Archives, American Philosophical Society)

Boston, January 22d, '50

Isaac Lea Esqr.
My dear sir,

I have received from Mexico three volumes, from their author, Don Lucas Alamán, which he desires me to present in his name to the American Philosophical Society. Sr. Alamán was formerly Minister of Foreign Affairs in Mexico. He is a man of distinguished ability, and of late years, since his retirement from office, has devoted himself to letters. The historical Dissertations contained in the two first volumes are of much value for the illustration of the Mexican annals, for which the writer had some peculiar advantages, as having under his care the archives of the family of Cortés. The other work—*Historia de Méjico* —embraces the modern history of that country, during the revolutions there from 1808 till 1820. It seems to me, from a cursory inspection, to be an important work, which must be read with interest by those who feel a curiosity in the subject.

I shall be obliged by your presenting these volumes in the name of Sr. Alamán to the society, and it will give me great pleasure if it will inscribe his name on the list of its honorary members—a distinction which I know will be very gratifying to him.[2] I shall be happy in such a case to be the medium of communicating it to him.

I pray you to excuse the trouble I give you; but as I am personally unacquainted with the librarian, and know the interest which you take in the affairs of the society, I take the liberty to address myself to you.

With much regard, I remain, my dear sir, Truly yours

WM. H. PRESCOTT

1. Isaac Lea (1792–1886), zoologist, author and publisher, was known to WHP through the American Philosophical Society.
2. Early in 1851 Alamán was elected to membership in the American Philosophical Society.

231.   To William Gardiner Prescott
                      (WHP Papers, Mass. Hist. Soc.)

Boston, February 3, 1850

My dear son,

The steamer sails on the sixth instant from this port, and this letter will make one of its sixty or seventy thousand talks between friends on different sides of the water. I suppose it will travel after you to Madrid, where I hope it will find you safe and sound after a tedious, and at this season, from the accounts we have of the snow in France, I fear formidable journey. We are enjoying very fine weather—at this date there is no snow worth speaking of on the Common, and it rained all this morning, at a temperature of 40°. I do not believe you have fared so well. We were very sorry to learn that your old enemy has taken you by the throat again. The Paris climate does not agree with you. And I fear that of Madrid, of which there is an old proverb, you know, will not be much better. But after you have seen enough of the society there—which may take five or six weeks—you will have a delightful season for the south; and I wish I had that carpet in the Arabian Tales, and I would set my foot on it, and be with you when you take that trip; for I should be travelling over my own ground again. I send you, by in large, however, a few additional letters of introduction, which Payson was kind enough to give me for you. They are to ladies, which is just what you want. Pray do not omit, so soon as you have seen the parties, to write him, giving some account of the manner in which they are received—and thank him, for he deserves it. It was his own doing, without any suggestion from me, of course.

In your letter to Elizabeth you give us a pretty fair account of your Paris experiences. Do you keep a journal? It is a great pity if you do not. You have had immense opportunities for seeing what is most worth seeing, and most difficult to be seen, in the way of society. And yet if you are too indolent to make memoranda of it, it will all run off like water from your memory. You can *always* save one hour for scribbling out of the four and twenty. And if you are confined to the house by weather or illness, what a clear field you have then for reminiscences. But I dare say you give a good many of these supernumerary moments to cramming for your tour. I dare say, too, you do not annihilate life in Europe by sleeping more hours than is necessary. You ought to be wide awake when there is so much to see, and to treasure up for the rest of your life. Your letters to your mother and me should by all means be very particular as to the persons. You see I had rather hear of persons than places, which last can be got in guide-books. Yet you have not told us as much of the people—some of them very interesting —whom you met in Paris. Pray take more time for your Spanish correspondence.

It is high time you should be in Spain. I want you to be among natives—not with a Yankee clique, who keep you still at home while you fancy yourself abroad. But enough of lecturing.

For domestic news, what is there? Your mother wrote to you of the deaths that have occurred, one after another, and I will not repeat them, but tell you of the more lively doings here. There has not been much gaiety this winter—no dances; you will find them in Spain—the land of the dance. There have been talking parties enough of late, which are as much to my taste as any other, not caring a button for either. Lizzie passed three days last week, together with Cora, Harriet Appleton, Augusta Peabody, and Miss Timmins, at Mr. Copley Green's. They had fine drives in the sleigh—billiards—pleasant dinners—&c. It is quite *a l'Anglaise*—the style of the establishment, not omitting that excellent feature in English country life—the family prayers.

Charles Perkins[1] has issued cards for a *matinee musicale* for tomorrow. He is composer and performer. Lizzie, Mrs. Hauteville, and I join forces and go. I am quite a connoisseur, you know. We have had no

matchmaking of late to stir us up. But *on dit* that your friend Dr.
Brooks is making the agreeable to Miss Timmins. It may, however,
only be a little flirtation between the parties. Another of your friends,
Benjamin Welles, is positively engaged to Mrs. Schemerhorn of New
York, by which he gets some money, I understand; and very likely
something better, in a good wife. We seem to be colonizing Boston
with New York lasses. Harry Ritchie passed last Sunday evening with
us, when we mustered some twenty, including Searses and Wormeleys.
He is a good fellow, in every sense, I believe. Your mother and I called
last week on our neighbors, Mr. and Mrs. Sargent of New York, who
were kind to you in Paris. We shall ask them to drop in on some Sunday evening. She is much liked here, and spoke very kindly of you.
Rogers (Jacob) called here the other morning, and told us all about
you. He says you will not be in a hurry to get home, he thinks. Well,
make the most of your funds and your time; but when you do come,
I hope it will give you as much pleasure as it will us, or your tour will
have been lost time. One of the best results of travel is to make a man's
country dearer to him than ever. Count Circourt wrote very kindly of
you to your Uncle Ticknor; said that you had formed a very correct
estimate of what you had seen abroad, but not at all to the disparage-
ment of your own country, which you seemed to prize as you ought.
Laudatus a laudato is a good thing.

Mrs. Sears has just sent in a note touching the purchase of some
Spanish fans for her and Ellen. I will remit forty dollars on account of
it to the Barings. The other charges you have incurred, you write, will
be settled separately with the Paris bankers. *Tant mieux.* Payson thinks
you had best send your purchases in Madrid home via Cádiz, to save
vexation of duties, &c., if you take them with you. Mr. Burton, to whom
you have a note—an old friend and kinsman of ours—will always take
charge of them at Cádiz. I have only to say, if you hear aught of your
Uncle Ticknor's book in Spain, do not omit to write it. It will please
him. Good-bye, dear Will. With ever so much love from your mother
and the household, I remain now and ever Your affectionate Father

WM. H. PRESCOTT

Mrs. Sears's note—
1 fan, dark top, ornamented with gold
Pearl sticks	do.	do.	do.
1 fan, dark top,	do.	do.	do.
Dark sticks	do.	do.	do.

$20 each; and if the slightest inconvenience to William to bring them
in his trunk, on no account to attempt it, as it is of no importance
whatever, and merely a fancy.

P.S. On reflection, I will enclose this letter in a common envelope with Payson's. Today, the 5th, the glass at 12°. Such are our changes; but no snow. In my letter I have only given you gossip of the town. Yet general politics are becoming interesting. There is a very bad feeling in Congress on the slave question between North and South. The Southerners fume greatly about a separation. The North has the power and the South the brag; but if the North push their power to extremes, some mischief may grow out of it. Mr. Clay has brought in a compromise bill, in reference to the various topics of initiation. It is to be hoped that there are moderate men enough in both parties to carry this or some other compromise through.[2]

Your mother desires me not to conclude without informing you that your friend Frederick Cunningham is to be married in a few weeks, and will live the first year with his father.

1. Probably Charles Callahan Perkins (1823–86), artist and author of works on art.
2. WHP engaged in no scholarly labor during the early months of 1850; indeed he even failed to make entries in his journal.

232.   To Richard Bentley
            (Richard Bentley Papers, Harvard College Library)

Boston, February 4th, 1850

My dear Sir,

I received by the last the copy of the new edition of *Ferdinand and Isabella*, for which I am much obliged to you. I shall be very happy to receive the copy of Murray's *Cities and Wilds of Andalusia*,[1] which you say you sent me, but which has not come to hand.

I shall be very glad to hear from you that the reduced size of the *Ferdinand* and the other works puts money into your pocket. I trust you will always keep a supply of the larger size on hand, if it be only to maintain the credit of the books—on which the cash, moreover, not a little depends.

I should be happy to contribute the notice you mention of Mr. Ticknor's book. But I have written one—a very long one—published in the last *North American Review*, which, should you ever go into another edition of my *Miscellanies*, might be incorporated with it.[2] (Would an edition in this smaller size not pay?) Review writing is so much out of my beat now, that I never fall into it, except from absolute necessity; as, when a friend puts to sea for the first time, one would give him a good breeze. In this case, I have blown my blast.

As to the portrait, it is in the hands of an engraver who is taking it

from the bust, and who works very slowly. But I can bide his time.
When it is done, I shall send it to you—and I like it—with much
pleasure.

I remain, my dear Sir, Very truly yours

WM. H. PRESCOTT

1. Cultivating the writer from whom he awaited a fourth history, Bentley
frequently sent WHP copies of titles which he had recently published.

2. A short review of Ticknor's book which appeared unsigned in the *Boston
Daily Advertiser* on January 1, 1850, was now expanded and sent to Bentley by
its author, WHP. The expanded version was published in *Bentley's Miscellany*,
XXVII (1850), 385–87. Soon new editions of Prescott's essays in both England
and America added as their fourteenth item WHP's assessment of Ticknor's
work which had appeared in the *North American Review*.

233.   To Susan Prescott
(WHP Papers, Mass. Hist. Soc.)

Baltimore, Thursday evening [April 11, 1850]

My dear Wife

I do not like to go to bed before writing you a line to tell you of our
whereabouts.[1] Although—to say truth—I am so tired that one eye has
gone to sleep already.

I dined at Bancroft's[2] on Tuesday—a lady dinner—of twenty persons
—extremely *recherché*—and elegant. I have seen nothing in better style
in New York. They were both very kind and hospitable. I handed in
the lady, who was very pleasant and full of anecdote, relating to her life
in England—of great interest to me.

Wednesday morning we flitted to Philadelphia—dined there at four
o'clock. Walked about the city—shopped—&c. In the evening, all to
the Museum, like ours. Amory grew tired—came home—and all went
to bed by eleven.

This morning rose betimes—came here by the rail-road without
accident or adventure. Found Kennedy[3] with his carriage at the depot
—went to our lodgings. Then the ladies went in his carriage (very kind)
about town. Amory and I walked with him. He dined with us at six
—and I was so tired that before he left, my eye-lids were continually
closing.

Tomorrow rise with the lark—and ho! for Washington. Elizabeth
and I dine tomorrow with Lady Bulwer,[4] and in the evening to the
President's levee,[5] all of us. On Saturday we all dine (except Cora)
with Winthrop,[6] who will have the English minister and lady, Ticknor
and Anika and I do not know who else.

Have you seen the report of the doings at the Maryland Historical Society?—and the handsome manner in which Bulwer spoke of me. You will find it probably in the *National Intelligencer*—of this week. So look at it—and read it to Mother.

We are all well. Charles Amory writes he found you not at all dull —and rejoicing in a dress-maker. Martha[7] is [a] treasure—to me especially. I am truly glad she came with us. Elizabeth and Amory are both well. With love to Mother—I am ever your affectionate

W. H. P.

1. On April 8, in a miscellaneous party that included daughter Elizabeth, son Amory, the Ticknors and others, WHP set out on a trip to Washington which consumed two weeks.

2. Upon their return from England the George Bancrofts took up residence in New York City.

3. I.e. John Pendleton Kennedy.

4. Sir Henry and Lady Bulwer then presided over the British legation in Washington.

5. Despite his lack of polish, President Zachary Taylor won the affectionate respect of WHP.

6. I.e. Robert Charles Winthrop of Boston.

7. Martha Babcock Greene Amory (1808–98), wife of WHP's brother-in-law Charles Amory.

234.   To William Gardiner Prescott
(WHP Papers, Mass. Hist. Soc.)

Boston, Sunday, April 28, 1850

My dear William,

Is this the last letter I shall send you? I suppose not, but your coming letters will determine. We shall all be glad to see you. We are now, or shall be tomorrow, without a son in our home. Amory sails tomorrow, at seven o'clock in the morning. He would have gone yesterday but the captain could not get his hands together. He sails in the "Orissa," a ship of six hundred tons belonging to Rollins and Atkins. He has an excellent captain, named Sears, who takes his wife with him. She is said to be a good sailor and a very nice person, and made the last voyage with him. A nephew of Mr. I. P. Davis, who was in Mills's counting-house, goes out also. He is a very good young man, educated, and a good companion for Amory. We thought it best that Amory should follow his inclinations in making this voyage to Calcutta, which would let him into the mode of transacting the India business, give him health, (and his lungs are not too strong), and employ him actively during a year, which at home would pass away almost in idleness; for as the oldest person in the counting-room, he would be pretty much master of his own time. He shows a manly spirit in going, and I have given him a little adventure to turn to the best account he can in Calcutta. Your mother feels very sad at the prospect of our desolation, but the prospect will brighten soon. Yet do not hurry home before your money is gone on this account. I would have you see all that your funds will allow you; as it may be your only chance for seeing the Old World —at least in the like case I have found it so. Amory desires me to say that if you write to him you must address to the care of "Baboos Radhakissen Mitter Rajkissen Mitter & Co., Calcutta," and *prepay the letter* when you mail it for Calcutta.[1]

I returned last week from a very pleasant excursion to Washington, which I made with Lizzie, Amory, and your Aunt Martha Amory. Your Uncle William Amory joined us at Baltimore. We passed a week in the American capital—heard the debates, and—at least one of us—saw the pistol drawn, not fired, in the Senate[2]—dined and danced and supped to our hearts' content. I began with a dinner at the English Minister, Sir Henry Bulwer—with Lizzie, and we ended with a dinner at the White House. It is a noble palace and handsomely furnished. "Rough and Ready" is a very pleasing old soldier—of kindly and most cordial manners—very simple, yet with nothing vulgar in his air. He told us that the first time he ever dined at the Presidential palace was in 1816, when a young man. He was invited by Madison, and when he came he thumped away at the door with his knuckles—never having seen a bell—till another gentleman arriving showed him how to pull it, and so brought the servants. That is an anecdote of the head of a great nation! The honors of the house are admirably done by his daughter, Mrs. Bliss, a lively and very handsome woman, and her husband, Colonel Bliss, a man of very gentlemanlike manners. I saw no one in Washington who interested me more than Mr. Clay. He dined with us at Sir Henry Bulwer's, on his seventy-fourth birthday. His manners are very courteous, and even cordial. He came to see us in our quarters more than once, and took much pleasure in talking with the ladies. I should have told you that Cora was of our party, though she did not visit with us. She is a dear, good girl, and a true friend of Elizabeth.

We passed four days in New York. I dined with two or three of your friends who gave me some account of your European ways—Mrs. Bancroft, Wainwright, and Minturn.[3] All concurred in speaking highly of you and of your gentlemanlike deportment, which pleased me much. Mrs. Bancroft is a great friend of yours, and she is really a charming woman. I had one of the most elegant dinner parties at her house which I saw in my tour. She occupies an excellent house in New York. At

Mrs. Minturn's I also had a very pleasant dinner—as pleasant as good
company and good cheer and a handsome establishment could make
it. Washington Irving dined with us there.

This is the sort of life you have been leading now for almost two
years—something too much of it. I found a fortnight long enough. You
are soon to return to another sort of life. You must look on these two
years as an episode to your regular existence. You have been a per-
petual guest at the feast of pleasure—but the pleasantest feast will cloy
in time, and pleasure when it is the business of life ceases to please.
You have mixed with men who, gay and careless as they may appear in
society, have had their working hours and working years to gain them
the distinction which gave them consequence in your eyes. Yet in
Europe there is a large class of *far-nientes,* who make a sort of society
of themselves, and whose demands have therefore created all the facilities for killing time, not demanded, and therefore not known in the
New World. Here every man that is a man is busy with something. The
few idlers are all to be noticed for their habitual discontent, their
grumbling, and their incessant change of place. But *coelum non ani-
mum,* &c. You have doubtless met some of these specimens on the other
side of the water—sometimes men of really fine parts, rendered useless
by the want of power to accommodate themselves to the usages and
actual condition of our state of society. And a fortunate state it is which
will not tolerate drones, or at least tolerates them only on the condition
of self-inflicted misery. Yet it is a hard thing for a young man to pass
from the gay society of Europe—and you have had an extra share of it
—to the quiet business occupations of our New England life. It will be
repulsive at first—and dreary from its monotony. This you will expect,
and make up your mind to. And, to a great extent, that must be the
case with the European traveller, if he is a man of business, a student,
or a politician—when he returns home from his travels. But never
fear. After the first plunge, you will get accommodated to the necessary
change, till the new and more profitable way of life will become necessary to your existence, and you will find your happiness where you
find your fame and fortune, and when you feel that you are pursuing a
career that must best answer the great ends of your being. You will
then look on the last two years as a beautiful vision, filling your mind
with agreeable images and a store of recollections that may not only
be agreeable but serviceable as affording you means of larger comparison and illustration for the practical duties of life. I have seen more
than one person—not fools in other respects—repine on returning
home because America was not Europe! As if, too, Europe on a holiday
were the same as working-day Europe. A young fellow on his travels is

enjoying one long holiday. But every schoolboy knows that vacations derive their value from term-times.

Monday.—At seven this morning Amory was summoned on board his vessel, and he went amidst our parting Goodbyes and God bless yous. But in half an hour he returned, as a heavy storm, set in from the north-east, made it impossible to sail. I shall keep this letter open to advise you of his actual departure.

Today I have an English gentleman—Mr. Twisleton—a brother of Lord Say and Sele to dine with me—with your Uncle Ticknor, Mr. Gray, your Uncle William Amory, and Hillard. Mr. Twisleton is a very accomplished and amiable man, an excellent specimen of British aristocracy. I believe there is nothing more to tell you. They say Mr. Thomas Perkins's estate turns out less than 50,000 dollars!—a wife and four children.

Monday, 4 o'clock, P.M. The wind has come round south-west, and Amory has just taken his departure, under a smacking breeze, leaving your mother, I fear, with too heavy a heart to dine with us. He first visits the Isle of France, which, as he spends a fortnight there, will prolong his voyage one month. So he will probably not be at home before the 1st of April.

With much love from the family, I remain, my dear son, always, Your affectionate father

WM. H. PRESCOTT

1. Amory did not attend college. At this time he was in his twenty-first year.

2. On April 17, 1850, Senator Foote of Mississippi had confronted Senator Benton of Missouri.

3. Robert Bowne Minturn (1805–66), merchant, shipowner and socialite in New York City. Quite soon he helped to arrange WHP's crossing to England.

235.   To Charles Sumner
               (Charles Sumner Papers, Harvard College Library)

Beacon Street, Tuesday Morning [c. April 30, 1850]

Dear Sumner,

Since you think so well of Gliddon's scheme, I will put my name down at Ticknor's bookstore.[1] It seems to me that $1200 is a round sum for a mummified Egyptian—though he were the slave of Pharaoh.

I returned last week from my Southern trip—passed a week in the American Metropolis—and did not see the pistol drawn in the Senate, though I did see many a cork drawn in the banquet hall from bottles well-charged with grape, or at least the juice of it. The result of all the hospitality I experienced is that I have come home Rough and

Ready to the backbone. Do you not admire my patriotism? If you were to spend half an hour with the old chief's daughter, who does the honors of the house, I think you would be a convert too. But I don't know. Are you not one of those unaccountables whom Man delights not, nor woman neither. Faithfully yours

WM. H. PRESCOTT

1. The well-known downtown Boston bookstore of William Davis Ticknor (1810–64), who was also prominent as publisher.

236.   From Harper & Brothers
(WHP Papers, Mass. Hist. Soc.)

New York, May 7, 1850.

Private
W. H. Prescott Esq.
Dear Sir,

We are about starting a Monthly Magazine, selected mostly from Foreign Periodicals. In the first Number we insert from the London Pictorial News an Engraving of a Bust of Mr. Alison[1] and also of Mr. Macaulay.[2] We are also having one made of your Bust, and wish some reading matter, as with the others, which we hope you will have furnished as early as convenient.[3] We presume you will readily find a copy of the last Number, with the Supplement, of the News, in Boston, for your guidance. Very respectfully Your Obedient Servants,

HARPER & BROTHERS

1. Archibald Alison (1792–1867), famed for his *History of Europe*. WHP met him in 1850.
2. Thomas Babington Macaulay (1800–1859) won renown with his *History of England*. WHP also met him in 1850.
3. WHP's likeness was reproduced and his career sketched in Volume I, Number 1, of *Harper's New Monthly Magazine* (June, 1850), pp. 138–39.

237.   To William Gardiner Prescott
(WHP Papers, Mass. Hist. Soc.)

Boston, May 14th 1850

My dear William,

You will be more surprised by the contents of this letter than any you have received for a long time, I fancy. At last the die is cast, the stateroom is taken and paid for; and I embark in the good ship "Niagara"—British Mail Packet—from New York on the 22d instant. Mr.

Kirk will come out with me, as I shall want a friendly pair of eyes, and he wants to see his fatherland. So this will make the trip as agreeable as any that takes me from home can be. The greatest pleasure in prospect is that of seeing you. Indeed I should not go unless you were to be there. But as the Spring comes round, I am continually talking, you know, of going, till they call it the Spring-halt; and now your mother, grandmother and all urge me so to make the most of your companionship that I shall be with you, God willing, in three weeks. If you are in London soon enough, can't you come to Liverpool for me? I have written to Mr. Lawrence to ask him to get rooms at the Clarendon or one of the best hotels[1] not far from him—a parlor and two bedrooms for you and me. I shall probably stay in London till the latter part of July—then see something of the English country till September, and return then with you, so as to get the Pepperell change of the leaf.

I have also asked Mr. Lawrence to engage me a good servant, as I shall want one capable of taking care of me and making me full as comfortable as in Beacon St.

I shall send a duplicate of this to Greene & Co., as it is possible you may return through France, but I trust not. I have no time to add anything before the letter can be copied and mailed. We are all well and with much love

I remain, my dear William Your affectionate father,

WM. H. PRESCOTT

P.S. Lizzie has gone to pass a few days with her friend Mrs. David Sears, and when she wrote her letter did not believe my poddering on the matter would result in this.[2]

1. WHP had rooms at Mivart's on Brook Street, close to Grosvenor Square.

2. At least four things contributed to WHP's rather sudden decision to visit England: (1) the recent trip to Washington, D.C., had been highly relished, (2) he was not immersed in any significant research and writing, (3) he was prodded toward transatlantic travel by Bancroft in New York and Twisleton in Boston, and (4) it was the best season of the year for travel.

238.   To George Bancroft
                  (Draft, WHP Papers, Mass. Hist. Soc.)

                                          Boston, May 14th '50

My dear Bancroft,

Did you ever think to hear of my packing up for the Atlantic trip? The time has come, however, and after a good deal of poddering and pondering, I have made up my mind to go in the very next steamer, that sails from New York—the "Niagara." I have written by telegraph today to our friend Minturn to ask him to get me a good stateroom with a couple of berths in it. Now it is possible he may not be in town. Could you do me the favor to see about the matter for me in case he is absent? Should I be able to get the said accommodations I shall come to New York on Monday, and, if you will allow me, on Tuesday, take a *family dinner* with you, in order to ask some scores of questions of your wife and you as to proprieties, *convenances* &c &c in the London world, which will much relieve me of awkward uncertainties that one feels in going to a strange place. Would that you both were in London now.[1]

Remember me kindly to her, and believe Faithfully yours,

WM. H. PRESCOTT

1. Minturn acquired the tickets, Bancroft gave the dinner, and WHP asked his many questions.

239.   From Edward Everett
(WHP Papers, Mass. Hist. Soc.)

Cambridge, U.S.A., 20 May 1850

My dear Prescott,

I enclose you letters to Mr. Macaulay, Lord Ashburton, Lord John Russell, and the Duke of Northumberland.[1]

I would with pleasure increase the number, but that I am certain no letters will be of any importance to you. If, however, you think of any person likely to be known to me, to whom you would prefer to take a line, do not hesitate to say so.

Wishing you all the enjoyment you deserve, I remain sincerely your friend.

[EDWARD EVERETT]

P.S. The letter to Lord John Russell is also a letter to his brother the Duke of Bedford.[2] Lady Ashburton is a daughter of Lord Sandwich. She is very clever; a great admirer of Carlyle.[3] Theirs is the only great house in which I ever saw him.

It would be proper before leaving a letter of introduction to seal it with some seal; not your own. To save time, I would in calling ask if the people are at home, sending in the letter and asking to see them. They will rarely be at home; but if they are, you have economized a day or two.[4]

1. William Bingham Baring (1799–1864), Baron Ashburton, son of the statesman of Webster-Ashburton Treaty fame.

Lord John Russell (1792–1878), statesman, was then Prime Minister and First Lord of Treasury.

Algernon Percy (1792–1865), sixth Duke of Northumberland.

2. Francis Russell (1788–1861), tenth Duke of Bedford.

3. WHP, on the other hand, was not an admirer of Carlyle.

4. Letters of introduction from former diplomats Everett and Bancroft, plus the friendship of Minister Lawrence, facilitated WHP's movements in English society.

240.   To William Howard Gardiner
(William H. Gardiner Papers, Mass. Hist. Soc.)

London, July 18, 1850

My dear William,

I send by this steamer a Stilton cheese for you—which I trust will come in good condition. The Stilton is admitted by the knowing ones here still to carry off the palm in the cheese line; and I know whom I am sending it to.

You are now at your pleasant country place, and I am preparing for expeditions into the country myself, after a week for Belgium—my *historical* ground. I have invitations to about thirty of the best places here. So I can pick for myself. I propose to go to Alnwick Castle, Howard Castle, Naworth Castle—on the border—the Duke of Argyll's at Inveraray, Lord Lansdowne's at Bowood. I have arranged to spend some time at these, and if I have time before September 7th—my embarking day—shall make the most of it for other places.[1] So I shall see John Bull under his best aspect in the country, as I have already seen him in town. I have been very industrious here, have breakfasted out pretty often, lunched out occasionally, *dejeuned* at 5 P.M. now and then, dined out every day, danced and routed it enough to turn the stomach of a young bachelor. I have seen daylight in the streets after a rout— not a row.[2] My present occupation is portrait sitting. I am a perfect sitter, having had long practice, and am now being done for a couple. One, by an artist named Richmond, is considered a perfect affair. So I am rewarded, though it is not for me, but for Lord Carlisle. It will be engraved in a large size, so you will judge for yourself. An artist here gets 50 guineas for allowing his work to be engraved—and the affair is his, not mine. The other picture, for a Mr. Stirling, is not so— successful.

Well, what shall I tell you of London life? A singular society it is —wealth, rank, fashion, beauty, scholarship, with a good share of pretension, arrogance, narrow-mindedness, triviality, &c. &c, with plenty of leisure to have them all jumbled together in every possible way, half a dozen times a day. But of one thing you are sure. You will always find luxury, splendid services, works of art, libraries, careful feed [*sic*]

(I am tired to death of the same things, however) in every house you visit. What strikes one most is the inexhaustible variety of persons and characters one meets with. All are drawn into this great vortex, and here they sail round and round, but in so many circles that you may not meet the same face again for weeks. There is considerable shyness in the English character, generally, with a good store of cordiality below the surface. The talk at table rarely flags, and at bachelor dinners, which are very rare, the noise is deafening. The constant familiarity with society puts every one at his ease. All talk politics—women and all. I have been here in a crisis, and I think the women were as busy as the men. The politics they talk are wholly English. They rarely send their views beyond the little island. If the United States were to go to the bottom of the sea, they would learn it in time by the effect it would have on their trade. They have a dim consciousness of a great and growing power in the West, which they don't much fancy; but few of them have very clear ideas as to the locality and history of the country. A lady told me the other day that she had never heard the name of Dr. Channing. She was a lively, intelligent young woman—the daughter of a bishop. If it had been Beelzebub, one would have thought she would have heard of his name. Lord Lyttleton[3] told me the same. His writings are chiefly circulated among Unitarians and a few more educated men who appreciate him. The bigotry of the English surpasses everything since the days of Ferdinand and Isabella. I have hit on an episcopal vein in London life, so I know it well. But I am going to breakfast, my last before leaving London for Belgium. I dine today with Lockhart—my last dinner here. He has interested me much. He is very unfortunate in his children—his son a good-for-nothing, his daughter in very doubtful health, and he a widower. But his conversation is very entertaining—of the past. Macaulay astonishes me—but he is oppressive. But I must bid you good-bye, dear William. Pray write me how things are going on in the New World. Remember me kindly to the Colonel, who I trust is in good health; and with my love to Caroline, believe me, dear William, Most affectionately yours,

W. H. PRESCOTT

1. WHP's tour of stately homes included these: Hams Hall, Warwickshire; Alnwick Castle, Alnwick, Northumberland; Inveraray Castle at Inveraray upon Loch Fyne; Naworth Castle in Cumberland; Castle Howard in Yorkshire; Chatsworth in Derbyshire; Trentham Hall, Staffordshire; and Ampthill. Other places received passing attention.

2. Accompanied by Kirk, his reader-secretary, WHP was able to write his wife often and at great length. At times Kirk was not alone in aiding this voluminous gossipy record of the trip.

3. George William Lyttleton (1817–76), sixth Baron Lyttleton.

241.   To William Amory Prescott
                          (WHP Papers, Mass. Hist. Soc.)

                                                    London, July 29th '50
My dear boy,

   I have just returned from an excursion which I have been making
with Mr. Kirk during the last week in Belgium and Holland, to look
over my historical ground of Philip II,[1] and I find a letter sent to me
for you from Lizzie which I enclose with this. I suppose it will tell you
pretty much the same sort of things which a letter from your mother
has told me. The letters from home make us feel how dear home is.
What a singular thing that a quiet family like ours should thus be
scattered abroad.

   I have been passing a very pleasant 6 weeks in London in company
of one kind or another nearly all the time. I have seen a great number
of interesting persons, and some rather tedious ones; and on the whole
I think I now understand pretty well what London society and London
life at the West End are made up of—a great deal of splendor, talent, education, luxury, dissipation and frivolity—good and bad mixed up, as in
all other places, but, from the great predominance of wealth, rank, and
fashion, showing all their peculiarities in stronger lights than elsewhere.
Among other of my adventures I have been made a doctor of laws at
Oxford—dressed up in a red scarlet gown in the dogdays—and have
appeared in gold-laced coat, white breeches, buckles, and sword, at the
Queen's concerts, drawing-room and ballrooms.[2] But I am tired of the
whole thing, and shall be truly glad when September comes to take
me to the bleak shores of New England again. I mean to have one
month's stay in Pepperell this autumn.

   Will, who is now in Paris, will join me tomorrow, and accompany
me to several places in the country. I am going to the Duke of Northumberland's, Duke of Argyll's, Lord Carlisle's, Lord Lansdowne's, and
one or two others.[3] Then ho! for home. I wrote you and sent some letters of introduction from Calcutta House 3 weeks since, which I trust
you have received. I hope you are deriving profit from your voyage in
every sense; and that while in Calcutta you are making yourself acquainted with everything that would interest an intelligent traveller
as well as a man of business, and that wherever you go, you will hold
fast by those principles in which you have been educated, and which
alone can secure your happiness in this world as well as the next.

   Always, dear Amory Your affectionate Father

                                                    WM. H. PRESCOTT

1. This hurried trip enabled WHP, for the only time in his life, to study some of the setting related to one of his histories.

2. The degree was conferred on WHP at Oxford on June 24; his presentation to Queen Victoria took place on June 20 at St. James's Palace.

3. George Douglas Campbell (1823–1900), eighth Duke of Argyll. His Duchess, Elizabeth Georgiana (1824–78), was the eldest daughter of the second Duke of Sutherland.

Henry Petty (1780–1863), third Marquess of Lansdowne, had his seat at Bowood.

242.   To Charles Sumner
(Charles Sumner Papers, Harvard College Library)

Trentham, September 2d '50

Dear Sumner,

I should sooner have written to express my sincere sorrow at the family affliction which has fallen on you. I had not the pleasure of knowing your brother, but from all accounts he was one whose death must make a mournful void in your domestic circle. But you have lived long enough to know where best to find your consolation.

Though I shall be at home by the first of October, it may please you to know something of my whereabouts, and what I have been doing. Indeed I promised our friend Lord Carlisle to write you some account of the doings at Castle Howard, as a thing that *would* interest you. But I see the papers are full of them, and you read all the English papers. He came to Naworth to meet me on my return from the Duke of Argyll's at Inveraray. It was very kind of him, as he was full of business for the coming visit. Naworth is a brave old place, which he has in a great measure restored since the damage by fire. It transports one back to the feudal times even more than Alnwick. The other place, Castle Howard, is a princely residence—one of the finest things in England. Nothing can be more grand than the gallery—150 feet long—where the dinner was served—with the display of paintings, sculptures, and books —both a library and a picture gallery. The little Queen I had the opportunity of seeing thoroughly,[1] as I sat within four [places] of her at table, and talked with her besides, as well as the prince, a well-informed, well-bred gentleman, who is doing all he can to overcome his necessarily insignificant position. He has succeeded in shining with something more than reflected light, by connecting himself with objects of national utility. The Queen has great merit on various accounts, and her example has done much for the nation. But she has not the talent of winning hearts. Her person is plain, her movements very graceful and dignified. But I will talk to you about their regalia, if you feel an interest in them, when we meet. The Queen, on her departure, gave a hundred pounds to be distributed among the house servants, and fifty among the grooms and stable gentry. This was princely. We had a grand ball the night after royalty had departed, and I renewed my youth by dancing three quadrilles and two contra-dances—the two last with the superb Duchess of Sutherland.[2] Indeed it was four in the morning when I wound up with Sir Roger de Coverley!

On my way to town, Will and I—for we keep together—visited Chatsworth,[3] where we were well regaled; for the Duke, who is absent, had written to have lunch provided for us, and the waters to play and the whole suite of rooms, private as well as public, to be thrown open to us. A lordly residence certainly—for a bachelor too.

This letter, begun at Trentham, is finished at London, where I returned today, September 4th. I passed a couple of days at Trentham —one of the most delightful Italianized seats in England,[4] where everything reflects the taste and luxurious contrivances of the beautiful genius of the place. Before leaving there I performed the royal ceremony of planting a tree—an evergreen to flourish *in perpetuo* in memory of the Western stranger. I cannot tell you the pleasure I have had under the roofs of the Howards—three of the family, with whom I have staid[5]—a noble and warm-hearted race indeed—as you will agree with me. I have now seen a fair specimen of English town life and country life. The last is by itself, and were I a good-for-nothing bachelor I should not so abruptly turn myself from it. You know how one house leads to another without end. But my time is nearly come, and I have time only for two or three other places. I believe I know most of the notabilities here worth knowing. The most interesting is the old 'Duke'[6]—so well preserved though a little deaf and bent. His mind untouched. Macaulay is a wonder in his way—especially in the way of memory. He is a perfect *tour d'esprit*. To think of a man's being able to repeat seven books of *Paradise Lost,* and most of the other five. Of all the loveable people—with the exception of the famille Howard, I have found nothing like the Milmans—the Dean and his wife, equally charming—and our friends the Lyells, true as steel, and by no means so hard. But I shall soon be where I can talk all my experiences and the results of them over with you *viva voce*. I have often found friends who ask after you, and express the hope of one day seeing you—and many a one who speaks of Longfellow as a familiar acquaintance whom they would like to take by the hand. His charming volumes are to be seen everywhere. One of them, a splendid copy of *Evangeline,* was paid me as a bet by a lady. He would meet with a cordial reception from those by whom he would most care to be received.

Addio dear Sumner. Pray remember me cordially to him and to Hillard, and believe me Ever faithfully yours

WM. H. PRESCOTT

[P.S.] I just saw old Rogers, for the last time—Cato the Censor Atticized. He was in his drawing-room, preparing to go to Brighton, and says he has humbugged the world this time.

1. A royal progress brought Queen Victoria and Prince Albert and their entourage to Castle Howard on August 27, 1850. Needless to say, the visit was much publicized.
2. Harriet Elizabeth Georgiana (1806–68), third daughter of the sixth Earl of Carlisle, was the wife of the second Duke of Sutherland.
3. Chatsworth, about twenty miles north of Derby, was an estate of the Duke of Devonshire.
4. Trentham Hall was a property of the Duke of Sutherland.
5. Here WHP refers to the Duchess of Argyll and the Duchess of Sutherland as well as the Earl of Carlisle.
6. Arthur Wellesley (1769–1852), first Duke of Wellington.

243.   To William Howard Gardiner
(William H. Gardiner Papers, Mass. Hist. Soc.)

Boston, September 30th [1850]

Dear Will,

Here I am. On tumbling out the contents of my trunks I find a waterproof coat—much in vogue now—which I got for the measure of "a stout gentleman" whom I love dearly, and also a cigar box of capacious dimension, suited to the said stout gentleman's infirmities—which he will oblige me by accepting as a souvenir of my last trip to London.[1]

With love to Caroline, I remain always Faithfully yours

WM. H. PRESCOTT

1. Sailing on the *Niagara,* the same vessel that had taken him to England, WHP had arrived in New York on September 27.

244.   To Henry Wadsworth Longfellow
(Henry W. Longfellow Papers, Harvard College Library)

Pepperell, October 7th [1850]

My dear Longfellow,

I have just returned from my English trip, and now that I am on my own heather again feel a strong desire to write you a note about what, after all, you know well enough already—the popularity of your name on the English side of the water. It is indeed very gratifying for a personal friend to see in what manner you are regarded and spoken of by the people whose education and social position make their opinions of great value to an author.

Your reputation has been on the increase rapidly and largely the last few years in England. Certain it is that your works are admired not only more than those of any American poet, but of any living English poet, as far as my experience goes. I have heard them quoted and sung and talked of, and great interest shown as to your personal habits, looks, manners &c. You know in what handsome forms your writings are published; and if you should travel there you would find in how cheap and popular forms they are to be found at all the railway stations. Your prose writings seem to be also in great favor, and your reputation in the land of our fathers is such as the most ambitious aspirant for literary laurels might well covet.

I have had a pleasant time and made many most agreeable acquaintances and some true friends, I trust. But the sight of the gray rocks of New England was grateful to me and I feel more like a man on my own heather than on the best that I have trodden abroad. Pray remember me most kindly to your wife and say to her that I saw her sister Mary[1] repeatedly, in good health and spirits, and believe me, my dear Longfellow, Very sincerely yours,

WM. H. PRESCOTT

[P.S.] I had a pleasant day here with Sumner yesterday, who left me this morning.

1. I.e. Mary Appleton Mackintosh, wife of Robert James Mackintosh and daughter-in-law of Sir James Mackintosh.

245.   To John Gibson Lockhart
(MS. 935, no. 43, National Library of Scotland)

Boston, November 26/50

My dear Mr. Lockhart,

Do you remember one day expressing a desire to me of being better acquainted with our canvas-backs? At all events I remember it, and I have taken the liberty to send you three brace of them by the steamer that takes this note. I do not know that I could send anything from our Yankee land which I would more willingly submit to your criticism— and it will give me only the more pleasure if you cut it up with a relish.

That the devil may not send cooks, I must warn you that the true way of roasting the canvas-back is to have them a little underdone—so that the juice shall run freely from them when carved. The birds are just now in the best order for eating, and these, with a number of their fellows who go out with them, were shot, three days since, at the mouth of the Susquehanna—a river which they frequent for the wild celery which grows on its borders. I hope they will come to you in good condition.

I am now in my winter quarters—the town—having secured a month, after my return, for the country—to see the autumn 'die like the dolphin'[1]—with all the bright variety of colors that belongs to our forest scenery after the frost has touched it. The past summer has filled my mind with pleasant reminiscences enamored of the English country life, like no other life in any other country, so complete and well-appointed with something to suit the taste of every one. The Englishman's castle is the true place to see him in. The word *home* means much more in your land than anywhere else, certainly.

Of all that I saw no place sticks in my memory like Abbotsford. Thanks to your kindness, I could take it leisurely, with all its sad and tender recollections—even to a stranger—without being hurried along in the train of sight-seers.

But I must not take up more of your time.[2]

And with my best wishes for your health and happiness I remain, my dear Mr. Lockhart Very sincerely yours

WM. H. PRESCOTT

1. Lord Byron's *Childe Harold,* canto iv, stanza 29, reads:
"Parting day
Dies like the dolphin, . . ."
2. Meanwhile WHP's correspondence, including more correspondents and inviting long letters, was taking up more of his time.

246.   To Ángel Calderón de la Barca
(Draft, WHP Papers, Mass. Hist. Soc.)

Boston, December 19th [1850]

My dear Calderón,

It did me good to see your handwriting again; for it seems to me as if I have been round the world—which most people would do easier than what I screwed myself up to do; for, as you know, I have been to Europe since I last had the pleasure of communicating with you. It is a thing I have been talking of every spring for I don't know how long, and I am not sorry that I worked my courage up to the proper point at last. I was absent between four and five months, reaching home the beginning of October. I should have written you sooner but I was not quite certain whether you as well as la Señora were not in Cuba. I passed three months in England—my object being to see its society, and I was pretty industrious while I was there. My first day in London I became acquainted with the Cabinet Ministers, at a dinner party, and their ladies; and while I remained there I was in a constant whirl of breakfasts, luncheons, dinners, and routs. So I think I saw London— that is to say a certain phase of it—very well for the time; and a wonderful place it is—such variety and brilliancy in the society. But the glory of England is not the town. I passed another six weeks in the country—at different seats—some of them the best worth seeing, I suppose, in England. That is the true place in which to see the Englishman —in his lordly halls, his magnificent parks, where he diffuses the generous hospitality of a great feudal proprietor, and enjoys the state of an independent potentate on his own princely domains. I passed some time in Scotland, and I think your wife will not disagree with me in thinking that there is more that touches the heart in the Scottish scenery—wild and picturesque as it is—than in the tamer beauty of England. I spent a week at Inveraray Castle, the Duke of Argyll's, amidst the heather, the bold lochs, and the Highland mountains. Then I visited some border castles—stayed with the Duke of Northumberland, at Alnwick,—where he was living in feudal pomp; and at Naworth Castle, a fine old place of Lord Carlisle's. Ten days I passed at Castle Howard, in Yorkshire—one of Vanbrugh's brilliant creations —and there I had the honor of being present at the royal visit—so that I had a rare opportunity of seeing the *crème de la crème*. I visited also several other places, in the south, among them Trentham, the Duchess of Sutherland's—a sort of fairy garden in which art, directed by the taste of its lovely proprietor, has mixed up the Italian with the English in a most enchanting way. But I will not weary you with a muster-roll of places. I did not find London very different from any other great capital, except that there was more of everything than is to be found anywhere else. But English country life, in this its most splendid form, with all the appliances of luxury, healthy recreation, and polished social intercourse, and its genial hospitality, is unique. John Bull certainly has a noble heart and a warm one, though there is sometimes an icy reserve formed over it which must be thawed out at the first.

I passed a week also in Belgium, to look up the localities in the

Netherlands, and did send a thought to Spain; but I had not the courage to prolong my stay sufficiently to go there. I met in London some congenial spirits, who hail Spain as a sort of fatherland—Ford and Stirling. I don't know that you know either of them. Both have written on Spanish subjects; both are men of ample fortune, in the best society of London; and their houses are filled with curious books and works of art from the Peninsula; and I found at their tables luncheons and dinners dressed *a l'Espagnol,* and delicate wines—which transported me for the time to the land of the hidalgo.

I mean to write your wife some further account of my experiences.[1] I have now returned to my armchair to gnaw upon the dry bones of Philip II.[2] I shall be very glad to receive Alamán's books. I wonder he had the good nature to send any to me since I have been able to do so little for him in the way of the translation.

Bulwer[3] dined with me when he was here the other day. He is an agreeable man of the world, but his constitution seems to be a good deal shaken. I suppose you and he now are on the most amicable footing. He will be able to make a report of us to you, as I saw a good deal of him. Could you think to say to him that Ames the artist has not yet been to see me about the Gonsalvo?

Adieu, my dear Calderón. Pray remember me most affectionately to your wife, who I hope is in good health after her Cuban escapade, and believe me now and ever Your faithful friend

WM. H. PRESCOTT

[P.S.] The box containing Alamán's books has come, all safe. What a quill-driver he is! He puts such tortoises as me to shame. I suppose he is one of those boiling spirits that must be doing something—making *pronunciamientos* or writing an account of them. The last, at all events, he does well. I have got him chosen a member of the Historical Society of Massachusetts and am en train for a similar honor from the Philosophical Society of Philadelphia. He has sent me three copies of tom. II and one of tom. III. Now a copy for each of these societies and one for myself would have required, instead, three copies of each volume. I suppose you can't rectify it.

1. The trip of 1850 had continuing significance for WHP, permeating his recollections and correspondence for months thereafter.
2. Achieving nearly nothing of a scholarly nature during the winter of 1850–51, WHP reminded himself, "The time taken to settle my wits after my voyage, and to get them into order for composition, may account in part for my laziness." See Prescott (Gardiner, ed.), *The Literary Memoranda,* II, 207.
3. I.e. Sir Henry Bulwer.

247.   From Richard Ford
                  (Extracts, WHP Papers, Mass. Hist. Soc.)

                                          London, December 23, 1850
                                                    123 Park Street

Mi más querido amigo

I have been a great wanderer since you left us, making tours into the
North and to the lakes with the Lovelaces. On my return I found your
kind and agreeable letter, giving so graphic an account of your return
to your native land, and I have since seen Dr. Holland,[1] who had the
last peep of you. Do not forget the *little* old country, or its many and
large friendships for you, now we feel that you are one of us. Your
letter has given many of your admirers sincere pleasure. I cannot help
enclosing you the answer Lady Mahon[2] sent me. You know *how beautiful, how charming* she is; and indeed it is one of your brightest triumphs in England to have gained her entire favor. Do you not
remember how you were struck with her, when you met her for the
first time at this house. I was sitting in Grosvenor Place the other day,
and we had a long, very long chat about you, and how great a favorite
you are among us all. Stirling is still at his ancestral castle in Scotland.

I have moreover to thank you for the *canvas back* ducks which have
flown fresh and sweet across the broad Atlantic. I had here last week
the Bunsens—the ex-Prussian Premier—Radowitz—the Milmans—
Lady Davy, Lady Eastlake[3] and other great friends and admirers of
yours, to feast on these delicacies of the new world, and you may depend
upon it the *donor* was not forgotten in our *cups;* how much we all
wished you had been among us.

                    .   .   .   .

The huge glass palace for the exposition of 1851 is rapidly rising.
We are not comfortable (*we* who look over the Park) at the thought of
the mob of next year. I suppose some of your countrymen will come
over. If I can be of any use to any of them, you know you have a *friend*
at 123 Park Street who will consider a recommendation from *you* as
the best *passport.*

                    .   .   .   .

Whenever I can be of the smallest service here, pray command me.
Your ever most sincere friend

                                                    RICH. FORD

1. Henry Holland (1788–1873), an eminent physician and a tireless traveler, first met WHP in London in 1850.

2. Lady Mahon (1815–73), wife of Philip Henry Stanhope (1805–75), who, styled Viscount Mahon between 1816 and 1855, later became Earl Stanhope.

3. Christian Karl Josias von Bunsen (1791–1860), Prussian diplomat and later Baron, served as ambassador in London from 1842 to 1854.

Joseph Maria von Radowitz (1797–1853), Prussian general and statesman.

Lady Davy was the widow of the famous chemist Sir Humphrey Davy.

Lady Elizabeth Eastlake (1809–93), wife of Sir Charles Lock Eastlake, edited her husband's works on art and also wrote works of her own on art criticism.

248.   To Richard Bentley
(Richard Bentley Papers, Harvard College Library)

Boston, U.S., May 20, '51

My dear sir,

My friend Mr. Parkman,[1] of this city, proposes to send out by this steamer the proofsheets of a new work of his relating to the occupation of this country by the French, and their intercourse with the Indians. His work leads him largely into an account of these sons of the forest, for which, as you are probably aware, he is better qualified than any good writer among us by his residence with them. I have seen some hundred and fifty pages of the book, and it seems to me to be written with much spirit, with many picturesque descriptions and stirring incidents—told in a skilful manner, that I should think would engage the interest of the reader. The rare materials from which the story is drawn gives it still higher value in an historical view. I cannot tell how much curiosity the English reader would feel in this portion of American history, or how far such a work would be a good book in the sense of the *trade*. I believe, from the specimen I have seen, it will prove a good book in every other sense, and as such, if you think it for your interest—of which you are much the best judge—I hope you will be able to make some arrangement with Mr. Parkman for the publication of it.[2]

With sincere regard, I am, my dear sir, Truly yours,

WM. H. PRESCOTT

1. Francis Parkman (1823–93), fellow Bostonian and fellow historian, was of the generation of WHP's children.

2. Bentley published Parkman's *History of the Conspiracy of Pontiac* in August, 1851.

249.   From Richard Bentley
                       (WHP Papers, Mass. Hist. Soc.)

                              New Burlington Street, May 22, 1851

W. H. Prescott
My dear Sir,

You will be rejoiced to hear that the vexed question of the right of foreigners to a copyright in their works in Great Britain has been decided in the affirmative by the Lord Chief Justice, Lord Campbell, and 5 other judges in a Court of Error, reversing the crude and hasty decision of the Chief Baron Pollock. Under the constant fear of unprincipled men taking advantage of that decision of the Chief Baron, it was almost impossible to venture on any works. Now, however, I breathe again; and although there is some notion of carrying the matter to the court of last resort—the House of Lords, I look upon this as mere vapouring of men who have been defeated in their mal-practices, and a little cool discussion with their counsel will take it out of them.

I am rejoiced on all account; for altho weak in regard to priority in the case of *Ferdinand and Isabella*[1] the pirates will not feel disposed to hazard that matter now.

It is very important that this matter has been settled before the publication of *Philip the Second*.[2] When is it likely that you would be thinking of putting that work (the first part, I mean) in the press? In the autumn it would appear with advantage if it suited your convenience.[3]

I have the honor to be, my dear Sir, Yours most faithfully

                                                  RICHARD BENTLEY

1. Special concern about *Ferdinand and Isabella* derived from the fact that it alone of all WHP's books had been published earlier in America than in England.

2. The copyright pendulum soon swung to the opposite extreme, distressing both Bentley and WHP.

3. At this time WHP had written only eight chapters, little more than 250 pages, of the book which Bentley desired.

250.   To Lady Mary E. Lyell
             (Transcript, Lady Lyell's Letterbook, WHP Papers, Mass. Hist. Soc.)

                                    Nahant, July 14th, 1851

My dear Lady Lyell[1]

It is an age since I have written or received a line from you. And now I do not know that this will reach you till long after its date, as I heard before leaving town from our friend Anna Ticknor that you were to make one of your geological escapades—in the direction of the Canaries. I suppose when you and your husband have looked up the rest of the planet our turn will come next, and you will be ready for another trip across the Atlantic. It is indeed but a trip. I have just returned from a tour quite as formidable. I have been passing some four weeks in an excursion to West Point, the Catskill, Trenton Falls, and Niagara. I took my youngest son and Elizabeth with me. Mr. and Mrs. Edward Perkins were of the party also, and Mrs. Peabody and her daughter—the fiancee of William.[2] So we had a very agreeable party, and took it leisurely. We passed two days in visiting some pleasant places on the Hudson, and three more we spent at Trenton. You remember that extraordinary spot, with the little river tumbling into cataracts of white and yellow foam, and cutting its way through walls of rock, which, as they are covered with evergreens, look like the castellated walls of some huge fortress. Then we gave a week to Niagara. A week is not too long for the father of cataracts. One cannot comprehend the wonderful scale on which Nature acts, in this most marvellous of her water works, in a few hours. It is a spectacle that grows on you —as the true sublime always does—the longer you dwell on it. Yet Tupper, the English bard of *proverbial* memory—pronounced it, in a poem which he let off on its borders the other day, "only beautiful!"

It is now more than a year since I landed on your hospitable shores, and about this time I was preparing for my little continental tour. Anniversaries bring with them more vivid recollections of the past— though it will require no such memento to stimulate my recollections of the dear friends and the pleasant hours I enjoyed in merry England.

What a glorious thing the Glass Palace has turned out—for all but Brother Jonathan's share of it. And yet there would have been no good ground for complaint or ridicule on that score, if he had not demanded such large accommodations prospectively. But the Yankees are apt to indulge in large anticipations—which to their credit, it must be admitted, are sometimes realized.

I heard of you before you left town at Lord Carlisle's. Did you see a picture of Niagara which I sent him? It was executed by a French artist, and was thought here as good as anything of the kind that had been done among us. He expressed to me when in England a desire to have such a painting, if I could meet with one good enough to hang on his walls. By the bye, I think the engraver of Richmond's portrait of me does not work as rapidly as the artist did. I hope he will do the thing as well, and I shall be content to wait for it. A letter which I had the other day from Lady Carlisle tells me that they are much concerned for the health of William Lascelles, her son-in-law. I should be sorry that her forebodings should prove true, for he is an excellent person, much beloved by his family. Is it true that Ford is wooing his third bride? Can you tell me any thing about her? I should not have supposed he was so much in love with Hymen. Rogers, I understand, resumes his breakfasts; so I suppose he does not mean to flinch before he has rounded his century. How I should like to be once more in that gay circle of wit, genius and genial hospitality, and to wind it up with a few weeks in the paradise of country life—English country life! But that will hardly be, and I must content myself with looking on the broad sea, as I now do, and hear the billows break on the beach, as they come rolling on from the Old World across the waters. Many a thought I send across to the friends on the other side, as I look on the wide waste from my rocky eyrie. You remember my cottage at Nahant, "Fitful Head" as we call it, and Norna had no wilder spot.

Will it be long before you see the dear good Milmans? When you do you will remember me most affectionately to them, though, if it be long, I shall remember myself first by a letter. But—I do not know how it is—one becomes a poor correspondent when there is no immediate call for writing. It is delightful to talk with a distant friend after one's pen is set agoing, but it is some effort to set it agoing. We put off writing till tomorrow, and tomorrow &c &c as Shakespeare says.

We like your Minister Bulwer, very much better than he has liked himself, for he seems to be used up in constitution. But in society he is very agreeable, and is a lively correspondent, and his dinner eloquence is admirable. We have all been in confusion, about the fugitive slave law, as you have heard from the Ticknors, who enter into the debate very warmly—which is more than I do. Politics are not in my line. Ticknor, you know, has a decided turn for them. Sumner, as you have heard, goes to the U.S. Senate—which he says he does not want. Few of his old friends want it either for him. Yet I shall not quarrel with him, as most of them have done, for his intemperate manner at expressing his opinions, in which opinions, however, I by no means concur. But life is too short, and our little town ought to be too small, for such feuds.

The Ticknors are rejoicing at Bellows Falls, on the Connecticut, where they have detected a first-rate hotel, in which the whole family are disporting themselves to their great content.

Adieu, dear Lady Lyell. Pray remember me most lovingly to your husband, to your good father, mother and sisters and believe me, now and always, most affectionately yours

1. The WHP-Lady Lyell correspondence represents the biggest two-party file among all of WHP's papers of the 1850's.

2. On November 6, 1851, William Gardiner Prescott was married to Josephine Augusta Peabody, daughter of the Joseph Augustus Peabodys of Salem.

251.   To Rufus Wilmot Griswold

(Special Collections Department, University of Kansas Library)

Pepperell, Mass. September 24th [1851]

My dear sir,

I hasten to answer your note (which I received but five minutes since, in the country, where I am passing the autumn) inviting me to attend a meeting for the purpose of doing honor to Mr. Cooper's memory.[1] Of course—even if I could otherwise have done it—it would be now too late for me, even with the aid of railroad wings, to attend your meeting on the 25th. But I assure you I sincerely sympathize in its object, and shall most cordially concur in any testimony of respect for a writer who has done so much for American literature—both at home and abroad. With great regard, I remain, my dear Mr. Griswold, Very truly yours,

WM. H. PRESCOTT

1. James Fenimore Cooper (1789–1851), the first significant American novelist to employ the American frontier and wilderness in his works, had recently died. No proof exists of WHP's enjoyment of Cooper's works, but, as in numerous other instances, the historian hailed any American achievement that added international stature to its literature.

252.   From Pascual de Gayangos

(WHP Papers, Mass. Hist. Soc.)

44 Half Moon St., Piccadilly, October 22, 1851

My dear friend

I have to apologize for not having written to you all this while, during my long visit to the English shores again. Whenever I am in dear old England, I feel great disinclination to return to my not less beloved country. I only wish it were in many respects like this!

As you may suppose my old friends have made much of me and though I only intended to stay two or three months, their kind and pressing hospitality has kept me for upwards of 5 months. Indeed I could only go by leaving behind, as a sort of pledge, my dear daughter—now a full blooming young lady of 15, and of course, I will return for her next season, unless some Englishman intends to rob me of my treasure.

In a case directed to friend Ticknor, you will find several numbers of the *Colección de documentos,* a rare volume of sermons preached at the *Honras* of Philip 2, and a little essay of mine upon a curious and obscure point of Spanish history.

Our Academy is now publishing a bulletin of its transactions, together with several important documents for the history of the Middle Ages. They intend at a later time to print papers relative to Charles V, Don John of Austria, and Philip 2°. I have subscribed both you and Ticknor to this collection which is not expensive, and comes out monthly, as in our wish to contribute materials for the history of Spain and our almost total want of funds, I know it is the wish of our body that all the members belonging to it should become subscribers. Would to God we were rich enough to distribute them gratis!

Stirling and Ford beg to be kindly remembered to you and with my best wishes for your success in your great, I should say immense literary undertaking,[1] believe me My dear friend always sincerely yours

P. DE GAYANGOS

P.S. I saw the other day at the British Museum an account of the death of Prince Don Carlos. I cannot say that it contains any new facts, but I am sure that it differs materially from any other I have read. If you wish I can have it transcribed for you as there is now in London a Spaniard who will gladly accept the job. I sail in a few days for Cádiz in a war steamer belonging to our government.

1. Still laboring to develop the kind of intellectual momentum required to complete his big project, WHP needed the kind of encouragement that this letter represented.

253.   From Abbott Lawrence
                (WHP Papers, Mass. Hist. Soc.)

London, December 12, 1851

William H. Prescott Esq.
  Boston, Mass.
My dear Prescott,

Upon the arrival of my son James last week, he made to us an announcement which was both new and agreeable. Of James I can speak in unqualified terms of approbation *as a man.* I have no hesitation in saying that I believe, whatever may be the expectations of Mrs. Prescott and yourself in regard to him as a son and husband, you will not be disappointed. Of Miss Elizabeth I know enough to *rejoice* that she is to be the wife of my son. It is a union in all respects satisfactory to me and mine—and I cannot but believe that it promises as much happiness to our children and respective families as can be looked for in this world.

It is a great matter to begin our career in the world with just views of life and living. I trust James and Elizabeth will remember that when they shall have been married they assume new responsibilities, taking as they must a new departure on the voyage of life, where they must judge and act for themselves, and by their actions they must be judged. You and I have lived long enough to have been taught something of the trials and troubles, and disappointments that environ poor humanity, sometimes from want of discretion, in others from want of principle, and sometimes from causes beyond the control of the wisest and the best. I will not on this occasion say more, than admonish our children to be moderate in all things—particularly in their views of living, and to commence the world in a manner that shall leave space for increase of expense, when it may be required and afforded. Upon this point I have no anxiety, well knowing that Mrs. Prescott has always had an eye to a liberal expenditure, guided by a judicious economy—which I am quite sure she has transmitted to her daughter.

Now my dear friend I sat down to write a few words expressing my satisfaction to Mrs. Prescott and yourself (and I must say to Madame Prescott) upon the happy event which is to bring us into more intimate relations—and not to inflict a *homily* upon life and living.

James is in Paris, where he will remain three or four days. I believe he intends to return about the 24th instant—if so he will probably be with you on *twelfth night*. I beg you to offer Mrs. Prescott—and to Madame Prescott my warmest regards, with my love and affection to Elizabeth[1]—and to Mr. William and Mr. Amory my kind remembrances—and for yourself I beg you to believe that I am now and always most sincerely Your friend

ABBOTT LAWRENCE

1. Elizabeth Prescott was married to James Lawrence (1822–75), the eldest son of the Abbott Lawrences, on March 16, 1852.

254.   To Jared Sparks
                 (Jared Sparks Papers, Harvard College Library)
                                              Boston, February 19th '52
My dear Sparks,

The good people of the town of Pepperell and the neighboring county are making an effort in the Legislature to get an appropriation for raising a monument to Colonel William Prescott. Of course the vexed question has arisen, Who was the Commander at Bunker Hill? The legislators are not quite so well informed on the historical matters of their country as on its actual condition—the prices of pork, poultry and a' that. To enlighten them, Mr. Bellows of Pepperell, formerly a member of the Senate, is appointed to prepare an argument, to be made *early next week* before this learned body, which I have no doubt he will do very well after a diligent perusal of Frothingham's "Siege of Boston," and one or two other works orthodox and germane to the matter.

Now my motive for boring you is that Mr. Bellows has seen me this morning and tells me that it would greatly strengthen his position if your testimony could be adduced in favor of it. Can you conscientiously—I mean with a historical conscience—say that you consider Colonel Prescott as the true commander at the Battle of Bunker Hill? Or as the actual commander in the redoubt? Or that you agree with the views expressed thereon by Frothingham in his book, which I suppose you have read? If your judgment leads you to assent to either of these queries, I shall take it very kind of you if you will address a line to Mr. Bellows (Hon. C. W. Bellows, Boston, Mass.) either directly to him or under cover to me, as soon as you get this. *Delay would defeat the object.* If you cannot assent to either of the queries, you of course will not trouble yourself with an answer at all. Do not allude to me in the answer, should you make one, as it would have more weight addressed directly to a party who has no interest in the matter. This is Mr. Bellows's suggestion—and seems reasonable—though any interest I have in the affair is not strong enough to desire to see any thing but the fair truth, whether written on stone or brass, or on the "Monumentum perennais" which the historian's hand piles up—the best monument of all.[1] Always Sincerely Yours

WM. H. PRESCOTT

1. Working more diligently and more successfully than he had for six years, WHP had exclaimed, on February 9, "Can I not bag 400 pages this year?" See Prescott (Gardiner, ed.), *The Literary Memoranda*, II, 210.

255.   From Lady Mary E. Lyell
                    (Extracts, WHP Papers, Mass. Hist. Soc.)

Mildenhall, Suffolk
1st July 1852

My dear Mr. Prescott

   It is only today that we have heard of your sad loss,[1] and it seems as if some letter Mrs. Ticknor had written me has never reached me, or indeed you may believe I should have written before, for you must know we sympathize in your sorrows as well as your joys. At your dear mother's age, it seemed almost unreasonable to expect it, but I did hope to have seen her once more. I shall always think of her great kindness to me. Hers was an enviable old age, so active and useful to the last, surrounded by those she loved best, and sympathizing in the enjoyments of her younger friends.

Today, I believe, you go to Nahant, where the fresh sea breezes will be good for you and dear Mrs. Prescott.[2] Perhaps you will be still there in the beginning of September when we reach Boston, for I must tell you now (what has been a secret for some time from all but our friends the Ticknors), that we are coming out this autumn to pass a few months in your country. It is only a fortnight since we have communicated this to any of our own family, as so many things may and do intervene, that we did not want to tell our plans before they were quite settled. We plan to be at home again before Christmas, but shall pass seven or eight weeks at Boston where Charles will give a course of lectures at the Lowell Institute. Before this, however, we plan to make some excursions to Nantucket, Martha's Vineyard and some other geological points, and if you should be at Pepperell, we should like to be a day or two there that we might see you in your home. But at any rate while we are at Boston we plan to use much of our time and see as much as we can of our old friends (I don't want to see any new ones).

.   .   .   .

Give my kindest love to Mrs. Prescott. Charles sends his to both of you and believe me, my dear Mr. Prescott Ever affectionately yours

MARY E. LYELL

[P.S.] If you are seeing or writing to the Ticknors, please say I have received her letter and will write by next mail.

1. In her eighty-fifth year, Mrs. William Prescott had died on May 17, 1852.
2. WHP had gone to Nahant on July 1. Three days later he wrote, "I miss the accustomed faces." See Prescott (Gardiner, ed.), *The Literary Memoranda,* II, 213–14. This proved to be his last summer at Fitful Head.

256. To Pascual de Gayangos
(The Hispanic Society of America; draft, WHP Papers, Mass. Hist. Soc.; and in Penney, *Prescott,* pp. 98–102)

Boston, July 11, 1852

Our letters, dear Gayangos, come as far apart as those of lovers after a quarrel. But you and I have not quarrelled—and never will, I imagine. In yours of the 9th of June, which I received last week, you speak of recopying the lost manuscripts. This is very kind of you, and like yourself. They will be welcome when they come—and that will be in good season; for I find that this history of *"el Prudente"* is, as you predicted, no summer day's work. I have been well at work last winter, and am now in my second volume—still in the Netherlands—drawing near to the coming of the "iron duke."[1] I am making up this portion of the story out of the letters of the actors—very little from chronicle or history. This furnishes the most authentic basis. But it is a work of more time; and whether it will be so taking with the public I know not. Bentley writes to learn when I shall be ready with another brace. But I do not mean to give him or any publisher the right to chide me for taking my ease, by tethering myself to a certain day. It would give me a fever.

You say that our friend Stirling is really set to work with his Donship of Lepanto. I did not know whether it was anything more than play—*pour s'amuser.* If I do not come out soon, all my fine feathers will be plucked beforehand, so I shall have little left that is new to make a show with. Another friend of mine is upon the history of Holland![2] But the world is wide; and there are many ways, *Dieu Merci,* of telling the same story. Besides I have not heard of any one who proposes to swallow the monster whole, as I do—horns, tail and all. They only cut delicate slices out of him, to suit a dainty appetite.

By the by, you mention that you have furnished Stirling with the manuscript of Father Angulo used by Sandoval, and that it contains an account of the mock funeral of Charles V. I have treated this as apocryphal in a chapter which I have devoted to the cloistered life of the Emperor. I should be much obliged, therefore, if you could send me in a letter, without waiting for the other manuscripts, that part of Angulo's narrative which relates to the funeral—with the title of the manuscript and the chapters, &c. for reference. I only desire what relates to this single subject—which of course will not cover much ground. You see I never leave off boring you.

How do you come on with Ticknor. The volume sent of the translation is a credit to all parties concerned, and to the Madrid press.[3] Could you not remember, when you send the manuscript you are recopying, to put with them the Madrid translation of the "Conquest of Peru." I suppose the translation is finished.[4] I have only received one volume, and that poorly got up. I think they might have given me a more respectable form. They have done better for me in Mexico, where the work has also been translated into Castilian.[5]

Burton writes me, in a letter received this week, that he advised you of his sending me a lot of sherry. It was the dark sherry, and I desired the best he could send. But it is nine years old, after all. Which do the *Madrileños* prefer of the sherry wines? Do you like the brown, as in England, almost the only kind I found there—or the lighter kinds, the Amontillado, &c? The latter I have with me in the country now, where I am passing the summer (though I date as ever from town, that you may direct to me in Boston.) It is a light summer beverage, but has an etherlike taste I do not wholly relish. What a land is that, where —not "the cypress and myrtle," as Byron sings[6]—but old manuscripts and old wines of the noblest kinds flourish side by side—the land of the hidalgo—the land that I love.

Fare thee well, my dear friend. With kind remembrances to your wife, believe me Always faithfully Yours

WM. H. PRESCOTT

P.S. Has Ford sent you his account of the Wellington diorama? How Ford loves the French!

You know that my son William is married, and established near me. I do not think that I have told you that my only daughter was married this spring to the eldest son of Mr. Lawrence, our Minister at London. Both the nuptials are as pleasing to me, as any such events can be—that make one's hearth and home desolate.—Once more *Amigo mio, Adios.*

1. The Duke of Alva (1508–83), the Spanish general who suppressed Dutch opposition (1567–73) with extreme cruelty, was often so labeled.

2. John Lothrop Motley (1814–77), destined to win fame for his studies of the Dutch, was that friend.

3. Gayangos was translating Ticknor's *magnum opus* on Spanish literature.

4. The first Spanish translation of the *Conquest of Peru* in Madrid was published in 1847–48 in two volumes.

5. In 1849, in two volumes, the translation by Joaquín García Icazbalceta was published in Mexico City, a second edition appearing there the following year.

6. Referring to Greece, Byron wrote in the *Bride of Abydos,* canto i:
"Know ye the land where the cypress and myrtle."

257.   From Henry Hart Milman
                    (WHP Papers, Mass. Hist. Soc.)

Deanery, St. Paul's, July 31, 1852

My dear Mr. Prescott

Do you remember on one of our very agreeable excursions a very gentlemanly clergyman, a Canon of Windsor, who shewed us over the beautiful St. George's Chapel—we both were grateful for his civility.

He writes me now that a son of his, a young sailor, has been seized with a love of letters, and when on service in the Pacific, was taken with a strong interest about the Peruvians—so much so that he is determined to make an antiquarian tour in that country. He proposes to seek his destination through the United States, and is naturally most anxious to become acquainted with the historian of Peru, who may furnish him with useful information, and indeed may almost give him instructions as to his mission. I scruple not [. . .] to introduce to you Mr. Clements Markham.[1] They are descendants of the Archbishop of York of that name. I have besides my respect for Canon Markham a sort of interest in the family—one of the sons, who was cut off by an early death, was the most intimate friend of one of my boys at Westminster.

I know not when this will reach you, but probably long before you will have heard of us from the Lyells.

We are now, though I date from St. Paul's, on our summer excursion—summer indeed, we have not for many years had such a continuance of hot weather. Our destination is Scotland. With Mrs. Milman's kindest remembrances, believe me, my dear Mr. Prescott Ever your attached friend

H. H. MILMAN

1. Clements Robert Markham (1830–1916), geographer and historian, was inspired by WHP's writing to dedicate his scholarly labors to South America.

258.   From William Stirling
(WHP Papers, Mass. Hist. Soc.)

128 Park Street, Grosvenor Square
November 8th, 1852

My dear Prescott

Here is my *Cloister Life of Charles V*[1]—a volume which will have some interest for you as treating of a subject and a time which falls within the noble track of history on which you are yourself engaged, and on which I hope you will shortly enlighten and delight us. For any criticism or remarks, which your intimate acquaintance with all the facts treated of, may enable you to make, I shall be truly obliged.

Since I last wrote to you, I have been elected member of our parliament for my native county of Perth—and am now in turn awaiting the opening of the campaign between Her Majesty's Government and Her Majesty's opposition. At present I am on the side of the former —though how soon I may have to cross the border is very uncertain.

Our friend Ford continues my neighbour, and has been visiting me in Scotland. I think all our other friends remain pretty much in *statu quo*. The Duke of Wellington is almost the only very remarkable loss which London has sustained since Peel's death, and your departure.

You will soon, I suppose, hear all the latest gossip of the town from Thackeray[2]—who left England the day before his novel of "Esmond" appeared. It is highly praised by the critics—and that part of the reading world who are tinctured with letters. But though shewing perhaps more literary ability than any of his previous writings, it is not likely to be as extensively popular. But the success of any work of fiction is likely to appear dwarfish beside the colossal pedestal at present occupied by Mrs. Beecher Stowe.

I hear there is a son of yours in town whose acquaintance I hope shortly to make. Believe me Ever yours very truly

WILLIAM STIRLING

1. This work by Stirling became one of the reasons why WHP, interrupting his labor on Philip II, also turned to the career of Charles V.

2. Before this letter reached WHP, he and Thackeray were renewing in Boston the acquaintance which had been initiated in London.

259.   To Richard Bentley
(Richard Bentley Papers, Harvard College Library)

Boston, November 26, '52

My dear sir,

Your letter of the 26th ultimo duly came to hand. In it you speak of sending the annual account to Colonel Aspinwall, which I suppose has been done.

I am sorry that my correspondence with Mrs. Stowe[1] has had no better result, as I see her next work advertized by some publisher—I forget whom—in the English papers. I told you, I believe, that I had not the honor of knowing the lady personally, and she has not made any reply to the letter which I wrote in answer to hers. I presume she had never any serious thought of an arrangement with you in the matter. But I do not know who her advisers are, or indeed anything of her, beyond what is published to the world. Her literary adventure is a miracle, for in a twinkling *Uncle Tom* has shot up into a celebrity equal to that reached by the best of Scott's novels, while in point of literary execution merely, it is not equal to the worst. It has shown what an antislavery chord John Bull as well as Brother Jonathan has in his bosom.[2]

Touching the contract of Philip the Second, it seems to me there is no occasion at present to bother our brains about the matter. I am getting on in a comfortable way, and if I stimulate myself by a contract it will, I fear, only create a nervous sensation such as I used to feel when I came tardily with my exercises to school. Of one thing you may be sure, if you are alive—and I trust the period is not so far off as to give any ground for apprehension on that score—I shall much prefer, for the sake of 'auld lang syne'—unless I feel very differently from what I now do—to deal with you to dealing with any other publisher.

With much regard, I remain, my dear sir, Very truly yours,

WM. H. PRESCOTT

1. In his letter of June 6, 1852, WHP had recommended to Bentley that he give consideration to Harriet Beecher Stowe's *Uncle Tom's Cabin*.

2. Within eighteen months of its introduction into England, *Uncle Tom's Cabin* was published in forty editions by eighteen different publishers in London. For a fuller statement of WHP's relationship to Bentley's effort to become her publisher, see Gardiner, "William Hickling Prescott: Authors' Agent," pp. 75–77.

260. Memorandum Concerning Expenses

(WHP Papers, Mass. Hist. Soc.)

[Expenses for 1852]

		Children	Total
January	2117.76	–0–	2117.76
February	710.80	2412.47	3123.27
March	808.60	353.00	1161.60
April	649.99	–0–	649.99
May	580.75	185.00	765.75
June	520.25	125.00	645.25
July	474.16	72.50	546.66
August	673.84	106.50	780.34
September	715.83	113.50	829.33
October	2012.42	–0–	2012.42
November	751.50	1300.00	2051.50
December	1685.15	70.00	1755.15
	11,701.05	4,737.97	16,439.02

Rent 2,000.00

Total 18,439.02

Add William's interest (omitted) 600.00

19,039.02

Charity and Presents amounted to 2163.00

Total 19,039.02—for 1852[1]

1. Obviously the expenses of a single year cannot be taken as "average" expenses; cf. item 271 *infra* for another annual statement of expenses. Certain observations, however, are in order concerning the expenses of 1852: (a) those related to the children covered Amory's travels, Elizabeth's wedding, and some of the expenses of William Gardiner Prescott's separate household; (b) WHP's expenses for his own household approximated $1000 per month, with the average higher for the months in Boston and lower for the seasons spent at Nahant and Pepperell.

261.   To Lady Mary E. Lyell

(Transcript, Lady Lyell's Letterbook, WHP Papers, Mass. Hist. Soc.)

Boston, March 1, 1853

Dear Lady Lyell,

By the last steamer I received a kind letter from you giving me the account of your visit to Lady Mary Labouchere's.[1] How it would have rejoiced me to be one of the party! With Lady Mahon you made such a charming trio! I do not know any spot I should like to wander over better than the precincts of the country churchyard. I thought the exact churchyard which the poet had in his mind was well ascertained, and that it was the one at Stoke. But it seems Dr. Hawtrey's[2] was a different affair—I had forgotten. Mentioning him reminds me of a promise I once made him to send him a Yankee copy of *Ferdinand and Isabella*. If you ever see him, could you not burden your memory with this—that I had not forgotten, but that I find the American edition is contraband, and cannot be passed into England even at the Author's desire—the gentlemen of the Custom House most unceremoniously disembowelling a copy as soon as it comes into their hands —which I much regret, as I do not like to fail in a promise.

Thank you, my dear friend, for your goodnatured attention to my whims as well as wishes in the portrait business. As to the "Esquire," I am glad you decided to lop it off. What should a Yankee democrat be doing with titles when royalist John Bull rejects them? Besides I have no legal right to it, never having taken the trouble to be sworn a justice of the peace, although I receive a commission every seven years regularly. I am delighted you are so well satisfied with the print that you can find no worse fault with it than that it will give only one expression of the features. If the artist has seized a good one, I am more lucky than I have usually been under the hands of the limner. I thought the original the best duplicate I have ever seen of myself. Time will make it less and less true, but not less true to the past, and I think I have given my last sitting. So old Time may work on me with his chisel as much as he likes.

I am sending this week a bust of myself to New York to garnish the "Prescott House"[3] which they write me will be open in June. Will you not take lodging there, when you make another visit to the New World? It is nearly opposite to the house where you were quartered last.

At length I have the pleasure to send you the little nothings by Bigelow Lawrence,[4] viz. a miniature pencil-case to be worn round the neck, for ornament more than use. Item—an ivory stylus, more for use than ornament (the worse for wear, having been pared away, as it required sharpening, an inch or more) with which I wrote all the *Conquest of Mexico*. I gave to dear Mrs. Milman the stylus that indited *Peru*. Anna Ticknor has the *Ferdinand and Isabella* one. My wife says she will not accept the one with which I am doing the *Philippics*. As that is agate pointed, I think it will be able to run off as long a yarn as I shall care to spin.

I do not know much news that will interest you. We are now, you know, in the midst of transition and in two days the *ins* will become *outs* and the *outs, ins*. General Pierce keeps his own counsel, (a miracle here) so well that no one can divine the cabinet that is to be. My friend Bancroft is, I understand, at Washington, to see, I suppose, if any trump will turn up in his hand. I hope not, for the sake of his History. But what is history to romance now-a-days! I received a letter yesterday from a Frenchman, St. Hilaire,[5] in which he prophesies that *Uncle Tom* will give the death blow to slavery in the U.S.! I had a letter by last steamer also from the Duchess of Sutherland, in which she speaks too of *Uncle Tom*. This did not surprize me. Strange that the English should not understand that three-fourths of the country, slaveholders and all, look on slavery as a deplorable evil. But how to rid ourselves of the cancer in the system—that is a problem, for the solution of which California might well be offered as a premium.

We are going on here in the regular way, dining and being dined. I do little of the latter. Tomorrow I have some bigwigs to feed with me, the Governor, the Chief Justice, his Excellency Abbott[6]—with four others, including our friends Gray and Hillard—a small party, and rather select. Ticknor could not come. He said he was tired of Excellencies and honors and a' that. Something in this certainly.

But I am abusing the privilege of twaddle. Pray remember me most cordially to your husband and your family, and believe me, my dear Lady Lyell, with kindest remembrances to my friends at the Deanery Always your affectionate

[P.S.] Susan desires me not to omit to give her warmest love to you.[7]

1. In 1852 Mary Matilda Georgiana (1823–92), sixth daughter of the sixth Earl of Carlisle, married Henry Labouchere. He later became the first Baron Taunton.

2. Edward Craven Hawtrey (1789–1862), provost of Eton.

3. Among the many things named in honor of WHP—literary societies, towns and capes, etc.—this appears to be the only hotel.

4. Probably Timothy Bigelow Lawrence (d. 1869), who had graduated from Harvard in 1846.

5. Augustin François César Prouvençal de Saint-Hilaire (1779–1853), French botanist.

6. I.e. Abbott Lawrence.

7. Tantalizing tidbits from certain of WHP's letters to Lady Lyell (items 261, 268, 272, 280 in this collection) are in Ticknor, *Prescott, passim.*

262.   From Colonel Thomas Aspinwall
(WHP Papers, Mass. Hist. Soc.)

London, 11 March 1853

Wm. H. Prescott Esq.

My dear Sir

I communicated your reply to Mr. Bentley as you desired in your letter of the 21st of last month. Today I have received his rejoinder, in which he declines to pay £600 for your interest in the *Ferdinand and Isabella* and *Miscellanies.*

You will probably derive a greater profit than £400 if the present arrangement remains undisturbed, although it will come by a protracted train of instalments. I did not like to say a word to you on the subject, lest it should rather embarrass than aid you; and besides I had given my views some time ago.

I am much gratified to learn that efforts are making in earnest at Washington for the establishment of an international copyright between the United States and this country.

Bentley was very anxious sometime since to *forestall* your Philip the 2d and said he should write you on the subject. You will judge for yourself whether it is best to give any pledge in his favor, or to have the work open to competition. You have a name and the publishers will be eager to turn it to their account, while Mr. Bentley will naturally be averse to relinquish the credit of ushering into the world the literary progeny of a distinguished habitué. It would be a blot on his escutcheon, if you were to graciously permit Mr. Murray to bear the name of "Prescott" on his colours.

I am, my dear Sir Ever most truly yours

THOS. ASPINWALL

[P.S.] A copy of Mr. Bentley's letter is enclosed.

263.   To Lady Mary E. Lyell

(Transcript, Lady Lyell's Letterbook, WHP Papers, Mass. Hist. Soc.)

Boston, March 28, [1853]

My dear Lady Lyell,

The prints have not turned up after all—though the steamer of the 5th has been in port a week, and has nearly discharged her cargo. I trust they will lie over now till the next Boston packet, or I shall not fare so well at the New York Custom House. I suppose Richmond has been a day too late.

But if my own phiz has not come to light, a much better one has in your pretty daguerreotype. How kind it was in you to remember your promise. It is so good—what they call a speaking likeness. Yet alas, it won't speak. How delicately it is touched with the painter's colors—the dress and the ornaments are better, I think, than we do them, and the sun must have thrown aside his English veil when he smiled on you, for it is a very bright impression. I do not know whether you will take it as a compliment, that good as the likeness is, we do not think it does you quite justice. I think people are apt to like to have it said that their portraits flatter them—strange enough.

I received by the same steamer several little souvenirs, among the rest one in the substantial form of a Stilton cheese, which I trust will turn out better than some you wot of. Old Lady Carlisle was kind enough to send me a copy of the illustrated edition of *Uncle Tom* with Lord Carlisle's preface, and Lady Mary Labouchere a volume of Gray with illustrations.

We have had a little excitement in our commonwealth from a proposal to merge the Athenaeum in the City library—that is not yet born. Ticknor wrote a circular showing the manifold advantages of such a measure. This brought down a sour rebuke from old Mr. Quincy, and a reply in which Ticknor had the better of his opponent, in temper decidedly. In the meantime, showers of missiles were let off on one side and the other in the papers and yesterday we had a meeting, particularly full, of the members—over 600—when a vast deal of patriotic glow was exhibited in favour of the time-honored institution, and after some sparring it was unanimously voted not to give up the old ship. I could not but think if a subscription paper had made its appearance how soon the hall would have been cleared of those zealous friends of the institution. I was one of those, however, who could not make up their minds to throw open the doors to the many-headed.

Since I last wrote, one of the events which it required no witch to predict has come to pass,—our Elizabeth has made me a happy grandfather. A bouncing boy—an infant prodigy of course and Lizzie in excellent health.[1] So thirty years and more—a generation are put on my shoulders! Shall you not regard me with more veneration hereafter?

I hope you and your husband are in perfect health. I see by your portrait that you have not pined since your return to the land of roast mutton. I think my commissions were enough to take down some flesh. In my next I shall tell you what I think of the print.

I have been listening to Moore's *Correspondence*. It has not cost the noble editor much sweat of the brain, I think. It gives one a good idea of Tom's heart. What a little name Tom is! "Your own Tom."! When you think of his warbling his songs, it reminds you of *tom-tit*. I wished, however, he had trusted more to these songs, and less to Lord Moira. The breath of patronage is not the atmosphere for true genius. On the whole, the best letters in the book—as far as I have read—only to 1812, are those of Miss Godfrey. Do you know any thing of her? Is she still extant?

Farewell, my dear friend. With kindest remembrances to your husband and your family, I remain, most affectionately yours[2]

1. James Lawrence, born March 23, 1853. A month later, on April 20, 1853, a granddaughter, Edith, was born to William and Augusta.

2. A week before writing this letter, WHP, in a moment of retrospective longing, had said, "The *last week* reviewed the industry of the *Peruvian*—golden age." See Prescott (Gardiner, ed.), *The Literary Memoranda*, II, 215.

264.   From R. Augustus Wight
(WHP Papers, Mass. Hist. Soc.)

Ellerlie, April 11th 1853

Wm. H. Prescott Esq.
Dear Sir,

Will you favor one of your younger readers with your autograph?

And will you allow him to return you his most hearty thanks and acknowledgments for having cured him of novel reading? I was a most desperate and determined peruser of the "yellow-covered" until my good sister Agnes gave me all your histories (superbly bound) and I confessed I wanted no better "novels." Dear Sir, you are a magician; again and again I go back and put myself under your delightful spell. Allow me to thank you and to love you for the good you have done me.

I want something that has been in your hands—that will serve to bring you nearer to me. Very respectfully,

R. AUGUSTUS WIGHT

265.   ## To Mary Elizabeth Wormeley
(Wormeley-Latimer Papers, Mass. Hist. Soc.)

Lynn,[1] August 1, 1853

My dear Lizzie,

I received the other day your note with the interesting account of the poor negro families which the late cruel law of Virginia parts asunder. Such a law will give work enough for the charitable; and the state should have accompanied it by another making an appropriation that might neutralize some of the ill effects of the former. But that, I suppose, they prefer leaving to their brethren in the North.

I have the pleasure of enclosing you a check for $25, which is little for the good work. But you are aware that applications in one form or another, and most of them for meritorious objects, are a pretty common thing in our good town of Boston, and absorb our means very thoroughly.

I have also the pleasure of sending £5 as the subscription of Lady Ellesmere to the same excellent object. Lord Ellesmere and his family[2] passed Friday with us at Lynn, and I spoke to Lady Ellesmere of your benevolent project—though without any idea of enlisting her sympathies in any practical way. But on her return to town, she sent me the enclosed with many expressions of interest in the cause. This was a very kind act, since it was certainly not her affair—except as the friend of humanity.

With kindest remembrances to your mother and sisters, I remain, dear Elizabeth,[3]

1. In the process of shifting his summer residence from Fitful Head to a less exposed setting, WHP was passing his first summer at Lynn on the mainland.
2. Francis Leveson-Gower (1800–1857) was the first Earl of Ellesmere. Lady Ellesmere was Catherine (1800–1886), daughter of the third Duke of Portland.
3. The signature has been cut off this letter.

266.   ## To Lady Mary E. Lyell
(Transcript, Lady Lyell's Letterbook, WHP Papers, Mass. Hist. Soc.)

Boston, September 13, 1853

My dear Lady Lyell,

Last evening I had the pleasure of receiving yours of the 23d August —and such a good letter, so full of facts—just the facts too that have interest for me. It is very kind of you to task your memory so pleasantly and profitably for me, who can give you so little in return.

We are just now in town—*in transitu*—those three or four horrid days of topsy-turvy confusion, when all the summer gear is to be turned off, and the trunks filled up again with the autumn liveries. Such a medley of things as are scattered about the room! My study looks like a pawnbroker's shop!

We have had an intense summer. Much as I like the new house, I don't know if I shall not be obliged to flit back again to Fitful Head. In that case I shall build a stone house there on a larger scale than the present. But Susan does not want to move from her present quarters, now that we are established in them. So I shall give them a fair trial. There is much that is charming in them. I have arranged to have a good bit of lawn got up for us, if possible, and quantities of trees dotted and clumped over the grounds—so when you return here in the course of the 19th century—you will have something more shady for a noontide stroll than the sands of the sea-shore.

I am glad that the Ellesmeres found Boston more to their taste than some other parts of the country—I did little enough for them.

So Macaulay will not probably come out till November of next year. It is just about the time when I shall be ready. For I find it will be expedient to enlarge the amount of my two first volumes, in order to bring in some interesting matter, for which I have materials, and which I think will be of service in conciliating the good will of the public. It is important that the leading volumes should take for the sake of their successors, as well as their own.

A day or more has passed since I wrote the preceding, during which I have been spinning round like a tee-totum. I have seen the Ticknors twice. They are in good condition, having just returned from their Lake George expedition. They told me that Mr. Norton[1] was dying —indeed by this time he is probably dead. He dies literally from want of breath, for there seems no disease on him but debility. He dies without having finished his great work on the Evidences. Two years ago I begged his friends to urge him not to postpone it, as he had already had a warning in a severe fit of illness. But I suppose he has never perfectly rallied. The translation of the Gospels and Acts is complete.

Hillard has come out with his book this week. It is a charming work, exhibiting his peculiarities of his mind—his relish for the beautiful, and his rich and glowing language. It is a pleasant book on a threadbare topic. Ticknor or Hillard, I forget which, is to send you a copy. I have sent one to the Duchess of Argyll and to Mrs. Milman— that the work may be known among good judges of literary merit. Could your husband—or rather, I think I had better speak to him myself. Will you, dear Lyell, when you happen to be at Murray's—to whom a copy has been sent out by this steamer—tell him something about Hillard—what a clever man he is in both the English and Yankee sense of the word—and how well he is qualified by the natural turn of his mind, and by his general cultivation, for such a work? It would predispose him in its favour, and at least lead him to give it a fair examination. There are so many books of travels.[2]

I must congratulate you on your visit to Osborne. You keep such high company, what with Queens and Presidents—that you will hardly feel at home with any thing less than a *chef d'etat*. I wonder what you told his Noble Highness anent the Crystal Palace of New Amsterdam. I am told it is filling up very finely—though somewhat of the latest.

And now, dear Lady Lyell, I believe I have spun my yarn—and told you nothing. But the New World is not the place for news. I wish you could be with us in the shades of Pepperell. We saw the Searses last evening and Ellen lamented she had seen so little of you, whom she was sure she would have liked so much. I have been very industrious since you went away and mean to keep the steam up in my autumn *villeggiatura*. With kindest remembrances to your family, believe me, my dear friend, always affectionately yours.

1. I.e. Andrews Norton.
2. WHP's unsigned review of Hillard's *Six Months in Italy* was published in the *National Intelligencer,* October 6, 1853, p. 2.

267.   From Fanny Calderón de la Barca
(Extracts, WHP Papers, Mass. Hist. Soc.)

Madrid, 3d November 1853

My dear Mr. Prescott

It was with great pleasure that Calderón received your kind letter of the 10th October a few days ago—and as he has not a *moment* unoccupied, he gives me the agreeable task of answering it. He lost not a *moment* in complying with Lady Lyell's desire that he would send letters of introduction for her husband—and he also wrote to herself, expressing the pleasure it gave him to be of use to her.

.   .   .   .   .

You have heard, I suppose, by the English or other newspapers, that Calderón continues Minister of State—the Conde de San Luis, Presidente del Consejo.

.   .   .   .   .

We on our side, if not as *importantly* occupied, are *unceasingly* so —visits without end to receive and to pay—and when it is not an Opera night, a reception—very informal, however, which lasts till about one in the morning. It is a curious life to lead for a time—but I do not think I should like it to last very long. I find Madrid wonderfully improved, and a splendid city, even after Paris.

The Queen,[1] whom I had not seen since she was thirteen, nine years ago, I think a very fine-looking woman—not critically handsome—but with a more beautiful expression than I almost ever saw in anyone— the sweetest and most *winning* smile—and a *true Queen* in dignity of manner. She is very tall and large, but carries off her size. She is kindness itself to Calderón—and as for him he is *enchanted* with her—and thinks her intelligence and knowledge of affairs quite wonderful. The first time Lydia and I were presented to her, we went in private—and nothing could exceed her kindness and cordiality. She remembered Kate perfectly—and asked many questions about her. The King[2] has a handsome face—but is very short and has a *squeaking* voice. The little Princess is a nice little thing with short brown hair who holds out her hand to be kissed quite as naturally as the Queen does. The Queen says that the *Infantita* has a fancy for Calderón, because children have an intuitive love for those who are good.

The arrival of Soulé made a *sensation—not* of an agreeable nature. The prejudice against him in this country from the Queen downwards is stronger than anything you can conceive. Calderón presented him, and Madame Soulé and the son had an audience some days ago. But I must say their position is most disagreeable—and it will require the greatest tact and conciliation on the part of Soulé to do away in the slightest degree with the impression caused by his speeches—especially his last in New York.[3] I am sorry for Mme. Soulé—as for him, he acted with his eyes open—and must take the consequences. The Queen, who has a curious degree of penetration *at first sight,* said to Calderón when he went out, "He has the face of a French republican—of the days of the Revolution."

As yet, Calderón has named no one to the United States. We waited for the arrival of Soulé, for his reception and discourse. It is *very* difficult to find the proper person.

.   .   .   .

Your friend Gayangos lives not very far from us—and we have seen him frequently. He talks a little of paying a visit to the United States one of these days—especially to *Boston,* of course.

.   .   .   .

You need not be surprised if you hear of this Ministry speedily breaking up with a *crash—after* the 19th. If it does, these three months I shall not forget. If Calderón finishes without any great *compromiso,* then I shall not be sorry to have had the experience of this kind of life. Today he was heartily wishing himself in a village by the seashore. We see a great deal of Martínez de la Rosa,[4] who at present is leading a quiet life—till the opening of the *dreaded Cortes.* We have been at a *bull-fight,* a scene of *barbaric magnificence.*

I fear I am writing a confused letter—as I am interrupted every moment—with "Señora—visitas"—and enters the Governess of the Infantas—the old Duchess of San Carlos—half a dozen ladies whose names I have not *caught,* and can only guess at—the *Introductor de Embajadores*—a little man with high-heeled boots and brushed-up hair, which he hopes will increase his height—I consult him upon every point of etiquette—General Concha, whom we all like—and so on. What are the *filibusteros* doing? I wonder if they miss Calderón? I show your picture to everybody and you are called *fino—inteligente —bondadoso* &c. But I need not tire you by *crossing.*[5] *Adios.* Remember me kindly to every member of your family—to Mr. and Mrs. Lawrence and *their* family—Mr. and Mrs. Ticknor &c—and believe me, dear Mr. Prescott Siempre su afectuosima amiga

FANNY CALDERON DE LA BARCA

[P.S.] If Mrs. Ritchie and Lilly are in Boston, will you give them my love. Of course Charles Sumner is in Washington.

1. Isabella II, born in 1830, reigned from 1843 to 1868, during which period reactionary forces usually were in control under constitutional forms.

2. Don Francisco de Asis, cousin of the queen, whom she had married in 1846.

3. Pierre Soulé (1801–70), blatant annexationist in reference to the troubled issue of Cuba, served as American Minister in Spain between October, 1853, and December, 1854.

4. Francisco de Paula Martínez de la Rosa Berdejo Gómez y Arroyo (1786–1862), politician and writer.

5. Fanny Calderón had turned several sheets of her letter 90 degrees and, using them a second time, had written over the previous portions of her letter.

268.   To Lady Mary E. Lyell

(Transcript, Lady Lyell's Letterbook, WHP Papers, Mass. Hist. Soc.)

Boston, December 25, 1853

A Merry Christmas to you, dear Lady Lyell and to Lyell too, and good orthodox mince pies to celebrate it with. I wonder where you are keeping it. Not where you will find it kept in as genial a way as in Old England. How much your countrymen, by the by, are indebted to

Washington Irving for showing the world what a beautiful thing Christmas is—or used to be—in your brave little island. I was reading his account of it this morning—stuffed as full of racy old English rhymes as Christmas pudding is of plums. Irving has a soul, which is more than one can say for most writers. It is odd that a book like this, so finely and deliberately executed, should come from the New World, where one expects to meet with hardly any thing more than the raw material.

We are to keep the high festival in Beacon Street—tomorrow. The Lawrences of each generation and all sexes, the Paiges ditto, our own children and David Sears, Jr. and *sposa* are bidden to the feast. So there will be no want of good company and I trust not of good cheer. I suppose you think that heretics like us have no right to meddle with Christmas at all. But I have always managed very cleverly in the matter —eating Thanksgiving at my father's and Christmas at my mother-in-law's. So I did not allow myself to be cheated by the old Puritans out of my mince pies. The last Thanksgiving we were all with Mr. Lawrence in Park St. How easily one's children bring one into new combinations!

I don't know any thing that has been stirring here of late that would have interest for you or us either—for that matter. It has been a quiet winter—quiet in every sense, for the old graybeard has not ventured to shake his hoary locks at us yet, or at least he has shed none of them on the ground, which is as bare as November. This is quite uncommon and very agreeable. But winter is not likely to rot in the sky—and we shall soon see the feathers dancing about us.

I suppose Anna has told you that the eldest son of Wm. Appleton went mad the other day, and is now in the asylum at Charlestown. His brother is also there, and both are tenants of a noble building which their father erected at his own expense, furnishing more ample accommodation to the inmates than the other buildings. This is his eldest son. But there is a taint of insanity in the mother's blood which all the ocean could not wash out. The father and two sisters died mad, and some others of her kin have lived so. Did your husband know Dr. Flagg, of this town, in Winter Street? He broke his neck by throwing himself out of a chamber window the other day, on a *flag*-stone in a delirium. I wonder how our lunatics compare with yours, as to numbers. I think, however, it would be difficult to tell, as your lunatics are not shut up. At least I met some in England going the rounds, whom we should think odd enough for a hospital. Yet I suspect our high-pressure atmosphere is very insanitying.

I have had another engraved portrait of myself sent me—the one I spoke to you of—not quite finished; when it is, I will send you a copy —being of octavo size—for a work in Philadelphia, and executed by Welch, who did the Washington head. The family think it good—for me in the dyspepsia. Lady Ellesmere sent me her portrait the other day. It was taken recently, and the engraving is prettily executed. It is altogether a domestic *fancy,* as her eyes are cast down on a huge bit of embroidery, as big as a baby, which she holds in her hands. It is not unlike, yet does not quite do her justice. The artist is Thorbush, engraved by Atkinson. She was still at Worsley, and the Argylls were with her.

By the by, talking of the Ellesmeres, reminds one of the gout, which seems to be a synonym of Lord Ellesmere. And that reminds me that a fortnight since my wife had an attack of the gout, the *veritable,* and no mistake. Dr. Jackson tended her, and subdued her by colchicum. It was in her right hand, so I make a point now when I touch the right to apologize. Did you ever hear any thing like it! so thin-blooded and temperate as she is—only one glass of wine *per diem* to dock off. I told Lady Ellesmere that I thought it must be some that her lord had left, out of his superfluity, for he seemed to have enough and to spare.

I believe your last arrangement is not to go through Madrid. I should like to have heard your Spanish experiences. The Calderóns would have been very glad to see you, and they are at the top of the world there. Madame Calderón wrote me the other day that Calderón had sent you some letters for the Canaries, and that she hoped they had not miscarried, but that she had not heard from you since. Will you excuse me for suggesting that a line to her from Teneriffe, in which you could mention the reception of them, (after you have seen some of the consignees,) would probably gratify her.

I must not conclude without congratulating you on the changes in the arrangement of your family circle—your sister's engagement, and your father's change of residence to the Regent's Park. The first is the greatest event, and yet the last will probably bring you the most happiness; for the one takes away a dear friend and the other brings him closer. But all seems to work well with you. It was so fortunate, your having the society of your brother-in-law and sister on this expedition. God bless you, my dear friend. Give my kindest remembrances to your husband. Pray remember the boulder, and beg him not to push you off the Peak of Teneriffe—and believe me, most affectionately yours

P.S. Thank you for your kind letter of November 17. Anna Ticknor, by your orders, asked me about some matters in it ten days before it arrived. It stuck somewhere unaccountably by the way.

P.P.S. December 27—There are six inches of snow on the ground.

Christmas went off merrily. Old Messrs. Lawrence and Prescott and Mesdames Lawrence and Prescott Scotch-reeling it till midnight.

P.P.P.S. I forgot to say that I have done with Turnbull, who has done me no harm, and no good either. He has done some good in this town, and though a humbug is by no means a quack.

269.   From Harper & Brothers
(WHP Papers, Mass. Hist. Soc.)

New York, December 28th 1853

W. H. Prescott, Esq.
  Boston

Dear Sir,

Notwithstanding our recent pressure and confusion,[1] we feel ashamed at not having acknowledged, before this, your very kind note of the 14th instant. We thank you for it, most heartily,—and for the kind and welcome expression of sympathy which it contained, and which, rest assured, was most thankfully appreciated.

The plates of all your works, we are happy to inform you, are *safe,* —and we intend to reprint from them as soon as we can possibly find presses and paper.

We shall be pleased to hear from you at any and all times,—and to receive any suggestions you may have to offer.

With respect, Your obliged friends,

HARPER & BROS.

1. On December 10, 1853, a devastating fire swept the establishment of Harper & Brothers.

270.   Memorandum Concerning Income
(WHP Papers, Mass. Hist. Soc.)

Income received 1853

National Insurance	628.00		
Fireman	600.00		
Hospital	400.00		
		Insurance	1,628.00
Amoskeag	960.00		
Jackson	–0–		
Lowell	450.00		
Nashua	360.00		

Boott	480.00		
Merrimac	800.00		
Stark	420.00		
Massachusetts	320.00		
Hadley	–0–		
Manchester	–0–	Manufacturing	3,790.00
Suffolk	690.00		
Metropolis	800.00	Banks	1,490.00
Copy Rights	3,505.00	Copy Rights	3,505.00
Lowell R.R.	450.00		
N.Y. Central	8,402.00		
Housatonic	–0–		
Berkshire	630.00		
Michigan	504.00		
Connecticut	120.00		
Wilmington	868.00		
N.Y. & N.H.	175.00		
Michigan Bonds	888.00		
Connecticut preferred	64.00		
N.Y. Central Bonds	210.00	Rail Roads	12,331.00
Beacon St.	1,850.00		
Cooper St.	439.00		
Salem St.	573.00		
Merrimac	144.00		
Nahant	400.00		
Pepperell	100.00		
Manchester Lands	–0–		
Lynn	552.00		
Smith	510.00		
Maine	100.00	Real Estate	4,668.00
William's note	600.00		
Amoskeag note	600.00		
Va. & Canada	200.00		
Col. Bank	84.00		
Worcester R.R.	73.00		
Bay State	180.00		

	Other Stocks	1,737.00
		29,149.00
	Debts, Interest	1,410.00
	Net Income	27,739.00*

* This owing to the great dividend on the consolidation of the N.
York Central R.R.

271.   Memorandum Concerning Expenses
               (WHP Papers, Mass. Hist. Soc.)

                    Expenses 1853

		Children	Total
January	2687.55	76.28	2763.83
February	844.17	–o–	844.17
March	890.06	1000.00	1890.06
April	1397.03	126.25	1523.28
May	1070.88	1000.00	2070.88
June	730.87	–o–	730.87
July	2069.32	–o–	2069.32
August	488.10	490.37	978.47
September	370.00	–o–	370.00
October	1001.86	5.00	1006.86
November	2560.33	5409.56	7969.89
December	481.61	120.00	601.61
	14,591.78	8,227.46	22,819.24

Included
    Lynn, house and grounds   1346.67
              furniture   522.51
                                     1869.18
    Amory   7927.46
    Also   2213.00   Charity
    Also   1300.00   Superfluities—extra
[on jacket]   Actual Expenses
                                 1852 — 19,000
                                  '53 — 26,100
                                  '54 — 22,170
                                       67,270

Included   Not included
   '53 — 1900 Lynn   10,000 — Elizabeth ⎱
   '54 — 1500 furniture   5,000 — William ⎰ when married
        — 4000 extra [?]

272.   To Lady Mary E. Lyell
(Transcript, Lady Lyell's Letterbook, WHP Papers, Mass. Hist. Soc.)

Boston, February 26, 1854

My dear Lady Lyell,

I don't know where this letter may find you. I suppose in the Canaries—the African isles. There will remain now only one other quarter
of the globe left unvisited by you. I believe you have never penetrated
into any part of Asia. I am sorry I am not likely to get a letter from the
Peak of Teneriffe. There could have been something sublime in that
date—like a note from the Pyramids! And while you are running such
a glorious orbit, my little circle is bounded by the domestic circle. So
what can I have to tell you that can interest one of such large cosmo-
politan ideas and experiences?

We have had as great variety in our winter, however—meteorologi-
cally speaking—as if we had travelled from Lapland to your little
Canaries—heavy snows and heavy rains alternately—thermometer at
zero when we go to bed and bouncing up above temperate before the
next day at twelve! It is as fickle as a woman's will—and the sex have
that privilege. Two days since we had a furious snow-storm, and while
I am writing a warm rain is coming down merrily.

We have not quite so much variety indoors—a pretty good round of
dinners in a small way, and some private theatricals, to break up the
monotony. On Tuesday (this is Sunday, and you see how well I spend
it) we have a dramatic exhibition at Dr. Cushing's in Watertown—
handbills printed, the scenic decorations, I am told, excellent—the
Germania band for the orchestra—one hundred and fifty spectators
—and three farces or vaudevilles, the actors our young people. I suppose Anna Ticknor has told you of some theatricals in which Lizzie
took a part, and very well. Though Macready said one day that he
never knew an amateur performer who could earn two and sixpence a
week on the stage. But there is a pleasure in their very unsophisticated-
ness. I went some years since with Mrs. Nathaniel Thayer (do you
know her? a charming little woman, daughter of the *patroon* of Albany,) to the theatre. It was the first time she had ever seen a play!
When one of the actresses was left alone on the stage, Mrs. Thayer
remarked to me "She felt for the poor lady, it must be so embarrassing
to her!" It was quite charming.

I dined with the Ticknors on Friday last—a snug little party—very
pleasant. Anna has been in good health this winter and in very good
spirits. Good kind friends they are; and if you want to find it out, be a
little ill or out of sorts yourself, and you will soon prove it. We had

quite a fright day before yesterday. My boy William took it into his head to top off a quantity of sugar of lead—which being wisely kept by his wife in a congress-water bottle he mistook for that agreeable beverage. The mistake was discovered before half the tumbler was emptied. And then such a fright! He sent to me for an emetic; and the servants went scampering after the Doctors—always out, of course, when wanted.

I ran at the top of my speed for an apothecary. Poor Will, meanwhile, examined the Encyclopedia, found *sugar of lead*—a slow but sure poison. Pleasant interval was it not! For three-quarters of an hour elapsed, when three of the faculty and an apothecary all bounced on the scene at once. And such a dosing—ipecac, sulphate of zinc, &c &c and the results left him as light and free of incumbrances as if he had been on a first voyage, two days out. So he is now all right again. But I don't think I have felt so uncomfortably for a long time as when I was running (and ruminating by the way) after the apothecary.

I have been tolerably industrious—for me—this winter, and I hope to be in condition to make a bow to the public by the end of the year.[1] But it is a far cry to Loch Awe. You have heard that my publishers the Harpers were burnt out last December. They lost about a million— one-third perhaps insured. It is said they have as much more left. I should have made [money] by the fire, as they had about half an edition of each of my books on hand, which they had paid me for. But I could not make money out of their losses, and I told them to strike off as many more copies without charging them. Ticknor did the same. If all their authors would do as much for them, they would be better off by at least a couple of hundred thousand dollars than their report now shows.

What a mess seems likely to come out of the Turkey business! His Czarship has met with a disagreeable surprise, no doubt, and if he goes further may fare worse. Yet his situation is more to be envied than that of Austria. How sharply Kossuth, Mazzini &c must be looking on the scene, biding their time. We are here just now all alive with the Nebraska question. Do you know what that is?[2] I suppose Anna keeps you booked up about the politics. Everett made a speech, good as far as it went, but some thought too temperate by half. A friend said, "He might just as well have put a little more milk into his water!"

Now I believe I have emptied my budgets of nothings. It is a shame to saddle you with postage for them. If letters paid according to their value, how light the tax would be! I have paid my share of postage, however, for printed matter, at least, have I not? How glad I should be to find a round sum charged for a letter from Teneriffe!

I wish you could return through Spain and see Calderón in his glory, as the premier, and Señora Fanny. They would be so kind to you and you would see Madrid, the Escorial, and a' that, under such advantages. The secret doors would fly open.

Good-bye, dear Lady Lyell. Susan desires kindest remembrances to you and your husband—pray give mine and

No se olvide jamás de su más afectísimo amigo Q.B.S.P.

GUILLERMO H. PRESCOTT

1. WHP completed the second volume, and with it five years of labor, in August, 1854. For his progress and problems in that interval, see Prescott (Gardiner, ed.), *The Literary Memoranda,* II, 218.

2. The Kansas-Nebraska bill, providing for popular sovereignty in the areas concerned regarding the question of slavery, was passed by the U.S. Senate late in May, after three months of bitter debate.

273.   To Alexander Burton

(O. D. Wilkinson Collection, The Historical Society of Pennsylvania)

Boston, February 26, 1854

My dear Mr. Burton,

You will think I am a regular *bon-vivant,* and love my bottle right well; for I am going to avail myself of your kind permission and ask you to do me the favor to send me some of the good Spanish wines. Not, however, of the same kind as what you last sent—which proves to be excellent in the way of dark sherry. What I now want is the lighter sort; and I shall be obliged if you will send me four quarter casks of Amontillado, and one of Manzanilla, for myself, my son, and my son-in-law, Mr. Lawrence. I will thank you to address them all to me, and draw on me as before for the amount. I presume the cost of these wines, of the best quality, will not be greater than that of the dark sherry of the best kind. I hope I am not giving you too much trouble in taking you literally at your word.

I hope your health has been good of late, and that you have not been plagued with rheumatism—which, I believe, is an old enemy of yours, as it is of mine. It is in the blood, and my son William has suffered from it this winter.

I have been pretty industrious, for me, of late, and hope I shall send into the world before next year some of the results of those manuscripts which you have been so kind as to send me from time to time, in the shape of a brace of volumes—the history of Philip el Prudente; when I shall have the pleasure to send you a copy. But it will be only the beginning of a work which I shudder to think may extend to two or three volumes more. But the history of that monarch is not only the history of Spain but of Europe; and there is no cramming it into a nutshell.

With constant regard, I remain, my dear Mr. Burton, Very truly your friend and kinsman

WM. H. PRESCOTT

274.   To Richard Bentley
(Richard Bentley Papers, Harvard College Library)

Boston, May 15, 1854

My dear Sir,

I have now brought my two volumes of the "History of Philip the Second" so nearly to a completion, being occupied with the closing chapters, that I can safely make an arrangement for the sale of them. Had Colonel Aspinwall remained in London, I should probably have left the matter to him; and I enclose you a note which I wrote some time since—intended to be presented by my agent to the English publishers,—giving a general view of the nature of the book. As I am now situated I shall negotiate the sale of the book myself.

One difficulty presents itself in the precarious nature of the existing copyright law, which is liable at any moment to be overthrown by a judgment of the House of Lords, to which I understand the question is now submitted. Any arrangement that I may make, therefore, must embrace the alternatives of my being able to give a copyright to the English publisher, or only such advantages as he may derive by my sending him sheets in advance as they are printed under my own eye here.

After the best information I can obtain on the subject I have made up my mind as to the probable worth of the book; and I offer it to you at the rate of One Thousand Pounds per volume; that is two thousand pounds for the two volumes first to be published, and one thousand pounds for each succeeding volume of the work.

This is on the presumption that I can give you a good copyright, which will be the case unless the last decision—of Lord Campbell I think it was—be reversed. As to the passage of an International Copyright Law, I have no faith in it at all.

In the other alternative of my being only able to send you the proofs in advance, I will furnish them to you for five hundred pounds a volume for the two first volumes and two hundred and fifty pounds for each succeeding volume of the work. The amount of the copyright—or of the sum paid for receiving the sheets in advance—as the case may be—to be paid one-half by a note of six months, the other half by a note of nine months, from the date of publication.

I have only to add that, as I have many friends, to whom I wish to present copies, I should stipulate to have twenty-four copies of the work of the largest size published given to me without charge.

As it would be difficult and annoying to carry on a correspondence about the matter at the distance by which we are separated, I have put the book at such a price as I believe it to be honestly worth. I shall be much disappointed if you do not accept the terms. After the long and friendly relations that have subsisted between us, I should regret to be obliged to carry my wares to another market. But I must frankly tell you that it will not be in my power to accept any modification of the terms proposed; and if you do not find it to your interest to accept them as they now stand, I shall, on receiving your reply, feel myself at liberty to dispose of the book *on the same terms* in another quarter.

As I am desirous of settling the affair, I shall be obliged by your giving me an answer *by return of mail.*

In giving you a preference in this offer, it is needless to say I have consulted only my own feelings towards you; and I hope you will believe me sincere when I repeat that I shall be under the necessity of considering an answer which does not explicitly accept, or which may propose *any modification of the terms* (either in regard to the sum to be paid for the copyright if it should appear, that I am able to give one, or in regard to the sum to be paid for the advance sheets—the stipulations on both points forming part of the same contract) *as equivalent to a rejection of them.*[1]

With sincere regard, I remain, my dear sir, Very truly yours

WM. H. PRESCOTT

1. Initiating what he hoped would be a pleasant, quick and profitable negotiation, WHP learned, in time, that the publication of his new work in England would be none of those things.

275.   To Fanny Calderón de la Barca
            (Draft, WHP Papers, Mass. Hist. Soc.)

Lynn, July 17, 1854

My dear Mme. Calderón,

This note will be handed to you by my son Amory—the little

"Judge," as Calderón used to dub him, though now not very little and still less of a judge. After a year passed in Europe, and another since at home, he goes to complete his survey of the Continent and as he has not been in Spain, he will probably pass the next winter there.[1] Would that I could be with him. But I am not a bachelor, to carry my household on my back, but a venerable grandpapa, with two generations below me gathered under my roof. Still the gray hairs have not come very thick though they do mount guard about the temples. Will you allow Amory to ask counsel of you how to proceed in a strange place where he is ignorant of the language, though I trust he has lived enough in Paris to turn his French to account.

I suppose you must be overwhelmed with occupations in your official position. Do Calderón and you like it as well as diplomacy? Not so well, I suspect, if you have to deal with ministers from the United States. Our two countries seem to be in awkward relations with each other. The matter is not mended by having a man at the head of our affairs who though from the North seems to be securing as large advantages for the South as if he had been born south of the Potomac. He is ogling Cuba most fearfully. I trust he will not be supported in it by your nation.[2] But when I see the rapacity in some quarters and the subserviency in others, I guess and fear.

Luckily I live in the 16th century. My Philip II will be launched here and in London next spring, I trust. I hope no filibusters in the shape of maudlin translators will fall on it, as they did on *Peru*. I had rather it should remain in the web of English undefiled, where it will at least furnish a draught for a few friends in Madrid whom I care most about.

The summer has scattered your friends here. The Ritchies are at Newport, the Ticknors on Lake George; we anchored on the seashore of Lynn,[3] in very comfortable quarters where I shall not despair of one day receiving you and Calderón. Pray remember me most warmly to him and believe me, my dear friend

1. At this time Amory was approaching his twenty-fifth birthday. In the course of his Asiatic and European rambles, Amory nourished an expanding wanderlust. Never in the years remaining to WHP did his younger son remain long in Boston.

2. The climax of Soulé's brusque diplomacy, the Ostend Manifesto, was at hand. As he had opposed Polk's expansionist policy in reference to Mexico in the previous decade, so WHP also opposed the Cuban policy of the Pierce administration.

3. This was WHP's second summer at Lynn, during which he and his family

so adapted themselves to it that the idea of returning to Nahant dropped from his thinking.

276.   From Harper & Brothers
(WHP Papers, Mass. Hist. Soc.)

New York, July 29th, 1854

Wm. H. Prescott, Esq.
Dear Sir,

Yours of the 19th is at hand. Absence from the City has prevented us from making an earlier acknowledgement of your favor.

Enclosed please to find our bookkeeper's Statement of the Account, &c. as requested. Should it require explanation or correction, we beg you will let us hear from you at your convenience. Your Draft upon us for the balance will be duly honored as usual.

We shall be happy to dispose of our interest in the plates of the "Miscellanies" at a reasonable rate,—say the price charged for stereotyping at Cambridge.[1]

Our Warehouseman being sick and absent, we are unable just now to ascertain the quantities of the respective works now on hand. He will probably be back shortly, however, when we shall be able to decide whether the copies already printed will probably meet the demand until the time referred to.

We of course deeply regret the breaking off of our business connexions with you,—so long and so agreeably maintained,—but do not in the least blame you for it.[2] You could not have consistently acted otherwise than you have under the circumstances. And we know of no Author whom we would rather see benefitted by the envy and spite of our rivals than yourself. You have always acted honorably and liberally towards us—and we shall ever entertain towards you sentiments of more than high respect and friendly regard. It will always afford us sincere pleasure to hear of, and to contribute to your success, prosperity, and happiness.

As ever,—with thanks and respect, Your Obedient Servants

HARPER & BROTHERS

1. Unlike his histories, for which he always completely controlled the stereotype plates, WHP initially owned only a half-interest in the plates for the *Miscellanies*. Preparatory to taking that title from the Harpers, he negotiated the purchase of their half-interest.

2. A Boston firm having outbid the New York house for WHP's new work, the historian was transferring all of his American publishing business to Phillips, Sampson and Company.

277.   To Harper & Brothers
                      (Draft, WHP Papers, Mass. Hist. Soc.)

                                              August 7, 1854
Dear Sirs,

I duly received your letter containing the statement of our account and I will draw for the balance, $2624.83, tomorrow. I am glad to see that the books continue to do so well.

When your warehouseman returns, I shall be much obliged by your favoring me with a statement of the number of copies of each of the works on hand, and by your advising me what quantity of each you think will probably carry you on till the latter end of March.

With respect to the *Miscellanies,* you offer your half of the plates on what seems to me to be very fair terms. But as I am at some distance from Cambridge, the most direct mode would seem to be to pay you what you charged for the plates yourself in your account with me. On December 1, 1845, you state the whole cost of the plates at $449.60 —making your half equal to $224.80—which sum I am willing to pay you for them. The first article, being the Life of Brown, I suppose you are aware, is from Sparks's *American Biography,* the copyright of which, I believe, belongs to you. As the plates would be of no use to me without the right of publishing this, I suppose you mean to accord it.[1]

It gives me great satisfaction that you have looked upon my new arrangement in the light in which you have; since it assures me that when our business connections are dissolved, the same friendly feelings will remain between us that have existed throughout our intercourse with each other.

1. The Harpers gave WHP the right to publish the material on which they held the copyright.

278.   From Richard Bentley
                      (WHP Papers, Mass. Hist. Soc.)

                      New Burlington Street, August 11, 1854
Dear Sir

You will regret to hear, that the House of Peers here has reversed the decision of the Court of Error; and disregarding the clearly expressed ruling of Lord Campbell, supported by the opinion of *a majority of the Judges,* has determined the question that a foreigner cannot hold copyright in Great Britain.

This revocation of a principle that I regarded *as established,* is a grievous blow to me, from the extensive dealings I have had with

American authors. But in no other case do I so much deplore this event, as with respect to your valuable works. Henceforward it seems, or rather it is clear, I must be content to share with those who are sure to compete actively with me any benefit which may accrue from the sale of your works and one of my first endeavours must be, not only to reduce considerably the selling price of the present editions, but to bring out others on the lowest scale of prices that will admit of remuneration, to prevent others from underselling me.[1]

Colonel Aspinwall has applied to me for the Accounts, and they have been this day forwarded to him.

The 4th account of the cheap Edition of *Ferdinand and Isabella* gives a profit to you of   £87. 6. 6.
and the 8th Account of *Miscellanies* 8vo.   4. 18. 8.
                                                            ―――――――――
                                                            92. 5. 2.

On the other hand, I am still a loser by the cheap Edition of *Miscellanies,* the deficit on the 3rd account being £25.19. – and by the 8vo Edition of *Ferdinand and Isabella* the 14th account showing a loss of £97.7.–.

This is a glorious time for unprincipled men or pirates. Is it too much to hope, that such a state of things might be terminated by an International Copyright Act?

I have the honor to be, Dear Sir Yours most faithfully

RICHARD BENTLEY

[P.S.] Mr. Brown is preparing for me the engravings for Philip II.

1. This about-face in the English courts disturbed WHP greatly. As Colonel Aspinwall's departure from London was imminent and the negotiation of a publishing arrangement rendered too tedious for his own direct correspondence, the historian soon found it necessary to locate another agent in London.

279.   To George Bancroft
                (George Bancroft Papers, Mass. Hist. Soc.)

Lynn, August 23, [1854]

My dear Bancroft,

You ask me to give you some information about a reader—in regard to which I have certainly had some experience. I have been usually in the habit of getting some young man when he graduates and engaging him to read for me three or four years during which he finds leisure time for studying his profession. Sometimes I have had gentlemen of the cloth, before they have wagged their powers in the pulpit. Once I had a lieutenant of marines; and once I remember I advertized and had a shower of applications by post, among them a lady who called herself widow with three children. I had a leaning toward her; but my wife said if I took any lady as a reader she would scratch her eyes out; so as I thought that would make two blind persons, instead of one, I gave it up. Yet Mr. Parkman, the historian of Pontiac, has found comfort, I believe, in a female reader. The compensation for a woman, I suppose, would be much less than that of a man. I have usually paid my readers from 450 to 500 dollars a year, for which they have given me five hours *per diem*. But for the last few years I have had an arrangement of a permanent character with Mr. Kirk, who acts as my reader and amanuensis.

As you say, I am approaching an historical crisis, and in the course of next spring hope to be delivered of a brace of volumes—no great affair after so long a period of gestation. The late decision in the House of Lords has cut off a good slice of my anticipated English profits. But I have somewhat provided against this ill wind by securing a good price for the advance sheets.[1]

I have been more fortunate in my arrangements here. I am going to tell you a secret, which you must tell to nobody but your wife. I am going to leave Harpers and connect myself with a Boston house. This I do not from any dissatisfaction with the Harpers, who have done well by me from first to last. But the offers I had for *Philip II* and the other works were of a kind I could not refuse. The Harpers themselves allow this; and we shall part, as we have lived, on the most amiable terms. The house is not your old firm, Little and Brown. I will tell you the particulars hereafter. At present I beg you to say nothing about it, I having no right to say so much.[2]

I rejoice you are so soon to reappear on the historic stage. With my sincere regards to your wife, believe me ever, dear Bancroft Faithfully yours

WM. H. PRESCOTT

[P.S.] Gayarré[3] spent an hour with me and I was only sorry he would not accept those hospitalities which I pressed upon him.

1. Ever sanguine, WHP was destined to disappointment concerning the income to be derived in this fashion.

2. On August 22, 1854, WHP wrote, "Finished last note of last chapter of Vol. 2d of *History of Philip the Second*." Continuing, he summarized his new contract: "By my new contract—to take effect on the publication of Philip II, —I am to receive $6000 for each of the vols. of that work. The publishers also agree to pay me $6000 a year for six consecutive years for the right to publish 3000 copies of each of my former historical works annually in 12mo." See Prescott (Gardiner, ed.), *The Literary Memoranda*, II, 218, 220. The full text of this agreement of August 5, 1854, the longest and most complex of all

WHP's publishing contracts, is in Gardiner, *Prescott and His Publishers,* pp. 302–9.

3. Charles Étienne Arthur Gayarré (1805–95), historian.

280.   To Lady Mary E. Lyell

(Transcript, Lady Lyell's Letterbook, WHP Papers, Mass. Hist. Soc.)

Boston, November 4, '54

My dear Lady Lyell

So here I am in winter quarters again—55 Beacon Street—with the old Common before me, shedding its faded honors on the pates of the respectable burghers who are strolling about its malls. Yet it seems somewhat too early to leave the country when the summer heat is in the town. The mercury stands at 70° in the shade at noon, or at least was as high as that for several days the last week and part of this. The seasons are decidedly out of joint. I hope it does not bode the end of the world. Though some score of both sexes, Millerites,[1] resting on that fond prediction took their station one evening last week in one of our squares all robed in white and ready to mount. But neither cloud, nor flaming chariot, nor wings nor balloon was in waiting to take them up. So they went home again, much chapfallen and probably supperless to bed! This kind of prediction comes round every year or two, and there is always found a fresh crop of fools to believe it. It is a good world after all, for there is not more than one knave to a hundred fools in it.

We passed a very quiet month in old Pepperell. Susan was so fatigued with the rather bustling life we led at Lynn that I proposed we should live like anchorites—bating the bread and water—in the country. So we had only the children and little ones. One friend—the ex-minister to England[2]—spent indeed a couple of days with us—Groton, the next town, you know, to Pepperell, was his birthplace. His father[3] was a lieutenant in my grandfather's regiment on the memorable day of Bunker Hill, when British tyranny was so well humbled, you recollect. The two brave companions-in-arms were great friends, and being neighbours often sipped their toddy together in the same room where their descendants took their champagne and sherry—the latter some of the good—I do not say the best, fruits of our glorious Revolution. It was rather interesting to think of it, was it not? But poor Lawrence went from us to Groton to pass a few days, and while there had a bad attack of—I don't know what—nor the doctors either—great pains in the chest—pressure on the head and insensibility. Yet they do not think it apoplectic in its character—but arising from a disturbance of the liver, to which he has been subject. Any way it is very alarming. It is the third attack of the kind he has had in six weeks, and it makes all his friends 'guess and fear.' for the future. He is now on a very careful regimen, and pays little attention to business or any thing that can excite him. His loss would be a great one to this community, and it certainly would be inestimable to his family. There are few whom I should be more sorry to part with, for besides good sense and large practical information, he has such a genial nature, with such frank and joyous manners as are not often found among us cold-blooded Yankees. I would not have you think from all this that he is at the point of death. On the contrary, I have just met him in the street, and looking very well. But his constitution is shaken.

We have been putting our house in Beacon Street in order this summer, getting up new curtains for the drawing-rooms, one set crimson damask, the other green ditto, with furniture to match, and new carpets in drawing-rooms, and library—all as fine as a Lord Mayor's show. I mean they shall last me till you come here again.

In coming from Pepperell I took a fancy to be weighed at the station —feeling that I was quite in flesh—not to an inconvenient degree— and found I had gained five pounds this summer. Not bad—but in getting on the platform my feet slipped and I sprained a thumb— luckily of the left hand. I neglected it until I was obliged to reduce the inflammation by leeches. It is still quite *hors de combat*—and a warning to all middle-aged gentlemen, or rather gents who have passed their *premiere jeunesse*—(that is better) not to be too antic—or they may prove themselves too antique for such capers. I had no idea what a useful member a thumb is—equal to any four of the digits at least.

Soon after our return to town your friends the governor-general of all the Canadas and lady turned up again—to my great satisfaction, as I wished to see them and have the opportunity of paying them some attention. I dined with them at the Ticknors day before yesterday and today they dine with us. We shall have a dozen more friends, the *famille* Sears, the elder and younger branches, the Ticknors supported by Hillard, and our brave ex-consul Aspinwall. Do you think it will be prim and prosy? I wish you and your husband were to help us out with it. I like the Heads[4] very much the little I have seen of them—well-bred, unaffected, and intellectual people, with uncommon good-nature for travellers, i.e. John Bull travellers. I must thank you heartily for your kindness in enabling me to meet the winter's cold by such comfortable socks. I enclose a draft for £1.10 being the amount of the bill you sent me. I have made it payable to Sir Charles, as the lady's existence, in money matters, is not recognized by the polite code of the Anglo-Saxons. I must thank you too for the pleasant Hungary volume you were so obliging as to send me at the same time. The sketch of Kossuth's personal character is extremely interesting—and for me I should be very glad to have the patriot succeed any where—except in this country.

I am going to press in a few days—a work of four months will see me, in stereotype—fixed as fate, and sometime in March, or perhaps by April Fool's day, I may hope to make my bow to the British lion. It is full time.

I told Rich the other day to get one of Richmond's portraits of me to give to a bookseller and he wrote me that the portraits were "not for sale in London, that they were American." What can this mean? Don't you suppose they are for sale?

But my dinner hour is approaching; yours is long since past. So I must bid you farewell, dear Lady Lyell, and beseeching kind remembrance to your husband in which Susan joins, as well as to yourself—I remain now and ever most affectionately yours

[P.S.] You will not forget to remember me kindly to our friends at the Deanery.[5]

1. Followers of William Miller (1782–1849), who had prophesied the end of the world in 1843 and 1844 and continued to believe in an early second coming of Christ.

2. I.e. Abbott Lawrence.

3. Samuel Lawrence (b. 1754).

4. Sir Edmund Walker Head (1805–68) and Lady Anna Maria Head. A brilliant scholar, Head was appointed Governor-general of Canada in September, 1854.

5. I.e. the Milmans.

281.   To George Stillman Hillard
        (DeCoursey Fales Collection, The New York Public Library)

                                  Beacon Street, November 15 [1854?]

My dear Hillard,

I have listened to your account of my "houses" in the volume which Putnam sent me last Saturday.[1] I have also read it since with my own eyes; so I can pronounce on it—though I suppose I may be regarded as a somewhat prejudiced judge. If the public are of my mind, they will think you have done nothing more graceful or with better effect in this way—[. . .] picturesque. You found good scope for variety of painting in town, country, and sea-side. I do not know which of these I like best. The country piece is quite in the Claude style—golden and glowing. But what do you mean by the "magnieloquent" tone about "mountains?" Let me tell you that Monadnoc[2] is as high as Mount Vesuvius, and if he could spew out an acre or so of lava on the neighbors now and then, would be quite as sublime. But we can't have every thing.

Then you have made a nice little group of family portraits—from old John, with his armor of proof, downwards. Your mention of my father is very grateful to my feelings, and shows your appreciation of his wise and benevolent character; and I must thank you for your kind word about my dear Mother. The public, I am sure, will ratify what you have said on both.

As to myself I only hope that the same well-disposed public may be content to see me through the same "gold-dust vapor" that you have done; but not in the medium of friendship, and I have no right to expect it.

Your piece is the longest in the beautiful volume, by which as far as the quality of the writing is concerned, both Putnam and the public, I believe, will be gainers.

Always dear Hillard most truly and affectionately Yours

WM. H. PRESCOTT

1. *Homes of American Authors, Comprising Anecdotical, Personal, and Descriptive Sketches,* written by various authors and published originally in 1854, contained a sketch of WHP's homes which had been written by George S. Hillard.

2. This impressive peak, some miles distant from the house at Pepperell, often drew the admiring gaze of the historian during his autumn stays in the country.

282. To S. Austin Allibone[1] *et al.*

(S. Austin Allibone Papers, AL276, The Huntington Library, San Marino, California. Reproduced by permission)

Boston, November 28, '54

Gentlemen,

My friend, Mr. Ticknor, informs me that you have written to him, requesting to be furnished with a memoir of him for your proposed publication of Allibone's Dictionary of English Literature. I shall be happy to write such a notice of him as you desire; and I shall be obliged by your letting me know what length you wish it to extend to, and at what time it will be necessary to send it to you. As I am very much occupied at present in getting a work through the press, I should wish to have as long a time as possible.[2] But whatever limits you fix, the article shall be punctually furnished at the time appointed. Your obedient servant

WM. H. PRESCOTT

1. Samuel Austin Allibone (1816–89), editor of *A Critical Dictionary of English Literature and British and American Authors* (3 vols., Philadelphia, 1858–71).

2. On this day, November 28, 1854, the printing of *Philip the Second* got underway: see Prescott (Gardiner, ed.), *The Literary Memoranda,* II, 220.

283.   From Anna Ticknor
(WHP Papers, Mass. Hist. Soc.)

Park Street, January 1, 1855

Dear William,

The multiplication of years carries a wonderful alchemy with it—it teaches us what is most worth having, as well as what is most durable; and amongst the few things that stand the severe test, old friends shine bright and distinct. It is a happiness to possess them, to have faith in them, to try to please them, and in this chilling season that freezes most things, it is pleasant to express the warmth of memory and affection. I would fain do it to you and Susan, as earnestly and warmly as I feel, but neither words nor things are fair types. You must believe in what is not expressed.

My little token is more ingenious than tasteful—it courts for me a thought, at the time you are most likely to feel kindly. When beauty and talent are by your side and you test your knife, and look round, let a stray thought travel to one who rejoices in your enjoyments.

May the years as they chase each other supply you and Susan with cheering substitutes for what they take, and may you both enjoy life while I have any. With love to my kind invisible friend Susan,[1] always

Dear William, faithfully and affectionately yours,

ANNA TICKNOR

1. Susan, the stay-at-home introvert, was much the reverse of the widely traveled extrovert Anna Ticknor.

284.   To S. Austin Allibone
(S. Austin Allibone Papers, AL280, The Huntington Library, San Marino, California. Reproduced by permission)

Boston, March 20, 1855

To S. Austin Allibone, Phila.

My dear sir,

I have had the pleasure of receiving some proofs of your new dictionary,[1] which I herewith return. I have read the articles you desired.

They are very elaborate, as is particularly true of that of Bacon, which is written with great circumspection, and as it seems to me in an impartial spirit. But if you go on at this rate, before you get through the alphabet you will turn out a library of volumes. Yours very truly

WM. H. PRESCOTT

P.S. I learn from Mr. Ticknor that his name is to be put to the article on me in Duyckinck's proposed work.[2] I think it will have an awkward effect for us to be chronickling each other. So that I should be better pleased not to appear as the author of the notice of him in your work.[3]

1. Allibone's *Critical Dictionary of English Literature.*

2. Ticknor's summary of WHP's career is in Evert A. and George L. Duyckinck, *Cyclopaedia of American Literature* (2 vols., New York, 1855), II, 235–42.

3. WHP's unsigned article on Ticknor appeared in Allibone, *Critical Dictionary of English Literature,* III, 2416–18.

285.   To Joaquín García Icazbalceta[1]
(Draft, WHP Papers, Mass. Hist. Soc.)

April 26, '55

Arranged with same person copied last batch of manuscripts which I sent you, and delivered him the manuscripts you have selected, which he is now employed upon. He computes that the whole number of pages will be about 400, and if it does not exceed that, he engages to do it for $100. The paper and other expenses may come to 5 more. I have attended to your request to have the paper of a smaller size. He tells me he shall have the whole done by September, when I will forward it according to your directions. You can send me a draft for $105 if you please at your leisure.

Sr. Ramírez, who filled the office of Minister of Foreign Relations in your country and who did me the honor to write some very excellent communications on the *Conquest of Mexico* has lately been in New York, where he wrote me he was to embark the next day for England. He considers that he has made some important discoveries in regard to the hieroglyphical writing of the Aztecs, as well as to their chronological system, and proposes to pass some 5 or 6 months abroad, where he can conduct his researches with the advantages of great libraries to assist him. He considers that he has ascertained the existence of phonetic characters among the ancient Mexicans.[2] Have you any knowledge yourself how he has succeeded in establishing this interesting point, which would raise the ancient races an important step in the scale of civilization.[3]

Believe me, my dear sir, with much regard Very truly yours

1. Joaquín García Icazbalceta (1825–94), leading Mexican student of historical bibliography in the nineteenth century, was inspired and assisted by WHP, especially as the Mexican gathered materials for his *Colección de documentos para la historia de México* (2 vols., México, 1858–66). García Icazbalceta's letters to WHP have been published in C. Harvey Gardiner (ed.), "Las cartas de Joaquín García Icazbalceta a William H. Prescott," *Boletín de la Biblioteca Nacional* (México), XIII, 4 (Oct.-Dec., 1962), 3–33.

2. José Fernando Ramírez (1804–71) made no such discovery concerning the Aztecs, but he did promote the publication of Diego Durán's *Historia de las Indias de Nueva España,* which had remained in manuscript for 300 years.

3. WHP concluded the second volume of his *Philip the Second* the day after he wrote this letter. In less than a month he had inaugurated a new project— "Have broken ground," he wrote, "on a *super-numerary Book* to be added to an edition of Robertson's *Charles V* containing a view of his Cloister Life— founded on the late researches in Simancas." See Prescott (Gardiner, ed.), *The Literary Memoranda,* II, 221.

286.   Memorandum Concerning Landscaping
(WHP Papers, Mass. Hist. Soc.)

For Lynn, 1856

1855. September 4: arranged with Mr. Pitman 100 trees about 8 feet high for $100, 25 shrubs additional included; 8 trees 8 inches diameter $125, in all $225. I to furnish the muck additionally—he to warrant for a year, to set out, stone, &c. —the large trees, elms—the others elms, Norway maples, sycamores, mountain ashes, Italian poplars—the 6 large elms on the eastern part of the ring, towards the house—2 ditto in a line east of great cherry tree. Mr. Pitman will furnish also honeysuckles for the porch, and one or two for the posts. He will trim off the dead wood &c. of the trees now standing—this last, as well as the muck, extra charges.

Also 12 elm trees of the size of those on opposite side of the road, to be planted along the street, about 15 apart—the trees on the line next the great cherry tree to be transplanted to the group before Reynold's pig-sty—also out of the 1/2 dozen trees to be set out between Mr. Custis's and my piazza—ditto on the road bordering on Reed's, and in the line betwixt me and his barn.

12 trees on road, price not mentioned—probably not far from smaller trees—stakes to be added.

287.   To Harper & Brothers

(J. Henry Harper, *The House of Harper—A Century of Publishing in Franklin Square* [New York, 1912], pp. 140–41)

September [?], 1855

Dear Sirs,

I have the pleasure of introducing to you Mr. Thomas Motley, Jr. who goes to your city for the purpose of making arrangements for the publication of a work by his brother, Mr. Lothrop Motley. He is a gentleman of high character and entire responsibility. His brother, Mr. Lothrop Motley, is now in Europe, where he has been engaged several years in the composition of a history of the Netherlands.

As he has been living in the midst of the scenes he describes, and with the best materials at his command, his works cannot fail to be of the most authentic character. Although I have not seen the manuscript, yet I cannot doubt, from his high parts and brilliant and attractive style, that his book will be one of great interest and importance. I hope therefore that you will give it a careful examination, and that he will be able to make an arrangement with you which will be satisfactory to both.[1]

I remain, dear Sirs, Very truly yours,

W. H. PRESCOTT

1. In the spring of 1856, Harper & Brothers published John Lothrop Motley's *Rise of the Dutch Republic*. WHP hailed Motley's labors, prior to its publication, in the preface of his own *Philip the Second*. A detailed statement of relations between WHP and Motley is in Gardiner, "William Hickling Prescott: Authors' Agent," pp. 79–83.

288.   From Russell Sturgis[1]

(WHP Papers, Mass. Hist. Soc.)

London, October 17, 1855

My dear Sir

I have safely *delivered* Don Felipe—and paid to Baring Brothers & Co. to your credit £250—Bentley being the purchaser. Routledge gave me to understand that he could not go beyond that price, under any circumstances. Trübner was very anxious Longman & Co. should have the book, but could get no *offer* from them, and wanted one from me to submit.

I enclose a note I had from Bogue, who would have liked the book, and who, though he offered but £250, I think might have been brought to £300, but even this would not have covered the difference (£50 a volume) you proposed to allow in Bentley's favor, so I doubt not you will be satisfied with the result.[2] I cannot help being glad that Bentley succeeded in getting the Cash, and secured the volumes, which he *glared* at like an *old lion* and carried off in triumph, expressing in the strongest terms his sense of your consideration for him. I enclose copy of my letter to him by which you will see I promise that no stray copy shall get abroad till 10, December. Yours very truly

RUSSELL STURGIS

I pointed out to Bentley the corrections you sent me at various times. —RS

P.S. Perhaps when some more volumes are ready, you will try the experiment of whether residence here during the process of publication will secure a copyright, and so make up for the small sum obtained for the two present volumes.

I was at the dinner given to Thackeray on his departure the other day—he has no arrangement for lecturing in Boston, which I am sorry for. I hoped he might have come under the wing of the "Lowell Institute." RS

1. Russell Sturgis (d. 1887), of Baring Brothers & Company, served as WHP's second and last literary agent in London.

2. WHP, far from satisfied, was disgruntled. Chaotic conditions in reference to copyright had dashed his hopes of £1000 per volume to the reality of £250 for both volumes. A fuller consideration of this tortuous and disappointing negotiation is in Gardiner, *Prescott and His Publishers*, pp. 88–95.

289. Memoranda Concerning Allowances for Sons
(WHP Papers, Mass. Hist. Soc.)

Allowances[1]

Boston November 2, '55

W. Amory Prescott

I have made a copy of this which I retain.

An arrangement between my father and myself as regards my allowance &c.

– – – – – – – – – – – – – – – – –

1st—My allowance to begin from the 7th of November 1855.

2 —For the first year I am to receive $3500. To be paid me as follows:

   $200 —for passage from Boston to Paris.

   $1575—in a Letter of Credit to be taken out with me on the 7th of November 1855.

$575 —on the 7th of February in a Letter of Credit
$575 —on the 7th of May   "   "   "
$575 —on the 7th of August   "   "   "

[3] After which I am to receive an allowance of Fifteen hundred dollars a year, so long as I remain from home, which will be subject to a deduction of one hundred dollars a year as interest on the money which I have borrowed. This money is to be paid me at intervals of every four months, in sums of $400 for the first four months, and $500 for the last eight months.

4—I understand that my father refuses to pay any debts of whatever nature they may be.

5—That he will not advance me the money oftener than it is due each quarter, or every four months. That in case he should see fit to withdraw my allowance at any time, he will be at liberty to do so.

_ _ _ _ _ _ _ _ _ _ _ _ _ _ _ _

Amory—Remittances to him in 1855-6-7

November 7, '55—I remit £90, which with £250 in Baring Bros. hands, will give Amory £327 = $1575 and leave a balance of £13 to settle interest &c. on past accounts, to be settled in next annual account of Baring Bros. & Co.

_ _ _ _ _ _ _ _ _ _ _ _ _ _ _ _

October 24, '56—I have written to Amory today to say that I agree to give him $600 in addition to the 1400 I was to remit to him the coming year—making $2000 in all, the whole sum to be paid quarterly, as follows:

| November 7, 1856, | $565 | February 7, 1857, | $435 |
| May 7, 1857, | $500 | August 7, " , | $500 |

I have added, at the end of his year I expected him to return and live at home, when I would allow him $1200, minus the 100 for the interest on his debt. Also that I would never pay a debt.

April, 1857. I have written to Amory that I shall pay him $500 a quarter, and take care of interest of his debt, so long as I am content he shall remain abroad.

_ _ _ _ _ _ _ _ _ _ _ _ _ _ _ _

1857—promised him 2000 per annum while away, payable 500 per quarter. Paid him in April, a month too soon, first 500, so pay henceforth July 7, October 7, January 7, April 7.

I am to pay *William* also 500 per quarter while away, viz. August 1, November 1, February 1, May 1.

— — — — — — — — — — — — — — — —

April 7, 1858—Henceforth allowance to Amory 1400 per annum (besides the 100 interest) or 3 payments, August 1, December 1, April 1 —two first 500 each and the last, April, 400.

— — — — — — — — — — — — — — —

June 1858—Hereafter I will pay him 375 every 3 months, viz: January 1, April 1, July 1, October 1 = 1500, besides the 100 interest.

1858—I pay *William* 425 February 1, May 1, August 1, November 1 = 1700 per annum

— — — — — — — — — — — — — — —

1. Whereby two pampered sons were enabled to postpone the day that might force them to face the responsibilities of adult manhood.

290.   From Richard Ford
                        (WHP Papers, Mass. Hist. Soc.)

                                    123 Park St., November 29, 1855
Dear Prescott

Don Felipe has duly arrived,[1] and has, you may be well assured, been right royally welcomed. I congratulate you most sincerely on this *obra grande*. I am charmed with the clear, elegant and sustained style in which you have given us so much new and real history. Verily you are the most good-natured of men to praise that poor creature Watson, whose nonsense you have extinguished.

I met Twisleton the other day, and cross-examined about you and your doings: his account was excellent. Your many friends here would have much rejoiced had all this copyright worry induced you to cross the Atlantic, and come over and settle these matters *en persona*. Bentley writes me no end of letters of the £1000 a year that he loses by the decision of the Lords, and he devoutly wishes *sus señorias al diablo*.

I pray you to extend to me your friendly indulgence, and kindly to forgive my apparent neglect in writing. The truth is that I have not been quite well for these last 4 or 5 months, and have sadly lacked energy and been afflicted with a sort of tintophobia; but I have often talked about you to mutual friends: to Gayangos who has been over here, and to Stirling, who is *picking* another plum out of Don Felipe. He is very busy with the epitome of Don John of Austria.[2] You really must get on and out with the rest of the Prudent king's history. When do you expect to complete the work? The Editor of the *Quarterly* is most anxious to know, and I am doubting whether to wait until the whole *obra* is completed, or to write a review, by way of instalment. Yet it is a cruel thing to approach so great a work and so large a subject in an imperfect manner. A worthy notice should offer to the public a broad sketch of the whole of your gigantic performance. It really is unbecoming to treat such a history by bits and starts by shred and patches.[3]

I again, humble I, have another reason for suggesting delay. You, no doubt, know how difficult it is to grapple with these undertakings when the mind is not at ease, and when time is swallowed up by business, and that the worst and most engrossing—*law business.*

My wife, by the sad death of her brother, has become the heiress of certain entailed estates, which just now entail on me infinite bother, and alas! I cannot, like *El Prudente,* manage all these matters with a "slip of paper."

How odd it is that the great historians of these times on both sides of the Atlantic, the Macaulays and Prescotts will bring out their works *in numbers* as it were, but so Gibbon and Hume doled out history in volumes, making this labour of love the occupation of a life—sure ground of immortality.

Excuse this scrawl from Your most sincere friend and adviser

RICH. FORD

1. After considerable delay, which Bentley had requested because of conditions in England which accompanied the Crimean War, the first two volumes of *Philip the Second* were published in London on October 30, 1855. Publication in America followed on December 10. Presentation copies, generously given and gratefully received, served to reintensify WHP's correspondence.

2. Probably *Don John of Austria, or Passages from the History of the Sixteenth Century,* which was not published in WHP's lifetime.

3. The piecemeal publication of *Philip the Second* posed for editors and reviewers a problem which no previous work by WHP had given them. The outcome, highly displeasing to the author, was a combination of delayed and brief notices rather than full and immediate reviews.

291. Memorandum Concerning Publishing Contract
(WHP Papers, Mass. Hist. Soc.)

January 14, 1856

Memorandum

Agreed with Messrs. Phillips and Sampson on the terms for publication of Robertson's *Charles the Fifth,* with continuation by me.[1] I to stereotype the continuation at my cost; Robertson's History ditto at cost of both parties equally; I to pay half the expenses and receive half the net profits on the sale of the work; they, however, to be exclusively responsible for bad debts and to charge no commissions; the work to continue with them as long as they publish *Philip II*, that is, in the same manner with the other historical works; I to be the sole proprietor of the copyright of my continuation; this contract not to be assigned to any other party; but in case of separation, which may take place for any of the causes that may authorize me to remove my other works as stated in the former contracts, I am to have possession of my own plates of the continuation, and also of the plates of Robertson's History on my paying the half of their original cost of these latter.

1. WHP's portion of this work had consumed twice as much time and filled three times the number of pages he had originally planned for it, eight months rather than four, and 200 pages instead of 70.

Late in January and throughout February, 1856, WHP labored on a memoir of his friend, the late Abbott Lawrence. Initially printed in the *National Portrait Gallery* (Philadelphia, 1856), it also was printed for private distribution.

292.   From Clements Robert Markham
                (WHP Papers, Mass. Hist. Soc.)

4 Onslow Square, London
March 5th 1856

My dear Mr. Prescott,

I have sent you a copy of my book about Peru,[1] containing the results of my investigations at Cuzco, more particularly as to the language and literature of the Incas. The last part gives a sketch of the history of Peru, in more modern times. The perusal of your charming "Conquest," at a time when I was serving on the West coast of South America, first gave me a wish to see Cuzco; and, steadily keeping this wish in view, I was on my road to gratify it when I had the pleasure of spending a few agreeable days at Pepperell, in 1852.

I hope parts of my book may amuse you, when they call your own labours on the same field of research to your memory.

With remembrances to Mrs. Prescott and your son, I remain Yours very sincerely

CLEMENTS R. MARKHAM

[P.S.] I have been charmed and interested with your *Philip II*. When is the next volume to appear?[2]

1. *Cuzco: A Journey to the Ancient Capital of Peru* (London, 1856).

2. For the question posed by friends, reviewers and publishers, WHP had no answer. He launched into the writing of the third volume of *Philip the Second* in March, 1856.

293.   To Charles Sumner
(Charles Sumner Papers, Harvard College Library)

Boston, March 13, '56

My dear Sumner,

I am very much obliged to you for the agriculturals which you have sent me, and which will serve me a good turn in Pepperell. Unluckily the prying fingers of the Post Office gentry broke open two of the parcels and spilt all the seeds. One of them was the spinach, which I value very much, and should be glad to get a new variety. If a similar parcel of that article should fall into your hands, and you could without much inconvenience forward it to me at your leisure, I should take it very kind of you. If you have none at hand don't think of it again. Thank you for the paper containing the parallel betwixt Macaulay and me. I like it none the less that the writer, in a truly patriotic vein, seems inclined to strike the balance in my favor.

We have been very dull here in the social way this winter. But ever since Lent has set in we have had a merry round of fêtes and dinners —and the last in the most improved form of civilization, with the ladies mingling equally with the men. I suppose the time with you grave senators is better occupied, in turning Kansas, if possible, into a slave state, and coddling up a little war with Great Britain. Always faithfully yours,

WM. H. PRESCOTT

[P.S.] Have you read the *Attaché in Madrid? On dit* that none but Madame Calderón could have written it.

294.   From Lucilla Stanley Lincolne
(WHP Papers, Mass. Hist. Soc.)

Surrey Street
Norwich, March 25th 1856

My dear Sir,

Though we are virtually perfect strangers to each other, yet my love and reverence for your genius has been so strongly aroused by the perusal of your works, that you stand high in the list of my *unknown* friends. I should not have ventured to trouble you thus, but for my anxiety on one point. I have just concluded the perusal of your volume of the reign of Philip II, published by Bentley, and so interested have I been in studying the various characters and scenes you describe, that it is to me an *acute* disappointment to find the history abruptly concludes thus, "But from these scenes of domestic sorrow it is time that we should turn to others of a more stirring and adventurous character." We are left in ignorance of the fate of the prince of Orange, the persecution of Perez, and the disentanglement of the various plots which deepen in interest as we proceed. May I beg of you to listen to the voice of your humble friend from across the wide Atlantic, and complete our obligations to you, by finishing the noble work you have begun? True, it will but add another leaf to the laurel garland you have already earned for yourself, but then it will be the completion of the rich series of histories you have already given us. My private circumstances are but moderate, yet I have managed to secure all the works you have already issued, and many an hour have I passed delightfully in their society, when worn out by my day's labours. Surely, it *is* "more blessed to give than to receive," and happy as I have been thus engaged, a still greater happiness must be yours, dear Sir, when you reflect on the gratification and instruction you have afforded thousands beside myself. And now, may I beg your pardon for this intrusion on your literary retirement? "Of friends, however humble, scorn not one;" [1] do not reject my request, I implore you, but show that you forgive me by complying with it. If you have not yet *published* the continuation, at least send me word that you are *writing* it. Or if our good American cousins are more highly favoured than we are, I should be most thankful to know the name of your publisher from whom I might procure it. A line from you, my dear Sir, would be a most valuable possession to me, whatever intelligence it might communicate, chiefly, if it told me that you had complied with my wish long ago, and that the envied volume was in existence.

Once more, pardon me for this liberty, and with the greatest feeling of respect for your genius (worthy only to be compared with our own Macaulay's) allow me to subscribe myself Most respectfully and sincerely yours

LUCILLA STANLEY LINCOLNE

1. William Wordsworth, in "To a Child, Written in Her Album," phrased it "Of humblest friends, bright creature! scorn not one."

295.   To Charles Folsom
                    (Charles Folsom Papers, Boston Public Library)

Beacon Street, [c. April 9, 1856]

Dear Folsom

I am much obliged to you for the friendly interest you take in the notice of *Philip* for the old North.[1] To speak candidly to you, I do not myself care a pinch of snuff about it: for the remarks contained in his little notice show that the opinions of the editor are quite as friendly to me as I could desire; and that the reasons I am not served up *in extenso* must proceed from any thing but a depreciation of the work. It, however, is not very creditable to a journal of the pretensions always maintained by the *North American* to overlook the literature which springs up under its own nose, especially when coming from one who has been one of the most copious contributors to its pages. But I doubt whether it will be worth while now to bother the editor with getting up a criticism—which if he is inclined to make, he can have a chance of doing when the next volume comes out; and some of us will be alive then I suppose.

Thank you for Bulfinch's erratas;[2] and pray thank him for me when you see him. A friend who points out an error does a kinder office than he who praises a merit. I shall not fail to profit by the corrections. How come they to escape the eye of your critical worship? I am more astonished that you should have overlooked the blunders than that I should have made them. But that is rather unfair, considering how many of my bad stitches you have had to take up, after all. I will take your hint and look to the plates. Always faithfully yours,

WM. H. PRESCOTT

1. The thirteen-line notice which began "We wait for the completion of this work, to review it," appearing in the April issue (pp. 573–74) of the *North American Review,* was upsetting to both Folsom and Prescott. The editor, apparently informed that the remainder of the work would not be forthcoming, included a longer consideration of the two volumes in the next issue, that of July, 1856, pp. 96–103.

2. Probably Thomas Bulfinch (1796–1867), whose volume *The Age of Fable* WHP had tried to bring to the attention of publisher Bentley.

296.   To Lady Mary E. Lyell
(Transcript, Lady Lyell's Letterbook, WHP Papers, Mass. Hist. Soc.)

Boston, June 9, 1856

My dear Lady Lyell

The steamer that follows the one which takes out this note to you will carry out our dear friends the Ticknors. It seems the last arrangement is that, instead of taking the quarters you had provided for them, they are to go to Twisleton's house—which, if I remember the locality right, (and I had when in London some pleasant meetings there, at one house and another) is a good way out of the reach of Bow Bells and not very near to you.

Lizzie[1] was married, you know, a little more than a fortnight since. The wedding was got up in very pretty style. There was quite a hot-house of flowers distributed through the house, and vases full of them were suspended before the windows and between the bookcases of the library, which was profaned by being turned into the supper-room. The whole was arranged with a good deal of taste; and the meeting had the cheerful, and indeed merry aspect which it ought to have, instead of the solemn air of a funeral which some people think it necessary to give to it, when the bride looks like a lamb led to the slaughter. The happy couple, who are to take the manse, begin life probably in better style than they will end it, and there are a good many degrees too between that and poverty. On the whole I believe it is an excellent connection, and promises well for all concerned.

We have had a stirring month, this last one, and very pregnant with mischief. The British minister is sent home in disgrace,[2] our Senator Sumner's head broken in the Senate,[3] the free people of Kansas bullied and bludgeoned and in fine blunderbussed out of the territory. One good thing has happened. Mr. President Pierce, the abettor, if not the author of most of this mischief, has had his congé, which will enable him to walk into his primitive obscurity, except so far as a bad name may be kept alive, in the pages of history. I think you knew Buchanan.[4] I have been told he found favor in London. I hope it is true, as it will be more likely to make him regard John Bull with a friendly eye. At all events he is a man of talent, and if he turns out a knave, it will be some credit to us that he does not prove a fool too. He has been nominated by the Democratic convention as their candidate—and a nomination by that party in the present state of things is next door to a coronation. I know you have seen Pierce, for I had the pleasure of being with you. You have not forgotten that memorable night, when we expended such a world of merriment under the very eyes of republican majesty; if majesty that can be called which had the unmistakeable look of a New Hampshire country attorney.

Have you not been greatly scandalized and shocked, as we have all been, by the martyrdom of poor Charles Sumner. He has indeed barely escaped with his life. 'Luke's iron crown' was nothing to the flagellation that rained upon his philanthropic pate. Even those who do not like Sumner as well as I do feel as if every blow had descended on old Massachusetts. This attempt to introduce club law into debate has excited a great commotion throughout the country—which the game now going on in Kansas does not help to allay. The presidential canvass comes in good time to give our thoughts another direction. But the signs of the times are very gloomy. Yet I have faith that we shall continue to hold together, precisely because the bonds that unite us are so loose that it will not be easy to snap them.

What will you say in England about your minister, and his little tail of consuls, sent home by the "Canada." Sober minded people here, I think, condemn the measure very generally. Those who think that Crampton did not act as discreetly as he should have done, still think that Lord Clarendon's[5] very courteous and indeed apologetic tone of communication should have met with a more courteous response than has been given to it by this abrupt dismissal of the Minister—a minister too who in his personal relations has won so largely on the regard of all who had public or private intercourse with him. Under all circumstances, however, it cannot go further than some retaliatory action in reference to Dallas.[6] The language employed by our government was at least well-bred—as well bred as it could be in the doing a discourteous act, and after a little dignified and very inconvenient coolness, I trust that our next administration and John Bull will shake hands as cordially as ever. The whole affair is regarded as a presidential manoeuvre, which, thank Heaven, has not helped the president to win his game.

I have been working pretty diligently for me the last three or four months, and in fact worked myself into an ugly fit of dyspepsia. But that has gone off. I was my own doctor on the occasion, and the medicine I administered was champaign, which in reasonable doses I have always thought had much virtue. We have had incessant rains here the last months. The *park* before my window wants only a flock of midland sheep upon it to be perfectly *a l'anglaise*. We shall go where there is water enough of another kind in a week, as we flit to Red Rock.[7] Meantime though I read tolerably hard by day, I indulge in a mild sort of dissipation in the evening. This evening the theatre— tomorrow a large dinner in the country at Mr. John Thayer's in honor of the young bridals—the next evening private theatricals at Mrs. Charles Amory's. So whoever gets broken heads we contrive to have our cake and ale, and ginger too, an' we like it.

My books have gone off merrily. My publishers account to me for thirty thousand volumes of the old and the new works, sold in the last six months. As they are all of the large 8vo size, this shows that our public loves *good* books—don't you think so?

William and his wife and children are to pass the summer with us at Lynn—that is, as much as will remain of it before they flit to the other side of the water. They are going to pass I don't know how long a time on the Continent. It will be a loss to us, as you may imagine. But I have still another little nest of children and grandchildren, who

I think will not take wing very soon. As one gets on in life the lesson he should learn, if he would bear up under his troubles, is not to have less love, but more philosophy.

Adieu, my dear friend. The day will never come when I shall not call you so. Pray remember me most kindly to your husband and your family and believe me, now and always Most affectionately yours

1. Eliza Sullivan Ticknor, who was the second daughter of George and Anna and ten years younger than WHP's favorite Anika, married William Sohier Dexter.

2. Sir John Fiennes Twisleton Crampton (1805–86), while serving as the English Minister at Washington, had encouraged the recruiting of Americans for service under the British flag during the Crimean War.

3. In mid-May, several days after his vigorous speech concerning Kansas, in the course of which he verbally blistered Senator Butler of South Carolina, Sumner was brutally caned by a kinsman of Butler, one Preston Brooks.

4. Turning to Buchanan as its candidate in the race of 1856, the Democratic party repudiated its one-term President Franklin Pierce. James Buchanan (1791–1868) had served as the American Minister in London for two years during the Pierce administration.

5. George William Frederick Villiers (1800–1870), fourth Earl of Clarendon, was the English Foreign Minister during the Crimean War.

6. George Mifflin Dallas (1792–1864) followed Buchanan in London in 1856, arriving there at the moment of the American demand for the recall of Crampton. The English government did not demand Dallas' dismissal and he served at the Court of St. James from 1856 to 1861.

7. This was the name of the summer residence at Lynn.

297.   To Lord Wensleydale[1]
              (Ticknor Collection, Archives, Dartmouth College Library)

                                              Boston, June 13, '56

My dear Lord Wensleydale

This note will be handed to you by my friend Mr. Ticknor who goes by the next steamer to Europe with his wife and daughter, and will probably pass some three weeks in London on his way to the Continent. They are friends with whom I have been most intimate from early days, and for whom I have the greatest regard, and I should not like to have them visit London without invoking for them some portion of that kindness which you and Lady Wensleydale bestowed so liberally on me.

With Mr. Ticknor's reputation you are doubtless well acquainted as the historian of Spanish literature, and the social position which he occupies in his own country is as eminent as the literary. Few persons who visit your shores from any part of the United States are as well

qualified to give and receive pleasure in an intercourse with the cultivated circles of your metropolis.

I suppose that the fiat has not yet gone forth against the grouse, and
that you have not flitted to the classic shades of Ampthill. Your birds
have a decided interest in long sessions.[2] It would be well for us if we
had game laws that would help to break up our sessions in Washington to send some of the members back to the woods, where they would
do themselves and their country more credit than in the halls of debate.

With very kindest remembrances to Lady Wensleydale, believe me,
my dear Lord Wensleydale, with the highest regards, Very truly yours

W. H. PRESCOTT

1. James Parke (1792–1868), eminent as barrister and judge, was created
Baron Wensleydale in January, 1856. WHP had enjoyed hospitality at his seat
at Ampthill Park.

2. Traditionally the grouse season opened with the prorogation of Parliament and the exodus of the social elite from London to their country places.

298.   To Richard Bentley

(Richard Bentley Papers, Harvard College Library)

Boston, August 4, '56

My dear sir,

I shall in the course of next November have something for the public which you may perhaps like to publish in London. Robertson's
History of Charles V terminates with the account of his reign; at least
only two or three pages, and those full of inaccuracies, are devoted to
an account of his life after his abdication. This was no fault of his;
for he could not get the materials for it, which were to be found in
archives of Simancas, and these were not opened until very recently to
the scholar. It was from these materials that both Stirling in London
and Mignet[1] in Paris made up their accounts of Charles V after his
retirement, and from similar materials I wrote a chapter on the same
subject in my *History of Philip the Second*.

As the reign of Charles the Fifth comes between those of Ferdinand
and Isabella and Philip the Second, of both of which I have written
histories, my publishers have thought that to supply the link in the
chain it would be well to reprint Robertson's *Charles V* with the uniform edition of my works, and containing an account of his life after
his abdication by way of completing Robertson's narrative. I have
accordingly done this, furnishing an amount of matter equal to about
200 octavo pages. I have made no alteration in Robertson's work, ex-

cept simply adding captions to the chapters to make it uniform with
my continuation, and having an index made for the whole work, which
will be, as it usually is, printed in 3 volumes 8vo. It will not appear
here before the 15th of November, and has not yet been advertized.
If you would like to have the work, I shall be obliged by your letting
me know what you are willing to pay for it on the delivery of the
sheets; and I shall be able to forward these, together with a printed
copy of the new edition of Robertson's *Charles the Fifth* immediately
after receiving your answer. This vessel will take out letters from me
to two other houses, making the same offer. There is so short a time
before the publication of the work that there will be no time for any
further correspondence in the matter; and I shall give the book, as I
have engaged, to whoever offers the highest terms for it. But should
you offer the same as the highest terms offered by either of the other
parties, I shall give you the preference. I have also had a new portrait
of Charles the Fifth prepared, which I can send with the work if you
desire it.[2]

I remain, dear sir, Very truly yours,

WM. H. PRESCOTT

1. F. A. M. Mignet, *Charles-Quint; son abdication, sa retraite, son séjour et
sa mort au Monastère de Yuste.*

2. Four weeks after writing this letter, on August 29, WHP completed the
correction of proofs for this work.

299.   To Josephine Augusta Prescott
                     (WHP Papers, Mass. Hist. Soc.)

Pepperell, October 15, '56

My dear Augusta,

It was very kind of you to send me such a nice letter giving us an
account of your doings in Paris.[1] I assure you you cannot be too
minute. We like to know all about you, however trivial, and about
William and the dear children. Little Edith is constantly in our minds;
and as to the trumpeter,[2] I suppose we must drop that name, since his
good conduct entitles him to promotion. I am glad you have found
for what a reasonable sum you can live in Paris. In all great cities a
person who is not obliged to move in a court circle may live as cheap
or as dear as he pleases. It requires only forethought and the power
of resisting. I suppose Amory by this time must have found out that
a dinner can be had for less than a napoleon, which he once wrote

me was the lowest sum possible for a gentleman. The Yankees in Paris have established a very ridiculous reputation in this line.

The death of poor Clara must have proved a great shock to you, as it did to all of us. I suspect life had little charms for her, and she has no doubt made a good exchange for it. But so young and so interesting, we may well mourn her loss. As to her father and mother, I tremble for the consequences—the one so excitable, the other already so much broken in health. I suppose they will not continue their voyage, if the telegraphic message reaches them in Halifax.

We are now at the Highlands, where the landscape is particularly beautiful this year. The rains have given us an English green, which, as if by a magician's wand, has been turned as far as the trees are concerned, in the course of a few days, into the greatest variety of rich and gaudy colors. James and Elizabeth, and their little menagerie,[3] are with us, as is also Elizabeth Lawrence—a most capital country girl, up to rambles of any extent, scaling stone walls, climbing fences, or making a foray upon the chestnuts. We are all hot with politics;[4] James delivered a discourse at Hollis this week, at which we all attended except your mother, coming home late at night in a rain storm. Little Jemmie is in fine feather. He was writing a note yesterday; and we asked him what he said. He answered, "Dear Deadens, I am in Pepperty. I saw a pretty calf; her name is Deadens." He often talks about the little darling. We lead a quiet life, though it was broken last week by two arrivals, who your mother says seemed to drop from the clouds. One Sir Henry Holland; and the next day an English traveller who footed it from the Junction. And this evening a letter has been sent to me introducing the editor of the "Times;" but it is much out of time for me in the woods. Your mother says if another one comes she goes to Boston. She has not strength for it; and when we come to Pepperell I want a quiet month for her to recruit in.

Tell William I have received the two months' rent from Little and paid the quarter's rent to Dalton, leaving about $100 to William's account. Tell him also I shall be glad to hear from him. As he has nothing to do but to amuse himself his silence will look as if he found other things more agreeable than writing home. This I should be sorry for. Your mother Prescott has not been very well this summer, though the air and living agree with her as usual in Pepperell. But she is full of sensitive apprehensions, which disturb her rest like real troubles. I trust she will mend in this respect. Amory is with you. I know that you and William will treat him lovingly. It is most important for him to be with you as much as possible. Adieu, dear Augusta. Kiss my dear

Edith and Will for me, and with your mother's and Lizzie's warmest love to you and William—to which add mine—believe me always Your affectionate father

WM. H. PRESCOTT

1. William and Augusta, accompanied by their two small children, had sailed for Europe in late summer. Once ashore they hastened to William's favorite city, Paris, where they were joined by Amory.

2. At this time Edith Prescott was three and one-half years old; her brother, William Hickling Prescott, born February 22, 1855, was a scant twenty months.

3. In addition to James, now three and one-half years old, James and Elizabeth Lawrence also had a second child, Gertrude, born February 19, 1855. The historian's love for his four grandchildren included a generous array of nicknames for them.

4. WHP supported and voted for John C. Frémont, the unsuccessful Republican candidate for the presidency.

300. From George Routledge[1]
(WHP Papers, Mass. Hist. Soc.)

2 Farringdon Street
October 31, 1856

W. H. Prescott Esqr.

Dear Sir

We have received all that is required for *Charles the Fifth*. As we publish in two volumes we have employed Dr. Nuttall to do new indexes. We hope to have the demy 8vo edition ready in about a week —the other three editions will follow at intervals of about ten days. It is not a common occurrence for an author to see four editions of the same book published almost simultaneously. We shall have great pleasure in forwarding copies of each when ready.

Specimens of all will be seen by the trade at our annual sale on Monday next—upon which occasion we give a grand banquet—and your books stand first in the Catalogue.

On November 6th (Thursday) we will send Mr. Russell Sturgis a check.[2]

When you have time perhaps you will let me know what progress you are making with the remaining volumes of *Philip the 2nd*—as I am disposed to make some liberal arrangement with you. Believe me, Dear Sir Yours very truly

GEORGE ROUTLEDGE

1. George Routledge (1812–88), best known for his cheap editions of classics, had become WHP's London publisher, having outbid Bentley for *Charles the Fifth*.

2. Routledge owed Prescott £110.

301. To Richard Chenevix Trench[1]
(Charles E. Feinberg, Detroit)

Boston, November 3, 1856

My dear sir,

I am much obliged to you for your kindness in sending me your little volume on the genius of Calderón,[2] which I should sooner have thanked you for; but I was desirous of reading it first, or rather of listening to it, which I have now done with great pleasure. I do not think that the English generally have shown any very great relish for Castilian literature, although some of the best histories of the political condition of Spain have come from your island. Your own contribution, therefore, to the stores of criticism on the literature of Spain is the more remarkable; and it must certainly command attention, from the temperance which you have shown in your analysis of the character and writings of Calderón, which so strongly contrasts with the exaggerated tone of his admirers, especially in Germany, and with the very low estimate of him in some other quarters. Although so great a favorite with his own nation, it would seem that it is not so easy for foreigners to place themselves in such a *rapport* with his peculiar genius as to be able to comprehend and to do justice to what is really deserving of admiration in his writings. To do this thoroughly one must understand the character of his nation and the age in which he lived. In your analysis it seems to me that you have shown an entire familiarity with both; and in the versions which you have given of his dramas, or portions of them, you seem to have entered very successfully into the spirit of the original. I feel that I have hardly a right to pronounce upon the composition of a scholar who has given so profound a study of the subject, with which I am imperfectly acquainted; but I was not willing to thank you for the volume without giving you the impression which the careful reading of it has made upon me.

I don't know that you have seen a volume of *Miscellanies,* consisting of literary essays, published by me a few years since. It contains some notices of Castilian and Italian literature, made mostly at an earlier day, which, in your leisure moments—if you ever have any—may possibly interest you. At all events they will prove my own appreciation of these beautiful literatures. I have directed my publisher, Mr. Bentley, to send you a copy, which you will oblige me by accepting. I have told him to send the 12mo edition, as it contains one article more than the other, being a review of my friend Mr. Ticknor's great work, to which I see you refer.

Believe me, my dear sir, with great respect, Your obedient servant,

WM. H. PRESCOTT

1. Richard Chenevix Trench (1807–86), a ranking English clergyman, possessed ranging literary interests and wrote on numerous and varied subjects.
2. *Calderón, His Life and Genius.*

302.   To Edward Everett

(Prescott's Letters 1827–58, Edward Everett Papers, Mass. Hist. Soc.)

Boston, November 18, 1856

Dear Sir:

You are respectfully invited to attend a meeting of AUTHORS, EDITORS, PUBLISHERS and BOOKSELLERS, of Boston and vicinity, at the Rooms of the New-England Emigrant Aid Company, No. 3 Winter Street, on Thursday next, the 20th instant, at 11 o'clock, A.M., to consult upon the best means for securing the blessings and privileges of Freedom to Kanzas.[1]

Hon. Eli Thayer, of Worcester, will address the meeting.

WM. H. PRESCOTT,
HENRY W. LONGFELLOW,
JAMES RUSSELL LOWELL,
NATHAN HALE,
THOMAS M. BREWER,
PHILLIPS, SAMPSON & CO.,
JOHN P. JEWETT & CO.,
CROCKER & BREWSTER,
GOULD & LINCOLN,
JAMES MUNROE & CO.,
CROSBY, NICHOLS & CO.,
BENJAMIN H. GREENE,
WHITTEMORE, NILES & HALL.

1. The various economic segments of Boston were attempting to raise a fund of $100,000.

303.   To George Routledge

(Draft, WHP Papers, Mass. Hist. Soc.)

Boston, December 19, '56

My dear sir,

I am much obliged to you for sending so promptly the copies of

Charles V. They are very prettily got up; and I see you have taken care to have the dates carefully entered and the whole work properly arranged. I don't know but it would have been wiser in the long run for us here to have brought out the book in two volumes, instead of three—especially as I have only one edition, and that the dearest for the purchaser. *Charles V.,* however, steps off very well, though by no means like his son Philip of pious memory. But every body who wants Robertson now and hereafter will be likely to give it the preference.

The other day my publishers received a letter from a London house, saying that it had obtained the opinion of counsel which satisfied them that if an American would take his book to Canada and remain there —in Montreal or Quebec, for example—while it was published, and sell the copyright to a publisher there, it might then be transferred to a publisher in London, who would thus get a sound copyright. This seems plausible, but a foreigner unacquainted with the English law on the subject cannot judge enough of it. The house proposed to negotiate with me on this basis. As the letter was addressed to my publishers here, I was not called on to give an answer. I mention this to you that you may satisfy yourself of the feasibility of this way of proceeding; and if you find it safe and we agree on the terms, I should not object to make a short visit to Canada, which I can do in twelve hours[1] —though it would take more than any of the brotherhood would offer me to cross the ocean for the purpose. Indeed Mr. Bentley offered to pay my expenses and the £500 per volume with half the profits beyond this forever (enclosing the guaranty of his "inspectors") if I would come to London when the two volumes of Philip were published. But I am too snugly anchored at home to allow myself to be knocked about on the salt water for a month for double the money.

I forgot to say that his Majesty the Emperor made his public entre into this capital on the 8th instant which I hope gives you time enough. I shall be obliged by your sending me the account of the copies for which I am your debtor. Add correction, *genius*, for *genus*. I remain, dear Sir, Very truly yours

WM. H. PRESCOTT

1. WHP would find no shortcut to a secure copyright abroad.

304.   To William Gardiner Prescott
(WHP Papers, Mass. Hist. Soc.)

Boston, December 29, '56

My dear William,

We have been much distressed to hear of the severe illness from which you have suffered. From Augusta's account, I suspect the foul fiend has never taken you by the throat so fiercely before. I fear there is something in the atmosphere of Paris that does not suit you. I hope this is not so, as you are so comfortably established there for the winter. Should you be attacked again, perhaps a prompt resort to the caustic may ward it off—not a very palatable remedy certainly. You found your dear little wife the best of nurses, for love will buy services that money can't.

We are here in pretty good health—though your mother is not so strong as I could wish. She has not much appetite; but it is in her favor that her rest at night is better than it has been for a long while; and this is very important. I have been somewhat teased with headaches, which Jackson considers rheumatic, affecting the neck as well as head. I have not given way to it, however, though I have been leading a very quiet life since my return to town. But I am now breaking out in the winter campaign of dinners and dances. We kept high festival, as your mother told you, I believe, at Christmas, and next week I dine with Mrs. Wadsworth, and Mrs. Sears, Jr.—having dined with the Senior last week, and refused three other invitations. Then we have a giant ball at Mrs. John Thayer's, and a New Year's ditto at Lapanti's, where we are invited by the managers, and a couple of festival New Year's trees,—so that I keep my footing in all the merry-making from the nursery upward. I have been working pretty fairly; and *Charles the Fifth,* with my tail-piece of 200 pages tagged on to him, made his bow to the Yankee public a fortnight since, and to John Bull early in November. It has gone off satisfactorily to my publishers, and has drawn forth some good-natured criticism—and I dare say ill-natured, though I have not heard of it—from the knights of the quill on both sides of the water. My *works,* as they are called, now swell to the respectable number of 14 volumes[1] 8vo—enough, if well written; and if not, *horresco.* It will be a heavy load, at all events, for Posterity, and it would not be a miracle if some of it never reached its destination.

We are now in quiet waters again, as the hurly-burly of the election is over. News of course is rather a scarce commodity. I have embarked 5000 dollars in Edward Dexter's boat, as you know. So far, it promises well. But it is a business that must be before long over done. Edward lives contentedly enough in his backwood's life, and Gordon, who went out to see, seems quite to envy him. Yet it is not a very luxurious life, for Edward and his partner rise long before daylight, and while one grooms and feeds the horse, the other chops the wood and kindles the fire. But they make merry over their hardships, and that is the true way to deal with them. The best example in this way is to be found in Dr. Kane's volumes. Have you read them? He has done us the honor to place our name among those that crown the cliffs and capes in the polar seas[2]—a compliment that makes one shudder to think of in the present state of the temperature.

Our poor friend Frank Gray is now dying by a slow and, during the last few days, a painful death. He has borne up under his long illness with wonderful patience and serenity. He is now unconscious, and can hardly continue four and twenty hours longer.

Our Sunday evenings are kept up in quite a spirited manner, and we have the accession this winter of pleasant visitors in Elizabeth Bigelow Lawrence and Emily Sears—to supply Augusta's vacancy. I am glad that Amory is near you, and, as I hope, constantly with you. It must be delightful to him, in his life of exile, to come on those again who are kith and kin, and for whom he can feel a true love and have it returned. This is home in a dreary land of strangers; and home is a word worth all the others in the language—for any one, at least, who has his heart in the right place. I am very glad to find that Augusta and you enjoy yourselves so well in Paris. The pleasure of all you see must be doubled by having her to see it with you. And much as we wish to have you near us, we shall be happy while you both are happy too. Augusta, by the by, has shown her usual taste in the selection of the toggery for your mother. Every article is a *bijou,* and gives complete satisfaction, and shows what Paris is good for. Young Childe, who comes in occasionally on a Sunday evening, is loud in his praises of the gay capital. Do you know him? He is very clever.

I am glad you received so much kindness from your friends in your illness. I expected nothing less from the Thorndikes—good and true friends of ours always. And Lady Lyell's aunt shows kindness from another quarter where I should count on it. Pray write to Lady Lyell and thank her—if you have found the acquaintance a pleasant one. On Martha you have a double claim, for she belongs to the *famille* Prescott—as well as Peabody.[3]

I want you to purchase some little affair that you think would please Edith—for 10 or 15 dollars, and give it to her from me, with the enclosed note, when you give it—as a little *souvenir.* As we are drawing on your purse by these letters, which we cannot pay for, I shall send Mr. Lowell this week fifty dollars for you to pay for postage this coming year and Edith's present—so that you may not be brought in debt by our scribbling.

Good-bye, my dear son. Pray remember me most kindly to the Thorndikes, and thank them for their kindness to you; also to Richard and Martha Rogers; and with a kiss to Augusta and to the bairns, and with the same from your mother, believe me always Your affectionate Father

WM. H. PRESCOTT

[P.S.] I had a letter, 14 close pages, from your Uncle Ticknor, last week—very pleasant—from Rome, where he winters.

December 30. I have just heard that poor Gray breathed his last at 8 o'clock last evening.

1. The total is derived as follows:

Ferdinand and Isabella	3	vols.
Conquest of Mexico	3	"
Miscellanies	1	"
Conquest of Peru	2	"
Philip the Second	2	"
Charles the Fifth	3	"
	14	vols.

2. Elisha Kent Kane's *Arctic Explorations, in the Years 1853, '54, '55.* Kane's map included a Cape Prescott at approximately 72°45′W and 79°40′N.

3. The former Martha Peabody had become Mrs. Richard Rogers.

305.   To Lady Mary E. Lyell
(Transcript, Lady Lyell's Letterbook, WHP Papers, Mass. Hist. Soc.)

Boston, February 9, 1857

My dear Lady Lyell,

I am not sure that I am not in your debt for more than one kind letter since I last wrote. But it is not worth while to be precise in the matter or to reckon up one's correspondence with a friend like a credit and debit account with one's banker. Of one thing I am quite sure, that one of your letters is worth any two of mine; for what can I tell you that will much interest you of this commonplace matter-of-fact land of ours where now that there is no president to fidget about, and no southern hero to cudgel Northerners in the Senate-chamber—for Brooks, you know, has gone to his account—we seem to be all going to sleep. I am afraid the readers of history and such "small deer" will be as drowsy as the rest. Yet I had a grand run last year certainly. You ask me if 40,000 volumes were sold in the United States alone of my works. The number was somewhat over that, exclusive of foreign sales. As my edition is of the large 8vo size—for I have not allowed my works to go into a smaller size yet, they come in a dear form to the reader. The books have been republished in England in two editions, in Germany and translated into four Continental languages,[1] and three translations of the *Mexico* and two of the *Peru* have appeared in the Castilian. I say nothing of Old England, where I had such a splendid copyright contracted for, when the House of Lords—Heaven forgive them!—kicked over as good a pail of milk for me as a history-monger could desire. You will not think I sound the trumpet so lustily for myself to any one but you. But you will not think it egotism if I talk to you as to my own kith and kin. You are much nearer to me than most of them, I ween.

It was a nice little note you so kindly sent me from Bowood—the place I missed seeing. I talked over your visit there with Elizabeth Lawrence, who passed some days with you in the same delightful spot. We often go over our merry times in Merry England. It is a great pleasure to me to have some one with whom I can compare reminiscences. I still keep up a correspondence—letters far between—with a few friends on the other side. One from Ford the other day spoke of himself as being on a severe regimen that looked to me rather serious. Some of my letters speak of Lord Ellesmere's illness as one that is by no means quieted, which I was very sorry to hear. I received last week a portrait of her mother from Lady Mary Labouchere—admirable—and giving the perfect expression of her serene and benevolent countenance, which has never faded from my memory.

I am sorry to see from your letters that your excellent mother has so long remained an invalid. From the way in which you speak of her, I trust her health will soon be restored to her. It is painful to think that one whose life seemed to pass in making others happy should have any thing to interfere with her own happiness.

We have been shuddering here under a perfectly Arctic winter. The mercury has made two dips into 12° and 14° *below* zero! in Boston and 20° and 30° in the country. At this present writing the capricious quicksilver has mounted to 50° and over. Our bodies should be made of well-seasoned timber. We have not been very merry within doors. Just now we have a little outbreak. The arrival of Mrs. Van Rensselaer —a charming woman. Do you happen to know her? from Albany—the wife of the patroon—has given us a little stir. She is to dine with us and a large company this week. These English dinners of both sexes are the only form of society which I affect. I have refused all *buffalo* feeds through the winter. In truth I have not been quite as well as usual, having been plagued with rheumatic headaches,[2] which compel me to lie on the sofa more or less of every day, and consequently to do little real headwork. I have changed my ordinary dinner hour to the old-fashioned early one, which I think has helped me. I believe when Nature made man, she filled up the cavity in his head-piece with a flimsy kind of composition by way of brains, not at all prepared to endure the wear and tear of the rest of the body. I was warning Agassiz[3] of this the other day—who trifles shockingly with his German *physique*. His wife told me that to draw his mind from his incessant labors, she gave him *Consuelo*[4] to amuse him. So he went to work, read in bed *all* the first and second night, and did not attempt to close his eyes till the third night! I think she might as well have left him to his turtles, which are to form the fascinating subject of the first volume of his *magnum opus*. You know our friend Gray left $50,000 for a Museum of Comparative Zoology in Harvard—doubtless carrying out the suggestions of his friend Agassiz.

Were you not surprised to learn that he had a collection of prints that cost $30,000, which he left also to Harvard, with $10,000 in addition to provide for keeping it in order?

I had an epistle of fourteen pages from Ticknor the other day. What a royal tour he has been making on the Continent.

I must not close without thanking you for the kindness of your aunt in Paris to my bairns. She sent the little ones Xmas presents. Was it not kind in her to think of them. But she has your blood in her veins. A letter from William this morning tells me he and Augusta have just been presented.[5] The empress recognized an old acquaintance in him at Madrid and his majesty did me the imperial honor to ask William to give his compliments to me. Pray remember me most kindly to Lyell, and to your own family and believe me, my dear friend Always most affectionately yours

P.S. My wife, hearing this letter read, begs that I will remind you that I have a wife, who also desires much love to you, and that I have been charged ditto by James and Elizabeth Lawrence, and by Mrs. Bigelow Lawrence—which she says as usual I should have forgotten to do without her help.

Have you read Motley's *Dutch Republic?* I wish you would tell me honestly how it has taken in London, and what they say of it. Does it bear out my prediction in my *Philip?*[6] I should like to hear from you in *confidence* about it. I am reading every page of Macaulay's last brace. Pity he has so good a memory. Don't you think it has led him to remember sometimes what his reader may forget? His powers appear only the more extraordinary that he can clothe with interest details so dry in themselves as those that are scattered over many of the pages.

1. I.e. German, Spanish, Italian and French.
2. Warnings of trouble ahead, these headaches persisted between December, 1856, and March, 1857.
3. Louis John Rudolph Agassiz (1807–73), Swiss-born Harvard naturalist.
4. George Sand's novel *Consuelo* is named for its Spanish singer-heroine.
5. An event of Sunday, January 18, 1857, the presentation of William and

Augusta to Emperor Napoleon III and his Empress is reported in detail in
young Prescott's letter of January 21–22 to his father.
   6. Motley's success in England was fantastic. How much of it was English
ratification of Motley's Protestant pro-Dutch outlook cannot be determined.

306.   To Josephine Augusta Prescott
                         (WHP Papers, Mass. Hist. Soc.)

                                                Boston, February 17, 1857
   Thank you, dear Augusta, a thousand times for the kind and interesting letter which you sent me from Paris last month. It was just
the kind of letter which I wish to receive, giving an account of you and
William and the bairns, and not telling me of the things which are
to be found in Murray's Guide Book, and which every traveller knows
by heart. We cannot hear too much of the little darlings. A peep into
the nursery is worth the best spectacle to us at home. From all accounts
Willie is turning out a miracle of beauty and sweet disposition. But
it will be long before he takes the place of my sweet little Edith in
my heart. Yet if he deserves half the good things that people who have
seen him speak of him, he will make us all very happy.
   What very nice accounts William and you have given us of the court
presentation. I feel very much flattered by the emperor's notice of me.
If William should ever have another audience of him, I beg he will
tell him how much honored I feel by his notice of so humble an individual. If *you think best,* you can tell him that should he ever come
here, we shall be very happy to have him dine with us *en famille* without ceremony. It is a pleasant thing for William that the empress
should have retained her recollection of him. I think the best thing,
however, said on the occasion was dear little Edith's question as to
whether her father was to be a coachman! It is a good satire, and ought
to find its way into *Punch.* I hope William will be as lucky as I was
in London, and sell his fine feathers when he has no longer use for
them at half price.[1] This reminds me of the secretaryship of legation,
which William wished me to interest myself to obtain if possible for
him. Had Fremont come into power—as it was known through the
papers that I supported him (though only by a silent vote), I might
possibly have stood some chance in preferring such a petition. But
in the present state of things it would be a mere waste of paper to
write about it. The quantity of applicants for every office great and
small in the gift of the government passes belief; and no one stands
the least chance of success who cannot show a list of services rendered
to the cause. I was requested a month since by a friend to whom I have

been under great obligations myself, and who fills a diplomatic post abroad, to prefer his claims, which are very considerable, to his remaining in his present post. Though I hate to ask a favor, especially of a man whom I have been opposed to, I wrote to Mr. Buchanan on the subject. He was polite enough to send me an answer, which however must have crushed the hopes of my transatlantic correspondent, whose name I am not at liberty to disclose.[2] Mr. Buchanan wrote that those who had been toiling to obtain the present glorious triumph of the democracy thought they had a better claim to the places in the gift of the government than those who having been abroad had no share in bringing about the victory. He accordingly advised the diplomat to return home. Yet this person is a democrat, and by his merits fully deserves the patronage of the party. I should be very glad, if William would like such an appointment, to have him in it; and however disagreeable to me to ask favors, I would overcome that repugnance to please him. But you see it would only expose me to the mortification of such an answer, or a more severe one. I have spoken on the subject to a friend well acquainted with the policy of the government in these matters; and I find his opinion to be precisely like my own. So there is no use in thinking more of the matter, at least in this king's reign.

Amory wrote the other day to his mother a letter in which, among other things, he remarked that the 24th of January had gone and that it was rather sad to find no one near him remembering his birthday, which he said now made him 28 years old. It is not so strange that no one should remember his birthday, since he has forgotten the date of it himself. He was not born on the 24th but the 25th of January, and in the year 1830, which makes him on his last birthday not 28, but 27 years old. Ask him to make a memorandum of this, or he may begin to feel old before his time. I wish you would thank him too in my name for the receipt which he so affectionately sent me for curing headache. I have no doubt it has great virtue, but I had about as lieve have the headache as take it. Indeed I have applied to no doctors. I have no great faith in the faculty, but shall watch my own symptoms. The best recipe I can find for it is a good dinner; and I have hardly been out till the last week for a month, refusing all buffalo parties. A visit of Mrs. Van Rensselaer here has set us all in motion. I have dined the last week at three large parties made in honor of her, and have felt better for it each time. But I do not allow myself to do any work at present—at least nothing more than a labor of love like this present writing. Your Aunt Martha comes off with her theatricals this week, and the next I am to be one of the spectators. Fanny Kemble[3] has begun a course of Shakspere Readings. The season tickets vanished like a flash of powder; but she was so polite as to send me a ticket for myself and friend for the whole course. In consequence there was a great pulling of caps among the ladies at Mrs. Wadsworth's last evening as to who that friend should be. So the possession of the golden apple will expose me to no little obloquy, I am afraid. It was an amiable thing in Mrs. Fanny, however, wasn't it?

Elizabeth Bigelow proves a great acquisition to our little circle. I don't know what news to tell you which you won't hear better from your mother, who is in excellent health, and seems to enjoy herself in the social doings. But I must close if I would be in season for the mail.

With much love to William and to Amory, who I hope visits you every day, and with ever so many kisses for the bairns,

Believe me, dear Augusta [. . . .][4]

[P.S.] Your mother Prescott desires me not to omit her love to you all. I think the turning of my little love-token for Edith into Mrs. Baibauld was making the best use of it.

Did I tell you that Samuel Eliot has a daughter?

Tell William that both the "Edinburgh" and the London "Times" have given favorable notices on the *Philip* and *Charles*—the "Times" quite emphatic and promising [. . . .] The date of this was January 12.

1. In Paris, as in London, presentation at Court necessitated special dress which was useless in normal circumstances. WHP's reference is to his experience of 1850.

2. I.e. Theodore S. Fay.

3. Frances Anne Kemble (1809–93), commonly called Fanny, resided and gave dramatic readings in the United States in the periods 1849–68 and 1873–78.

4. The complimentary close and signature have been cut from the letter, apparently to satisfy someone's desire for WHP's autograph signature.

307. To Robert Anderson Wilson[1]

(Copy, WHP Papers, Mass. Hist. Soc.)

To Mr. Wilson
Boston, April 8, '57
(Keep for present)

My dear sir,

I have had the pleasure of receiving your note today, in which you say you propose to write a history of the conquest of Mexico without the fable, and ask me if I now have any authorities on this subject that I can lend you. To take you literally I should say that I have no such authorities; for mine all relate to the conquest with the fable. I should be very happy, however, to send you such as I have were they not still necessary to me. I have made many alterations and corrections in the volumes since the first edition appeared, and shall probably have occasion to make many more. To do this, and to verify my own statements I cannot well part with my authorities; and though I have achieved the conquest of Mexico I do not think it would be prudent to disband my forces while my position is assailed by such a bold antagonist as you.[2] Though some of the works could not be easily replaced, yet fortunately the most popular and important ones may be readily obtained from public libraries.

I am much obliged to you for the offer of Mme. Calderón's travels. But my stray volume has turned up again, and I have no occasion to avail myself of your politeness.

Believe me, dear sir, Very truly yours,

WM. H. PRESCOTT

1. Robert Anderson Wilson (1812–72), author of several unreliable works on Mexico, simultaneously sought WHP's aid and attacked his writing.

2. Wilson's *A New History of the Conquest of Mexico,* a major attack upon WHP's work, was published in 1859, after WHP's death. However, George Ticknor and John Foster Kirk vigorously defended WHP in print.

308.   To Lyman C. Draper[1]
(Draper–Wisconsin Historical Society Correspondence, Wisconsin Historical Society)

Boston, May 28, '57

L. C. Draper Esqr.
My dear sir,

I have had the pleasure of receiving from you in behalf of the Historical Society of Wisconsin the two volumes of the general history of your state[2]—a work which, from the inspection I have as yet been able to give it, appears to me highly creditable to its author, and one which must entitle both him and the Historical Society to the gratitude of coming generations. Your own pamphlet on the capital of Wisconsin is filled with matter of the greatest interest.[3] It is a fortunate thing to find in our young states men who combine knowledge and talent with the leisure to place on record important facts relating to their early history.

I did myself the pleasure some time ago to send one of my works to be placed on the shelves of the Historical Society. I have now taken the liberty to order my booksellers, Phillips, Sampson & Company, to forward a copy of my last book, *Philip the Second,* to your address; and I should be much obliged by your giving it a place next its predecessor. My publisher will send it by the first opportunity; but as this may not presently occur, I shall be obliged to you if you will let them or me know of any way in which it can be forwarded, without charge to the Society, in which case I shall at once avail myself of it. With much regard, I remain, dear sir, Very truly yours

WM H. PRESCOTT

1. Lyman C. Draper (1815–91), energetic and able Secretary of the State Historical Society of Wisconsin from 1854 to 1886.

2. Probably volumes 1 and 2 of the *Collections of the State Historical Society of Wisconsin.*

3. The forty-eight-page study entitled *Madison, the Capital of Wisconsin* was published in 1857.

309. To George E. Ellis[1]

(George E. Ellis Papers, Mass. Hist. Soc.; and in *Proceedings* of the Massachusetts Historical Society, XIII [Boston, 1875], 246–49)

Boston, June 1st, 1857

My dear Mr. Ellis,

I hope I have not abused your patience in delaying so long to give you the information which you desired respecting the *modus operandi* in my historical composition. My defective eyesight has rendered it somewhat peculiar. But I suspect most of the peculiarities have been already noticed by me on other occasions.

I suppose you are aware that, when in College, I received a blow on the eye which deprived me of the use of it for reading and writing. An injudicious use of the other eye, on which the burden of my studies was now wholly thrown brought on a rheumatic inflammation, which deprived me entirely of sight for some weeks. When this was restored the eye remained in too irritable a state to be employed in reading for several years. I consequently abandoned the study of the law, on which I had entered; and as a man must find something to do I determined to devote myself to letters, in which independent career I could regulate my own hours with reference to what my sight might enable me to accomplish.

I had early conceived a strong passion for historical writing, to which perhaps the reading of Gibbon's *Autobiography* has contributed not a little. I proposed to make myself an historian in the best sense of the term, and hoped to produce something that Posterity would not willingly let die. In a memorandum book as far back as the year 1819 I find this desire intimated; and I proposed to devote ten years of my life to the study of ancient and modern literatures,—chiefly the latter —and to give ten years more to some historical work. I have had the good fortune to accomplish this design pretty nearly within the limits assigned. In the Christmas of 1837 my first work, the *History of Ferdinand and Isabella* was given to the public.

During my preliminary studies in the field of general literature my eyes gradually acquired so much strength that I was enabled to use them many hours of the day. The result of my studies at this time I was in the habit of giving in the form of essays in public journals, chiefly in the *North American,* from which a number—quite large enough—have been transferred to a separate volume of *Miscellanies.* Having settled on a subject for a particular history, I lost no time in collecting the materials, for which I had some peculiar advantages. But just before these materials arrived my eye had experienced so severe a strain that I enjoyed no use of it again for reading for several years. It has indeed never since fully recovered its strength, nor have I ever ventured to use it again by candlelight. I well remember the blank despair which I felt when my library treasures arrived from Spain, and I saw the mine of wealth lying around me which I was forbidden to explore. I determined to see what could be done with the eyes of another. I remembered that Johnson had said in reference to Milton that the great poet had abandoned his projected History of England, finding it scarcely possible for a man without eyes to pursue an historical work requiring reference to various authorities. The remark piqued me to make the attempt.

I obtained the services of a reader, who knew no language but his own. I taught him to pronounce the Castilian in a manner suited, I suspect, much more to my ear than to that of a Spaniard; and we began our wearisome journey through Mariana's noble history. I cannot even now call to mind without a smile the tedious hours in which, seated under some old trees on my country residence, we pursued our slow and melancholy way over pages which afforded no glimmering of light to him, and from which the light came dimly struggling to me through a half intelligible vocabulary. But in a few weeks the light became stronger; and I was cheered by the consciousness of my own improvement; and when we had toiled our way through seven quartos, I found I could understand the books when read about two-thirds as fast as ordinary English. My reader's office required the more patience of the two. He had not even this result to cheer him in his labor.

I now felt that the great difficulty could be overcome, and I obtained the services of a reader whose acquaintance with modern and ancient tongues supplied, as far as it could be supplied, the deficiency of eye-sight on my own part. But though in this way I could examine various authorities, it was not easy to arrange in my mind the results of my reading drawn from different and often contradictory accounts. To do this I dictated copious notes as I went along, and when I had read enough for a chapter—from thirty to forty, or sometimes fifty pages in length—I had a mass of memoranda in my own language, which would easily bring before me at one view the fruits of my researches. These notes were carefully read to me; and while my recent studies were fresh in my recollection, I ran over the whole of my intended chapter in my mind. This process I repeated at least half a dozen times —so that when I finally put my pen to paper, it ran off pretty glibly, for it was an effort of memory rather than creation. This method had the advantage of saving me from the perplexity of frequently referring to the scattered passages in the originals; and it enabled me to make the corrections in my own mind which are usually made in the manu-script, and which, with my mode of writing,—as I shall explain, would have much embarrassed me. Yet I must admit that this method of composition, when the chapter was very long, was somewhat too heavy a strain on the memory to be altogether commended.

Writing presented me a difficulty even greater than reading. Thierry, the famous blind historian of the Norman Conquest, advised me to cultivate dictation; but I have usually preferred a substitute that I found in a writing-case made for the blind, which I procured in Lon-don forty years since. It is a simple apparatus, often described by me for the benefit of persons whose vision is imperfect. It consists of a frame of the size of a sheet of paper, traversed by brass wires, as many as lines are wanted on the page, and with a sheet of carbonated paper, such as is used for getting duplicates, pasted on the reverse side. With an ivory or agate stylus the writer traces his characters between the wires on the carbonated sheet, making indelible marks, which he can-not see, on the white page below. This treadmill operation has its defects; and I have repeatedly supposed I had accomplished a good page, and was proceeding in all the glow of composition to go ahead, when I found I had forgotten to insert a sheet of my writing paper below, that my labor had all been thrown away and that the leaf looked as blank as myself. Notwithstanding these and other whimsical distresses of the kind, I have found my writing-case my best friend in my lonely hours; and with it I have written nearly all that I have sent into the world the last forty years.

The manuscript thus written, and deciphered—for it was in the nature of hieroglyphics[2]—by my secretary, was then read to me for corrections, and copied off in a fair hand for the printer. All this, it may be thought, was rather a slow process, requiring the virtue of patience in all the parties concerned. But in time my eyes improved again. Before I had finished "Ferdinand and Isabella," I could use them some hours every day. And thus they have continued till within a few years, though subject to occasional interruptions, sometimes of weeks, and sometimes of months, when I could not look at a book. And this circumstance, as well as habit—second nature—have led me to adhere still to my early method of composition. Of late years I have suffered, not so much from irritability of the eye as dimness of the vision; and the warning comes that the time is not far distant when I must rely exclusively on the eyes of another for the prosecution of my studies. Perhaps it should be received as a warning that it is time to close them altogether.

But I have inflicted on you enough of my egotism—quite enough, I imagine, to make you repent having shown any curiosity respecting my method of composition.[3]

With much regard, I remain, dear Mr. Ellis, Very truly yours

WM. H. PRESCOTT

1. George Edward Ellis (1814–94), a Boston theologian with a scholarly interest in history, was a long-term friend of WHP.

2. This term, often employed by WHP, exaggerates the nature of his writing on the noctograph. It varies considerably in its legibility, but the writing is rarely impossible to read.

3. This letter represents the best unified statement by WHP of his method of composition.

310.   To Moses Dresser Phillips[1]

("Autograph Letter and Engraved Portraits of William H. Prescott the historian, compiled by Abram E. Cutter," Boston Public Library)

Lynn, August 21, '57

Dear sir,

I am at this moment engaged in the bloody battle of Lepanto; and I think it would be hardly fair to my Spanish friends if I were to leave them in the lurch and go about some other business.[2]

When I spoke of writing, it was only a few pages, such as would authorize you to mention my name on your list of contributors. When I last saw you I mentioned that I thought the best way of doing this would be to furnish you with part of a chapter, equal perhaps to a dozen or fifteen or twenty pages, of my history—which I flatter myself would have more interest for the public than any hoozymoozy nonsense which I could manufacture. Whether it would not be better to wait until nearer the publication of the book you can judge. But when I come to town, which will be by the middle of next month at farthest, I will see you about it.[3]

I am glad to see that the Star of the West beams so brightly on you and Mr. Sargent. I hope that some of its genial rays may fall upon me. Very truly yours,

WM. H. PRESCOTT

1. Moses Dresser Phillips (1813?–59), partner in the publishing house of Phillips, Sampson and Company, was the member of the firm with whom WHP principally dealt.

2. About to launch *The Atlantic Monthly*, Phillips, Sampson and Company sought to couple WHP's name with the first issue of that publication.

3. The unsigned article "The Battle of Lepanto," *The Atlantic Monthly*, I, 2 (December, 1857), 138–48, was WHP's contribution.

311.   To John Lothrop Motley
               (Draft, WHP Papers, Mass. Hist. Soc.)

Lynn, September 8, '57

My dear Motley,

I have the pleasure to enclose you a letter received last week from Gayangos which will tell its own story.[1] He seems not certain when he expects to be in London. If you can communicate with his daughter, whom I mentioned to you in my note the other day, she doubtless will give you the time, and you certainly had better see him if possible. With respect to his proposal for me to determine the compensation, I would willingly do it, but it would obviously be of no use. I could tell what the worth of the copying is, as there is a regular price for all that. But I have no means of determining the value of his time or the difficulties he has to overcome in deciphering manuscripts &c. If the thing were left to me the course I should take would be to inquire what he thought the time and labor worth and accept his estimate as the right one. This is in fact the way I have always dealt with him, remitting him say £100 or 200 for which he gave me an accounting from time to time. He is a gentleman whom I should trust entirely for the estimation of his own services which in my judgment have been always very reasonable. The expense for copying is as cheap in Spain as in any part of Europe. There are two ways in which you might proceed in order to regulate your own expenses. First by naming a sum which you would not have him exceed; and secondly by obtaining accounts from him from time to time which would show you how you stand. A word to the wise—I shall not charge you for my advice. Do not trouble yourself to return the letter.

What a nice humbug that dinner of yours with C. King.[2] Amory told me about it.

1. Continuing his research in Spanish history, Motley had sought WHP's aid in ferreting out manuscripts in Spain.

2. Probably Charles King (1789–1867), President of Columbia College in New York City between 1849 and 1864.

312. Memorandum Concerning Publishing Contract
(WHP Papers, Mass. Hist. Soc.)

December 11th, 1857. Told Mr. Phillips that if these times[1] continued I should be perfectly willing to do whatever was reasonable in regard to the guaranty of $4000 a year on the sales of the old books.[2]

I said I thought the 3d volume of "Philip" would be ready by June; and at all events had very little doubt that it would be ready by October. But told him he must not understand this as in a respect a promise on my part, as I could never consent to be a bookseller's hack.

1. The publishing industry had become peculiarly sensitive to the general economic depression of 1857.

2. Initially WHP's contract had called for $6000 annually from these titles. He already had made a considerable concession to his publishers.

313.   From Moses Dresser Phillips
(WHP Papers, Mass. Hist. Soc.)

Tuesday, December 30, 1857

My Dear Sir,

Mr. Kirk handed me your very kind note yesterday, but I was too much occupied to reply. Pray be assured the delay was not because I did not at once feel this renewed act of great kindness and generosity.

It is true that my settlement of the late account was based wholly upon your figures as you say, and not that I have even now looked into the contract. It is entirely sufficient for me that you interpret or state it to be so.

But now what shall I say more than to thank you for your generous surrender of so much that belongs to you?

I will tell you what I will say. I will promise to *try* to make it good to you in my future efforts for the sale of your works.

I reminded you the other day of your voluntary alteration of the original contract and told you how many times I had told of it—as illustrating your desire for exact justice,—and with your leave I shall, as I may have occasion, relate these fresher circumstances also, as showing how careful you are that no interest of yours shall ever bear unpleasantly (though it be a contract) upon your publishers.

I said before and I now repeat that such has never in any single instance been my experience before.

And now in return for all this I can promise but one poor return and that is that as in times past, so shall your interests in the future have my first—highest and paramount consideration and exertions —and if there is any world and money left, we will make a good return.

Tendering you the compliments of the Season, I am Very truly yours

M. D. PHILLIPS

314. To William Gardiner Prescott
(WHP Papers, Mass. Hist. Soc.)

Boston, January 31, 1858

My dear William,

I send you enclosed a bill drawn in your favor by the Thayers on M. Calmont Bros. & Co. at 60 days for £122. 14s. 6d, the equivalent of the six hundred dollars for allowance and rent. I don't know why you put it at 60 days. If you had not given such precise instructions, I should have sent you a draft on Munroe by Mr. Hall, as I have done to Amory, which I believe would be as safe as any other that could be given. Business is anything but brisk here; but a feeling of confidence is generally coming; stocks of all kinds, including manufactures and railroads, are slowly rising; there is a superabundance of specie, and money may be had at easy rates. Yet many a gallant boat has capsized and gone to the bottom, beyond the reach of fair winds and sunny skies to set it agoing again. You will find two or three of your friends who are condemned to a lamentable change in their way of life. Some of your shaky manufacturing stocks seem to be looking better in the world. The Pacific quoted at 25 per cent, and Middlesex, which you hold as security, I believe, quoted at 23. There is a general feeling that the times are mending, but it must be slow rising from a paralysis. Books are in the category of superfluities, and will make no figures until people have money to throw away. My third volume is so well advanced that in a few months I could send it to the press. But I shall not put out on such a stagnant sea as we have now. Yet my publishers still keep above water, which is something more than the Harpers can boast. You ask me to let you know something about my account with Phillips and Sampson the last year. They had paid me about $7000 when the crisis came on—since which they have not earned a hundred, nor do I expect that they will earn anything of consequence, certainly for six months to come. And the same, I believe, must be said of all cotton and woollen manufactures for the first half of the present year. We may then hope that things will take a better turn. *Quién sabe?* I parted this week with 40 shares in the New York Central at 80—a rise, however, of 30 per cent since this great agony.

How much news you pick up in Paris! You speak of the Thayers as if it were doubtful whether enough would remain to pay Francis anything. Nat Thayer,[1] the other day, speaking of his actual losses to me made them out as inconsiderable in comparison with the amount of his property; and no one, I believe, doubts the firm having a very large capital. John's property remains in the firm for five years.

Hard as the times are the town is not willing to give up its cake and ale; and gatherings under the name of 'bread and butter parties,' 'whist parties,' 'the lancers,' &c keep us quite lively. Some of these, like the 'lancers,' are for the young fry, who take it out in dancing. The others, mere *conversazioni*, where they have only talk and ice creams, Roman punch, sandwiches, different kinds of game, oysters in their varieties, champagne, &c &c—on the economical scale to suit the times. Some call them 'poverty parties.' Did you hear of the happy saying of Miss Winthrop and Bob Sears. She was speaking of her having had rather a slow time at some place, where she said "she was pretty much occupied with teaching two *fossils* to dance—David Sears and James Lawrence." She forgot that her auditor was a Sears. He did not, and reported the pleasant remark, quite, I am told, to the young lady's discomposure. Poor Sears is indeed a fossil—at least his legs are in a fair way to become such, from the fierce attacks he has of sciatica. For the last fortnight he has been in constant suffering. I fear the only remedy for him is rest from his labors, which are wearing him out. The best remedy would be a trip to Europe, for a year at least. They leave us next week for their splendid residence, which, with all their retrenchments, will cost them too much.

Young Sears has been playing the agreeable, with serious intentions they say, to Miss Mary Peabody. The lady, it is thought, looks amiably upon him. It would be a good thing all round.

I was sorry to learn that dear Augusta has been so plagued with nervous headaches. I had a pleasant account of you both from Lady Lyell. I think Mrs. Peabody is very desirous to join you, if she can reconcile it with prudence. If you can do the same and Augusta can spare you, we should be delighted to see you at Red Rock next summer, where [. . .] promises to get me up a lawn. Mrs. Peabody has not been in robust health this winter, and I do not doubt that the voyage would be of service to her as well as the society of Augusta and the bairns—bless the little souls.

Pray thank Edith for her affectionate letter which Jemmie enjoyed as well as her grandpapa. The pretty daguerreotype of herself and Willy is a great comfort to us.

I am sorry not to have been able to send you my portrait for Bañue-los, whom I like too well not to be too happy to send it. If Mrs. Peabody goes out, it will give me the means of doing so.

Richard Rogers was here today, and I think he feels disappointed at not having heard from you lately. You had better write him if you are his debtor. Our Sunday evenings have been very flourishing this winter; and among others, your friend Frank Brooks and his interesting wife have come and talked about you and Augusta.

Our life here goes on in much the same quiet train as usual; and that I believe is the best way for us. Your dear mother's health has been better than it has been for some years, and I have had but little head-ache to bother me. Perhaps it is the mild weather, in which we have had the advantage of you in Paris. But I am getting prosy. Remember me kindly to the Thorndikes; and with love to my dear daughter Augusta and the sweet little bairns, and to Amory, who, I trust, was not troubled by my last letter—the only one I could write.

I remain—now and ever Your affectionate father

WM. H. PRESCOTT

1. Nathaniel Thayer (1808–83), financier and philanthropist, whose wedding WHP had attended in 1846 near Albany, New York.

315.   From George Bancroft
                         (WHP Papers, Mass. Hist. Soc.)

                                   New York   February 18/58

Dear Prescott,

I have heard with more pain than I can express, that you have been ill.[1] If you love me, let your secretary write me word that you are better, that you have not been very ill, that you are now well.

Will the sight of a proof sheet cheer or alarm you? Here is the way in which I introduce the hero of Bunker Hill to the nearer acquaintance of my readers; claiming their sympathy in advance.

I come out May 1, and then and now and always dear Prescott Am most truly yours

GEO. BANCROFT

1. On February 4, 1858, WHP had suffered a stroke of apoplexy. For some time both his vision and power of motion were affected, but he gradually recovered his strength.

316.   From R. H. Major
                      (WHP Papers, Mass. Hist. Soc.)

British Museum
February 20th, 1858

Sir,

By desire of the Council of the Hakluyt Society, I take the liberty of addressing you with a request.

At a meeting of the Council on Monday last, it was proposed by Mr. Wentworth Dilke,[1] who, I believe, is known to you, and seconded by Sir David Dundas that I should write begging your kind cooperation in editing a translation of the so-called "Carta quinta" of Cortés. The document has been already translated, subject to revision, by Mr. Steel of the Spanish Consulate, but the Council feeling the importance of a fitting introduction to a document of the kind, have hoped that you might kindly afford them the advantage of your distinguished name and pen in this portion of their undertaking.[2] I beg leave to enclose a prospectus of the Society, a set of whose publications are possessed by the Boston Athenaeum Library.

Trusting that you will pardon the boldness of this request in consideration of its object, I have the honor to be, Sir, with great respect, Your faithful servant,

R. H. MAJOR
Honorary Secretary of the Hakluyt Society

1. Charles Wentworth Dilke (1789–1864), an English critic and antiquarian, edited the *Athenaeum* between 1830 and 1846.

2. WHP politely declined this proposition. When the Hakluyt Society brought it to fruition some years later, Pascual de Gayangos performed the service which had hopefully been assigned to WHP.

317.   To Charles Sumner
              (Charles Sumner Papers, Harvard College Library)

Boston, February 26, '58

My dear Sumner,

Many thanks to you for your kind note. The enemy is put to rout —the only traces of him that remain are the loss of a few proper names out of my vocabulary and a slight increase of opacity in the eye, which annoys me when I attempt to read. But I am confident that either these things will mend or I shall get accustomed to them.

Another consequence I must not omit—a vegetable diet and potations of water. I shall do better for my friends.

With the hope that your health continues steadily to improve, I remain always, dear Sumner, Very affectionately yours,

WM. H. PRESCOTT

318.   To George Bancroft
(George Bancroft Papers, Mass. Hist. Soc.)

Boston, April 17, '58

My dear Bancroft,

Thank you for so kindly sending me the little gem of Historic criticism—for the word "great" comprehends every thing, and belongs only to the dead. A foreigner is one remove short of death, and may sometimes get it.

I confess my weakness—at the ripe age of 62—which I shall be on the 4th of next month—of being pleased with flattering criticism. I wish I could reach the loftier position of looking down with equanimity on censure and abuse. I remember Irving's telling me he made it a point never to read anything like ill-natured criticism; and I have more than once followed his example. One might be content to take the bitter, if it brought any good with it. *Fas est [et] ab hoste doceri.* But my experience is that it only spoils the temper—without mending the manner—much less the morals. The only reformation worth much—literary or moral—must come from within.

I give you joy at having washed your hands of the printers' devils. I am just beginning the dirty work, though I do not propose to launch my argosy before December.

With love to your wife, believe me now and ever, dear Bancroft, Very affectionately yours,

WM. H. PRESCOTT

319.   To Charles Folsom
(Charles Folsom Papers, Boston Public Library)

Boston, April 22, '58

Dear Folsom,

So we have now fairly begun our corrections.[1] Your proofs came in season for me yesterday; but that there may be no delays hereafter, it is better that I should state to you what would be the latest hour at which they can reach me and give me time for corrections. I think you must consider three o'clock on the day after you get the proofs from Metcalf as the latest hour when they should be put into my hands. I can do nothing with them after the sun has set, and the Cambridge wagon calls for them early on the following morning. I hope that this arrangement will always be convenient for you. By this arrangement the batch you receive from Metcalf this morning should be put into my hands tomorrow by three o'clock, and so on. Always yours,

WM. H. PRESCOTT

[P.S.] I believe I told you the quantity you will receive is ten pages every other day.

1. The production of the stereotype plates for the third volume of *Philip the Second* was underway.

320.   To William Gardiner Prescott
                (WHP Papers, Mass. Hist. Soc.)

Boston, April 26, 1858

My dear William,

I enclose you a draft on M. Calmont at 60 days sight as you desired, for £185.15.7d—equal to nine hundred dollars. I paid nine per cent for the exchange, which they assured me at Thayers was less than they had been selling bills for, and was as low as they should furnish a bill for £10,000. Of this amount 500 are for the quarterly allowance; 95 for the rent of your house; 200 for the candelabra for Elizabeth; 40 for some articles which Elizabeth will write you about; 14 for some little matters for Anna Ticknor, of which she also advises you by this steamer. The remainder, amounting to some 50, you will take for yourself, as I doubt not you will find occasion for it. I wish I could send you more. Since the bill was received from Thayers it occurred to your mother to send for a dozen of fine cambric pocket handkerchiefs as a present for your Aunt Dexter.[1] She wishes them to be plain except that the initials E. D. may be prettily embroidered on one of the corners. If it should not be convenient for you to pay for the handkerchiefs, pray let me know the *damage* and I will send out the money which your mother does not wish to amount to a great sum.

Yesterday we had the pleasure of receiving yours of the [blank] instant. I am much obliged by your affectionate cautions about the premature exercise of my wits. What you say is very sensible. But the exercise I give them will, I think, do me no harm; and Jackson, who is a better judge, thinks so too. I am now putting the 3d volume of *Philip* through the press—not more than five pages a day—moderate work, and not very exciting. To do nothing but sit still and suck one's thumbs would kill me with *ennui;* and one might as well die of apoplexy as ennui. Indeed it would be better and much more creditable to die in harness. But in truth I hope to live many years; and if the foul fiend threatens me again I shall hope to scare him away with a book in one hand and a carrot in the other, and if he lingers I will pelt him with potatoes. I have great confidence in a vegetable diet, and begin to look down with compassion on those carnivorous people who live in ignorance of the nice things which a little culinary science may make out of vegetable—especially in the way of soups.

So you leave for home, you think, by the 14 of August. We shall be right glad to see you all again; and I hope you will have staid long enough to have had your fill of the Old World and not long enough to have lost your relish for your own country.

I don't know what news to tell you that will much interest you. Yet there are three brace of lovers who have become engaged the last week —all of whom you know: James Codman and Miss Henrietta Sargent; Edward Codman and Miss Leslie Tilden; Charles Eliot and Miss Peabody, eldest daughter of the late Rev. Mr. Peabody.

As you stay till August, Augusta and the bairns will have time to throw off the whooping-cough and come home in good condition to be benefitted by the voyage and change of climate. Nothing can be finer than the last month has been. I hope the good weather will not be worked up before your arrival.[2]

With love and kisses to Augusta and the bairns, in which your mother joins, believe me always, my dear son, Your affectionate father

WM. H. PRESCOTT

1. I.e. Elizabeth Dexter.
2. Early autumn found WHP rejoicing that all of his children and grandchildren were close at hand.

321.   From Moses Dresser Phillips
           (WHP Papers, Mass. Hist. Soc.)

Saturday Morning, June 12/58

My Dear Sir

Presuming the inclemency of the weather will prevent your coming out today—I have filled a check for one-half the balance of the account, and added the interest to the other half for the time taken and enclose the note for that.

Do not trouble yourself about any acknowledgement of them. We can adjust that, and the contract matter together.

For these repeated concessions and accommodations on your part, I have no parallel in my business relations,—and the only poor promise I have in return for them is that if I live, it shall be my endeavor to show that your munificence has not been thrown away.

What I shall want afterwards I am sure I don't know—but I *do* want to live to show the world what can be done with that great Post Octavo scheme. Leaving "Uncle Tom's Cabin" out of the way, and then I shall beat the world in a three or five years stretch,—i.e. in the number of volumes sold from *one pen.*

What my ambition will be afterwards I don't know—but that I have and that I shall do.

May you and I and the *Atlantic Monthly* all live to tell the world of it when it is done.[1] Very truly yours

M. D. PHILLIPS

P.S. The engraver I intended to have call on you is not in town today.

1. The next year, instead of contributing to the realization of this dream of success, brought death to WHP and Phillips and bankruptcy to the publishing house of Phillips, Sampson and Company.

322.   To Charles Folsom
                (Charles Folsom Papers, Boston Public Library)

Lynn, June 30, [1858]

Thank you, dear Folsom, for the correction of the swaddling clothes blunder, which I have set right, preferring the clothes to the leading-strings, as the language of Don John.

I would suggest to you that in some of your longer notes, written *calamo currente,* you subside into an infinitesimally small hand, somewhat annoying to eyes—or rather half an eye—like mine. I don't want letters as big as a sign-board's, but such as a Christian gentleman may reasonably demand who would not shorten his days by endeavoring to decipher the hieroglyphics of the writer.

I congratulate you that we get on as rapidly as when I was in Boston —"*rapido si, ma rapido con leggi*"—you love a quotation. Those who have said you were not the most punctual of men know nothing about it, and I will take up the gauntlet for you on this quarrel whenever you desire it. Thine always

WM. H. P.

323.   To George Routledge
                  (Draft, WHP Papers, Mass. Hist. Soc.)

                                    Boston, September 20, 1858
My dear sir,

I have had the pleasure of receiving your letter of the 3d instant in which you offer me 260 guineas for the advance sheets of the 3d volume of my *Philip the Second*,[1] on the condition that you are to have the remaining volumes on the same terms. This stipulation seems to me a reasonable one. It must not, however, be forgotten, as among possible, though by no means probable, contingencies, that before the completion of the work an international copyright treaty may be brought about between England and America, and in that event it must, of course, be understood that no condition in regard to sending forward the sheets of volumes still to appear will be of any force, and that I shall be at full liberty to dispose of the copyright to the highest bidder. But I should, in this case, as a matter of courtesy, give the refusal right to the publisher of my third volume at the price originally offered by you, namely £1000 a volume, the price which Mr. Bentley has since more than once informed me he should be happy to pay for the work if a copyright could be secured.

With this explanation, which will doubtless accord with your own views, I now accede to your proposal and send by this steamer the sheets of the 3d volume, with daguerreotypes of two portraits to be engraved for it. You will please acknowledge the receipt of the parcel without delay. A duplicate copy will follow by the steamer of next week. I may add that from all I have gathered from quarters where I thought the best information was to be had on the subject, I do not at present see the least reason to hope for an arrangement between the two governments in regard to copyright.

The offer made me for this volume by Mr. Bentley was nearly double the amount of yours but it was accompanied with a condition which I regarded as inadmissible, in regard to a priority of publication. As I stated to you in my last, the book will appear here on December 15th, and must not be published in England before December 17th.

I had forgotten to state in my last that the work will be completed in two more volumes, making five in the whole.

P.S. If you preferred to bring out the volume on the 12th instead of the 17th of December, I would make arrangements for its appearance here on the 10th, as indeed this earlier date would be rather more agreeable to me. Be so good as to let me know in your reply which day will suit you best. I shall hope to hear from you by return of mail.

1. Russell Sturgis had again served as WHP's literary agent in London. Bentley, publisher of the first two volumes of *Philip the Second* and an unsuccessful bidder for the third volume, was thoroughly enraged.

324.   To William Howard Gardiner
             (William H. Gardiner Papers, Mass. Hist. Soc.)

Beacon Street, October 30, 1858

Dear William,

I returned to town yesterday, in as good condition as usual, after breathing for six weeks nothing but mountain air and eating vegetables. I heard from Davis that you were in town, and as I wished to see you I called at the office, but was not fortunate enough to find you. The point on which I wished to talk with you was this:—Some twenty years ago, at a time when Robbins was in one of his financial perplexities, I joined with some other gentlemen in lending him a sum of money—my share being $2000—for which we received security in the shape of a mortgage—as well as I can recollect—on the Grafton property, but learning some time afterwards that I had thereby made myself responsible for the debts of the company, in the same manner as if I had been a proprietor, I insisted on giving up my claim, and no doubt signed a discharge to that effect, though I have no distinct remembrance of having done so. The property is now about to be sold; and Mr. Parsons informs me that the purchaser requires a discharge from me, in the form of a quitclaim deed, that which I before gave not being, I suppose, to be found. Of course I can have no objection to do this, if it is merely the simple transaction which it appears to be. The question is whether my signing this deed at present may not carry with it the implication that I have up to this time had an interest in the property, with the personal liability that would belong to such interest. I am almost ashamed to have delayed the proceedings by this scruple. But having seen more than one instance of the ill effects of ignorance combined with haste (and I have plenty of the former in matters of this kind), I have preferred to have your opinion before taking the step required of me; and I should therefore be obliged by your letting me know—as early as convenient, in order that I may not increase the delay more than is necessary—whether you see any objection to my signing the enclosed deed. Always faithfully yours,

WM. H. PRESCOTT

325. From Richard Bentley

(Extracts from complete text in R. Bentley [ed.], *Correspondence of William H. Prescott, Esq. with Richard Bentley, from August, 1856, to November, 1858* [n.p. (1859)], pp. 14–16)

New Burlington Street, November 9, 1858

Sir,

Your letter of the 21st September, in reference to the disposal of the Third Volume of the Memoirs of "Philip the Second" has both surprised and grieved me more than I can express;—surprised me, because it has never been my misfortune in a long life to have experienced treatment so incompatible with the usages of men of letters in this country; and grieved me, because least of all did I expect, after the frank nature of our past intercourse, such a total forgetfulness on your part of the obligations which such a connexion involved.

.   .   .   .

But what am I now to think of the injury thus coolly inflicted upon me? What I feel I will not express, lest I should use language which I am unaccustomed to employ, even under excitement; but I must take leave to tell you, that every one who has read our correspondence agrees with me, that no such thing could possibly occur among English gentlemen.

Upon any future occasion when you may think of publishing in this country, I must beg leave to be spared a renewal of correspondence.[1]

That others may not be led into similar losses, by conduct of the like nature, I shall feel myself justified in submitting this letter either to my friends, or to the public, as I shall deem expedient.[2]

I am, Sir, Your obedient servant,

RICHARD BENTLEY

1. Except for this termination of his relations with Bentley, WHP had known completely harmonious relations with every one of his publishers.

2. In 1859 Bentley published *Correspondence of William H. Prescott, Esq. with Richard Bentley, from August, 1856, to November, 1858,* which WHP did not live to see. The absence of the original of this letter of November 9, 1858, from the Prescott papers suggests that its contents so pained the historian that he caused it to be destroyed.

326. To Oliver Wendell Holmes[1]

(Oliver Wendell Holmes Papers, The Library of Congress)

Beacon Street, December 28, '58

My dear Dr. Holmes,

I am truly obliged to you for the beautiful present you have sent me of the *Autocrat*. The volume is got up in a style of the most perfect elegance and taste. The dress is just what it should be for a work in which a sound philosophy and acute criticism are conveyed under the playful and popular garb of a literary lounger.

Phillips has officiated as your midwife as well as mine in bringing our literary bantlings into the world; and as he has just delivered my muse of another of her numerous progeny, I hope you will allow me to send it to you as a memento of our simultaneous appearance before the public.

With great regard believe me, my dear Dr. Holmes, Very sincerely yours

WM. H. PRESCOTT

1. Oliver Wendell Holmes (1809–94), physician, poet, essayist and novelist.

327.   From Lady Mary E. Lyell
               (Extracts, WHP Papers, Mass. Hist. Soc.)

53 Harley Street, London
30th December 1858

My dear Mr. Prescott,

Before the old year closes, I must write to you once more. I hope the New Year will bring me a letter from you, and what a joyful New Year's gift it would be if you accede to our proposal. However I hardly expect you will do that at once. It is long to look forward, but when the fine weather comes on and short passages across the ocean, I do trust and hope that pleasure is in store for us. . . . We are not going out of town this Christmas we have so many family meetings instead. We have been to horsemanship and Dickens' readings and Albert Smith. The worst of going out in the evenings is that it breaks into our reading *Philip* which I am reading aloud to Charles and which we are both delighted with. We generally contrive to get a little every day. Charles must thank you for himself. I have heard it highly spoken of by the Dean, Sir Henry Hallam and Lord Macaulay. I daresay they may have told you so themselves. I am very much struck in the account of the rise of the Moriscoes of the similarity to our Indian rebellion—the cruelty on both sides and the secrecy. I have heard no one say so, but it seems to be as if it might have been written for it. Perhaps all rebellions are alike when there is a subject and a dominant race.

I have not yet bought your socks, but shall do so very soon—unless you tell me you will come and choose them yourself. The patterns I have are 2 and 3. I don't understand the V marked on them but that is of no consequence. You were sad when you last wrote at Washington Irving's illness and Mr. Thorndike's death.

.   .   .   .

The Twisletons are at Bowood—Lord Lansdowne has just sent us a basket of game, very welcome for the hospitalities of this season. The Milmans dined with us lately, both very well. He said he was going to write to you. Charles is much occupied with his Etna paper still. He wisely determines not to hurry. He works so steadily every day that he certainly ought not to overdo it. I told you he had received the Copley Medal. As soon as the President's speech is printed I will send you a copy. I am longing to hear again from Anna Ticknor, tell her please. When next you write I wish you could mention the John A. Lowells,[1] of whom we have not heard for an age. Another thing, I should be so much obliged if you would learn for me about John Cameron, our former servant, now with Mr. Nathan Appleton.[2] We heard he had broken his leg and was in the hospital. I do hope he will not be lame and unfit for service. This will not give you trouble, I think, when you are walking along sunny Beacon Street. We have always pleasant news from Berlin, all well there. I hope Mr. James Lawrence continues to improve and all the rest are well. My kind love to Mrs. Prescott, believe me ever, my dear Mr. Prescott Affectionately yours

MARY E. LYELL

[P.S.] I send you heartfelt wishes for every good this world can give in 1859.

1. Probably John Lowell (1824–97), jurist.
2. Nathan Appleton (1779–1861), along with his brother Samuel, pioneered in the manufacturing of cotton cloth.

328.   To George Routledge
                 (Draft, WHP Papers, Mass. Hist. Soc.)

Boston, January 11, 1859

My dear Sir,

I have had the pleasure of receiving yours of the [blank], and have drawn as you desire me on your name in New York for £267—and the draft has been duly accepted.

You ask me when I shall be likely to have another volume ready for the press. I cannot say. I have not broken ground on it yet;[1] but shall soon do so. It must depend on my health, which is good now. But the warning which I got last winter makes me more cautious than I used to be. I should be sure that any thing I write, as Scott used to say, shall smell of apoplexy.

I am glad that the present volume has gone off as well as you anticipated. I should suppose that all who have got the two elder brothers would want this—sooner or later—as well as the two that are to come.

I am obliged to you for offering to execute any little commission I may wish in the great Babylon. I have written him, but to send some copies of my books, notifying me of the cost, and I will pay it to your house in New York.

I should like to send the three volumes of *Philip* to [blank].

Also another set of the three volumes of *Philip* to Mons. le Comte Albert de Circourt, aux soins de le Comte Adolphe de Circourt, 11 Rue de [. . .], Paris, paying the charges on them if you can do so for me.

I am glad that you have made an agreement with Bentley and bought the plates of the two prior volumes. This guaranties you from any interference on that quarter—as it possibly will from any other.

I have not yet received the copy of the 8vo edition of the volume 3d which you mention having sent me, care of Ticknor and Field, who had not got them yesterday. I wish you would send me, in addition, a copy of the cabinet edition of the 3d volume of *Philip* and a complete set of the *Mexico,* cabinet edition.

I remain dear Sir, Very truly yours

1. Once the third volume of *Philip the Second* was behind him, WHP, instead of plunging into the next one, had turned to revising his *Conquest of Mexico*. See Prescott (Gardiner, ed.), *The Literary Memoranda,* II, 230.

329.   To William Amory Prescott
                   (WHP Papers, Mass. Hist. Soc.)

Boston, January 22, 1859

My dear Amory,[1]

It was very kind of you to write me such a pleasant letter, giving me so minute an accounting of your doings in the great metropolis. You have been more busy there than we have, and show as long a roll of dinners and dances as could be expected in Paris or London. Some of the persons you have visited are old friends of mine, whose faces I should like to look on again. We should probably find one another the worse for wear. It is a wound to one's *amour propre*—to borrow an old phrase of yours—to see an old friend after a long separation. The face of one serves as a looking-glass for the other. I was much obliged by your thinking of the books for me. I have learned that they have all now reached their proper destinations, except that to Mr. Davis, which I gave fresh orders to be delivered to him.

We sent on a bevy of ladies, Amorys and Lawrences, as a contribution to the Batchelors' ball in Philadelphia—a day or two since. It was going a good way for any lady out of her teens to find a place to hop in. I hope you had too many agreeable engagements in New York to allow you to take the expensive trouble of making one of the party.

But are you not soon thinking of returning to the Yankee capital? You will find there, in Beacon Street, more love—and that is the best thing in this world—than you will be likely to meet with in all the other streets and towns in the world besides.

The increased illness of your Aunt Mary has thrown a cloud over us. I had sent out invitations for a little dinner—Lord Frederick C., Lord Radspark, Ticknor, Hillard, your Uncles William and Charles [. . .][2] excuse ourselves from receiving them. I was much chagrined in regard to Lord F., who brought me a note from Lord Carlisle. But during the first part of the week I was prevented by an ague, which put me *hors de combat,* and I could receive no one; and now the condition of your aunt's health makes it equally impossible. She still lingers, but a day or two must close the scene of her long and patient sufferings.

Adieu, my dear son. With your mother's love, believe me always [. . .][3]

1. Returned from Europe and unable, or unwilling, to settle in Boston, WHP's younger son was in New York City.

2. At this point the manuscript has been cut.

3. Another piece has been cut from the manuscript, this one apparently to yield WHP's autograph.

330.   To Sir Charles Lyell
(Transcript, Lady Lyell's Letterbook, WHP Papers, Mass. Hist. Soc.; and extracts in Ticknor, *Prescott,* p. 440)

Boston, January 23, 1859

My dear Sir Charles,

I have had the pleasure of receiving your friendly letter of December 31st and must thank you for another, in which you so kindly invited my wife and me to visit you in England. Nothing, you may well believe, could give her and myself greater pleasure than to pass some time under your hospitable roof, which would afford me the inexpressible satisfaction of taking some friends again by the hand, whose faces I would give much to see. But I have long since abandoned the thought of crossing the great water, and the friends on the other side of it are, I fear, henceforth to find a place with me only in the pleasures of memory. And pleasant recollections they afford, to fill many an hour, which the world would call idle, for there is neither fame nor money to be made out of them. But one who has crossed sixty (how near are you to that ominous line?) will have found out that there is something of more worth than fame or money in this world.

I was last evening with Agassiz, who was in capital spirits at the prospect of opening to the public a project of a great museum, for which Frank Gray, as I suppose you know, left an appropriation of fifty thousand dollars. There will be a subscription set on foot, I understand, for raising a similar sum to provide a suitable building for the collection—a great part of which has already been formed by Agassiz himself—and the governor,[1] at a meeting of the friends of the scheme held the other evening at James Lawrence's, gave the most cordial assurances of substantial aid from the state. Agassiz expressed the greatest confidence to me of being able in a few years to establish an institution which would not shrink from comparison with similar establishments in Europe. He has been suffering of late from inflammation of the eyes, a trouble to which he is unaccustomed, but for which he may thank his own imprudence.

I am glad to learn that you are pursuing with your usual energy your studies of Etna. The subject is one of the greatest interest. I must congratulate you on the reception of the Copley medal. However we may despise or affect to despise the vulgar *volitare per ora,* it is a satisfaction to find one's labors appreciated by the few who are competent to pronounce on their value.

You have seen the accounts of Everett's arrangement with the editor of the New York *Ledger*. Odd enough, and opens to him the widest field for talking with his countrymen. He means to give them, I am told, some lectures on their conduct, which they may profit by if they like. I doubt if his gentle nature is made of stuff stern enough for that. Did you see a discourse of Lord Carlisle on the Yankee character lately delivered by him at Hull? It was copied—or extracts made from it—in one of our papers, with a liberal commentary on it. I sent the paper to him. It will be easier to detect our faults, I suspect, than to correct them.

We are in a very quiet, prosperous way just now—precisely that in which people are apt to be most saucy. The government seems to be ogling Mexico on the one side, and coquetting with Cuba on the other. Its way of dealing with the latter is charming. I wonder, if John Bull should insist on buying Maine to annex to Canada, whether we would or no—what would come of it. Such a notion might find a good place in *Punch*.

I hope you will have received by the last steamer a new portrait of my phiz. It was taken for the *Eclectic Review* in New York and engraved by a good artist in Philadelphia. As it is considered here the best likeness that has been taken of me of late, I thought your wife might like to see how old Time has been nibbling on my superficies since she saw me last. Mrs. Prescott does not like it, because it is so true.

Good-bye, my dear Lyell, with kindest remembrances to your wife, believe me, always Faithfully yours

1. Nathaniel Prentiss Banks (1816–94), a Republican, served as Governor of Massachusetts from 1858 to 1861.

331.   To William Amory Prescott
       (Copy, Ticknor Collection, Archives, Dartmouth College Library)

Boston, January 25, '59

My dear Amory[1]

Your mother desires me to thank you for your kind note, which she could not well do herself, having some engagements which prevent her. This is the day of your Aunt Mary Dexter's funeral, which took place at three in the afternoon. She died as you probably know, on Saturday night, after a confinement to her chamber of two months, which she has borne with the greatest sweetness and resignation. The services were performed at Trinity Church and it was a touching thing to see your Uncle Thomas looking like a broken-hearted old man, preparing to set out alone the remainder of his journey. They had lived forty years together. The evening of life is coming over those of our generation, and we must be prepared to say farewell to one another.[2]

WM. H. PRESCOTT

1. Probably WHP's last letter.
2. Having recently bid farewell to so many, WHP was prepared. His own death came on January 28, 1859, the result of another apoplectic stroke.

Appendix

---

332. **Last Will and Testament of William H. Prescott[1]**
(Probate Court, Suffolk County, Massachusetts)

I William H. Prescott, of Boston in the County of Suffolk, make this my last will and testament.

First – I direct my executor to pay all my just debts.

Second Item: – I give to my sister, Catharine Elizabeth Dexter[2] five hundred dollars, together with any such book or trinket as she may choose from my effects to keep as a token of my love.

Third Item: – I give to my friend Mrs. Anna Ticknor, wife of George Ticknor, one hundred dollars, to be laid out by her in some token of my sincere affection for her.

Fourth Item: – I give to each of my friends George Ticknor, William H. Gardiner and William Amory any work out of my library which they may respectively choose, to be kept in token of our old friendship.

Fifth Item: – I give to my brother-in-law Franklin Dexter one hundred dollars as a token of my regard.

Sixth Item: – I give to my cousins Miss Harriette and Miss Anna Prescott, daughters of the late Dr. Oliver Prescott, two hundred dollars each.

Seventh Item: – I give to my mother's half brother Thomas Hickling Esq. of St. Michaels in the Azores two hundred dollars.

Eighth Item: – I give to Nathan Webster, who formerly lived in my father's family, fifty dollars.

Ninth Item: – I give to J. Foster Kirk, my reader, three hundred dollars.

Tenth Item: – I give to the President and Fellows of Harvard College my collection of books and manuscripts relating to the reigns of Ferdinand and Isabella, as registered on a catalogue of mine entitled—"A catalogue of works relating to the reigns of Ferdinand and Isabella." This collection is curious, and difficult to procure, and may be of some value in a library which I believe does not contain complete materials for foreign history of any period, however limited in extent.

Eleventh Item: – I give to the Boston Athenaeum a book in my library called "The Antiquities of Mexico," in seven volumes folio, edited by Augustin Aglio.

Twelfth Item: – Subject to the foregoing donations, I give to my wife Susannah the free choice of such books as she may first select out of my library; and I then give to my eldest son, William G. Prescott, one hundred volumes, such as he may next select therefrom; after which I give to my daughter Elizabeth one hundred volumes thereof such as she may next choose; and thereafter I give to my son William Amory Prescott one hundred volumes to be chosen by him from the said library; and all the rest of my library, after the above selections, I give to my said children to be equally divided among them. But I recommend that my other historical collections, both printed and manuscript, namely, the collections described in my catalogue as "Works relating to Mexico and Peru," and that described as "Works relating to Philip the Second," be kept entire, and each disposed of as a whole by sale to some public institution in this country if any shall desire to purchase it, and otherwise that it be sent to England and sold there. And I request my friend George Ticknor to take the trouble of disposing of these collections, the cost of each appearing in my account books.

Thirteenth Item: – The sword which belonged to my grandfather Colonel William Prescott, worn by him in the battle of Bunker Hill, I give to the Massachusetts Historical Society as a curiosity suitable to be preserved among their collections; and the sword which belonged to my wife's grandfather Captain Linzee of the British Royal Navy, who commanded one of the enemy's ships lying off Charlestown during the same battle, I give to my wife.[3]

Fourteenth Item: – I give to my wife Susannah, for her own use forever, ten thousand dollars to be paid her in one year after my decease, with interest from my decease. I also give her my household furniture, plate, and wearing apparel; and direct that my wine be equally divided between her and my children who may survive me.

Fifteenth Item: – I give the old family farm situated in the towns of Pepperell and Hollis to my eldest son William Gardiner Prescott, and the male heirs of his body forever to hold the same in tail male; and in default, or on failure of male issue of my said son, I give the remainder of said estate to my youngest son William Amory Prescott, and the male heirs of his body forever, to hold the same in tail male; and in default or on failure of male issue of my said youngest son, I give the remainder of said estate to my heirs at law, to their own use in fee simple forever.

Sixteenth Item: – I give and devise to my friends George Ticknor and William Amory my mansion house in Beacon Street, Boston, and all other real estate wheresoever situated whereof I may die seized, except the said farm at Pepperell, together with such of my personal estate as may be selected to compose the particular trust funds hereinafter mentioned, to hold to them and the survivors of them, and his heirs, executors or administrators, the said personal estate upon the trusts hereinafter declared respecting the said particular trust funds, and the said real estate upon the trusts following, namely;—The said Trustees, and their successors in said trust, shall constantly keep the said mansion house insured against loss by fire, so long as they shall hold the same in trust; and they shall permit my said wife to use and occupy the said mansion house during her life, if she shall elect so to do; and in that event, so long as she shall continue her election to occupy, or to have the right of occupying, said house, she shall keep the same in good repair, except in the case of loss by fire, and the value of the use of said mansion house, so long as my said wife may occupy the same, shall be reckoned as part of the income of the trust fund hereinafter established for her benefit, at the rate of twelve hundred dollars a year only, whatsoever may be the appraised value of said house, and the trustees shall pay one-half only of the taxes, which shall be lawfully assessed thereon out of the income of her said trust fund, and the other half of the said taxes, together with the expense of insurance against loss by fire, shall be apportioned equally among the owners of the beneficial interest in the reversion of said mansion house, and shall be paid by my said trustees out of the income of the trust funds hereinafter established for their benefit, in proportion to their respective interests in said reversion;—but if, by the death of either of my children, or otherwise it shall happen that any person or persons, for whose benefit no trust fund shall be held by my said trustees under the subsequent provisions of this will, should become entitled to a share of said reversion, the just proportion of taxes and insurance which may fall to such share shall be paid by the trustees out of the income of the trust fund established for the benefit of my wife, so that my said trustees may always have the means in their own hands of paying such taxes and insurance;—and whensoever the said house shall be leased, with my wife's consent, in such manner, that twelve hundred dollars a year shall be payable to her out of the rents, as hereinafter provided, the trustees shall charge one-half of the taxes to her and may pay the other half as well as the expense of insurance out of the surplus rents of said estate, beyond said sum of twelve hundred dollars; but whensoever it shall be leased under such circumstances that no part of the rents of said house shall be payable to my wife, or that the whole net rents shall be payable to her, in either of these cases, the whole expense of taxes, insurance and repairs shall be paid out of the rents; —and my said wife shall signify to my said trustees in writing, whensoever they shall call upon her so to do, her election whether or not she will occupy the said house, and may also at any time thereafter signify to them in writing her subsequent election no longer to occupy the same, if she prefer to live elsewhere, or she may signify her election that the same should be leased for a limited term, with a right on her part to return to the said house at the expiration of such lease; and I hereby authorize and empower my said trustees, and their successors in said trust, to lease the said house at any time during the life of my wife when she shall desire it, on such terms as they may deem expedient, but in such case my wife is to receive out of the rents and profits of said estate the sum of twelve hundred dollars a year only, and all the residue of the net income derived therefrom is to be distributed by my said trustees to the persons who shall be entitled under this will to the beneficial interest in the reversion of said mansion house; and I further authorize and empower my said trustees, and their successors in said trust, to lease from time to time, and also to sell and convey, at such time or times as they in their discretion may deem most for the interest of my estate, all the real estate herein devised to them, except the said mansion house during my wife's life, if she shall elect to occupy or to keep the right of occupying the same upon the terms aforesaid, and also in that event to sell and convey the said mansion house in like manner with my said wife's consent and concurrence, but not otherwise, during her life; and after her decease, whether in my lifetime or afterwards, or whensoever her estate and interest in said house shall otherwise determine, to sell and convey the same, whensoever they shall deem it expedient so to do; and the purchasers of the said mansion house, and of the other real estate aforesaid, whensoever sold by my said trustees, shall hold the same free and discharged from all trusts, and without any obligation to see to the application of the purchase money.—And the said trustees, so long as they may hold any parcel of productive real estate herein devised to them, are further empowered to appropriate the same at their discretion towards the formation of either of the particular trust funds hereinafter mentioned and thereafter to hold and dispose of the same as part of such trust fund according to the uses and purposes thereof as hereinafter declared; and in case of a subsequent sale of any real estate constituting a portion of said trust fund the proceeds shall be appropriated in like manner to the uses and purposes of said fund; but in case of a sale under the power herein given of any parcel of real estate not so appropriated, and whether productive or unproductive, the proceeds may be applied at the discretion of the trustees towards the formation of either of said trust funds, until the same shall have been fully formed, and thereafter such proceeds shall be paid over to my children, and the issue of any child deceased, or to such other persons as may at the time be entitled thereto under the provisions of this will concerning the disposition of the final residue of my estate; and all rents and profits of real estate, while held by the said trustees, except as before directed concerning the mansion house, shall be accounted for and paid over, either as part of the income of the particular trust fund to which it may belong or else as the property of the persons entitled at the time to the final residue of my estate; and my intention is that all the productive real estate herein devised to my said trustees shall be appropriated by them as part of the particular trust funds, unless they shall think it more advantageous that the same should be sold; and my further direction is that all the real estate not so appropriated and whether productive or unproductive, except the mansion house during my wife's life, if she elects to keep the right of occupying it, shall be sold, either before the formation of the trust funds hereinafter mentioned, or within one year next after the formation thereof, unless my trustees shall think the time unfavorable for such sale;—But if my said trustees shall not exercise the said power of sale in respect to all or any of the said real estate within one year after the formation of said particular trust funds, in that case upon and after the expiration of said year, they shall hold the said real estate to the use of the same persons, and in the same proportions, as would then be entitled thereto by the clause of this will disposing of my residuary estate; and in respect to all or any of the said real estate except the said mansion house during the continuance of my wife's estate and interest therein, and also in respect to the said mansion house, subject to her right and interest therein, the said trustees, whensoever they may deem it expedient so to do, may terminate their said trust by a release and conveyance of all their right, titles and interest therein, to the same persons, and in the same proportions, as would be entitled thereto, if the said trust had then otherwise terminated by its own limitation.

Seventeenth Item: – In addition to the legacy of ten thousand dollars and the use of the said house, as above provided, I give to my said wife the interest of sixty thousand dollars at the rate of five per cent per annum commencing at my decease, and to be paid to her from time to time, and as she may require the same by my executor or administrator, until my estate shall be so far settled that the fund hereinafter mentioned shall be formed and set apart for my wife's benefit.

Eighteenth Item: – So soon as it shall be found safe and convenient in the settlement of my estate to form and set apart the trust funds hereinafter mentioned, my will is that my executor or administrator shall for that purpose make a complete inventory of all my estate real and personal, which shall come to his knowledge, excepting household furniture and other chattels herein specifically bequeathed, and shall cause the value thereof to be ascertained by suitable appraisers, who shall be selected and agreed upon by my said executor or administrator and the trustees acting under this will; my intention being that they shall not be bound to select for this purpose one set of appraisers for all the property, but may select such persons as they may consider to be competent judges of any one species or item of property to appraise the fair value thereof, and other persons to appraise the fair value of any other species or item of property comprising part of my estate; and if, after paying all the particular legacies herein bequeathed, and allowing for and deducting all debts that may remain unpaid, my whole remaining estate, according to the inventory and appraisement aforesaid, shall be found to amount to not less than two hundred and sixty thousand dollars, nor more than three hundred and ten thousand dollars, in that case a trust fund of eighty thousand dollars is to be formed, in the manner hereinafter directed, for the benefit of my wife, should she survive me, so long as she may live; but if the value of my whole estate shall be found to exceed three hundred and ten thousand dollars, in that case the said trust fund shall be increased to eighty-five thousand dollars; and if on the other hand the value thereof shall be found to be less than two hundred and sixty thousand dollars, in that case the said trust fund shall be diminished to seventy-five thousand dollars. And the said trust fund shall be formed as follows—In the first place, my said mansion house in Beacon Street, Boston, if my wife shall elect to occupy or to have the right of occupying the same, on the terms before stated, shall constitute a part of said fund, and shall be taken therefor at a valuation of twenty thousand dollars only, whatever may be the true appraised value thereof—Secondly, the said George Ticknor and William Amory, trustees as aforesaid, and their successors in said trust, may, if they shall see fit, select and set apart as another portion of said fund any other productive real estate above devised to them whereof I may die seized, estimating the same at its true appraised value, and they may set apart and appropriate in like manner the proceeds of any real estate by them held—Thirdly, the same trustees may also select, either in lieu of such real estate, or in addition thereto, so much of the personal property, at its appraised value, as may suffice to make up the said fund, and my executor or administrator shall upon request transfer the same to the said trustees. But the said trustees shall not be bound to take and hold as part of the said trust fund any specific property, real or personal, held by me at my decease, except the said mansion house if my wife shall elect to have the use thereof upon the terms aforesaid. And should she not so elect, they may take the said mansion house at its true appraised value as part of the said trust fund, or not, as they in their discretion may think best. And the said trustees in lieu of taking specifically at its appraised value any real or personal property left by me, and holding the same as a part of the said trust fund, may at their discretion require that so much as may be needful make up the said fund, in whole or in part, shall be paid to them in money, and to be by them invested in such other property as they may think more advisable to hold for the said trust; and in such case my executor or administrator shall sell so much of my personal estate as may be needful to raise the requisite sum and pay over the same to the said trustees. And the same trustees shall hold the property composing the said fund, whether real estate, or specific personal property, or money, upon the special trusts hereinafter mentioned and no other, to wit, upon trust to place and keep the money out at interest, on mortgages, or other good security, or otherwise to invest the same, either in real estate, or in public stocks, or stocks of incorporated companies, or upon suitable contracts of deposit with the Massachusetts Hospital Life Insurance Company, as they in their discretion may think most advisable, with power to change investments whensoever they may deem it expedient to do so, and for that purpose to sell and convey any of the said trust property free and discharged from all trusts in the hands of the purchaser, and without any obligation on his part to see to the application of the purchase money; and upon the further trust to collect from time to time all the rents and profits, interest, dividends, and income, which shall accrue from the said trust property; and after paying all taxes, insurance and other reasonable charges or expenses incident to the care and preservation of the said trust property, and to the due execution of the said trust, to pay over from time to time in quarterly or other convenient terms of payment, the whole net residue of the income of said trust fund to my said wife, Susannah, during her life, upon her sole and separate receipt or order in writing, notwithstanding any future coverture, provided however that my said wife, occupying the said mansion house, shall have the use thereof as an equivalent for twelve hundred dollars only of the said income, and one-half of the taxes lawfully assessed thereon, so long as said house shall compose a part of said trust fund at the said valuation of twenty thousand dollars, and so long as my wife shall continue to occupy the same; and whensoever the said house, composing a part of the said trust fund at the said reduced valuation, shall be leased to any other person, so much only of the rents and profits thereof as shall equal the said sum of twelve hundred dollars a year and one-half of the taxes shall be accounted for to my said wife as part of the income of her said trust fund, and the residue of the said rents and profits and taxes shall be distributed and accounted for, to and with the owners of the beneficial interest in the reversion of said mansion house, or otherwise as before directed; but if the said house shall at any time be taken and held as part of the said trust fund at its true appraised value, my wife not electing to occupy the same, the net rents thereof, whether more or less than the said sum of twelve hundred dollars a year, shall be accounted for and paid over to my said wife as part of the income of her trust fund; and at the decease of my said wife the capital of said trust fund shall be disposed of as is hereinafter directed in the clause of this will concerning the disposition of the final residue of my estate.

Nineteenth Item: – After the formation of the said trust fund for my wife's benefit, all the remaining property, real and personal, in said inventory, excepting the farm at Pepperell, and excepting so much of said inventory as may be needful to pay any debts or legacies that may remain undischarged, shall, together with the reversion of said trust fund at my wife's decease, be divided at the appraised value into so many equal shares as I may leave children of our said marriage, or issue of any such child deceased, such issue having the same share which his, her or their parent would have been entitled to if living, and to share the same equally among them; but in estimating the said shares, and dividing the property, due allowance is to be made for any advance to either of my children or grandchildren, and the same shall be accounted as debts due to my estate and payable out of their respective shares, provided that the same be endorsed by me on this instrument as an advance made to such child or grandchild, or else be witnessed by a promissory note of the party to be charged therewith; and no sum of money, or other property which has been, or may hereafter be paid or given by me, in my lifetime to or for any child or grandchild, shall be treated as an advance in the division of the property which I may leave at my decease, nor constitute in any other form a claim against such child or grandchild, unless the same shall either be endorsed by me on this instrument as an advance to such child or grandchild, or shall be witnessed by his or her promissory note.

And my will is, and I hereby order and direct, that, out of the respective shares of my children in the said property, a trust fund shall be formed and held by my said trustees for each of my children, during his or her life, in manner following; that is to say, a fund of twenty-five thousand dollars in amount shall be held in trust for the benefit of my eldest son William Gardiner Prescott, during his life, should he survive me; and a like fund of fifty thousand dollars in amount, excepting as is hereinafter provided, shall be held in trust for the benefit of my youngest son William Amory Prescott, during his life, should he survive me; and three-fourths parts of the share of my daughter Elizabeth, wife of James Lawrence, shall be held in trust for her benefit, during her life, should she survive me; and I hereby devise and bequeath to the said George Ticknor and William Amory, and the survivor of them, and his heirs, executors or administrators, to hold upon the trusts hereinafter declared, so much of my estate as shall be needful to form the said trust funds respectively, and I direct my executor, or administrator, to transfer to my said trustees, or their successors in said trust, such portion of my personal estate as they may select to hold specifically at their appraised value, as part of the said trust funds, any or either of them; and so far as they may not elect to receive specifically, at their appraised value, portions of my personal estate, sufficient to make up the said funds, nor appropriate therefor at its appraised value, as I hereby empower them to do, any productive real estate herein devised to my said trustees, or the proceeds of any real estate by them held, I direct my executor or administrator to sell so much of my personal estate as may be needful, and to pay over to my said trustees so much money, in addition to the real estate or its proceeds so appropriated by my said trustees, and the personal estate so specifically selected by me and transferred to them, as shall suffice to complete the formation of said funds; and the said trustees shall hold the property composing said funds respectively upon the following trusts, and no other; that is to say, they shall put out at interest, on mortgages, or other good security, all moneys composing the capital of either of said trust funds, or they shall otherwise invest the same, either in real estate, or in public stocks, or the stocks of incorporated companies, or in suitable contracts of deposit with the Massachusetts Hospital Life Insurance Company, as they in their discretion may think most expedient; and they shall from time to time, whensoever and so often as they may think it expedient, sell and convey any real or personal estate composing part of either of the said trust funds, so as to be free and discharged from all trust in the hands of the purchaser, and without any liability on his part to see to the application of the purchase money, and they shall invest and reinvest from time to time in manner aforesaid the proceeds of such sales, with full power to change investments at their discretion; and they shall from time to time collect all rents, profits, interest, dividends, and income of the said trust property, and after paying therefrom all taxes, insurance and other reasonable charges and expenses incident to the care and preservation of said trust property, and the due execution of the said trusts respectively, they shall pay over the residue of the said income as follows; that is to say, in respect to the trust funds of each of my said sons, the net income thereof shall be paid over, in quarterly or other convenient and fixed terms of payment, to the son who is entitled thereto, during his life, either personally, or upon his written order, or receipt, dated and made after such income shall have become due and payable; and in respect to the trust fund of my said daughter, the net income thereof shall be paid over to her in like manner, either personally, or upon her separate order, or receipt, in writing, made and dated as aforesaid; and in such manner as to be free from the control of her present or of any future husband, and in no way liable for his debts; and neither of my said children shall have any power to control or dispose of either capital or income of his or her trust fund otherwise than by testamentary disposition, as hereinafter provided, or by orders and receipts for the income made and dated after the same shall have become due and payable; and the said trustees shall hold the capital of the said trust funds respectively upon the further trust to convey, transfer and pay over the same, at the decease of my said children respectively, to such person or persons, in such proportions, and under such limitations as each of my said children, in respect to his or her trust fund, by his or her last will and testament, or in the case of my daughter by any instrument in writing in the nature of a last will and testament, which, her coverture notwithstanding, she is hereby expressly empowered to make, shall give, direct, limit, or appoint the same; and in default of such testamentary appointment, the said trustees shall convey, transfer and pay over the said capital of each of my said children, at his or her decease, to his or her lawful issue him or her surviving, and the lawful issue of his or her children deceased in equal shares, the issue of any such deceased child, through all the degrees, to take equally among them by representation the share which his, her or their parent would have been entitled to if living; and if there be no issue him or her surviving, and no testamentary disposition or appointment, in that case, the trust capital of my child so dying, shall be equally divided between his or her mother and brothers or mother, brother and sister, as the case may be, and the lawful issue of any brother or sister deceased, who shall take by representation, through all the degrees, and equally among those in equal degree, the share which his, her or their parent would have been entitled to if living, and the share so accruing to the issue of any brother or sister deceased shall be conveyed, transferred, and paid over immediately to such issue; and the share so accruing to either of my sons shall be paid over immediately to him; but three-fourths of the share so accruing to my said daughter shall be added to the capital of the trust fund held for her benefit, and shall be held, managed and disposed of, during her life, and at her decease, in the same manner as is herein directed concerning her original trust fund, and the remaining fourth part only shall be paid over immediately to her; and the whole share which may accrue to my wife shall be added, in like manner, to the capital of the trust fund held for her benefit, and shall be held, managed and disposed of during her life and at her decease in the same manner as is herein above directed concerning the original trust fund established for her benefit; and if at the decease of either of my children, without issue him or her surviving, and without any testamentary disposition or appointment of the capital of his or her trust fund, there should be no brother, nor sister, nor issue of a deceased brother or sister then living, the said trustees shall dispose of the said capital in the same manner as is hereinafter directed concerning the disposition of my estate in case of the decease of all my children, and all their issue in my life time. But if at the division of my estate into shares as above directed, the whole property set apart for the share of my son William Amory Prescott, exclusive of his reversionary interest in his mother's trust, should not equal in value the sum of fifty-five thousand dollars, so as to give him, after setting apart his said trust fund of fifty thousand dollars, a sum of five thousand dollars, at least, in immediate possession, independently of any advance he may have had from me in my life time, my will is that, in this event, the said trust fund shall be so far diminished during his mother's life, that he may receive in immediate possession the said sum of five thousand dollars, or its equivalent; and I direct my executor or administrator, to pay or transfer that amount to him for his own use, and to pay or transfer the balance only of his share of the said remaining property to the said trustees to hold for his benefit during his mother's life, and that at her decease so much of his reversionary interest in the trust fund reserved for the benefit of his mother as may be needful shall be added to his trust fund, so as to make the same thereafter of the full value of fifty thousand dollars, to be held in trust for him during his life, and to be disposed of at his decease, in the same manner as is above provided.

Twentieth Item: – Subject to the foregoing trusts for the benefit of my wife and children during their respective lives, I give, devise and bequeath all the residue and remainder of my estate, real and personal, including the reversion of the trust fund set apart for my wife during her life, to my three children above named, and their heirs, for their own use; to be divided between them in such manner that each of my children, if all shall survive me, may have so much of my estate as, with the addition of the trust fund established for his or her benefit, shall constitute one full third thereof; and in case of the decease of either of them in my lifetime, leaving lawful issue him or her surviving; and living at my decease, I give, devise and bequeath the share which said deceased child would have taken, or would have had the use of, if living, to his or her issue, equally among those in equal degree, children in all cases taking by representation the share of their deceased parent; but in case my child so dying should leave no lawful issue, or such issue should not be living at my decease, I give, devise and bequeath his or her said share to his or her surviving brothers, or brother and sister, or brother, or sister only, as the case may be and the lawful issue of any brother or sister deceased, such issue taking by representation the share of the deceased parent. And in case my wife should not survive me, then all the property which might otherwise have been seen apart to form the trust fund for her benefit is to be distributed immediately to and among my said children, and the issue of any child deceased standing in the place of the deceased parent, saving and reserving only the several trust funds for each of my children out of their respective shares as above provided. And in case all of my children and their issue who may survive me should afterwards die in the lifetime of my said wife, and any of the trust funds established for the benefit of my children, or any other of the trust property aforesaid should remain in the hands of the trustees above named, and their successors in said trust, in such event, upon and after the decease in my wife's lifetime of the longest liver of the said children and of their issue, the said trustees shall from time to time, by quarterly or other convenient terms of payment, pay over to my said wife, during her life, upon her own sole and separate order or receipt, notwithstanding any future coverture, the whole net income of all the trust property so remaining in their hands, to whichsoever of the several trust funds aforesaid the same may belong, excepting so far as the same may have been other-wise lawfully appointed by the last will and testament, or other instru-ment in the nature thereof, of either of my said children, in cases where such testamentary disposition would be effectual under the fore-going provisions; and in case all my children and their issue should

die in my lifetime, my wife surviving me, in that event, I devise and
bequeath all my property and estate to the trustees beforementioned,
and their successors in said trust, to hold and manage the same in
trust for my wife during her life, with like powers of sale, investment
and reinvestment as are above given in relation to the particular fund
established for her benefit, and to pay over in like manner to her the
whole net income thereof during her life; and upon the decease of my
said wife, none of my said children or of their issue her surviving,
whether they have died in my lifetime or afterwards, the said trustees
shall assign, transfer and pay over one-half part, not exceeding eighty
thousand dollars of all the trust property remaining in their hands, and
not otherwise effectually disposed of by any last will and testament, or
instrument in the nature thereof, of either of my said children, and
if said half should exceed eighty thousand dollars, then they shall assign, transfer and pay over the amount of eighty thousand dollars, to
such person or persons in such manner and upon such limitations, as
my said wife by her last will and testament, or by any instrument in
the nature thereof which, notwithstanding any future coverture, she
is hereby expressly empowered to make, may give, direct, limit or appoint the same; and in default of such testamentary appointment,
they shall assign, transfer and pay over the said half part of the said
trust property, or the said amount of eighty thousand dollars thereof,
as the case may be, to the person or persons who at the time of her
decease would be entitled by law as her nearest of kin to succeed to
her property had she died unmarried and intestate on that day; and
all the residue of said trust property they shall in like manner assign,
transfer and pay over to the person or persons who would at the same
time be entitled by law, as my nearest of kin, to succeed to my property had I died intestate on the same day; and in like manner if neither
my wife, nor either of my children, nor any issue of either of them
should survive me, in that event, I give eighty thousand dollars to my
wife's nearest of kin living at my decease, and the residue of my estate
to my nearest of kin.

Twenty-first Item: – Having entire confidence in the ability and integrity of my friends herein named as trustees, I direct that no bond
shall be required of them for the faithful execution of their trusts; and
if either of them shall decline the trust, or die, resign, or be removed,
before the trusts shall be fully executed, I request the Judge of Probate
for the County in which this will shall be proved, upon the application
of the other trustee, or of any cestuique trust, to appoint in his stead
a suitable person to be a co-trustee, who shall be entirely acceptable
to the surviving or remaining trustee, and also to such of the cestuique

trusts as may be of age, such trustee, so appointed, to be exempted from giving bond according to law, if the surviving or remaining trustee, and all the cestuique trusts who are of age, shall assent thereto, and signify the same in writing to the Judge of Probate; and I direct such conveyances and assignments to be made by the trustee who shall decline, resign, or be removed, and by the remaining or surviving trustee to the new trustee, who shall be appointed, as shall vest the estate and property in him, jointly with the other trustee, to hold upon the trusts herein expressed, in like manner as if he had been named herein; and if both the trustees herein named should decline the trust, or die, resign, or be removed, before the trusts should be fully executed, I request that two suitable trustees may be appointed in their place, with like exemption from giving bonds as aforesaid, on the same conditions, my intention being, that there shall always be two trustees for the trusts herein created; and I hereby grant to the trustee or trustees, who shall be duly appointed, the same powers which have been granted to the trustees herein named; and I further order that one trustee, whether herein named, or hereafter appointed, shall not be answerable for the neglect, misdoings or default of another but each only for his own wilful negligence, act or default.

Twenty-second Item: – It is my intention herein that all real estate, which I may hereafter inherit, purchase, or acquire, and die seized of, shall pass by this will as if I were now possessed of the same.

Lastly: – I hereby revoke all former wills, by me made, and declare this only to be my last will and testament, written on four sheets of paper, and I appoint William H. Gardiner, of Boston, Esquire, sole executor thereof.

In testimony whereof I have written my name on each of the three sheets hereto annexed, in the margin and have hereunto set my hand and seal this fifth day of January in the year of our Lord one thousand eight hundred and fifty-four.

Signed, sealed, published and declared, by the said testator as and for his last will and testament, in presence of us, who, at his request and in his presence and in the presence of each other have hereunto subscribed our names, as attesting witnesses thereof

(s) Wm. H. Prescott

The following alterations being first made. *Interlined and inserted*

—1st sheet, the word "she"—3rd
sheet "three fourths of," "interest."
Altered—1st sheet, word "reversion"—2nd sheet, word "place"—
3rd sheet, "limitations"— also
1st sheet the word "three"
  (s) J. L. English
  (s) W. N. Davis
  (s) H. M. Aborn

This is a codicil to my will dated the fifth day of January eighteen
hundred and fifty-four, and hereto annexed.

First: – In addition to all devises, legacies and bequests, in my said
will, to or for the benefit of my eldest son Wm. Gardiner Prescott, I
release and acquit to him a debt of ten thousand dollars for moneys
lent or advanced to him to be used in business, for which I hold his
promissory note; and the same is not to be charged to him in estimating his share of my estate; anything in the nineteenth item of my
said will to the contrary notwithstanding; and in case the said debt
should be paid to me by my said son in my lifetime, I give to him the
sum of ten thousand dollars to his own use, in addition to the other
devises, legacies and bequests in my said will.

Second: – In respect to the trust fund created in my said will for the
benefit of my youngest son, William Amory Prescott, I direct that in
case of the decease of his mother in my lifetime, or if she should survive
me, then upon her decease, whensoever the same may happen, the said
trust fund for the benefit of my said youngest son shall be increased
from fifty thousand dollars mentioned in my said will to sixty thousand
dollars, to be held, managed and disposed of by the same trustees, in
the same manner, and upon the same trusts, as are named and declared
in my said will respecting the said fund of fifty thousand dollars.

Hereby ratifying and republishing my said will, except so far as it is
altered by this codicil, I declare this to be a codicil thereto, written
wholly on one sheet of paper.

In testimony whereof I have hereunto set my hand and seal this
fifteenth day of March in the year of our Lord eighteen hundred and
fifty-four.

Signed, sealed and published and   (s) Wm. II. Prescott
declared to be a codicil to the last
will and testament of the said
testator, in our presence, who at
his request, and in his presence

and in the presence of each other,
have hereunto subscribed our
names as the attesting witnesses
thereof.

(s) J. L. English
(s) W. N. Davis
(s) H. M. Aborn

This is a second codicil to my last will and testament, dated the fifth day of January, eighteen hundred and fifty-four and hereto annexed.

First: – The legacy of fifty dollars, given by the eighth item of my said will to Nathan Webster, is hereby increased to one hundred dollars.

Second: – The legacy of two hundred dollars, given by the sixth item of my said will to my cousin Harriet Prescott, is hereby increased to four hundred dollars, one half payable as soon as may be, the other half in one year after my decease.

Third: – The legacy of three hundred dollars, given by the ninth item of my said will to my reader J. Foster Kirk is to be paid to him as soon as may be after my decease; and I hereby give to him a further legacy of five hundred dollars, payable one-half in six months, and one-half in one year, after my decease; but both the said legacies of three hundred dollars and five hundred dollars are hereby made dependent upon the condition that the said legatee shall continue to be in my service, as reader, at the time of my decease.

Fourth: – Whereas by my said will I have devised and bequeathed, both real and personal estate, to George Ticknor and William Amory, and the survivor of them, to hold upon certain trusts therein declared, I now hereby nominate and appoint my son-in-law, James Lawrence, to be a third trustee thereof until the distribution of my estate into the particular trust funds mentioned in my said will, and thereafter to be a third trustee of each of the said funds, except that which is established for the benefit of my daughter Elizabeth, wife of the said Lawrence; and I do hereby devise and bequeath the same real and personal estate to the said Ticknor, Amory and Lawrence, the survivors and last survivors of them, and his heirs, executors and administrators, to hold and dispose of, upon the same trusts, and with the same powers, and according to the same limitations, and for the same uses and purposes as are declared, limited and appointed by my said will; except that the particular trust fund created for the benefit of my said daughter Elizabeth shall immediately upon the formation thereof be transferred to the said Ticknor and Amory to hold and manage the same separately from the said Lawrence, for the benefit of my said daughter, upon the trust heretofore declared concerning the same; and except, also, the other particulars in which the said trusts, powers, limitations, uses or purposes set forth in my said will may be revoked, altered or modified by this codicil; and it is not my intention by the appointment of such third trustee to make it imperative that there shall always be three trustees to execute any of the said trusts, two being in my judgement sufficient therefor; but in case of a vacancy, by death, resignation, or otherwise, the two surviving, or remaining trustees, may cause the same to be filled, or not, as they shall think best, taking care only that there shall always be two trustees capable of acting for each of the said trust funds, and that whenever a vacancy occurs, by the death, resignation, or otherwise, of one of the two, the survivor shall, as soon as may be, cause such vacancy to be filled; and successors in the said trust shall always be appointed in the manner provided in said will, and shall have all the powers given to the original trustees above-named.

Fifth: – Whereas, by the fifteenth item of my said will, a certain farm therein mentioned is devised to my eldest son, William Gardiner Prescott, in tail male, with remainders over, as therein set forth, now I do hereby revoke the said devise, and in lieu thereof, I devise the same farm to the abovenamed Ticknor, Amory and Lawrence, the survivors and last survivor of them, and his heirs, upon the trust nevertheless that during the life of my said son, the said trustees shall take the rents and profits thereof, and dispose of the same, in the same manner as is hereinafter provided concerning the income of the trust fund directed by my will, and by this codicil, to be formed for the benefit of my said son, with full liberty, however, to the said trustees, to permit my said son at their discretion, from time to time, and for so long a time as they may see fit to use and occupy the said farm rent free;—and upon and after the decease of my said son, they shall hold the fee of the said farm, to the use of his eldest son, and the heirs male of the body of this eldest son of my said son, with remainder to the second and other sons successively of my said son, and the heirs male of their bodies respectively forever, in tail male;—and in default or on failure of male issue of my said eldest son, I give the remainder in fee simple to my daughter Elizabeth and her heirs.

Sixth: – Whereas by the nineteenth item of my said will, I directed the formation of a particular trust fund of $25,000. only in amount for the benefit of my eldest son, William Gardiner Prescott, and a like fund of $50,000 in amount for the benefit of my youngest son, William

Amory Prescott, and by the effect of the same and of divers other items and clauses of my will, the residue of their respective shares of my estate, subject to the appropriation for the benefit of their mother, during her life, and their reversionary shares in the particular trust fund established for her benefit, and their shares and interests in other property, which might accrue to them respectively, from time to time, according to the provisions of my said will, upon the happening of the events therein mentioned, were to be conveyed, transferred, delivered, and paid over to my said sons respectively, for their own use, and as their own absolute property, now, in lieu thereof, I hereby provide and declare my will to be that the whole share of each of my sons, in my estate, including his share in the reversion of the particular trust fund established for the benefit of my wife, and whatsoever else, may at any time accrue and become payable to, or the property of my said sons, or either of them, under and by virtue of the provisions of my will, except moveables specifically bequeathed to them, and except as is hereinafter provided, shall be held in trust, for their benefit respectively, during their respective lives; and I hereby devise and bequeath the same to my trustees abovenamed, the said Ticknor, Amory and Lawrence to hold, manage and dispose of both principal and income during the lives of my said sons respectively, upon the same trusts, and in like manner, as is provided in my said will respecting the said particular trust funds of $25,000 and $50,000 except as may be otherwise directed in this codicil, concerning the disposition of either the principal or the income of the several increased trust funds, hereby created for the benefit of my said sons respectively. And whensoever, in my said will, I have directed my trustees to release, convey, deliver, or pay over any property other than rents, profits, interest and income to either of my said sons, I now order that instead thereof, they shall add the same to the trust fund held for his benefit; and that all his share, of rents, profits, interest or income shall be disposed of as hereinafter directed.

Seventh: – In respect to the net income of the particular trust fund held for the benefit of my said eldest son, William Gardiner Prescott, I direct that the same shall be paid over, by the trustees thereof, either to my said son, or to his wife, or to his children, any or either of them, according to the discretion of my said trustees; or that the same shall be otherwise appropriated, in such manner as my said trustees shall see fit, for the support and benefit of my said son and his family, during his life; and the property, composing the capital of said fund, at the decease of my said son, shall be disposed of according to his will, if any; and in default of a will, the same shall be disposed of in like manner as is directed in my will concerning the capital of the fund of $25,000 excepting that whatsoever may accrue thereby to my youngest son William Amory Prescott is to be added to the trust fund held for his benefit, instead of being delivered, or paid over to him for his own use.

Eighth: – In respect to the income of the trust fund held for the benefit of my youngest son William Amory Prescott, the same is to be paid over to him at the times, and in the manner, directed in my said will; and in respect to the property, composing the capital of said fund at the decease of my said son, the same is to be disposed of as follows: —if my said son shall hereafter marry, and leave either a widow, or lawful issue him surviving, the whole of the said property shall be disposed of as he by his last will and testament may direct; but, in such case, should he die intestate, the whole property shall go to his widow and children, or if there be no children, to his widow, brother and sister, or other heirs under the statute of distribution and descents, in the same manner, and proportion, as if the said property were vested in him, and in his own possession at his decease;—but in case my said son should die unmarried, or should not leave at his decease, either a widow, or lawful issue him surviving, in such case one-half only, in value, of the said property shall be disposed of, as he, by his last will and testament may direct; and the other half shall go in the same manner as is provided by my will, respecting the fifty thousand dollar trust fund, in the event of his dying without issue and without a testamentary appointment; excepting, that whatsoever may accrue, by any of the foregoing provisions to my eldest son, William Gardiner Prescott, is to be added to the trust fund held for his benefit, instead of being delivered, or paid over to him, for his own use. And so, if my said youngest son should leave no will, and no widow, or lawful issue, him surviving, the whole of said property is to go as is provided by my will, respecting his trust fund there mentioned,—in the event of his dying, without issue and without a will, excepting as aforesaid, concerning what may thereby accrue to my said eldest son.

Ninth: – In ascertaining the shares of my children, respectively, as provided in my said will, and also in ascertaining and setting apart the amount or proportion thereof, which is to be held in trust for their benefit, I now declare my will to be, as follows. By a former codicil dated the fifteenth day of March eighteen hundred and fifty-four, I have released to my said eldest son a debt of ten thousand dollars, therein described, as witnessed by his promissory note for that sum, but erroneously so described, inasmuch as said debt is in fact witnessed by his two promissory notes of five thousand dollars each. That release

I hereby confirm; the same being grounded on the consideration, that I have heretofore advanced to, or paid for, each of my other children, sums not charged to them as an advance, but equal in amount to the debt so released. I have further advanced, or become liable for, divers sums, on account of my said eldest son, to be by him used in the business of the late firm of Henshaw and Prescott, amounting in the whole to the sum of twenty-five thousand dollars, or thereabouts, for which I hold the notes and securities of said house, now insolvent, proveable as a debt against their assets, and entitled to such dividends as may be paid thereon. In respect to this debt, my will is, that after crediting whatever may be received thereon from the assets of Prescott and Henshaw, and whatsoever else may otherwise be paid, or recovered, on this account from either of the partners, the balance unpaid, beyond the sum of eight thousand dollars which I hereby give up and release to my said son, whether said balance be discharged by the effect of the insolvent law, or not, is to be treated as an advance to my said eldest son, to be repaid out of his share of my estate, but without interest, and in manner following,—in case his mother should survive me, five thousand dollars of the said advance, should so much remain unpaid beyond the eight thousand dollars above released, shall constitute a charge against his reversionary interest in the particular trust fund established for her benefit, and the payment thereof out of his share of my estate, shall be deferred until the final distribution of said trust fund at his mother's decease, and the said principal sum, without interest is then to be taken out of his reversionary share of said fund, and the residue, if any, of my said advance to my said son, is to constitute a charge upon, and be taken out of his share of my estate, at the first distribution thereof; but if my wife should not survive me, or should die before the first distribution of my estate, in that case, the whole of my said advance to my said son, beyond the sum of eight thousand dollars above released, is to constitute a charge upon and be taken out of his share of my estate, at the first distribution thereof; and all the residue of my said eldest son's share of my estate, is in either case, to be held in trust for his benefit as above provided. And in respect to my youngest son William Amory Prescott, I direct that when his share of my estate shall be ascertained, at the first distribution thereof, the sum of ten thousand dollars shall be paid to him in money or its equivalent, for his own use, provided his mother be not then living; but if his mother be then living, five thousand dollars only shall be paid to him for his own use, out of his share, at the first distribution of my estate, and five thousand dollars more, shall be paid to him, in like manner, at his mother's decease, out of his reversionary share in the trust fund established for her benefit; and all the residue of my said youngest son's share of my estate is, in either case, to be held in trust for him as above provided.

Hereby republishing my said will and the former codicil thereto, and satisfying and confirming the same in all particulars, except in so far, as it is by this instrument revoked, altered or modified, I declare this to be a second codicil to my said will, wholly written on one sheet of paper bearing my signature thereon.

In witness whereof I have hereunto set my hand and seal, at Boston, this eighteenth day of December in the year of our Lord eighteen hundred and fifty-five.

Signed, sealed, published and   (s) Wm. H. Prescott
declared by the testator to be a
codicil to his last will and
testament, before us, the subscribing witnesses, who in his presence,
and in the presence of each other,
and at his request, have hereunto
subscribed our names, as the attesting witnesses thereof.

The following interlineations
being first made—"beyond the sum
of eight thousand dollars which I
hereby give up and release to my
said son; whether said balance be"
—"should so much remain unpaid
beyond the eight thousand dollars
above released"—"if any"—
"beyond the sum of eight thousand
dollars above released."—
"Whether" being erased.

(s) J. L. English
(s) H. M. Aborn
(s) Wm. Nye Davis

This is a third codicil to my will dated the fifth day of January A.D. 1854 and hereto annexed.

First: – Whereas it may be doubtful whether the provisions of my said will and former codicil concerning my mansion house in Beacon Street, in Boston, as therein expressed may be understood to embrace the stable in rear of said house, and constituting a part of the same lot, but not of late used by me, in connection with my said house, now for the removal of all doubts in the premises, I hereby declare my intention to be, that my wife shall have the same use and control during her life of the said stable, as of the mansion house itself, without paying any additional rent therefor, and that the said stable shall be deemed to be an appurtenance of the said house, and that all the provisions of my said will and former codicils, relating to the disposition of said house, shall be construed in like manner, and with the same effect, as if the said stable had been therein expressly mentioned in connection therewith.

Second: – In regard to the bequest to my wife of household furniture, plate and wearing apparel, by the fourteenth item of my said will, my intention is to bequeath to her, and I hereby do bequeath to her for her own use and disposal, not only household furniture properly so called, but all pictures, busts and moveables of every description, in either of my dwelling houses, except such as are otherwise specifically bequeathed by the same, or some other clause of my said will, or by any codicil thereto; not intending, however, hereby to revoke or alter the former provisions of my will regarding a distribution of my wine, or the disposition of my books and manuscripts, or any specific bequest therein contained to any other person than my said wife, and not intending to include in the term moveables, any moneys, or securities for money, or evidences of property, or other papers of pecuniary value.

Third: – Whereas by the effect of my said will and former codicil, the whole share of my eldest son William Gardiner Prescott, in my estate is directed to be held in trust for his benefit during his life, and this provision was founded upon the consideration of his liability for the debts of the late mercantile house of which he was a member, and whereas my said son has since obtained a full discharge from his said liability, I now direct that in respect to his share in my estate, the provisions of my said will and codicil shall be so far altered and modified, that two-thirds only of his said share, shall be held upon the trusts therein declared for his benefit during his life, and that the remaining one-third part thereof, shall be paid and delivered to him, as his own absolute property; that is to say, after the formation of the trust fund directed by my said will and codicils to be formed for the benefit of my wife, in case she survives me; one-third of his share of the remaining estate, not included in said trust fund for my wife, shall be paid and delivered to him so soon as shall be convenient in the distribution and settlement of my estate, and at or after the decease of his mother, whensoever the same may happen, one-third of his share of the property set apart for her trust fund, shall be paid and delivered to him so soon as shall be convenient in the distribution of the capital of said trust fund; and in case my wife shall not survive me, one-third of my said son's whole share of my estate shall be paid and delivered to him so soon as shall be found convenient in the distribution and settlement of my estate; but the remaining two-thirds of his share of my estate before and after the distribution of his mother's trust fund, and also in case no such fund should be formed, shall be held in trust for his benefit during his life, and both the capital and income thereof, shall be in all respects managed and disposed of during his life, and at his decease by the same trustees, and in the same manner, as is directed by my said will and former codicils, concerning his whole share in my estate. But in respect to the share of my daughter Elizabeth, my will is, that one-fourth part only of her share in my estate distributable in her mother's lifetime, and one-fourth part only of the property held in trust for her mother, and distributable at her mother's decease, shall be paid over and transferred to my said daughter as her own absolute property, and that the remaining three-fourths parts of her said share shall be held in trust for her benefit during her life, and that both the capital and the income of her said trust fund shall be in all respects managed and disposed of during her life, and at her decease, by the same trustees and in the same manner as is directed by my said will and former codicils.

And in respect to the share of my son William Amory Prescott, my will is, that ten thousand dollars only thereof shall be paid or delivered to him as his own absolute property, namely five thousand dollars as soon after my decease as may be convenient in the settlement of my estate, and five thousand dollars at the decease of his mother and the distribution of the trust fund formed for her benefit, and in case of her death before me, or before the formation of such trust fund, the whole ten thousand dollars shall be paid and delivered to him, as soon as may be convenient in the settlement of my estate; but all the residue of the share of my said son, is in either case, to be held in trust for his benefit during his life, and the capital and income thereof shall be managed and disposed of during his life, and at his decease, by the same trustees, and in the same manner, as is directed by my said will and former codicils.

And whereas by the effect of my will and former codicils, a difference is made in the disposition of what may accrue to my daughter, and what may accrue to either of my sons from the division of a trust fund held for the benefit of either of my children, who shall die intestate and without issue, now for the purpose of placing my sons and my daughter on an equality in that respect, and to remove all doubts concerning my intention in respect to the disposition of the property held in trust for either of my children so dying intestate and without issue, I hereby declare my will to be as follows: Whensoever either of my children for whom property is held in trust under the provisions of my will, shall die intestate in respect to such property, and without issue him or her surviving, all the property so held in trust for the child so dying, shall be equally apportioned between his or her mother, brother and sister, or mother and brothers as the case may be, and the issue of brother or sister deceased, standing in the place of and taking the share of the deceased parent; and whatsoever shall thus accrue to the issue of one of my children deceased, shall be paid and delivered to such issue in discharge of the trust to that extent; but whatsoever shall thus accrue to my wife, or daughter or either of my sons, shall not be paid over and delivered to them or either of them, but shall be transferred and added to the trust funds held for them respectively, and shall be managed and disposed of both capital and income, in all respects, as is directed concerning their original respective trust funds.

Fourth: – Whereas since the date of my last preceding codicil I have purchased from William C. Stimpson and George Linder assignees of the joint and separate estate of Henshaw and Prescott, all the interest of my said son William Gardiner Prescott in the estate bequeathed by his late grandmother Hannah R. Amory to my wife Susan, and her issue, and all his interest in the furniture and other chattels then situated in his house numbered Forty in Chestnut Street, Boston, subject to a certain mortgage thereon to John A. Lowell, all which property is more particularly described in the deed of said Stimpson and Linder to me, now I hereby bequeath to my said son, as a particular legacy, whatsoever property I may hold at my decease acquired by my said purchase from his assignees, so that the same may not be reckoned as part of my general estate in estimating the shares of my children therein, but is to be regarded as an additional bequest to my said eldest son;—and hereby confirming all former releases of claims against my said son for advances in my lifetime, I now release to him in addition thereto whatsoever balance may remain unpaid on the debt of the said firm of Henshaw and Prescott, which would have constituted a charge, by the effect of my said will and former codicils, on my said son's share of my general estate.

Fifth: – I hereby revoke the several clauses of my said will and former codicils which relate to the old family farm at Pepperell, and in lieu thereof I now devise the said farm to the said Ticknor, Amory and Lawrence, my trustees abovenamed, the survivors and last survivor of them and their and his heirs, but upon trust to preserve and effectuate all contingent estates and uses hereinafter created; that is to say, should my eldest son William Gardiner Prescott survive me, they shall hold the said farm to the use of my said eldest son and the heirs male of his body forever, successively in tail male, meaning that the same shall always descend to the eldest lineal male heir exclusively, in right of primogeniture, and according to the course of descent in tail male by the common law of England, so long as the entailment shall remain unbroken, by any act adequate to defeat the same, by the Statutes of this Commonwealth, and in case my said eldest son should die in my lifetime leaving male issue me surviving, the said trustees shall hold the said farm to the use of his eldest son me surviving, and the heirs male of his body forever, in tail male successively, according to the like law of primogeniture, and course of descent as aforesaid, with remainder to the said trustees to hold the same to the use of the second and other sons successively of my said eldest son, and the heirs male of their bodies respectively forever, according to the same law and course of descent; and in default, or on failure at any time of male issue of my said eldest son; I devise the said farm to the same trustees abovenamed for the contingent uses following; that is to say, if at my decease, my second son, William Amory Prescott, shall be living in this country, or if being abroad he shall return to this country, within one year after my decease, and if in either case he shall within one year after my decease declare in writing under his hand by some suitable instrument deposited for record in the Registry of the same Court of Probate wherein my will shall be proved, his intention bona fide to make this country thereafter his usual place of abode, in such case, upon and after the making and depositing of such instrument in manner aforesaid, the said trustees shall hold the said farm to the use of my said second son and the heirs of his body forever, in tail male successively, according to the like law of primogeniture, and course of descent as aforesaid; and in default of the performance of said condition, and also in case of its performance, in default; or on failure thereafter of male issue of my said second son, the said trustees shall take and hold the said farm to the use of my daughter Elizabeth and her heirs in fee simple.

Sixth: – The furniture of my house at Pepperell and all stock, farming utensils and other chattels appertaining to said farm, I bequeath to the person in whom the use or equitable estate above devised shall first vest, requesting that the same, so far as may be consistent with the free use thereof by the owner for the time being, may be transmitted to succeeding owners of the estate.

Seventh: – I hereby declare that in adding James Lawrence by a former codicil to the trustees named in the original will, my intention was, and if not already sufficiently implied, I now provide that he, and any successor to him in the trust, who may be appointed in the manner therein directed, shall be exempted from the giving of bonds to the Judge of Probate, in like manner, as the original trustees and their successors, are exempted in express terms.

Hereby republishing my said will, and the former codicils thereto, and notifying and confirming the same in all particulars, except in so far, as it is by this instrument revoked, altered or modified, I declare this to be a third codicil to my said will, wholly written on one sheet of paper bearing my signature thereon.

In witness whereof I have hereunto set my hand and seal, at Boston this twenty-fifth day of March in the year of our Lord eighteen hundred and fifty-seven.

Signed, sealed, published and de-   (s) Wm. H. Prescott
clared by the testator to be a codicil
to his last will and testament before us, the subscribing witnesses
also at his request, in his presence
and in the presence of each other,
have hereunto subscribed our
names as the attesting witnesses
thereof. Item Sixth being written
in the margin before signing.
"Now" also being interlined.
  (s) J. L. English
  (s) Wm. Nye Davis
  (s) H. M. Aborn

This is a fourth codicil to my will dated the fifth day of January eighteen hundred and fifty-four.

Whereas my said will, as originally framed, directed that, out of the share in my estate of my eldest son William Gardiner Prescott, twenty-five thousand dollars should be retained and held in trust for him during his life; and that out of the share of my youngest son William Amory Prescott, fifty thousand dollars should be so retained and held in trust for him during his life; but, by the second codicil thereto added, it was directed that the whole share of each of my said sons should, with certain exceptions, be so held in trust; and afterwards, by a third codicil, these provisions were again so far modified, that two-thirds only of my said eldest son's share are to be held in trust for his benefit, and that, of my said youngest son's share, ten thousand dollars only is to be paid over to him at the times therein mentioned,

and the whole residue is to be held in trust for him during his life;—
and whereas the causes which led to the said provisions in regard to the
share of my eldest son have since been effectually removed,—

Now I do hereby alter and modify the said provisions as follows:—

So far as they relate to and affect the share of my said eldest son;
my will now is, that no part of the same shall be retained and held in
trust for his benefit, but that the whole of his said share (subject only
to the provisions concerning a trust fund for his mother, distributable
at her decease,) shall be transferred and paid to my said son, absolutely,
for his own use, and I devise and bequeath the same to him and his
heirs accordingly.

But, so far as the said former provisions relate to and affect the
share of my said youngest son, the same are to remain in full force and
without alteration.

Hereby ratifying and republishing my said will, and the former
codicils thereto, in all other particulars, except in so far as it is by
this instrument revoked, altered, or modified, I declare this to be a
fourth codicil to my said will, wholly written on one sheet of paper,
bearing my signature thereon, and annexed to the said will and former
codicils.— In witness whereof I have hereunto set my hand and seal
this twenty-first day of August, in the year of our Lord eighteen hundred and fifty-eight.

Signed, sealed, published, and   (s) W. H. Prescott
declared to be, by the testator, a
codicil to his last will and testament, before us the subscribing
witnesses, who, at his request,
and in his presence, and in the
presence of each other, have
hereunto set our names as the
attesting witnesses thereof.
"Dollars" interlined.
  (s) J. L. English
  (s) Wm. Nye Davis
  (s) H. M. Aborn

1. Written January 5, 1854, this document is accompanied by codicils dated
March 15, 1854, December 18, 1855, March 25, 1857, and August 21, 1858.

2. Her first name, seldom used, was spelled variously as Cathcrine and
Catharine.

3. Both swords now constitute an honored exhibit of the Massachusetts
Historical Society.

Index

Accounting: house repairs, 234–36
Acknowledgments, x–xv
Adams, John Quincy: described, 58n3
Adams, Sir William: oculist, 15, 16n2; advice of, 23; fee of, 23; mentioned, 16
Agreement: for reader-secretary, 241, 242n2, 251; with Robert Carter, 241; with John Foster Kirk, 251
Alamán, Lucas: books by, 281–82; described, 303; mentioned, 135, 137n2
Alison, Archibald: historian, 291, 291n1
Allibone, S. Austin: letters to, 347, 348–49; mentioned, 348n1
American Philosophical Society: presentation copy, 211; mentioned, 129, 281
American Stationers' Company: publisher, 115n1; mentioned, 121, 122n1
Amory, Charles: described, 64, 65n2; mentioned, 287, 287n7
Amory, Susan, 30, 31n1. *See also* Prescott, Susan Amory
Amory, William: travel companion, 77–78; postscript by, 79; trustee, 404ff.; mentioned, 64, 65n3, 107, 262, 288
Aspinwall, Colonel Thomas: literary agent, 107n3, 112n1, 140, 201–2, 221–22, 222n1; letters to, 112, 204–5; letters from, 156–58, 201–2, 209–10, 221–22, 238–39, 244–45, 321; commission, 157, 158n1; son, 157, 158n2; on copyright, 321; leaves London, 337; mentioned, 159, 244, 317, 342
Asylum for the Blind: bequest, 90,

91n2; activity, 142–43; mentioned, 71, 72–73
Azores: described, 5–11; government, 9

Bache, Franklin: letter to, 129
Baltimore: described, 59
Bancroft, George: letters to, 46–47, 56, 76–77, 88–89, 101–3, 108–9, 292–93, 342–43, 389; historian, 47n1, 171; translator, 56, 56n3; article by, 76–77, 77n1; books by, 89, 89n2, 96, 182, 186; reviews *Ferdinand and Isabella*, 121, 122n2; encouragement by, 134; abridgment by, 176; letters of introduction by, 272; letters from, 272, 387; dinner, 286, 287n2; mentioned, vi, 123, 128, 129n2, 209n2, 320
Beckwith, Dr. John: presentation copy, 243
Bentley, Richard: publisher, 112, 113n2; letters to, 117–18, 139–41, 181–82, 268, 285–86, 305, 317–18, 337–38, 363–64; opinion concerning, 129; seeks book, 158, 159n2, 285, 286n1; letters from, 158–59, 249, 278–79, 306, 341–42, 395; at mercy of, 202; schedule for *Conquest of Peru*, 239, 240n1; on copyright, 306, 306nn1,2, 341–42, 342n1; declines proposition, 321; offer declined, 393; enraged, 394n1, 395, 395n2; mentioned, vi, 137, 193, 209, 232, 351–52, 366n1
Bethune, George Washington: presentation copy, 243, 243n6; mentioned, 275
Biographers: named, vi
Books: purchased, 28, 53, 54, 73–74, 81–83; received, 60, 66, 67, 69, 79, 103; ordered, 60–61, 66, 68–69, 70–

Books (*continued*)
  71, 71n2, 75, 80, 84, 85, 87, 92–94,
  95, 97–98, 99–100, 104
Boston Athenaeum: purchases by, 55;
  supported, 322; bequest, 403; mentioned, 50, 50n1, 84, 85n1, 88
Boston Daily Advertiser, 119n2
Boston Public Library: cooperation
  of, xi
Bowen, Francis: editor, 264; letter to,
  275–76; mentioned, 69n
Boys' Asylum: manager, 38–39; mentioned, 39n1
Bradford, Thomas G.: borrows book,
  113; letter to, 113; mentioned,
  113n1
Brevoort, Henry: friend, 191, 192n4;
  presentation copies, 231, 242
Brooks, John: governor of Massachusetts, 14, 14n2
Brown, James: letter to, 174; mentioned, vi, 174n1, 182
Bulfinch, Thomas: book by, 359n2
Bunker Hill Monument Association:
  fair, 160–61, 164n7; mentioned,
  89n4, 90
Burton, Alexander: kinsman, 167n1;
  aid by, 336; letter to, 336–37; mentioned, vi, 284
Busson: reader-secretary, 30
Butler, Caleb: book by, 250, 250n2;
  letter to, 250; mentioned, 250n1

Cabot, Dr. Samuel: letter to, 219;
  mentioned, 219n1
Calderón de la Barca, Ángel: Spanish
  diplomat, 127, 128nn2,3; books for,
  128; presentation copy, 243; letter
  to, 301–3; mentioned, 133, 135, 137,
  153
Calderón de la Barca, Frances: letters
  to, 159–64, 338–39; letters from
  172–73, 326–28; life in Mexico, 172–
  73; books by, 196, 357; life in Madrid, 326–28; politics in Spain, 326–
  28; mentioned, vi, 164n1
Calhoun, J. Edward: presentation
  copy, 243, 243n7
Carey, Henry: presentation copy,
  231, 232n4, 243

Carlisle, Earl of: guest of, 296–97;
  mentioned, 184n1. *See also* Morpeth, Lord
Carlisle, Lord. *See* Carlisle, Earl of
Carlyle, Thomas, 293, 294n3
Carroll, Charles: visited, 59, 60n1
Carter, Robert: agreement with, 241;
  reader-secretary, 241, 242n1
Catherwood, Frederick, 203, 204n3,
  226
Channing, William Ellery: letter to,
  130–31; clergyman, 131n1; mentioned, vi, viii
Charles the Fifth: contract for, 355–
  56; publication day, 369; opinion
  concerning, 369, 377; mentioned,
  370
Circourt, Count Adolphe de: reviews
  by, 140, 141n3, 221, 221n1; articles
  by, 221, 221n1; letter from, 221; suggestion of, 221, 221n2; mentioned,
  284
Clay, Henry: described, 57, 58n2; mentioned, 288
Clergymen: named, vi
"Club": publication by, 31; nature,
  31n3; meetings, 45, 123, 124; wine
  for, 197; mentioned, 128
Club-Room: periodical, 31; poems
  sought for, 32; article in, 33; publication, 33; promotion, 34; demise,
  35n2
Codicils: first, 416–17; second, 417–22;
  third, 422–27; fourth, 427–28
Cogswell, Joseph Green: letters to,
  138–39, 240–41; presentation copies,
  231, 242; mentioned, 47, 48n6, 56,
  109, 139nn1,2
Collis, James: clerk-secretary, 7
Commonplace book: maxims in, 35–
  36; religious beliefs, 36–37; course
  of studies, 37; memorandum, 38;
  studies, 40; musings, 40–41
Composition: maxims on, 35–36; rules
  regarding, 36n3
Congress: described, 58n3
Conquest of Mexico: writing initiated,
  145n5; American contract for, 201,
  201n3; Aspinwall negotiates publication, 201–2; publication, 202–4,
  206–7; contract for, 205n1; critical

readings, 206, 206n1; index, 206; English edition, 209; income from, 211, 211n3; American edition, 211n1; opinions, 212–13, 214–15, 218–19, 221; compared with *Ferdinand and Isabella*, 213; popularity, 213, 213n1; physical appearance, 220; French translation, 221, 221n3; as standard, 238, 239, 239n3; mentioned, 237

Conquest of Peru: publication, 237–38, 238n1; stereotype plates, 239; opinions, 242, 245–47, 258–59; presentation copies, 242–43; publication day, 243n1; English edition, 244, 249, 249n1; Dutch edition, 252, 253n4; German edition, 263; Spanish editions, 263, 314, 315nn4,5

Contracts: for books, 110n2; with Bentley, 113n3, 209, 210n1; with Little, Brown and Co., 138n2; terms, 201, 201n3, 209, 210n1; for *Conquest of Mexico*, 205n1, 209, 210n1; for *Miscellanies*, 222n1; for *Conquest of Peru*, 237–38, 238n2, 239nn1,2; with Phillips, Sampson and Company, 343–44n2

Cooke, Robert: letter from, 204–5

Cooper, Sir Astley Paston: surgeon, 15, 16n1; fee, 23

Copyright law: in America, 147–48, 152–53

Correspondents: English, vi; French, vi; German, vi; Italian, vi; Mexican, vi; Spanish, vi

Course of studies, 37

Cumplido, Ignacio: presentation copy, 242; publisher, 243n2

Dexter, Edward: nephew, 257, 258n4

Dexter, Elizabeth Prescott, 60, 192. *See also* Prescott, Catherine Elizabeth

Dexter, Franklin: articles by, 31, 31n5, 34; as critic, 36; lawyer, 280; bequest, 402

Dexter, George M.: accounting by, 234–36: mentioned, 236n1

Dexter, Gordon: nephew, 271, 272n4; mentioned, 278

Dickens, Charles: letter to, 196–97; mentioned, vi, 197n1

Draper, Lyman C.: letter to, 378–79; books by, 379nn2,3; mentioned, 379n1

Dufief, Nicolas Gouïn: author, 7, 12n4

Dunham, Samuel Astley: historian, 130–31, 131n2

DuPonceau, Peter Stephen: presentation copy, 211; letter to, 211–12; mentioned, vi, 211, 211n2

Dwight, Henry: friend, 44, 45n1

Eberty, Dr. H.: letter from, 263–64; translator, 263–64, 264n1

Edgeworth, Maria: novelist, 144n3; admired by, 245–47; letter from, 245–47; mentioned, vi

Edinburgh Review: read, 42

Eliot, Samuel Atkins: historian, 240–41, 241n1; books by, 268, 268n1, 270

Eliot, William Havard: friend, 44, 45n1

Elliott, Dr. Samuel Mackenzie: oculist, 187–89, 189n1; presentation copy, 243

Ellis, George E.: letter to, 379–82; mentioned, vi

English, James Lloyd: reader-secretary, 46n2, 47n3

Engravings: ordered, 84–85, 98, 99nn3,4

Everett, Alexander Hill: letters to, 48–49, 51–53; letter from, 49–50; book by, 56, 56n2; mentioned, vi, 49n1, 53, 135

Everett, Edward: article by, 35, 35n1; letters to, 54, 62–63, 368; politics, 90, 91n4, 98–99, 103, 103n6; assistance of, 166n3, 179, 180n4; described, 180, 335; diplomat, 209–10, 210n3; president of Harvard, 262, 262n1; letter from, 293; mentioned, vi, 400

Expenses: statements of, 22–30, 318, 333

Farre, Dr. John Richard: physician, 15, 16n1; fee, 23

Fay, Theodore Sedgwick: letter to, 212; opinion of Harpers, 227; mentioned, vi, 212nn1,3

Felton, Cornelius Conway: letter from, 101; mentioned, vi, 101n1

Ferdinand and Isabella: opinions, 107, 111–12, 131n2, 142, 156, 192; plans for, 107; publication discussed, 108–9; production, 109, 110, 111, 113–14, 114–15, 117, 117n3, 119–20, 121; proofs, 112; preliminary copy, 120; publication day, 122, 123n1, 124; promotion, 122–23; sale, 125; errata, 125–26, 126n2, 127; American editions, 126, 126n1, 127, 127n2, 142, 142n1, 146–47, 147n1; English editions, 140, 141nn2,4, 158, 159n1, 181–82, 222, 278, 285; Italian edition, 155, 155n2, 252; inspires poetic drama, 173; as standard, 203, 205, 207; proposition concerning, 216–17, 217n1; offered to Harpers, 220, 220n1

Fernández de Navarrete, Martín: assistance of, 50, 50n4, 136, 144, 145n1; letter to, 144–45; mentioned, vi

Fisher, Dr. J. C.: article by, 35, 35n1

Folsom, Charles: letters to, 110, 111, 113–14, 114–15, 115–17, 119–20, 120–21, 121, 121–22, 124, 125–26, 126, 127–28, 128–29, 137–38, 141–42, 197, 207, 240, 358–59, 389–90, 392; reputation as editor, 114n2; paid, 207, 240, 240n1; mentioned, vi, 110, 110n1, 197n1

Folsom, George: book by, 203, 204n4; mentioned, 204, 204n2

Ford, Richard: scholar, 142, 142n2; medal, 158, 181; letters from, 192–93, 227–28, 304, 354–55; invitation by, 193, 193n4; book by, 227–28, 228n1; acknowledges gift, 304, 354; prospective article by, 354–55, 355n3; mentioned, vi, 277, 303, 310

French, Benjamin Franklin: historian, 216, 216n1

Fribourg: servant, 30, 30n5

Frisbie, Levi: Harvard faculty, 4, 5n5

Gales and Seaton: letter to, 224; publishers, 224n1

Gallatin, Albert: visited, 190; ethnologist, 217–18, 218n1; letters to, 217–18, 253–55; mentioned, vi

Gallenga, Antonio. *See* Mariotti, Luigi

García Icazbalceta, Joaquín: letter to, 349–50; book by, 350n1; mentioned, vi

Gardiner, John S. J.: dinner, 4, 5n6; mentioned, 19

Gardiner, William Howard: prospects, 4, 5n6; critic, 36; reviews *Ferdinand and Isabella*, 114, 114n1, 121, 122n3, 124; letters to, 118–19, 206, 294–95, 299, 394; corrects *Conquest of Mexico*, 206, 206n1; letter from, 212–13; opinion of *Conquest of Mexico*, 212–13; on style, 213; gifts for, 299; bequest, 402; executor, 415; mentioned, vi, 115

Gayangos, Frances de: letter from, 262–63; mentioned, vi, 263n1

Gayangos, Pascual de: letters from, 149–51, 309–10; offers aid, 149–51; assistance of, 151n1, 152n4, 167, 383; letters to, 167–70, 177–80, 313–15; book by, 168, 170n2, 178; in Africa, 262–63; in England, 309–10; translator, 314, 315n3; mentioned, vi, 182, 227, 327, 354, 388n2

Gibbon, Edward: historian, 41, 41n3; inspired by, 199

Goodhue, Jonathan: letters to, 72–73, 106; presentation copy, 242; mentioned, vi, 73n1, 128

Gray, Francis Calley: friend, 43, 44n8; politics, 52, 90, 90n3; death, 371–72; mentioned, 109

Gray, John Chipman: shares expenses, 24; article by, 34; mentioned, 15, 21

Greenwood, Francis William Pitt: letter to, 33; article by, 33, 33n2; mentioned, 33n1

Griffin, George: friend, 191, 192n7

Griswold, Rufus Wilmot: presentation copy, 243, 243n4; letter to, 309

Hall, Jonathan Prescott: presentation copy, 243, 243n3

Halleck, Fitz-Greene: biography of, viii; letter to, 32; mentioned, vi, 32n1

Hamilton, John Church: presentation copy, 231, 232n3, 243; letter from, 268–69; mentioned, vi

Harper, Fletcher: letter to, 231; mentioned, 231n1

Harper & Brothers: letters from, 200–201, 216–17, 291, 331, 340; letters to, 202–4, 210–11, 220, 237–38, 239–40, 242–43, 249, 341, 351; proposition by, 216–17; opinion concerning, 223, 226, 227n2; launch magazine, 291, 291n3; fire, 331, 331n1; mentioned, vi, 201n1

Harris, Thaddeus William: letter to, 159; librarian, 159, 159n1

Harvard College: cooperation of, x–xi; news, 64, 65n6; bequest, 402–3; mentioned, 66

Hawthorne, Nathaniel: political post, 273, 273n2; mentioned, 273n1

Hickling, Amelia: aunt, 6, 12n2

Hickling, Harriet: opinion of, 6; aunt, 10, 11, 12n2

Hickling, Thomas: grandfather, 6, 10, 12n3

Hickling, William: uncle, 16, 16n3

Hillard, George Stillman: book by, 148, 148n2, 325, 326n2; articles by, 213, 214n1, 346–47, 347n1; letter from, 213–14; letter to, 346–47; mentioned, vi, 215, 275

Historians: named, vi

Holmes, Oliver Wendell: letter to, 395–96; mentioned, vi, 396n1

Hone, Philip: described, 191, 192n5; presentation copy, 242

Howe, Samuel Gridley: letters to, 142–43, 145–46; mentioned, 73n4

Hughes, Christopher: presentation copy, 243, 243n5; letter to, 244

Hume, David: historian, 41, 41n3

Icazbalceta, Joaquín García. See García Icazbalceta, Joaquín

Income: annual, 331–32

Indexer: John Langdon Sibley, 109, 109–10n2, 115

Invoices: books, 53, 73–74, 74n1, 81–83, 86–87

Irving, Washington: writings, 67, 67n1; kindness, 138–39, 139n2; letter to, 152–53; on copyright, 154; presentation copy, 243; dinner, 270; mentioned, vi, 85, 153–54n1, 191

Jackson, Dr. James: physician, 11, 12n15; mentioned, 330

Kennedy, John Pendleton: friend, 244, 244n1, 286, 287n3

Kent, James: jurist, 191, 192n6

Kirk, John Foster: agreement with, 251; reader-secretary, 251, 251nn1,2; trip to England, 295n2; defense by, 378n2; bequests, 402, 417; mentioned, 343, 384

Kirkland, John Thornton: president of Harvard, 4, 5n3; clergyman, 12n8; marriage, 52

Knapp, Jacob Newman: teacher, 3, 3n2, 19

Lawrence, Abbott: diplomat, 310–11; letter from, 310–11; health, 344–45; memoir, 356n1; mentioned, 277, 278n3, 292, 294n4, 320

Lawrence, Elizabeth Prescott: trust fund for, 410ff. See also Prescott, Elizabeth

Lawrence, James: described, 310–11; health, 397; trustee, 417ff.; mentioned, 79n1, 400

Lea, Isaac: letter to, 281–82; mentioned, 282n1

Leatham, Willam Henry: letter from, 173; poet, 173, 173nn1,2; mentioned, vi

Lembke, Friedrich Wilhelm: aide, 164, 165n17; mentioned, 137n4, 139, 166, 169

Lieber, Francis: book by, 131–32, 147; letters to, 131–32, 147–48, 154–55, 170–71, 174–76, 185–87, 226–27; presentation copy, 211; mentioned, vi, 132n1, 152, 184n1

Lincolne, Lucilla Stanley: letter from, 357–58; mentioned, vi

Little, Brown and Co.: *Ferdinand and Isabella,* 141–42; letter to, 146–47; mentioned, 220

Lockhart, John Gibson: described, 294; letter to, 300–301; mentioned, vi, 64, 65n4, 69, 70, 71n1

Longfellow, Henry Wadsworth: biography of, viii; guest, 107; letters to, 184, 230, 299–300; reputation in England, 298, 300; mentioned, vi, 107, 107n2, 197

Lunt, George: reader-secretary, 46, 47n2

Lyell, Sir Charles: letter to, 399–401

Lyell, Sir Charles and Lady Mary E.: mentioned, 185, 187n4, 194

Lyell, Lady Mary E.: letters to, 306–8, 319–20, 322–23, 324–26, 328–31, 334–36, 344–46, 359–62, 372–74; letters from, 312–13, 396–97; social gossip, 397; mentioned, vi

Lyman, Theodore: friend, 11, 12n14

Macaulay, Thomas Babington: historian, 185–86, 291, 291n2; style, 267; book by, 270; opinion concerning, 295, 298

Major, R. H.: letter from, 388

Manuscripts: bibliography of, xiii–xv

Mariotti, Luigi: letter to, 182–83; mentioned, 183n1, 186–87

Markham, Clements Robert: introduced, 315–16, 316n1; book by, 356, 356n1; letter from, 356

Marryat, Frederick: novelist, 129, 129n4

Mason, William Powell: friend, 4, 5n7

Massachusetts Historical Society: cooperation of, x; bequest, 403, 428n3

Maturin, Edward: letter to, 223; novelist, 224nn1,2; book by, 224n2; mentioned, vi

Mayer, Brantz: letter to, 218–19; mentioned, vi, 219n1

Mears, Grenville: letter to, 218

Memoranda: concerning articles, 38; concerning eyes, 187–89; concerning personal regimen, 255, 255nn1,2; concerning expenses, 318, 319n1, 333; concerning income, 331–33;

concerning landscaping, 350; concerning allowances for sons, 352–54; concerning publishing contract, 355–56, 384

Metcalf, Keith and Nichols: letter to, 206–7

Mexico: questions about, 162–63, 165n14

Middleton, Arthur: at Harvard, 4, 5n2; in Spain, 98, 99, 106, 166–67; letter from, 166–67; presentation copy, 211; mentioned, vi, 190

Mignet, François Auguste Marie: archivist, 179, 181n5; letter to, 224–25

Miller, General William: visitor, 161, 164n10; letter from, 258–60; on war with Mexico, 259

Milman, Henry Hart: review by, 215, 216n2; letter from, 315–16; mentioned, vi, 298, 308

Miscellanies: publication, 231, 231–32n2; promotion, 238; reception, 240, 240n2, 249; English edition, 249; stereotype plates for, 340, 340n1, 341; presentation copy, 367–68; mentioned, 285

Moore, Thomas: quoted, 30, 31n2

Morghen, Rafaelle: prints by, 18, 20n2, 26

Morpeth, Lord: letter from, 214–15; mentioned, 194. *See also* Carlisle, Earl of

Motley, John Lothrop: historian, 314, 315n2; book by, 351n1, 374, 375n6; letter to, 383–84; mentioned, vi

Murray, John: publisher, 202, 202n1; on copyright, 204; proposition by, 204–5, 205n1

Napier, Macvey: letter to, 225–26; publishes "correction," 226n2; mentioned, 226n1

Navarrete, Martín Fernández de. *See* Fernández de Navarrete, Martín

Nichols, George: letter to, 205

Noctograph: used, 20n6, 381

North American Review: articles in, 38, 38n1, 46n1, 54, 62–63, 63n1, 71, 71n1, 124n1, 276n1, 380; opinion concerning, 52, 119, 359; reviews

Ferdinand and Isabella, 114n1; inquiry about, 117; reviews *Conquest of Mexico,* 214n1; reviews *Philip the Second,* 359n1; mentioned, 31n4, 36, 36n2, 64, 65n7, 88, 97, 99, 103
Novelists: named, vi

Ogden, Rollo: biography by, viii
Otis, Edmund B.: reader-secretary, 207, 207n1

Palfrey, John Gorham: *North American Review,* 121–22, 122n4; mentioned, 92, 92n4, 128, 129n2
Papers: nature, v–vii
Parker, Daniel: visited, 27, 30n2
Parkman, Francis: historian, 305, 305n1; book by, 305, 305n2
Parkman, Dr. George: murder, 279–81; mentioned, 281n1
Parsons, Gorham: letter to, 38–39
Parsons, Theophilus: article by, 31, 31n5; letters to, 34, 44, 44–45; mentioned, vi
Peabody, Captain Joseph: of Salem, 3, 3n2
Peabody, Joseph Augustus: friend, 3, 3n2
Peck, Harry Thurston: biography by, viii
Penney, Clara Louise: book by, viii
Philip the Second: publication, 355nn1,3; review, 358–59, 359n1; opinions, 377, 396; production, 389–90, 391, 392; publication schedule, 393; presentation copies, 398
Phillips, Moses Dresser: letter to, 382–83; launches *The Atlantic Monthly,* 383n2; letters from, 384–85, 391–92; death, 392n1; mentioned, 383n1
Phillips, Sampson and Company: bankruptcy, 392n1; mentioned, vi, 340n2
Pickering, John: letter from, 111–12; reviews *Ferdinand and Isabella,* 112n2, 120–21; mentioned, vi, 112n1
Pickman, Haskett Derby: friend, 8, 12n7
Poets: named, vi

Poinsett, Joel Roberts: letters to, 133–34, 134–37; politician, 134nn1,5,6; mentioned, vi, 75, 75n1
Politicians: named, vi
Politics: American, 52, 53n5, 76–77, 90, 98–99, 176, 176n4, 222, 236, 261–62, 273, 285, 308, 320, 335, 336n2, 360–61, 362nn3,4, 365, 366n4, 368, 375–76, 400–401; European, 335
Polk, James K.: letter to, 236; mentioned, vi
Portraits: for histories, 169, 177–78
Portuguese nation: character, 8, 10
Practices: editorial, ix–x
Preble, Caroline: friend, 16, 16n4. *See also* Wormeley, Caroline Preble
Prescott, Catherine Elizabeth (sister): letter to, 3; watch, 27. *See also* Dexter, Elizabeth Prescott
Prescott, Catherine Greene Hickling (mother): letters to, 5–12, 14–16, 18–20; instructions from, 17; letters from, 17, 20–21, 228, 248; postscript by, 229; household role, 248; death, 312–13, 313n1; mentioned, 12n1, 60, 248n2
Prescott, Catherine Hickling (daughter): birth, 44, 44n2; death, 67n1; mentioned, 58, 58n4
Prescott, Edward Goldsborough (brother): oration by, 102, 103n3; debts, 218; death, 218n1; mentioned, 4, 5n9, 19
Prescott, Elizabeth (daughter): marriage, 311n1; mentioned, 79, 79n1, 153, 154n7, 192, 200, 200n3, 228, 241, 241n2, 248, 248n3. *See also* Lawrence, Elizabeth Prescott
Prescott, Josephine Augusta (daughter-in-law): letters to, 364–66, 375–77
Prescott, Dr. Oliver, 8, 12n9
Prescott, Susan Amory (wife): religious beliefs, 37n2; letters to, 56–58, 58–60, 77–78, 79, 189–92, 228, 248, 286–87; nature, 58n5, 348, 348n1; household role, 248, 249n4; health, 330, 370; bequests, 402ff.; trust fund for, 407ff. *See also* Amory, Susan
Prescott, Dr. William, ix

Prescott, William (father): letters to, 4, 5–12, 14–16, 18–20, 22–30; letters from, 12–14, 17–18, 21–22; advice by, 13–14; law office, 46; investments, 88–89, 89n1; Harvard, 194n1; death, 222n2; estate, 222–23; mentioned, viii, 5n1, 60, 200n1, 218

Prescott, Mrs. William (grandmother), 11, 12n13

Prescott, William Amory (son): nickname, 200n1; watch, 251; social nature, 256, 257, 269–70; hunter, 276; sails to India, 287–88, 290; letters to, 296, 398–99, 401; trip to Europe, 338–39, 339n1; allowances, 352–54; in Europe, 365, 371; birthday, 376; in New York City, 398–99, 399n1; bequests, 403ff.; trust fund for, 410ff.; mentioned, 79, 79n1, 153, 154n7, 290n1

Prescott, William Gardiner (son): letters to, 194–95, 197–99, 199–200, 208, 229, 251–53, 255–57, 260–62, 265–67, 269–71, 276–78, 279–81, 282–85, 287–90, 291–92, 369–72, 385–87, 390–91; at Harvard, 197, 199n1, 208, 209n1; health, 265, 282, 369–70; legationship, 266; visits Bentley, 278–79; marriage, 309n2; accident, 335; allowances, 353–54; plans, 361; trip to Europe, 364–66, 366n1; at French Court, 375, 377n1; bequests, 403ff.; trust fund for, 410ff.; mentioned, 58, 58n4, 195–96nn1,2,3, 230n2, 253n1, 364, 365, 366, 374, 374–75n5

Prescott, William Hickling: articles by, xvii–xx, 45, 46n1, 62–63, 90, 91n1, 91–92, 92nn1,2, 104–5n2, 115–17, 117n2, 118, 172n4, 183n2, 196, 197n2, 219, 275–76, 277, 285, 286n2, 326n2, 349n3, 356n1, 382, 383n3; advice for, 13–14; aids Rich, 69, 69n3; affection for grandfather, 89, 89n5, 312; aids institute for blind, 142–43; asks aid, 159, 179–80, 181nn8,9, 205, 293, 312, 398; abridges *Ferdinand and Isabella*, 176, 177n5; advises son, 194–95, 198–99, 199–200, 200n2, 229, 251–

53, 253n8, 257, 271, 272n2, 277, 283, 289–90; aids F. Calderón de la Barca, 196, 197n3; advises Lieber, 226–27; aids novelist, 232, 234n3; aids S. A. Eliot, 240–41, 268; acknowledges gifts, 250, 260, 285, 357, 367, 378, 395–96; amusement, 256; as correspondent, 257n1; aids Alamán, 282, 282n2; at Castle Howard, 297–98, 299n1; aids F. Parkman, 305; autograph sought, 323; aids García Icazbalceta, 349, 350n1; aids J. L. Motley, 351, 383–84, 384n1; aids Bulfinch, 359n2; alters contract, 384, 384nn1,2; air of resignation, 401; attends funeral, 401

biographies of, vii–viii; buys prints, 18; bet paid, 34; borrows book, 43; book invoices, 53, 73–74, 81–83, 86–87; begins writing *Conquest of Peru*, 219n2; begins work on *Philip the Second*, 249n1; buys stereotype plates, 341; begins *Charles the Fifth* project, 350n3; books by, 372n1

correspondents, vi; confusion of names, viii–ix; chronology, xvii–xx; career interest, 6; concerning room, 21; commonplace book, 35–36, 36n1, 36–37, 38, 40, 40–41; concerning archives, 137n5; compares societies, 190–91; correspondence increases, 247n2, 301n2; check, 324; celebrations, 328–29; cancels dinner, 399

described, v, 79, 79n2; desires illustrations, 94, 95n3; declines to continue as trustee, 145–46; daily routine, 189; describes Gallatin, 190, 192n2; describes New York society, 190–91; declines committee appointment, 194, 194n1; declines historical theme, 216: denies bigotry, 218–19; death of father, 222n2; describes Beacon Street residence, 228, 228n1; disappointed, 352n2; describes Pepperell, 365; declines proposition, 388n2; declines invitation, 399–400; death, 401n2

editor, 32, 33; executor, 222–23, 223n2

financial interests, 44–45, 45n2; flattery by, 107, 107n1, 110, 111n5, 115, 115n2, 138, 138n4, 392; friendship with Sumner, 274–75

gifts for children, 59; gifts for, 227, 247; grandchildren, 322–23, 323n1, 361–62, 364–66, 366nn2,3, 387, 391, 391n2; generosity, 384–85, 392

Harvard, 4, 121, 121n1, 402–3; health, 5–8, 10, 12, 14–15, 46n2, 48–49, 49n4, 54, 68, 69n2, 77, 187–89, 225, 240n2, 257, 262, 361, 370, 373, 374n2, 379–82, 387, 388n1, 388–89, 390–91, 397; humor, 52, 53n7, 137, 138n1, 343; horseman, 91n5; honorary memberships, 129, 141, 141n2, 155, 155n1, 224–25, 225n1; honorary degrees, 171n1, 183–84, 187n2, 209, 209n2, 296, 297n2; honors on title pages, 182, 182n1; honors, 185, 187n2, 320, 321n3, 371, 372n2; house repairs, 234–36, 236n2

inspired by S. Johnson, 49, 49n3; institution for blind, 71, 72–73, 73n2, 90; investments, 96, 96n1, 331–32, 370; inactivity, 285n2, 303n2; inspired by E. Gibbon, 379

journal, 22n1

letters from, 3, 4, 5–12, 14–16, 18–20, 22–30, 31, 32, 33, 34, 34–35, 38–39, 41–43, 44, 44–45, 45, 46–47, 48–49, 51–53, 54, 54–55, 56, 56–58, 58–60, 60–62, 62–63, 63–65, 66–67, 67–69, 69–71, 71, 72–73, 74–75, 76–77, 77–78, 79–80, 83, 83–85, 85, 87–88, 88–89, 90–91, 91–92, 92–94, 95, 96, 97–98, 98–99, 99–100, 101–3, 103–4, 105–6, 106, 107, 107–8, 108–9, 109, 110, 111, 112, 113, 113–14, 114–15, 115–17, 117–18, 118–19, 119–20, 120–21, 121, 121–22, 122–23, 124, 124–25, 125–26, 126, 127, 127–28, 128–29, 129, 130, 130–31, 131–32, 132, 133–34, 134–37, 137–38, 138–39, 139–41, 141, 141–42, 142–43, 143, 144–45, 145–46, 146–47, 147–48, 152–53, 154–55, 159, 159–64, 165, 167–70, 170–71, 174, 174–76, 177–80, 181–82, 182–83, 184, 185–87, 189–92, 194, 194–95, 196–97, 197,

197–99, 199–200, 202–4, 205, 206, 206–7, 207, 208, 210–11, 211–12, 212, 216, 217–18, 218, 218–19, 219, 220, 223, 224, 224–25, 225–26, 226–27, 229, 230, 230–31, 231, 236, 237–38, 239–40, 240, 240–41, 242–43, 244, 249, 250, 251–53, 253–55, 255–57, 260, 260–62, 264–65, 265–67, 268, 269–71, 272–73, 273–75, 275–76, 276–78, 279–81, 281–82, 282–85, 285–86, 286–87, 287–90, 290–91, 291–92, 292–93, 294–95, 296, 297–99, 299, 299–300, 300–301, 301–3, 305, 306–8, 309, 311–12, 313–15, 317–18, 319–20, 322–23, 324, 324–26, 328–31, 334–36, 336–37, 337–38, 338–39, 341, 342–43, 344–46, 346–47, 347, 348–49, 349–50, 351, 357, 358–59, 359–62, 362–63, 363–64, 364–66, 367–68, 368, 368–69, 369–72, 372–74, 375–77, 377–78, 378–79, 379–82, 382–83, 383–84, 385–87, 388–89, 389, 389–90, 390–91, 392, 393–94, 394, 395–96, 397–98, 398–99, 399–401, 401; letters to, 12–14, 17, 17–18, 20–21, 21–22, 49–50, 100–101, 101, 107, 111–12, 149–51, 155–56, 156–58, 158–59, 166–67, 172–73, 173, 183–84, 192–93, 200–201, 201–2, 209, 209–10, 212–13, 213–14, 214–15, 216–17, 221, 221–22, 222–23, 227–28, 232–33, 238–39, 244–45, 245–47, 248, 249, 258–60, 262–63, 263–64, 267–68, 268–69, 272, 278–79, 291, 293, 304, 306, 309–10, 310–11, 312–13, 315–16, 316–17, 321, 323, 326–28, 331, 340, 341–42, 348, 351–52, 354–55, 356, 357–58, 366, 384–85, 387, 388, 391–92, 395, 396–97; love of history, 40; love of poetry, 44n9, 184; lends books, 113, 217–18; "literary loafing," 123–24n6, 208n1, 240n2; letters of introduction by, 174, 174n2, 251, 351; letters of introduction for, 294n4

marriage of, 34n2; manager of Boys' Asylum, 38–39, 40n3; musings, 40–41; Mexican project, 126n1, 129n5, 133–34, 134–37, 139, 159, 168–69, 181; memoranda by, 187–89, 318, 319n1, 331–33, 333, 350,

Prescott, W. H. (*continued*)
352–54, 355–56, 384

newspaper, 119n2; Nahant, 161, 164n9, 313n2; needs encouragement, 310n1; negotiates sale of book, 337–38, 338n1

on travel, 41, 41n5; on phrenology, 58–59; opinion of Canadians, 78; on book design, 96, 96n4; opinion of the sea, 108, 109n1; on American critics, 119, 119n5; opinion of R. Ford, 142; on copyright, 147–48, 148n1, 152–53, 154–55, 253–55, 255n1, 337–38, 369, 369n1, 373; on politics, 154–55, 176n4, 224, 261–62, 266, 273, 285, 339, 339n2, 375–76; on English criticism, 165, 166n2; on civilization, 170–71; opinion of Bentley, 174, 174n4; on reviewing, 175–76, 176nn2,3; offers loan, 177; on society, 185, 187n3, 260–61; opinion of Macaulay, 185–86, 267; on spelling, 200; on Greek language, 208; opinion of Kingsborough's work, 217, 218n2; opinion of English publishers, 254; on translations, 255; on international organization, 274; on English life, 276, 278n1, 294–95, 308; opinion of Clay, 288; opinion of Taylor, 288, 290–91; on marriages of children, 315; opinion of *Uncle Tom's Cabin*, 317; offers to sell contract, 321; on literary patronage, 323; on wines, 336; offers *Philip the Second* to publishers, 337–38; on reader-secretary, 342–43; opinion of Ticknor, 362–63; offers *Charles the Fifth* to publishers, 363–64; opinion of P. de Gayangos, 383; on depression of 1857, 385–86; on literary criticism, 389

papers, v–vi; publication in England, 62, 62n1; progress with *Ferdinand and Isabella*, 88n1, 90, 93, 102–3, 103n4, 104, 107; preliminary printing, 93, 95n1; Phi Beta Kappa, 101n2; presentation copies, 122, 124, 125n2, 128, 130n2, 132n2, 134, 135, 141, 155, 166, 192, 193n6, 211, 225, 231, 244, 258, 354, 367–68, 378–79, 396, 398; promotion ideas, 122–

23, 123nn2,4, 182, 182n2, 210, 238; praises Lieber, 131–32; progress with *Philip the Second*, 144, 164, 170n9, 178–79, 250, 250n1, 258n6, 275n2, 306n3, 312n1, 314, 323n2, 335, 336, 336n1, 343n2, 346, 348n2, 350n3, 356n2, 384, 389, 397; progress with *Conquest of Mexico*, 153, 178, 180n3, 186, 187n5, 196; progress with *Conquest of Peru*, 153, 220n1, 228–29n1; Pepperell, 165; praises Longfellow, 184; preface to *Life in Mexico*, 196; praises Sparks, 216; personal regimen, 255, 255nn1,2; praises Whipple, 260; praises Sigourney, 264–65; praises Hawthorne, 272–73; praises oration by Sumner, 273–74; Parkman murder case, 279–81; praises Alamán, 281–82; portraits of, 294, 307, 329–30, 401; presented at English Court, 296; praises Cooper, 309, 309n1; praises Hillard, 346–47; progress with *Charles the Fifth*, 356n1, 364n2; praises Motley, 374; property question, 394

quotes Burns, 138; quotes Pope, 175, 176n1; quotes Horace, 193, 193n2; quotes Rogers, 215, 216n3; quotes Lord Morpeth, 216n3; quotes General Miller, 260n1; quotes Byron, 301, 301n1, 315, 315n6

reputation, v; reading, 7, 42–43, 43n1; religious beliefs, 36–37, 37nn1,2; role of reviews, 41; recommends a clergyman, 76–77; reads manuscript of novel, 231; reviewer, 265n1; refuses modern Mexican theme, 269n1; reasons for trip to Europe, 292n2; reflections on England, 301, 373; refuses to make contract, 317–18; residence at Lynn, 324, 324n1, 339–40n3, 350; research methods, 379–82, 382n3; relations with publishers, 395n1; revising *Conquest of Mexico*, 398n1

studies, 40, 40n2; seeks advice, 88–89, 108–9, 394; speech requested from, 101, 101n3; society, 103n5, 261, 320, 345, 357, 370, 373; spelling, 116, 117n1; social gossip, 160, 176, 255–57, 260–62, 266, 269–71, 277, 279, 283–84, 307–8, 319–20, 322–23, 324–26, 328–31, 334–36, 339, 344–46, 359–62, 364–66, 370–71, 373–74, 386–87, 391; seeks aid, 205, 206n1, 212, 250; summary of experience, 208; subscription, 224; sends gift, 300–301; sons pampered, 352–54, 354n1; sale of books, 361, 372, 385–86

trips to Europe, 5n10, 15–16, 17n5, 20n6, 30n6, 291–92, 294–95, 295n1, 296, 297–99, 302, 303n1; trips to Washington, 56–58, 58–60, 236, 286–87, 287n1, 288; trips to Niagara Falls and Canada, 77–78, 307; trustee of Athenaeum, 85n1; trip to Connecticut, 174–75; trip to New York City, 189–92; trips to New York City and Philadelphia, 241n2, 269–70; translators, 264n1

unwilling to enter into contract, 249, 249n1; urged to write biography of Scott, 269

views on death, 105–6; visits Belgium, 296, 297n1

will, 402–28

Printers: Folsom, Wells and Thurston, 121, 121n3

Prints: bought in Florence, 26

Publishers: named, vi

Quincy, Josiah: letter from, 209; president of Harvard, 209, 209n1

Randolph, Theodorick Tudor: friend, 8, 12n6

Ray, Mrs. Richard: presentation copy, 242

Ray, Robert: presentation copy, 231, 242

Reader-secretaries: Collis, 7; McCandlish, 16; Busson, 30; duties, 46; salaries, 46, 241, 251; George Lunt, 46, 47n2; James Lloyd English, 46n2; search for, 46–47; Thomas Andrew Watson, 230, 230n1; agreements, 241, 251; Robert Carter, 241, 242n1; John Foster Kirk, 251, 251n2,

295n2, 378n2, 402, 417; problems of, 380

Rich, Obadiah: invoices from, 53, 73–74, 81–83, 86–87; letters to, 54–55, 60–62, 66–67, 67–69, 69–71, 74–75, 79–80, 83, 83–85, 85, 87–88, 92–94, 95, 97–98, 98–99, 99–100, 103–4, 250; appointed consul, 100; letter from, 100–101; book by, 102, 104, 104n3; mentioned, vi, 49, 50, 51, 53, 53n1, 65, 247

Richardson, John P.: letter from, 183–84

Robertson, William: historian, 41, 41n4, 168, 170n6; book by, 363–64

Rogers, Samuel: biography of, viii

Roman Catholic Church: rites, 8–9

Routledge, George: letter from, 366; publishes Charles the Fifth, 366, 367n2; letters to, 368–69, 393–94, 397–98; publishes Philip the Second, 393; mentioned, vi, 366n1

Saunders, Frederick: of Harpers, 243, 243n8

Sears, David, II: letter from, 222–23; mentioned, 223n1

Shattuck, Dr. George C.: letter to, 130; mentioned, 130n1

Sibley, John Langdon: indexer, 109, 109–10n2, 115, 206

Sigourney, Lydia Howard Huntley: presentation copy, 211, 211n4; letter to, 264–65; mentioned, vi

Slavery: view on, 57

Soulé, Pierre: in Spain, 327, 328n3

Sparks, Jared: letters to, 31, 34–35, 45, 63–65, 71, 90–91, 91–92, 96, 105–6, 107, 107–8, 109, 122–23, 216, 311–12; historical labors, 47, 48n5, 52, 109; books by, 96, 115–17, 118; advice from, 104; death of wife, 105–6; letter from, 107; opinion of Ferdinand and Isabella, 107, 107n1; assistance of, 166n3; president of Harvard, 262, 262n2, 266; mentioned, vi, 31, 31n1, 63, 171, 209n2

Stephens, John Lloyd: presentation copy, 231; mentioned, 200, 201n2, 226, 255

Stereotyping: of book, 108, 108n2, 109, 110n3, 114–15, 390n1; plates bought, 340–41; mentioned, 128n2, 201, 237

Stirling, William: book by, 267, 268n2, 316, 317n1; letters from, 267–68, 316–17; historical labors, 354, 355n2; mentioned, vi, 268n1, 277, 303, 310, 314

Story, Joseph: letter to, 124–25; death, 230, 230n2; mentioned, 125n1, 215

Stowe, Harriet Beecher: book by, 317–18, 318n2; recommended, 317–18, 318n1

Stuart-Wortley, Lady Emmeline, 272, 272n1

Sturgis, Russell: letter from, 351–52; literary agent, 351–52, 352n1, 394n1; negotiates sale of *Philip the Second*, 351–52

Sullivan, William: letter to, 132; mentioned, 132n1

Sumner, Charles: biography of, viii; letters to, 143, 165, 194, 273–75, 290–91, 297–99, 357, 388–89; travel companion, 236n1; goes to Senate, 308; attacked, 360; mentioned, vi, 144n1, 149, 193, 212, 215, 227, 275n1

Swan, Timothy: letter from, 33

Taylor, Zachary: visited, 286; mentioned, 288

Tefft, Israel K.: letter to, 141; mentioned, 141n1

Ternaux-Compans, Henri: scholar, 169, 170n5

Thacher, Samuel Cooper: clergyman, 8, 12n8

Thackeray, William Makepeace: novelist, 317, 317n2

Ticknor, Anna: health, 334; letter from, 348; bequest, 402; mentioned, vi, 43, 44n6, 192, 267, 267n1, 359

Ticknor, Anna (daughter), 208, 209n3

Ticknor, George: biography by, vii–viii; biography of, viii; advice from, 27; letter to, 41–43; assistance of, 46–47; books, 49; travel companion, 57, 58n1, 59; trips by, 57, 58n1, 59, 102, 109, 359, 372; promotes *Ferdi-*

nand and Isabella, 88–89; on Spanish literature, 176, 186; book by, 275, 277; translated, 314; biographical sketch, 347; writes biographical sketch, 349, 349n2; letter of introduction, 362–63; defense by, 378n2; bequest, 402; trustee, 404ff.; mentioned, vi, 30n3, 66, 130, 130n2, 143, 149, 160, 165, 175, 208, 221, 230–31, 247, 308, 310

Treadwell, Mrs.: of Boston, 7, 11–12, 12n5

Trench, Richard Chenevix: book by, 367, 368n2; letter to, 367–68; mentioned, 368n1

Trust funds: established, 404ff.

Twisleton, Edward Turner Boyd: friend, 281, 281n4, 290, 354

Tytler, Patrick Fraser: letter from, 155–56; historical labors, 156; mentioned, vi, 156n1

United States Literary Gazette: article in, 44, 44nn1,3

Van de Weyer, Sylvain: diplomat, 179, 181n6

Vatican: account of, 19

Verplanck, Gulian Crommelin, 191, 192n8

Wainwright, Jonathan Mayhew: clergyman, 189, 192n1; presentation copy, 231, 242

Walsh, Robert: opinion concerning, 52; mentioned, 47, 47–48n4, 65

Ward, Samuel: presentation copy, 243; mentioned, 106, 106n2

Ware, Henry: Harvard faculty, 4, 5n4

Ware, John: article by, 31n5, 34

Warren, Henry: article by, 31, 31n5

Watson, Thomas Andrew: reader-secretary, 230, 230n1

Webster, Daniel: visited, 57; on copyright, 154; letter to, 272–73; mentioned, vi

Webster, John White: murderer, 279–81; mentioned, 281n2

Wells, Charles: letter to, 33

Wensleydale, Lord: letter to, 362–63

Wheaton, Henry: diplomat, 212, 212n2

Whipple, Edwin Percy: book by, 260, 260n2; letter to, 260; mentioned, 260, 260n1

Wight, R. Augustus: letter from, 323; seeks autograph, 323; mentioned, vi

Will: text, 402–16; witnesses, 416, 417, 422, 427, 428; first codicil, 416–17; second codicil, 417–22; third codicil, 422–27; fourth codicil, 427–28

Wilson, Robert Anderson: letter to, 377–78; book by, 378n2; mentioned, vi, 378n1

Winthrop, Robert Charles: dinner, 286; mentioned, 277, 278n5

Wolcott, Roger: book by, viii; cooperation of, x

Wolf, Ferdinand: librarian, 179, 181n7

Wormeley, Caroline Preble: friend, 128, 129n3. See also Preble, Caroline

Wormeley, Mary Elizabeth: letters to, 230–31, 324; book by, 231n2; letter from, 232–33; proposed dedication by, 232–33; mentioned, vi, 231n1

Young, Alexander: letter to, 127; mentioned, vi, 127, 127n1